Global Issues

Global Issues

THIRD EDITION

CQ PRESS

A Division of Congressional Quarterly Inc. Washington, D.C.

SELECTIONS FROM **THE CQ RESEARCHER**

CQ Press
1255 22nd Street, N.W., Suite 400
Washington, D.C. 20037

(202) 729-1900; toll-free, 1-866-4CQ-PRESS (1-866-427-7737)
www.cqpress.com

♾ The paper used in this publication exceeds the requirements of the American National Standard for Information Sciences—Permanence of Paper for Printed Library Materials, ANSI Z39.48-1992.

Printed and bound in the United States of America

07 06 05 04 03   5 4 3 2 1

A CQ Press College Division Publication

Director	Brenda Carter
Acquisitions editor	Charisse Kiino
Marketing manager	Rita Matyi
Production editor	Belinda Josey
Cover designer	Kimberly Glyder
Composition	Olu Davis
Print buyer	Margot Ziperman
Sales manager	James Headley

Library of Congress Cataloging-in-Publication Data

Global issues: selections from The CQ researcher— 3rd ed.
    p. cm.
Includes bibliographical references and index.
  ISBN 1-56802-873-3 (alk. paper)
  1. Globalization. 2. International relations. 3. Security, International. I. CQ Press. II. CQ researcher. III. Title.
JZ1318.G558 2004
327—dc22

                              2003023659

Contents

INTERNATIONAL POLITICAL ECONOMY

Annotated Contents

The 16 *CQ Researcher* articles reprinted in this book have been reproduced essentially as they appeared when first published. In a few cases in which important new developments have since occurred updates are provided in the overviews highlighting the principal issues examined.

CONFLICT, SECURITY, AND TERRORISM

North Korean Crisis

While a U.S.-led coalition fought to topple Saddam Hussein's regime in Iraq, a dangerous foreign policy crisis was brewing on the Korean Peninsula. In fall 2002, Kim Jong Il resumed North Korea's program to develop nuclear weapons in violation of the Nuclear Non-Proliferation Treaty and a 1994 agreement with the United States to freeze the program in exchange for food and energy assistance. The Bush administration rejects North Korea's call for bilateral negotiations to resolve the crisis, arguing that to accept would be caving in to "nuclear blackmail." Instead, it insists on including regional Asian powers in talks. Administration critics say that ignoring North Korea—which may have enough material to build at least one nuclear weapon and could soon produce many more—is a recipe for war.

Weapons of Mass Destruction

First came the attacks on September 11, 2001, killing more than 3,000 people. Then mysterious letters laced with deadly anthrax spores took five more victims. For all their devastation, however, these attacks pale in comparison to the mayhem that terrorists could unleash with deadlier weapons. In fact, intelligence officials say that al Qaeda leader Osama bin Laden has pursued nuclear and biological weapons and that weapons-grade nuclear material in the former Soviet Union could fall into the wrong hands. International treaties have sought to curb the proliferation of weapons of mass destruction, but diplomacy alone may not be enough. As the Department of Homeland Security works to shore up defenses, the Bush administration wants to double the anti-terrorism budget.

Future of NATO

President George W. Bush's Iraq policy has exacerbated long-standing tensions between the United States and its allies in the North Atlantic Treaty Organization (NATO), established after World War II to counter the Communist bloc. The administration's go-it-alone stance in foreign policy prompted France and Germany to lead unsuccessful efforts to thwart Bush's plans to attack Iraq. Some experts say the rift is proof that the alliance has outlived its mandate, while NATO supporters say it remains a vital bulwark against terrorism and other threats to democracy. Meanwhile, some critics are asking whether the United States' allies should speed up weapons modernization to better collaborate with the Pentagon's technologically sophisticated equipment. Others say NATO is fast evolving into little more than a political forum.

New Defense Priorities

After the Cold War, the Pentagon began downsizing its forces and developing high-tech, mobile weapons designed to deal with "rogue" states, like Iraq—less powerful than the Soviet juggernaut but still able to attack the United States and its allies. The September 11 attacks forced Pentagon planners back to the drawing board to develop new strategies and weapons. Defense Secretary Donald H. Rumsfeld wants to further transform the military to enable it to counter emerging threats from unconventional forces like al Qaeda. Meanwhile, President Bush put his new preemptive strike strategy into practice by deposing Iraqi president Saddam Hussein, despite the opposition of most U.S. allies.

Policing the Borders

To keep the United States safe from terrorists, customs and immigration agents must monitor 7,500 miles of land and sea borders, dozens of airports, and 300 official ports of entry. They also monitor the 11 million trucks, 2.2 million rail cars, and 7,500 foreign-flagged ships that enter the country each year. In addition, they oversee the 31 million non-citizens—mostly tourists—who visit each year. After September 11, President Bush formed the Department of Homeland Security, and Congress passed sweeping legislation giving police and intelligence agencies more power to monitor U.S. borders. Experts disagree over which security steps would be most cost-effective and least disruptive to trade and Americans' daily lives, and civil libertarians warn that some proposed measures—such as linking driver's licenses to a national database and targeting certain ethnic groups—would undermine civil liberties.

INTERNATIONAL POLITICAL ECONOMY

Oil Diplomacy

The United States depends on imported oil to satisfy more than half its voracious appetite for petroleum and petroleum products. Despite efforts to diversify oil suppliers and conserve energy after the 1973 Arab oil embargo, growing energy consumption all but forces the United States to continue relying on Middle Eastern oil. That reliance is likely to continue despite the war with Iraq and growing anti-American sentiment in the region. The Bush administration proposes reducing U.S. dependence on foreign oil by intensifying domestic production in Alaska and other environmentally sensitive areas. Critics contend that the thirst for oil was behind the administration's plan to invade Iraq as well as its willingness to repeat Cold War patterns and maintain close relations with dictatorial regimes accused of human-rights abuses.

Japan in Crisis

Once the economic envy of the world, Japan now is entering its second decade of nearly continuous recession, with no end in sight. Unemployment, homelessness, and crime are on the rise, and the banking system is lurching toward collapse under the weight of a trillion dollars in bad loans. Even the election in 2001 of Prime Minister Junichiro Koizumi on a radical reform platform has produced little change, owing in part to the power of special interest politics. Japan also must deal with the economic costs of an increasingly aging population and growing competition from neighboring countries. Meanwhile, since the September 11 attacks on the World Trade Center and the Pentagon, the United States has pressured Japan to help in the war against terrorism, triggering a debate within the country over its long-standing prohibition against sending troops into overseas combat.

Foreign Aid After Sept. 11

As U.S.-led forces continue to wage the Bush administration's war on terrorism, calls are mounting for the United States to attack terrorism on another front: by boosting foreign aid. A coalition of international humanitarian agencies wants the United States and other industrial nations to double their aid levels as a way to alleviate the poverty, disease, and illiteracy they say fan the flames of terrorism. They focus their call on the United States, which spends less on aid as a percentage of national income than any industrial nation. Critics say foreign aid has done little to improve living standards in the developing world, often lines the pockets of corrupt government officials, and does not address the true causes of anti-U.S. sentiment.

DEMOCRATIZATION

Rebuilding Iraq

In the wake of the fall of Baghdad, U.S. and British efforts to rebuild Iraq face daunting problems. An independent task force warns of a "steady deterioration in the security situation" due to escalating guerrilla attacks against coalition forces. Thus far, restoration of security and basic services has been delayed, fueling anti-Americanism among a frustrated Iraqi public. Some experts question a recent decision to purge experienced government officials who belonged to the ruling Baath Party. Others argue that coalition efforts would be bolstered if other countries and the United Nations played a greater role in restoring Iraq's infrastructure and government. Meanwhile, many worry that Iraq will not be able to transition to a stable democracy—a concern dismissed by President Bush.

Emerging India

With more than a billion people, India is the world's second most populous country and its largest democracy. Sweeping economic reforms and the development of high-tech industries in recent years have given the nation new optimism for the future, but poverty, food shortages, and violence between Hindus and Muslims continue to plague India. Some observers fear the country's hallowed tradition of pluralism and secular government is at risk. Another flashpoint is the Muslim-majority province of Kashmir, where a separatist movement is supported by Pakistan, India's nuclear-armed neighbor and enemy. Meanwhile, India, also a nuclear power, is seeking a permanent seat on the U.N. Security Council, an effort that is coinciding with a warming in U.S.–Indian relations due in part to India's support for the U.S. war on terrorism.

Trouble in South America

New problems—including the financial collapse of Argentina—have obliterated the last decade of economic growth in South America and pushed the continent into recession. Some economists blame the International Monetary Fund and other multilateral lenders for the decline, arguing that they forced South America's fragile economies to adopt free trade and other market-oriented policies without fully considering the consequences. Defenders of the banks' policies blame the region's economic woes on huge budget deficits and corruption. Meanwhile, leftist guerrillas continue to terrorize Colombia, and political turmoil, especially in Venezuela, has led some experts to worry about the survival of democratic gains made throughout South America in the 1980s and 1990s.

Aiding Africa

Liberia's descent into chaos is the latest chapter in the tragic history of sub-Saharan Africa. For decades, the world's poorest region has been battered by famine, AIDS, and horrific civil wars that have killed or maimed tens of millions of people. Some Africa-watchers now contend that the continent's prospects are looking up, and that with increased Western financial assistance Africa will become more democratic and prosperous in the coming decades. Other experts argue that even recent positive steps, like shifts toward democracy in the 1990s, have stalled. Moreover, they warn that sending foreign aid to Africa is a waste of money. Meanwhile, the deployment of U.S. troops in war-torn Liberia has sparked debate over whether the United States should intervene in nations of questionable strategic importance.

HUMAN RIGHTS

Torture

The war on terrorism has sparked a new debate in the United States over the use of torture to extract information thought necessary to protect public safety. In the wake of the September 11, 2001, attacks, some government officials believe that using physical force against suspected terrorists is justified, especially if they may know about planned future attacks. Others reject torture as unreliable and an affront to legal and civilized norms of behavior. Meanwhile, the State Department's annual human rights report documents the continuing state-sanctioned use of torture in more than 100 countries on five continents. The report—and now the fall of Saddam Hussein's regime in Iraq—has intensified the call by some human rights groups for Western countries to arrest the leaders of nations that brutalize their own citizens.

Ethics of War

The war on terrorism unleashed by the September 11, 2001, attacks raised questions about how civilized nations should confront enemies that flout established international humanitarian law. Amnesty International and other groups contend the United States is violating the Geneva convention—which mandates humane treatment of civilians and prisoners of war (POWs)—by relocating captives from the war in Afghanistan and holding them incommunicado. The Bush administration says these al Qaeda and Taliban prisoners do not warrant POW status because they did not represent legitimate states. Meanwhile, religious leaders said attacking Iraq would not constitute a "just war" because Saddam Hussein did not pose an imminent threat. Others argued that Hussein must be confronted because he had used weapons of mass destruction before and would do so again.

HEALTH AND THE ENVIRONMENT

Bush and the Environment

Since taking office, President Bush has sought to reverse an array of regulations and long-standing environmental protection laws. Administration officials say many of the old rules actually were harming the environment and the economy—such as by permitting delays in removing flammable deadwood from forests or by barring oil and gas production on public land. Bush also repudiated the Kyoto Protocol, an international treaty to slow global warming. Conservationists say such actions jeopardize the progress made in restoring environmental health since the passage of bedrock environmental protection laws more than 30 years ago. They also contend the president's policies favor the energy industry and others that have long chafed at environmental regulations.

Fighting SARS

In November 2002, a deadly, new form of pneumonia—severe acute respiratory syndrome—broke out in southern China. By the time Chinese authorities acknowledged the SARS outbreak four months later, it had spread beyond China's borders. To date, SARS has afflicted thousands in 32 countries; hundreds have died. Public health experts around the world are scrambling to eradicate the epidemic and develop vaccines to prevent future outbreaks. In the United States, critics say the outbreak is a wake-up call concerning underfunding of the public health system. Meanwhile, some health experts worry that Americans may not be willing to accept quarantines and other strict measures needed to stop a SARS epidemic. They want to give the World Health Organization the power to intervene in any country that fails to take appropriate action.

Preface

As the world's peoples become increasingly interconnected, scholars, students, policymakers, and journalists deliberate questions that have global significance. Can the United States keep weapons of mass destruction out of the country? Should WHO intervene in countries that fail to halt the spread of infectious diseases? Will Africa's recent democratic gains be sustained and expanded? Ideas, products, and services are exchanged so rapidly today that they routinely have international consequences. Thus, more than ever, Americans are aware of, and engaged with, issues that have effects beyond our own borders. Educators can help prepare their students for living in a global community by introducing them to such issues.

This reader is a compilation of 16 recent reports from *The CQ Researcher*, a weekly policy backgrounder that concentrates on bringing complicated and controversial issues into focus. Balanced accounts about trade and economic relations, the protection of human rights, the preservation of the environment, and the security of a country's people and resources allow instructors to explore these kinds of tough questions in a thorough manner, challenging students to enter into the dialogue and form their own views. The *Researcher* presents students with an array of questions guaranteed to get them thinking about problems that engage thoughtful people around the world.

The readings in this new edition of *Global Issues* add color and depth to our understanding of the impact of globalization by introducing students to the range of opinion on topics making headlines worldwide. Each report objectively chronicles and analyzes past actions as well as current and possible future political maneuvering. *Global Issues* is designed to encourage discussion, to help readers think critically and actively about the world, and to facilitate further research. It provides clear, real-world examples that add substance and detail to college courses while showing students how the policy debate affects their lives and their futures.

The collection is organized into five subject areas that span a range of important international policy concerns: conflict, security, and terrorism; international political economy; democratization; human rights; and health and the environment. It is an attractive supplement for courses on world affairs in political science, geography, economics, and sociology. Interested citizens, journalists, and business and government leaders also will turn to *Global Issues* to familiarize themselves with key issues, actors, and policy positions.

THE CQ RESEARCHER

The CQ Researcher was founded in 1923 under a different moniker: *Editorial Research Reports.* ERR was sold primarily to newspapers, which used it as a research tool. The magazine was given its current name and a design overhaul in 1991. Today, *The CQ Researcher* is still sold to many newspapers, some of which reprint all or part of each issue, but the audience for the magazine has shifted significantly over the years. Today many more libraries subscribe, and students, not journalists, are the primary audience.

People who write for the *Researcher* often compare the experience to drafting a college term paper, and indeed, there are many similarities. Each report is as long as many term papers—about 11,000 words—and is written by one person.

Like students, staff writers begin the creative process by selecting a topic. Working with the publication's editors, the writer chooses a subject that has policy implications and about which at least some controversy exists. After a topic is approved, the writer embarks on a week or two of intense research. Articles are clipped, books ordered, and information gathered from a variety of sources, including interest groups, universities, and government. Once a writer feels well enough informed about the subject, he or she begins a series of interviews with experts—academics, officials, lobbyists, and practitioners. Each piece usually requires a minimum of ten to fifteen interviews. Particularly complex subjects call for more. After much reading and interviewing, the writer begins to put the report together.

CHAPTER FORMAT

Each issue of the *Researcher*, and therefore each selection in this book, is structured in the same way, beginning with an introductory overview of the topic that briefly touches on the areas that are explored in greater detail in the rest of the chapter.

Following the introduction is a section that chronicles the important debates in the field. The section is structured around "issue questions," such as Can Iraq be transformed into a stable, pro-Western democracy? Should the United States consider military action to halt North Korea's nuclear program? This section is the core of each chapter: the issues are often controversial and usually are the subject of much argument among people involved with the field. Hence, the writer never provides conclusive answers. Instead, a range of opinion is presented.

Following these questions and answers is the "Background," which provides a history of the issue being examined. This look at important events and actions offers insight into how current policy has evolved. An overview of existing policy and important developments follows "Current Situation." Each selection ends with "Outlook," which addresses the near future of the topic or debate.

All selections contain features that augment the main text, and each includes two or three sidebars on issues related to the topic. "At Issue" gives the floor to two outside experts with opposing responses to a relevant question. This "yes–no" feature is an effective starting point for class discussion. Also included are a chronology of important dates and events and an annotated bibliography that details some of the sources in writing the article.

ACKNOWLEDGMENTS

We wish to thank many people for helping make this collection a reality. Foremost is Tom Colin, editor of *The CQ Researcher*, who gave us his enthusiastic support and cooperation as we developed this collection. He and his talented staff of editors and writers have amassed an award-winning library of *Researcher* reports, and we are privileged to have access to that rich cache. We also gratefully acknowledge the advice and feedback from the scholars who commented on our plans for the volume. Some readers of this collection may be learning about

The CQ Researcher for the first time. We expect that many of them will want regular access to this excellent weekly research tool—winner of the American Bar Association's 2002 Silver Gavel Award. Anyone interested in subscription information or a no-obligation free trial of the *Researcher* can contact CQ Press at www.cqpress.com or 1-866-4CQ-PRESS (1-866-427-7737, toll-free).

We hope that you are as pleased with the third edition of *Global Issues* as we are. We welcome your feedback and suggestions for future editions. Please direct comments to Charisse Kiino, at CQ Press, 1255 22nd Street, N.W., Suite 400, Washington, D.C. 20037, or ckiino@cqpress.com.

—*The Editors of CQ Press*

Contributors

Thomas J. Colin, managing editor, has been a magazine and newspaper journalist for more than 25 years. Before joining Congressional Quarterly in 1991, he was a reporter and editor at the *Miami Herald* and *National Geographic* and editor in chief of *Historic Preservation.* He holds a bachelor of arts degree in English from the College of William and Mary and a bachelor's degree in journalism from the University of Missouri.

Mary H. Cooper specializes in environmental, energy, and defense issues. Before joining *The CQ Researcher* as a staff writer in 1983, she was a reporter and Washington correspondent for the Rome daily *l'Unità.* She is the author of *The Business of Drugs* (CQ Press, 1990). She is also a contract translator–interpreter for the U.S. State Department. Cooper graduated from Hollins College with a degree in English.

Patrick Marshall, a freelance writer in Bainbridge Island, Washington, has written about public policy and technology for more than twenty years. He is the reviews editor at *Federal Computer Week* and a technology consultant for the *Seattle Times.* He holds a bachelor's degree in anthropology from the University of California, Santa Cruz, and a master's degree in foreign affairs from the Fletcher School of Law and Diplomacy.

David Masci specializes in social policy, religion, and foreign affairs. Before joining *The CQ Researcher* as a staff writer in 1996, he was a reporter at CQ's *Daily Monitor* and *CQ Weekly*. He holds a bachelor of arts in medieval history from Syracuse University and a law degree from George Washington University.

1

North Korean Crisis

Mary H. Cooper

President Bush looks through bulletproof glass across the demilitarized zone into North Korea during a visit to South Korea in February 2002. Bush has condemned the North for abusing its people and trying to build nuclear weapons. But North Korean leader Kim Jong Il says Bush's statements and policy changes amount to a policy of aggression.

AFP Photo/Luke Frazza

From *The CQ Researcher*,
April 11, 2003.

The bombs dropping in Iraq this week are real. But Pentagon planners also worry about the fictional scenario known as Operation Plan 5027:

Along the heavily guarded demilitarized zone (DMZ) between North and South Korea, deadly chemicals released by a barrage of North Korean artillery shells doom 630 South Korean and American soldiers to a grisly death. Other rounds pound South Korea's capital, Seoul, 30 miles to the south. Then tanks — carrying North Korean soldiers clad in chemical-protection gear — roll into Seoul.

The invasion would be over within hours — but the victory short-lived. Superior U.S. and South Korean firepower would drive the invaders back across the DMZ in a day or two. But an estimated 1 million people, mostly civilians in Seoul, would be killed.

While American troops in Iraq move into Baghdad, the Pentagon's nightmare scenario for the Korean Peninsula may be inching closer to reality. And because North Korea may already possess at least one nuclear weapon, in the event of war it likely would prove a more dangerous adversary than Iraq.

"The situation in Korea is infinitely more serious than in Iraq right now," says Kurt Campbell, program director for international security at the Center for Strategic and International Studies (CSIS). "It is probably one of the most serious foreign-policy crises that the United States has faced in a decade."

The Korean crisis has been building since March 2001, when President Bush repudiated the policy of engagement toward North Korea crafted by his predecessor, Bill Clinton. Under the Agreed Framework signed by Clinton and North Korean leader Kim Jong Il in 1994, the North agreed to freeze its program to develop nuclear weapons in exchange for vitally needed fuel and food and construction of two nuclear power plants. Clinton's policy of engagement, coupled with South Korea's "sunshine policy" of gradual reconciliation with the North, eased the tensions that had gripped the peninsula since the Korean War ended in 1953. [1]

At about the same time the negotiations were being completed, however, U.S. intelligence agencies began receiving new evidence that North Korea had developed one, perhaps two, nuclear bombs in violation of its commitments under both the Framework and the 1985 Nuclear Non-Proliferation Treaty (NPT). Clinton decided to rely on diplomacy to convince the North to abandon its nuclear ambitions, a position Bush has emphatically rejected.

"The Bush administration thought the Clinton approach to North Korea was servile," says Selig S. Harrison, chairman of a group of Korea experts who recommend changes to current U.S. North Korea policy and director of the Asia program at the Center for International Policy. [2] "It didn't reflect the fact that we're the boss. The whole idea of the agreement was repugnant to the Bush administration."

"We have no illusions about this regime," said Secretary of State Colin L. Powell. "We have no illusions about the nature of the gentleman who runs North Korea. He is a despot, but he is also sitting on a failed society that has to somehow begin opening if it is not to collapse." [3] Powell added that the administration was extremely concerned about North Korea's "efforts toward development of weapons of mass destruction and the proliferation of such weapons and missiles and other materials to other nations, not only in the region but around the world."

The North s Focus on Nuclear Weapons

Facilities to research, develop and produce nuclear fuels and weapons are thought to be scattered throughout North Korea, including several in Pyongyang, the capital. After decades of mismanagement, North Korea relies heavily on international food aid while spending needed capital maintaining its large army and developing long-range missiles and nuclear, chemical and biological weapons. Last December, North Korea expelled U.N. monitors and repudiated a 1994 agreement that shut down its nuclear reactors, intensifying fears it would produce nuclear weapons.

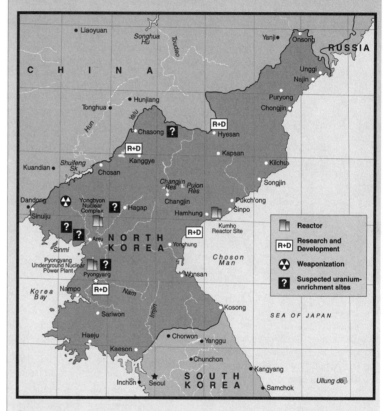

Sources: CIA, *The World Factbook 2002*; Center for Non-Proliferation Studies

Because of North Korea's apparent violation of the '94 agreement, both the Clinton and Bush administrations delayed construction of the two promised power plants to pressure the government to allow inspections of its nuclear facilities. As of early 2003, the plants were far from completion. [4]

Bush's condemnation of North Korea — officially known as the Democratic People's Republic of Korea

North Korea at a Glance

North Korea, one of the world's most highly controlled and isolated economies, faces desperate conditions. Industrial capital stock is nearly beyond repair, and industrial and power output have declined. Despite a good harvest in 2001, the nation faces its ninth year of food shortages. Massive international food aid since 1995-96 staved off mass starvation, but the population remains vulnerable to prolonged malnutrition. The regime recently has emphasized earning hard currency, developing information technology, addressing power shortages and attracting foreign aid, but without undergoing widespread market-oriented reforms. Last year, heightened political tensions with key donor countries and general donor fatigue reduced desperately needed food aid.

Area: 47,386 sq. mi., slightly smaller than Mississippi.

Geography: Strategic location bordering China, South Korea and Russia; the mountainous interior is isolated, sparsely populated.

Natural resources: coal, lead, tungsten, zinc, graphite, magnesite, iron ore, copper, gold, pyrites, salt, fluorspar, hydropower.

Population: 22.2 million (July 2002 est.)

Life expectancy: 71.3 years

Religion: traditionally Buddhist and Confucianist, some Christian and Chondogyo (Religion of the Heavenly Way)

Government: authoritarian socialist; Kim Jong Il has ruled since his father and the country's founder, Kim Il Sung, died in 1994.

Capital: Pyongyang; population, 2.5 million (2002 est.)

GDP: $22 billion; growth rate, 1%; per capita, $1,000 (2002 estimates).

Labor force: 9.6 million; agricultural 36%, non-agricultural 64%

Industries: military products, machine building, electric power, chemicals, mining, metallurgy, textiles, food processing, tourism.

Agriculture: rice, corn, potatoes, soybeans, pulse, cattle, pigs, eggs.

Exports: $826 million (2001 est.); minerals, metallurgical products, manufactures (including armaments), textiles, fishery products; main partners: Japan 36.3%, South Korea 21.5%, China 5.2% (2000)

Imports: $1.8 billion (2001 est.); petroleum, coking coal, machinery and equipment, textiles, grain; main partners: China 26.7%, South Korea 16.2%, Japan 12.3% (2000).

Source: CIA, *The World Factbook 2002*

(DPRK) — intensified after the Sept. 11, 2001, terrorist attacks in the United States. In his January 2002 State of the Union address, the president branded North Korea, Iraq and Iran as an "axis of evil" bent on obtaining weapons of mass destruction to use against the United States and its allies.

Moreover, two key Pentagon documents issued last year specifically linked North Korea to contingencies that might call for pre-emptive military action, possibly including the use of nuclear weapons. [5]

Then last summer, when *The Washington Post's* Bob Woodward interviewed Bush, he reported that the president nearly jumped out of his chair when asked about Kim. "I loathe Kim Jong Il!" Bush shouted. "I've got a visceral reaction to this guy because he is starving his people. And I have seen intelligence on these prison camps — they're huge — that he uses to break up families and to torture people. . . . Maybe it's my religion," said Bush, who often invokes his Christian faith, "but I feel passionate about this." [6]

In response to Bush's policy changes, North Korea accused the United States of reneging on its 1994 commitment to build the two nuclear plants — desperately needed to power the country's collapsing industries and farms — and declared that Bush's policies and statements amounted to a threat of aggression.

"A dangerous situation where our nation's sovereignty and our state's security are being seriously violated is prevailing on the Korean Peninsula due to the U.S. vicious, hostile policy towards the DPRK," the government said on Jan. 10. "After the appearance of the Bush

North Korean soldiers march in Pyongyang on March 26, 2002. After World War II, North Korea poured its resources into creating a million-man army equipped with some 11,000 artillery pieces. Now leader Kim Jong Il is thought to be developing nuclear weapons.

made Scud missiles on a Yemen-bound North Korean freighter. In February, North Korea reactivated its 5-megawat reactor at Yongbyon, which can produce enough plutonium to produce up to six nuclear weapons. (*See story, p. 12.*) On March 1, four North Korean fighter jets shadowed a U.S. spy plane in international airspace off North Korea's coast, the first such incident since 1969. Later that month, North Korea launched two cruise missiles into the Sea of Japan — an act that Pyongyang has frequently employed to express its displeasure with policies of the U.S. or its allies in the region.

Today, Washington and Pyongyang are at an apparent stalemate. North Korea wants the United States to resume food and energy assistance, promise not to invade and participate in bilateral negotiations, which the Bush administration rejects as caving in to "nuclear blackmail" and "rewarding bad behavior." Washington says North Korea must first shut down its nuclear-weapons program and insists on including South Korea and the other regional powers — China, Japan and Russia — in any talks.

The war with Iraq has further complicated the policy dilemma. North Korea declared on March 21 that the U.S.-led operation to topple Saddam Hussein would have "disastrous" consequences and accused the United States of pushing the Korean crisis toward an "explosive phase." Moreover, many analysts believe that while the world is watching Iraq, North Korea will restart its Yongbyon plutonium-reprocessing plant. [8]

"We should be prepared for North Korea to try to take advantage of our distraction in Iraq," says Michael Levi, director of the Federation of American Scientists' Strategy Security Project. "I don't know exactly what they would do, perhaps restart their reprocessing plant. But certainly they'd like to be getting more attention."

For the moment, the U.S. is standing firm. "The administration has decided that we shouldn't be cowed into submission or forced into dialogue, and that we should actually stand them down," says Victor D. Cha, an associate professor at Georgetown University's School of Foreign Service and an administration adviser on Korea. "If that fails, then we're looking at isolation and containment. And if that fails, or if the North is found to be exporting weapons of mass destruction, then I think a military option will get talked about a lot more."

Indeed, says Michael A. McDevitt, director of the Center for Strategic Studies at the Center for Naval

administration, the United States listed the DPRK as part of an 'axis of evil,' adopting it as a national policy to oppose its system, and singled it out as a target of pre-emptive nuclear attack, openly declaring a nuclear war." [7]

Many analysts say North Korea's fear of U.S. aggression is genuine. "From the North Korean point of view, the United States would like to bring about the downfall of their government as a totalitarian regime that we don't like," Harrison says. "They also think the [new] national security doctrine legitimizing the idea of a pre-emptive military strike against any country we think might be a threat was definitely targeted toward them."

Tensions had escalated even more last October, when State Department officials traveled to Pyongyang, the capital, to present evidence that North Korea had a secret program to enrich uranium that could be used for nuclear weapons. North Korea acknowledged the U.S. claim that it had a uranium-enrichment program, though it denied it was for making nuclear weapons. However, it subsequently announced it was pulling out of the NPT and expelled International Atomic Energy Agency (IAEA) monitors from its plutonium-reprocessing facility at Yongbyon. The U.S. and its allies promptly stopped fuel oil shipments to North Korea.

Relations quickly deteriorated further. In December a U.S. Navy ship temporarily seized 15 North Korean-

AFP Photo/Goh Chai Hin

Analyses, "The beginning of wisdom in dealing with North Korea is the realization that there are no good choices — only bad and less-bad choices. You don't want to reward bad behavior, and clearly North Korea has been doing really dumb, bad things.

"So the options you face are either rewarding bad behavior by going into negotiations or refusing to negotiate, which allows North Korea to control the process, continue doing bad things and escalate tensions."

As the political stalemate drags on, these are some of the questions being asked:

Does North Korea's nuclear program pose an immediate threat to the United States?

The North Korean government admitted last fall that it has conducted a clandestine program to develop nuclear weapons, in violation of both its 1994 Agreed Framework with the United States and the NPT, which it signed in 1985. Analysts now suggest it may be on the verge of producing nuclear weapons from either enriched uranium or reprocessed plutonium, or both.

Even if the regime halted its weapons programs tomorrow, U.S. intelligence suggests it already has enough fissile material for at least one nuclear bomb. "North Korea probably has one or two nuclear weapons," says Levi of the Federation of American Scientists. "That's the most obvious danger."

South Korea and Japan also think North Korea has nuclear weapons. And recent reports suggest the Bush administration has quietly acknowledged that reality and shifted its efforts from blocking North Korea's development of nuclear weapons to stopping it from exporting them. [9]

It is uncertain how soon Pyongyang could add to its nuclear arsenal. The Yongbyon reactor, deactivated under the 1994 agreement, could be restarted quickly and used to reprocess the plutonium contained in some 8,000 spent fuel rods stored at the site. "The plutonium reprocessing is probably much closer to realization than the uranium-enrichment program," Levi says. "They would simply take material that had been generated by operating the nuclear reactor over a decade ago and in six months convert it into as many as six nuclear bombs."

Uranium enrichment is a more complex process, but easier to hide from spy-satellite cameras. Analysts believe several enrichment labs may be hidden around the country, including underground facilities. But North Korea would be unable to produce uranium-based weapons for at least another year, most experts say.

But James A. Kelly, assistant secretary of State for East Asian and Pacific affairs, recently told the Senate Foreign Relations Committee the enriched-uranium issue is not "somewhere off in the fog of the distant future." Rather, he said, "it is only probably a matter of months, and not years, behind the plutonium." [10]

Further fueling America's anxiety, CIA Director George J. Tenet told a congressional panel last month that North Korea's Taepodong-2 ballistic missile — which could carry a nuclear warhead — is capable of reaching the Western United States. [11] However, the missile has never been tested — casting doubt on its ability to actually reach such a distant target.

Some experts downplay Pyongyang's nuclear threat. Using nukes to drive the Americans out of South Korea would be suicidal, they point out, because a large portion of the peninsula would be destroyed or contaminated with deadly radioactive fallout. It also would invite U.S. retaliation in kind.

"If they wanted to damage the South, they could do it with artillery," says Georgetown's Cha, noting North Korea has about 11,000 missiles.

Alternatively, North Korea could attack the United States and its allies indirectly by providing the weapons to terrorist organizations like al Qaeda. "With the six or seven nuclear weapons it could have in a year or so, North Korea could carry out a test explosion, target South Korea and Japan, hold a few bombs in reserve and even sell plutonium to eager buyers," wrote Robert J. Einhorn, a senior CSIS adviser who served as assistant secretary of State for non-proliferation in the Clinton administration. "Within several more years, it could be producing large quantities of fissile material from its uranium-enrichment plant and three plutonium reactors." [12]

But other experts discount the threat. "In the short run, you don't have to worry about North Korea selling off its nuclear material," says David Albright, president of the Institute for Science and International Security, a Washington think tank. "Because it is extremely worried about being attacked by the United States, I find it very difficult to believe North Korea would sell any of its precious plutonium to a terrorist group." Albright estimates that Pyongyang could develop no more than five to eight nuclear weapons by the end of this summer. "That's not very many if you're facing an invasion by the United States."

The State of Nuclear Proliferation, 2001

The 1968 Non-Proliferation Treaty restricts Nuclear-Weapon States status to nations that "manufactured and exploded a nuclear weapon or other nuclear explosive device prior 1 January 1967." The CIA estimates that North Korea has diverted enough plutonium to develop one or two nuclear weapons.

Recognized Nuclear-Weapon States (NWS)	No. of strategic warheads	Unrecognized Nuclear-Weapon States	Estimated no. of warheads	States of Immediate Proliferation Concern	Recent Adherents to the Non-Proliferation Treaty
China	300	India	45-95	Iran	Algeria, Argentina,
France	Less than 500	Israel	75-125	Iraq	Belarus, Brazil,
Russia	6,094 deployed	Pakistan	30-50	Libya	Kazakhstan, South
United Kingdom	Less than 200			North Korea	Africa, Ukraine
United States	7,295 deployed				

Source: Arms Control Association, March 12, 2003, www.armscontrol.org

Nonetheless, many experts say it would be foolhardy to dismiss the hostile statements coming out of Pyongyang today as groundless bluster. "North Korea has been systematically shedding any inhibitions about building nuclear weapons," says McDevitt of the Center for Strategic Studies. "They've walked away from the Agreed Framework, they've told the IAEA inspectors to get out of Yongbyon and they've said they were leaving the NPT. Now there's a big question as to whether we can get them out of the [nuclear] game."

Indeed, some longtime observers say it may already be too late. "This is not just a bluff," says Donald P. Gregg, president of the Korea Society and a former U.S. ambassador to South Korea. "The Bush administration says it will not allow North Korea to become a nuclear power. Now that they've announced that they're going to become one, the question [for Washington] becomes: 'What are you going to do about it?'"

Should the United States hold bilateral talks with North Korea?

Since Pyongyang acknowledged its uranium-enrichment program last October, it has called on the United States to sign a non-aggression treaty promising not to attack North Korea and to enter into direct, bilateral negotiations to resolve tensions between the two nations. The Bush administration has emphatically rejected the proposal, especially in light of steps taken by North Korea to accelerate its weapons program.

"Each of these North Korean provocations is designed to blackmail the United States and to intimidate our friends and allies into pushing the United States into a dialogue with the North — giving the North what it wants, and on its terms," said Assistant Secretary of State Kelly. "We tried the bilateral approach 10 years ago, by negotiating the Agreed Framework. . . . And we found the North could not be trusted. This time, a new and more comprehensive approach is required." [13]

The Bush approach to negotiations with North Korea would include South Korea and Japan — the United States' principal allies in Northeast Asia — as well as China and Russia, both of which have historic ties to North Korea and are eager to remain the region's only two nuclear powers. (*See sidebar, p. 8.*)

Many experts outside the administration fault Bush for ignoring North Korea's call to the negotiating table. "The administration has made a mistake by equating diplomacy with appeasement," says Campbell of CSIS. "Diplomacy was invented to deal with unpleasant people and circumstances, the very situation we're facing in North Korea. Among all the bad options on the Korean Peninsula — including war, serious proliferation problems and the prospect of triggering regionwide insecurity — diplomacy is really the only way to go."

Campbell does not dismiss the administration's goal of multilateral dialogue, but he says bilateral talks are a necessary first step. "Direct, bilateral negotiation is the way forward toward progress on multilateral talks," he says. "Direct talks are essential to bringing our allies together for potentially more serious options if things go poorly in those negotiations."

Some experts say bilateral talks could not only resolve the nuclear crisis but also pave the way for more sweeping changes on the peninsula. "If we can get this nuclear issue behind us and normalize relations with North Korea, maybe they'll begin to open up," says McDevitt. "Maybe they'll begin to change their economy, as the Chinese did. Maybe things will turn out so well we can get to a state of peaceful coexistence between the two Koreas."

Continuing to reject Pyongyang's call for bilateral talks and a non-aggression treaty could backfire on the administration, some experts say. "It's quite clear to me that if we do not talk directly to them and answer their security concerns, North Korea will at some time this year announce that it is going to build nuclear weapons," says former Ambassador Gregg. "I am told that there is still a window of time, but that that window is not going to stay open too much longer."

With its hands full in Iraq, however, the Bush administration is showing little inclination to shift its hard-line stance. "There is zero support for a proactive engagement of North Korea," says L. Gordon Flake, executive director of the Mansfield Center for Pacific Affairs, which promotes cooperation between the United States and Asia. "There are some who are willing to deal with the North Koreans if they unilaterally capitulate on their nuclear program. But no one in the administration thinks that we should approach the North Koreans with a plan, that we should try to engage them — no one in this administration, period."

Supporters of the administration's position say acceding to Pyongyang's demands for both a non-aggression treaty and bilateral talks would severely limit Washington's hand. "People who say we must negotiate with the North Koreans also say we have to renounce the use of force and the threat of sanctions," says administration adviser Cha. "That's a very difficult position to negotiate from."

The supporters also contend that accepting bilateral talks would relieve South Korea, Japan, China and Russia — who don't want North Korea to become a nuclear power — from taking responsibility for the outcome. "If this were something that didn't directly affect the security interests of all the countries in the region, then you might be able to say that it's alright to leave the United States to deal with it alone," Cha says. "There are some countries that would like the problem to just go away and free-ride off the United States. But these are all grown-up countries now, and the administration is on the right track by pushing the multilateral effort and trying to get other countries on board."

Should the United States consider military action to halt North Korea's nuclear program?

For many months after citing the Pyongyang regime as part of an "axis of evil" bent on destroying the United States, President Bush took pains to reassure North Korea the United States had no plans to attack. But the president recently has hardened his stance toward North Korea.

"I still believe this [crisis] will be solved diplomatically," Bush said in February. But for the first time, he also hinted at the possibility of further action if diplomacy fails. "All options are on the table, of course," he added. Underlining the president's statement, White House spokesman Ari Fleischer said the United States has "robust plans for any contingencies" involving North Korea, including the use of force. [14]

Concerned that Kim might try to take advantage of the diversion of U.S. forces to the Middle East, the Pentagon in early March deployed 24 long-range bombers to Guam, within striking distance of North Korea. While still hoping to halt North Korea's nuclear program through diplomatic efforts, the president said, "If they don't work diplomatically, they'll have to work militarily." [15]

Likely military scenarios include a "surgical" strike at the Yongbyon reactor. But even if it destroyed the facility, critics say it probably would not end Pyongyang's nuclear capability. "Even if there were only one plutonium-reprocessing program, North Korea could reconstitute the program in a matter of years," says Levi of the Federation of American Scientists. "There isn't a military option that provides the same comprehensive solution that diplomacy might."

Moreover, Levi adds, taking out Yongbyon would not affect what experts say is North Korea's highly secret uranium-enrichment program, which may include numerous underground locations. "It's very hard for us to verify how far along they are because we don't know where the uranium facilities are," Levi says. "That means there is no military option short of regime change that will completely remove the North Korean nuclear threat."

Global Nuclear-Weapons Stockpiles

The 1968 Nuclear Non-Proliferation Treaty (NPT) recognizes the five permanent members of the U.N. Security Council — the U.S., Russia, France, United Kingdom and China — as Nuclear-Weapon States, or countries that had "exploded a nuclear weapon" before Jan. 1, 1967.

The treaty designated the International Atomic Energy Agency (IAEA) as the monitoring agency. Countries that signed the NPT agreed to refrain from producing or stockpiling nuclear weapons. [1]

The NPT, which now has 187 signatories, has the broadest support of any arms-control treaty. Only four countries — Cuba, India, Israel and Pakistan — have not signed the pact. Of these, only Cuba has not actively developed a nuclear capability.

But the near-unanimous global support for the NPT in principle has not removed the threat of nuclear proliferation. According to the Nuclear Threat Initiative, a nonprofit organization founded by media mogul Ted Turner and former Sen. Sam Nunn, D-Ga., "More than a decade after the end of the Cold War, there are still some 30,000 strategic and tactical nuclear weapons in the world (mainly in U.S. and Russian arsenals). "The world's stockpiles of separated plutonium and highly enriched uranium (HEU) are estimated to total some 450 metric tons of military and civilian separated plutonium, and some 1,600 tons of HEU — enough to make nearly a quarter-million nuclear weapons." [2]

India, Israel and Pakistan are believed to possess finished nuclear weapons or components that could be rapidly assembled. In 1998, India and Pakistan — engaged in a longstanding border dispute — acknowledged their nuclear status. Israel, the only other unrecognized nuclear state, began developing its nuclear capability in the 1950s with French assistance. The United States has refrained from pressing its chief Middle Eastern ally to end its nuclear program, and Israel has never acknowledged its arsenal, estimated at 75 to 125 warheads.

North Korea, along with Iraq, Iran and Libya, are "states of immediate proliferation concern" — believed to be seeking a nuclear capability in violation of the NPT. In 1993, North Korea announced that it would withdraw from the treaty, but rescinded that decision after signing the 1994 Agreed Framework with the United States, promising to freeze its nuclear program in exchange for food and fuel assistance.

However, citing its right to self-defense after the Bush administration's condemnation of North Korea as part of

---

[1] Unless otherwise noted, information in this section is based on Arms Control Association, "The State of Nuclear Proliferation, 2001," www.armscontrol.org. For background, see Mary H. Cooper, "Non-Proliferation Treaty at 25," *The CQ Researcher*, Jan. 27, 1995, pp. 73-96.

[2] Nuclear Threat Initiative, "Controlling Nuclear Warheads and Materials: The Global Threat and Urgent Steps to Address It," www.nti.org.

Critics of the military option say that despite its much-vaunted ability to fight two wars simultaneously, the United States may not be up to the task as long as the fighting continues in Iraq. "In foreign affairs, Washington is chronically unable to deal with more than one crisis at a time," wrote former Secretary of State Warren Christopher nearly three months before the invasion of Iraq. "While Defense Secretary Donald H. Rumsfeld may be right in saying that our military can fight two wars at the same time, my experience tells me that we cannot mount a war against Iraq and still maintain the necessary policy focus on North Korea and international terrorism." [16]

In any event, North Korea repeatedly has warned that an attack on its nuclear facilities would trigger all-out war, the consequences of which would be catastrophic, even if Pyongyang did not use a nuclear bomb, military experts warn.

North Korea has more than 8,000 artillery pieces deployed along the DMZ as well as 70 percent of its 1.2 million troops. "Military pre-emption has an incredibly high risk of starting another Korean war," says McDevitt, of the Center for Strategic Studies. "Unlike other areas of the world, the geography of the Korean Peninsula is such that North Korea could lash out immediately and cause a lot of death and damage in the South. It would not be hard to destroy that reprocessing plant militarily. It's the consequences that you have to be able to deal with."

an "axis of evil," North Korea in 2002 again announced it was withdrawing from the NPT. The United States estimates that North Korea has enough fissile material to make one or two nuclear bombs.

Iraq was trying to develop nuclear weapons when Israeli air strikes destroyed its French-supplied reactor in 1981. Iraq was ordered to disarm after the 1991 Gulf War, but shortly after the war IAEA inspectors discovered a large, secret nuclear-weapons program in violation of the NPT. By 1998, when Iraqi leader Saddam Hussein expelled the inspectors, the IAEA had concluded that Iraq was no longer able to produce nuclear weapons. During their recent return to Iraq, halted before the March 19 U.S.-led invasion, weapons inspectors failed to turn up fresh evidence of Iraqi non-compliance with the NPT, despite U.S. and British allegations that Iraq was seeking nuclear weapons.

The United States believes that Iran, which shares a border and longstanding animosity with Iraq, is also secretly pursuing a nuclear-weapons program, although the IAEA still considers it in compliance with the NPT. Since the mid-1990s, Russia has assisted Iran in building nuclear-power plants, but acceded to U.S. demands not to sell the Iranians uranium-enrichment technology that could be used to build weapons.

Russia also has begun discussions to help Libya modernize its nuclear reactor. The United States suspects that Libya is trying to build nuclear weapons. On a positive note, seven countries have forsaken nuclear weapons over the past decade. Belarus, Kazakhstan and Ukraine, which inherited weapons stockpiles from the Soviet Union when it collapsed in 1991, have returned the nuclear weapons to Russia and joined the NPT as independent countries. South Africa, which developed six nuclear bombs in the 1980s, dismantled its arsenal and declared itself nuclear-free in 1994. After the discovery of its nascent program in 1991, Algeria renounced nuclear weapons and acceded to the NPT in 1995. Argentina and Brazil ended their programs and signed the NPT in the late 1990s.

But there is lingering concern about the potential theft of poorly guarded nuclear weapons and fissile material in the former Soviet Union. Since 1992, the United States has spent some $4.1 billion to secure nuclear weapons and material stored there. Much of the money has gone to the Defense Department's Cooperative Threat Reduction program, created by legislation sponsored by Nunn and Senate Foreign Relations Chairman Richard G. Lugar, R-Ind.

But House Republicans, claiming the program has failed to gain sufficient Russian support, have blocked a Bush administration request to expand the program and spend up to $50 million in fiscal 2003 and 2004 to secure weapons of mass destruction materials outside the former Soviet Union, including in Iraq. [3]

Concern about nuclear proliferation has mounted since the Sept. 11, 2001, terrorist attacks. "We are in a new arms race between terrorist efforts to acquire nuclear, biological and chemical weapons and our efforts to stop them," said Nunn. [4]

---

[3] See David Ruppe, "U.S. Response: House Rejects Bush Cooperative Threat Reduction Request," *Global Security Newswire*, April 2, 2003.

[4] Nunn addressed the World Affairs Council in Washington, D.C., Oct. 22, 2002.

BACKGROUND

Korea's Roots

North Korea emerged from the ashes of World War II in 1945 to become one of the most enduring vestiges of the Cold War. But the culture and political ideology of the communist state are unique, owing as much to the Korean Peninsula's troubled history as to Cold War rivalry. Indeed, the authoritarian, paternalistic, isolationist and highly militaristic regime that rules North Korea today has its roots in Korea's troubled dealings over the millennia with its powerful neighbors — China, Russia and Japan. [17]

For many years, Korea managed to ward off Western encroachment, which began in earnest with U.S. Navy Commodore Matthew C. Perry's opening of Japan to foreign trade in the mid-19th century. Indeed, Americans' first attempt to penetrate Korea's isolation ended badly. In 1866, when the U.S.S. General Sherman steamed up the Taedong River to the outskirts of Pyongyang, local inhabitants burned the ship and killed all its crew. North Korea's late leader, Kim Il Sung, claimed that his great-grandfather participated in that attack, now celebrated as a heroic victory against foreign invaders.

Korea's isolation was short-lived. Japan annexed the peninsula in 1910 and turned it into a colony whose nat-

CHRONOLOGY

1940s-1980s *Korean War ends in a stalemate, and a tense standoff on the Korean Peninsula ensues.*

Aug. 11, 1945 As World War II draws to a close, U.S. officials decide to divide Korea into Soviet and U.S. zones, separated along the 38th parallel. In September, 25,000 American soldiers occupy southern Korea.

May 1948 U.N.-supervised elections result in the creation of the Republic of Korea (South Korea).

Sept. 9, 1949 The People's Democratic Republic of Korea — North Korea — is established with guerrilla leader and Korean Workers' Party head Kim Il Sung as its leader.

June 1950 North Korean forces invade South Korea. Although U.S.-led United Nations forces repel the invasion, hostilities continue until July 27, 1953, when the two sides sign an armistice.

1965 Soviet engineers help build North Korea's nuclear reactor at Yongbyon.

1984 North Korea tests missiles based on Soviet Scud technology.

1985 North Korea signs the 1968 Nuclear Non-Proliferation Treaty (NPT).

1990s *The United States and South Korea try to ease tensions on the Korean Peninsula through a policy of engagement with North Korea.*

March 12, 1993 As one of his last major acts before handing over the country to his son, Kim Jong Il, Kim Il Sung announces his intention to withdraw from the NPT.

Oct. 21, 1994 The United States and North Korea sign an Agreed Framework in which Pyongyang promises to adhere to the NPT and freeze its nuclear-weapons program in exchange for food and energy assistance.

1998 North Korea test-fires a longer-range Taepodong-1 missile over Japan.

2000s *The Bush administration shifts U.S. policy toward North Korea.*

October 2000 During the Clinton administration's waning days, Secretary of State Madeleine K. Albright makes a historic visit to North Korea but fails to reach an agreement that would halt North Korea's exports of missile technology to Pakistan and other countries. North Korea's second in command, Vice-Marshal Jo Myong Rok, visits Washington and signs a joint non-aggression pact. North Korea agrees to a moratorium on long-range missile tests and continues the freeze at Yongbyon.

March 2001 President Bush repudiates the Agreed Framework and Clinton's engagement policy toward Pyongyang.

Sept. 11, 2001 Members of the al Qaeda terrorist organization kill some 3,000 Americans in New York City, the Pentagon and rural Pennsylvania.

January 2002 In his State of the Union address, Bush lumps North Korea with Iraq and Iran as an "axis of evil" bent on obtaining weapons of mass destruction to use against the United States and its allies or provide to anti-American terrorists.

October 2002 A U.S. State Department delegation to Pyongyang confronts North Korea with evidence that the regime has started a uranium-enrichment program in violation of the 1994 agreement. North Korea acknowledges the program and says it will withdraw from the NPT.

Feb. 7, 2003 Bush for the first time suggests that the United States may consider the use of military force to halt North Korea's nuclear program.

March 1, 2003 Four North Korean fighter jets shadow a U.S. spy plane in international airspace off the North Korean coast. North Korea launches two cruise missiles into the Sea of Japan.

March 12, 2003 Central Intelligence Agency Director George J. Tenet tells a congressional committee that North Korea possesses the missile technology to reach the Western United States.

March 19, 2003 The United States leads an invasion of Iraq to topple its leader, Saddam Hussein. North Korea declares that the U.S.-British operation will have "disastrous" consequences and accuses the United States of pushing the Korean crisis toward an "explosive phase."

ural resources would help build the Japanese war machine. Korea's occupiers industrialized the peninsula, building factories, roads and hydroelectric dams and laying the foundations of later private industrial development in the south and state-controlled industry in the north.

The colonial experience, which ended with Japan's defeat in World War II, left a lasting impression of national humiliation that would feed Korean aspirations for independence.

Korean resentment of its colonial status fueled intermittent protests and insurrections that were brutally suppressed by Japanese administrators. Exiled to China and the Soviet Union, some of the dissidents, including Kim Il Sung, gained military training. After Japan annexed Manchuria in 1931, the rebel leaders returned to the region and led guerrilla actions against the Japanese occupation forces, which had a profound influence on North Korea's military and ideological development. Indeed, Kim and his resistance compatriots would occupy most leadership positions in North Korea for the next 50 years.

Korean War

Even before World War II ended, the United States and its allies began deliberating the future of Korea. At a meeting in Cairo, Egypt, in December 1943, they endorsed President Franklin D. Roosevelt's vague proposition that upon Japan's defeat Korea would become independent "in due course." The Roosevelt administration also reversed traditional American non-involvement in Korean affairs by defining security on the peninsula as important to postwar Pacific — and therefore U.S. — security.

On Aug. 11, 1945, War Department officials, without consulting Korean or Soviet officials, made the fateful decision to divide Korea into Soviet and U.S. zones separated along the 38th parallel. In early September, 25,000 American soldiers occupied southern Korea, ending the hated Japanese occupation of the peninsula. But they immediately faced opposition among Koreans who saw the U.S. presence as a continuation of colonialism and resented the notion that they were not ready for independence. Meanwhile, Soviet forces occupied Korea north of the 38th parallel and brought with them Kim Il Sung and other communist leaders who had left the country during the Japanese occupation.

Soviet leader Josef Stalin had quietly accepted the partition of Korea, but U.S.-Soviet relations quickly chilled. Although Korea was home to one of the oldest communist movements in Asia, the United States saw the emergence of communist leanings in the South in late 1945 as evidence of a Soviet plan to dominate the entire peninsula.

In 1947, President Harry S Truman called for the containment of communism within existing boundaries — the so-called Truman Doctrine. The U.S. won United Nations support for U.N.-supervised elections for all of Korea if the Soviet Union approved the plan. When it didn't, elections were held in the South in May 1948, resulting in the establishment of the Republic of Korea and the ascendance to power of Syngman Rhee, the first of several authoritarian leaders who would rule South Korea for the next three decades. [18]

Kim, meanwhile, had emerged as the leader of the communist movement that consolidated power in the North and established a central government in February 1946. Over the next year, land and industries were nationalized and brought under a system of central planning along the Soviet model. Bolstered by his earlier activities as a nationalist guerrilla, Kim became highly popular, far more than the new leaders in the South, who were regarded by many Koreans as puppets of the American colonial occupiers.

Kim strengthened his hold with the merger of communist parties in 1949 into the Korean Workers' Party, which dominated the new Democratic People's Republic of Korea (DPRK) from its founding on Sept. 9, 1948, three weeks after the Republic of Korea's formation.

In contrast to Soviet-supported regimes in Eastern Europe, Kim's brand of communism was no mere copy of the Soviet model — partly because of Stalin's withdrawal of Soviet forces from Korea in 1948. Kim infused a singularly Korean theme into his communist system through the adoption of *chuch'e* ideology. Defined roughly as keeping foreigners at arm's length, *chuch'e* appealed to the traditional Korean ideals of self-reliance and independence. Kim put his doctrine into action in 1955, when he distanced his regime from the Soviet Union, and throughout his rule by subjecting North Koreans to continual political indoctrination.

In 1949, Kim had himself named *suryng*, an old Korean word for "leader" that was modified to mean "great leader." That year he began condemning South Korea as a puppet state.

Does North Korea Have the Bomb?

The Bush administration and many non-governmental experts say North Korea already has enough fissile material to make two nuclear weapons and may be on the threshold of making many more. But the self-imposed isolation and secretiveness of the regime in Pyongyang make estimates sketchy at best. [1]

North Korea appears to possess the technology to produce nuclear weapons using two different materials — reprocessed plutonium and enriched uranium. Both techniques require the ability to mine and mill uranium.

To make a plutonium-based bomb, milled uranium is processed into reactor fuel and "burned" in a reactor. Plutonium is then extracted from the spent fuel and formed into the core of a fission-implosion weapon. High explosives are used to initiate the fission process that ends with the nuclear explosion.

A uranium-based bomb contains milled uranium that has been enriched to produce a Hiroshima-sized blast or an even more destructive weapon. An advanced uranium-based weapon would include tritium, a radioactive gas that can enhance the bomb's power.

Korea-watchers are most immediately concerned about North Korea's ability to reprocess plutonium from some 8,000 spent nuclear fuel rods stored near the 5-megawatt Yongbyon nuclear reactor. Under the 1994 Agreed Framework with the United States, Pyongyang shut down that reactor in exchange for U.S. food and fuel assistance.

Both sides abandoned the agreement last October, however, after Pyongyang admitted to U.S. State Department officials that it had launched a uranium-enrichment program. The Yongbyon facility, together with a smaller research reactor, could reprocess enough plutonium to build up to 50 bombs a year if North Korea can overcome technical problems at its antiquated plants and bring them both up to full operation. [2]

The status and location of North Korea's uranium-enrichment program are unknown, but experts believe it may be able to produce about 100 kilograms of weapons-grade uranium a year by 2005, at the earliest.

---

[1] Information based on "North Korean Nuclear Capabilities," Nuclear Threat Initiative and Center for Non-Proliferation Studies, www.nti.org.

[2] See Glenn Kessler and Walter Pincus, "N. Korea Stymied on Plutonium Work; Reprocessing Lab Called Antiquated," *Washington Post*, March 20, 2003, p. A24.

Although neither Seoul nor Pyongyang recognized the 38th parallel as a legitimate boundary, historians generally blame the North — and not the South — for the outbreak of the Korean War. Bolstered by some 100,000 war-trained forces and support from China and, to a lesser degree, the Soviet Union, North Korean forces invaded South Korea on June 25, 1950, and took control of all but a small corner of southeastern Korea around the port city of Pusan.

In September, U.N. and South Korean forces led by U.S. Gen. Douglas MacArthur drove out the invaders. The war dragged on for another three years, costing the lives of some 800,000 Koreans on both sides of the parallel, 115,000 Chinese and 37,000 Americans and laying waste to much of the peninsula. An armistice was signed in the summer of 1953 recognizing the de facto division of Korea.

Military Ambitions

The war's conclusion 50 years ago this July 27 came not with a peace treaty but with an armistice that merely suspended the hostilities and separated the two sides at the 38th parallel. To bolster South Korea's military forces, the United States retained a sizable military presence in South Korea, backed by naval forces in the Pacific and, ultimately, its superpower nuclear deterrent. Faced with such a formidable adversary, North Korea poured its resources into creating one of the most militarized societies on Earth — eventually building a million-man army equipped with some 11,000 artillery pieces.

It was not long before the North sought to move beyond its conventional arsenal. As early as 1964, Pyongyang set up a nuclear-energy research complex at Yongbyon, where the Soviets built Korea's first nuclear reactor a year later. A plutonium-reprocessing plant and other support facilities appeared over the next two decades.

Despite signing the NPT in 1985 — which barred signatories without nuclear weapons from developing them — barely two years later Pyongyang began hindering U.N. inspections of its nuclear facilities to ensure compliance with the treaty. The IAEA inspectors did not gain access to North Korean nuclear facilities until May 1992. Amid intelligence reports that North Korea was secretly continuing its nuclear program at clandestine sites, their findings were inconclusive.

Besides pursuing a nuclear capability, North Korea also is believed to have developed biological and chemical weapons beginning in the early 1980s, even though in 1987 it acceded to the 1972 Biological and Toxin Weapons Convention banning pathogens for military uses. But, according to the Washington-based Nuclear Threat Initiative, North Korea produced weapons containing anthrax, botulinum toxin and plague. [19]

The group also estimates that North Korea has 12 chemical-weapons plants producing some 4,500 tons of mustard, phosgene, sarin and other chemicals — and that annual production could reach 12,000 tons in case of war. Unlike the United States, North Korea never signed the 1993 Chemical Weapons Convention, which bans chemical weapons and provides for monitoring compliance, including intrusive inspections and allowances for sanctions and the use of force against violators. In addition, North Korea's thousands of artillery systems can deliver chemical weapons into the DMZ and Seoul. [20]

Since the 1970s, military experts say North Korea has been developing missiles capable of reaching targets beyond the range of conventional artillery. By 1984, it had tested a ballistic missile based on the Soviet Scud technology, and it has since produced several types of missiles, including 100 of the advanced, 800-mile-range Nodong. The even longer-range Taepodong-1 failed during a 1998 test launch, while the newer Taepodong-2, which potentially could reach the U.S. West Coast, is reportedly almost ready for testing.

Although there is no evidence that North Korea has exported its weapons of mass destruction, it has sold its missile technology to several countries, including Egypt, Iran, Libya, Pakistan, Syria and Yemen.

Hardship and Repression

Missile sales are among North Korea's few sources of hard currency. The government maintains a strict policy of self-sufficiency, even in the face of economic collapse since the early 1990s. The Soviet Union's demise and the rejection of the communist model throughout Eastern Europe at the beginning of the decade abruptly halted North Korea's main source of fuel oil and coal to generate electricity, power industrial plants and make fertilizers.

Moreover, a series of droughts and floods destroyed much of its agricultural output. Food shortages began in the early 1990s with the loss of electricity-driven irrigation systems and fertilizers. As the government continued to allocate most food and consumer goods to the military, the shortages produced a nationwide famine that prompted many foreign governments, including the United States, to ship food to North Korea. Up to 3.5 million North Koreans, out of a pre-famine population of some 22 million, are believed to have succumbed to malnutrition and starvation. [21]

North Koreans who try to flee their plight have little hope of success. Most try to wade across the icy Tumen River into China, where an estimated 300,000 North Koreans have quietly settled among the region's ethnic Koreans. Many are abused and exploited. Others are aided by foreign Evangelical Christian missionaries, who help them escape to South Korea via an "underground railroad." [22]

But China, eager to prevent a destabilizing influx of millions of North Koreans, refuses to grant them refugee status. Appeals for asylum in the Japanese consulate in China also go unheeded, with North Korean refugees often dragged from the gates of the consulate. [23]

The vast majority of would-be refugees are arrested and forcibly repatriated to North Korea, where they face imprisonment and sometimes execution. [24]

According to the U.S. State Department's 2002 human rights report, the North Korean government has detained 150,000 to 200,000 political prisoners in prisons and forced-labor or "re-education camps." North Koreans can be detained indefinitely without a trial for "crimes against the revolution," such as speaking with South Koreans, reading foreign literature or practicing Christianity. Defectors and refugees, the report says, tell of extrajudicial killings and "disappearances" and prisoners — including newborn babies — being routinely executed. Others are beaten, sexually assaulted, tortured and used as guinea pigs in experiments using chemical and biological warfare agents, the report says. [25]

Evangelical Christians and missionaries from the United States, South Korea and around the world are par-

North Korean leader Kim Jong Il toasts Secretary of State Madeleine K. Albright during her historic visit to Pyongyang, on Oct. 24, 2000. She failed, however, to convince Kim to stop exporting missile technology to Pakistan and other countries.

ticularly upset about the alleged persecution of Christians in North Korea, which with the South was once a Christian stronghold in Asia. South Koreans claim an estimated 6,000 Christians are imprisoned in the North, although a State Department report on religious freedom says there is "no reliable information" on how many religious prisoners are in North Korea. However, defectors say Christian prisoners are considered insane, and their families are "identified for extermination for three successive generations," according to the report. [26]

Agreed Framework

On March 12, 1993, as one of his last major acts before handing the country over to his son, Kim Il Sung withdrew from the NPT, thus ending North Korea's commitment not to develop nuclear weapons. The announcement sparked concern throughout the region that Pyongyang would join China and Russia to become Northeast Asia's third nuclear power and fuel a regional arms race that might include South Korea and Japan.

After 18 months of bilateral negotiations aimed at ending the crisis, led by former President Jimmy Carter, the United States and North Korea signed the Agreed Framework on Oct. 21, 1994. [27] "This agreement will help achieve a longstanding and vital American objective — an end to the threat of nuclear proliferation on the Korean Peninsula," then-President Clinton said on Oct. 22.

Pyongyang agreed to remain a party to the NPT and freeze the construction and operation of nuclear reactors capable of producing weapons-grade material in exchange for a U.S. promise to provide two nuclear-power reactors to generate electricity. Pending completion of the reactors, considered to be proliferation-resistant, the United States would supply North Korea with heavy fuel oil to meet its energy needs. A new international consortium — the Korean Peninsula Energy Development Organization (KEDO) — was created to implement the agreement.

The agreement committed both sides to remove barriers to full economic and diplomatic relations. To that end, the Clinton administration relaxed longstanding U.S. economic sanctions against North Korea, including the Trading with the Enemy Act and the Defense Production Act — both in place since 1950 — and the 1979 Export Administration Act. The agreement left in place bans on government military assistance and U.S. exports to North Korea of military and "dual-use" items — goods produced for civilian purposes but potentially adaptable to military use. The agreement also committed both countries to keep the Korean Peninsula free of nuclear weapons, including a U.S. promise to "provide formal assurances" not to threaten or attack North Korea with nuclear weapons.

The Agreed Framework identified several specific obligations for both parties. North Korea agreed to freeze operation of its 5-megawatt reactor and plutonium-reprocessing plant at Yongbyon and halt construction of a 50-megawatt reactor at Yongbyon and a 200-megawatt plant at Taechon. Both of the larger reactors would have to be dismantled entirely before the United States would complete the second reactor. North Korea also agreed to "can" all spent fuel from its reactor at Yongbyon, pending its eventual removal from the country, and allow IAEA inspectors complete access to all nuclear facilities.

For its part, the United States agreed to set up KEDO, which it did on March 9, 1995, to provide fuel oil and assistance in implementing the agreement. KEDO, which includes the 15-member European Union and 12 other countries, delegated to Japan and South Korea responsibility for financing and building the two 1,000-megawatt, nuclear-powered reactors at a cost of $4 billion.

After numerous delays, ground was broken at the site in the North Korean coastal city of Kumho in August 2001, and initial construction began a year later. To compensate for the loss of electricity generation caused by the shut-down of North Korea's existing nuclear plants, the agreement committed the United States and its KEDO partners to provide 500,000 metric tons of heavy fuel oil until the new power reactors came on line.

But another crisis had erupted in August 1998, when North Korea test-fired its Taepodong-1 medium-range ballistic missile over Japan. That test, paired with evidence that North Korea was developing a long-range missile that could reach the United States, prompted calls to abandon the Agreed Framework. Clinton established an outside policy review committee, chaired by former Defense Secretary William J. Perry. The committee issued a joint U.S.-South Korean-Japanese statement in May 1999, calling on North Korea to verifiably eliminate its nuclear-weapons and missile programs in return for a U.S. affirmation that it had no "hostile intent" toward North Korea.

The Clinton administration's policy of engagement with North Korea provided the security guarantee that enabled South Korean President Kim Dae Jung to advance his "sunshine policy" of phased reconciliation with North Korea. The first North-South summit meeting, held in Pyongyang on June 13-15, 2000, paved the way for numerous follow-up official contacts, exchanges of letters between family members separated since the Korean War and the return, in 2002, of several Japanese citizens kidnapped decades earlier by North Korea. The two governments agreed to reopen rail and road links across the border and once again allow South Korean tourists to visit scenic Kumgang Mountain, just inside North Korea. North Korea announced plans to establish two special economic zones, similar to those that launched China's trade boom in the late 1970s, at Kaesong and Sinuiju. [28]

In October 2000, as the Clinton administration drew to a close, Secretary of State Madeleine K. Albright made a historic visit to North Korea. She failed, however, to reach an agreement that would halt North Korea's exports of missile technology to Pakistan and other countries.

The same month, North Korea's second in command, Vice-Marshal Jo Myong Rok, visited Washington and signed a joint communiqué in which both countries promised: "Neither government would have hostile intent toward the other." North Korea also agreed to a moratorium on tests of long-range missiles and continued the freeze at Yongbyon. Improving relations between North and South Korea culminated in a now-controver-sial summit meeting between the leaders of the two countries. [29] Finally, in an effort to ease relations with Japan, North Korea returned several Japanese citizens who had been kidnapped several decades earlier.

CURRENT SITUATION

Bush's About-Face

The easing of tensions on the Korean Peninsula was short-lived. In March 2001, two months after his inauguration, Bush stunned South Korean President Kim during a visit to Washington by repudiating his "sunshine policy." Bush's reversal essentially halted further improvements in North-South relations. Bush then repudiated the seven-month-old U.S.-North Korea joint communiqué abjuring hostile intent.

Bush's antipathy toward both the North Korean regime and the Clinton administration's engagement with it mounted after a December 2001 report by the National Intelligence Council. It revealed that U.S. intelligence agencies had concluded in the mid-1990s that North Korea had produced enough fissile material to assemble one, possibly two, nuclear weapons in violation of its NPT commitments. [30]

Several months later, U.S. intelligence agencies discovered that Pakistan, which had joined the nuclear club in the late 1980s, had provided Pyongyang with materials for a highly enriched uranium production facility. In exchange, North Korea helped Pakistan build a version of its Nodong medium-range ballistic missile, which Pakistan test-fired in 1998. The missile could be armed with a nuclear warhead and could reach deep into India, Pakistan's longstanding, nuclear-armed adversary.

In the year following the Sept. 11 terrorist attacks in the United States, the Bush administration issued three major policy statements identifying North Korea as a significant threat to U.S. security that the United States was prepared to address, militarily if necessary.

First, the "Nuclear Posture Review," a long-range planning document submitted to Congress on Dec. 31, 2001, cited North Korea as a potential target of a U.S. nuclear strike. "In setting requirements for nuclear-strike capabilities, distinctions can be made among the contingencies for which the United States must be prepared," the document states. "Current examples of immediate contingencies include an Iraqi attack on Israel or its neighbors, a

AFP Pool Photo/Chien-min Chung

Secretary of State Colin Powell meets with South Korean President Roh Moo Hyun at the presidential Blue House in Seoul, on Feb. 25, 2003, during Powell's efforts to build international support for U.S. efforts to disarm Iraq and North Korea.

North Korean attack on South Korea or a military confrontation over the status of Taiwan. . . . North Korea, Iraq, Iran, Syria and Libya are among the countries that could be involved in immediate, potential or unexpected contingencies. All have longstanding hostility toward the United States and its security partners; North Korea and Iraq in particular have been chronic military concerns. All sponsor or harbor terrorists, and all have active weapons of mass destruction and missile programs." [31]

Second, in his 2002 State of the Union address, Bush identified North Korea, Iraq and Iran as enemies. "States like these, and their terrorist allies, constitute an axis of evil, arming to threaten the peace of the world," Bush said. "By seeking weapons of mass destruction, these regimes pose a grave and growing danger. They could provide these arms to terrorists, giving them the means to match their hatred. They could attack our allies or attempt to blackmail the United States. In any of these cases, the price of indifference would be catastrophic. . . .

I will not stand by, as peril draws closer and closer. The United States of America will not permit the world's most dangerous regimes to threaten us with the world's most destructive weapons." [32]

Finally, in September, Bush's message assumed more concrete form in an updated version of the country's "National Security Strategy," the first to incorporate the policy implications of the Sept. 11 terrorist attacks. For the first time, the doctrine envisioned a first-strike strategy against terrorist organizations and "rogue states," including Iraq and North Korea.

"We must be prepared to stop rogue states and their terrorist clients before they are able to threaten or use weapons of mass destruction against the United States and our allies and friends," the document stated. [33]

Pyongyang's Response

The Bush administration's shift from a policy of engagement to what Cha of Georgetown calls "hawk engagement" has prompted North Korea to respond with a series of belligerent statements and actions. [34] When Assistant Secretary of State Kelly led a delegation to Pyongyang last October to confront the regime with evidence that it had started up a uranium-enrichment program, North Korea readily acknowledged it, abandoned the NPT and expelled the IAEA inspectors monitoring Yongbyon for treaty compliance.

North Korea has cited the Bush administration's policy statements to explain its insistence on a new non-aggression pact and its call for immediate bilateral negotiations to defuse tensions on the peninsula. As Washington demurred, Pyongyang turned up the heat, sending four MIGs to shadow a U.S. spy plane off the North Korean coast and launching two cruise missiles into the Sea of Japan.

The regime's rhetoric has been as provocative as its actions. "The U.S. loudmouthed 'development of nuclear weapons' by the DPRK is nothing but a subterfuge to internationalize its moves to pressure and isolate the DPRK and ignite a new war of aggression against it," the official news agency stated recently. "It is quite senseless and unreasonable for the U.S. to insist that the DPRK poses a 'nuclear threat' to the U.S. . . . The U.S. is well advised to give up its stand to stifle the DPRK and properly approach dialogue and thus fulfill its responsibility as the direct party concerned with the settlement of the nuclear issue on the peninsula." [35]

Should the Bush administration hold bilateral talks with North Korea?

YES
Sen. Richard G. Lugar, R-Ind.
Chairman, Senate Foreign Relations Committee
From a statement before the committee, March 6, 2003

The events of the last several weeks have confirmed and reconfirmed how volatile . . . the situation on the Korean Peninsula has become. The North Korean regime has taken highly provocative actions toward the United States and its neighbors. All of us remain concerned about the potential for miscalculation that could lead to a deadly incident or broader conflict.

North Korea . . . requires immediate attention by the United States, thoughtful analysis about our options and vigorous diplomacy to secure the cooperation and participation of nations in the region. Compared to most nations, our information on North Korean decision-making is scant. The actions of the North Korean regime and the military often stray from a course that we perceive as consistent with rational self-preservation. But we must . . . avoid simplistic explanations of North Korean behavior. . . .

In 1994, the United States and North Korea signed the Agreed Framework — the agreement under which North Korea was to shut down its nuclear facilities in return for shipments of heavy oil and the construction of two light-water nuclear reactors. . . . The Clinton administration had hoped to secure a freeze of North Korea's nuclear program and to prevent it from producing weapons-grade plutonium. It also intended that the Agreed Framework would be the basis for ongoing contacts with Pyongyang. But these goals have not been realized, and circumstances require the United States to develop a new approach.

The Bush administration has been reluctant to agree to a bilateral dialogue with North Korea until the regime satisfies U.S. concerns over its nuclear program. The administration has instead focused on proposals for multilateral talks involving North Korea and other countries. Multilateral diplomacy is a key element to any long-term reduction of tensions on the Korean Peninsula. But it is vital that the United States not dismiss bilateral diplomatic opportunities that could be useful in reversing North Korea's nuclear-weapons program and promoting stability. We must be creative and persistent in addressing an extraordinarily grave threat to national security.

While some American analysts oppose any dialogue with North Korea . . . I do not believe we have the luxury to be this absolute. The risks are too immediate, and the stakes too high. The United States must maintain military preparedness and should not tolerate North Korea's nuclear-weapons programs.

But the mere initiation of a bilateral dialogue, with American authorities concurrently consulting with the South Korean government, does not compromise our national-security interests.

NO
James A. Kelley
Assistant Secretary of State, East Asian and Pacific Affairs

From testimony before the Senate Foreign Relations Committee, March 12, 2003

We tried the bilateral approach 10 years ago, by negotiating the U.S.-[North Korea] Agreed Framework. . . . In 1993 and 1994, and over the past decade . . . we found the North could not be trusted. This time, a new and more comprehensive approach is required. The stakes are simply too high. . . .

To achieve a lasting resolution, this time the international community, particularly North Korea's neighbors, must be involved. While the Agreed Framework succeeded in freezing the North's declared nuclear-weapons program for eight years, it was only a partial solution of limited duration. That is no longer an option.

That is why we are insisting on a multilateral approach, to ensure that the consequences to North Korea of violating its commitments will deny them any benefits. . . . It was easier for North Korea to abrogate its commitments to the United States under the Agreed Framework, thinking it would risk the condemnation of a single country. In fact, the past six months have shown that the international community is united in its desire to see a nuclear weapons-free Korean Peninsula. . . .

If our starting point for a resolution is a multilateral framework, we believe that this time it will not be so easy for North Korea — which seeks not only economic aid but also international recognition — to turn its back on all its neighbors and still expect to receive their much-needed munificence. This would further North Korea's own isolation, with an even more terrible price to be paid by its people, who are already living in abject poverty and face inhumane political and economic conditions.

States cannot undertake this task alone. International institutions, particularly the International Atomic Energy Agency and the U.N. Security Council, will have an equally crucial role to play. Thus . . . we are moving forward with plans for multilateral, rather than bilateral, talks to resolve this issue. But the rubber hits the road when we are faced with violations of those agreements and commitments. Moreover, it is important to underscore that multilateral support for such regimes, as reflected in the [Nuclear Non-Proliferation Treaty], is critical.

We must, in dealing with North Korea, be mindful that other would-be nuclear aspirants are watching. If North Korea gains from its violations, others may conclude that the violation route is cost-free. Deterrence would be undermined, and our non-proliferation efforts — more critical now than ever — would be grossly jeopardized.

Even before the spy plane incident — but after Bush began suggesting that he would consider using military force to halt North Korea's nuclear-weapons program if diplomacy failed — the Pentagon sent two-dozen B-52 and B-1 long-range bombers to the Western Pacific island of Guam. White House officials said the deployment was to discourage North Korea from invading South Korea while the bulk of U.S. forces were fighting in the Iraq war, which began March 19.

"These moves are not aggressive in nature," Pentagon spokesman Lt. Cmdr. Jeff Davis insisted. "Deploying these additional forces is a prudent measure to bolster our defensive posture and as a deterrent." [36]

Policy Debate

As media attention focuses on Iraq, the crisis on the Korean Peninsula has escalated largely out of the public eye. But Korea experts and lawmakers are debating what the United States should do to resolve the crisis before it erupts into hostilities. A year ago, a task force of academics, former ambassadors and government officials began work on policy options. In February they recommended direct negotiations with North Korea aimed at ending Pyongyang's nuclear ambitions and providing more food and fuel for its starving population.

According to Harrison, chairman of the task force, the Bush administration must first drop its insistence on multilateral talks with North Korea and accede to their demand for direct, bilateral negotiations. "We're the ones that North Korea is afraid of," Harrison says. "Their whole policy of pursuing a nuclear-weapons option reflects the fact that they feel they have to deter us from both a possible pre-emptive military strike and pressure to bring down the regime."

The task force also endorsed a joint U.S.-North Korean declaration of non-aggression, which would become permanent upon the dismantlement of North Korea's nuclear-weapons program. "The declaration would also include a pledge to respect North Korea's sovereignty, meaning we won't try to bring about their collapse," Harrison says. "That way we would address their security concerns in the broadest sense."

Only then, he says, would the administration's multilateral approach come into play. "There could be regional security guarantees and economic cooperation that would help North Korea," Harrison continues. "The problem is the Bush administration's attitude.

What they have in mind is the use of multilateral action to pressure North Korea with no incentives — just all sticks and no carrots. So North Korea has no intention of going into such a multilateral gathering unless it has inducements attached to it."

Harrison says Bush's call for multilateralism in dealing with North Korea may fall on deaf allied ears, after the administration eschewed multilateral actions and opinions regarding the U.S. invasion of Iraq, which was widely criticized in the U.N. Security Council. "The Bush administration is not really embracing multilateral cooperation; they're embracing multilateral action under U.S. leadership to confront, isolate and pressure North Korea," Harrison says. "Just as they're trying to enlist the United Nations to do what [the U.S.] wants [in Iraq], they're trying to enlist the countries of the region to do what [America] wants — not as a way of accommodating other countries or taking action that reflects a common position on policy."

Indeed, when Secretary of State Powell visited East Asia to win support for U.S. policy toward North Korea, he failed to gain any pledges from China, Japan or South Korea, which would play key roles in Bush's multilateral approach to the North Korea problem. In South Korea, Powell attended the swearing-in ceremony for newly elected President Roh Moo Hyun. Roh, who had run on a platform stressing rapprochement with North Korea, won handily amid growing anti-American sentiment in South Korea. Although Powell announced the United States would resume shipments of food aid to North Korea, which it had suspended two months earlier in retaliation for Pyongyang's resumption of its nuclear program, Roh said the issue "must be dealt with through dialogue." [37]

Some Korea experts say the key to resolving the Korean crisis is to find a middle road between acceding to North Korea's demands for bilateral talks and Bush's hard-line alternatives. "Don't bomb and don't grovel," says Henry D. Sokolski, executive director of the Nonproliferation Policy Education Center, who was deputy Defense secretary for non-proliferation policy during the administration of President George Bush. "This would be a lot easier if the administration had a unified view on North Korea, but they're still divided pretty seriously between those who want to patch things over and please most of the governments in the region over the short run, and those who essentially are less concerned about them and want to put the North Korean regime out of commission."

In Sokolski's view, the United States could gain regional support for ending Pyongyang's nuclear-weapons program by taking smaller steps, such as helping Japan end North Korea's shipments of illegal methamphetamine to Japan, a trade that reportedly nets the North Korean military some $8 billion a year in hard currency. [38]

"Modest steps such as these could provide U.S. leadership in the region," he says. "We need to start with what the market will bear, which is not bombing. But it also is not accepting a non-aggression pact with North Korea."

OUTLOOK

Iraq War's Impact

Predictions of a North Korean military attack on South Korea to coincide with the U.S.-led invasion of Iraq thus far have proved wrong. Indeed, Pyongyang has been uncharacteristically silent in recent weeks, despite warnings that it would consider U.S.-South Korean military exercises as evidence of plans to invade North Korea. In addition to the 37,000 U.S. troops stationed in South Korea, some 5,000 American soldiers joined South Korean troops in the country's annual war games, which took place without incident from March 4 to April 2.

Pyongyang also stopped short of retaliating against Japan for its planned launch of a spy satellite. Instead of testing another long-range ballistic missile as it did in 1998, North Korea in late March fired a short-range, surface-to-ship missile that landed harmlessly off the North Korean coast.

But experts warn that the lull in hostile actions emanating from Pyongyang may be short-lived. "North Korea has some hard-liners that would make Americans turn white," says Albright, of the Institute for Science and International Security. "It's clear that they're hostile to the United States, and some of them probably would like to start a war right now. This is a very serious situation."

Barring an immediate escalation of tensions by Pyongyang, the war against Iraq makes it likely the Bush administration will continue to ignore North Korea's demands for the time being. But there is little hope that the nuclear crisis on the Korean Peninsula will subside on its own.

"Deferring the problem will not remove the risk of war in Korea," says McDevitt of the Center for Strategic Studies. "Long after the situation in Iraq is settled, the same dilemmas that we face today in thinking about military coercion in Korea will remain. Those dilemmas are not going to change."

Administration critics fear that the war in Iraq will only embolden would-be nuclear powers to hasten their nuclear programs. "Our attention is going to be occupied in Iraq for quite awhile, beyond the military confrontation," says Levi of the Federation of American Scientists.

Levi fears that the Iraq war by itself is sending the wrong message, not only to North Korea but also to other countries that either have or are considering obtaining nuclear weapons. "The administration also now has to worry about Iran, which is on the brink, and it may have to expand the 'axis' [of evil] if Libya makes significant strides in the next couple of years. The lesson of all this to other countries is to get nuclear weapons faster."

The most pessimistic observers fear that the United States may well be facing a war with North Korea. "We have backed ourselves into a polemical position where we cannot and will not back down," says Flake of the Mansfield Center. "We're not going to reward their bad behavior, we're not going to give into blackmail and we're going to continue to increase pressure.

"For their part," he continues, "the North Koreans are hard-wired for paranoia, and there's almost nothing we could do at this point that would cause them to give up their nukes. So, I expect that we're going to see a gradual ratcheting up of the pressure, and eventually someone is going to cross the line. The most likely scenario at this point is a war."

The Bush administration continues to express optimism that the crisis can be resolved diplomatically. "I think we're chipping away at this one, despite some of the criticism that is leveled at us that we won't simply . . . get in the room with the North Koreans," Secretary of State Powell said recently.

"We have a position, they have a position, and we are trying to find a way forward. I think the overall situation has improved . . . in that the tension has been lowered." [39]

NOTES

1. For background, see Kenneth Jost, "Future of Korea," *The CQ Researcher*, May 19, 2000, pp. 425-448.

2. "Turning Point in Korea: New Dangers and New Opportunities for the United States," Task Force on U.S. Korea Policy, February 2003.

3. Powell testified March 8, 2001, before the Senate Foreign Relations Committee.

4. See Phillip C. Saunders, "Confronting Ambiguity: How to Handle North Korea's Nuclear Program," *Arms Control Today*, March 2003, p. 11.

5. For background, see Mary H. Cooper, "New Defense Priorities," *The CQ Researcher*, Sept. 13, 2002, pp. 721-744.

6. Quoted in Richard Wolffe, "Who Is the Bigger Threat?" *Newsweek*, Jan. 13, 2002, p. 20. See also Bob Woodward, *Bush At War* (2002), p. 340.

7. North Korea's statement was published Jan. 10, 2003, by KCNA, the state news agency.

8. Published by KCNA, March 21, 2003. See also "North Korea Delays Inter-Korean Talks, Citing Military Tensions," *The New York Times*, March 23, 2003, p. A47.

9. See Doug Struck and Glenn Kessler, "Foes Giving In to N. Korea's Nuclear Aims," *The Washington Post*, March 5, 2003, p. A1.

10. Kelly testified March 12, 2003, before the Senate Foreign Relations Committee.

11. Tenet testified March 12, 2003, before the Senate Armed Services Committee.

12. Robert J. Einhorn, "Talk Therapy," *The New York Times*, Feb. 12, 2003, p. A37.

13. Kelly testified March 12, 2003, before the Senate Foreign Relations Committee.

14. Bush made his comments Feb. 7, 2003, in response to reporters' questions at the Treasury Department. Fleischer spoke Feb. 6. See "Bush: 'All Options on Table' on N. Korea," The Associated Press, Feb. 8, 2003.

15. Bush spoke with reporters on March 3, 2003. See "N. Korean Jets Stalk U.S. Plane," *Los Angeles Times*, March 4, 2003, p. A1.

16. Warren Christopher, "Iraq Belongs on the Back Burner," *The New York Times*, Dec. 31, 2002, p. A19.

17. Unless otherwise noted, material in this section is based on "North Korea — A Country Study," Library of Congress, June 1993.

18. For more information on Korea's postwar history, see Selig S. Harrison, *Korean Endgame* (2002).

19. "North Korea Overview," *Nuclear Threat Initiative*, January 2003.

20. For background, see Mary H. Cooper, "Chemical and Biological Weapons," *The CQ Researcher*, Jan. 31, 1997, pp. 73-96.

21. Marcus Noland, Sherman Robinson and Tao Wang, "Famine in North Korea: Causes and Cures," Institute for International Economics, 1999.

22. See Valerie Reitman, "Leading His Flock of Refugees to Asylum," *Los Angeles Times*, Oct. 27, 2002, p. A1.

23. James Brooke, "A Human Face on North Koreans' Plight," *The New York Times*, Aug. 15, 2001, p. A6.

24. See Human Rights Watch, "The Invisible Exodus: North Koreans in the People's Republic of China," November 2002.

25. The report can be found at www.state.gov/g/drl/rls/hrrpt/2001/eap/8330.htm.

26. Quoted in Doug Struck, "Keeping the Faith, Underground; N. Korea's Secret Christians Get Support From South," *The Washington Post*, April 10, 2001, p. A1.

27. Information in this section is based on "The U.S.-North Korean Agreed Framework at a Glance," Arms Control Association, January 2003.

28. See Jost, *op. cit.*

29. Howard W. French, "Former Leader Is Caught Up In South Korean Maelstrom," *The New York Times*, April 6, 2003, p. A12.

30. National Intelligence Council, "Foreign Missile Developments and Ballistic Missile Threat Through 2015," December 2001, p. 11. The council provides strategic analyses for the Central Intelligence Agency and other U.S. intelligence agencies.

31. U.S. Defense Department, "Nuclear Posture Review Report," Jan. 8, 2002, p. 16.

32. Bush delivered his State of the Union address on Jan. 29, 2002.

33. The White House, "National Security Strategy of the United States," September 2002, p. 18.

34. Victor D. Cha, "Korea's Place in the Axis," *Foreign Affairs*, May/June 2002, p. 81.

35. Korea News Service (KCNA), March 17, 2003.

36. See David E. Sanger and Thom Shanker, "U.S. Sending 2 Dozen Bombers in Easy Range of North Koreans," *The New York Times*, March 5, 2003, p. A1.

37. See Doug Struck, "Powell Makes Few Gains on Asia Tour," *The Washington Post*, Feb. 26, 2003, p. A16.

38. See Henry Sokolski, "Curbing the North Korean Threat: The U.S. Must Stop Aiding Its Military," *National Review Online*, March 10, 2003.

39. Powell spoke March 29, 2003, during an interview by *The New York Times*, posted on the State Department's Web site, www.state.gov.

BIBLIOGRAPHY

Books

Harrison, Selig S., *Korean Endgame: A Strategy for Reunification and U.S. Disengagement*, Princeton University Press, 2002.
A longtime Korea-watcher, who played a key role in talks leading to the 1994 nuclear freeze accord with North Korea, presents a detailed history of the peninsula and recommends how to forestall the North's nuclear-weapons program.

Noland, Marcus, *Avoiding the Apocalypse: The Future of the Two Koreas*, Institute for International Economics, 2000.
Noland examines three concurrent crises on the Korean Peninsula — the U.S.-North Korean nuclear confrontation, famine in North Korea and the financial crisis in South Korea.

Sokolski, Henry D., *Best of Intentions: America's Campaign Against Strategic Weapons Proliferation*, Praeger Publishers, 2001.
The executive director of the Nonproliferation Policy Education Center presents an exhaustive history of U.S. efforts to halt the spread of strategic weapons since World War II.

Woodward, Bob, *Bush At War*, Simon & Schuster, 2002.
The legendary Washington reporter describes the evolution of President George W. Bush's foreign policy after the Sept. 11, 2001, terrorist attacks in the United States, including his attitudes about North Korea.

Articles

Brooke, James, "A Human Face on North Koreans' Plight," *The New York Times*, Aug. 15, 2001, p. A6.
Brooke documents the hardships and repression suffered by North Koreans who try to flee the country.

Cha, Victor D., "Korea's Place in the Axis," *Foreign Affairs*, May/June 2003, pp. 79-92.
A Georgetown University professor and Bush administration adviser on Korea endorses the current U.S. stance toward North Korea, which he describes as "hawk engagement" to distinguish it from the Clinton administration's more accommodating "engagement" policy.

Garfinkle, Adam, "How to Overthrow Pyongyang — Peacefully," *The New Republic*, Nov. 4, 2002.
The editor of The National Interest writes that concern over North Korea's nuclear-weapons program underscores the justification for invading Iraq to prevent Saddam Hussein from developing a nuclear capability.

Hersh, Seymour M., "The Cold Test," *The New Yorker*, Jan. 27, 2003, pp. 42-47.
The Bush administration's intense focus on overturning the Iraqi regime has undermined U.S. policy toward North Korea, described as "a mixture of anger and seeming complacency."

Hertzberg, Hendrik, "Axis Praxis," *The New Yorker*, Jan. 13, 2003.
President Bush's lumping together of North Korea, Iraq and Iran — three disparate countries — as a homogeneous "axis of evil" has led to what the author calls "a fairly comprehensive botch" of U.S. policy toward these countries, especially North Korea.

Kim, Suki, "A Visit to North Korea," *The New York Review of Books,* **Feb. 13, 2003, pp. 14-18.**
A Korean-American visits North Korea and finds what she describes as an alien culture based primarily on obeisance to the reclusive country's leader, Kim Jong Il.

Saunders, Phillip C., "Confronting Ambiguity: How to Handle North Korea's Nuclear Program," *Arms Control Today,* **March 2003, p. 11.**
Accepting bilateral negotiations with North Korea, rejected by the Bush administration as caving in to nuclear blackmail, would offer political benefits that probably would not result from engaging other regional powers in multilateral talks.

Reports & Studies

Human Rights Watch, "The Invisible Exodus: North Koreans in the People's Republic of China," November 2002.
The independent human rights monitoring group documents extensive mistreatment of North Korean refugees attempting to flee famine in their country, only to be forcibly repatriated by the Chinese government.

Niksch, Larry A., "North Korea's Nuclear Weapons Program," Congressional Research Service, Sept. 21, 2001.
The Library of Congress' research branch reviews North Korea's efforts to develop nuclear weapons and U.S. responses.

Task Force on U.S. Korea Policy, "Turning Point in Korea: New Dangers and New Opportunities for the United States," February 2003.
A group of Korea experts call on the United States to take up North Korea's invitation to start bilateral talks with the aim of formally ending the Korean War, reducing the U.S. military presence in South Korea and dissuading North Korea from pursuing nuclear weapons.

For More Information

Arms Control Association, 1726 M St., N.W., Washington, DC 20036; (202) 463-8270; www.armscontrol.org. A nonpartisan organization dedicated to promoting effective arms control policies.

Center for Strategic and International Studies, 1800 K St., N.W., Suite 400, Washington, DC 20006; (202) 887-0200; www.csis.org. A research organization dedicated to providing insights and policy options on strategic global issues.

Federation of American Scientists, 1717 K St., N.W., Suite 209, Washington, DC 20036; (202) 546-3300; www.fas.org. A research and educational organization that supports global nuclear disarmament.

Institute for Science and International Security, 236 Massachusetts Ave., N.E., Suite 500, Washington, DC 20002; (202) 547-3633; www.isis-online.org. Dedicated to stopping the spread of nuclear weapons.

Korea Society, 950 Third Ave., Eighth Floor, New York, NY 10022; (212) 759-7525; www.koreasociety.org. Promotes better U.S.-Korea relations.

Korean Central News Agency, Democratic People's Republic of Korea; www.kcna.co.jp. North Korea's state-run news agency.

Mansfield Center for Pacific Affairs, 1401 New York Ave., N.W., Suite 740, Washington, DC 20005; (202) 347-1994; www.mcpa.org. Promotes understanding and cooperation between the United States and Asia.

Nonproliferation Policy Education Center, 1718 M St., N.W., Suite 244, Washington, DC 20036; (202) 466-4406; www.npec-web.org. Supports a more robust nonproliferation policy.

2

Weapons of Mass Destruction

Mary H. Cooper

A letter suspected of containing anthrax is examined at Fort Detrick, the Army's biomedical research facility in Maryland. It was addressed to Sen. Patrick Leahy, D-Vt., and FBI officials said it was from the same person who sent anthrax-laden letters to Sen. Tom Daschle, NBC News and *The New York Post.*

It sounds like the plot of the latest Bruce Willis thriller, but security experts say the scenario is far closer to reality than to Hollywood:

A cargo ship glides into New York Harbor. Before customs agents can come aboard for inspection, a nuclear bomb hidden in one of the containers stacked on deck explodes.

The blast and heat from the 12.5-kiloton weapon instantly incinerate 52,000 people. Another 10,000 die quickly of radiation sickness, and 200,000 eventually succumb to the effects of radioactive fallout. Farther from the blast site, hundreds of thousands of survivors develop radiation sickness. About 1,000 hospital beds are destroyed in the blast, and 8,700 more become too radioactive to use, leaving the city's health system overwhelmed.

Such nightmare scenarios are no longer considered far-fetched. Indeed, the above account appeared in an article about nuclear terrorism in the authoritative *British Medical Journal* not long after the Sept. 11 terrorist attacks killed more than 3,000 people. [1]

If the attacks taught anything, security experts say, it is that terrorists would not hesitate to wield nuclear, biological and chemical weapons — so-called weapons of mass destruction — against the United States.

"I have no idea whether one type of weapon is more likely than another," says Richard Falkenrath, senior director of policy and plans at the Office of Homeland Security, a White House agency set up in the wake of the Sept. 11 attacks. "But clearly there are certain biological and nuclear scenarios that exceed just about anything you can think of."

Americans recently got a real taste of what a biological attack

From *The CQ Researcher,*
March 8, 2002.

Six Diseases Get 'Highest Threat' Rating

Smallpox, anthrax and four other biological agents merit the highest priority for public-health preparedness because of their potentially lethal impact in the event of a bioterrorist attack, according to the federal Centers for Disease Control and Prevention. The CDC says small-scale bioterrorism events "may actually be more likely" but that health agencies "must prepare for the still-possible large-scale incident that could undoubtedly lead to catastrophic public-health consequences."

Evaluating Potential Bioterrorism Threats
(Ranked from highest threat [xxx] to lowest [0])

Disease	Public-Health Impact		Dissemination Potential	
	Disease	Death	Production	Person-to-Person
Smallpox	x	xx	x	xxx
Anthrax	xx	xxx	xxx	0
Plague	xx	xxx	xx	xx
Botulism	xx	xxx	xx	0
Tularemia	xx	xx	xx	0
Viral hemorrhagic fevers	xx	xxx	x	x

Note: The selection of the agents was not based on likelihood of their use but on the impact of their use on public health.
Source: U.S. Centers for Disease Control and Prevention, "Public Health Assessment of Potential Biological Terrorism Agents"

could do. In early October, letters laced with deadly anthrax spores were sent to three news organizations and two members of Congress.* The attacks killed five people, sickened 17 others and prompted some 30,000 postal workers and others at risk of exposure to seek treatment. The attacks also raised anxiety levels across the country, as Americans came to view their daily mail deliveries with apprehension.

But far more staggering devastation could be unleashed by other biological, chemical or nuclear weapons. Chemical weapons used by Iraqi President Saddam Hussein in the 1980s not only decimated Kurdish communities in his own country but reportedly caused genetic malformations that will persist for generations. In the absence of an effective vaccine or treatment, an outbreak of smallpox caused by terrorists

theoretically could infect hundreds of thousands of people — and would kill about a third of its victims.

Traditionally, the United States has relied heavily on diplomacy to keep smallpox and other lethal substances out of enemy hands. Several treaties drawn up over the past half-century require member countries to limit or destroy their nuclear, biological and chemical weapons. (*See chart, p. 34.*) But some treaty signatories nonetheless continued making chemical and biological weapons. And terrorists, by definition, flout internationally accepted norms of behavior.

Ultimately, keeping weapons of mass destruction away from terrorists is only as effective as the security around a nation's arsenals. After the Soviet Union's collapse, Russia's sophisticated military complex fell into disrepair, and some of its nuclear material went missing, despite U.S.-backed efforts to safeguard it. Moreover, thousands of scientists in the country's nuclear and biochemical weapons programs were suddenly unemployed, making them ripe targets for countries — or even terrorist groups — eager for their expertise.

* The crisis began on Oct. 5, when a photo editor at *The Sun,* a supermarket tabloid, died from an anthrax-laced letter. Letters were also sent to Senate Majority Leader Tom Daschle, D-S.D., Sen. Patrick Leahy, D-Vt., NBC-TV newsman Tom Brokaw and *The New York Post.*

Although Russian officials continue to deny that any of their nuclear weapons are missing, at least one former Russian general has claimed that a 10-kiloton nuclear device is gone. [2] And the National Intelligence Council, an umbrella group of intelligence analysts, told Congress last month that "weapons-grade and weapons-usable nuclear materials" have been stolen on at least four occasions from Russian institutes. [3]

"They could get it from anybody they could bribe," an American official told *The Washington Post* recently, referring to the possibility that Osama bin Laden — the alleged mastermind of the Sept. 11 attacks — or his al Qaeda operatives could obtain a nuclear or radiological weapon from former Russian scientists. [4]

The federal government now believes, according to *The Post*, that al Qaeda probably has acquired lower-level radionuclides that could be used for a "dirty bomb." The Post reported that President Bush has given nuclear terrorism priority over every other threat facing America, and that hundreds of radiation sensors have been deployed at national borders and around the District of Columbia. [5]

However, President Bush recently identified Iran, Iraq and North Korea as the most dangerous sources of nuclear, biological or chemical weapons, calling the three countries an "axis of evil." In particular, Bush warned them against supplying terrorists with weapons. "One of the worst things that could happen in the world is terrorist organizations mating up with nations which have had a bad history and nations which develop weapons of mass destruction," he said. "We . . . must make it clear to these nations they've got a choice to make. And I'll keep all options available if they don't make the choice." [6]

As the lethal legacy of both World War II and the Cold War, nuclear weapons conjure up familiar fears of massive, instant global devastation and lingering fallout from missile attack. But without missiles, terrorists with nuclear weapons would cause far less mayhem. Experts say terrorists would most likely detonate a small nuclear weapon delivered as a truck bomb or suitcase bomb, or aboard a cargo ship. Or terrorists could explode a less complex "dirty bomb," made by "wrapping" radioactive material — nuclear waste from hospitals or power plants — around conventional explosives. Terrorists also could cause devastating radiation releases by attacking nuclear power plants or the radioactive wastes stored in pools on their grounds. [7]

Chemical weapons would be easier for terrorists to acquire than nuclear material because dangerous chemicals have many industrial applications. In the United States alone, more than 800,000 plants produce potentially lethal chemicals. In 1985, the Japanese religious group Aum Shinrikyo released deadly sarin nerve gas in the Tokyo subway, killing a dozen people.

Most experts agree, however, that the most fearsome biological weapon, by far, is smallpox. Unlike anthrax, which usually only sickens those who come in direct contact with its spores, smallpox is highly contagious. Because infected individuals are contagious for 12 days before they show symptoms, they could unwittingly spread the disease to many others. And, because routine smallpox vaccinations ceased in the 1970s, when an aggressive global campaign wiped out the naturally occurring disease, few young people today are immune to the disease. Moreover, health experts do not know whether those vaccinated decades ago retain any immunity. There is no treatment for smallpox; once infected, about one person in three will die.

"Putting all of these things together, I would say that on anybody's hit list smallpox is always among the top two or three," says Anthony S. Fauci, director of the National Institute of Allergy and Infectious Diseases (NIAID), the federal agency in charge of developing vaccines for infectious diseases, including those spread by bioweapons.

"Prior to Sept. 11, it was quite realistic that we would be facing possibly a substantial bioterrorism threat," Fauci says. "Sept. 11 really drilled home to us that there are real people out there who have the destruction and the terror of the United States as their main objective."

Indeed, the recent discovery of documents in houses once occupied by bin Laden and al Qaeda members in Afghanistan suggests that the terrorist organization was well on its way toward stockpiling biological weapons. CIA Director George J. Tenet said the documents "show bin Laden was pursuing a sophisticated biological-weapons research program." [8]

The new evidence has heightened concerns over bioterrorism as never before. "In the past, only a few terrorist groups have acquired and used unconventional weapons, and nearly all have encountered major technical hurdles in doing so," said Jonathan B. Tucker, director of chemical and biological nonproliferation at the Monterey Institute's Center for Nonproliferation Studies. "Nevertheless, the anthrax attacks against the

Nuclear Sabotage and "Dirty" Bombs

The chances are slim that terrorists could obtain a nuclear weapon and the long-range missile to deliver it, security experts say.

More conceivably, terrorists could detonate a nuclear device aboard a ship docked in a busy port or a truck in an urban area, causing catastrophic damage. Even with stepped-up border security since Sept. 11, the U.S. Customs Service is only capable of inspecting about 2 percent of the 600,000 cargo containers that enter American ports each day. [1]

It would be much easier for terrorists to obtain radioactive material from civilian power plants or hospitals and "wrap" it around conventional explosives. Such "dirty bombs" would fall far short of the devastation resulting from a nuclear explosion, but, nonetheless, could spread deadly radiation over several city blocks.

"The nuclear device is a weapon of mass destruction," explained Siegfried Hecker, former director of the Los Alamos National Laboratory, one of three Energy Department facilities responsible for maintaining U.S. nuclear weapons. "Dirty bombs are weapons of mass disruption, in terms of frightening people, the cleanup and the potential economic consequences." [2]

Concern about dirty bombs mounted in mid-February,

when U.S. forces thought they had discovered evidence in Afghanistan that Osama bin Laden's Al Qaeda terrorist organization had acquired nuclear materials. Upon analysis, however, the contents of three suspicious canisters proved harmless. But officials cautioned that bin Laden had been trying to obtain nuclear materials for more than a decade and may indeed have developed the capability to make a nuclear device. [3]

Russia, with its stockpile of nuclear weapons and fissile materials — not to mention its contingent of poorly paid nuclear scientists — is a tempting target for would-be nuclear terrorists. When the Soviet Union fell apart a decade ago, it left a military complex in disarray. To prevent terrorists from stealing nuclear weapons from Russia's arsenal, Sens. Sam Nunn, D-Ga., and Richard G. Lugar, R-Ind., sponsored legislation in 1991 that established a program to help Russia secure and destroy much of its nuclear arsenal. The Nunn-Lugar Cooperative Threat Reduction program has helped deactivate 5,700 nuclear warheads in the former Soviet Union. [4]

Experts say it would be much harder for terrorists to steal any of the 6,000 U.S. nuclear weapons, especially with security now tighter around nuclear weapons facilities since Sept. 11. John Gordon, administrator of the National

[1] For background, see Patrick Marshall, "Policing the Borders," *The CQ Researcher*, Feb. 22, 2002, pp. 145-168.

[2] Quoted in Guy Gugliotta, "Technology of 'Dirty Bomb' Simple, but Not the Execution," *The Washington Post*, Dec. 5, 2001.

[3] See Thom Shanker, "U.S. Analysts find No Sign bin Laden Had Nuclear Arms," *The New York Times*, Feb. 26, 2002.

[4] See Peter Grier, "Loose Nukes," *The Christian Science Monitor*, Dec. 5, 2001.

United States indicate that terrorist use of biological weapons is no longer theoretical. Bioterrorism is a clear and present danger." [9]

On March 1, *The Washington Post* revealed further evidence of the government's concern about terrorism. President Bush, shortly after the attacks, dispatched a "shadow government" of about 100 senior civil servants to live and work in two underground bunkers in undisclosed locations on the East Coast, the paper reported. [10] The move — activating a plan initially devised by former President Dwight D. Eisenhower to ensure the continuity of the federal government in the event of a nuclear attack — was unprecedented. The plan wasn't even activated during the 1963 Cuban missile crisis.

In addition, states are preparing for potential biochemical weapons attacks by considering model legislation — recommended by the Centers for Disease Control and Prevention (CDC) — granting public health officials sweeping powers to use state militias to seize private property and take control of all roads, public areas, food, fuel, clothing and other commodities, including "alcoholic beverages, firearms, explosives and combustibles," and to vaccinate, isolate or quarantine individuals to prevent the spread of contagious disease during state-declared health emergencies. [11]

But some experts discount the danger. "A lot of people are overreacting," says Amy Smithson, director of the Chemical and Biological Weapons Nonproliferation

Nuclear Security Administration, dismisses the notion that terrorists could access the nation's nuclear weapons facilities. "The sites that store weapons and material are the most highly protected in the nation," he wrote. "They are not places a terrorist could attack with any real expectation of success." [5]

Far more vulnerable, according to critics of the U.S. nuclear power industry, are the country's 103 operating nuclear power plants and the outdoor pools where more than 40,000 tons of spent nuclear fuel rods are stored, many near cities. Since Sept. 11, officials have been concerned that terrorists could try to fly a fully fueled airliner into a nuclear power plant, causing a catastrophic release of nuclear contamination. As a result, security has been beefed up at nuclear plants around the country. [6]

The nuclear power industry now insists that its plants and 130 storage facilities are secure. But many neighbors of nuclear plants are taking no chances and are stockpiling potassium iodide, which is thought to protect against radiation-induced thyroid cancer, to use in the event of an accident or attack. [7]

President Bush recently designated Yucca Mountain in Nevada as the nation's official nuclear-waste repository. Under construction for more than a decade, it will permanently store 77,000 tons of waste deep inside the mountain, including the spent fuel from nuclear power plants and military nuclear waste. "Proceeding with the repository program is necessary to protect public safety, health and the nation's security," Bush wrote in a Feb. 15 letter notifying Congress of his decision.

The facility faces stiff opposition from Nevada officials, who say it poses unacceptable health risks to state residents. They also say transporting nuclear waste to Yucca Mountain in trucks or on trains would present opportunities for sabotage that could expose many other people to deadly radiation.

"This is the stuff of our worst nightmares," said Las Vegas Mayor Oscar Goodman, who has asked a U.S. Circuit Court of Appeals to stop the transfer because it would cause "immediate and irreparable harm" to the region. [8]

Arjun Makhijani, president of the Institute for Energy and Environmental Research, a nonprofit group in Washington, says the only sure way to prevent nuclear terrorism is to phase out nuclear energy gradually by closing each plant as its operating license comes due for renewal. "I don't think there is really any way to sensibly make nuclear power secure against this kind of attack," he says.

But Mitch Singer, spokesman for the Nuclear Energy Institute, the industry's main lobbying group, says, "There have been over 3,000 shipments of spent fuel in this country to date over the last 30 years or more, and there hasn't been any accident that has resulted in a breach of any of the fuel itself."

---

[5] From a letter to *The Washington Post*, Feb. 16, 2002.

[6] For background, see Mary H. Cooper, "Energy Security," *The CQ Researcher*, Feb. 1, 2002, pp. 73-96.

[7] See Randal C. Archibold, "In Shadow of Reactors Parents Seek Peace of Mind in a Pill," *The New York Times*, Jan. 21, 2002.

---

[8] See John J. Fialka, "Nevada Puts on the Gloves in Preparation to Fight Bush's Rule on Nuclear Waste," *The Wall Street Journal*, Feb. 19, 2002.

Project at the Henry L. Stimson Center, in Washington. "While we need to be aware of these threats, we also need to be cognizant of the challenges [terrorists face] in overcoming the technical hurdles" in acquiring weapons of mass destruction. "Fear is not conducive to good policy-making and good programs."

What experts do agree on is that an attack would sorely test the nation's understaffed and underfunded public-health system. Public hospitals have been facing financial woes ever since Congress in 1997 ordered $118 billion cut over five years from Medicare, the government-subsidized health-insurance program for the elderly. The nation's serious nursing shortage would further undercut the response to a bio-chemical attack. [12]

"Some people have the tendency to deny the danger and ask, 'Who's going to attack us in Peoria?' " says Mohammad N. Akhter, executive director of the American Public Health Association (APHA). "They think this is only a problem with the big cities. The reality is that terrorists can attack anywhere. No national plan for preparedness can succeed without local preparedness."

The Bush administration says protecting America from weapons of mass destruction is one of its top priorities. [13] Immediately after Sept. 11, Bush sought and received congressional approval for $40 billion in emergency funds to combat terrorism. Lawmakers then approved a $3.7 billion supplemental request for countering bioterrorism. In his fiscal 2003 budget proposal,

Border Security Gets Biggest Budget Chunk

President Bush proposes to spend $38 billion on homeland defense in fiscal 2003, almost twice the amount budgeted in 2002. About 45 percent of the money is for border security and biological terrorism.

President Bush's Homeland Security Budget, 2003

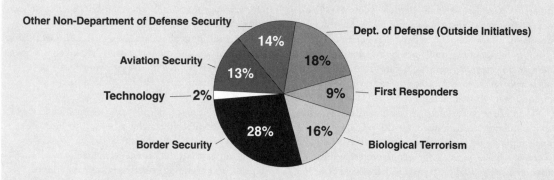

Other Non-Department of Defense Security — 14%

Dept. of Defense (Outside Initiatives) — 18%

Aviation Security — 13%

Technology — 2%

First Responders — 9%

Border Security — 28%

Biological Terrorism — 16%

Budgets for Anti-Terrorism Spending	2002 Budget	Post-9/11 Supplement (in $millions)	Proposed 2003 Budget
Supporting First Responders Police, firefighters and emergency medical personnel	291	651	3,500
Defending Against Biological Terrorism Enhancing medical communications and disease-surveillance capabilities; building a National Pharmaceutical Stockpile	1,408	3,730	5,898
Securing Borders Additional funding for the Customs and Immigration and Naturalization services and Coast Guard	8,752	1,194	10,615
Technology To track short-term foreign visitors, share security information with states and localities and protect the information infrastructure	155	75	722
Aviation Security Airport protection	1,543	1,035	4,800
Non-Dept. of Defense More agents for FBI, Drug Enforcement Agency and expansion of Citizens Corps	3,186	2,384	5,352
Department of Defense Pentagon and military base security; domestic combat air patrols	4,201	689	6,815
Total	$19,535	$9,758	$37,702

Source: White House, "Securing the Homeland; Strengthening the Nation," Feb. 4, 2002

Bush now is asking Congress for $37.7 billion for homeland security, $5.9 billion of which would go toward defending against biological weapons — more than four times the 2002 level.

As policy-makers consider plans to improve U.S. defenses against terrorist attacks, these are some of the issues they will consider:

Do terrorists already possess weapons of mass destruction?

Policy-makers have worried about nuclear weapons falling into terrorists' hands ever since the Soviet Union collapsed, ending the Cold War. During the ensuing economic crisis in Russia, thousands of nuclear scientists once responsible for the huge Soviet nuclear arsenal had few prospects for employment, making them ripe targets for states or groups seeking nuclear weapons.

The United States launched programs to remove Russian nuclear material from circulation and negotiated further U.S.-Russian nuclear-arms reductions. But many experts say that more needs to be done. "People know that there is a market for nuclear materials, and to this day we don't know where all of the materials from the former Soviet Union are," says Tarek N. Rizk, spokesman for Physicians for Social Responsibility, which supports the elimination of nuclear weapons. "To me, that says there is enough of a risk to say we should be acting fast."

Intelligence experts say there is no clear evidence that terrorists possess nuclear weapons or even enough nuclear material to construct a "dirty" radiation bomb. But uncertainty surrounds the status of biological and chemical weapons.

Last fall's anthrax attacks used a strain of the deadly bacterium that disappeared from the Army's bioweapons research facility in Ames, Iowa, at least a decade ago. [14] Even more worrisome is the lax security at bioweapons facilities in Russia, where scientists continued working on weapons-grade anthrax long after the country promised to stop such research. [15]

Some say the Japanese cult that released sarin gas in the Tokyo subway probably came closest to developing chemical weapons of mass destruction. During the trial of the group's leaders, they disclosed they were also trying to develop other chemical and biological weapons.

So far, says Smithson, terrorists have been unable to overcome several formidable technical obstacles to harnessing the full potential of biological weapons. "Governments have had to employ hundreds, if not thousands or tens of thousands of scientists, to figure all this out," she says. "Technical advances have made some aspects easier, but even terrorist groups specifically recruiting scientists are likely to run right smack into some of these technical hurdles."

For instance, microbes are hard to turn into biological weapons because they often perish when exposed to sunlight, water and other natural elements. Complex lab techniques are often needed to freeze-dry or otherwise weaponize these organisms. Unless they cause contagious disease in humans, microbes are hard to disperse broadly enough to cause much harm.

The anthrax attacks involved the use of weaponized spores, treated to withstand environmental exposure and delivered as a fine powder to maximize inhalation into the lungs, where anthrax is most deadly. Even so, the attacks only killed five people.

"Whoever is behind the anthrax letters obviously has significant technical skill," Smithson says. "But that was not a mass dispersal or a mass casualty-delivery attempt. It was about fear, not about killing lots of people."

But Fauci of the National Institute of Allergy and Infectious Diseases takes a different lesson from the anthrax attacks. "True, this was not a mass attack, but it certainly underscored the potential for a mass attack," he says. "If the same amount and grade of anthrax that was in the Daschle letter had been put into the ventilation intake system of the Hart Senate Office Building or the Washington Metro or the New York City subway, you would have had many, many more deaths. Hundreds, if not thousands of people could have gotten sick."

The discovery of the documents showing al Qaeda's interest in acquiring biochemical weapons disturbs many experts. Compounding their concerns, Italian police on Feb. 20 arrested a group of Moroccans with possible links to al Qaeda, who possessed a cyanide compound, documents and maps indicating plans to poison water supplies serving the American Embassy in Rome. [16]

While biological weapons pose a greater potential for widespread destruction, Smithson is more concerned about terrorists' access to chemical weapons. "A group that is intent on causing mass casualties is going to take the easiest route to do that," she says. "That's why terrorists turn most frequently to conventional bombs." According to her research into terrorist incidents over the past 25 years, more than 60 percent of attempts involving biological substances have failed to harm anyone. "If . . . my objective is causing mass casualties, then I'm going to do it the easier way," she says. "And that would involve sabotage of chemical plants. Think Bhopal."

In 1984, in one of the largest industrial accidents in history, 40 tons of methyl osicyanate leaked from a Union Carbide pesticide plant in Bhopal, India, killing nearly 4,000 people and seriously injuring 200,000. "There are over 850,000 facilities in [the U.S.] that produce, process, consume and store hazardous and extremely hazardous stuff," Smithson says. "Bad stuff can do just as horrible things to the human body as a classic nerve agent like sarin."

As in India, many U.S. chemical plants are in or near cities. [17] And sabotaging a chemical plant, she says, would pose fewer technical obstacles than producing a chemical weapon. For instance, she estimates it would take a small terrorist group — importing small quantities of precursor chemicals to avoid detection — 18 years to produce the two tons of sarin needed to kill 10,000 people. [18]

But acquiring weapons of mass destruction is only part of the challenge for terrorists: They must deliver them in ways that kill the most people, Smithson says. After the Sept. 11 attacks, authorities closed down small airports after reports that terrorists had tried to gain access to crop-dusters. But Smithson says it would be hard for terrorists to spread chemical or biological agents with crop-dusters because they are hard to maneuver and their sprayer nozzles must be carefully calibrated to be effective. [19]

Despite the technical barriers, there is growing official recognition of the threat of bioterrorism. A recent assessment by the CIA and 10 other U.S. intelligence agencies concluded that the United States is more likely to sustain a nuclear, biological or chemical attack at the hand of terrorists using trucks, ships or airplanes than one by a foreign country using long-range missiles. A similar report two years ago mentioned such a scenario only in passing. [20]

Should individual Americans try to reduce the risk of exposure to weapons of mass destruction?

In the early 1960s, when the Cold War seemed on the verge of escalating into a nuclear holocaust, thousands of Americans set aside food and water in basement fallout shelters, and schools taught children to "duck-and-cover" under their desks.

After Sept. 11, some local public health authorities distributed pamphlets outlining steps individuals should take that recalled some aspects of those earlier, perhaps naive, civil defense exercises. The Northern Virginia Regional Commission, whose jurisdiction includes the Pentagon, mailed all households in the area a 12-page pamphlet advising residents to put in an emergency supply of food, water and other goods, identify a windowless, upstairs room (chemicals tend to sink, it says) and be ready to seal themselves inside using wet towels and duct tape around any openings in case of chemical attack. The pamphlet includes tips on how to handle suspicious mail, what to do in case of evacuation and how to cope with a loss of power.

Some public health experts say these common-sense steps, which would serve equally well in a natural disaster, are even more essential at a time of heightened concerns about terrorism. Unlike a missile attack by a nuclear power, which at least would be detected some minutes in advance by U.S. radar, a terrorist attack likely would come without warning.

"A terrorist can strike anytime, anyplace with almost any weapon," says Falkenrath, of the Office of Homeland Security. "The odds of them hitting any one particular location are pretty low, but it could happen to anyone, anytime."

That unpredictability and the lack of warning that are the hallmarks of terrorist attacks become even more ominous if they involve biological or even chemical weapons. "In a bioterrorist attack, there would be no big bang, no smoke, no fire, no flash of lightning," says Akhter of the APHA. "A very important part of the responsibility of government and local health departments is to educate the public about what the threats are and to have every household do a few things to prepare themselves, such as having a working flashlight, a transistor radio for listening to the news and an adequate supply of food."

"We also need to make sure at the local level that we take the necessary steps to safeguard our children at school," Akhter says. In a biological or chemical attack, simply staying indoors may be the best way to avoid exposure to lethal substances. "So we have to make sure that the school systems are ready to keep children after school or even at night in case of attack, that the teacher will stay there and they have adequate supplies of water and food to feed the kids, because the safest thing to do is leave them where they are, rather than try to go and get them, exposing them to the outside."

The threat of biological or chemical terrorism has prompted many people to take more aggressive steps to protect themselves. Since September, Army surplus stores have sold out of gas masks, hazardous-materials suits and other personal-security equipment. Gas masks, which cost up to $500, are in huge demand, storeowners say, despite warnings that most of them require training and special fitting to use effectively and in any case would not protect against many chemicals. [21]

Some people began hoarding Cipro and other antibiotics after last fall's anthrax attacks, in case supplies ran out in a future epidemic. But health professionals warn against taking antibiotics in the absence of the disease, because it encourages development of antibiotic-resistant bacteria. [22]

Concern about the possible use of smallpox as a bioweapon has led to demands that the government make its limited supply of vaccines available immediately to those who want them. (*See "At Issue," p. 39.*) Current supplies of smallpox vaccine, which can cause serious side effects and is not currently available to health-care providers or to the public, would provide immunity for only about 15 million people. The government has ordered 209 million doses, but they are not expected to be available before the end of the year.

Meanwhile, government researchers will soon announce the results of an emergency study to determine whether existing vaccines could be successfully diluted to cover all 275 million Americans. "There's no question that the dilutional study is going to be successful," says Fauci, who expects to publish the final results this month. "This will give us enough to vaccinate everyone by the end of 2002, for sure."

But some experts argue that modern nuclear, biological and chemical weapons, if used by terrorists, are less amenable to individual civil defense tactics than they were during the Cold War, when the threat was primarily from other governments. An enemy government would most likely launch such a weapon via a long-range missile, giving the U.S. military time to spot it, respond in kind and warn the American public.

"Right now, we are woefully underprepared for a terrorist attack with weapons of mass destruction," says Rizk of Physicians for Social Responsibility. "But we don't believe that you could ever be fully prepared for something like this." For example, instead of worrying about how to survive nuclear terrorism, he says, "we should have stronger security at our nuclear power plants

and worry less about what happens when they have a meltdown or an explosion from a terrorist attack."

Will the administration's proposed defenses against weapons of mass destruction be effective?

In response to Sept. 11, President Bush created the Office of Homeland Security to coordinate the efforts of some 45 federal agencies involved in defending against terrorism, from the FBI and CIA to firefighters, health workers and other local "first responders" to an attack.

In addition, after the anthrax attacks Congress approved Bush's $9.7 billion supplemental request for homeland defense, including the $3.7 billion supplemental request for combating bioterrorism.

Bush's budget request for fiscal 2003, which begins Oct. 1, calls for doubling the amount spent this year for homeland security, to $38 billion. He also wants to quadruple current spending — $1.4 billion in 2002 — for countering bioterrorism, to $6 billion. Some 20 departments and agencies would receive anti-bioterrorism funding to strengthen a broad range of efforts, including training of first responders, improved communications, decontamination research and stockpiling vaccines. "It's money that we've got to spend," Bush said. "It's money that will enable me to say we're doing everything we can to protect America." [23]

Critics charge that the administration is throwing money at the bioterrorism problem and that few of the agencies are equipped to absorb such large sums. "To spend more on cutting-edge biomedical research is one thing," an editorial in *The Washington Post* said. "To ramp the bioterrorism research budget of the National Institute for Allergic and Infectious Diseases from $36 million to $441 million in a single year is quite another. Such bonanzas will strain even the most effective of competitive grant operations. Though the direction is right, the potential lurks in this bioterrorism bonanza for catastrophic waste." [24]

Recipients of the largess strongly deny the charge. "Whenever there's federal money to be had, there are always people who say you got too much," says Fauci, whose agency would receive the bulk of the $1.75 billion Bush has sought for the National Institutes of Health to research human immunity and microbes that could be weaponized to cause widespread disease. "We've been preparing for this, and we have a strategic plan and a research agenda. Those who say we cannot well spend it

C H R O N O L O G Y

1910s-1960s *Major powers produce nuclear, chemical and biological weapons.*

April 22, 1915 German troops release chlorine gas at Ypres, Belgium, killing thousands of French soldiers. By the end of World War I, chemical weapons kill almost 100,000 people and injure more than a million.

1925 The United States and other countries sign the Geneva Protocol, which bans the use of chemical and bacteriological weapons as "justly condemned by the general opinion of the civilized world."

November 1969 President Richard M. Nixon declares that the United States will not retaliate in kind against an enemy attack using biological or chemical weapons and unilaterally disbands the U.S. biological-weapons program. In February 1970, he broadens unilateral action to include not only germs, such as anthrax, but also toxins from living organisms.

1970s *Treaties strengthen limits on access to weapons of mass destruction.*

1972 The U.S. and Soviet Union sign landmark treaties to curb the nuclear arms race. They also join more than 100 other countries in signing the Biological and Toxin Weapons Convention (BWC) banning the possession of lethal biological agents except for research into vaccine development and other defensive programs. After the World Health Organization eradicates naturally occurring smallpox, the U.S. ceases routine vaccinations.

1975 The U.S. Senate ratifies the Geneva Protocol.

April 1979 An anthrax outbreak in Russia kills 64, suggesting the Soviet Union has continued its biological-weapons program in violation of the BWC.

1980s-1990s *Concern mounts over weapons of mass destruction.*

1983 Iraqi President Saddam Hussein begins using chemical weapons against Iran in a war that will continue until 1988. During the same period, he uses poison gas and possibly anthrax to kill Kurdish civilians in northern Iraq.

March 20, 1985 The Japanese cult Aum Shinrikyo releases sarin gas in the Tokyo subway, killing a dozen people.

1991 Sens. Sam Nunn, D-Ga., and Richard Lugar, R-Ind., cosponsor legislation creating the Cooperative Threat Reduction program, designed to destroy or deactivate nuclear warheads left remaining in the former Soviet Union. U.S. troops in the Persian Gulf War against Iraq are equipped with gas masks and protective clothing and vaccinated against anthrax, despite the vaccine's potentially harmful side effects.

April 1992 Russian President Boris N. Yeltsin announces that Russia will halt its biological-weapons program.

January 1993 The Chemical Weapons Convention is presented for signature at the United Nations. Unlike the BWC, the treaty includes extensive provisions for monitoring compliance.

1998 Iraq expels U.N. inspectors sent to monitor the country's nuclear, biological and chemical weapons programs as part of the agreement ending the gulf war.

2000s *The threat of nuclear or biochemical terrorism mounts after terrorist attacks kill thousands.*

Sept. 11, 2001 In the first major terrorist attack on U.S. soil, hijackers crash three airliners into the World Trade Center in New York City and the Pentagon, killing more than 3,000 people.

October 2001 Anonymous, anthrax-tainted letters kill five Americans and injure 17 others. The federal government begins a series of warnings to Americans about future terrorist attacks.

March 1, 2002 *The Washington Post* reports that since Sept. 11 a "shadow" government of about 100 top officials has been dispatched to live and work in underground bunkers to ensure the continuity of government in the event of a nuclear attack on the nation's capital.

. . . should see what we're doing before they make statements like that."

Some experts say more money needs to go to firefighters and other first responders, especially since the economy went into a recession last year, reducing expected state tax revenues and forcing many states to radically cut back on spending. Local health and emergency agencies complain most about the lack of adequate resources, according to Smithson of the Stimson center. "The jury's still out on what the administration is proposing" she says. "Some of the right words are being said about the need to get resources to the locals, but I'm not at all sure that this is what's going to happen."

Other critics want a greater emphasis on programs to protect against potential nuclear attacks, such as the Cooperative Threat Reduction program designed to keep leftover Soviet weapons out of terrorists' hands. The so-called Nunn-Lugar program — after former Sens. Sam Nunn, D-Ga., and Richard Lugar, R-Ind., cosponsors of the 1991 legislation creating it — has helped destroy or deactivate more than 5,000 Russian warheads. After Bush took office in January 2001, however, he asked Congress to cut spending for these programs, and funding was slashed by 75 percent.

Now the administration wants Congress to jack up the funding for Nunn-Lugar again, but critics say it's too little, too late. "Unfortunately, we've left the barn door open for a couple of years," says Rizk of Physicians for Social Responsibility, who criticizes the administration's controversial decision to abandon the 1972 Anti-Ballistic Missile Treaty and build a missile defense system to protect the United States from long-range nuclear attack. [25] "We're still concerned that $8 billion would be spent on national missile defense, and less than $2 billion on total cooperative threat-reduction programs, which are a much better investment," Rizk says. "The Cooperative Threat Reduction programs were all done as a partnership with Russia, but the Bush administration is much more comfortable with a unilateral style."

Bush critics say the same preference for unilateralism over international cooperation was evident in the president's Jan. 29 State of the Union address, when he dubbed Iran, Iraq and North Korea an "axis of evil" and issued a thinly veiled threat of military reprisal if they supplied such weapons to terrorists.

"[S]ome governments will be timid in the face of terror," he said, "and make no mistake about it: If they do not act, America will. Our . . . goal is to prevent regimes that sponsor terror from threatening America or our friends and allies with weapons of mass destruction."

Bush's speech drew largely negative reactions. In Iran, hundreds of thousands of protesters participated in anti-U.S. demonstrations in February marking the 23rd anniversary of the Islamic revolution. During a three-country Asian tour, Feb. 17-22, aimed largely at bolstering support for his war on terrorism, Bush faced the biggest anti-American demonstration in years in South Korea. The critics said alienating North Korea undermined President Kim Dae Jung's "sunshine policy" of friendly diplomacy and economic assistance toward the north. [26]

European leaders, who supported the U.S. war against terrorists in Afghanistan, are especially critical of what they now see as a unilateralist approach to dealing with terrorism. French Foreign Minister Hubert Vedrine called the president's approach "simplistic." Germany's Joschka Fischer said NATO allies would not go along with any U.S. unilateral action against other countries. "All European foreign ministers see it that way," Fischer said. "That is why the phase 'axis of evil' leads nowhere." [27]

BACKGROUND

Germ Warfare

Germ and chemical warfare was common long before the 20th century. [28] Poisoning wells and dumping plague-infested corpses over the walls of cities under siege was widely practiced in European wars, even before the nature of contagion was understood. In pre-Revolutionary America, British soldiers knowingly spread smallpox among hostile Native Americans by giving them germ-contaminated blankets, wiping out untold numbers of Indians. By accidental introduction and conscious spread as a bioweapon, smallpox helped determine the course of North American history. [29]

But it wasn't until World War I that biochemical warfare became an integral part of the modern arsenal. The first large-scale use of chemical weapons occurred on April 22, 1915, when German troops released deadly chlorine gas at Ypres, Belgium, killing thousands of French soldiers deployed downwind. Two years later, Germany introduced deadly mustard gas into its arsenal. By the end of the war, chemical attacks had killed almost 100,000 people and injured more than a million. Germany also spread anthrax to kill the Allies' horses and mules.

Many Nations Have Biochemical Weapons

In his recent State of the Union address, President Bush singled out three countries — Iran, Iraq and North Korea — as an "axis of evil," claiming they were developing weapons of mass destruction. In reality, such weapons are in the arsenals of at least two-dozen countries, despite international treaties barring or limiting their development. Eight governments are known to possess nuclear weapons: the United States, Russia, Britain, France, China, Pakistan, India and Israel. The extent of biological or chemical weapons proliferation is less certain, because they are easier to conceal. Many countries have discontinued their biological weapons programs but maintain supplies for research purposes. According to the Center for Nonproliferation Studies at the Monterey Institute of International Studies, the following countries had, or still have, bio-chemical weapons programs or probable arsenals:

Country	Action on Chemical (CWC) or Biological Weapons (BWC) Conventions	Past and Present Programs	
		Chemical Weapons	**Biological Weapons**
Canada	Ratified both	Former program: Mustard, phosgene and lewisite	Former program: Anthrax
China	Ratified CWC; acceded to BWC	Probable	Probable
Egypt	Not a party to either	Probable mustard, phosgene, sarin, VX	Probable
Ethiopia	Ratified both	Probable	
France	Ratified CWC; acceded to BWC	Former program: Mustard, phosgene	Former program: Potato beetle
Germany	Ratified both	Former program: Phosgene, cyanide, mustard, tabun, sarin, soman	Former program: Glanders, anthrax
India	Ratified both	Former chemical weapons program	
Iran	Ratified both	Known: Mustard, sarin, hydrogen cyanide, cyanogen chloride, phosgene	Probable: anthrax, foot and mouth disease, botulinum toxin, mycotoxins
Iraq	Acceded to CWC; ratified BWC as condition of end to 1991 Persian Gulf War	Past, possibly resumed: Mustard, sarin, tabun, VX, Agent 15	Past, possibly resumed: Anthrax, botulinum toxin, ricin, aflatoxin, wheat cover smut.

Source: "Chemical and Biological Weapons: Possession and Programs, Past and Present," Center for Nonproliferation Studies, Monterey Institute of International Studies, www.cns.miis.edu

But the world recoiled at the use of chemicals and germs in battle. In 1925 the Geneva Protocol banned the military use of chemical and bacteriological weapons, which it said were "justly condemned by the general opinion of the civilized world."

The ban on biological and chemical weapons applied to their military use, but not to their possession. Indeed, from the 1930s on the United States and other industrial countries continued to conduct research and development programs, which produced the deadly nerve agent sarin and other lethal chemicals.

Despite its lack of enforcement provisions, the protocol succeeded in deterring most countries from using chemical and biological weapons. During World War II, Japan was the only country known to have used biological weapons. Japanese aircraft dropped bacteria-laced bombs, feathers and cotton wadding over China, killing

Country	Action on Chemical (CWC) or Biological Weapons (BWC) Conventions	Past and Present Programs	
		Chemical Weapons	**Biological Weapons**
Israel	Not a party to either	Probable	
Italy	Ratified both	Mustard, phosgene	
Japan	Ratified both	Phosgene, hydrogen cyanide, mustard, lewisite, chloropicrin	Former programs: Anthrax, plague, glanders, typhoid, cholera, dysentery, paratyphoid
Libya	Not party to CWC; acceded to BWC	Known: Mustard, sarin, tabun, lewisite, phosgene	
Myanmar (Burma)	Not a party to either	Probable	
North Korea	Not party to CWC; acceded to BWC	Probable (adamsite, mustard, hydrogen cyanide, cyanogen chloride, phosgene, sarin, soman, tabun, VS)	
Pakistan	Ratified both	Probable	
Russia (former Soviet Union)	Ratified both	Probable (Novichok binary nerve agents, sarin, soman, mustard, lewisite, phosgene, VX analogue)	Former programs: Smallpox, plague, tularemia, glanders, Venezuelan equine encephalitis, anthrax, Q fever, Marburg virus
South Africa	Ratified both	Thallium, CR, paraoxon, mustard gas	Former programs: Anthrax, cholera, plague, salmonella, gas gangrene, ricin, botulinum toxin
South Korea	Ratified both	Past, possibly resumed	
Syria	Not a party to either	Probable (mustard, sarin, VX)	
Taiwan	Not party to CWC; ratified BWC	Probable	
United Kingdom	Ratified both	Former programs: Phosgene, mustard, lewisite	Former programs: Anthrax
United States	Ratified both	Former programs: Mustard, sarin, soman, VX, lewisite, binary nerve agents	Former programs: Venezuelan equine encephalitis, Q fever, tularemia, anthrax, wheat rust, rice blast
Yugoslavia	Acceded to CWC; ratified BWC	Former programs: Sarin, mustard, tabun, soman, VX, lewisite, BZ, CS tear gas	

some 700 Chinese with plague. Japan also used chemical weapons against China during the war, as did Italy against Ethiopia. [30]

By this time, the United States, Germany, Japan, Britain, Canada and the Soviet Union all had developed biological and chemical weapons. The United States justified its programs on the premise that it needed to have the weapons on hand to retaliate in kind if an enemy used them in an attack.

During the Cold War, even as the nuclear arms race accelerated, both the United States and the Soviet Union accelerated their bio-chemical-weapons programs. The main U.S. germ research facility was the Army's sprawling complex at Fort Detrick, Md. Until the late 1950s, the Army even tested the potential lethality of these weapons by spreading harmless chemicals and germs in a number of U.S. cities.

One of the products of this program was Agent Orange, a defoliant sprayed over vast swathes of jungle during the Vietnam War to expose Viet Cong hideouts. Critics later linked the herbicide to cancer and other serious diseases among Vietnam veterans. [31]

Anti-Proliferation Efforts

President Richard M. Nixon slowed the escalating biochemical arms race in November 1969. He not only declared that the United States would not retaliate in kind against an enemy attack using such weapons but also unilaterally disbanded the U.S. biological-weapons program. In February 1970 he broadened the unilateral action to include not only germs like anthrax but also toxins produced from living organisms, such as botulinum toxin and staphylococcal enterotoxin B.

The Nixon administration also led the call for a new treaty to ban germ warfare. In 1972, the United States, Soviet Union and more than 100 other countries signed the Biological and Toxin Weapons Convention, the first treaty to prohibit the possession of an entire class of weapons, except for research into defensive programs, such as vaccine development. [32]

The Senate ratified the accord on Dec. 16, 1974, and Nixon's successor, President Gerald Ford, signed it on Jan. 22, 1975. The government then suspended the bioweapons program at Fort Detrick, although it would continue to research defenses against biological attack. The program, newly named the Army Medical Research Institute of Infectious Diseases, focused on developing vaccines and equipment to detect biological agents and prevent infection.

Efforts to restrict chemical weapons also advanced during the 1970s. Ford declared that the United States would never use herbicides or tear gas in an offensive manner in war. The U.S. Senate finally ratified the Geneva Protocol in 1975, after senators were given assurances it would not constrain production of tear gas, nonlethal herbicides and other industrial chemicals.

But the treaties were little more than declarations of goodwill. Neither contained enforcement provisions, and because production of germs and chemicals could be concealed in ordinary commercial buildings, countries could violate the treaties without detection. Indeed, an outbreak of anthrax in Sverdlovsk, Russia, that killed at least 64 people in April 1979 was the first clear sign that the Soviet Union had continued its biological-weapons program, although Soviet authorities attributed the outbreak to tainted meat.

In 1992, however, Russian President Boris N. Yeltsin conceded that deadly spores had leaked from a munitions factory. He also announced that Russia would halt the biological-weapons program the Soviets had continued in violation of the treaty.

To strengthen the Biological Weapons Convention, treaty signatories launched a series of review conferences and agreed to confidence-building measures including exchanges of information on national programs to defend against bioweapons attack. They also agreed to immediately notify the World Health Organization of future outbreaks of life-threatening infectious diseases to prevent their spread.

Much of the impetus behind the new arms-control efforts stemmed from concern that biological and chemical weapons, because they are relatively cheap to produce, would proliferate beyond the industrial powers, becoming a "poor man's atom bomb."

By the 1980s, adherence to the Geneva Protocol's ban on chemical and biological weapons clearly was eroding. In 1983, Iraq began using chemical weapons against Iran in a war that continued until 1988. From 1987-2000, Iraq also used poison gas and possibly anthrax to kill Kurdish civilians in northern Iraq. [33] As a result, U.S. forces in the 1991 Persian Gulf War against Iraq were equipped with gas masks and protective clothing. They also received vaccines against anthrax, despite its purported potential for harmful side effects.

Impact of Gulf War

After the gulf war, the United States and other Western countries called for a new treaty banning chemical weapons and allowing inspections of facilities suspected of producing chemical weapons. In addition, signatories could impose sanctions and even military force against violators. On May 13, 1991, President George Bush declared that the United States would renounce the use of chemical weapons for any reason once such a treaty took effect. The Army began destroying its stockpiles of sarin and other deadly chemicals maintained for retaliation against a chemical attack.

In January 1993, the Chemical Weapons Convention was presented for signature at the United Nations. It requires signatories to declare all past and current chemical weapons programs and has about 200 full-time inspectors. [34]

Efforts soon got under way to give teeth to the Biological Weapons Convention as well, but to little avail. To date, 144 countries have signed and ratified the treaty, including Iraq — but not Syria or Israel, which are believed to have biological arsenals. But enforcement has proved elusive. A draft document calling for a new monitoring regime to enforce the ban failed to win the support of the United States and other industrial nations, after drug companies claimed that proposed random inspections could reveal commercial secrets.

Last fall, the United States effectively scuttled the six-year effort to strengthen the convention. The U.S. delegation at international negotiations proposed terminating the negotiations, arguing that the proposed enforcement provisions were too weak to prevent bioweapons proliferation. Organizers then suspended further negotiations until at least November 2002. [35]

Efforts to curtail further proliferation of biological and chemical weapons have focused on Iraq, which has maintained and used both, even though it signed the treaties banning them. After the gulf war, the United Nations set up a special commission to inspect Iraqi factories suspected of producing weapons of mass destruction. U.N. inspectors concluded that Iraq was still producing the nerve gas VX, as well as anthrax, botulinum toxin and other biological weapons.

But Saddam expelled the inspectors in 1998, charging that the delegation included American spies, and U.S. officials claim he most likely has resumed his banned weapons programs.

When asked recently if U.N. inspectors should return to Iraq, Secretary of Defense Donald H. Rumsfeld said that in the intervening four years the Iraqis "have advanced their weapons of mass destruction programs. They've had years to take advanced technology underground, to hide things, deny things, create mobility where they can actually keep [the weapons] moving ahead of the inspectors."

Thus, if the U.N. decides to send weapons inspectors back into Iraq, it would have to be with "a much more intrusive inspection regime," Rumsfeld said. [36]

"Dark Winter"

Several incidents over the past few decades have heightened security experts' concern that terrorists pose the greatest threat of using weapons of mass destruction.

In September 1984, nearly a thousand residents of The Dalles, Ore., fell ill from food poisoning. A year later, investigators discovered that followers of the Bhagwan Shree Rajneesh, the leader of a religious cult, had laced restaurant salad bars with salmonella in a scheme to win a local election by preventing opponents' supporters from voting. The group had obtained the salmonella — and more lethal germs — simply by ordering them from the American Type Culture Collection, now in Manassas, Va., which supplies laboratories with germs used in research and diagnostic tests.

A decade after the Oregon attack, on March 20, 1995, Japan's Aum Shinrikyo cult launched its far more lethal attack in the Tokyo subway system at the height of the morning rush hour. Investigators later discovered that the group was trying to develop a range of biological and chemical weapons, using air-filtration equipment and other supplies ordered from the United States. They had bought an Australian sheep farm, where they tested nerve gas on animals, and before the subway attack, cult members had used chemicals to kill several people in Japan. They even sent representatives to Zaire during the 1992 outbreak of Ebola in search of samples of the deadly virus.

In June 2001, partly in response to such attacks, four academic and research organizations launched "Dark Winter," a war game to determine the impact of a biological attack using smallpox. Within 13 days of the "release" of smallpox in downtown Oklahoma City, investigators said the disease had theoretically spread to 25 states and 15 countries. They concluded that such an attack would result in "massive civilian casualties, breakdown in essential institutions, violation of democratic processes, civil disorder, loss of confidence in government and reduced U.S. strategic flexibility abroad." [37]

In February 2001, an al Qaeda turncoat testified that the terrorist network was trying to develop weapons of mass destruction. Questioned about his role in the bombings of two American embassies in East Africa in 1998, Ahmed al-Fadl said the group already had made lethal chemical weapons and had tried to obtain nuclear material. [38]

CURRENT SITUATION

Anthrax Lessons

Last October, still reeling from the Sept. 11 terrorist attacks, the country was hit by the most serious domestic bioterrorist incident to date. The attack began when an employee of American Media Inc., a tabloid newspaper publishing company in Boca Raton, Fla., received the first of a series of anthrax-laced letters. By Oct. 4, an employee had died, and the FBI had quarantined the building. Because anthrax normally strikes cattle, few health-care professionals recognized the human symptoms of the disease, either in its less serious cutaneous form or in its highly lethal inhalation form, contracted when spores reach the lungs.

Over the next month, four more anthrax-laced letters were mailed — two to journalists in New York City, and two to senators in Washington. Before it was over, five people had died from inhalation anthrax, another 17 had developed the disease, and doctors had prescribed antibiotics to more than 30,000 others — mostly postal workers — thought to have been exposed to the spores. Besides the toll on human life, the attack cost untold millions in cleanup and other costs — $10 million alone to decontaminate the Senate's Hart Office Building, which was closed for 96 days.

Authorities still don't know who sent the anthrax letters, although the FBI has narrowed its investigation to about 20 people who may have had the means and motive. [39] In retrospect, the attacks taught public health planners some important lessons about the nature of anthrax and how to deal with future attacks involving weapons of mass destruction.

"Our tool kit for dealing with anthrax — diagnostic tests, therapeutics and vaccines — are all from the Cold War," says Falkenrath of the Office of Homeland Security. "They were all developed before the biomedical revolution, and they're really inadequate. Our scientific understanding of the infectiousness of these agents — their lethality, susceptibility to treatment and dispersal through the atmosphere — wasn't as good as we'd like them to be, and it wasn't at our fingertips as quickly as we wanted."

The CDC came under heavy criticism for failing to react quickly to the anthrax crisis. Director Jeffrey P. Koplan announced on Feb. 21 that he would resign in March. [40]

Evidence suggesting that the anthrax used in the attack came from one of six U.S. government labs prompted calls for tighter security. The Army, which maintains the biggest facility, has denied allegations by former employees that germs at the lab had been stolen or misused, but it says security has been tightened since the attacks. [41]

Budget Increases

Defending against future terrorist attacks is a key goal of the Bush administration's $2.13 trillion budget agenda for 2003. Presented on Feb. 4, the spending blueprint included funds to beef up patrols at the borders, airports and seaports to keep known terrorists out of the country and to interdict any attempts to smuggle weapons. The request includes $5.9 billion to fight bioterrorism. Added to the $3.7 billion in emergency funds Bush got from Congress last fall, it brings the total amount requested since Sept. 11 for preventing bioterror to nearly $10 billion — a sevenfold increase over the $1.4 billion initially approved for 2002.

A big chunk of the money — $1.75 billion — would significantly boost the current $200 million annual bioterrorism research budget, used to study microbes that could be used as bioweapons and to develop vaccines to prevent their spread and therapies to treat their victims.

Advances in genetic engineering greatly complicate that job. Although it would be hard to genetically engineer a microbe to bypass the immunity conferred by an effective vaccine, says Fauci of the Institute of Allergy and Infectious Diseases, the gene technology exists today to make a microbe insensitive to drug treatments. "That's why we're putting a lot of resources into doing the genomic sequencing of all these microbes," he says. "We need to have more than one class of antibiotics against a particular agent, so if somebody does genetically engineer it, we will have several other options of drugs."

The president has also sought money to improve early detection of disease outbreaks. "We've got to be able to talk to each other better," Bush said during a visit to a disease-surveillance center at the University of Pittsburgh. "We were able to save lives during the anthrax outbreak, but some infections were identified too late, and some people were too badly infected to save." [42]

As the lead agency in dealing with terrorist attacks, the Federal Emergency Management Agency (FEMA) would receive $6.4 billion — more than twice its current budget — for training first responders and other readiness measures. FEMA would spend more than $230 million to expand the Citizen Corps, a volunteer emergency-response effort championed by Bush. The budget also calls for $10 million to set up a centralized facility to train federal anti-terrorism forces to respond to

Should the federal government control access to vaccines against smallpox and other bioweapons?

YES Centers for Disease Control and Prevention (CDC)

From "Interim Smallpox Response Plan And Guidelines," Jan. 23, 2002

Many biological agents could be used to attack civilians; however, only a few, such as smallpox virus, have the ability to cause illness or panic to the extent that existing medical and public health systems would be overwhelmed. . . .

The possibility of using smallpox virus as a bio-terrorism agent and the potential for its rapid spread have prompted the updating of a response plan previously developed by the CDC during the 1970s. This updated plan incorporates and extends many of the concepts and approaches that were successfully employed 30 to 40 years ago to control smallpox outbreaks. These overall concepts for outbreak containment contributed greatly to the eventual global eradication of smallpox. . . .

Smallpox vaccine is a highly effective immunizing agent. It is a live-virus vaccine composed of vaccinia virus, an orthopoxvirus that induces antibodies that also protect against smallpox. . . .

As this plan states, the first and foremost public health priority during a smallpox outbreak is control of the epidemic. . . . Any vaccination strategy for containing a smallpox outbreak should utilize the "ring" vaccination concept. This includes isolation of confirmed and suspected smallpox cases with tracing, vaccination and close surveillance of contacts to these cases as well as vaccination of the household contacts of the contacts. Vaccinating and monitoring a ring of people around each case and contact will help to protect those at the greatest risk for contracting the disease as well as form a buffer of immune individuals to prevent the spread of disease. This strategy would be more desirable than an indiscriminate mass-vaccination campaign for the following reasons:

- Focused contact tracing and vaccination combined with extensive surveillance and isolation of cases were successful in stopping outbreaks of smallpox during the eradication program without the need for indiscriminate vaccination.
- Adverse events would be expected to be higher in an indiscriminate vaccination campaign due to vaccination of persons with unrecognized contraindications, such as HIV or AIDS.
- Current supplies of smallpox vaccine would be exhausted quickly if an indiscriminate campaign were utilized, potentially leaving no vaccine for use if smallpox cases continued to occur.
- Mass vaccination would require a very large number of health-care/public health workers to perform vaccination and deal with the higher number of adverse events.

NO J. Donald Millar
Vice Chair, Public Health Policy Advisory Board, Cato Institute

From "Free To Choose The Smallpox Vaccine," Jan. 4, 2002

The government should . . . make the smallpox vaccine available to the public on a voluntary basis. People will be free to choose to take it or not. . . .

Health and Human Services Secretary Tommy Thompson has vowed that there will be a vaccine dose set aside for "every man, woman and child."

Put special emphasis on the "set aside" part of that vow, because neither the legislation nor Bush administration guidelines would make the vaccine available to the public until there is a confirmed smallpox outbreak. Why would the federal government — as the sole owner of a highly effective smallpox preventative measure — sit on its stockpile until a number of Americans actually become victims?

The stated reason for withholding the vaccine is that it has potential side effects if widely administered, especially for persons with HIV/AIDS.

That philosophy stands in remarkable contrast to the traditional "ounce of prevention" public-health credo. Consider the statement made several years ago by former CDC Director David J. Sencer, who headed the agency when it spearheaded the World Health Organization's global smallpox-eradication program: "Stockpiling antibodies in the body is preferable to stockpiling vaccines on warehouse shelves."

To be sure, the danger posed from side effects is to be taken seriously. But for those people not infected with HIV/AIDS, the vaccine's risks are both known and negligible. Instead of prohibiting the destruction of the disease until smallpox is unleashed on America, would it not be better for the federal government to inform the public of the risks and benefits offered by the vaccine, and then allow each individual to decide whether or not to avail himself of its protection?

This is a classic case for informed consent, decentralized decision-making and individual weighing of the tradeoff between the small risk of an attack and the small risk of terrible side effects from vaccination. Moreover, if enough people voluntarily choose to get vaccinated, terrorists might well judge that such an attack isn't worth their while.

The idea that the government would withhold the only effective means of protecting the population from a terrible disease until an epidemic is confirmed is new to public health. Prevention, in the new concept, obviously has no meaning for the "sentinel" Americans who will become ill and die of smallpox as the trigger for the government's response. That is not good public health, and is certainly not good protection from bioterrorism.

biochemical or radiological attacks. That's in addition to $17.5 million spent on the project since Sept. 11. Homeland Security Director Tom Ridge reportedly is considering locating the facility at a former nuclear test site in Nevada, where federal training of first responders has already begun. [43]

But some public health experts warn against counting on a centralized emergency unit in a terrorist attack using weapons of mass destruction.

"Look at what happened in New York City," says the Stimson Center's Smithson. "Lives were saved on Sept. 11 by firefighters, police, paramedics and physicians who were there or could get there from Manhattan and neighboring jurisdictions, not some federal rescue unit from across the country. The same will hold true in a chemical disaster, because the response timeline is so short to make a difference in saving lives."

Vaccine Controversy

The administration's new budget calls for hundreds of millions of dollars to expand the National Pharmaceutical Stockpile, including enough antibiotics to treat 20 million people exposed to bacterial diseases such as anthrax and plague, as well as vaccines against anthrax and smallpox. [44]

"We need a better anthrax vaccine, and we need a vaccine for tularemia, and then there's the ever-frightening Ebola," Fauci says. "We're also working on drugs to treat people who get infected, either because they were not vaccinated or because they were vaccinated and the vaccine failed."

Faced with the specter of a terrorist attack with highly contagious smallpox, the Bush administration is circulating a new model law to help states set parameters for exercising police powers to prevent the spread of disease. The law includes provisions governing the seizure and destruction of contaminated property, confiscation of drugs and vaccines and the vaccination, quarantine or isolation of individuals who may have been exposed to disease.

The prospect of forced vaccination worries health activists concerned about the side effects and effectiveness of many vaccines, including those against anthrax and smallpox. The stockpiled smallpox vaccine, for instance, was originally developed in the early 20th century, long before safer, more modern vaccine technologies evolved.

During the global campaign to eradicate smallpox, the CDC estimated that the smallpox vaccine could cause one death per million vaccinations among those who have never received the vaccine. But the current adverse-reaction rate is likely to be higher because more people today have compromised immune systems due to HIV, AIDS, leukemia, lymphoma or immunosuppressive drugs. [45]

Partly because of concerns about the safety of the existing vaccine, some groups oppose mandatory vaccination once the vaccine becomes available to the public, including the nonprofit National Vaccine Information Center, which lobbies for safer childhood vaccines and informed consent prior to vaccination.

"While it is critical for the U.S. to have a sound, workable plan to respond to an act of bioterrorism, as well as enough safe and effective vaccines stockpiled for every American who wants to use them, there are legitimate concerns about a plan that forces citizens to use vaccines without their voluntary, informed consent," said center founder Barbara Loe Fisher." [46] She is particularly concerned that people with compromised immune systems, such as AIDS sufferers, should not be forcibly vaccinated.

Georgetown University law Professor Lawrence Gostin, who wrote the model law, says those fears are unwarranted. "No one can be forced to be vaccinated or treated if they are particularly susceptible to harm or injury," he says. "If such individuals were infectious, they would be quarantined."

"The vaccine does have some degree of toxicity that would make it problematic to vaccinate immuno-suppressed people, including those who are on certain drugs, the very old, the very young and pregnant women," Fauci says. "But if you're in the middle of an epidemic, those toxicities, on balance, are trivial compared with what the scourge of the epidemic would be."

Legal experts tend to agree. "Personal rights in the United States are fundamental, but they're not absolute," Gostin says. "It would simply be wrong to make the claim that any person can be free to do whatever they want, irrespective of the harm that they do to the community. If someone is infectious or potentially infectious, it just defies logic and common sense to suggest that they could be free from measures to prevent the spread of their infections, such as vaccination, treatment or even isolation or quarantine."

Gostin largely blames anti-government sentiment for the public health system's lack of readiness for dealing with a contagious disease such as smallpox.

"What's gotten us in the difficulties we're in now is the anti-government, anti-taxation, anti-regulation and literally anti-public health attitude that has prevailed of late," he says. "We have the public health system that we deserve because the country has let it atrophy from neglect. Individuals are not going to be able to protect health and security. They have to have some trust in government."

OUTLOOK

States' Role

Just how prepared the United States will be for another terrorist attack will depend in part on how soon it comes. Since last fall, the FBI has issued four alerts to the American public. The most recent one is due to expire on March 11 — the six-month anniversary of the attacks. The military campaign against al Qaeda and its Taliban protectors in Afghanistan is largely complete, and many al Qaeda operatives are now in custody at the U.S. base at Guantanamo Bay, Cuba.

But the threat of further terrorist attacks remains. Bin Laden's whereabouts are unknown, and other potential adversaries appear ready to take his place in masterminding further action against the United States. Abu Zubayadah, one of bin Laden's lieutenants, has reportedly emerged as al Qaeda's new chief of operations and may be organizing new attacks. [47]

Judging from their swift passage of earlier counter-terrorism legislation, lawmakers are likely to approve most of the president's latest request for anti-terrorism funds. But it is unclear how quickly those funds will find their way into effective readiness programs at the state and local levels, where the first response to attack would take place.

For now, state governments are studying how to improve their contingency planning and establish effective surveillance systems to detect disease outbreaks. Georgetown's Gostin says about half the states are considering the model law he authored and predicts that New York, California and most other big states will adopt some of his proposals this year.

But for now, he points out, "Most states don't even require reporting for many or most of the critical agents of bioterrorism." In addition, because of privacy rights in many states, he says, public health authorities cannot even share disease data with emergency-management or law-enforcement officials.

Some experts say public acceptance of such measures will depend in large part on efforts to better inform citizens now — before a crisis hits — about weapons of mass destruction and what would have to be done to curtail the damage.

"There are good public health reasons for the policies in place now, and there should be a degree of open-mindedness to modify these policies depending on how the situation evolves," says Fauci of the Institute of Allergy and Infectious Diseases. "For that to happen, we need to hold an open forum to inform the American public and answer their questions before an epidemic breaks out."

NOTES

1. Ira Helfand, Lachlan Forrow and Jaya Tiwari, "Nuclear Terrorism," *British Medical Journal*, Feb. 9, 2002, pp. 356-359.

2. Robert D. McFadden, "Tip on Nuclear Attack Risk Was Kept from New Yorkers," *The New York Times*, March 4, 2002.

3. Barton Gellman, "Fears Prompt U.S. to Beef Up Nuclear Terror Detection," *The Washington Post*, March 3, 2002.

4. *Ibid.*

5. *Ibid.*

6. From Bush's State of the Union address, Jan. 29, 2002, and comments at the White House, Feb. 13, 2002.

7. For more information on nuclear power plant security, see Mary H. Cooper, "Energy Security," *The CQ Researcher*, Feb. 1, 2002, pp. 73-96.

8. Tenet testified Feb. 6, 2002, before the Senate Select Committee on Intelligence.

9. Tucker testified Nov. 7, 2001, before the Senate Governmental Affairs Subcommittee on International Security, Proliferation and Federal Services.

10. See Barton Gellman and Susan Schmidt, "Shadow Government Is at Work in Secret," *The Washington Post*, March 1, 2002.

11. See "The Model State Emergency Health Powers Act," A Draft for Discussion, The Center for Law and the Public's Health, Georgetown and Johns Hopkins universities, http://www.publichealth-law.net/MSEHPA/MSEHPA2.pdf

12. For background, see Adriel Bettelheim, "Hospitals' Financial Woes," *The CQ Researcher*, Aug. 13, 1999, pp. 689-704, and "Reconciliation Package: Spending Cuts," *1997 CQ Almanac*, pp. 2.47-2.61.

13. For background, see David Masci and Kenneth Jost, "War on Terrorism," *The CQ Researcher*, Oct. 12, 2001, pp. 817-848.

14. See Rick Weiss and Joby Warrick, "Army Lost Track of Anthrax Bacteria," *The Washington Post*, Jan. 21, 2002.

15. Fred Guterl and Eve Conant, "In the Germ Labs: The former Soviet Union Had Huge Stocks of Biological Agents," *Newsweek*, Feb. 25, 2002.

16. See Richard Boudreaux, "Four Terror Suspects Arrested in Italy," *Los Angeles Times*, Feb. 21, 2002.

17. See James V. Grimaldi and Guy Gugliotta, "Chemical Plants Are Feared As Targets," *The Washington Post*, Dec. 16, 2001.

18. See Amy E. Smithson and Leslie-Anne Levy, "Ataxia: The Chemical and Biological Terrorism Threat and the US Response," Henry L. Stimson Center, October 2000.

19. For more information, see "Frequently Asked Questions: Likelihood of Terrorists Acquiring and Using Chemical or Biological Weapons," The Henry L. Stimson Center, www.stimson.org.

20. Central Intelligence Agency, National Intelligence Estimate, "Foreign Missile Developments and the Ballistic Missile Threat Through 2015," released Jan. 9, 2002. See also Walter Pincus, "U.S. Alters Estimate of Threats," *The Washington Post*, Jan. 11, 2002.

21. See Jacob H. Fries, "At Spy Stores, Era of 9/11, Not 007; Customers Now Want Gas Masks Instead of Camera Pens," *The New York Times*, Feb. 20, 2002.

22. For background, see Adriel Bettelheim, Drug-Resistant Bacteria," *The CQ Researcher*, June 4, 1999, pp. 473—96.

23. Bush spoke at the University of Pittsburgh's Realtime Outbreak and Disease Surveillance Center, Feb. 5, 2002.

24. "Bioterrorism Bonanza," *The Washington Post*, Feb. 6, 2002.

25. For background, see Mary H. Cooper, "Bush's Defense Strategy," *The CQ Researcher*, Sept. 7, 2001, pp. 689-712.

26. See Clay Chandler, "Thousands in Seoul Protest Bush's Visit," *The Washington Post*, Feb. 21, 2002. For background, see Kenneth Jost, "Future of Korea," *The CQ Researcher*, May 19, 2000, pp. 425-448.

27. See Peter Finn, "Europe Adamantly Opposed to Any U.S. Attack on Iraq," *The Washington Post*, Feb. 17, 2002.

28. For background, see Mary H. Cooper, "Chemical and Biological Weapons," *The CQ Researcher*, Jan. 31, 1997, pp. 73-96.

29. See Elizabeth A. Fenn, *Pox Americana* (2001), p. 29.

30. See Leonard A. Cole, *The Eleventh Plague* (1997), p. 8.

31. For background, see David Masci, "Legacy of the Vietnam War," *The CQ Researcher*, Feb. 18, 2000, pp. 113-136.

32. See Judith Miller, Stephen Engelbert and William J. Broad, *Germs* (2001), p. 63.

33. See Cole, op. cit., pp. 91-93.

34. See Matthew Meselson, "Bioterror: What Can Be Done?" *The New York Review of Books*, Dec. 20, 2001, pp. 38-40.

35. See Mike Allen and Steven Mufson, "U.S. Scuttles Germ Warfare Conference," *The Washington Post*, Dec. 8, 2001.

36. Rumsfeld appeared on CBS' "Face the Nation," Feb. 24, 2002.

37. ANSER Institute for Homeland Security, "Dark Winter," www.homelandsecurity.org. The Center for Strategic and International Studies, the Johns Hopkins Center for Civilian Biodefense Studies and the Oklahoma National Memorial Institute for the Prevention of Terrorism also hosted the game.

38. For more on al-Fadl's testimony, see Daniel Benjamin and Steven Simon, "A Failure of

Intelligence?" *The New York Review of Books*, Dec. 20, 2001, pp. 76-79.

39. See Judith Miller and William J. Broad, "U.S. Says Short List of 'Suspects' Is Being Checked in Anthrax Case," *The New York Times*, Feb. 26, 2002.

40. See Robert Pear, "Embattled Disease Agency Chief Is Quitting," *The New York Times*, Feb. 22, 2002.

41. See Joy Warrick, " 'No One Asked Questions,' " *The Washington Post*, Feb. 19, 2002.

42. Bush spoke at the University of Pittsburgh's Realtime Outbreak and Disease Surveillance Center, Feb. 5, 2002.

43. See Tom Gorman, "Ridge Sees Nevada Site as Fit for Anti-Terrorism Center Training," *Los Angeles Times*, Feb. 21, 2002.

44. See David E. Sanger, "Bush Plans Early Warning System for Terror," *The New York Times*, Feb. 6, 2002.

45. From the "Interim Smallpox Response Plan & Guidelines," Jan 23, 2002, Centers for Disease Control and Prevention Web site, http://www.bt.cdc.gov/DocumentsApp/Smallpox/RPG/index.asp, visited March 1, 2002.

46. Barbara Loe Fisher, "Smallpox and Forced Vaccination: What Every American Needs to Know," *The Vaccine Reaction*, winter 2002.

47. See Philip Shenon and James Risen, "A Nation Challenged: Bin Laden's Network," *The New York Times*, Feb. 14, 2002.

BIBLIOGRAPHY

Books

Alibek, Ken, and Stephen Handelman, *Biohazard: The Chilling True Story of the Largest Covert Biological Weapons Program in the World — Told from Inside by the Man Who Ran It*, Delta, 2000.
Since moving to the United States, Alibek, who ran the Soviet Union's biological weapons program, describes the extent of the secret program and reveals how much of the anthrax and other deadly germs have gone missing.

Cole, Leonard A., *The Eleventh Plague: The Politics of Biological and Chemical Warfare*, W. H. Freeman, 1997.
The author describes a wide range of chemicals and microbes that countries have produced to make weapons and the treaties designed to curtail their use.

Falkenrath, Richard A., Robert D. Newman and Bradley A. Thayer, *America's Achilles' Heel*, MIT Press, 1998.
Falkenrath, senior director of policy and plans at the newly created Office of Homeland Security, and his co-authors present a comprehensive analysis of the threat of weapons of mass destruction and examines how these weapons could be used against the United States.

Fenn, Elizabeth A., *Pox Americana: The Great Smallpox Epidemic of 1775-82*, Hill and Wang, 2001.
A catastrophic epidemic of smallpox swept across North America, spread in part by the intentional infection of Native Americans by British soldiers in an early use of bioterrorism.

Gostin, Lawrence O., *Public Health Law: Power, Duty*, Restraint, University of California Press, 2001.
The government's inherent responsibility to protect Americans' health means privacy rights may have to take a back seat to the public good in case of a potentially catastrophic attack requiring quarantine, vaccination and other intrusive action. Gostin, a professor at Georgetown University, has written a model law for states to use in drawing up their own preparedness plans.

Miller, Judith, Stephen Engelberg and William Broad, *Germs: Biological Weapons and America's Secret War*, Simon & Schuster, 2001.
For decades the United States and the Soviet Union built large quantities of biological weapons, largely without public knowledge. Research into deadly microbes has continued, enabling scientists to prepare for a possible bioterrorist attack.

Articles

Easterbrook, Gregg, "The Big One," *The New Republic*, Nov. 5, 2001, pp. 24-26.

A nuclear explosion — even one involving a crude atomic bomb like the ones the United States used to destroy Hiroshima and Nagasaki, Japan, during World War II — could destroy Washington, D.C., and kill most of America's leaders.

Garwin, Richard L., "The Many Threats of Terror," *The New York Review of Books,* **Nov. 1, 2001, pp. 16-19.**
The catastrophe wrought by last fall's terrorist attacks pales when compared to what could happen if terrorists used more powerful weapons. A 10-kiloton nuclear explosive detonated in a typical city would kill at least 100,000 people, while highly contagious microbes such as smallpox would kill a third of the people who became infected.

Gerberding, Julie Louise, James M. Hughes and Jeffrey P. Koplan, "Bioterrorism Preparedness and Response: Clinicians and Public Health Agencies as Essential Partners," *Journal of the American Medical Association* **(JAMA), Feb. 20, 2002, pp. 898-900.**
Learning from the anthrax attacks of last fall, local health departments, hospitals and doctors should recognize the broad array of symptoms that could result from exposure to deadly pathogens and coordinate a rapid response to future bioterrorist attacks.

Homer-Dixon, Thomas, "The Rise of Complex Terrorism," *Foreign Policy,* **January/February 2002.**
Globalization and technological advances have not only raised living standards but also made it easier for terrorists to obtain and use lethal weapons.

Reports and Studies

Smithson, Amy E., *Ataxia: The Chemical and Biological Terrorism Threat and the U.S. Response,* **Henry L. Stimson Center, 2002.**
A recognized national expert on the biochemical threat to the United States assesses the effectiveness of federal, state and local preparedness to deal with such an attack.

United Nations Development Program, "The Human Consequences of the Chernobyl Nuclear Accident: Strategy for Recovery," Jan. 22, 2002.
The 1986 accident at the Ukraine nuclear power plant caused some 2,000 cases of thyroid cancer, a figure that could reach 10,000.

For More Information

American Public Health Association, 800 I St., N.W., Washington, D.C. 20001; (202) 777-2534; www.apha.org. Group of health-care professionals and public-health officials that researches responses to outbreaks of communicable disease.

Chemical and Biological Weapons Nonproliferation Project, Henry L. Stimson Center, 11 Dupont Circle, Suite 900, Washington, D.C. 20036; (202) 223-5956; www.stimson.org. Assesses readiness for responding to a potential bio-chemical attack.

National Institute of Allergy and Infectious Diseases (NIAID), National Institutes of Health, 31 Center Dr., MSC-2520, #7A03, Bethesda, Md. 20892-2520; (301) 496-5717; www.niaid.nih.gov. Researches prevention and treatment of infectious diseases and potential bioweapons, such as smallpox.

Office of Homeland Security, The White House, 1600 Pennsylvania Ave., N.W., Washington, D.C. 20500; (202) 456-1414; www.whitehouse.gov/homeland. New executive agency that coordinates nation's responses to terrorist attacks.

3

Future of NATO

Mary H. Cooper

British soldiers protect other NATO peacekeepers during rioting in Mitrovica, Kosovo, in February 2001. NATO supporters say the half-century-old military alliance remains a vital bulwark against terrorism and other threats to democracy, but critics say the split in NATO over the Bush administration's plans to invade Iraq is dramatic proof that the alliance has outlived its mandate and is no longer relevant in today's world.

From *The CQ Researcher*, February 28, 2003.

World War II finally had ended, but now there was a new threat to peace: The Soviet Union was eyeing Eastern Europe. Fearful of another global conflagration, the United States and many of its allies banded together once again.

Thus was born the North Atlantic Treaty Organization (NATO).

Fast-forward to Sept. 11, 2001. The deadly attacks prompted President Bush's war on terrorism, and then his call for the removal of Iraqi leader Saddam Hussein, whom he accused of supporting terrorists. Bush's aggressive stance placed the United States squarely at odds with some of its closest NATO allies.

"No one can assert today that the path of war . . . might lead to a safer, more just and more stable world," said French Foreign Minister Dominique de Villepin to a round of applause at a Feb. 14 meeting of the United Nations Security Council. Addressing U.S. assertions that Iraq supports the al Qaeda terrorist organization, de Villepin insisted, "Nothing allows us to establish such links." [1]

Echoing the French diplomat's sentiments, millions of protesters filled the streets of cities throughout Europe — as well as the United States — on Feb. 15. The largest demonstrations were in the capitals of America's staunchest NATO allies — Britain, France, Germany and Italy. In London, an estimated 750,000 protesters staged what was believed to be the largest demonstration in Britain's history to denounce President Bush's war plans and British Prime Minister Tony Blair's support for them. In Rome, nearly a million protesters filled the streets. The anti-war rally in Berlin was the largest since protesters tore down the Berlin Wall in 1989. [2]

The international public's rejection of Bush's call for "regime

NATO Expands into Eastern Europe

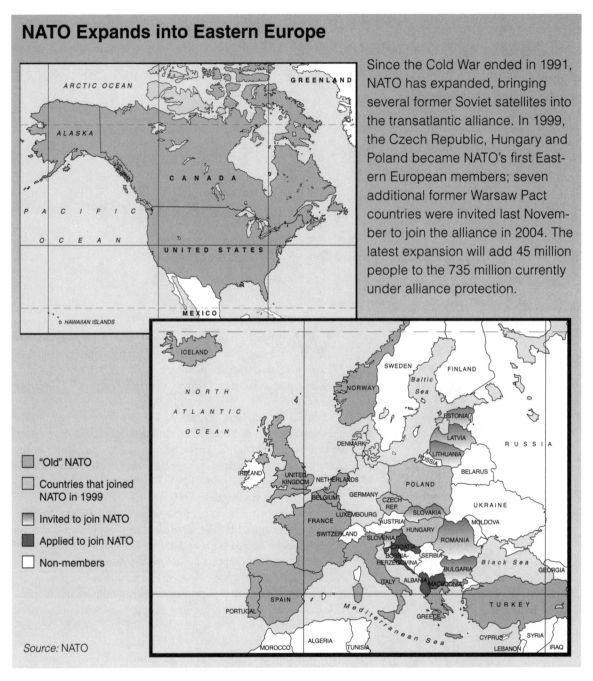

Since the Cold War ended in 1991, NATO has expanded, bringing several former Soviet satellites into the transatlantic alliance. In 1999, the Czech Republic, Hungary and Poland became NATO's first Eastern European members; seven additional former Warsaw Pact countries were invited last November to join the alliance in 2004. The latest expansion will add 45 million people to the 735 million currently under alliance protection.

"Old" NATO

Countries that joined NATO in 1999

Invited to join NATO

Applied to join NATO

Non-members

Source: NATO

change" in Iraq followed an unprecedented split within NATO the week before, when France, Germany and Belgium blocked a U.S. request that NATO transfer military equipment to protect longstanding alliance member Turkey in case a war in neighboring Iraq spilled over the border. The three countries argued that such action would merely accelerate — and indeed be seen as NATO endorsement of — what they consider an ill-advised war. The rare display of defiance of U.S. military leadership has plunged the alliance, the world's most powerful regional military coalition, into one of its deepest crises ever.

The situation is prompting some experts to ask whether the 54-year-old alliance can weather the rapidly changing security environment in an age of terrorism.

Moreover, as NATO expands eastward into former Soviet-controlled regions, some critics say its new members — many of them militarily weak — are transforming the military alliance into a political club with little real power.

Charles Grant, director of the Center for European Reform, a London think tank, says the crisis within NATO is symptomatic of a wider transatlantic rift. "While the argument on Iraq is very bad for NATO, it's also very bad for the European Union (EU), the United Nations and — more important — the transatlantic relationship," he says. "It's bad for everything, really."

Dissent within NATO is nothing new, of course. The alliance arose from the ashes of World War II, with a mandate to — as the saying goes — ensure Europe's security by keeping the Americans in, the Germans down and the Russians out. America's overwhelming military power occasionally conflicted with Europe's focus on economic development, causing periodic spats within NATO. However, the alliance weathered its differences and helped keep the peace in Western Europe until the collapse of the Soviet Union in 1991 ended the Cold War.

Today, however, the mission that once united the NATO allies is unraveling over the new threats they face — such as international terrorism — and differences over how to deal with them.

"After the Cold War, everyone breathed a sigh of relief that NATO had made it through the 1990s, but that was just the beginning," says Celeste A. Wallander, a senior fellow at the Center for Strategic and International Studies (CSIS) in Washington. "It was always clear that NATO was about more than the Soviet threat, but unfortunately terrorism took the transatlantic alliance by surprise. Even after Sept. 11, NATO members focused too much on their national interests in fighting terrorism and didn't use the opportunity to think comprehensively about our joint vulnerability."

That failure has become apparent since January 2002, when President Bush identified Iraq, Iran and North Korea as an "axis of evil" that supports international terrorism and called for the overthrow of Hussein. Not only

is Iraq developing banned nuclear, biological and chemical weapons, the administration asserted, but unless Hussein is disarmed he could hand over such weapons to al Qaeda and other terrorist organizations. Under U.S. pressure, the United Nations Security Council last November passed Resolution 1441, calling on Hussein to hand over any weapons of mass destruction and allow weapons inspectors to verify compliance with the order, or face "serious consequences."

The Bush administration says Hussein has had enough time to comply and is trying to assemble a "coalition of the willing" to join the United States in overthrowing the regime and destroying any banned weapons discovered in Iraq. After U.N. weapons inspectors reported limited progress in their mission to Iraq, Secretary of State Colin L. Powell said, "These are all tricks that are being played on us. These are not responsible actions on the part of Iraq. These are continued efforts to deceive, to deny, to divert, to throw us off the path." [3]

But America's NATO allies remained divided over how to resolve the Iraq question, even though a majority of the 19 members support a U.S.-led invasion of Iraq. France and Germany, however, adamantly oppose action, barring more concrete evidence of Iraqi weapons of mass destruction and absent a new Security Council resolution authorizing military action. And in NATO, all decisions must be made by consensus, with all members agreeing to any alliance action.

The split within NATO reflects the widening rift between the United States and its allies since Bush became president. [4] To the dismay of many U.S. allies, Bush has renounced the Kyoto treaty to curb global warming, dismissed South Korea's diplomatic opening to North Korea, abandoned a prominent U.S. role in resolving the Israeli-Palestinian conflict, refused to join the International Criminal Court and withdrawn from the Anti-Ballistic Missile Treaty — all high priorities in Europe.

Finally, the administration's consideration of launching a pre-emptive strike against Iraq added to the allies' commonly held perception that Bush has adopted a unilateral defense posture that ignores NATO's role. The Europeans were alarmed further by the administration's National Security Strategy, issued last September. It reiterated Bush's pre-emption policy — even in the absence of imminent attack — and stated that the future goal of

Is a Bigger NATO Better?

Recent and proposed NATO expansions include 10 former Soviet-bloc countries. Besides the irony of former communist enemies joining America's key defensive alliance, the expansions present serious challenges for the alliance.

For one thing, the new members don't bring much military muscle to the table. Of the former communist states invited to join NATO since the end of the Cold War in 1991, only Poland and Romania maintain standing armies of more than 100,000 troops. And the new members' combined defense spending added just $7.4 billion to the $461 billion spent by NATO countries in 2000. [1]

Meanwhile, the sheer increase in NATO's ranks adds more bureaucratic weight to an organization that by all accounts is already bogged down by numerous committees and missions. In addition, the organization's consensus decision-making can be a time-consuming process — all the more so with 10 new members.

"NATO is not a four-letter synonym for efficiency," says Anthony H. Cordesman, a military analyst at the Center for Strategic and International Studies (CSIS) and former NATO staff member. "It can't be; it's an alliance of too many countries."

Expansion has also raised concern about NATO's commitment to two of its core principles: adherence to democratic institutions and respect for human rights. Some critics say that in the rush to incorporate its former adversaries, NATO has ignored some of the new members' records on corruption and human rights.

"NATO needs to have an expulsion mechanism for members who just don't qualify anymore," says Celeste A. Wallander, an expert on NATO, Russia and Eastern Europe at CSIS. She cites nagging instances of political corruption or the continued influence of Soviet-era security forces that supposedly were dismantled long ago in several new NATO states, including the Czech Republic, Hungary and Romania. [2]

"They say what needs to be said to get in, and then they don't live up to it," she says.

Not all new members are tarred with the same brush, however. "Lithuania has made great progress toward dealing with its past in the Holocaust, and Poland has been an incredibly constructive new member of NATO," Wallander adds. "So it's not all negative, but there are some problems."

The 10 former Soviet states that have turned to NATO for their security since the end of the Cold War include Poland, Hungary and the Czech Republic, which joined in 1999. Then, at NATO's November meeting in Prague, seven other Eastern European countries — Bulgaria, Romania and Slovakia, the former Soviet Baltic republics of Estonia, Latvia and Lithuania, as well as the former Yugoslav republic of Slovenia — were invited to join in May 2004. If all goes according to plan, NATO's membership would jump to 26 countries — up from 16 during the Cold War.

Expansion proponents say the seven prospective new members could strengthen the alliance in several ways. Adding the Baltic republics extends NATO to Russia's western border, a step adamantly opposed by Moscow until it reached comprehensive cooperation agreements with NATO and the United States. [3] Slovakia's entry brings the rest of the former Czechoslovakia — split in two when Slovakia and the Czech Republic parted peacefully 1993 — into the alliance. Moreover, Romania and Bulgaria will constitute NATO's easternmost boundary, providing strategically important access to the Black Sea. Meanwhile, Slovenia, the first of the former Yugoslav republics to join, will extend NATO's reach southward into the Balkans.

"Prague was truly a transformational summit — for NATO's members, for the invitees and for the wider Euro-Atlantic community," said NATO Secretary General George Robertson. "NATO has moved decisively to make real a longstanding goal: to create a Europe truly whole and free, united in peace, democracy and common values, from the Baltics to the Black Sea." [4]

---

[1] NATO figures, found at www.nato.int/docu/review/2002/issue3/english/stats.html.

[2] Celeste A. Wallander, "NATO's Price: Shape Up or Ship Out," *Foreign Affairs*, November/December 2002, pp. 2-8.

[3] For background, see David Masci, "The Future of U.S.-Russia Relations," *The CQ Researcher*, Jan. 18, 2002, pp. 25-48.

[4] Robertson addressed the Bulgarian parliament in Sofia on Feb. 17, 2003.

U.S. policy is to maintain military primacy as the world's only superpower and to discourage the emergence of any rival superpower. [5]

The administration's call to arms against Iraq has intensified the rhetoric on both sides of the Atlantic. Defense Secretary Donald H. Rumsfeld ruffled feathers when he dismissed France and Germany as part of the "old Europe" that the United States could do without in the war on terrorism by relying on Italy, Spain, the Czech Republic and other states in the "new Europe." He later equated Germany with Cuba and Libya as countries that obstruct U.S. plans for Iraq. [6]

European analysts say such comments only worsen already-frayed transatlantic relations. "Public opinion in every European country, including Britain and Turkey, is extremely hostile to military action," Grant says. "It's not because people in Europe are stupid or misguided or foolish. It's because nobody has really made a convincing case to them that Iraq is a present and immediate threat to them or to the world."

Some longstanding supporters of the transatlantic alliance are calling for a truce in the war of words. "We have to understand that people with strong political convictions can come to different conclusions," says Karsten D. Voight, coordinator for German-American affairs at the German Foreign Office in Berlin. "What we need across the Atlantic is a kind of rhetorical disarmament in both directions."

Beyond the current rift over Iraq and responses to terrorism, some analysts say the NATO allies need to reflect on their post-Cold War missions. "It's true that the Soviet Union and the Warsaw Pact are gone," says Anthony H. Cordesman, a military analyst at the Center for Strategic and International Studies who served on NATO's international staff during the Cold War. "We have absorbed the enemy, and as a result, a lot of the imperatives have changed. Now that the catalyst that has kept us united has disappeared, there's a need for really hard debate among the partners."

Here are some of the questions being debated:

Is NATO still relevant?

After World War II, the NATO allies banded together to stop the Soviet Union's westward expansion and ensure the survival of democratic institutions and economic reconstruction in Western Europe.

The demise of the Soviet Union in 1991 and the inte-gration of a unified Germany into a peaceful and prosperous Western Europe marked the fulfillment of NATO's original goals. The United States has emerged from the Cold War as the world's sole superpower, and some American critics of the alliance say NATO is more of an impediment than an asset in meeting today's threats to security. The watershed event, they say, was the 1999 U.S.-led NATO operation to drive Serb forces out of Kosovo (*see p. 55*). Although the operation was ultimately successful, critics say disagreements within the alliance hampered its effectiveness.

"I don't think NATO will act collectively very often, if at all, because it's so hard to get so many countries in agreement on anything," says Max Boot, a national security analyst at the Council on Foreign Relations, a think tank in New York City. "It's very hard to make targeting decisions in wartime by committee. The difficulty is only growing because France and Germany are off the reservation now, actively opposing American policy on a host of issues and trying to set themselves up as rival power centers. That paralyzes the ability of NATO to act as a collective entity."

Kosovo taught Europeans a different lesson about the evolving nature of NATO. Even though the alliance works by consensus, with each member enjoying an equal voice in decision-making, European observers say the United States took over the military operation.

"The Americans were frustrated to discover that NATO was a multilateral organization, while the Europeans were equally frustrated to find that, in reality, NATO was totally unilateral," says Guillaume Parmentier, director of the French Center on the United States, a research institute in Paris. "Kosovo was meant to be a NATO operation, but the Europeans discovered that the term 'NATO operation' actually meant an American operation."

European observers are all too aware that U.S. "hyperpower," as the French dub American military might, threatens to make the alliance less useful to the United States than it may be to Europe. In fact, the 15-member European Union is developing a defense structure outside NATO, which will replace NATO peacekeeping operations in Macedonia this year. [7] But even with a much weaker NATO, the European allies are in no position to go it alone in the face of a major security threat.

"There's no doubt that in some ideological quarters

U.S. Spends Most on Defense

The United States accounts for more than half of the $488 billion in military expenditures by NATO member countries. America's $322 billion annual defense budget is almost 10 times the budget of Britain — NATO's next-largest military spender.

Defense Spending by NATO Members, 2001

Country	Population (in millions)	Defense spending ($ Billions in 2001)	Defense spending (as % of GDP)	Active Forces	Reserve Forces
Belgium	10.2	3.0	1.3%	39,400	100,500
Canada	31.7	7.7	1.1	56,800	35,400
Czech Republic	10.2	1.2	2.2	53,600	0
Denmark	5.3	2.4	1.5	21,400	64,900
France	59.3	32.9	2.6	273,700	419,000
Germany	82.4	26.9	1.5	308,400	363,500
Greece	10.7	5.5	4.8	159,200	291,000
Hungary	10.0	0.9	1.8	33,800	90,300
Iceland	0.3	N.A	N.A	0	0
Italy	57.2	21.0	2.0	230,400	65,200
Luxembourg	0.4	0.1	0.8	900	0
Netherlands	15.9	6.3	1.7	50,400	32,200
Norway	4.5	3.0	1.8	26,700	222,000
Poland	38.8	3.4	2.0	206,000	406,000
Portugal	9.9	2.2	2.0	43,600	210,900
Spain	39.7	6.9	1.2	143,500	328,500
Turkey	67.7	7.2	5.0	515,100	378,700
U.K.	58.9	34.7	2.5	211,400	247,100
U.S.	281.4	322.4	3.2	1,367,700	1,200,600
Total:	**794.5**	**$487.8**	**N/A**	**3,742,000**	**4,455,800**

Source: The International Institute for Strategic Studies, *The Military Balance 2002-2003*

close to the Bush administration you hear some public doubts about the value of NATO," observes Voight. "Some Europeans are now more interested in NATO than some Americans. Indeed, it's quite clear that most Europeans would like NATO not only to continue but also to be relevant in solving new challenges."

Despite French and German reluctance to support U.S. plans to oust Hussein, the Bush administration has taken steps to strengthen NATO's ability to face new challenges. For example, the United States strongly supported a proposal approved last November to build a NATO rapid-reaction force that could move quickly to put down conflicts on NATO's periphery before they escalate into wars.

But few observers think the new force will strengthen Europe's hand within NATO. "It's been said that NATO is no longer a pact; it's a pool," says Lawrence J. Korb, director of national security studies at the Council on Foreign Relations and former assistant Defense secretary during the Reagan administration. "The United States wants to draw on the military assets of the member countries as it sees fit."

Because membership in the new rapid-reaction force is voluntary, NATO is now "a coalition of the willing," Korb says. "It's basically not really an alliance any more."

The war on terrorism has cast further doubt on NATO's military relevance. "The attacks of Sept. 11 could have been prevented by better intelligence-gathering, sharper police work, proper airport security, a more watchful immigration service and greater vigilance among ordinary citizens," writes Deaglan de Breadun, an Irish columnist. "NATO is no more suited to this job than a bear is to catching wasps." [8]

Even if NATO is less relevant as a military alliance, supporters say it remains a vital link between North America and Europe. "It's regrettable that people don't understand that what makes NATO work is the whole package," says Wallander of the Center for Strategic and International Studies. "It's not just about interoperability, the joint command that allows the militaries to train together, or the fact that the United States can count on its NATO allies for overflight and basing rights. There is also a unity of political purpose and common values.

"NATO members come to the table with the presumption that they see security in common ways and that they can find ways to work together to address security concerns, and that sets it apart from most international organizations."

Should America's allies assume a stronger military role within NATO?

For much of the Cold War, U.S. critics of NATO complained that the allies were freeloading on the United States. "It's grow-up time," quipped then-Rep. Patricia Schröeder, D-Colo., chiding the Europeans for not contributing enough to NATO's defense during the 1980s. At the time, the critics pointed out, the United States was spending more on NATO defense than all the other alliance members combined — at a time of widening federal budget deficits.

Calls for burden-sharing largely faded away after the Soviet Union disintegrated. Indeed, NATO members — including the United States — cut defense spending, downsized their military forces and closed bases in Europe. But the United States, as the world's sole remaining superpower, maintained its overwhelming military force.

The United States spent about $322 billion on defense in 2001, nearly twice the $165 billion all the rest of NATO spent combined. The U.S. also spent a greater percentage of its gross domestic product (GDP) — 3.2 percent — on defense than all other NATO members except Greece and Turkey. [9]

Since the 1991 Persian Gulf War, the Defense Department has spent billions on advanced communications equipment and high-tech weapons, such as armed unmanned aircraft and "smart" bombs that find their targets with the help of remote-guidance systems. The result has been a widening technological gap between U.S. and allied forces (*see pp. 59-60*).

Some experts say anxiety over that technological gap underlies much of the anti-American feeling about U.S. plans to invade Iraq. "The allies are not so much rattled about U.S. pre-emptive policy as they are about the enormous gulf that has opened up between the United States and the rest of its NATO allies," says Michael J. Glennon, a professor of international law at Tufts University's Fletcher School of Law and Diplomacy. "This gap became evident for the first time in Kosovo, when they saw the tremendous leap that the United States had taken since the gulf war."

Henning Riecke, a senior research fellow at the German Council on Foreign Relations in Berlin, says the military-technology gap has been putting stress on the alliance for years and is getting more and more pronounced. "It was a problem during the campaigns against Serbia," he says, "and it became even more obvious when the NATO partners were only marginal participants in the air war in Kosovo."

Even America's perennial good neighbor, Canada, shares the concern about the military gap and the allies' weakening clout. "After a couple of decades of defense spending cuts, we don't have much of a military left up here in Canada," says Rudyard Griffiths, executive director of the Dominion Institute, a Toronto think tank. "Canada's role within NATO today is uncertain, not in terms of our willingness, but in terms of what we can bring to the table, and therefore the commensurate influence we have within the alliance."

As the allies have fallen behind in military technology, U.S. reliance on them in military operations has dwindled. "The fact that the American military is so much more sophisticated means that the Europeans are even less important for the United States with regard to today's operations against weapons of mass destruction and terrorism," Riecke adds.

No one expects the allies to come close to equaling the United States' military clout. "Nobody in Europe believes that Europe can provide a counterweight to the United States in hard military power," says Grant of the Center for European Reform. But the allies have specialized forces that can carry out specific missions to complement U.S. offensive capability. "What the Europeans can do quite well and have large numbers of soldiers for is peacekeeping. Some of the Europeans are much more experienced than the Americans in this, and they do it quite well. What they can't do is the high-intensity warfare."

The military-technology gap has widened largely because of the allies' unwillingness to cut back their generous education, health and welfare programs in favor of hefty increases in military spending. European Union domestic social spending averaged 25 percent of GDP in 1997, the most recent data available, compared with 16 percent in the United States. [10]

"The Europeans are not going to substantially increase their military spending because to do so, particularly in a time of economic crisis, would mean cutting back dramatically on their welfare programs, and they're simply not willing to make those tradeoffs," Glennon says.

"The military gap is too big to be bridged, so we shouldn't expect the Europeans to spend enough money to catch up with the Americans," Riecke says. "The only thing we can hope for is to slow down the speed of its widening."

The NATO allies are trying to do just that — by making their troops and equipment work more efficiently with U.S. forces, by pooling their military resources to reduce redundancy and by training specialized forces to cover niche areas, such as peacekeeping or countering biological or chemical warfare. "Not everybody has to do all of the tasks of a military force," Riecke says. "Instead of trying to close the technology gap, we're trying to become more interoperable with the United States."

While such changes will come slowly, they are not insurmountable, NATO backers insist. "We just got through a fairly complex air operation in Kosovo, and while it did not go smoothly, it also didn't go all that badly," Cordesman says. "There's a lot of room for improvisation and adaptation."

Will NATO's expansion strengthen the alliance?

When NATO expanded eastward after the Cold War, bringing three former Soviet satellites into the transatlantic alliance, Russia initially opposed the move as an encroachment on its sphere of influence. But improving U.S.-Russia relations paved the way for a series of agreements between Russia and NATO on military cooperation that mitigated Russian opposition to NATO's expansion.

In 1999, the Czech Republic, Hungary and Poland became NATO's first Eastern European members. In November, with the Bush administration's full support, seven additional former Warsaw Pact countries were invited to join the alliance: Bulgaria, Estonia, Latvia, Lithuania, Romania, Slovakia and Slovenia. They are expected to become full members in May 2004, bringing NATO membership to 26. At least three more nations — Albania, Croatia and Macedonia — have applied for membership and are being considered for future accession.

"America is very pleased by today's decision," Bush said on Nov. 21, 2002, in Prague after NATO announced the latest expansion. "By welcoming seven members, we will not only add to our military capabilities, we will refresh the spirit of this great democratic alliance."

Although NATO was created as a military alliance, its recent expansion was motivated more by political aims. "NATO is not a true military alliance anymore; it doesn't have a common enemy," says Korb of the Council on Foreign Relations. "Expansion is a way to integrate the former members of the Warsaw Pact, and even Russia, into Europe. The new members really don't have much to add militarily, and you can't station forces on their territory without angering Russia. So NATO is no longer so much about collective defense as it is about collective security."

Eastern European countries are clamoring for admission to NATO, Korb explains, because it's the only door open to Western economic and political benefits. "NATO is allowing countries that can't get into the European Union to become part of Europe," he says. Unlike EU membership, which requires countries to adopt broad and painful economic reforms, Korb says, "You can join NATO without really having to do much. The Czechs, for example, have done literally nothing militarily since they joined."

Meanwhile, the administration's strong support of NATO expansion has paid off in support from some NATO members for Bush's war plans against Iraq.

"Countries like Spain, Italy, Poland, Hungary and the Czech Republic are much more amenable to contributing a small piece of a larger puzzle," says Boot of the Council on Foreign Relations. "Also, they don't have the grand ambitions of dominating the world scene that Paris seems to have. The new members of NATO are very much pro-American, so they are a real reservoir of support for us on the continent."

Expansion is likely to leave the United States with an ever-stronger grip over NATO decision-making. "Because the new members of NATO will contribute only marginally to enhancing NATO's military prowess, their addition underscores its transition from a military alliance to a political club," says Tufts' Glennon. "The bigger the committee becomes, the more unwieldy it becomes, and the more resistant the United States will be in the future to running wars through that particular committee. There are just too many fingers on the trigger."

Indeed, some European observers see America's support of NATO expansion as a cynical means of weakening European obstacles to its own agenda. "By inviting seven countries to join NATO, Bush killed seven birds with one stone," editorialized the Slovenian daily, *Delo*. "The East is at its climax; the United States has gained its most pro-American allies, its most faithful front in the war against terrorism; Europe is humiliated; NATO is marginalized and demoralized; and Bush — with his war — is on top, the leader of the world." [11]

Whatever Washington's true motives for backing NATO's expansion, America's longstanding allies — including "old Europe" — view expansion as a beneficial part of the unification process that has been under way for decades through the European Union.

"We always saw NATO enlargement and EU enlargement as two parallel elements of a Europe whole, undivided and free," says Voight of the German Foreign Office. "We are overcoming not only centuries, but 2,000 years, of European conflict — a pattern of European behavior that forced the United States to come to Europe in military form in two world wars."

Voight advises patience in weighing the potential contributions of an expanded NATO to global security. "We are now striving to project stability outside of Europe, which is where the United State wants us to do more," he

says. "I agree with the Americans, but it will take time before we achieve a more united voice in Europe. I see this as a challenge, but not hopeless. I'm optimistic in the longer run and realistic in the short run."

BACKGROUND

Cold War Alliance

When World War II ended in 1945, European countries were eager to demobilize and turn their energies to economic recovery. But the Soviet Union — a vital wartime ally — thwarted those plans when it began expanding its sphere of influence westward, manipulating the installation of communist governments in Eastern Europe. [12]

Following the Soviet blockade of Berlin in 1948, the United States, Canada and 10 European countries * sought to counter Soviet expansion. The North Atlantic Treaty, signed on April 4, 1949, in Washington, D.C., committed them to defend one another from attack and firmly established the transatlantic link by permanently tying the security of North America to that of Europe. At the same time, NATO was created as the treaty's organizational structure.

The treaty derived its legitimacy from Article 51 of the United Nations Charter, which affirms the right of independent states to individual or collective defense. [13] The treaty's central tenet, laid out in Article 5, states that an armed attack on one or more members of NATO will be deemed an attack against them all. Member countries agreed to develop and maintain their own military defenses and to conduct collective defensive operations in the event of attack on another member. They also agreed to adhere to democratic principles of government and further the cause of human rights. The North Atlantic Council, the alliance's top decision-making body, was set up as a forum for political consultations at NATO headquarters in Paris.

The treaty's Article 10 allowed the alliance to invite other European states in a position to contribute to the collective security. Greece and Turkey joined in 1952, after rebuffing Soviet advances. The Federal Republic of Germany — West Germany — joined in 1955. Spain

---

* The 10 were Belgium, Denmark, France, Iceland, Italy, Luxembourg, the Netherlands, Norway, Portugal and the United Kingdom.

CHRONOLOGY

1940s-1980s *Soviet expansion into Eastern Europe leads to the East-West standoff known as the Cold War and the creation of NATO.*

April 4, 1949 The United States, Canada and 10 European countries sign the North Atlantic Treaty, promising to protect each other against attack.

February 1952 Greece and Turkey join NATO.

1954 European countries establish the Western European Union, a common-defense agreement.

1955 West Germany joins NATO.

1966 President Charles de Gaulle pulls France out of NATO's military command.

1979 The United States deploys nuclear missiles at U.S. bases in Europe, fueling a European anti-nuclear peace movement.

1982 Spain becomes NATO's 16th member.

1987 The Intermediate-Range Nuclear Forces Treaty calls for the elimination of all land-based, short- and intermediate-range U.S. and Soviet nuclear missiles from Europe.

1990s *NATO allies struggle to identify the alliance's security role in the post-Cold War era.*

November 1989 East Germans tear down the Berlin Wall — the Cold War's most visible symbol.

Oct. 3, 1990 East and West Germany merge into the democratic Federal Republic of Germany.

1991 The United States leads an international force, including some NATO members, in repelling an Iraqi invasion of Kuwait.

Dec. 31, 1991 The Soviet Union breaks up, ending Cold War and the Warsaw Pact.

January 1994 NATO creates the Partnership for Peace (PfP), aimed at developing military cooperation with its former Warsaw Pact adversaries.

May 1995 NATO embarks on its first military operation, launching air strikes against Serb ground forces in Bosnia.

1997 NATO and Russia sign the NATO-Russia Founding Act establishing a framework for security cooperation.

March 1999 U.S.-led NATO forces drive Serb troops out of Kosovo to try to halt the genocide of Muslim Kosovars.

April 1999 NATO marks its 50th anniversary by enlarging its membership to include the Czech Republic, Hungary and Poland — the first former Soviet-bloc countries to join the alliance.

2000s *NATO confronts terrorism and weapons proliferation.*

Sept. 11, 2001 Terrorists crash airliners into the World Trade Center, Pentagon and Pennsylvania countryside. NATO allies offer to defend the United States.

Oct. 7, 2001 The United States and Britain attack Afghanistan, rebuffing NATO's offer to help oust the Taliban regime and track down terrorist leader Osama bin Laden.

September 2002 The Bush administration announces that pre-emptive strikes will be part of its national-security strategy.

Nov. 8, 2002 The United Nations Security Council passes Resolution 1441, calling on Iraq to hand over any weapons of mass destruction it may possess, or face "serious consequences."

Nov. 21-22, 2002 At its summit meeting in Prague, NATO invites Bulgaria, Estonia, Latvia, Lithuania, Romania, Slovakia and Slovenia to join the alliance.

March 1, 2003 Chief U.N. arms inspector Hans Blix will report on Iraqi compliance, an assessment that may prove key in shaping support for a U.S.-British resolution authorizing the use of military action against Iraq.

May 2004 NATO membership is scheduled to expand to 26 countries following referenda in the seven new alliance candidates.

became NATO's 16th member in 1982, after the right-wing regime of Gen. Francisco Franco was replaced by a democratic government.

With European nations busy rebuilding their economies and political institutions, the United States assumed the dominant military role within the alliance from the first. The European Economic Community — later renamed the European Union — was the key to improving economic and political relations on the continent. [14] As part of the rebuilding process, European countries in 1954 established the Western European Union (WEU), a common-defense agreement. But throughout the Cold War, Europe looked to NATO — and primarily the United States — for protection from the principal perceived threat to their security, the Soviet Union.

From the beginning, the imbalance in military power between the United States and its allies strained transatlantic relations. Indeed, at the end of World War II, the United States was the only NATO member with nuclear weapons. It was soon joined, however, by Britain and France.

NATO's first major crisis came in 1956, when British and French forces, over strong U.S. opposition, temporarily seized the Suez Canal after Egypt nationalized the vital shipping route.

A deeper breach came in 1966, when French President Charles de Gaulle, eager to maintain French sovereignty over its nuclear and other military assets in the face of what he saw as Anglo-American domination of the alliance, pulled out of NATO's military command and requested the removal from France of allied installations and bases not under direct French control.

By 1967, U.S. and other alliance troops and equipment had been moved from France to bases in West Germany and other nations, and NATO headquarters shifted from Paris to Brussels. France maintained its NATO membership, however, including its commitment to the common defense.

In 1979, in an effort to counter Soviet intermediate-range nuclear missiles, the United States stationed nuclear Pershing and cruise missiles at U.S. army bases in Europe. The deployment fueled an anti-nuclear peace movement centered in West Germany and Britain that quickly spread throughout the continent, undermining NATO cohesion. It also energized U.S.-Soviet arms-control negotiations, culminating in the 1987 Intermediate-Range Nuclear Forces Treaty, which banned land-based, short- and intermediate-range nuclear missiles. West

French President Jacques Chirac (left) and German Chancellor Gerhard Schröeder meet in Berlin on Jan. 23, 2003, when they reiterated their anti-U.S. position that Iraq needs to be disarmed "by peaceful means."

AFP Photo/Patrick Kovarik

Germany, where most of the U.S. nuclear weapons were deployed, embarked on a policy of détente with the Soviet Union in an effort to reduce East-West tensions and thus reduce the risk of war.

NATO's ability to weather the tensions in transatlantic relations began to pay off in the late 1980s. Under the leadership of President Mikhail S. Gorbachev, the Soviet Union adopted a policy of *perestroika*, relaxing political controls and introducing limited market reforms to revive the country's moribund economy. The uprising of Eastern Europeans against their Soviet-supported rulers culminated in 1989, when East Germans tore down the Berlin Wall — the Cold War's most visible symbol.

The European Union Spreads Its Wings

Like NATO, the European Union (EU) has been expanding into the former Soviet sphere of influence, approving applications last December from the Czech Republic, Estonia, Latvia, Lithuania, Hungary, Poland, Slovenia and Slovakia.

But some of the EU's new members — after decades under authoritarian communist rule — strongly disagree with some of its old members on what to do about Iraqi dictator Saddam Hussein.

"We are not joining the EU so we can sit and shut up," Czech Foreign Minister Cyril Svoboda said recently. Indeed, many EU applicants — which generally support Bush's desire to effect a "regime change" in Iraq — complained that France, which opposes the war, had shut them out of the debate. [1]

Both supporters and opponents of Bush's policy within the EU have been criticized for failing to respect the organization's goal of forging a common foreign policy by consulting with fellow EU members before stating their views. After German Chancellor Gerhard Schröeder and French President Jacques Chirac repeatedly voiced their opposition to Bush's war plans, eight other EU leaders assured Bush of their support. [2]

"Before we say we're not going to go to war, even when there is a U.N. mandate to do so, as Schröeder did, we should consult the other Europeans," says Henning Riecke, a senior research fellow at the German Council on Foreign Relations in Berlin. "We should at least acknowledge that we are taking these positions outside the EU. This repeated circumvention of procedures inside the EU is very frustrating, and it should remind the Europeans that they have a long way ahead if they want to come to unity."

Other observers downplay the significance of the rift over Iraq and are more sanguine about the European Union's future.

"The Europeans have done an admirable job of getting their house in order," says Michael J. Glennon, a professor of international law at Tufts University's Fletcher School of Law and Diplomacy. "If one thinks about the way the world should look 200 years from now, one would look to the European Union as a kind of model."

Like NATO, the European Union traces its roots to the immediate post-World War II period. But while NATO was dedicated to providing security for war-torn Western Europe, the European Economic Community (EEC) — the EU's precursor — aimed to remove trade barriers and hasten economic development.

Over time, the EEC's six founding members — Belgium, France, Italy, Luxembourg, the Netherlands and West Germany — added new countries and created new institutions to bind its members closer together. In 1979, EEC citizens elected representatives to a new European Parliament to deal with community affairs. In 1992, in recognition of the organization's growing political role, members changed the organization's name. In 1999, 11 of the 15 EU members adopted a single currency, the euro. The United Kingdom, Sweden, Denmark and Greece opted out of the common currency. Greece later adopted the euro, and Sweden is in the process of doing so, bringing to 13 the number of countries that will have replaced their national currencies with the euro. [3]

Since the Cold War ended in 1991, 13 countries have applied to join the EU, nine of them former Soviet republics or allies. To gain admission, applicants must adopt sweeping political and free-market economic reforms, a daunting process for countries whose economic and political institutions were based on a communist model for a half-century.

If voters in those countries approve membership, they will officially join the EU in 2004. The EU postponed admission for Bulgaria, Romania and Turkey, citing their failure thus far to meet admission criteria.

Although the EU and NATO are entirely separate organizations, 11 EU members belong to the transatlantic military alliance. Economic-policy hurdles to EU membership make joining NATO easier for some countries. For instance, Turkey has been a NATO member since 1952; Bulgaria and Romania were invited to join the military alliance last November.

"It's much easier to come into NATO than into the EU," Riecke says. "It will take quite a while before Bulgaria, for example, joins Europe because it is so far behind economically."

---

[1] Quoted by Keith B. Richburg, "EU Unity on Iraq Proves Short-Lived," *The Washington Post*, Feb. 19, 2003.

[2] Jose Maria Aznar, Jose-Manuel Durao Barroso, Silvio Berlusconi, Tony Blair, Vaclav Havel, Peter Medgyessy, Leszek Miller and Anders Fogh Rasmussen, "United We Stand," *The Wall Street Journal*, Jan. 30, 2002.

[3] For background, see Mary H. Cooper, "European Monetary Union," *The CQ Researcher*, Nov. 27, 1998, pp. 1025-1048.

On Oct. 3, 1990, East Germany merged with the Federal Republic. The same year, NATO and the Warsaw Pact states signed the Treaty on Conventional Armed Forces in Europe (CFE), which set limits on non-nuclear weapons on the continent, and called for a policy of non-aggression.

After Iraq's invasion of Kuwait on Aug. 4, 1990, the United States led a coalition force to drive out the invaders in early 1991. Although NATO was not involved directly in Operation Desert Storm, as the Pentagon dubbed it, several members participated, and the alliance deployed troops in neighboring Turkey — a longstanding NATO member — to demonstrate the collective-defense commitment in case the conflict spread.

On Dec. 31, 1991, the Soviet Union broke up, and with it the Warsaw Pact. By 1992, the former super-power had devolved into a single powerful successor state — Russia — and a loose aggregation of former Soviet republics known as the Commonwealth of Independent States. The former Warsaw Pact allies of Eastern Europe, meanwhile, had shifted their focus westward, adopted democratic governments and begun reforming their economies on the capitalist model.

NATO had emerged victorious from the 40-year Cold War without firing a shot.

Changing Vision

Amid the celebrations over their Cold War victory, NATO leaders initially lost sight of the fact that the Soviet Union's demise eliminated the alliance's principal reason for being. But the 1990s soon presented a set of unforeseen threats to European security that posed new challenges to NATO's cohesion.

Ironically, NATO's first major challenge stemmed directly from the dissolution of the very East-West divide that had prompted NATO's creation nearly a half-century earlier. In 1991, a series of bloody wars broke out in the Balkans, as Croatia and then Bosnia-Herzegovina, successor republics of communist Yugoslavia, struggled against Serbia for independence. Although NATO was well equipped to stop the massacre of Muslims in Bosnia, the allies disagreed over their new mission, and many were reluctant to intervene in areas outside NATO territory.

By the next year, the NATO and WEU allies finally had decided to support peacekeeping operations in the Balkans. NATO ships helped enforce U.N. sanctions barring arms deliveries to Serbian forces in Bosnia, and

NATO warplanes tried, with little success, to protect U.N.-defined "safe areas" inside the country from geno-cidal attacks by the Serbs. Finally, in May 1995, NATO launched air strikes against Serb ground forces — the first offensive military operation in NATO history. NATO also deployed thousands of troops to monitor and enforce the so-called Dayton peace accords, which settled the conflict. [15]

One of the alliance's key goals in the post-Cold War era has been to improve relations with its earlier nemesis, Russia, and the other former Soviet republics and Eastern European countries. Building on the 1975 Helsinki Accords, which set standards for basic human rights and created the Conference on Security and Cooperation in Europe (CSCE), NATO and Russia agreed to such measures as information-sharing on military assets, advance notification of military maneuvers and arms control. In January 1995, the CSCE formally became the Organization on Security and Cooperation in Europe (OSCE).

In November 1991, the confidence-building process was advanced when NATO established the North Atlantic Cooperation Council to encourage more detailed exchange of military information with Russia and its former allies. In January 1994, NATO took the process yet another step further by setting up the Partnership for Peace (PfP), aimed at developing true military cooperation with its former adversaries as well as non-allied Western European countries. Under this program, NATO and 27 PfP members * conducted joint military exercises, and PfP forces joined NATO's peacekeeping mission in Bosnia. Improved relations with Russia culminated in 1997, with the NATO-Russia Founding Act, which established a framework for security cooperation.

In April 1999, at its 50th anniversary summit in Washington, NATO enlarged its membership for the first time in 17 years when three PfP members — the Czech Republic, Hungary and Poland — became the first former Soviet-bloc countries to join the alliance, pushing the North Atlantic community's boundary some 400 miles eastward.

---

* The 27 original PfP members were Albania, Armenia, Austria, Azerbaijan, Belarus, Bulgaria, Croatia, Czech Republic, Estonia, Georgia, Hungary, Kazakhstan, Kyrgyz Republic, Latvia, Lithuania, Moldova, Poland, Romania, Russia, Slovakia, Slovenia, Switzerland, Tajikistan, Macedonia, Turkmenistan, Ukraine and Uzbekistan.

NATO also adopted a new initiative aimed at improving the ability of alliance forces to work together more efficiently and modernize their arsenals to face new security threats.

NATO operations had long been plagued by incompatible communications equipment and weaponry, making coordinated maneuvers difficult at best. Moreover, allied forces were still dominated by the tanks and other heavy weapons designed to thwart a Soviet ground invasion of Europe. Future conflicts would likely involve regional flareups or local terrorist incidents requiring lighter and more nimble, flexible forces that could be deployed quickly, even to distant battlefields. A key goal of the new initiative was to strengthen European military assets, which had fallen behind U.S. weaponry in quality and firepower after decades of lower defense spending.

Also in 1999, NATO overcame nearly a decade of indecision and debate over its role in the ongoing crisis in the Balkans and engaged in an offensive war to halt the killing and expulsion of ethnic Albanians in the Serb province of Kosovo by forces loyal to Serb leader Slobodan Milosevic, now on trial for war crimes in The Hague, Netherlands.

The Kosovo aerial bombing campaign began on March 24 and ended 78 days later with the retreat of Serb forces, the installation of a NATO-led international peacekeeping force and the establishment of a U.N.-sponsored international administrative body to govern the province.

The allied mission was not, however, a complete success. While NATO forces suffered only two casualties, the reliance on air attacks caused hundreds of civilian casualties and extensive damage to towns throughout the province. [16] NATO forces followed their operation in Kosovo with a successful mission to disarm rebels seeking to overthrow the government in neighboring Macedonia in 2001.

CURRENT SITUATION

Threat of Terrorism

Just as the NATO allies were becoming willing to undertake out-of-area missions in the Balkans, they also faced a pernicious new challenge: terrorism. Indeed, the 19 Arab men who killed more than 3,000 people on Sept. 11, 2001, were armed with nothing more than box cut-

ters when they crashed four hijacked airliners into the World Trade Center, the Pentagon and a field in rural Pennsylvania. NATO, with its nuclear arsenal, heavy tanks and smart bombs, was powerless against such unconventional tactics.

America's allies reacted to the attacks — ascribed to Saudi expatriate Osama bin Laden's Islamist al Qaeda organization — by invoking Article 5 of the North Atlantic Treaty, declaring that an attack on one member was an attack on all. "Nous sommes tous des américains" (We are all Americans) proclaimed the French daily *Le Monde*, echoing the solidarity expressed throughout Europe immediately after the attacks. The transatlantic goodwill lasted for several weeks, as President Bush put together a coalition to go after bin Laden, then headquartered in Afghanistan, and the Islamist Taliban regime that was protecting him.

But U.S.-allied relations began to fray as the time for military action grew near. Mindful of the difficulties experienced in the joint NATO effort in Kosovo, the Bush administration rebuffed offers by its NATO allies to participate in the mission.

"The military in the United States didn't want to use NATO in Afghanistan because they felt the alliance was too multilateral," says Parmentier, of the French Center on the United States. "I wasn't surprised at all when the Americans did that," he adds, acknowledging NATO's inefficiency. "NATO is organized in such a way that the military part does political work, and the political part does military work, and of course that doesn't work well.

"What surprised me was the contempt some in the Defense Department expressed, which was totally unnecessary. They could have been polite about it; in fact, they should have been, for their own interest."

Compounding the allies' sense of rejection was the Bush administration's formal adoption of a policy of preemption in September 2002. While several of Bush's predecessors, including John F. Kennedy and Bill Clinton, had acknowledged that the United States might be forced to attack a hostile power to prevent imminent aggression against America or its allies, none had adopted pre-emption as official policy.

Some experts say the administration's move was little more than a long-overdue formal recognition of the United States' de facto status as the world's lone superpower. "The truth hurts," says Glennon of Tufts University. "In the Bush administration's favor is this perhaps ingenuous belief on its part that we can afford to be straightforward and candid about our deeper motives, and that the rest of the international community is able to deal with that."

Indeed, some Europeans acknowledge that their governments failed to appreciate the changed security environment after the Sept. 11 attacks. "Nine-eleven did a lot to make Americans understand how vulnerable they are," says Riecke of the German Council on Foreign Relations. "In the 1990s, everybody in Europe was anxious that the Americans would focus too much on the military and too little on the non-military, diplomatic means of conducting foreign policy. But in the end, this amounted to complacency on our part."

To many observers in Europe and the United States, however, the pre-emptive strategy is part of a go-it-alone trend in American defense policy that accelerated after the terrorist attacks. "For the first time since the dawn of the Cold War, a new, grand strategy is taking shape in Washington," wrote G. John Inkenberry, a professor of geopolitics and global justice at Georgetown University, a year after the attacks. "It is advanced most directly as a response to terrorism, but it also constitutes a broader view about how the United States should wield power and organize the world order.

"According to this new paradigm," Inkenberry continued, "America is to be less bound to its partners and to global rules and institutions while it steps forward to play a more unilateral and anticipatory role in attacking terrorist threats and confronting rogue states seeking weapons of mass destruction. The United States will use its unrivaled military power to manage the global order." [17]

Prague Summit

NATO heads of state met in Prague last Nov. 21-22 to formally begin admitting seven new East European members. The three Baltic states — Estonia, Latvia and Lithuania — became the first former Soviet republics to join the alliance. Also invited were three former Warsaw Pact members — Bulgaria, Romania and Slovakia (formerly part of Czechoslovakia) — and the former Yugoslav republic of Slovenia. This latest expansion, scheduled to be completed in time for the next NATO summit in March 2004, would add 45 million people to the 735 million currently under alliance protection. [18]

The Bush administration strongly supports NATO enlargement, but critics say it will only hamper the

Czech paratroopers participate in the August 2001, NATO peace-keeping mission in Macedonia. In 1999, the Czech Republic was one of three countries to become NATO's first Eastern European members.

alliance's effectiveness — as well as U.S. security. "With this latest round of expansion, NATO will have 26 members, and at least three more are poised for admission in coming years," wrote Sen. Christopher J. Dodd, D-Conn. "Unless changes are made to strengthen the ability of NATO to act, there is little to prevent the diminution of its power and effectiveness as a military alliance, which would leave America, Europe and the world far worse off in the long run." [19]

Responding to such concerns, summit participants produced a commitment to modernize alliance forces to improve the rest of NATO's ability to work with the technologically advanced U.S. military. The "Prague Capabilities Commitment" identified 400 specific areas for improvement, including biochemical- and nuclear-warfare defenses, surveillance, command-and-control communications and combat effectiveness. America's allies agreed to acquire more large transport aircraft, refueling aircraft and air-launched, precision-guided munitions.

Members also agreed to create a new NATO response force, with technologically advanced, interoperable munitions and equipment for air, land and sea capabilities. The new force is to be flexible enough to move quickly and incorporate technology enabling the alliance to work together in meeting such new security threats as terrorism and regional conflicts that threaten European stability.

AFP Photo/Stephen Jaffe

Secretary of State Colin L. Powell (right), accompanied by NATO Secretary-General George Robertson, tells reporters on Feb. 20, 2003, that the U.S. will not improve its offer of $6 billion in aid to Turkey in exchange for basing rights for a possible invasion of Iraq. NATO members had opposed aid to the longtime NATO member because members felt it indicated support for action against Iraq. However, NATO recently decided to send purely defensive equipment, such as AWACS radar-surveillance planes and Patriot missile systems.

Military experts welcome NATO's modernization effort, but many, including Korb of the Council on Foreign Relations, say there has been little to show for it thus far. "The gap between the United States and Europe is so great technologically that it's almost impossible for us to work together," he says.

Despite such misgivings, NATO is participating in new operations. Britain and Turkey took command of a 22-nation peacekeeping force in Kabul, the Afghan capital, in December 2001 — the first NATO mission outside Europe. On Feb. 10, Germany and the Netherlands assumed control of the force. Last month, allied soldiers fought alongside American and Afghan troops to put down a rebel assault in southeastern Afghanistan. For Norway, it was the first time its planes had carried out combat bombings since World War II. [20]

But it is too soon to expect the allies — even such NATO powers as Germany — to do much more. "Thirteen years after the fall of the Berlin Wall, Germany's military forces are still largely structured to defend against Soviet tanks streaming across the Fulda Gap," wrote Heidi Reisinger, a research fellow at the

German Academy of the Federal Armed Forces for Information and Communication. Because all of NATO Europe possesses only 11 long-range aircraft (compared with more than 250 in the United States), she wrote, "Berlin has to rely on a private, London-based company that rents the Germans Ukrainian and Russian transport aircraft. If things in Afghanistan go badly and Germany needs to make a 911 call . . . it will have to be routed through the switchboard at the White House." [21]

Crisis Over Iraq

Allied anxiety over U.S. military superiority and President Bush's preference for unilateral action has intensified the current policy dispute over the administration plans to invade Iraq.

At last November's Prague summit, NATO allies issued a joint statement supporting U.N. Security Council Resolution 1441, calling on Iraq to disarm and committing the alliance to "take effective action to assist and support the efforts of the U.N. to ensure full and immediate compliance by Iraq." [22] But NATO's consensus soon fell apart over how to back up that statement in the face of continued Iraqi stonewalling over its weapons programs and Bush administration plans to force compliance by military means.

Seen from Europe, where most governments base their foreign policy more on "soft power" (diplomacy and development assistance), America's focus on military might — "hard power" — is misplaced. They point to a longstanding pattern of U.S. spending that favors weaponry over foreign aid. Continuing that trend, Bush has requested $399.1 billion for the military in fiscal 2004 — $16.9 billion above current spending.

"For many Europeans, it is strange to see that the United States is paying close to 10 times as much on defense as Germany, while spending so little for development aid and international institutions," Riecke, of the German Council on Foreign Relations, says. "They wonder: Wouldn't it be cheaper to buy Iraq than bomb it?"

Adding fuel to the debate is a clash of deeply held moral convictions on both sides of the Atlantic. Many of Bush's strongest supporters are religious conservatives who see the Iraqi regime as a threat to Israel as well as the United States. Much of the European opposition to Bush's war plans, however, has its roots in the peace movement of the 1970s and '80s, which grew out of

Does the Bush administration's foreign policy undermine NATO?

YES Sen. John Kerry, D-Mass.
Candidate for the Democratic Presidential Nomination

From a Speech at Georgetown University, Jan. 23, 2003

The Bush administration's blustering unilateralism is wrong, and even dangerous, for our country. In practice, it has meant alienating our longtime friends and allies, alarming potential foes and spreading anti-Americanism around the world. Too often, administration officials have forgotten that energetic global leadership is a strategic imperative for America, not a favor we do for other countries.

Leading the world's most advanced democracies isn't mushy multilateralism — it amplifies America's voice and extends our reach. Working through global institutions doesn't tie our hands — it invests U.S. aims with greater legitimacy and dampens the fear and resentment that our preponderant power sometimes inspires in others. In a world growing more, not less, interdependent, unilateralism is a formula for isolation and shrinking influence.

As much as some in the White House may desire it, America can't opt out of a networked world. . . . And those who seek to lead have a duty to offer a clear vision of how we make Americans safer and make America more trusted and respected in the world.

What America needs today is a smarter, more comprehensive and farsighted strategy for modernizing the greater Middle East. It should draw on all of our nation's strengths: military might, the world's largest economy, the immense moral prestige of freedom and democracy — and our powerful alliances.

Let me emphasize that last asset in this mission: our alliances. This isn't a task that we should or need to shoulder alone. If anything, our transatlantic partners have a greater interest than we do in an economic and political transformation in the greater Middle East. They are closer to the front lines; more heavily dependent on oil imports; prime magnets for immigrants seeking jobs; easier to reach with missiles and just as vulnerable to terrorism.

Meanwhile, NATO is searching for a new mission. What better way to revitalize the most successful and enduring alliance in history than to reorient it around a common threat to the global system that we have built over more than a half-century of struggle and sacrifice?

The administration has tried to focus NATO on the Middle East, but its high-handed treatment of our European allies, on everything from Iraq to the Kyoto climate-change treaty, has strained relations nearly to the breaking point. We can do better. With creative leadership, the U.S. can enlist its allies in a sustained, multilateral campaign to build bridges between the community of democracies and the greater Middle East — not just for them, but for us.

NO Colin L. Powell
Secretary of State

From a Speech to The World Economic Forum, Davos, Switzerland, Jan. 26, 2003

More than a half-century ago, the United States helped rescue Europe from the tyranny of fascism that had led to World War II. We stayed to help Europe regain its vitality. We supported and continue to support a strong, united Europe and congratulate Europeans on the recent enlargement of the European Union.

Americans and Europeans together built the greatest political-military alliance in history. NATO was at the core of our efforts to keep the peace in Europe for more than four decades. The Cold War ended, and yet 10 nations have joined the alliance since the Cold War's end. Why were they so anxious to join? And why do still others wait on the list to become members of this grand alliance?

The answer, I think, is rather simple. They want to join to be part of Europe, a Europe whole and free, but they also want to be part of a body that links the United States and Canada to Europe. They want to be part of a transatlantic community, a transatlantic community that at one and the same time promotes peace, prosperity and democratic values — the power of men and women to choose, to sustain government of the people.

Now, I'm aware, as everyone in this room is aware, that Americans and Europeans do not always see things the same way in every instance. . . . Problems with some of our friends across the Atlantic go back a long time, more than two centuries by my count. . . . Yet the marriage is intact, remains strong [and] will weather any differences that come along because of our mutual shared values.

Differences are inevitable, but differences should not be equated with American unilateralism or American arrogance. Sometimes differences are just that — differences. On occasion, our experiences, our interests, will lead us to see things in a different way. For our part, we will not join a consensus if we believe it compromises our core principles. Nor would we expect any other nation to join in a consensus that would compromise its core principles. When we feel strongly about something, we will lead. We will act even if others are not prepared to join us.

But the United States will always work, will always endeavor, to get others to join in a consensus. We want to work closely with Europe, home of our closest friends and partners. We want to work closely with Europe on challenges inside Europe and beyond, and you can trust us on that.

U.S. Air Force

The Predator, an unmanned reconnaissance drone that is used by the United States in Afghanistan and over southern Iraq, is armed with short-range missiles. The NATO allies fear that because U.S. military weaponry is so much more technologically advanced than Europe's, the alliance is less important to the United States in fighting terrorism.

church-based opposition to the arms race. "There are no two parts in our debate who are more apart from one another than those who have strong moral and religious convictions, meaning the religious right in the United States and the Christian left in Germany," says Voight of the German Foreign Office. "Both groups argue in moral terms, but they argue against one another."

As the rhetoric in the Iraq debate between the United States and its opponents has become more heated, several NATO allies have cast their votes firmly with the Bush administration. "Our strength comes in our unity," wrote the leaders of Spain, Britain, the Czech Republic, Denmark, Hungary, Italy, Poland and Portugal in an open letter published in *The Wall Street Journal.* Echoing the Bush administration's warning, they continued, the transatlantic relationship "must not become a casualty of the current Iraqi regime's persistent attempts to threaten world security." [23] The letter followed French and German pledges to use their seats on the Security Council to at least delay, and possibly block, U.N. authorization for a strike on Iraq.

Many Europeans, including some who are not opposed to intervening in Iraq, are offended by Defense Secretary Rumsfeld's offhand remarks about "old Europe" and his lumping Germany together with Libya and Cuba as countries that obstruct America's war on terrorism. "Every time Rumsfeld opens his mouth he

damages America's reputation," says Grant of the Center for European Reform. "He's incredibly good at upsetting people. Though his comment about 'old Europe' was actually perfectly accurate, it wasn't the wisest thing to say when you're trying to build a coalition."

The only high administration official who commands broad respect in Europe is Secretary of State Powell, who until recently tended to sympathize with most allies' desire to pursue diplomacy as long as possible to rid Iraq of its weapons of mass destruction.

"If it weren't for the tireless work of Colin Powell, we wouldn't have a transatlantic relationship at all," Grant says. "As far as we can see, the whole relationship has been propped up by Powell on the American side. Throughout this debate, the administration's diplomacy has been inept, especially when it has been done by people other than Powell."

America's North American NATO ally, Canada, tends to look more toward Europe in the dispute over U.S. policy toward Iraq. "One of the problems of U.S.-Canada relations, going back to your Revolution, has always been that Canadians are pretty wary of the 850-pound gorilla south of the border," says Griffiths of the Dominion Institute in Toronto. "When it starts acting up, we start becoming very cautious. The Canadian public is always suspicious of Americans, and Bush hits a lot of our stereotypes of an American president from Texas. There's an old Canadian adage that it's better for the Americans not to be talking about you, and if Rumsfeld told [Prime Minister Jean] Cretien it's time to pull up his socks and deliver, the political reverberations up here would be immense."

At home, the Bush administration has enjoyed strong support in Congress for its war plans. Last October, Congress authorized the use of military force against Iraq, and few legislators raised serious objections. The consensus in Washington is beginning to erode, however. [24]

Few legislators are as outspoken in their criticism of Bush's policy on Iraq — and its treatment of America's allies — as Sen. Robert C. Byrd, D-W.Va. "This administration has called into question the traditional worldwide perception of the United States as a well-intentioned peacekeeper," he said. "This administration has turned the patient art of diplomacy into threats, labeling and name-calling of the sort that reflects quite poorly on the intelligence and sensitivity of our leaders, and which will have consequences for years to come. . . .

"We may have massive military might," Byrd continued, "but we cannot fight a global war on terrorism alone. We need the cooperation and friendship of our time-honored allies, as well as the newer-found friends whom we can attract with our wealth."

OUTLOOK

Political Fallout

If NATO fails to agree on how to deal with Iraq, experts worry that the crisis will spill over into the political landscape of some of America's longstanding allies, such as Britain, Italy and Spain. The leader with the most at stake is British Prime Minister Blair, whose staunch support of Bush's Iraq policy has cost him dearly. Since the massive anti-war demonstrations in London on Feb. 15, Blair's approval rating has sunk to about 35 percent. [25]

"People in America don't realize that not only British public opinion but also [Blair's] own political party hate this war," says Grant of the Center for European Reform. Under Britain's parliamentary system, the prime minister presides at the pleasure of the majority party. "If the war turns out to be anything other than short and relatively painless, he'll cease to be prime minister," says Grant, himself a Blair supporter. "The risks he is taking are absolutely enormous."

Blair's ouster, in turn, could spell trouble for the Bush administration. His replacement would be the Labor Party's second in command, Gordon Brown, who shares Blair's support of Britain's "special relationship" with the United States, but not his affinity for military solutions. "Brown is a bit of a pacifist who doesn't believe in military spending and doesn't like warfare," Grant says. "With Brown in charge, Britain will not be willing to fight alongside America nearly so much as it has done with Blair."

German Chancellor Schröeder, too, may pay a price for his opposition to U.S. policy. At a recent conference in Germany, Marine Gen. James Jones, the new U.S. military commander in Europe, suggested that the United States was considering moving some of its 100,000 troops currently based in Germany to new "lily pad" bases in Eastern Europe, which could serve as launching areas for rapid deployment to the Middle East or Africa. [26]

Jones did not suggest that the plan was aimed at punishing Schröeder for his criticism of U.S. policy on Iraq, and some German observers downplay the significance of Jones' comments. "Such a move may be possible in 10 years," says Riecke, of the German Council on Foreign Relations. "But Germany has a certain level of infrastructure that makes it very useful for the Americans to stay here." However, a significant drawdown of the U.S. forces could harm the German economy, which already suffers from one of Europe's highest unemployment rates, and possibly undermine Schröeder's already tenuous support at home.

Two Paths?

Despite the seriousness of the rift between the United States and its allies over Iraq, few observers predict it will render NATO obsolete. "NATO is still valuable," says Wallander of the Center for Strategic and International Studies. "It's possible that NATO and the transatlantic community could emerge stronger from however the policy on Iraq works out, but only if the members of NATO recognize that the security challenge of the 21st century is bigger than Iraq. Iraq is just one case of what's going to be our threat environment for at least the next decade."

But it's far from certain what role the alliance will play in the new security environment. "It's easier to describe what NATO won't be doing than it is to describe what NATO will be doing," says Glennon of Tufts University. Just a decade ago, there was talk of using NATO as kind of a standby reserve force ready to back up U.N. Security Council resolutions. "Kosovo effectively ended that dream, because rightly or wrongly, the United States lost enthusiasm for NATO military operations. So NATO almost surely will not be engaged in out-of-area operations."

Other analysts say the allies have a basic choice to make over NATO's future role. "NATO is at a crossroads," says Parmentier of the French Center on the United States. "The easy path would be to make NATO into more of a political organization that would discuss matters of mutual concern. With so many new countries joining, it's quite easy to see it becoming a sort of forum.

"But there is a harder path," Parmentier says, "which would emphasize the military side of NATO. That would make NATO into a more effective organization by pooling military forces and placing them at the service of its members."

However NATO evolves, many predict it will continue to serve the main purpose its founders had in mind. "NATO will never be a four-letter word for efficiency because it's an alliance of too many countries," says the CSIS' Cordesman. "But NATO's actual purpose is to bring Europe together and bridge East and West. It's nice to have allies with us in Iraq — it would probably be nice to have them in Antarctica, too — but it's vital to have them in Europe."

NOTES

1. De Villepin spoke Feb. 14, 2002.

2. See Glenn Frankel, "Millions Worldwide Protest Iraq War," *The Washington Post*, Feb. 16, 2003.

3. Powell addressed the U.N. Security Council on Feb. 14, 2003, after reports by chief U.N. arms inspector Hans Blix and International Atomic Energy Agency Director Mohamed El Baradei.

4. For background, see Mary H. Cooper, "Transatlantic Tensions," *The CQ Researcher*, July 13, 2001, pp. 553-576.

5. The strategy paper can be found at www.white-house.gov/nsc/nss9.html.

6. Rumsfeld testified Feb. 5, 2003, before the House Armed Services Committee.

7. "EU, in First Military Mission, Will Keep Peace in Macedonia," The Associated Press, Jan. 27, 2003.

8. Deaglan de Breadun, "Bigger, Not Better, at Fighting Terror," *The Irish Times*, Nov. 25, 2002.

9. International Institute for Strategic Studies, *The Military Balance 2002-2003*, (2002), p. 332.

10. Organization for Economic Cooperation and Development, *Annex to OECD*, "Society at a Glance: OECD Social Indicators," 2001.

11. *Delo* (Ljublijana, Slovenia), Nov. 22, 2002, cited in *World Press Review*, February 2003, p. 24.

12. For background, see Mary H. Cooper, "Expanding NATO," *The CQ Researcher*, May 16, 1997, pp. 433-456.

13. For background, see Mary H. Cooper, "United Nations at 50," *The CQ Researcher*, Aug. 18, 1995, pp. 729-752.

14. For more information on the European Union's development, see Mary H. Cooper, "European Monetary Union," *The CQ Researcher*, Nov. 27, 1998, pp. 1036-1038.

15. For background on Bosnia and war crimes, see Kenneth Jost, "War Crimes," *The CQ Researcher*, July 7, 1995, pp. 585-688, and Mary H. Cooper, "Women and Human Rights," *The CQ Researcher*, April 30, 1999, pp. 353-376.

16. For an analysis of NATO's intervention in Kosovo, see Ivo H. Daalder and Michael E. O'Hanlon, *Winning Ugly: NATO's War to Save Kosovo* (2000).

17. G. John Inkenberry, "America's Imperial Ambition," *Foreign Affairs*, September/October 2002, p. 49.

18. Figures from NATO's Web site, www.nato.int.

19. Christopher J. Dodd, "NATO: The More the Murkier," *The Washington Post*, Nov. 27, 2002.

20. See Carlotta Gall, "U.S. and Its Allies Fight Rebel Force on Afghan Peaks," *The New York Times*, Jan. 29, 2003.

21. Heidi Reisinger, "Note to Gerhard: This Is Getting Embarrassing," *The Washington Post*, Nov. 24, 2002.

22. "Prague Summit Statement on Iraq," Nov. 21, 2002. NATO press release 133, www.nato.int.

23. Jose Maria Aznar, Jose-Manuel Durao Barroso, Silvio Berlusconi, Tony Blair, Vaclav Havel, Peter Medgyessy, Leszek Miller and Anders Fogh Rasmussen, "United We Stand," *The Wall Street Journal*, Jan. 30, 2002.

24. See Niels C. Sorrells, "Senate Democrats Press for Diplomatic High Ground on Iraq," *CQ Weekly*, Feb. 8, 2003, pp. 358-360.

25. See Glenn Frankel, "Blair Under Siege Over Stance on Iraq," *The Washington Post*, Feb. 19, 2003.

26. See Peter Grier and Faye Bowers, "Roles on Iraq May Reshape NATO," *The Christian Science Monitor*, Feb. 12, 2003.

BIBLIOGRAPHY

Books

Asmus, Ronald D., *Opening NATO's Door*, Columbia University Press, 2002.
While serving as a State Department official in the Clinton administration, the author strongly advocated NATO's expansion as a way to enhance stability in Eastern Europe after the Soviet Union broke up. He describes the diplomatic process that led to improved relations between the alliance and Russia as well as the accession of Poland, the Czech Republic and Hungary in 1999.

Boot, Max, *The Savage Wars of Peace: Small Wars and the Rise of American Power*, Basic Books, 2002.
The author chronicles the United States' repeated use of military force throughout its history and concludes that intervention is justified to ensure freedom in foreign countries because "a world of liberal democracies would be a world much more amenable to American interests than any conceivable alternative."

Daalder, Ivo H., and Michael E. O'Hanlon, *Winning Ugly: NATO's War to Save Kosovo*, Brookings Institution Press, 2000.
Two military experts analyze NATO's first military offensive, launched on March 24, 1999, to drive Serb forces out of Kosovo. The aerial bombing campaign succeeded, but lasted longer than expected, failed to immediately halt the Serbs' expulsion of Muslim civilians and pointed up shortcomings in NATO's ability to act as a cohesive military force.

Sloan, Stanley R., NATO, *The European Union and the Atlantic Community: The Transatlantic Bargain Reconsidered*, Rowman & Littlefield, 2002.
A veteran NATO observer presents a critical history of the alliance and calls for a new treaty to accommodate the post-Cold War security environment.

Articles

Gordon, Philip, "Bridging the Atlantic Divide," *Foreign Affairs*, January/February 2003, pp. 70-83.
The director of the Brookings Institution's Center on the United States and France warns that the escalating tensions between the Bush administration and its European counterparts threaten to weaken the strong bonds both sides need to defend against terrorism and other threats to security.

Grant, Charles, "The Troubled State of Transatlantic Relations," *Global Agenda*, 2003.
The author says policy differences over the Israeli-Palestinian conflict and Iraq, a widening military gap and Europe's failure to adequately confront terrorism are aggravating transatlantic tensions that undermine NATO's effectiveness.

Kagan, Robert, "Power and Weakness," *Policy Review*, June/July 2002.
The author touched a raw nerve in Europe by asserting that Europeans' preference for diplomatic solutions to crises is the inevitable result of Europe's loss of military power, while the United States' willingness to assert its military might stems from its emergence as the world's sole superpower.

Lambert, Richard, "Misunderstanding Each Other," *Foreign Affairs*, March/April 2003, pp. 62-74.
Print and broadcast media commentators are fanning animosity between the United States and its European allies, turning to longstanding stereotypes to emphasize differences in viewpoint rather than seeking the common ground needed to improve relations.

Nordhaus, William D., "Iraq: The Economic Consequences of War," *The New York Review of Books*, Dec. 5, 2002, pp. 9-12.
A Yale University economics professor estimates that even a short, victorious war to oust Iraqi leader Saddam Hussein would cost $121 billion, including military, peacekeeping, reconstruction and nation-building. A more protracted war that ended badly for the United States could cost as much as $1.6 trillion, a staggering amount if shouldered by America alone.

Zakaria, Fareed, "Our Way," *The New Yorker*, Oct. 14 & 21, 2002, pp. 72-81.
America's military dominance, decried in France as "hyperpower," may threaten U.S. security over time. "The Soviet Union was feared by its allies; the United States was loved, or, at least, liked," the author notes. "Look who's still around."

Reports and Studies

European Institute, "Transatlantic Interoperability in Defense Industries: How the U.S. and Europe Could Better Cooperate in Coalition Military Operations," September 2002.
The report addresses a key challenge to the NATO allies' ability to work together. The lack of common standards and communications capability impeded allied effectiveness in Kosovo and contributed to the U.S. decision to virtually exclude its NATO allies from last year's operation in Afghanistan.

NATO Office of Information and Press, "NATO Handbook," 2001.
This exhaustive review of the transatlantic alliance's history and organization includes texts of treaties and descriptions of NATO's numerous programs and missions.

For More Information

Atlantic Council of the United States, 910 17th St., N.W., Suite 1000, Washington, DC 20006; (202) 463-7226; www.acus.org. Promotes constructive U.S. leadership and engagement in international affairs, based on the central role of the Atlantic community.

Center for Defense Information, 1779 Massachusetts Ave., N.W., Suite 615, Washington, DC 20036; (202) 332-0600; www.cdi.org. Advocates a strong defense while opposing excessive weapons expenditures and policies that increase the risk of war. Web site provides data about NATO troop levels and spending.

Center for Strategic and International Studies, 1800 K St., N.W., Suite 400, Washington, DC 20006; (202) 887-0200; www.csis.org. A research institute that studies a range of strategic international issues.

Council on Foreign Relations, 58 East 68th St., New York, NY 10021; (212) 434-9400; www.cfr.org. A nonpartisan foreign-policy think tank.

European Institute, 5225 Wisconsin Ave., N.W., Suite 200, Washington, DC 20015-2014; (202) 895-1670; www.europeaninstitute.org. A public-policy organization devoted to transatlantic affairs.

North Atlantic Treaty Organisation, Blvd. Leopold III, 110 Brussels, Belgium; www.nato.int. Web site containing a wealth of information about NATO's history, organization and mission.

U.S. Department of Defense, European and NATO Affairs, The Pentagon, Washington, DC 20301-2400; (703) 697-7207; www.defenselink.mil. The Defense Department's Web site provides information on U.S.-NATO relations and troop strength.

4

New Defense Priorities

Mary H. Cooper

Secretary of Defense Donald H. Rumsfeld calls for transforming the military to enable it to counter "asymmetric" threats from unconventional forces like the al Qaeda Islamic terrorist organization. The administration applied some of its new military priorities in the war to oust Iraq's Saddam Hussein, who President Bush said was developing weapons of mass destruction.

From *The CQ Researcher,*
September 13, 2002 (Revised June 2003).

During the Cold War, the U.S. military amassed an arsenal of unprecedented power, including thousands of nuclear weapons, bombers, aircraft carriers, tanks and submarines. But nothing about the Sept. 11 terrorist attacks on New York City and the Pentagon corresponded to the conventional, dooms-day war scenarios anticipated by the Pentagon — a Soviet land invasion of Europe or nuclear missile attack against the United States.

Nevertheless, President George W. Bush responded to the attacks in a conventional manner. He declared a "war on terrorism" and sought international support for military action. Then he mounted a U.S.-British offensive against the alleged mastermind of the attacks, Saudi exile Osama bin Laden, his Islamic terrorist organization al Qaeda and its Taliban supporters in Afghanistan. [1]

Although Operation Enduring Freedom used some of the Pentagon's most sophisticated new communications systems and "smart" weapons, many al Qaeda leaders escaped capture. The operation succeeded in toppling the Taliban, but Bush's larger war on terrorism continues amid questions about U.S. preparedness for such unconventional combat.

"As the cliché goes, the generals are always preparing for the last war," said Ranan R. Lurie, a senior associate at the Center for Strategic and International Studies (CSIS). "But there will never be a war that is so different from previous wars as this one is, and we would be extremely irresponsible not to recognize that fact."

But almost two years after Sept. 11, it is still unclear how the attacks will affect U.S. defense policy. In his first effort to adapt strategy and weaponry to a rapidly changing international security environment, Defense Secretary Donald H. Rumsfeld emphasized

U.S. Strength vs. Potential Enemies

The United States far surpasses in manpower and materiel the countries historically identified by the Department of Defense as potential enemies. Moreover, the comparison understates the full military strength of the U.S. because of the higher capability of U.S. weaponry, training and communications, according to the independent Center for Defense Information.

	Active Troops	Reserves	Heavy Tanks	Armored Vehicles	Planes	Helicopters	Warships
U.S.	1,400,000	1,200,000	8,303	24,075	9,030	6,779	200
Iran*	513,000	350,000	1,135	1,145	269	718	8
Iraq	429,000	650,000	2,200	4,400	350	500	--
Libya	76,000	40,000	2,210	2,620	594	202	4
North Korea	1,100,000	4,700,000	3,500	3,060	1,167	320	29
Sudan	104,500	--	170	488	46	28	--
Syria	316,000	396,000	4,850	4,785	640	221	2

*Iran has been historically defined as a potential U.S. enemy, but the Department of Defense removed Iran from the list in March 1999.

Sources: Center for Defense Information, *Military Almanac 2001-2002*, based on data from U.S. Department of Defense and the International Institute for Strategic Studies

the need to "deter and defeat" unconventional adversaries like bin Laden. He called for a stronger homeland defense and preparations for countering "asymmetric" warfare — unconventional attacks by forces, like al Qaeda, which cannot match the United States' military strength on the battlefield. [2] Indeed, the Sept. 11 hijackers were not regular soldiers, and their commanders acted on behalf of no recognized government.

Since the attacks, Bush has requested, and obtained from Congress, an immediate infusion of money to conduct the war on terrorism. Lawmakers approved a record $382.2 billion military-spending measure for fiscal 2003 — a 10 percent, or $34.4 billion, increase over 2002. The Pentagon has requested $399.1 billion for fiscal 2004, a 4.4 percent increase over last year. [3]

Rumsfeld's Pentagon is forging ahead with efforts to build what Rumsfeld says will be a more flexible, mobile military capable of using the latest technology to quash the kinds of asymmetric warfare likely to threaten national security in the future.

"Big institutions aren't swift on their feet," Rumsfeld said on Sept. 3, 2002. "They're ponderous and clumsy

and slow." A terrorist organization, meanwhile, "watches how you're behaving and then alters and adjusts at relatively little cost, [in] relatively little time, [with] relatively little training to those incremental changes we make in how we do things." [4]

The solution, Rumsfeld said, is to change the way the U.S. military does things. "Business as usual won't do it," he said.

In the process, Rumsfeld is planning to scuttle some traditional weapons, such as the Crusader, a heavy cannon designed for old-style battlefield combat. Eliminating the $11 billion program — which is already under way — may be the first of several major changes in ongoing weapons systems. The latest "defense planning guidance," which lays out the administration's defense investment priorities for fiscal 2004-2009, calls for the review — and possible elimination — of several other major systems now considered outmoded for future combat scenarios (*see p. 78*).

Aside from the expanded spending bill, however, there are few signs that the attacks have prompted major defense-policy changes. "Although Sept. 11 has created a greater sense of threat and a greater willingness to spend money on national security, the long-term plans of the military establishment's senior policymakers have changed relatively little in response to Sept. 11," said Loren B. Thompson, a defense analyst at the Lexington Institute, a think tank in Arlington, Va. "Judging from the defense planning guidance, what they're trying to achieve and what priorities they plan to pursue are remarkably similar to the goals and terminology used prior to Sept. 11."

Bush's most visible defense-related initiative is the new Department of Homeland Security — a massive, $34.7 billion undertaking to merge some 170,000 federal workers from 22 agencies into a new, Cabinet-level agency dedicated to protecting the United States from terrorist attack. [5]

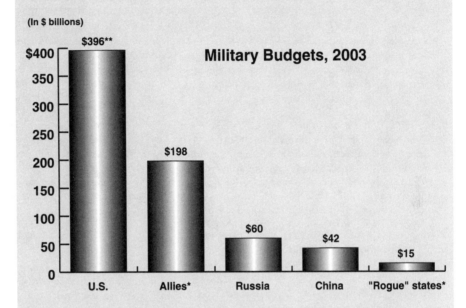

U.S. Military Spending Dwarfs Other Nations

The proposed U.S. military budget for 2003 exceeds the combined military budgets of the world's other major powers and the "rogue" nations identified as potential enemies by the Defense Department.

(In $ billions)

Military Budgets, 2003

- U.S.: $396**
- Allies*: $198
- Russia: $60
- China: $42
- "Rogue" states*: $15

*Allies include the NATO countries, Australia, Japan and South Korea. Rogue states are Cuba, Iraq, Iran, Libya, North Korea, Sudan and Syria.

**Includes requests for Energy Department nuclear-weapons programs and military construction in addition to the core Defense Department budget request.

Source: Center for Defense Information, *Military Almanac, 2001-2002,* based on data from the International Institute for Strategic Studies and the Department of Defense.

"But that is almost entirely separate from the military establishment," Thompson said. "Defense spending has increased, but for the most part not because of Sept. 11. So it is somewhat misleading to think that the surge in money for homeland security is synonymous with increased defense spending."

But others warn against radical changes in the Pentagon's ongoing effort to transform the military. "There is danger in taking an overly militarized view of the war on terrorism," said Joseph Nye, dean of Harvard University's John F. Kennedy School of Government. "It's important to realize that the military is only a part of what is needed to protect against terrorism, and maybe not even the dominant part."

Nye, who served as assistant Defense secretary for international security affairs under former President Bill Clinton, says the attacks did not significantly change the nature of emerging post-Cold War threats to U.S. security — such as the possibility that Iraq and other so-called rogue states may be developing nuclear weapons. "We have to have an intelligent defense strategy" to deal with such threats, he said.

In fact, Bush's recent war to effect "regime change" in Iraq represents one of the major shifts in the administration's military policy. Bush has often warned that he would consider preemptive strikes against any states or terrorist groups trying to develop nuclear, biological or chemical weapons — so-called weapons of mass destruction — that could be used against the United States.

Bush's Go-It-Alone Nuclear Policy

The Bush administration's call to overthrow Iraqi President Saddam Hussein — suspected of developing nuclear weapons for possible use against the United States or its allies — represents a radical departure in U.S. arms-control policy. That policy, in essence, called for negotiation rather than unilateral action.

During the Cold War, the United States and the Soviet Union developed a series of negotiated agreements to avert a potentially catastrophic nuclear exchange. Those treaties included the 1972 Anti-Ballistic Missile Treaty (ABM) and the SALT I and II treaties, negotiated in the 1970s and 1980s.

When the Soviet Union dissolved in 1991, the SALT treaties became obsolete, and the United States and leaders of the new Russia negotiated new treaties, starting with the 1991 Strategic Arms Reduction Treaty (START I). It limited each side to 6,000 warheads and 1,600 long-range bombers and missiles. The treaty also applied to the Soviet successor states of Russia, Ukraine, Belarus and Kazakhstan, then the repositories for the former Soviet arsenal. [1]

As bilateral relations steadily improved, the United States and Russia agreed to further nuclear-arms reductions. In January 1993, even before START I took effect (December 1994), they signed START II, which called for nearly halving each country's strategic nuclear warheads, to 3,500. The U.S. Senate ratified the treaty in January 1996, the Russian legislature in 2000.

In March 1997, President Bill Clinton and Russian President Boris Yeltsin agreed to begin negotiations on START III, once START II entered into force. The new treaty would have reduced each side's nuclear arsenals to 2,000-2,500 warheads and set limits on shorter-range, or tactical, nuclear weapons.

By 2001, when President Bush took office, START II had yet to enter into force. As a critic of traditional arms-control policy, Bush strongly supported the accelerated construction of a national missile-defense system. But the ABM Treaty prohibited such a nationwide defensive system, on the theory that it would spark the building of more nuclear arms to overcome it.

The ABM Treaty allowed each country to install a single missile-defense site, with no more than 100 interceptors, provided they did not provide nationwide coverage. The treaty was part of a broad agreement limiting both sides' ballistic-missile arsenals. (The 1979 SALT II Treaty contained a second set of limits, but the Senate refused to ratify it after the Soviets invaded Afghanistan in 1980.)

On Dec. 13, 2001, Bush announced his intention to unilaterally withdraw from the ABM Treaty, calling it out of date. Over Russian objections, the United States officially withdrew from the treaty on June 13, 2002.

At the same time, Bush announced — again unilaterally — plans to continue reducing the U.S. nuclear arsenal. Instead of pursuing his predecessor's efforts to conclude START III, Bush bypassed the negotiation process and declared that the United States would cut its nuclear arsenal to below the levels agreed to under START II. Russia,

---

[1] Information in this section is based in part on Amy F. Woolf, "Nuclear Arms Control: The U.S.-Russian Agenda," Congressional Research Service, June 13, 2002.

"We must . . . confront the worst threats before they emerge," Bush told the graduating class of West Point on June 1, 2002. "In the world we have entered, the only path to safety is the path of action. And this nation will act."

Preemptive-strike proposals stem from frustration over the U.S. military's inability to prevent the Sept. 11 attacks as well as from fear that in the era of the suicide bomber, America's longstanding strategy of deterrence may not be enough.

"Most countries are deterred from attacking us, even if they have nuclear weapons, by the fact that we also have nuclear weapons and could do considerable damage to them," said Peter W. Galbraith, a professor at the

National War College, which trains senior Pentagon officers. But al Qaeda has "no return address," he pointed out. "If they smuggle [a nuclear weapon] in and blow it up in Washington or New York, we can do nothing to hit back except what we've been trying to do, apparently unsuccessfully, for the last year, which is to get Mr. bin Laden, dead or alive."

Bush enjoyed widespread bipartisan support for his military actions in Afghanistan following the Sept. 11 attacks. But the war to oust President Saddam Hussein of Iraq, absent overt aggression against the United States, raised concerns at home and abroad. Senate Foreign Relations Committee Chairman Joseph R. Biden Jr., D-Del., held a hearing on the issue several months before

however, called for a formal, bilateral agreement binding the two sides to any further nuclear arms reductions.

On May 24, 2002, Bush and Russian President Vladimir Putin signed a new Strategic Offensive Reductions Treaty. Known as the Treaty of Moscow, it calls for cuts in each country's deployed nuclear warheads to between 1,700 and 2,200 by the end of 2012. As the Senate prepares to consider the treaty, Senate Foreign Relations Committee Chairman Joseph Biden Jr., D-Del., and some other lawmakers are pressing for controls on short-range nuclear warheads as well. Russia's stockpile of thousands of tactical weapons is poorly guarded, and lawmakers worry that terrorists could obtain some warheads and make easily concealed "suitcase bombs" that could be detonated in a U.S. city. [2]

Meanwhile, the administration has stated it will not seek ratification of the 1996 Comprehensive Nuclear Test Ban Treaty (CTBT). By prohibiting all nuclear tests, the treaty aims to halt the improvement of existing nuclear arsenals and the development of new nuclear weapons. Signed by

Iraq's Saddam Hussein meets in August with Foreign Minister Sheikh Hamad of Qatar, the first Gulf state to re-establish ties with Iraq after the 1991 gulf war.

President Clinton and 164 other countries, it would enter into force after ratification by the 44 countries that already have nuclear weapons or nuclear reactors. To date, 31 have done so, including Russia, the United Kingdom, and France.

In the United States, critics have argued that some signatories might secretly test weapons or improve their nuclear stockpiles while the treaty-abiding United States would be left with a deteriorating arsenal. On the basis of these objections, the Senate rejected the treaty in 1999.

But a panel of experts convened by the National Academy of Sciences recently found that fear unfounded. "We judge that the United States has the technical capabilities to maintain confidence in the safety and reliability of its existing nuclear weapon stockpile under the CTBT," the panel concluded, "provided that adequate resources are made available." [3]

Although the administration will not seek ratification of the CTBT, it says it intends to observe a nuclear-testing moratorium in place since October 1992.

[2] See Miles A. Pomper, "U.S.-Russia Nuclear Arms Treaty Debated," *CQ Weekly*, July 13, 2002, p. 1897.

[3] National Academy of Sciences, "Technical Issues Related to the Comprehensive Nuclear Test Ban Treaty," July 31, 2002.

the U.S. Invasion began in March. "I want [administration officials] to define their objectives in Iraq," Biden said. "I want to know what scenarios there are for eliminating the chemical and biological weapons that Iraq may use if we attack. I'd like to know how important our allies are in this." [6]

In response to such concerns, Bush announced on Sept. 3 he would not take action before seeking the approval of Congress. Later, he discussed his concerns about Iraq with leaders from Britain, France, Russia, China and other nations. Only Britain agreed to join the United States in the war.

As lawmakers debate the nation's post-9/11 defense policy, these are some of the issues being considered:

Should the United States embrace the preemptive-strike doctrine?

President Bush has described Iraq, Iran and North Korea as part of an "axis of evil" bent on destroying the United States and its allies. Iraqi President Hussein rose to the top of that list, the administration said, because he had biological and chemical weapons, was developing nuclear weapons and allegedly supported anti-U.S. terrorist groups.

The president's father, former President George Bush, ousted Iraq from Kuwait in 1991 but stopped short of invading Baghdad and going after Hussein. [7]

Hussein defied a United Nations resolution mandating inspections of suspected Iraqi nuclear, biological and

Defense Dominates Discretionary Spending

Defense spending is expected to comprise 18 percent of the nation's $2.1 trillion budget this fiscal year. However, military spending comprises almost half of the $792 billion the nation spends annually on discretionary items, such as foreign aid.

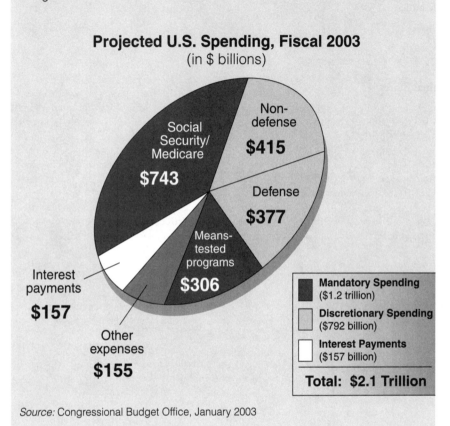

Projected U.S. Spending, Fiscal 2003
(in $ billions)

Non-defense
$415

Social Security/ Medicare
$743

Defense
$377

Means-tested programs
$306

Interest payments
$157

Other expenses
$155

Mandatory Spending
($1.2 trillion)

Discretionary Spending
($792 billion)

Interest Payments
($157 billion)

Total: $2.1 Trillion

Source: Congressional Budget Office, January 2003

turned up the rhetorical heat against Iraq. "It's the stated policy of this government to have a regime change," Bush said on July 8, 2002. "And we'll use all the tools at our disposal to do so." Earlier that year, the president reportedly signed an order directing the Central Intelligence Agency (CIA) to initiate a covert program to overthrow Hussein. [8]

To justify such an offensive, the administration articulated a new preemptive doctrine allowing the president to initiate military action — without congressional approval — against rogue states with weapons of mass destruction.

"Deterrence — the promise of massive retaliation against nations — means nothing against shadowy terrorist networks with no nation or citizens to defend," the president said at West Point. "If we wait for threats to fully materialize, we will have waited too long. [O]ur security will require all Americans to . . . be ready for preemptive action when necessary to defend our liberty and to defend our lives."

In fact, preemption isn't a new doctrine, said the war college's Galbraith. "It's long been the case that if we thought that someone was about to attack the United States we would take action against them," he said. "This is an evil regime that has practiced genocide against its own people, would do it again if unrestrained and certainly is going to cheat on every agreement it has made with regard to weapons of mass destruction. The Iraqi

chemical weapons production sites — a provision of the peace agreement Iraq signed when it surrendered. The second Bush administration charged that Iraq continued to develop weapons of mass destruction despite U.N. economic sanctions intended to force Hussein to readmit weapons inspectors.

After the 1991 Persian Gulf War, the U.S. sought to prevent further Iraqi aggression. Britain and the United States enforced "no-fly" zones designed to keep Iraqi forces out of northern and southern regions of the country, home to persecuted Kurdish and Shiite Muslim populations.

But after the Sept. 11 attacks, the administration

people will be very supportive of our taking action to liberate them."

Galbraith wonders, however, about the administration's logic of announcing — and then debating — preemptive action. "It doesn't make sense to announce it, particularly if you're dealing with someone like Saddam Hussein," he said. In fact, he added, announcing it in advance removes any reason for Hussein "not to use whatever weapons he has."

Supporters of Bush's emerging preemptive-strike policy argue that terrorist organizations and hostile governments that threaten the United States are unlikely to respond to traditional methods of deterrence.

"There is no give and take between such regimes and our country," said Lurie of the CSIS. The fact that North Korea, Iran and Iraq either have or are developing nuclear weapons and are hostile to the United States fully justifies a preemptive doctrine, he added. "The danger is immense. I would hate to see a situation where people are standing around scratching their heads, if they still have heads, and wondering, 'Why didn't we see it coming?'"

But preemptive action may have unintended consequences, critics say. Because it would permit the United States to launch a military operation unilaterally, the doctrine would alienate longstanding U.S. allies and may undermine the credibility of the United Nations and other international institutions, which the United States helped build. Indeed, widespread opposition from France, Germany and other allies to the U.S.-led war has produced the biggest strains in transatlantic relations since the end of World War II.

"It is not only politically unsustainable but diplomatically harmful," wrote G. John Inkenberry, a political science professor at Georgetown University. "And if history is a guide, it will trigger antagonism and resistance that will leave America in a more hostile and divided world." [9]

Others are more concerned about the administration's suggestion that a preemptive strike against Iraq might involve the use of nuclear weapons. After the gulf war, the Iraqi military moved some of its essential communications — and weapons — into deep underground bunkers. To destroy those installations, the Pentagon called for developing small, "bunker-busting" tactical nuclear warheads. [10]

"Tac-nukes," as they are called, were first developed as a last-resort defense against a massive Soviet invasion of Europe. They have never been used, and critics warn that deploying such nuclear weapons would lower the threshold for the future use of similar or even more lethal weapons. Although none were used in the war against Iraq, Congress has approved funds to develop nuclear bunker busters in the 2004 budget.

"It is politically inconceivable that the United States could ever be the first to use nuclear weapons," Galbraith said, adding that it would also be "militarily disastrous" for the United States. "If you have, as we do, the most powerful conventional forces in the world, the last thing you want is for it to become acceptable for people to ever think about using nuclear weapons against our forces."

Moreover, said Michael E. O'Hanlon, a senior fellow at the Brookings Institution, it is doubtful that conditions favorable to implementing a nuclear first-strike would ever arise. "You'd have to have Saddam deep in some underground bunker out in the middle of nowhere, where prevailing winds would not carry the fallout toward major cities," he says. "He's more likely to be where there are a lot of civilians, because that's his best defense against attack.

Supporters of preemption say the changing security environment warrants an equally radical shift in thinking. "During the Cold War, we had one enemy that mattered, and we relied on deterrence because we couldn't defend ourselves against a large Soviet attack," said the Lexington Institute's Thompson. "Today, we not only have other options, but we've also got lots of other enemies, and we don't understand some of them. So the administration's basic logic is valid: Not only are new enemies less predictable, but they may be less deterrable. So just trying to discourage aggression isn't enough any more."

Should the pentagon play a bigger role in homeland security?

Traditionally, the Defense Department was charged with defending the United States abroad while a broad array of agencies protected Americans on U.S. soil. Tragically, the Sept. 11 attacks revealed a gaping hole in that division of labor.

The Bush administration responded immediately by creating the White House Office of Homeland Security, headed by former Gov. Tom Ridge of Pennsylvania. On

June 6, 2002, Bush proposed transforming the office into a new, Cabinet-level Department of Homeland Security, merging all or parts of the 22 agencies that protect the United States from terrorist attacks. Congres approved the new department, and Ridge was sworn in as its secretary on Jan. 24, 2003.

The Pentagon has a limited role in the new department, due in large part to the longstanding legal separation of military and police functions. The 1878 Posse Comitatus Act prohibited using military forces for domestic law enforcement. Adopted in response to excesses by federal troops deployed in the South during Reconstruction, the law has been amended to allow for limited military involvement in drug interdiction and a few other exceptions.

Pentagon officials traditionally have opposed exceptions to the law, fearing domestic assignments could weaken the military's readiness overseas. However, the terrorist attacks blurred that distinction. While the attacks took place on U.S. soil, they were conducted by foreign nationals and supported by overseas leadership and funding. As a result, the military was immediately pressed into service after the attacks: Air Force jets patrolled over American cities while National Guard troops guarded airports and assisted at border checkpoints.

The administration, eager to strengthen local defenses against terrorist attack, has asked for a review of the law's ban on domestic military involvement.

The Pentagon's new domestic role is managed through the recently created office of the assistant secretary of Defense for homeland security. But Air Force Gen. Ralph E. Eberhart, who heads the Northern Command, created after Sept. 11 to boost domestic security, is among a handful of military brass who advocate amending the law to enhance the military's contribution to homeland defense. "My view has been that Posse Comitatus will constantly be under review as we mature this command," he said.

The command, which began operations Oct. 1, 2002, at its headquarters in Colorado Springs, is authorized to deploy military personnel to back up domestic agencies such as the FBI and the Federal Emergency Management Agency (FEMA), as needed in emergencies. [11]

Some experts say the ban on military involvement in domestic law enforcement is a waste of vital military know-how and manpower. "Our Department of De-fense has more tools, training, technology and talent to help combat the terrorist threat at home than any other federal agency," said Sen. Joseph I. Lieberman, D-Conn., chairman of the Senate Armed Services Airland Subcommittee. He would give the 460,000-member National Guard — essentially a 50-state militia that can be mobilized in state and national emergencies — an especially prominent role in homeland security.

"Our military has proven capable of brilliance beyond our borders," Lieberman said. "Now we must tap its expertise and its resources within our country by better integrating the Defense Department into our homeland security plans." [12]

But some experts agree with Pentagon officials who say the line between the military and law enforcement should remain strong. "The job of the Pentagon is to deter and defeat adversaries," said Thompson of the Lexington Institute. "Dragging them into an already overcrowded homeland defense arena would be a big mistake. We really don't need aircraft carriers defending our coastlines."

Other experts want the National Guard and the reserves to focus primarily on external threats, because that's where the risk is most serious. "If there is a catastrophe here at home, the National Guard is not going to be on hand quickly enough to be the most important player in the first few hours after an attack," said O'Hanlon of the Brookings Institution. "It's going to be local fire, police and rescue personnel. These first responders should get most of the resources, and the Guard should remain focused primarily on overseas combat."

Would a national missile-defense system protect the United States?

In one of the first major arms-control agreements of the Cold War era, the United States and the Soviet Union agreed to refrain from building defenses against the biggest perceived threat of the time — a massive nuclear attack by one superpower against the other. By prohibiting defenses against such a nuclear holocaust, the 1972 Anti-Ballistic Missile (ABM) Treaty assured each Cold War adversary that the other side was essentially defenseless. Moreover, the strategy — known as Mutual Assured Destruction (MAD) — theoretically reduced the incentive to build more nuclear weapons. [13]

Toward the end of the Cold War, however, President Ronald Reagan rejected the ABM Treaty's logic and called for the development of a space-based system capable of intercepting incoming missiles. Although critics ridiculed the plan as technically unfeasible — dubbing it "Star Wars" after the popular movie of the time — the Strategic Defense Initiative received funding that continued even after the Soviet Union's collapse in 1991. President Clinton later endorsed a more limited approach aimed at deflecting attacks from hostile states like Iraq, Iran and North Korea that had or were developing nuclear weapons.

George W. Bush entered the White House promising to remove the main legal obstacle to missile defenses by jettisoning the ABM Treaty altogether, which he did, effective June 14, 2002. The next day, on June 15, construction began on a missile-defense facility at Fort Greely, Alaska, the first component of a larger system that could total $238 billion by 2025. [14]

The attacks of Sept. 11 merely confirmed the views of missile-defense critics who had warned all along that long-range missiles no longer posed the biggest threat to U.S. security and that defending against them entailed huge technical obstacles.

"President Bush will not and cannot deploy any meaningful missile defense anytime this decade," wrote Joseph Cirincione, an analyst at the Carnegie Endowment for International Peace, who argues that the program has greater political than practical value. "Missile defense plays well for the Republicans. It shows that President Bush is keeping the faith with the Reagan revolution, and it remains an applause line for his core, conservative constituency." [15]

Harvard's Nye argues that the missile-defense program would be useless against today's immediate threats. "The idea of being able to defend ourselves against missiles from second-tier states at some point in the future is a worthy objective," he said. "The key questions are how much you spend, how fast you develop the program and how effective it will be."

Nye worries that emphasizing missile defenses may divert resources away from other weapons of mass destruction, such as nuclear "suitcase" bombs that could be smuggled across inadequately policed borders. "The danger is that we spend a lot of money nailing the door shut while leaving the windows open," he said.

Moreover, he said, "Getting rid of the ABM Treaty may make people think that other threats have gone away, and they haven't."

Some missile-defense advocates say that the terrorist attacks strongly suggest the program's design should be altered. O'Hanlon of Brookings supports a "relatively small" system, partly to avoid fueling a nuclear arms race with China, which has a limited nuclear arsenal.

But, he concedes, the threat from China is "not so dire as to constitute [an] urgent reason for investing huge numbers of national security dollars."

In addition, huge technical obstacles to developing an effective missile-defense system remain. "The administration is probably right that countries that don't now have missiles will be more inclined to acquire them if we are defenseless," said Thompson of the Lexington Institute. "But that doesn't address the main question, which is whether the defenses will work, and on that the jury is still out."

Like O'Hanlon, Thompson worries that a major missile-defense system would spur China to expand its nuclear arsenal. "But the missile defense system we are planning to deploy, at least during the Bush years, will be very modest," Thompson said. "It could cope with a North Korean missile attack or a handful of missiles accidentally launched by China or Russia, but not much else."

Meanwhile, Thompson echoed the skeptical views of many defense experts on both sides of the debate. "Although missile defense is still a worthwhile undertaking, Sept. 11 essentially confirmed the critics' complaints that there are many other ways that we could be attacked."

BACKGROUND

Post-Cold War Shift

The ongoing evolution in U.S. military strategy dates from the Soviet Union's collapse in December 1991. [16] Besides ending the Cold War, it abruptly eliminated the rationale for America's military strategy since the end of World War II.

The United States and the communist-led Soviet Union spent the early years of the Cold War in a race to build nuclear arsenals. As it became clear that neither country could defeat the other without destroying itself in the process — the MAD notion — they negotiated a series of bilateral arms-control agreements to slow the arms race. (*See sidebar, p. 70.*)

CHRONOLOGY

1950s-1970s *Cold War shapes U.S. defense policy; superpowers sign nuclear arms control treaties.*

1972 The U.S.-Soviet Anti-Ballistic Missile (ABM) Treaty is signed, prohibiting the superpowers from erecting a ballistic missile-defense system.

1973 War Powers Resolution calls for Congress and the president to share in decision-making over going to war.

1980s-1990s *As the Cold War winds down, hostile "rogue" states and Islamic terrorists replace the Soviet Union as the United States' main security concern.*

1991 The U.S. leads an international coalition to drive Iraq from Kuwait. The Soviet Union collapses in December, ending the Cold War. U.S. and Russia sign START I treaty limiting nuclear weapons.

1993 The first major study on transforming the military after the Cold War reaffirms the "two-war strategy" — calling for military preparedness to fight two regional wars at once. In January, Russia and the U.S. sign START II, calling for halving each country's nuclear warheads. On Feb. 23 Arab terrorists bomb the World Trade Center, killing six and injuring 1,000.

1994 The National Defense Authorization Act orders a Pentagon review of broad strategic goals every four years. U.S. forces withdraw from Somalia on March 25 after 18 American soldiers are killed during a failed U.N. peacekeeping mission. U.S. troops oust a Haitian military regime that had seized power from the elected president.

June 25, 1996 Terrorists bomb U.S. military barracks in Saudi Arabia, killing 19.

1997 The first Quadrennial Defense Review (QDR) directs the military to prepare for a broad range of conflicts and threats. Critics say retaining the two-war strategy fails to consider new security threats, such as terrorism, requiring more mobile forces.

August 1998 On Aug. 7, terrorists bomb U.S. embassies in Tanzania and Kenya, killing 224; U.S. retaliates on Aug. 20 by attacking al Qaeda camps in Afghanistan.

1999 The United States leads a NATO campaign to halt Serb repression of ethnic Albanians in Kosovo. Critics blame civilian casualties on the U.S. military's reluctance to place troops on the ground.

2000s *Continued terrorist attacks prompt changes in defense policy.*

Oct. 12, 2000 *USS Cole* is bombed in Yemen by militant Muslims, killing 17.

January 2001 President George W. Bush asks for the largest defense budget increase since the 1980s and orders review of the nation's military capability.

Sept. 11, 2001 Al Qaeda terrorists attack World Trade Center and the Pentagon, killing 3,000.

May 8, 2002 Defense Secretary Donald H. Rumsfeld says he wants to cancel the $11 billion Crusader cannon, one of several weapons systems that critics say are ill-suited to current threats.

May 24, 2002 U.S. and Russia sign Treaty of Moscow, calling for more cuts in nuclear arms.

June 1, 2002 Bush announces plans to use preemptive strikes against states or terrorist groups trying to develop weapons of mass destruction.

June 13, 2002 Bush withdraws U.S. from ABM treaty.

July 8, 2002 Bush says his government wants "a regime change" in Iraq.

Sept. 4, 2002 Bush promises to ask Congress and the U.N. Security Council for approval to attack Iraq.

Sept. 12, 2002 Bush is scheduled to address the U.N. General Assembly to present his case for attacking Iraq.

March 20, 2003 The United States and Britain invade Iraq and topple the government of President Saddam Hussein.

May 1, 2003 Bush declares victory in Iraq.

The Cold War also shaped the superpowers' arsenals of non-nuclear weapons. Assuming that the biggest threat was a massive land invasion of Warsaw Pact forces across West Germany's Fulda Gap, the United States arrayed heavy tanks, artillery and ground troops along the so-called Iron Curtain — the border between Soviet-dominated communist Eastern Europe and democratic Western Europe.

As the superpowers refrained from direct hostilities in Europe, the Cold War devolved into a series of U.S.-Soviet proxy wars in Africa, Asia and Latin America — wherever socialist- or communist-leaning rebels were active in a country run by a pro-U.S. government. These far-flung conflicts and face-offs required the deployment of troops and equipment at military bases around the world.

The prevailing military doctrines were containment and deterrence. Containment — a term coined in 1947 by U.S. diplomat George F. Kennan — called for preventing the Soviet Union from expanding beyond a handful of bordering countries, which together became known as the Communist Bloc. Deterrence, reflecting President Theodore Roosevelt's admonition to "speak softly and carry a big stick," called for building a military strong enough to dissuade the enemy from attacking.

But both doctrines became less relevant after democratically elected governments replaced the communist regimes in the former Soviet states and Eastern Europe. U.S. policymakers anticipated a hefty "peace dividend" — more funds for domestic needs — as overseas military commitments, military bases and defense spending were cut. The transformation left Pentagon planners scrambling to define new strategies for dealing with a radically different set of security concerns.

Some of these threats had been emerging even before the Soviet collapse, as Iraq, North Korea and a few other regional powers began building arsenals of advanced conventional weapons and, in some cases, weapons of mass destruction. [17] To cope with the threat of what the State Department called rogue states, Pentagon planners began assembling the forces necessary to prevail against two regional powers simultaneously. They also began shifting procurement priorities from massive tanks and artillery to lighter, more mobile weapons that could be quickly transported from bases in the United States.

AFP Photo

AFP Photo/Chris Bouroncle

Weapons of Choice

In an effort to save money, the Pentagon is retaining the less-expensive F-35 Joint Strike Fighter (top), while some older warplanes may be dropped or phased out. Pentagon planners also may shelve plans to replace the Navy's nine *Nimitz*-class aircraft carriers (bottom) with a new generation of nuclear-powered carriers.

Iraq's Hussein put the new plans to the test in 1990, when he invaded Kuwait, launching the Persian Gulf War. Equipped with the latest in high-technology hardware, from night-vision equipment to precision-guided "smart" bombs, the 500,000 U.S. and allied forces of Operation Desert Storm drove Iraq out of Kuwait in just seven weeks in 1991.

The United States' first major post-Cold War conflict also revealed some weaknesses in the new U.S. strat-

Getty Images

Despite calling for a sweeping transformation of the U.S. military, the Bush administration has canceled only one major weapon system to date — the Crusader, a heavy cannon designed for old-style battlefield combat. Defense Secretary Donald H. Rumsfeld asked that the $475 million initially requested for the $11 billion Crusader program in 2003 be used instead to speed development of lighter, more mobile artillery.

egy. Lightly armed 82nd Airborne Division soldiers — who were deployed early — were vulnerable to Iraqi attack for weeks before more heavily armed reinforcements could arrive by ship. In addition, several "smart" bombs missed their targets and killed civilians, and Iraqi Scud missile launchers evaded detection long enough to cause significant damage in Israel and Saudi Arabia.

There was another problem with the smart bombs and other precision weapons that could be employed far from the battlefield. While they kept U.S. combat casualties to a minimum, they also fostered a reluctance to

place U.S. troops in harm's way. It was this caution, critics say, along with fears that Iraq might disintegrate, that led then-President George Bush not to pursue Iraqi troops to Baghdad.

Clinton's Changes

President Clinton (1993-2001) continued the process of "transforming" the military. During his administration, calls mounted for more than just modernization but for a true revolution in military affairs that would incorporate rapidly developing technology into weapons systems and adjust strategy to accommodate them.

Such a technological transformation would be as revolutionary as the introduction of gunpowder or the development of aircraft carriers before World War II. Military planning, advocates said, should acknowledge that future adversaries, unable to match the United States' overwhelming force superiority, would try to use surprise and unconventional uses of the weapons at hand to engage the world's sole superpower in "asymmetrical" warfare.

However, the most visible changes during this period were in so-called force downsizing. The Clinton administration closed 97 major bases — including 24 in California and seven in Texas — and downsized 55 others. Gen. Colin L. Powell, then-chairman of the Joint Chiefs, supported the development of a "base force" — the minimum number of troops and weapons needed to protect U.S. national interests while maintaining enough capacity to win two major regional wars simultaneously.

In 1993, the first major study on transforming the military after the Cold War — the so-called Bottom Up Review — reaffirmed the two-war strategy, despite criticism that it was unrealistic and expensive to fund, and supported a controversial new role for the military as peacekeepers. [18]

Meanwhile, the Clinton administration faced several military challenges that tested the president's goal of broadening the role of U.S. forces to include peacekeeping and other non-traditional missions. These would take U.S. troops to parts of the world where the United States had little or no prior military presence. On March 25, 1994, one such operation ended in disaster, when U.S. forces withdrew from Somalia after 18 American soldiers were killed during a failed U.N. peacekeeping mission in Mogadishu. A more successful operation came on Sept. 19, 1994, when

Clinton sent troops to Haiti to oust a military regime that had seized power from the elected president.

A congressionally mandated commission reassessed the international-security environment as part of the 1994 National Defense Authorization Act and recommended retaining the two-war standard. But in view of the rapidly changing global situation — including regional conflict in the Balkans and threats from Iraq and North Korea — the commission suggested that the Pentagon review its broad strategic goals every four years. In 1996, Congress agreed with the panel and required the Defense Department to con-

U.S. Military Manpower Has Declined

The number of active-duty military personnel declined and then leveled off in the post-Cold War period. High levels in previous years reflect the world wars and the Korean and Vietnam wars.

(In millions)

U.S. Active-Duty Military Personnel, 1918-2002

2.9, 0.34, 12.0, 1.6, 3.6, 2.8, 3.5, 2.2, 1.8, 1.5, 1.4, 1.4, 1.4

1918 1920 1945 1947 1952 1962 1968 1987 1992 1996 1998 2000 2002

Source: Center for Defense Information, *Military Almanac, 2001-2002*

duct a comprehensive examination of America's defense needs at four-year intervals.

The first Quadrennial Defense Review (QDR), issued in 1997, directed the military to prepare for a variety of conflicts and threats, ranging from illegal drug trafficking to terrorism to major wars. But because it kept the two-war standard for determining force strength, critics continued to accuse the Pentagon of exaggerating defense needs to meet budget targets.

Congress had stepped into the debate in 1996 when it passed the Military Force Structure Review Act, which created another panel to assess ongoing defense policy changes. The following year, the National Defense Panel challenged the two-war scenario as a Cold War holdover and faulted the 1997 QDR for failing to adequately plan for the kind of military transformation required to deal with future challenges, such as asymmetric threats.

To pay for new weapons better suited for dealing with

the emerging threats, the panel also asked the Pentagon to consider scaling back or eliminating several programs that critics said were either too expensive or antiquated "legacy systems," such as the Army's Crusader artillery vehicle, the Comanche helicopter, the Navy's last *Nimitz*-class aircraft carrier and several tactical, or short-range, aircraft.

By the end of the Clinton administration, some of the Pentagon's efforts to transform the military had begun to bear fruit. In early 1999, Clinton ordered U.S. forces to lead NATO's Operation Allied Force to halt Serb repression of ethnic Albanians in Kosovo. The almost exclusive use of air power and precise munitions enabled the allies to prevail in 11 weeks with few U.S. casualties. However, the deaths of some 500 civilians from stray bombs once again demonstrated the shortcomings of such heavy reliance on long-distance warfare.

Operation Allied Force also demonstrated the limited usefulness of some Cold War systems, such as the Army's

European Allies Oppose Attack on Iraq

Almost from the moment President Bush took office last year, America's European allies have accused him of adopting unilateral defense and foreign policies. One of the sole exceptions to such complaints was the outpouring of sympathy and solidarity after the Sept. 11 terrorist attacks.

Bush has strained transatlantic relations by rejecting several international agreements that enjoy broad support in Europe — including the Kyoto treaty to slow global warming, the U.S.- Soviet Anti-Ballistic Missile (ABM) Treaty and the treaty creating the new International Criminal Court.

Now, his insistence on preemptive U.S. military action to overthrow Iraqi leader Saddam Hussein has injected a new source of tension between the United States and its military allies in the North Atlantic Treaty Organizaton (NATO).

Ever since the president's father — President George Bush senior — led a broad, U.N.-sanctioned coalition to expel an Iraqi invasion of Kuwait in 1991, America's staunchest ally in the quest to contain Iraq has been Britain. Since the Persian Gulf War, British and U.S. air forces have jointly enforced "no-fly" zones over northern and southern Iraq to prevent Iraq from threatening its neighbors and persecuting Kurdish and Shiite Muslim minorities. Since 1998, U.S. and British aircraft have stepped up their attacks on Iraqi ground installations, completing more than 40 so far this year alone.

On Sept. 10, in one of his strongest statements yet, British Prime Minister Tony Blair called Hussein "an international outlaw" and said he believed it was right to deal with the Iraqi leader through the United Nations. "Let it be clear," Blair said, "that he must be disarmed. Let it be clear that there can be no more conditions, no more games, no more prevaricating, no more undermining of the U.N.'s authority. And let it also be clear that should the will of the U.N. be ignored, action will follow." [1]

America's other NATO allies have been adamantly opposed to military action against Iraq from the start. It's not that the Europeans are unconcerned about threats posed by Iraq, but they insist on obtaining a clear mandate from the international community before undertaking any military action. French President Jacques Chirac, who on Aug. 29 criticized "attempts to legitimize the use of unilateral and preemptive use of force" in Iraq, argues that the U.N. Security Council must approve any military operation. German Chancellor Gerhard Schroeder opposes an attack even with U.N. blessings, and indeed has made his opposition to invading Iraq a part of his current campaign for reelection. The goal, he said, should be to pressure

---

[1] Quoted in Terrance Neilan, "Blair Says 'Action Will Follow' if Iraq Spurns U.N. Resolutions," *The New York Times online*, Sept. 10, 2002.

---

big tanks, which were too wide and heavy for Kosovo's narrow roads and rickety bridges.

Bush's Priorities

During the 2000 presidential campaign, candidate George W. Bush criticized then-President Clinton for underfunding U.S. defenses and failing to prepare both military strategy and weaponry for 21st-century contingencies. He repeatedly promised the military, "hope is on the way."

Upon taking office in January 2001, Bush ordered Rumsfeld to conduct a comprehensive review of the nation's military capability. "To meet any dangers, our administration will begin building the military of the future," Bush said after asking for the biggest increase in

military spending since President Ronald Reagan's massive Cold War buildup in the 1980s. "We must and we will make major investments in research and development." [19]

High on Bush's priority list was the national missile-defense system. Although Clinton had supported research into a similar system, he had opposed its actual development because the ABM Treaty banned such systems. Declaring the treaty obsolete, Bush abandoned the agreement and pushed ahead.

When the Pentagon released its second Quadrennial Defense Review on Sept. 30, 2001 — barely two weeks after the terrorist attacks — its central objective was to "deter and defeat adversaries who will rely on surprise, deception and asymmetric warfare to achieve their objec-

Hussein to allow weapons inspectors — whom he expelled in 1998 — back into Iraq, not to go to war regardless, as Vice President Dick Cheney has suggested. "The problem is that [Cheney] has or seems to have committed himself so strongly that it is hard to imagine how he can climb down. And that is the real problem, that not only I have but that all of us in Europe have."

Non-European voices have been equally forceful. "We are really appalled by any country, whether it is a superpower or a poor country, that goes outside the United Nations and attacks independent countries," said former South African President Nelson Mandela. Russian Foreign Minister Igor Ivanov warned, "Any decision to use force against Iraq would not only complicate an Iraqi settlement but also undermine the situation in the gulf and the Middle East." The Arab League warned that an attack on Iraq would "open the gates of Hell" in the Middle East. Foreign ministers from 20 Arab states called for a "complete rejection of

British Prime Minister Tony Blair, left, meets with President Bush at Camp David in early September. Blair supports military action against Iraq only if the U.N. fails to resolve the conflict.

threats of aggression against some Arab countries, in particular Iraq." [2]

Joseph Nye, dean of Harvard University's John F. Kennedy School of Government, says European allies might support U.S. action if the emphasis were not just on changing the regime but rather on stopping Hussein from obtaining weapons of mass destruction. "That means going through the U.N. inspection system and proving that he's not living up to his multilateral commitments, that he's developing nuclear weapons and that those pose an imminent threat," says Nye, who was former President Bill Clinton's assistant secretary of Defense for international security affairs. "Those are the key steps for gaining international support."

---

[2] Quoted in Nicholas Blanford, "Syria worries US won't stop at Iraq," *The Christian Science Monitor*, Sept. 9, 2002.

---

tives," said Rumsfeld. "The attack on the United States on Sept. 11, 2001, will require us to move forward more rapidly in these directions, even while we are engaged in the war against terrorism." [20]

But many defense analysts were disappointed that the QDR lacked clear recommendations on how to achieve such a radical shift in focus.

"There is nothing in the QDR that envisions a significant increase in the new war-fighting technologies everyone agrees are critical," wrote Steven J. Nider, director of foreign and security studies at the Progressive Policy Institute, a liberal think tank. Calling the review "maddeningly vague," he charged the Rumsfeld Pentagon with the same inertia that had stymied change since the end of the Cold War. [21]

"More than just a broken campaign promise," he concluded, "it represents a missed opportunity to reshape our military to wage a new kind of war against new threats and enemies."

CURRENT SITUATION

Afghanistan Victory

The most salient lesson learned from Operation Enduring Freedom is that it was an astounding success, said Lurie of the CSIS. "What happened in Afghanistan was definitely an American victory," he said. "Someone may still be shooting a mortar here and there, but the fact of the matter is, we took over Afghanistan in a

AFP Photo/David Marck Jr.

U.S. soldiers search for enemy forces in eastern Afghanistan in March, 2002. Despite its success in routing the Taliban, Operation Enduring Freedom fell short of its primary objective, capturing Osama bin Laden and destroying his terrorist organization. Critics say the United States' unwillingness to commit adequate manpower to the Tora Bora campaign allowed Taliban and al Qaeda forces to slip away.

few weeks, something that the Soviets couldn't do in 10 years."

Thanks to the Bush administration's coherent reaction to the Sept. 11 attacks, "Every country now knows what to expect if it allows its own forces or terrorists acting from its territory to attack the United States," Lurie said. "As the old saying goes, 'If you can't kill the lion, don't sting it.'"

Enduring Freedom also introduced several innovations in hardware and tactics. Special-operations forces used laser range-finders and global-positioning systems to help pilots home in on and destroy targets with much greater precision even than during the Gulf War. [22] Unmanned aerial vehicles (UAVs), together with older imaging satellites and the Joint Surveillance Target Attack Radar System, enabled U.S. commanders to obtain vital information about remote battlefield conditions without placing American pilots in danger. And improvements in communication networks relayed the information faster than ever.

Moreover, for the first time unmanned planes, like the CIA's Predator UAVs, were used offensively to fire Hellfire air-to-surface missiles at enemy targets. And precision weapons — such as laser-guided missiles and JDAMS (guided bombs better suited to poor weather) — were first used as the predominant form of ordnance fired on enemy targets.

With the hostilities winding down, Pentagon planners said they had learned several lessons that would guide them in further transforming the military. Brookings' O'Hanlon argues that the mission's success depended not so much on the latest aircraft, ships and ground vehicles, as on improved communications, better-prepared troops and more coordination between special-operations forces on the ground and Air Force and Navy aircraft.

"It's dangerous to infer too much from one conflict, especially in this situation, where the Taliban really didn't have good air defenses," O'Hanlon said. "But I would still argue that Operation Enduring Freedom makes the case for smart munitions being very effective, and sometimes being good enough that you don't need to have the fanciest airplane from which to drop them."

But others warn about the unwillingness to commit adequate manpower to complete the job. "Instead of putting American troops on the ground in the Tora Bora campaign, which would have been costly and might have involved more casualties, we relied on Afghan allies who were hardly tested," said Galbraith of the National War College. "These guys weren't trained, and they operated in the Afghan manner, which is to serve whomever pays the highest price. They simply let the al Qaeda people slip away. There should have been more U.S. forces up there to seal up the escape routes."

Galbraith also questions the growing reliance on high-technology munitions. "There's a belief that high-tech is a magic wand, and that's not true because it depends on intelligence, which is never going to be that good," he said.

Galbraith cites the tragic U.S. bombing of a July 1 wedding party in Oruzgan Province, killing at least 54 civilians. American forces reportedly mistook the traditional firing of rifles into the air by wedding guests for an al Qaeda attack.

"You're just not going to ever get 100 percent intelligence as to whether something is a wedding or a gathering of [Taliban leader] Mullah Omar and his buddies," Galbraith said. "[So,] troops on the ground are probably essential."

Indeed, despite its success in routing the Taliban, the Afghanistan campaign fell short of its primary objective, capturing bin Laden and destroying his organization.

Some critics contend that no matter how well equipped, the U.S. military cannot win this kind of war on

Are the Pentagon's efforts to transform the military on track?

YES Paul Wolfowitz
Deputy Secretary of Defense

From Testimony Before The Senate Armed Services Committee, April 9, 2002

Our overall goal is to encourage a series of transformations that, in combination, can produce a revolutionary increase in our military capability and redefine how war is fought. . . .

Long before Sept. 11, the department's senior leaders — civilian and military — began an unprecedented degree of debate and discussion about where America's military should go in the years ahead. Out of those intense debates, we agreed on the urgent need for real changes in our defense strategy. The outline of those changes is reflected in the Quadrennial Defense Review (QDR) and the 2003 budget request. . . .

Setting specific transformation goals has helped to focus our transformation efforts, from investments to experimentation and concept development. The six goals identified in the QDR are:

- To defend the U.S. homeland and other bases of operations, and defeat nuclear, biological and chemical weapons and their means of delivery;
- To deny enemies sanctuary — depriving them of the ability to run or hide — anytime, anywhere;
- To project and sustain forces in distant theaters in the face of access-denial threats;
- To conduct effective operations in space;
- To conduct effective information operations; and,
- To leverage information technology to give our joint forces a common operational picture. . . .

Taken together, these six goals will guide the U.S. military's transformation efforts and improvements in our joint forces. Over time, they will help to shift the balance of U.S. forces and capabilities. U.S. ground forces will be lighter, more lethal and highly mobile. . . . Naval and amphibious forces will be able to assure U.S. access even in area-denial environments, operate close to enemy shores and project power deep inland. Air and space forces will be able to locate and track mobile targets over vast areas and strike them rapidly at long ranges without warning. . . .

Even as we fight this war on terror, potential adversaries scrutinize our methods, they study our capabilities, they seek our weaknesses. . . . So, as we take care of today, we are investing in tomorrow. We are emphasizing multiple transformations that, combined, will fundamentally change warfare in ways that could give us important advantages that can help us secure the peace.

We realize that achieving this goal requires transforming our culture and the way we think. We must do this even as we fight this difficult war on terrorism. We cannot afford to wait.

NO Andrew F. Krepinevich
Executive Director, Center for Strategic and Budgetary Assessments

From Testimony Before The Senate Armed Services Committee, April 9, 2002

While the Defense Department's rationale for transformation is persuasive, its process for effecting transformation is more difficult to discern and, hence, to evaluate. A transformation process is needed to validate vision, to identify the best means for addressing critical challenges and to determine if opportunities can be realized. . . .

The process should enable feedback on transformation initiatives (for example, new operational concepts, doctrines, systems, networks, force structures). This will enable senior Defense leaders to gauge whether the transformation path being pursued is, in fact, the correct path, or to make the appropriate adjustments if it is not. Such a process can help inform choices about investments in future capabilities — R&D, procurement, personnel and force structure — so as to reduce uncertainty in a resource-constrained environment.

Unfortunately, the Defense Department's modernization strategy today remains much the same as it was during the Cold War era, with its emphasis on large-scale, serial production of relatively few types of military systems and capabilities. To the extent possible, we should avoid premature large-scale production of new systems . . . until they have clearly proven themselves helpful in meeting critical operational goals. . . .

The United States military must transform itself, and it must begin now. As [Defense] Secretary [Donald] Rumsfeld has said, "Transformation is not a goal for tomorrow, but an endeavor that must be embraced in earnest today. The challenges the nation faces do not loom in the distant future, but are here now."

To its credit, the Bush administration has both clearly defined what transformation is, and provided a persuasive case as to why the world's best military needs to transform. Unfortunately, it has not yet developed either a transformation strategy or a process to ensure that transformation will come about. This is most clearly demonstrated in the absence of plausible service and joint war-fighting concepts for addressing the new, emerging critical operational goals, and finds its ultimate expression in the administration's program and budget priorities, which for the most part sustain the course set by the Clinton administration. . . .

If the Defense Department fails to seize the opportunity to transform our military — we run a very real risk of investing a substantial sum of our national treasure in preparing our military to meet the challenges of today, and yesterday, rather than those of tomorrow. Should that occur, payment could be exacted not only in lost treasure but also in lives lost.

its own. "The military solution was very good in toppling the Taliban, but not at getting rid of al Qaeda, which still has cells in some 50 countries," says Harvard's Nye. "The only way you're going to get rid of them is through very careful intelligence-sharing with many other countries."

But other countries may not be so willing to share intelligence if another potentially sweeping change in Pentagon planning and missions is adopted. Rumsfeld reportedly is considering expanding the role of special-operations forces to capture or kill al Qaeda leaders.

Such clandestine missions — usually limited to the CIA under legally defined conditions — could potentially involve U.S. combat forces in covert actions inside countries with whom the United States is not at war, without the knowledge or consent of the local governments. Pentagon officials reportedly said the expansion of the military's role into covert missions could be justified as "preparation of the battlefield" in the war against terrorists who do not recognize national boundaries. [23]

Defense Budget

The Bush administration has called for speeding plans to transform the military. In 2002, for example, it canceled the $11 billion Crusader cannon. Rumsfeld asked that the $475 million initially requested for the Crusader in 2003 be used instead to speed development of lighter artillery weapons for the Army. [24]

"So little is certain when it comes to the future of warfare, but on one point we must be clear," Rumsfeld wrote in defending his decision to drop the program. "We risk deceiving ourselves and emboldening future adversaries by assuming [the future] will look like the past. Sept. 11 proved one thing above all others: Our enemies are transforming. Will we?" [25]

Besides the Crusader, four other major programs may be sacrificed in the interest of transformation, though the Pentagon has deferred a final decision on their fate. The list includes key weapons currently under development by all four branches of the armed services.

For instance, the F-22 fighter — designed to replace the Air Force's F-15 — may be dropped in favor of the cheaper F-35 Joint Strike Fighter, which is already under development. The Marine Corps' V-22 Osprey, which has a tilt rotor that enables it to land and take off like a helicopter and fly like a plane, also is under review. Development of the Osprey has been plagued by accidents that have cost the lives of 23 servicemen. The Army is also scrutinizing its

Comanche helicopter, another troubled program under development for nearly two decades and still at least 10 years from becoming operational. Finally, Pentagon planners are eyeing the Navy's proposed CVNX nuclear-powered aircraft carriers, designed to replace the nine *Nimitz*-class carriers deployed beginning in 1975.

"The administration [believes] the world is changing very rapidly and that something more than evolution [in strategy and weapons design] is required to prepare for future threats," said Thompson of the Lexington Institute. He sees two problems with the administration's approach.

"First, they don't have a clear idea of what the future threat is," he said, "so there's a danger that much of what they do may be inappropriate. Secondly, it's much easier to kill programs . . . than to build a legacy of replacement programs, which takes more time than a single administration has to complete. So the danger is that the Bush administration will be all too effective at eliminating key programs and not effective at all at building a foundation for modernization that is sustained by its successors."

Some experts applaud Rumsfeld's decision to terminate the Crusader as a step in the right direction. "Up to now, every service has been getting their dream piece of equipment, and killing the Crusader dealt a blow at that trend," Harvard's Galbraith said. "It certainly hasn't completely transformed the military, but looking for lighter, more mobile forces is the right idea."

Galbraith is less supportive of the administration's $7.8 billion request for the national missile-defense program, which Congress is expected to approve in full. [26] "The threat isn't a rogue country firing off a missile, because wherever that missile comes from it's going to have a return address," he said. "The real threat is that somebody will acquire or build a nuclear weapon, smuggle it into the country and set if off in Manhattan or Washington, and we won't know where it came from."

In his view, a far better use of those funds would be to develop technologies to detect nuclear weapons and inspect everything that enters the country. "I'm no techno-wizard," he said, "but I sense that money spent that way would be much better than on a missile defense that deals with a very unlikely threat."

Other experts say the Pentagon has not fully applied the lessons of either Desert Storm or Enduring Freedom to the military budget. "I would put more money into munitions, command-and-control networks, information processing and unmanned aerial vehicles and less into the major combat platforms that are carrying those smaller capabilities," O'Hanlon of Brookings said.

Lurie of the CSIS agrees that large weapons systems continue to receive an inordinate share of the defense budget.

"I would like to see a much bigger chunk dedicated to intelligence," he said. "That is probably our most crucial weapon to counter terrorism."

OUTLOOK

Lessons from Iraq

The past year has put the Bush administration's defense priorities under the spotlight. Faced with growing concern in Congress about the potential risks involved in preemptively attacking Iraq, administration officials insisted that Hussein possessed chemical, biological and nuclear weapons and that the risks of inaction were far greater.

Left to deploy nuclear weapons, Vice President Dick Cheney warned, the Iraqi leader would "seek domination of the entire Middle East, take control of a great portion of the world's energy supplies, directly threaten America's friends throughout the region and subject the United States or any other nation to nuclear blackmail." [27]

Bush assured legislators he would seek congressional approval before taking action against Iraq and consulted with the other members of the United Nations Security Council — the leaders of Russia, China, Britain and France — to explain his position. [28] Finally, the president presented his case to the United Nations in New York on Sept. 12 — the day after the one-year anniversary of the terrorist attacks.

In effect, Bush was seeking approval from Congress, the country and America's allies for his preemptive-strike policy. "We're in a new era," Bush said. "This is a debate the American people must hear, must understand. And the world must understand, as well, that its credibility is at stake." [29]

As the months wore on, Bush's argument swayed many in the United States, but hardly anyone else. He won overwhelming approval in Congress for a war resolution, and he convinced the Security Council to unanimously adopt Resolution 1441, ordering Iraq to fully and voluntarily disclose the status of its weapons programs. Even after the war began, he kept the unwavering support of the American people, who backed the conflict by a ratio of three-to-one.

But Bush's determination to proceed with the invasion even after weapons inspectors failed to disclose evidence that Iraq possessed weapons of mass destruction alienated many of America's traditional allies. After France and Germany condemned the administration's preemptive war plan, the United States was left with just Britain as a major partner in what Bush called the "coalition of the willing" to invade Iraq. Fellow NATO member Turkey refused to let U.S. forces use its territory across the border from Iraq as a staging area for the impending invasion.

On March 20, Operation Iraqi Freedom began with heavy air strikes, dubbed "shock and awe," against military targets in Iraq, followed by a ground invasion of coalition tanks from Kuwait northward toward Baghdad, the Iraqi capital. From the beginning, critics charged that Rumsfeld had placed too great an emphasis on high-tech weaponry and left ground forces with too few troops. But Iraq's armed forces failed to mount a strong counterattack, and Baghdad fell to coalition forces within weeks. On May 1, Bush formally claimed victory.

In the end, the United States lost just 110 in Operation Iraqi Freedom, fully a quarter of whom died in non-combat accidents. Supporters of Rumsfeld's military transformation attribute the rapid victory and lack of massive casualties to the United States' advanced, satellite-assisted communications equipment, advanced aircraft and smart munitions.

But the military victory left the administration with the much more arduous task of rebuilding Iraq, devastated not only by the war but also by decades of authoritarian rule. Indeed, the post-war mission may prove to be a far greater challenge than the war itself.

Bush has long criticized the use of American troops in peacekeeping operations in the Balkans and elsewhere. But U.S. allies contribute the bulk of peacekeepers now deployed in Afghanistan.

"You would have to assume that we'd be looking at a multiyear stability operation that would make the efforts in the Balkans look relatively modest by comparison," Brookings' O'Hanlon said.

The United States provides about 15 percent of peacekeeping forces in the Balkans. "We'd have to be closer to 25 percent of the total force in Iraq because it would be seen as very much our war," O'Hanlon predicted. "We couldn't do what we've done in Afghanistan and essentially ask our allies to do the whole thing for us."

Indeed, while transatlantic relations have improved somewhat since the war's end, the job of peacekeeping and nation-building in Iraq has fallen squarely on the shoulders of the United States and Britain. Some 150,000 U.S. soldiers — and only 12,000 allied troops — remain in Iraq, helping restore basic services, hunting for weapons of mass destruction and acting as policemen in anticipation of a new civilian government that can take over these missions. That could take months or even years, analysts predict. Meanwhile, persistent attacks on U.S. troops have prompted the military to launch a new mission, dubbed Operation Desert Scorpion, to aggressively hunt down Hussein supporters and beef up humanitarian aid to win over Iraqi public opinion.

Although a majority of Americans still support the military action in Iraq, the administration is coming under scrutiny by critics who charge that Bush misled Americans about the dangers posed by Hussein's regime. Nine weeks after the war's end, the United States had failed to produce clear evidence that Iraq possessed weapons of mass destruction.

NOTES

1. For background, see David Masci and Kenneth Jost, "War on Terrorism," *The CQ Researcher*, Oct. 12, 2001, pp. 817-848.

2. Donald H. Rumsfeld, Foreword, *Quadrennial Defense Review Report*, Department of Defense, Sept. 30, 2001, p. iv.

3. See Carl Hulse, "Senate Easily Passes $355 Billion Bill for Military Spending," *The New York Times*, Aug. 2, 2002.

4. " 'The American People Have Got the Staying Power for This,'" *The New York Times*, Sept. 3, 2002.

5. Adriel Bettelheim, "Congress Changing Tone Of Homeland Security Debate," *CQ Weekly*, Aug. 31, 2002, pp. 2222-2225.

6. See James Dao, "Senate Panel to Ask Bush Aides to Give Details on His Iraq Policy," *The New York Times*, July 10, 2002.

7. Mary H. Cooper, "Energy Security," *The CQ Researcher*, Feb. 1, 2002, pp. 73-96.

8. See Bob Woodward, "President Broadens Anti-Hussein Order," *The Washington Post*, June 16, 2002.

9. John G. Inkenberry, "America's Imperial Ambition," *Foreign Affairs*, September/October 2002, p. 45.

10. See William J. Broad, "Call for New Breed of Nuclear Arms Faces Hurdles," *The New York Times*, March 11, 2002.

11. Quoted by Eric Schmitt, "Wider Military Role in U.S. Is Urged," *The New York Times*, July 21, 2002.

12. Lieberman addressed a June 26, 2002, forum on homeland security sponsored by the Progressive Policy Institute.

13. For background, see Mary H. Cooper, "Missile Defense," *The CQ Researcher*, Sept. 8, 2000, pp. 689-712.

14. See Pat Towell, "Bush Wins on Missile Defense, But With Democratic Stipulation," *CQ Weekly*, June 29, 2002, pp. 1754-1757.

15. John Cirincione, "No ABM Treaty, No Missile Defense," *Carnegie Analysis*, June 17, 2002, www.ceip.org.

16. This section is based in part on Mary H. Cooper, "Bush's Defense Strategy," *The CQ Researcher*, Sept. 7, 2001, pp. 689-712.

17. For background, see Mary H. Cooper, "Weapons of Mass Destruction," *The CQ Researcher*, March 8, 2002, pp. 193-216.

18. Unless otherwise noted, information in this section is based on Jeffrey D. Brake, "Quadrennial Defense Review (QDR): Background, Process, and Issues," *CRS Report for Congress*, Congressional Research Service, June 21, 2001.

19. Speech at the American Legion convention, San Antonio, Texas, Aug. 29, 2001.

20. Rumsfeld, *op. cit.*, p. iv.

21. Steven J. Nider, "New Military Strategy Falls Short," *Blueprint Magazine*, Nov. 15, 2001.

22. Unless otherwise noted, information in this section is based on Michael E. O'Hanlon, *Defense Policy Choices for the Bush Administration*, Second Edition (2002), pp. 99-102.

23. See Thom Shanker and James Risen, "Rumsfeld Weighs New Covert Acts by Military Units," *The New York Times*, Aug. 12, 2002.

24. See Pat Towell, "Crusader May Be Precursor to More Defense Cuts," *CQ Weekly*, July 20, 2002, pp. 1963-1967.

25. Donald Rumsfeld, "A Choice to Transform the Military," *The Washington Post*, May 16, 2002.

26. See Pat Towell, "Missile Defense Money Pivotal for House and Senate Conferees," *CQ Weekly*, Sept. 7, 2002, pp. 2321-2322.

27. Cheney addressed a convention of veterans in Nashville, Tenn., on Aug. 26, 2002. See Elisabeth Bumiller and James Dao, "Cheney: Nuclear Peril Justifies Iraq Attack," *The New York Times*, Aug. 27, 2002.

28. Elisabeth Bumiller, "President to Seek Congress's Assent Over Iraq Action," *The New York Times*, Sept. 5, 2002.

29. Bush's remarks are found at www.whitehouse.gov/news/releases/2002/09/20020904-1.html.

BIBLIOGRAPHY

Books

Butler, Richard, *Fatal Choice: Nuclear Weapons and the Illusion of Missile Defense*, Westview, 2002.
The former head of the U.N. Special Commission on Iraqi weapons programs argues that the Bush administration's plan to build a missile-defense system will only prompt China and other countries to build more nuclear weapons.

Cohen, Eliot A., *Supreme Command: Soldiers, Statesmen, and Leadership in Wartime*, The Free Press, 2002.
A defense analyst argues that the Powell doctrine has severely limited the military's ability to defend U.S. national interests. Attributed to Secretary of State Colin Powell, the doctrine directs the U.S. to abstain from foreign military incursions unless vital national interests are at stake and to use overwhelming force once it decides to act.

O'Hanlon, Michael E., *Defense Policy Choices for the Bush Administration (2nd ed.)*, Brookings Institution, 2002.
A Brookings analyst argues that the Bush administration, despite promises of a radical overhaul, has essentially continued the "transformation" begun by its predecessors.

Articles

Boyer, Peter J., "A Different War," *The New Yorker*, July 1, 2002, pp. 54-67.
The Army, with its legacy of heavy, slow-moving weapons, is the target of much of Defense Secretary Donald Rumsfeld's campaign to revolutionize the military, including increased reliance on long-distance precision strikes using Navy and Air Force aircraft and weapons.

Carr, David, "The Futility of 'Homeland Defense,' " *The Atlantic Monthly*, January 2002, pp. 53-55.
Carr argues the U.S. cannot defend itself completely against attacks involving nuclear, biological or chemical weapons, which could be smuggled in shipping containers, without destroying its free-trade policy.

Homer-Dixon, Thomas, "The Rise of Complex Terrorism," *Foreign Policy*, January/February 2002, pp. 52-62.
The Sept. 11 attacks offer a glimpse of future terrorist actions, a University of Toronto political scientist writes. Wealthy countries, with their widespread energy and industrial facilities, provide myriad targets for far more devastating attacks.

Kagan, Fred, "Needed: A Wartime Defense Budget," *The Wall Street Journal*, April 3, 2002.
A military historian argues that the U.S. armed forces have been so profoundly weakened over the past decade that they will be unable to conduct future operations, including an incursion against Iraq, unless defense spending grows by at least triple the $150 billion increase requested this year by President Bush.

Nather, David, "For Congress, a New World — And Business as Usual," *CQ Weekly*, Sept. 7, 2002, pp. 2274-2288; 2313-2322.
Nather's comprehensive report leads off the magazine's Special Report on congressional and defense issues on the one-year anniversary of the Sept. 11 terrorist attacks. Topics covered include President Bush's efforts to sell lawmakers on preemptive strikes against Iraq, missile defense and Attorney General John Ashcroft and national security.

Perry, William J., "Preparing for the Next Attack," *Foreign Affairs*, November/December 2001, pp. 31-45.
Former President Clinton's Defense secretary says the most immediate threat to the U.S. is a small nuclear or biological weapon unleashed in a major city, and that the best defense is vigorous efforts to halt weapons proliferation.

Wallerstein, Immanuel, "The Eagle Has Crash Landed," *Foreign Policy*, July/August, 2002, pp. 60-68.
A Yale University historian argues that the U.S., like all other great powers before it, is destined to decline in power, and indeed has been losing ground since the 1970s.

Weinberg, Steven, "Can Missile Defense Work?" *The New York Review of Books*, Feb. 14, 2002, pp. 41-47.
A Nobel laureate in physics argues that the national missile-defense system being pursued by the Bush administration will not work against the most dangerous threat — an accidental launch of one of Russia's 3,900 nuclear warheads — and may prompt other countries to develop or expand their own nuclear arsenals.

Reports and Studies

Grimmett, Richard F., "War Powers Resolution: Presidential Compliance," *Issue Brief for Congress*, Congressional Research Service, updated June 12, 2002.
The 1973 War Powers Resolution, meant to ensure that the president and Congress share in war-making decisions, is coming under scrutiny once again as President Bush contemplates action against Iraqi leader Saddam Hussein.

U.S. Department of Defense, "Quadrennial Defense Review," Sept. 30, 2001.
The Bush administration's first QDR provides few major changes from earlier calls for "transforming" the military by developing more flexible, high-tech weapons to deal with new threats to U.S. security.

For More Information

Brookings Institution, 1775 Massachusetts Ave., N.W., Washington, DC 20036; (202) 797-6000; www.brook.edu. An independent research organization devoted to public policy issues.

Center for Defense Information, 1779 Massachusetts Ave., N.W., Washington, DC 20036; (202) 332-0600; www.cdi.org. A nonpartisan, nonprofit educational organization that focuses on security policy and defense budgeting.

Center for Strategic and International Studies, 1800 K St., N.W., Washington, DC 20006; (202) 887-0200; www.csis.org. A bipartisan organization that analyzes challenges to U.S. national and international security.

Council on Foreign Relations, 58 E. 68th St., New York, NY 10021; (212) 434-9400; www.cfr.org. A nonpartisan research organization dedicated to increasing America's understanding of the world and contributing ideas to U.S. foreign policy.

Lexington Institute, 1600 Wilson Blvd., Suite 900, Arlington, VA 22209; (703) 522-5828; www.lexingtoninstitute.org. A nonprofit, nonpartisan organization that supports a limited role for government and a strong military.

Nuclear Threat Initiative, 1747 Pennsylvania Ave., N.W., 7th floor, Washington, DC 20006; (202) 296-4810; www.nti.org. Co-chaired by Ted Turner and Sam Nunn, this nonprofit organization works to reduce the global threats from nuclear, biological and chemical weapons.

U.S. Department of Defense, Washington, DC 20301-7100; www.defenselink.mil. The Pentagon's Web site is the most complete source of DOD information.

5

Policing the Borders

Patrick Marshall

A Customs Service agent inspects the seal on a cargo container in the port of Miami. Agents monitor more than 6 million containers of cargo brought to U.S. ports yearly by 7,500 foreign-flag ships. About 2 percent are x-rayed or physically inspected.

From *The CQ Researcher,*
February 22, 2002.

Foreign visitors to the United States are expected to fill out their entry forms accurately. When Khalid Al Midhair and Nawaq Alhamzi arrived, they noted they would be staying at an unspecified Marriott Hotel in New York City.

Shortly before the Sept. 11 terrorist attacks, the two Arab men were identified as potential terrorists, but when FBI agents went looking for them the addresses proved bogus. Midhair and Alhamzi eventually surfaced — they were among the hijackers on the American Airlines plane that slammed into the Pentagon. [1]

In the wake of the attacks, whatever comfort Americans took from the two oceans buffering them from the rest of the world suddenly vanished. As the deaths of more than 3,000 people tragically underscored, America is as vulnerable to terrorists as any country in the Middle East or Europe.

What had gone so wrong? Why had 19 Arab men with terrorist ties been allowed into the country? How had all of them managed to carry box cutters aboard commercial airliners? And why hadn't the CIA, FBI and other government intelligence agencies been able to track down those that had been identified?

The attacks put the nation on high alert. Airports shut down; ships with potentially dangerous cargo, such as liquefied natural gas, were blocked from ports; National Guardsmen patrolled power plants, reservoirs, borders, airports and major bridges. Greyhound even stopped running buses. [2]

Then, without warning, anthrax-tainted letters began arriving at government and news organization offices around the country, eventually killing two postal workers.

Soon afterward, more sweeping responses were ordered.

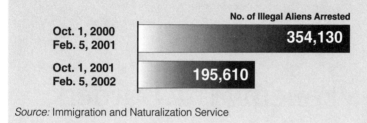

Illegal Apprehensions Dropped After Sept. 11

The number of illegal aliens apprehended by U.S. Border Patrol agents along the 2,000-mile Southwest border with Mexico plummeted 45 percent after the terrorist attacks. Officials say increased patrol efforts help account for the drop, as well as the depressed U.S. economy and increased optimism in Mexico.

No. of Illegal Aliens Arrested

Oct. 1, 2000 Feb. 5, 2001	354,130
Oct. 1, 2001 Feb. 5, 2002	195,610

Source: Immigration and Naturalization Service

President Bush formed a new Homeland Security Office to find answers and coordinate a response. Legislators summoned experts from the responsible agencies and quickly passed legislation giving police agencies more power to fight terrorism. And the administration started the process of funneling more money to border-security agencies.

Debate still rages over how best to reduce threats to the nation's security, but experts agree that border security is one of the keys. The task is massive. In addition to policing the nation's 7.500-mile-long borders with Mexico and Canada, agents from the Customs Service and Immigration and Naturalization Service (INS) must monitor the 11 million trucks and 2.2 million rail cars that enter the United States every year, plus 7,500 foreign-flag ships that make 51,000 calls in U.S. ports.

The job includes responsibility for the more than 31 million non-citizens who enter the country each year — who are supposed to notify the INS when their visas expire or when they change addresses, jobs or schools.

It's an uphill battle, in the view of Stephen E. Flynn, a senior fellow in the National Security Studies Program at the Council on Foreign Relations and a commander in the U.S. Coast Guard.

"As Americans now contemplate the road ahead, they need to accept three unpleasant facts," he wrote recently. "First, there will continue to be anti-American terrorists with global reach for the foreseeable future." [3]

Secondly, "These terrorists will have access to the means — including chemical and biological weapons —

to carry out catastrophic attacks on U.S. soil.

"And third, the economic and societal disruption created by both the Sept. 11 attacks and the subsequent anthrax mailings will provide grist for the terrorist mill."

But many experts say the U.S. must also focus on border security in other nations. "All of us are thinking about a more layered approach to the border," says an official at the Office of Homeland Security, who asked that his name not be used. "Before, we were working with a paradigm based on the war against drugs: If drugs reached the border, that was OK, because if we found the drugs at the border and confiscated them, they didn't get to the end user.

"But today we have the threat of weapons of mass destruction reaching our borders. As soon as they get close to our borders they can be harmful. That's one of the reasons we need to push our borders out" and work with border security in other nations.

To bolster border security, anti-terrorism experts have called for several immediate improvements, including:

- better intelligence gathering on visa applicants;
- increased data-sharing among federal agencies;
- closer scrutiny of incoming cargo;
- stronger security measures at the borders; and
- computer tracking of immigrants and visa holders after they've arrived in the United States.

President Bush's 2003 budget proposes about $11 billion for border security, including $380 million for the INS to build a state-of-the-art visa-tracking system, and an increase of $619 million for the Customs Service's inspection budget.

But experts disagree over which steps would be the most cost-effective and the least disruptive to trade and Americans' daily lives.

"How much should we spend, and how many liberties should we curtail, in an attempt to stop terrorists?" asks Sam Francis, a syndicated columnist who has written extensively on domestic terrorism. "Congress is going to have to look at some of the proposed systems, and they're going have to answer that question. At this point, there's just a lot of chest thumping. Nobody wants to be seen as soft on terrorism."

Dennis McBride, president of the Potomac Institute for Policy Studies in Arlington, Va., says, "Basically, we need a cost analysis of where we're putting our assets. This is a war, and we have to take a warlike approach and be systematic."

Flynn argues that the goal of such an assessment should be keeping America's infrastructure functioning rather than preventing all terrorist acts. "It is inevitable that we will have breaches of security," he explains. "When we do the postmortem, it is important that we see the event as a result of a correctable security feature, not the absence of security."

On Sept. 11, Flynn notes, "we assumed that we had no credible airport security anywhere, and so we grounded all flights and basically had to go back to square one." The goal should be to strengthen the system enough so [the entire system] doesn't have to shut down when a terrorist incident occurs, he says.

Security officials say they generally feel confident that the government has responded well to the terrorism challenge up to this point, but largely through efforts that will be very difficult to maintain without dedicating additional resources.

"Since Sept. 11, there have been some huge efforts by the border agencies to improve our security, but it's not sustainable," says the Office of Homeland Security official. "For starters, the Customs and INS agents on the borders are burning out. That's why the president has asked for the additional funds."

Meanwhile, civil liberties advocates warn that certain proposed security measures — such as instituting a national ID card and enforcing immigration laws by targeting certain ethnic groups — would undermine some of Americans' most cherished civil liberties. [4] (See "At Issue," p. 105.)

As policy-makers discuss how to protect America's borders, here are some of the key questions they are asking:

Can the United States track foreign visitors effectively?

When Americans learned that 13 of the 19 terrorists involved in the Sept. 11 attacks had entered the country legally and that three of them had overstayed their visas, the public immediately wanted to know how visas are issued by the State Department and then monitored by the INS after the visa holder enters the United States.

"What went wrong in the issuance of valid visas that

A gamma-ray imaging device scans a truck passing through U.S. Customs at the U.S.-Mexico border crossing in Laredo, Texas. Unlike older technologies using x-rays, the new technology uses low radiation doses and doesn't require a special enclosure. Trucks are scanned for contraband, mis-manifested cargo, explosives and weapons.

permitted these 13 terrorists to legally enter the United States?" Sen. Dianne Feinstein, D-Calif., asked Mary Ryan, assistant secretary of State for consular affairs, during Senate hearings last October. "Or do you view their entry as acceptable risk?" [5]

"We had no information on them whatsoever from law enforcement or from intelligence," Ryan replied. "So they came in. They applied for visas. They were interviewed. And their stories were believed. Like most Americans, I was surprised at how much we learned about some of these terrorists in the immediate aftermath of the Sept. 11 atrocities. And the question in my own mind is, 'Why didn't we know that before Sept. 11?' "

Ryan's question was rhetorical. Her department knows very well why they didn't have the information they needed to filter out the terrorists before granting them visas: Federal agencies, such as the CIA and the FBI, didn't share the information they have about visa applicants.

"We have had a struggle with the law enforcement and intelligence communities in getting information," Ryan complained. "I've tried, we've tried in the Bureau of Consular Affairs . . . to get . . . information from the FBI. We were constantly told we were not a law-enforcement agency, and so they couldn't give it to us. Other agencies fear compromise of sources and methods." [6]

Indeed, many intelligence experts argue that the FBI and the CIA might have been able to thwart the Sept. 11 attacks had they worked together more closely. The critics blame the lack of cooperation on several factors, including U.S. laws — especially grand jury secrecy laws — that prevent the FBI from sharing information with the CIA and other intelligence agencies.

Just six weeks after the attacks, however, Congress revamped some of the secrecy laws. A sweeping new anti-terrorism bill — the USA Patriot Act — now allows the FBI to share secret grand jury evidence with the CIA and other agencies dealing with national security without first obtaining a court order (see page 103). [7]

Attorney General John D. Ashcroft says the new law "takes down some of the walls" between the FBI, the CIA and the INS. "We are working very aggressively to coordinate our informational capabilities so [agencies] in one part of the government that have information can make that information available to, and valuable to, others," Ashcroft said after the Patriot Act was signed on Oct. 26. [8]

There have been other changes since the attacks. Law enforcement and intelligence agencies have nearly tripled their contributions to the database used by consular officials to screen visa applicants, according to the Bureau for Consular Affairs. The database contains an estimated 5.7 million records on aliens in or applying to enter the United States, generated primarily from visa applications and supplemental information from other federal agencies. The information is now being shared with the INS, the agency that decides whether to admit visa holders to the United States.

In addition to the tens of millions of legal visa holders in the United States, the INS estimates that 6 million to 7 million people are in the country illegally, 41 percent of whom have overstayed their visas. At a minimum, that would mean tracking some 2.4 million people.

Some critics of the visa system say that even when agencies have had all the information they need about applicants, the criteria for granting visas and permitting entry to the United States are too loose. Currently, individuals can be denied visas for a variety of reasons, from having a contagious disease or a criminal record to having committed or planned to commit a terrorist act.

However, once inside the United States, visa holders are not monitored unless they are under investigation by a federal law-enforcement agency, such as the FBI or the

Drug Enforcement Administration. But because one of the Sept. 11 attackers was in the country on an expired student visa, many have called for stricter monitoring.

"The State Department needs to be given sweeping authority to keep out anyone who belongs to the 'Death to America Club,'" says Mark Krikorian, executive director of the Center for Immigration Studies, an immigration policy think tank. "If you're an enemy of America, I'm not really interested in whether you've killed anybody or not — you have no business being here."

However, others see serious problems with the current procedure for putting foreigners on a "lookout list" of individuals who should be denied admission.

"We're concerned that people might be put on the list not because of involvement in a terrorist group but because of their political views or because their government just doesn't like that person," says Timothy Edgar, legislative counsel at the American Civil Liberties Union (ACLU). "That happened back in the Cold War days, when we had grounds of inadmissibility based on being a member of the Communist Party or advocating communism and so forth. [Such practices] interfere with American citizens' right to hear that person."

The INS faces challenges even more daunting than those facing the State Department. Due to limited resources and, some critics say, poor planning, even if the agency had good information about dangerous individuals headed for our borders, the service would be hard-pressed to prevent them from entering the country or to track and deport those who do get in.

"On Sept. 10," notes Flynn of the Council on Foreign Relations, "just over 300 U.S. Border Patrol agents supported by a single analyst were assigned the job of detecting and intercepting illegal border crossings along the entire, vast 4,000-mile land and water border with Canada." *

While patrols have been beefed up significantly since Sept. 11, no one seriously believes any number of border agents can prevent a determined terrorist from entering the United States. What's more, recent experience has shown that even when the Border Patrol catches a criminal alien, he may be released because of lack of data coordination between agencies.

---

* Of the Immigration and Naturalization Service's 9,824 Border Patrol agents, 9,500 are assigned to the U.S.-Mexico border.

Such was the infamous case of the "Railway Killer," a rail-hopping Mexican named Angel Maturino Resendiz, alias Rafael Resendez-Ramirez, who eventually confessed to murdering at least eight people along railway lines in three Southwestern states. When Maturino was still at large, Houston police had contacted the INS about him, but the agency failed to put an alert for him in the Border Patrol's primary database. Thus, when he was caught trying to enter the United States in El Paso, Border Patrol agents didn't know he was wanted for murder and sent him back to Mexico. A few days later, he re-entered the country and murdered again. He eventually surrendered in 1999.

Congress responded to the incident by ordering the government to merge the fingerprint files of the FBI and the INS, but the two databases still are not linked.

And that wasn't the first time Congress had ordered better tracking of alien entries and exits. In the Illegal Immigration Reform and Immigrant Responsibility Act of 1996, lawmakers mandated that a computerized system be established for tracking aliens whose visas have expired. But after border-area business groups complained it might delay cross-border shoppers, Congress never appropriated enough money for it and later watered it down so it doesn't apply to most land-border entries into the United States (*see p. 101*).

Glenn Fine, inspector general of the Department of Justice, found that the INS had not properly managed another entry and exit system mandated by Congress, despite having spent $31 million on the pilot program.

As a result, Fine told a congressional hearing recently, the INS is virtually incapable of tracking those who overstay their visas and has no way to apprehend them. "Our review found that the principal INS system for tracking these overstays, the non-immigrant information system, was not producing reliable data, either in the aggregate or on individuals," Fine said. "We also found that the INS had no specific enforcement program to identify, locate, apprehend and remove overstays, and that using the INS data was of little use for locating them." [9]

James Ziglar, who was appointed INS commissioner two months before the hearing and only a month before the Sept. 11 attacks, admitted the agency has many holes to plug, but said they've been trying.

"There are lots of things that we need to change, but the idea that this organization is sitting around and doesn't care and hasn't been approaching these problems is not true," Ziglar told senators.

More than 3 million vehicles a year pass U.S. Customs before driving through the Detroit-Windsor tunnel at the Canada-U.S. border crossing. Customs agents nationwide annually monitor more than 11 million trucks and 2.2 million rail cars crossing the borders.

Can the United States keep weapons of mass destruction out of the country?

Keeping terrorists out of the United States is only half the battle; they also must be prevented from bringing in lethal biological agents or other weapons. For the U.S. Customs Service, the Treasury Department agency that handles property searches at the borders, the challenge is at least as daunting as the challenge facing the INS.

Part of the challenge is understaffing. For example, observes Flynn of the Council on Foreign Relations, the number of customs inspectors on the U.S.-Canadian border was reduced by about 25 percent from 1985 to 2000, even as trade between the two nations increased from $116.3 billion to $409.8 billion. [10]

The Customs Service also faces serious challenges in monitoring America's ports. "At many ports, access is virtually uncontrolled," F. Amanda DeBusk, a former member of the Interagency Commission on Crime and Security in U.S. Seaports, told a Senate hearing last December. [11]

Tens of Millions of Visitors

More than 31 million non-immigrant aliens were admitted to the United States in 1999, the most in history. The typical non-immigrant is a tourist or business person who visits for a few days to several months.

Non-immigrants admitted to U.S.
(in millions)

1975	7.0
1981	11.8
1985	9.7
1990	17.7
1995	22.6
1999	31.4

Source: Immigration and Naturalization Service

"Access is overseen by contract security personnel, who, like airport baggage screeners, receive low wages and little training," said Argent Acosta, a customs official in New Orleans." [12] And the ranks of customs agents at the ports are just as decimated as they are along the borders, he pointed out.

"Despite the huge increases in trade since I started with customs in 1970, the number of customs inspectors at the Port of New Orleans has dropped from approximately 103 in 1970 to 29 this year," Acosta said, pointing out that with its current staff, the service is only capable of inspecting about 2 percent of the 600,000 cargo containers that come into the nation's seaports each day.

U.S. Customs Commissioner Robert C. Bonner later took issue with Acosta's use of the 2 percent figure, say-

ing it was unfair to use the "startling statistic" without explaining the complex process used by customs inspectors to carefully target which shipments to inspect among the $1.2 trillion in goods processed by the service each year.

"An effective border strategy requires a thoughtful approach that relies only in part on physical examinations of cargo," Bonner said in a Feb. 16 *Washington Post* Op-Ed article.

The service also combines "good intelligence, advance-arrival information, state-of-the-art inspection technology, strong industry-government partnerships, a well-trained work force and sophisticated systems to exchange and analyze mountains of data," Bonner said.

"We follow a complex process that requires far more than mere physical examination to prevent terrorists or their weapons from entering the United States," he said. [13]

But the agency had warned earlier that it was woefully understaffed and underfunded. According to a February 2001 study, in order to meet its mission requirements, the service said it needed an additional 14,777 positions — mostly inspectors — over its fiscal 1998 base of 19,428 positions. [14]

And it is not just lack of manpower that hampers the Customs Service, critics say. Like the INS, the service lacks information about land and sea shipments because it has inadequate databases and outdated equipment.

"The world may be well into the electronic age, but the U.S. Customs Service is still struggling with paper-based systems," Flynn wrote. "For years, its proposed [data-modernization] projects have run aground on the twin shoals of flat federal budgets and industry disputes over the timing, format and quantity of data it should provide to customs in advance." [15]

Last April, the Customs Service received the seed money to start modernizing its database, but completion is years away. In the interim, according to Flynn, "inspectors will have to rely on only the bluntest of data-management tools." [16]

Customs Service officials are optimistic, despite the challenges. While conceding that the current system "is clearly on overload," Deputy Assistant Commissioner John Heinrich says the situation is improving rapidly. Besides increasing staffing since Sept. 11, Heinrich says, all ports of entry on the northern border — many of which were frequently unstaffed before Sept. 11 — are being "hardened," or made more secure.

Critics Advocate Immigration Limits

Critics of U.S. immigration policy argue that the Sept. 11 terrorist attacks tragically proved that the country needs to clamp down on legal as well as illegal immigration.

"The numbers of immigrants are such that the government has lost the capacity to monitor who is here, and under what conditions," says Daniel Stein, executive director of the Federation for American Immigration Reform. "The numbers are too high. The exploded numbers of the aliens fighting to stay in the country have hamstrung the whole enforcement apparatus of the Immigration and Naturalization Service" (INS).

In fact, according to INS figures, the number of legal immigrants has been steadily falling. From an all-time high of more than 1.5 million in 1990, the number dropped to 646,568 in 1999, the most recent year for which totals are available. [1] At the same time, however, non-immigrant visitors, such as tourists, business people and students, rose sharply. In 1999, 31.4 million visitors were admitted, compared with 17.6 million in 1990.

The number of immigrants isn't the critics' only concern. Some argue that immigrant communities in the United States offer a haven for terrorists.

"Immigrant sub-cultures, not just Islamic or Arabic but many different cultures, provide comfort and anonymity for potential terrorists," says political columnist Sam Francis. "Obviously, most of the people in the subculture communities are not terrorists, and most of them are not sympathetic with terrorists. But the community itself provides cover and a kind of sanctuary for terrorists."

Mark Krikorian, executive director of the Center for Immigration Studies, agrees. "Immigrant communities serve as the sea within which terrorist fish swim," he says, much as Italian communities in major U.S. cities once served as "incubators" for the Mafia. It was only when

immigration from Italy was reduced, Krikorian says, that people in the communities began to assimilate into the broader American society. "The Mafia lost the incubator they benefited from and the FBI was, little by little, able to penetrate the group," Krikorian says.

Krikorian argues that lower levels of immigration today would have a similar impact. "Today, Muslim communities form unwitting cover for terrorists, and promoting the assimilation of the recent immigrants in these communities can only make it more difficult for terrorists who operate in these communities to use them as hosts," he says. "A reduction in immigration is naturally going to allow assimilation to operate more thoroughly, and that will have national-security benefits."

But civil liberties advocates reject proposals that single people out by race or national origin, and especially those that target legal immigrants for special attention. "We had a terrible legacy in this country of discriminatory immigration policy," says Timothy Edgar, legislative counsel for the American Civil Liberties Union. "It would be a huge mistake for this country to assume we're going to come up with a list of pariah countries in the Islamic world that can't get access to the United States."

In fact, Edgar says, terrorists don't always come from a specific country or group of countries. For example, he says, recent terrorist incidents have involved an American — Oklahoma City bomber Timothy McVeigh — and a man from Great Britain, Richard Reid, who was recently arrested on board a U.S. airliner after trying to ignite explosives in his shoes.

Edgar suspects other motives lie behind suggestions to reduce legal immigration. "I think the basic impetus behind some of these proposals has nothing to do with enforcing immigration laws," he says. "It stems from a vague anxiety that immigrants are more likely to be dangerous."

Judith Golub, senior director for advocacy for the American Immigration Lawyers Association, agrees. "We are a nation of immigrants," she says. "The only way to enhance our security is to target only those who plan to do us harm, and those are terrorists, not immigrants."

---

[1] *1998 Statistical Yearbook of the Immigration and Naturalization Service*, Department of Justice, November 2000, p. 19.

And new technology will extend the range of existing personnel. "We're going to install new gates and extensive video systems so that remotely we can see what is happening at ports of entry after they've been closed [for

the night] and the gates have been shut," Heinrich says.

In addition, the purchase of new x-ray and gamma-ray detectors will make it possible to examine more containers with fewer inspectors, he says.

Policing the Borders — at a Glance

- Of the 9,824 Immigration and Naturalization Service (INS) Border Patrol agents, 9,500 are assigned to the U.S.-Mexico border.
- INS agents arrested 1.2 million people who tried to enter the United States illegally last year. For every one person arrested, an estimated three more enter the United States undetected.
- There are 300 official ports of entry into the United States, but only 5,113 INS immigration inspectors. Last year they made more than a half-billion inspections at all border crossings.
- The 1,977 INS special agents posted worldwide are authorized to arrest non-citizen criminals and also investigate alien-smuggling cases, counterfeit immigration documents, foreign-based organized-crime syndicates and gang activities.
- The INS has 2,618 adjudication officers to consider petitions for immigration benefits. Last year, 7.3 million applications for immigration benefits were filed — not counting a half-million citizenship applications.
- About 640 INS deportation officers are responsible for tracking 314,000 aliens who have ignored deportation orders.
- The INS has 371 asylum officers who process more than 66,000 requests for asylum each year.
- The Customs Service collected $24 billion in duties, excise taxes, fees and penalties on imported and exported goods and services in fiscal 2000.
- The Customs Service has 7,562 inspectors, 588 canine enforcement officers and 1,030 import specialists.
- Customs agents inspected cargo (including 5.7 million seagoing containers) on 964,447 aircraft, 11.2 million trucks, 2.3 million rail cars and 214,610 vessels in fiscal 2001.

"The deployment of this additional technology . . . will enable us to examine in a matter of minutes an entire 40-foot container or an entire truckload of merchandise," Heinrich says. "Had we used simple, backbreaking labor, the time would be two to three hours."

In fact, Heinrich promises, at some ports inspectors will be able to increase by a factor of two or three the amount of "high-risk" cargo they can inspect from questionable shippers or lax foreign ports.

Flynn agrees that things have improved since Sept. 11, but he warns that there is still "virtually no security" at many ports, and that land entry points are similarly porous. If there were a terrorist incident at a port, he warns, it could lead to a "tremendously costly" shutdown of all ports, as it did for aviation on Sept. 11.

Most of the measures implemented since Sept. 11 have been too narrowly focused, Flynn says. "Ultimately," he says, "we need to go toward a point of origin and bring security to what we call the supply chain," by beefing up the security measures in place in other countries that ship to the United States.

Kim E. Petersen, executive director of the Maritime Security Council, an industry group, agrees.

"It was erroneous for the Office of Homeland Defense to consider U.S. ports as the first line of defense against weapons of mass destruction," Petersen says.

"The fact is, our first line of defense must be the ports of origin [because] we haven't been that good about identifying problem [domestic] ports."

Petersen argues that industry and the government need to work together to establish minimum-security standards for foreign ports, including tougher requirements for cargo manifest reporting and inspection. "If a particular port is identified as noncompliant, then, just as the Federal Aviation Administration does now, the U.S. government would impose sanctions up to and including a prohibition of shipments coming directly from that port," Petersen says.

"Otherwise, we're at the mercy of shipments coming into the United States," he continues. "In the case of a weapon of mass destruction, we won't discover it until it actually exists within our ports, and that is an unacceptable risk."

Customs officials say they agree with the concept. Heinrich says such a program would require "deploying our own officers as analysts in foreign countries, sharing of technology that we're using here and working closely with those governments to identify cargo shipments before they actually are placed on the vessel."

But Heinrich concedes that it won't happen overnight. "It will be two to three years before we can say with certainty that the threat has been reduced about as significantly as we can expect," he says.

And while many of the proposed measures may be costly, Petersen points out that in addition to increased security, they will provide across-the-board benefits to ports, shippers and the nation's economy.

"These very same measures would also help prevent theft of cargo and other crimes," he says. "Literally tens of billions of dollars are lost worldwide through cargo theft. It would be cost-effective for many ports to enact these measures, and I expect they'll be far more receptive than many people suppose."

Should lawmakers create a new border security agency?

President Bush created the Office of Homeland Security and tapped then-Gov. Tom Ridge, R-Pa., to develop and coordinate a comprehensive national strategy against terrorist attacks. Without a congressional mandate, however, policy experts say the office largely depends upon presidential coattails for influence, because it has no direct authority over any of the agencies involved in protecting the borders and very little experience in dealing with the issues.

"Let's face it, Tom Ridge's office is brand new," said INS Commissioner Ziglar. "They are still getting organized, and they don't have anybody over there who are experts on immigration, customs [or] border enforcement. That's why they necessarily have to rely on us." [17]

Ridge acknowledges the problem and has proposed combining the agencies responsible for border enforcement. "There may be some fusion of these agencies," he said. "We need to change our border strategy so there is only one face greeting people, instead of the way it is now where one agency looks in the trunk and another looks in the back seat. But I know my colleagues resist this consolidation." [18]

Indeed, the president's 2003 budget proposals did not include such a request. "The administration is convinced that we basically have a very good system," says McBride of the Potomac Institute. "They give me no reason to think that they want to re-examine our philosophy of security."

However, the Bush administration has proposed restructuring the INS so that its enforcement functions are separate from its visa and other administrative functions.

But House Judiciary Committee Chairman James Sensenbrenner Jr., R-Wis., says the INS restructuring plan is inadequate. "It does not go far enough for the rescue mission that is needed — both on the enforcement side and the immigration-services side," Sensenbrenner said at a Nov. 14 press conference. "I fear this proposal will follow its administrative-restructuring predecessors in making little impact and possibly making things worse at the agency. We must remember that the current INS is the direct product of previous INS administrative-restructuring efforts." [19]

Instead, Sensenbrenner wants to abolish the INS and create an Agency for Immigration Services. Besides dividing enforcement functions from service functions, his proposed legislation would raise the agency's profile by putting an associate attorney general for immigration affairs at its helm, a position higher than the current INS commissioner.

Rep. Tom Tancredo, R-Colo., says Sensenbrenner's plan doesn't go far enough.

"There's something big-time wrong with the INS," Tancredo says and calls for an entirely new agency with broader responsibilities. Tancredo has introduced a bill to combine the responsibilities of the INS, the Customs Service, the Coast Guard and other agencies into a new National Border Security Agency.

"Right now, you can go to an entry point on the border and look at lines of cars coming in, each to a different station. Each of those stations might be manned by a different agency," Tancredo explains. "People sit in the hills around the portal with binoculars, trying to figure out which agency is manning which station. If they're smuggling drugs, they'll pick one line, and if they're smuggling people they'll pick a different line. That's how goofy it is.

"You could dump a zillion dollars into this system, and it would all be sucked up by inefficiency," he continues. "We should not add more money to this. The problem is lack of coordination, lack of a single line of authority and lack of direction."

But Tancredo is not hopeful about the prospects for his bill.

"When you're fighting the chairman of the committee, the president of the United States and all the agencies, I'd say the chances are slim to none," Tancredo says.

But, he warns, "If we don't do anything to shore up our borders and something else happens as a result of that inability or inaction, then we're not just responsible, we're culpable."

C H R O N O L O G Y

1875-1892 *Labor unrest and concern about an influx of Asians spur restrictive policies.*

1875 The Immigration Act of 1875 imposes the first significant federal controls on immigration, mainly by prohibiting new Asian laborers.

1882 The Immigration Act of 1882 sets a 50-cents per immigrant head tax. The first of several Chinese Exclusion Acts limits Chinese immigration. Similar legislation in 1884 and 1888 bars ethnic Chinese.

Jan. 1, 1892 Ellis Island in New York Harbor becomes the primary entry point for immigrants.

1917-1930 *Postwar fears of foreign agitators trigger immigration backlash.*

1917 The Immigration Act of 1917 imposes the first literacy test on immigrants and a head tax on Canadian and Mexican immigrants.

1921 The 1921 Emergency Immigration Restriction Act establishes the first quotas on the number of people admitted from each country or region.

1924 Congress creates the U.S. Border Patrol. The 1924 Immigration Act sets new quotas on immigrants from specific countries.

1940-1965 *Cold War politics influences immigration policy.*

1940 The Immigration and Naturalization Service is transferred to the Department of Justice. The Alien Registration Act requires all aliens — visitors as well as immigrants — to register and anyone over 14 to be fingerprinted.

1950 Internal Security Act includes political "subversives" among the list of excludable aliens.

1952 Influenced by Cold War political concerns, the Immigration and Nationality Act sets pro-Europeans immigration quotas.

1965 The 1965 Amendments to the Immigration and Nationality Act replaces the immigration quota system with ceilings on the number of entrants from the Eastern and Western Hemisphere.

1980-2000 *High immigration levels spur calls for restriction.*

1986 Immigration Reform and Control Act sanctions employers who knowingly hire illegal aliens.

1990 The Immigration Act of 1990 significantly increases the number of immigrants allowed into the country and prohibits exclusion because of beliefs, statements or associations.

1996 The Illegal Immigration Reform and Responsibility Act of 1996 provides increased funding for the Border Patrol, tougher penalties for illegal entry and added grounds for excluding aliens.

2001-2002 *Terrorism on American soil causes tighter border security.*

Sept. 11, 2001 Terrorists crash two airliners into the World Trade Center and one into the Pentagon; a fourth crashes in a Pennsylvania field.

Oct. 8, 2001 President Bush creates the Office of Homeland Security.

Oct. 26, 2001 Bush signs the USA Patriot Act allowing the FBI to share secret grand jury evidence with the CIA and other agencies without first obtaining a court order.

Dec. 19, 2001 The House passes by voice vote the Enhanced Border Security and Visa Reform Act, strengthening the foreign-student tracking system and once again requiring an automated entry-and-exit tracking system for all non-citizens entering and exiting the country, except for Canadian nationals. It also requires all visas and passports of immigrants and visitors to be tamper-resistant, machine-readable and contain biometric identifiers, such as fingerprints. It bars visas for anyone from countries that sponsor terrorism and authorizes 2,000 more INS inspectors and investigative personnel over the next five years.

BACKGROUND

Open-Door Policy

Border control meant two things to the newly independent American colonies: repelling invading armies and enforcing duties on imported goods.

The threat of invasion was of real but limited concern. For a European army to invade meant assembling a mighty fleet, and the only country at the time capable of doing that was England, which was licking its wounds following its defeat in the American war for independence. Thus, the new nation's primary military concern was policing the borders against Indian raids — deadly nuisances, to be sure, but not ultimately threatening to the country's security.

More of a threat was the nation's impending bankruptcy. On July 4, 1789, in an effort to put the country on a firmer financial footing, Congress passed the Tariff Act, which authorized the collection of duties on imported goods. A few weeks later, lawmakers passed legislation creating the U.S. Customs Service to collect the duties. In its first year, the service was the primary source of revenue for the federal government, collecting more than $2 million.

For nearly 125 years, customs funded virtually the entire government, and paid for the nation's early growth and infrastructure. The territories of Louisiana and Oregon, Florida and Alaska were purchased; the National Road from Cumberland, Maryland, to Wheeling, West Virginia, was constructed; and, the Transcontinental Railroad stretched from sea-to-sea. Customs collections built the nation's lighthouses; the military and naval academies; and the City of Washington. The new nation that once teetered on the edge of bankruptcy was now solvent. By 1835, customs revenues alone had reduced the national debt to zero!

In addition to collecting duties from law-abiding importers, the Customs Service — along with the Coast Guard and other agencies — apprehended smugglers trying to evade duties or smuggle illegal goods into, or out of, the country. During the War of 1812, for example, American profiteers took cattle to Canada illegally to sell to British troops. But because of the long and mostly unguarded land border, customs officers barely made a dent in the illegal cattle trade.

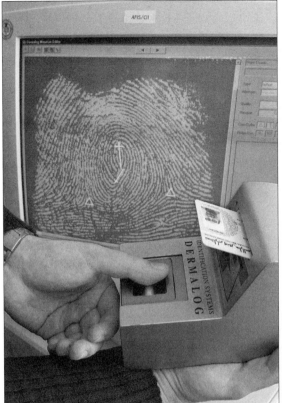

A fingerprint reader made by a German firm checks a passenger's thumbprint against the print on his passport. Legislation passed by the House would require that visas and other identification documents issued by the U.S. and other countries contain such "biometric" information.

The young country was just about as hungry for workers as it was for revenue, so immigration control was not an issue. Indeed, getting to the New World was still a relatively expensive proposition, which meant that hordes of uneducated people from the Old World did not threaten to flood the gates. For the most part, new arrivals were either relatively affluent immigrants or indentured workers and slaves. Laws restricting immigration were not seen as necessary. In 1793, in fact, President George Washington announced an open-door immigration policy.

While Congress wouldn't restrict immigration for almost 100 years, it was only five years until lawmakers, worried that radical supporters of the French Revolution

U.S. Targets Mideast 'Absconders'

The Justice Department in late January ordered anti-terrorism officials to target Middle Easterners who have ignored deportation orders, according to a confidential memo obtained by *The Washington Post*.

Out of the estimated 314,000 so-called absconders at large in the United States, federal officials are targeting approximately 6,000 individuals from countries on the list as being hospitable to al Qaeda, the terrorist organization headed by Osama bin Laden.

Special apprehension teams of agents from the Federal Bureau of Investigation, the Immigration and Naturalization Service and other agencies are being assembled, according to the Post. Absconders who are picked up will be detained and interviewed, and the memo directs investigators to encourage absconders to cooperate by referring to rewards being offered and the possibility of obtaining S Visas, which are given to immigrants who provide information to authorities that is helpful in criminal investigations. [1]

According to the memo, the government already has compiled a database of information gathered from recent interviews with thousands of Middle Eastern men who were invited to come forth voluntarily after the Sept. 11 attacks. Information gleaned from those apprehended and interrogated for failure to respond to deportation proceedings will be added to the database.

"We can't go after 314,000 people at a time, so it only makes sense to prioritize them in a way that makes sense from a law-enforcement perspective," a senior Justice Department official told the *Post*. "If we didn't do this, then we should be criticized." [2]

Meanwhile the administration is drawing criticism for targeting those from Middle Eastern countries.

"It's a fishing expedition," says Timothy Edgar, legislative counsel of the American Civil Liberties Union. "This is the biggest racial-profiling effort on the part of the government in decades."

Edgar says that the people who will be arrested and detained will be people for whom there is no indication that they are involved in terrorism. "It has become clear that it has nothing to do with enforcing immigration laws and has everything to do with selectively providing a pretext to aggressively investigate, interrogate and prosecute people based solely on their national origin," he says. "You really have to question whether this is the right use of limited government resources. This is a real blunderbuss approach."

But columnist Sam Francis argues that citizens should be more concerned about Americans' civil liberties than those of illegal aliens. "Frankly, we've allowed immigration to get out of control at this point," he says. "The result is that we're facing potential restrictions on our own civil liberties to control the situation. I don't think that's a good thing. I'd rather control immigration and have our civil liberties more secure."

---

[1] Dan Eggen, "Deportee Sweep Will Start With Mideast Focus," *The Washington Post*, Feb. 8, 2002, p. A1.

[2] *Ibid.*

---

might agitate in the United States, passed the four Alien and Sedition Acts of 1798. The controversial laws — later largely overturned — required a 14-year residency before immigrants could become citizens; allowed the president to expel aliens in the event of war or when they represented a threat to security; and made it a crime — for citizens as well as for aliens — to criticize the government.

Despite the new concerns, the government didn't begin recording the names of newcomers until 1819, when the Steerage Act required ship captains bringing immigrants to submit passenger lists to the Customs Service.

Federal Controls

The Immigration Act of 1875 marked the real beginning of federal controls on immigration. Among other things, the act prohibited the importation of Asian laborers without their consent and barred convicted felons and prostitutes from entering the country.

In 1882, Congress passed the first major restriction on immigration, the Chinese Exclusion Act. The law established a head tax of 50 cents per immigrant and banned "lunatics" and other individuals who might become public charges. Over the next 10 years, virtually all legislation related to immigration focused on controlling the flow of Chinese "coolie" labor. Subsequent

Exclusion Acts in 1884 and 1888 progressively expanded the restrictions from Chinese nationals to all individuals of Chinese extraction.

By 1891, anti-Catholic sentiment, coupled with business interests' concern that radical immigrants were behind the nation's rising labor activism, spurred passage of the Immigration Act. While the act extended exclusion of immigrants to the indigent and those with contagious diseases, it also created a superintendent of immigration in the Department of the Treasury. Soon after, the office was transformed into the Bureau of Immigration, the predecessor of the INS, with orders to deny entry to paupers, polygamists, the insane and persons with contagious diseases.

Until well after the turn of the century, immigration was generally easy to control since transportation was still relatively costly, and there were few entry points to the United States. The main public concern was not terrorists or criminals, but mass influxes of uneducated workers. On Jan. 1, 1892, the primary entry point for immigrants became Ellis Island. Sitting in the middle of New York Harbor, the facility was easy to control.

The only potentially uncontrollable area at the turn of the century was the long border with Mexico, which became a conduit for illegal Chinese laborers and Europeans who feared rejection at Ellis Island. Mounted guards were assigned to patrol the southern border, but the new patrol initially consisted of only a few dozen men and was not particularly effective.

World War I marked a turning point for America as a world power, and for U.S. concerns about immigration. The war's end brought special worries about the threat of radicalism, particularly after the Russian Revolution in 1917. The high levels of immigration from poorer Eastern and Southern European countries just before the war were cut dramatically during the war, and afterward, by restrictive — some would say racist — immigration legislation. The Immigration Act of 1917 imposed a literacy test intended to turn back some of the new, more impoverished immigrants, barred Asian immigrants from permanent residency and, for the first time, imposed a head tax on immigrants from Canada and Mexico.

Two major pieces of legislation in the 1920s — the 1921 Emergency Immigration Restriction Act and the 1924 Immigration Act — for the first time established quotas on immigrants from specific countries and regions. The new caps helped spark an immediate increase in illegal immigrants, which in turn prompted Congress to pass legislation creating the U.S. Border Patrol in 1924.

Growing Concern

World War II marked another turning point in U.S. immigration policy. In 1940, as part of a new wartime focus on controlling immigration, Congress transferred the INS to the Department of Justice. At the same time, the new Alien Registration Act required all aliens — visitors as well as immigrants — to register with the government. Those over 14 years of age had to be fingerprinted. Members or former members of prohibited organizations (especially communist organizations) were excluded from the country.

In 1965, amid charges that immigration quotas were biased against non-whites, lawmakers eliminated the system of visa quotas based on an applicant's country of origin. Instead, they set a ceiling on entrants from the Eastern Hemisphere and the Western Hemisphere, with a maximum of 20,000 visas to be granted per year to applicants from any single country.

Illegal aliens were the primary target of the sweeping 1986 Immigration Reform and Control Act. For the first time, both civil and criminal penalties were set for employers who knowingly hired illegal aliens. Largely as a tradeoff for the new penalties, however, Congress raised the official ceiling to 540,000 legal immigrants annually.

The 1986 law represented a response to public concerns over growing levels of both legal and illegal immigration. Between 1940 and 1991, legal immigration rose from 70,756 to a high of 1.8 million. [20] Expulsion of illegal aliens also increased over the same period by a factor of about 10. [21]

The number of foreign visitors also increased dramatically, rising from 6.3 million in 1975 to 11.8 million in 1981 and 1982. In 1999, there were more than 31 million non-immigrant arrivals. [22]

Public opinion polls throughout the 1980s and '90s showed a clear preference for restricting immigration. "Strong and increasingly well-organized public support for new restrictions on both legal and illegal immigration, coupled with Republican victories in both the House and the Senate in 1994, signaled that the immigration policy debate in the United States would likely be entering a new era of restrictionism," writes Debra L. DeLaet, a professor of political science at Drake University in Des Moines, Iowa. "Indeed, within two years, the new Republican Congress pushed through two significant pieces of legislation designed to reduce immigration to the United States." [23]

Sweeping New Laws

The Welfare Reform Act of 1996 denied federal benefits to legal and illegal immigrants. That same year, the Illegal Immigration Reform and Responsibility Act provided increased funding for the Border Patrol, increased penalties for illegal entry and added to the list of grounds for excluding aliens.

The new legislation also ordered the attorney general to develop within two years a computerized database showing when non-citizens enter and exit the country, so the INS could track visitors who had overstayed their visas.

Canadian officials and American merchants along both the northern and southern borders quickly attacked the tracking provision, saying it would disrupt America's ever-increasing cross-border traffic and trade with Mexico and Canada. The opponents convinced border-state lawmakers to try to gut the provision. And some lawmakers from northern-border states, like Michigan, where the automobile industry depends on just-in-time delivery of parts and materials from Canadian plants, wanted to repeal it altogether.

Then Sen. Spencer Abraham, R-Mich., currently Secretary of Energy — was among those who tried to get the tracking system scrapped. Abraham, who was chairman of the Senate Immigration Subcommittee, said the law would create 24-hour backups at U.S.-Canada bridges. "That would be unbearable, and the border would be effectively closed," Abraham said. [24]

In the end, Congress did not repeal the law but delayed its implementation for 30 months. But the issue remained contentious, especially since the country was experiencing a robust economy with unprecedented high employment. Employers were anxious to get as many immigrant workers into the country as possible.

"There was a general reluctance to enforce the laws regarding visa over-stays," remembers Daniel Stein, executive director of the Federation for American Immigration Reform (FAIR), which lobbies for tougher immigration controls.

Then in May 2000, Congress passed a compromise bill that fundamentally changed the tracking program by prohibiting the INS from requiring individuals to obtain any new documentation as part of the automated entry and exit system. In essence, it exempted Canadians — who do not need visas to drive across the border — from the bill's requirements. Congress also refused to fund creation of the database. Critics say the measure prevented the entry-exit tracking system from being properly implemented at the nation's land border entry ports.

"They tried to gut it without formally repealing it," Krikorian says. That is particularly true for traffic coming in from Canada, where, he says, liberal asylum procedures make the country a haven for terrorists.

But lawmakers from northern and southern states were happy. "The implementation of this system would have resulted in intolerable traffic delays and congestion at our borders," said Rep. Solomon Ortiz, D-Texas, then chairman of the Congressional Border Caucus. [25]

Political science Professor DeLaet concluded that "proposals for a computerized national registry database, a national identification card and stronger border control and enforcement measures are likely to be significant issues in the perennial debate [over] U.S. immigration policy." [26]

CURRENT SITUATION

Administration Action

When security officials sought to provide a higher state of security at land border crossings following the Sept. 11 attacks, massive traffic delays occurred. Long delays at the Canadian border in inspecting trucks carrying auto parts, for example, caused the temporary shutdown of assembly plants in Detroit. And the bureaucratic difficulties encountered in deploying National Guard troops to help with the job contributed to the problem of overlapping agency roles and jurisdictions.

Since Sept. 11, all federal agencies dealing with border security have shifted their primary missions. The Customs Service — which previously focused on collecting duties and interdicting contraband and drugs — now is focusing on preventing terrorists from smuggling chemical, biological or nuclear weapons or their components into the country in cargo, postal shipments or personal luggage.

The INS, whose primary mission was to manage the flow of immigrants and visitors to the United States, is under pressure to institute organizational reforms that will keep terrorists out of the country, improve databases, improve integration with other agency databases and separate its service and enforcement functions.

As part of the $2.2 billion increase in border-security spending requested by the Bush administration, the INS enforcement budget would be increased by $1.2 billion, $380 million of which is earmarked to implement the non-citizen entry-exit tracking system mandated in 1996. In addition, the administration wants to increase the Customs Service budget by $619 million, and the Coast Guard's security-related budget by $282 million.

Immigration reform groups complain that the budget does not beef up the agency's domestic-enforcement capabilities enough. "The administration is tinkering on the edges of the issue in a very lukewarm way," says Stein of FAIR.

FAIR and other immigration reform groups charge that the administration's border-protection policy is caught between two conflicting goals — one related to national security and one to politics. The administration wants to secure the borders against terrorists, while at the same time it wants to loosen immigration controls on Mexican immigrants, they say.

Before Sept. 11, Bush had indicated he would support an amnesty program for undocumented Mexicans already living and working in this country, a proposal sought by Mexican President Vicente Fox. 27 Fox had addressed a joint session of Congress on Sept. 5, and his visit was expected to spur liberalization of U.S. immigration laws.

"The president is trying to satisfy conflicting political objectives," Stein says. "You can't say you are a national-security president and then continue to support a system whereby you don't know who is in the country. These are totally irreconcilable goals." Under the amnesty program, he says, "You never really find out who these people are."

Bush and congressional leaders have assured pro-immigrant groups that they will not abandon the move toward liberalizing immigration laws. The issue speaks to a growing Hispanic electorate whose votes are sought by both parties. 28

Congress Responds

Just six weeks after the Sept. 11 terrorist attacks, Congress sent legislation to President Bush giving new powers to the government to fight terrorism. Included was broad, new authority allowing law enforcement officials to conduct searches and detain suspects, one of several requests made by Attorney General Ashcroft. The president signed the USA Patriot Act on Oct. 26.

Although the bill was tempered somewhat by more liberal members of Congress, especially Senate Judiciary Committee Chairman Patrick Leahy, D-Vt., it gave Ashcroft much of what he had asked for, including provisions that:

- Grant INS and State Department personnel access to the FBI's database and the Wanted Persons File for the purpose of checking the criminal history of a visa applicant;
- Give law enforcement the authority to conduct "secret searches" of a suspect's residence, including computer files;
- Allow the attorney general to detain any non-citizen believed to be a national security risk for up to seven days. After seven days, the government must charge the suspect or begin deportation proceedings;
- Allow authorities to track Internet communications (e-mail) as they do telephone calls;
- Broaden the grounds for excluding terrorists and aliens with ties to terrorist organizations; and,
- Direct the attorney general to implement fully and expand the foreign student tracking system.

Lawmakers are now considering legislation addressing several additional aspects of border protection. At least a dozen narrowly focused bills have been introduced, but the House has passed a comprehensive bill — HR 3525 — that would:

- Increase the number of border inspectors and provide more training;
- Improve technology and expand data-sharing among federal agencies;
- Remove the 45-minute time limit on INS inspections of people on incoming foreign flights;
- Restrict visas issued to individuals from countries designated as sponsors of international terrorism;
- Create terrorist "lookout committees" at U.S. embassies abroad;

- Tighten the student visa system by requiring schools to report to the government when foreign students do not report for class;
- Require that identification documents, such as passports and visas, issued by other countries contain "biometric information," such as fingerprints, by October 2003; and,
- Require airplanes and passenger ships arriving from other countries to provide passenger and crew lists to immigration officials before arrival.

The legislation passed by voice vote on Dec. 19, but it is blocked in committee in the Senate, where a similar bill has been negotiated — after much compromise — by Sens. Edward M. Kennedy, D-Mass., Sam Brownback, R-Kan., Jon Kyl, R-Ariz., and Feinstein. The law, which is strongly supported by the families of victims killed on Sept. 11, is expected to eventually pass the Senate and clear Congress.

The compromise bill contains the policy of exempting Mexicans and Canadians from the entry and exit visa system. "In the face of clear threats, they continue to take the short-range view, and they stall, stall, stall until the situation becomes intolerable," says a frustrated Stein, who charges that Congress is "capitulating to business interests" such as meatpackers and restaurant owners who resist "any kind of tightening of the labor market."

"It's maddening," he says. "Congress is constantly cheering the primacy of border commerce over the national security."

OUTLOOK

Civil Liberties

Ironically, notes Flynn of the Council on Foreign Relations, the tragic events of Sept. 11 revealed that America's economic and political openness and success also increased the nation's vulnerability. "For years, U.S. policy-makers, trade negotiators and business leaders have operated on the naive assumption that there was no downside to building frictionless global networks of international trade and travel," he writes. " 'Facilitation' was the order of the day.

"Inspectors and agents with responsibility for policing the flows of people and goods passing through those networks were seen as nuisances at best — and at worst, as

barriers to competitiveness who should be marginalized, privatized or eliminated wherever possible." [29]

The laissez-faire mindset made it relatively easy for potential terrorists to gain access to the country and to operate inside our borders, notes Stein of FAIR.

"One miscreant can get into the country and wind up perpetrating the murder of millions of people," he warns. "We're in what appears to be a protracted clash of civilizations. As long as we have to deal with these real and present threats — and we probably will for the rest of our lives — the immigration issue will never be seen the same again."

How much are Americans willing to change the way they live and do business in order to protect themselves? Krikorian at the Center for Immigration Studies says that tracking the millions of visitors to the United States is crucial to the nation's security. The most effective, practical way to track them, he says, is through the use of a secure driver's license.

Going after foreign visitors who overstay their visas is "difficult and time-consuming," Krikorian says, "but it's possible and feasible."

But the ACLU's Edgar urges caution in taking steps that might erode Americans' constitutional rights. "The greatest concern, first of all, is preserving the privacy of everyone in the country, particularly American citizens, and insuring against a national ID proposal," Edgar says. "We're also concerned about the possibility of 'mission creep' — that once we create the infrastructure of a vast computer database to track immigrants, we would also be able to track citizens."

No matter what steps are taken, security experts warn that the nation faces an uphill battle. "One characteristic of terrorists is that they want to meet the challenge," says McBride of the Potomac Institute. "As you raise the bar — and all these [anti-terrorist] measures are going to raise the bar — we're going to attract a more serious contender. The more serious contender is not going to just take a building out. A more serious contender is going to do something more destructive, and that worries me a lot."

McBride says his one hope is that if we can raise the bar enough, the cost of undertaking a major terrorist action may be too high for individual terrorist groups. "Diplomatic and other approaches are going to reduce the probability of state sponsorship," McBride says. "That's the good news."

Should driver's licenses be linked to a national database and used as ID cards?

YES Daniel Stein
Executive Director, Federation for American Immigration Reform

Written for The CQ Researcher, February 2002

There was a time in this country when most of us were born, lived and died in the same town where everybody knew us. We went to church with the local shopkeeper, bowled with the local bank president and called the cop on the beat by his first name. In that America, our face was all the identification we needed.

We don't live in that world anymore. Our ability to function in today's world depends upon being able to identify ourselves with a high degree of certainty to complete strangers.

Because we no longer know the people we deal with, we have come to rely on the government to vouch for our identity. The merchant who takes your check may not know you, but your driver's license assures him that the state knows who you are. In order for our society and economy to function efficiently, the information the state has must be reliable and accessible.

Mobility is not restricted to decent, upstanding people. The terrorists who murdered some 3,000 people on Sept. 11 succeeded in part because no database exists in the United States that can differentiate between people who belong here and those who do not.

These 19 terrorists were able to obtain Social Security numbers and driver's licenses (many issued under aliases) because there was no way to verify that they were illegally in the United States.

Identity fraud and identity theft are problems for law enforcement and an impediment to commerce. We need to correct the serious flaws in our identity process that endanger people's physical and economic security.

That must begin with the Social Security Administration confirming that applicants for an ID number are legally present in the United States and that the identity given is not an alias.

States could then rely on the Social Security number when issuing the second important identity document — the driver's license. Adding biometric information and including it on a common database used by all 50 states would create a high degree of certainty that a driver's license truly is a reliable form of identification. That's why the recent proposal developed by the American Association of Motor Vehicle Administrators deserves federal and state support.

We are already using these documents to identify ourselves. With the addition of technological features, we could close many of the loopholes that terrorists and other criminals use to their advantage, without any intrusion into the lives of law-abiding Americans.

NO Katie Corrigan
Legislative Counsel American Civil Liberties Union

Written for The CQ Researcher, February 2002

The recent proposal put forward by the American Association of Motor Vehicle Administrators to standardize driver's licenses nationwide and link state licensing databases into one giant integrated information bank is nothing less than a de facto national ID. Regardless of recent protestations that this plan is nothing like a national ID scheme, clearly this is a case of "if it walks like a duck and quacks like a duck, it must be a duck."

Considered side by side, the motor vehicle proposal and a national ID scheme are nearly identical. Each would require the establishment of a giant information bank accessible nationwide, and each would deploy a universal identification card of standard design across the country. Furthermore, the motor vehicle proposal and a national ID scheme also have exactly the same problems, including, most crucially, that they would both be ineffective in the fight against identify theft and terrorism.

Not only would the actual card be built upon a shaky foundation of easily forged or stolen documentation (Social Security cards, birth certificates), but a card touted as tamper-proof, especially one with biometric identifiers, could lead our nation to a false sense of security and would actually exacerbate the problem of identity theft. Consider the consequences if a thief steals someone's name and then walks around with an ID containing the stolen name with the thief's fingerprint. How difficult would it be for the victim to reclaim his identity?

The very idea of a national ID — or the standardized driver's license — should be anathema to a free society. One of the first principles of American democracy is the idea that we have the right to be immune from intrusive government — that we have the "right to be left alone."

That's why such a broad array of organizations signed onto a letter to the White House opposing the proposal. In addition to the ACLU, signatories included the Eagle Forum and Free Congress Foundation, as well as privacy groups, consumer-advocacy groups and conferences of state legislators from both sides of the political aisle.

Since Sept. 11, the United States has been engaged in widespread reflection on what it is about this country that we defend and celebrate. While civil libertarians want security as much as anybody else, we do not believe we must sacrifice our freedom to secure our safety. And in the final analysis, a national ID scheme of any form will guarantee us neither freedom nor safety.

NOTES

1. Nancy San Martin, "INS System Simply Can't Keep Up with Immigrant Tracking," *Knight Ridder Tribune Business News*, Sept. 27, 2001.

2. David Masci and Kenneth Jost, "War on Terrorism," *The CQ Researcher*, Oct. 12, 2001, pp. 817-848.

3. Stephen E. Flynn, "America the Vulnerable," *Foreign Affairs*, Jan. 1, 2002.

4. David Masci and Patrick Marshall, "Civil Liberties in Wartime," *The CQ Researcher*, Dec. 14, 2001, pp. 1017-1040.

5. Senate Judiciary Subcommittee on Technology, Terrorism and Government Information hearing on "Technological Help for Border Security," Oct. 12, 2001.

6. *Ibid.*

7. For background, see Brian Hansen, "Intelligence Reforms," *The CQ Researcher*, Jan. 25, 2002, pp. 49-72.

8. *Ibid.*

9. Senate Judiciary Subcommittee on Technology, Terrorism and Government Information, op. cit.

10. Flynn, *op. cit.*

11. Testimony before Senate Committee on Government Affairs hearing on "Weak Links: Assessing the Vulnerability of U.S. Ports and Whether the Government is Adequately Structured to Safeguard Them," Dec. 6, 2001.

12. *Ibid.*

13. Robert C. Bonner, "The Customs Patrol," *The Washington Post*, Feb. 16, 2002.

14. "U.S. Customs Service Resource Allocation Model Fact Sheet," February 2001, http://www.customs.gov/about/pdf/ram1.pdf.

15. Flynn, *op. cit.*

16. *Ibid.*

17. Joel Brinkley and Philip Shenon, "Ridge Facing Major Doubts on His Ability," *The New York Times*, Feb. 7, 2002.

18. *Ibid.*

19. http://www.house.gov/judiciary/ news111401b.htm

20. *1998 Statistical Yearbook of the Immigration and Naturalization Service*, Department of Justice, November 2000, p. 15.

21. *Ibid.*, p. 212.

22. *Ibid.*, p. 122.

23. Debra L. DeLaet, *U.S. Immigration Policy in an Age of Rights* (2000), p. 103.

24. Quoted in Catherine Strong, "Congress must undo controversial border provision slipped into a massive 1996 bill," The Associated Press, Oct. 4, 1998.

25. Quoted in Gary Martin, "Tracking plan gets House OK; INS system to follow foreigners' entries, exits," *San Antonio Express-News*, May 26, 2000.

26. *Ibid.*, p. 116.

27. For background, see David Masci, "U.S.-Mexico Relations," *The CQ Researcher*, Nov. 9, 2001, pp. 921-944.

28. For background, see David Masci, "Hispanic-Americans' New Clout," *The CQ Researcher*, Sept. 18, 1998, pp. 809-832.

29. Flynn, *op. cit.*

BIBLIOGRAPHY

Books

Borjas, George J., *Heaven's Door: Immigration Policy and the American Economy*, Princeton University Press, 1999.
A professor of public policy at the John F. Kennedy School of Government at Harvard University offers a thorough and insightful discussion of immigration's economic impact on the United States and how economic issues frame the overall debate over immigration policy.

DeLaet, Debra L., *U.S. Immigration Policy in an Age of Rights*, Praeger, 2000.
A professor of political science offers a cogent historical discussion of the development of immigration policy, including an examination of the impact of immigration policies on civil rights and, conversely, the impact of civil rights concerns on immigration policy.

Gimpel, James G., and James R. Edwards Jr., *The Congressional Politics of Immigration Reform,* **Allyn and Bacon, 1999.**
Gimpel, a professor of government at the University of Maryland, and Edwards, a former congressional staffer, have produced a detailed history of immigration legislation in Congress.

Mills, Nicolaus, ed., *Arguing Immigration: The Debate Over the Changing Face of America,* **Touchstone, 1994.**
This collection of essays by academicians, policy-makers and social commentators largely focuses on whether Americans should welcome immigrants or not, with additional contributions on such topics as the debate over a national ID card.

Reimers, David M., *Unwelcome Strangers: American Identity and the Turn Against Socialism,* **Columbia University Press, 1998.**
A professor of history at New York University explores the arguments of groups that advocate restrictions on immigration levels.

Articles

Brinkley, Joel, and Philip Shenon, "Ridge Facing Major Doubts on His Ability," *The New York Times,* **Feb. 7, 2002.**
Two reporters offer a number of interviews with key players to substantiate the argument that Tom Ridge, head of the Office of Homeland Security, faces an uphill battle in fulfilling his mandate to coordinate federal anti-terrorism policies among more than a dozen federal, state and local agencies.

Corn, David, "Ridge on the Ledge," *The Nation,* **Nov. 19, 2001, p. 19.**
Will the Homeland Security chief be an effective overseer or another spinner?

Eggen, Dan, "Deportee Sweep Will Start With Mideast Focus," *The Washington Post,* **Feb. 8, 2002.**
Eggen relates the contents of a confidential Justice Department memo obtained by the Post that details a plan to round up Middle Easterners who have ignored deportation orders.

Flynn, Stephen E., "America the Vulnerable," *Foreign Affairs,* **January 1, 2002.**
A senior fellow in the National Security Studies Program at the Council on Foreign Relations critiques the administration's responses to the terrorist attacks on Sept. 11. He urges the government to select future measures with a view not to preventing all future attacks — a goal he says is impossible — but to minimizing the disruption that will occur after an attack.

Waller, Douglas, "A Toothless Tiger? Bureaucratic barriers could thwart Tom Ridge's chance to be an effective antiterror czar," *Time,* **Oct. 15, 2001, p. 78.**
In the three weeks since Bush tapped Ridge to head his new Office of Homeland Security, the unified front against terrorism has started to develop some cracks.

Reports and Studies

1998 Statistical Yearbook of the Immigration and Naturalization Service, **Department of Justice, November 2000.**
This 294-page annual report offers a wealth of statistical information on current and historical levels of immigration and INS actions.

Krouse, William J., and Raphael F. Perl, "Terrorism: Automated Lookout Systems and Border Security Options and Issues," Congressional Research Service, June 18, 2001.
This report examines options and issues related to tightening border security by improving the "lookout" systems employed by the State Department and the INS to exclude individuals known to be members or supporters of foreign terrorist organizations from entry into the United States.

"Report on Crime and Security in U.S. Seaports," Interagency Commission on Crime and Security in U.S. Seaports, fall 2000.
A commission established by President Clinton in April 2000, long before the terrorist attacks of Sept. 11, 2001, finds lax security measures in the United States.

For More Information

Alexis de Tocqueville Institution, 1446 E St., S.E., Washington, D.C. 20003; (202) 548-0006; www.adti.net. A public policy think tank that seeks to increase public understanding of the cultural and economic benefits of immigration.

American Immigration Lawyers Association, 918 F St., N.W., Washington, D.C. 20004; (202) 216-2400; www.aila.org. Founded in 1946, the AILA includes over 7,800 attorneys and law professors who practice and teach immigration law. The related American Immigration Legal Foundation "promotes an alternative to the anti-immigrant messages produced by opponents of newcomers in America" through education and litigation.

Center for Immigration Studies, 1522 K St., N.W., Suite 820, Washington, D.C. 20005; (202) 466-8185; www.cis.org. The CIS is a nonpartisan, nonprofit research organization founded in 1985 devoted exclusively to studying the impact of immigration on the United States. CIS "seeks fewer immigrants but a warmer welcome for those admitted."

Federation for American Immigration Reform (FAIR), 1666 Connecticut Ave., N.W., Suite 400, Washington, D.C. 20009; (202) 328-7004; www.fairus.org. FAIR is a nonprofit public interest organization that lobbies in favor of strict limits on immigration.

Immigration History Research Center, http://www1.umn.edu/ihrc/index.htm#top. An international resource on American immigration and ethnic history based at the University of Minnesota.

Immigration Index, http://www.immigrationindex.org/. An online resource for issues related to immigration.

Lutheran Immigration and Refugee Service, 700 Light St., Baltimore Md. 21230; (410) 230-2700; www.lirs.org. Advocates for refugees and other migrants.

National Council of La Raza, 1111 19th St., N.W., Suite 1000, Washington, D.C. 20036; (202) 785-1670; www.nclr.org. Monitors legislation and lobbies on behalf of Latinos in the United States.

National Immigration Forum, 220 I St., N.E., Washington, D.C. 20002; (202) 544-0004; www.immigrationforum.org. Advocates pro-immigration policies.

National Immigration Law Center, 3435 Wilshire Blvd., Suite 2850, Los Angeles, Calif. 90010; (213) 639-3900; http://www.nilc.org. NILC is a national support center that promotes the rights of low-income immigrants.

U.S. Customs Service, Office of Public Affairs, 1300 Pennsylvania Ave. N.W. Room 6.3D, Washington, D.C. 20229; (202) 927.8727; www.customs.ustreas.gov. The Customs Service is the primary enforcement agency protecting the nation's borders. Part of the Treasury Department, it is the only border agency with an extensive air, land and marine interdiction force.

U.S. Immigration and Naturalization Service, 425 I St., N.W., Suite 7100, Washington, D.C. 20536; (202) 514-1900; www.ins.usdoj.gov. The Department of Justice agency that administers and enforces U.S. immigration and naturalization laws.

6

Oil Diplomacy

Mary H. Cooper

Anti-war protesters in New York City last November oppose President Bush's plan to overthrow oil-rich Iraq. Critics say America's need for oil lies behind the possible invasion as well as the friendly relations it maintains with nations that have been questionable allies in the war on terrorism or are accused of human-rights abuses. The administration says its concern in Iraq is eliminating Saddam Hussein's weapons of mass destruction.

From *The CQ Researcher*, January 24, 2003.

Following in the footsteps of world leaders like Russia's Vladimir Putin and China's Jiang Zemin, Crown Prince Abdullah of Saudi Arabia journeyed to Crawford, Texas, last April to meet with President Bush at his 1,600-acre ranch.

"I was honored to welcome Crown Prince Abdullah to my ranch . . . a place where I welcome very special guests to our country," Bush said later that day. "We spent a lot of time alone, discussing our respective visions, talking about our families. I'm convinced that the stronger our personal bond is, the more likely it is relations between our countries will be strong." [1]

The president's warm embrace of the Saudi leader struck many observers as inappropriate in the wake of the Sept. 11, 2001, terrorist attacks. Fifteen of the 19 Islamic extremists who crashed hijacked airliners into the World Trade Center and the Pentagon were Saudis, a fact the Riyadh government was slow to acknowledge. And when the Bush administration froze the assets of organizations and individuals believed to have ties to Osama bin Laden and his al Qaeda terrorist organization, the Saudi government initially failed to cooperate. Moreover, while expressing outrage at the attacks, Saudi leaders continued to tolerate anti-American teachings in *madrassas*, schools funded by Saudi charitable contributions, at home and overseas.

Few would disagree with the notion that U.S. diplomatic priorities around the world center on America's need to maintain the oil lifeline. The United States is by far the world's largest consumer of oil, a fact that shows no sign of changing. The wildly popular sport-utility vehicle (SUV) and other gas-guzzlers now account for more than half of new-car sales. Domestic oil reserves are dwindling fast,

OPEC Produces 40 Percent of World's Oil

The Organization of Petroleum Exporting Countries (OPEC) — including Venezuela, Nigeria and the Persian Gulf nations — produces about 40 percent of the world's oil. Russia, the United States and other non-OPEC nations produce the rest. OPEC's disproportionate influence on prices and supplies has prompted the U.S. and other industrial countries to seek new oil sources outside OPEC.

World Oil Production
(In thousands of barrels per day)

OPEC	**26,044**
Major OPEC producers	
Persian Gulf nations	17,437
Venezuela	2,701
Nigeria	2,102
Libya	1,308
Indonesia	1,274
Non-OPEC producers	**40,355**
Major non-OPEC producers	
Russia	7,298
United States	5,827
China	3,360
Mexico	3,168
United Kingdom	2,244
World Total	**66,399**

Source: Energy Information Administration, *Monthly Energy Review*, December 2002; online at www.eia.doe.gov/emeu/mer/inter.html

senior fellow at the Cato Institute, a conservative think tank in Washington, D.C. "It's the world's major holder of oil resources. There's no doubt that the friendliness of the U.S. relationship with Riyadh flows out of the desire to maintain access to oil."

Today, the United States imports more than half of the oil it consumes, a percentage expected to rise to 64 percent by 2020. And, despite efforts to develop oil sources away from the politically volatile Middle East, the United States still relies on oil from the region for a fifth of its imports. [2]

As the Bush administration prepares for possible war against Iraq, concern is mounting that the United States may be in for a new energy crisis, reminiscent of two oil "shocks" in the 1970s that saw oil prices increase nearly sevenfold. Not that Iraq wields much of an oil weapon, despite sitting astride the world's second-largest oil reserves after Saudi Arabia. Its oil exports have been limited to a bare minimum in the wake of the 1991 Persian Gulf War and Iraq's subsequent refusal to allow thorough U.N. inspections for weapons of mass destruction.

Thus, even a complete shutdown of Iraq's current production of 2.5 million barrels a day may have little impact on world oil markets. "Iraqi oil is important, but it's more important for Iraq than for the rest of the world," says John Lichtblau, a leading oil analyst and chairman of the nonprofit Petroleum Industry Research Foundation in New York City. "The rest of the world can live without Iraqi oil."

But Iraqi output is not the only uncertainty in the outlook for world oil supplies. A labor strike in Venezuela has halted exports from America's fourth-largest foreign oil supplier since early December. Strike leaders, who want to end the presidency of populist

so the United States grows more dependent on foreign oil each year.

But critics say the United States' growing need for oil is behind the administration's willingness to maintain friendly relations with Saudi Arabia and other allies with either poor human-rights records or questionable efforts to aid the U.S. war on terrorism. Moreover, the critics say Iraq's massive oil reserves, not concern about Iraq's weapons of mass destruction (WMD), are driving U.S. plans to invade Iraq.

"The United States is friendly with the Saudis for one reason and for one reason only," says Doug Bandow, a

Hugo Chávez, have declared that no resumption of oil exports can be expected before Feb. 2. Bush administration officials have suggested that any military operations against Iraq may begin in February as well, meaning that oil exports from both Iraq and Venezuela could be suspended at the same time.

Thus, at a time of unusual uncertainty, U.S. diplomacy is clearly targeted at ensuring access to oil. But critics insist the Bush administration may be going too far in accommodating unsavory regimes just to keep the oil flowing. Perhaps the biggest example, they say, is the House of Saud, America's second-largest oil supplier, which maintains an iron grip over the country, bans political opposition and rigidly suppresses women's rights. "You don't have to have the prince out to the ranch and have cuddly sessions with him talking about how wonderful everybody is," Bandow says. "We certainly should be willing to push for human rights."

Critics like Bandow say America's relentless quest for oil is compromising its reputation as the world's leading champion of democracy and human rights. Diplomacy fueled by oil interests only aggravates anti-American sentiment abroad, they say, by resurrecting the Cold War specter of a United States espousing democracy and human rights abroad while bankrolling unsavory dictators just because they were anti-communist.

Critics also worry about the U.S. government's recent efforts to establish more friendly relations with corrupt leaders in poor West African nations and the Caspian Sea area — potential new sources of sizable oil reserves — to fill the potential gap caused by a prolonged disruption of Persian Gulf oil. (*See sidebar, p. 112.*)

For example, President Nursultan Nazarbayev of Kazakhstan, a key oil producer in the Caspian Sea region, is widely regarded as a despot whose nation is

Canada Is Top U.S. Supplier

The United States imports more oil from Canada than from any other nation, including Saudi Arabia. Only two Middle Eastern nations rank among the nine biggest U.S. suppliers.

Biggest U.S. Oil Suppliers
(In thousands of barrels per day)

* Based on average amounts in the first 10 months of 2002

Source: Energy Information Administration, *Monthly Energy Review*, December 2002

infamous for human-rights abuses. He is currently under investigation by federal prosecutors who charge that he accepted bribes in exchange for U.S. oil-company concessions during the 1990s and lobbied the Bush White House to halt the inquiry. [3]

"History shows that oil producers don't fare as well in terms of democracy or economic well-being as non-oil producers," says Arvind Ganeshan, director of the business and human-rights program at Human Rights Watch, an international advocacy group. "The bulk of them, including the major oil producers, don't have a very good record on human rights, particularly in terms of democratic accountability."

In West Africa, for instance, the countries that stand to profit the most from developing and selling oil to con-

Search for Non-OPEC Oil Pays Off

The rise of Islamic extremism among some of the leading members of the Organization of Petroleum Exporting Countries (OPEC) has intensified concern about U.S. dependence on Middle Eastern oil, especially since the terrorist attacks of Sept. 11, 2001.

Of OPEC's 11 members, all but two — Nigeria and Venezuela — are predominantly Muslim. Violence by religious extremists has broken out in several member countries, including Indonesia and Nigeria, and threatens to destabilize Saudi Arabia and other key Persian Gulf producers.

Since the 1973 Arab oil embargo against the United States, a frantic search for non-OPEC oil supplies has paid off. Major new oil deposits were found in Alaska's North Slope, Mexico and the North and Caspian seas. As a result, the share of U.S. oil imports that come from OPEC producers has fallen from 70 percent to 40 percent since 1977.

Diversification has been made possible by technological advances in oil-detection and drilling equipment. Seismic devices allow geologists to find deposits that once lay undetected beneath thick layers of non-porous rock, and horizontal-drilling technology enables oil companies to reduce costs and speed production by tapping a number of deposits from a single bore. Most important, floating platforms and equipment that can probe ever-increasing depths for underwater deposits have made the largest discoveries accessible for extraction.

The most recent major oil find is in the Atlantic Basin, a vast region of underwater oil deposits stretching from Latin America to West Africa. The only OPEC member that stands to benefit from oil drilling in the basin is Nigeria. Non-OPEC West African nations that may profit from the expected bonanza include Angola, which has the most promising reserves, Ivory Coast, Sierra Leone, Equatorial Guinea, Congo, Namibia and Gabon.

On the other side of the ocean, Brazil and, to a lesser extent, Argentina have most of the Latin American portion of the reserves. [1] Experts are uncertain just how much oil these countries may produce. Brazil stands to quadruple its output by 2020, to 4.1 million barrels a day. But that probably won't be available for export because it will be needed to meet Brazil's domestic oil needs.

---

[1] Information on the Atlantic Basin is found in Energy Information Administration, *International Energy Outlook 2002*, pp. 35-36.

---

sumers like the United States — including Nigeria, Angola and Equatorial Guinea — are among the world's poorest countries, and some have been embroiled in civil unrest, widespread corruption and blatant human-rights violations.

In Nigeria, a member of the influential Organization of Petroleum Exporting Countries (OPEC), lawmakers have threatened to impeach President Olusegun Obasanjo more than once for allegedly violating the constitution, abetting corruption and allowing ethnic massacres by the military. Angola's 4.1 million displaced people, uprooted by a long-running civil war that ended last year, are routinely subjected to physical harassment and abuse by security forces. And in Equatorial Guinea, where the State Department closed the U.S. Embassy for eight years in part to protest the government's rampant abuses, "human-rights abuse went unabated in 2002," Human Rights Watch reports. [4]

Critics like Ganeshan say both the U.S. government and American oil companies with production-sharing or joint-venture arrangements in foreign countries can help improve economic and social conditions in countries that supply oil to the U.S. market. "Companies have an obligation to ensure that their operations respect human rights," Ganeshan says. "The U.S. government can press for transparency and accountability in how governments receive and spend oil money."

For now, though, most criticism centers on U.S. relations with Saudi Arabia. "Unfortunately, our dependence on relatively inexpensive Saudi oil has caused successive U.S. administrations to adopt what might be called a 'see-no-evil' attitude toward the kingdom's efforts to manage and suppress potentially threatening internal opposition by encouraging virulent hostility towards America and her allies, most especially Israel," said Frank J. Gaffney Jr., president of the conservative

West Africa is a different matter, however. Angola may more than quadruple its output by 2020, judging from the positive findings of exploratory probes. The impoverished country's economy, devastated by civil war, is unlikely to be able to absorb much of the oil it produces for the foreseeable future.

West Africa's oil is an attractive target for U.S. oil companies because it is a light, high-quality variety. Also, the region lies just on the other side of the Atlantic Ocean, only days away from East Coast ports, with no perilous choke points like the Middle East's Straits of Hormuz standing in the way of tanker traffic.

It's uncertain how the Atlantic Basin reserves will affect U.S. oil diplomacy. While they appear likely to reduce U.S. energy dependence on OPEC and the Middle East, there are other concerns surrounding relations with the region's governments. Human-rights advocates are calling on the U.S. government to break with the priorities of a century of oil diplomacy to address the extreme poverty and widespread human-rights abuses that have afflicted most emerging oil producers of West Africa.

Compounding the region's social and economic ills is pervasive corruption among government leaders, a situation that is unlikely to abate with an influx of oil money.

"In countries where power is concentrated in the hands of just one or a few individuals, adding the economic power that flows from control over oil revenues is a tremendous disincentive to accountability," says Arvind Ganeshan, director of the business and human-rights program at Human Rights Watch, an advocacy group. "If the government is the biggest political actor and the biggest company in town, which dictator wants to give that up?"

But Ganeshan says there are steps the United States could take to improve so-called transparency and accountability in the way host governments use the investments they receive from foreign oil companies and the revenues they receive from selling oil. "That can be done through bilateral diplomacy," he says. "Washington also can encourage the World Bank and the International Monetary Fund [IMF] to insist on that."

The IMF is in a particularly strong position to enforce accountability, he says, because it has the authority to call for audits into government finances and has a code of good practices for fiscal transparency.

Finally, Ganeshan says, as a key element of its oil diplomacy the U.S. government should enlist the help of American oil companies in these countries. "Washington should press very strongly for human-rights improvements and accountability," he says. "But it also should press American companies to maintain the highest human-rights standards possible in their operations."

Center for Security Policy and a former Reagan administration Pentagon official. "Clearly, we can no longer afford to indulge in such a dangerous stance." [5]

But others say the criticism of Saudi Arabia is overblown. Saudi leaders are helping ensure America's energy security by trying to maintain calm in world oil markets, they point out. On Jan. 12, Saudi-led OPEC announced it would increase production to compensate for the potential loss of Iraqi and Venezuelan exports.

"Saudi Arabia holds more than a quarter of the world's proven oil reserves, and as such has more capacity than anyone else to affect the oil supply," says Shibley Telhami, a Middle East expert at the University of Maryland. "If the Saudis chose to play the game irresponsibly, they could flood the market, throw a lot of people out of the oil business and then dominate the market themselves. But they have chosen to play largely a moderating role in the oil arena."

The administration also cites the Saudi's cooperation in allowing U.S. troops to be stationed on Saudi soil — a move that has triggered strong condemnation from Osama bin Laden. As confrontation with Iraq draws more imminent, these are some of the questions being asked about U.S. oil diplomacy:

Is American concern about weapons of mass destruction in Iraq a smokescreen for a grab for Iraq's oil?

The Bush administration's march toward war with Iraq began in earnest on Jan. 29, 2002, with the president's State of the Union address. In it, he branded Iraq, Iran and North Korea as an "axis of evil" bent on developing weapons of mass destruction to use against America and its allies or to supply to terrorists.

"States like these, and their terrorist allies, constitute an axis of evil, arming to threaten the peace of the world," Bush said. "By seeking weapons of mass destruc-

Nigerian villagers celebrate last December after Chevron-Texaco agreed to spend $100 million building a modern town in the oil-rich Niger Delta. The local Itsekiri people had blocked production facilities to protest the U.S. oil giant's failure to share its profits from the region's oil.

tion, these regimes pose a grave and growing danger. I will not wait on events, while dangers gather. I will not stand by, as peril draws closer and closer. The United States of America will not permit the world's most dangerous regimes to threaten us with the world's most destructive weapons."

Last October, Bush singled out Iraq as the most immediate threat to U.S. interests and defiantly dismissed U.N. efforts to halt weapons development in Iraq. Instead he called for a "regime change" in Baghdad. "The stated policy of the United States is regime change," Bush explained, "because, for 11 years, Saddam Hussein has ignored the United Nations and the free world, [and] we don't believe he is going to change." [6]

Although in the past Hussein has had programs to develop nuclear, biological and chemical weapons — and indeed used gas in 1988 to massacre separatist Kurds in northern Iraq — the administration has yet to present to the public clear evidence that Iraq has or is pursuing such a capability today.

The lack of proof prompts some critics to charge that Bush's concern about weapons masks another agenda — gaining control of Iraq's vast oil reserves, the world's second-largest after Saudi Arabia. "Weapons of mass destruction don't have much to do with this at all," says Mark Weisbrot, co-director of the Center for Economic and Policy Research, a liberal think tank. "There have been 230 weapons inspections now, and they haven't found anything. On the other hand, controlling the world's oil resources always has been a major strategic goal of the U.S. government."

Meanwhile, uncertainty over the stability of Saudi Arabia, the world's leading oil producer, has mounted since the Sept. 11 terrorist attacks and repeated threats from terrorist leader bin Laden against the regime for allowing the United States to base troops on Saudi soil. That makes it all the more important for the United States to gain access to Iraq's crude, Weisbrot says. "The administration doesn't know how long the Saudi regime is going to last, so they need another stable place where they can be based and control oil reserves. What's important here is the strategic power that comes from controlling oil resources."

Pulitzer Prize-winning *New York Times* columnist Thomas L. Friedman agrees that oil would be high on the list of U.S. objectives in any war on Iraq. "Any war we launch in Iraq will certainly be — in part — about oil," he wrote recently. "To deny that is laughable."

Moreover, Friedman said war would be justifiable, so long as it spawned a democratic government in Iraq and meaningful efforts to conserve energy in the United States. "I have no problem with a war for oil — provided that it is to fuel the first progressive Arab regime and not just our SUVs, and provided we behave in a way that makes clear to the world we are protecting everyone's access to oil at reasonable prices — not simply our right to binge on it." [7]

But protesters in European capitals recently brandished anti-war placards demanding "No blood for oil." [8] A recent Pew Research Center poll found that more than half the people in Russia, France and Germany thought "the U.S. wants to control Iraqi oil." [9]

Even in Britain, where Prime Minister Tony Blair has been Bush's strongest ally against Hussein, public opinion is divided over the true reasons why Bush and Vice President Dick Cheney — both former oil-company executives — are bent on targeting Iraq. "American oil companies stand to gain billions of dollars in the event of a U.S. invasion," wrote British columnist Robert Fisk. "Once out of power, Bush and his friend could become multibillionaires on the spoils of this war." [10]

These suspicions are even more pronounced in the Middle East, where anti-U.S. sentiment runs even higher because of the Bush administration's support of Israel's relentless suppression of the Palestinian uprising. "Clearly, oil is seen as a key factor in the region," says Telhami of the University of Maryland. "But, even worse, the common wisdom in the Middle East is that all of this is an effort to serve Israeli interests," since Israel has been attacked by Iraq in the past. "This is even more serious to people in the region than just the assumption that U.S. policy is based simply on oil."

But Secretary of State Colin L. Powell flatly rejects that notion. "The oil fields are the property of the Iraqi people," he said recently on NBC's "Meet the Press. "If a coalition of forces goes into those oil fields, we would want to protect those fields and make sure that they are used to benefit the people of Iraq and are not destroyed or damaged by a failing regime on the way out the door." [11]

Even if the United States takes control of Iraq's oil fields, it could require years and up to $40 billion to rehabilitate the country's aging oil infrastructure, bring it back into full production and develop new fields. [12] Such a monumental investment to control oil — that wouldn't even be available for years — would not justify conducting a military campaign, some experts say.

"No U.S. administration would launch so momentous a campaign just to facilitate a handful of oil-development contracts and a moderate increase in supply — half a decade from now," wrote Daniel Yergin, chairman of Cambridge Energy Research Associates. [13]

Oil-industry representatives agree that the benefits to Western oil companies would be far outweighed by the risks of war. "If we really wanted the oil, we could do a deal with Hussein right now, but that's not in our national interest," says John Felmy, chief economist at the American Petroleum Institute. He emphasizes that Iraq wants to sell more oil but is constrained by U.N. sanctions. "Oil is not even relevant to policy toward Iraq," he says. "Statements to the contrary are just ludicrous."

Should Saudi Arabia be held more accountable for its role in the spread of Islamic fundamentalism?

Since the Sept. 11 terrorist attacks, intelligence officials and Middle East experts alike have scrutinized U.S.-Saudi relations in an effort to understand why so many of the hijackers — as well as bin Laden — were Saudis. Of particular interest has been Islam's Wahhabi sect, a uniquely Saudi Arabian fundamentalist branch of the faith and a key institutional ally of the ruling House of Saud. Wahhabi clerics teach anti-American attitudes in Saudi-funded Islamic schools — known as *madrassas* — around the world.

"It is violent, it is intolerant and it is fanatical beyond measure," wrote Stephen Schwartz, author of a recently published book on Wahhabism and a convert to Islam. "Not all Muslims are suicide bombers, but all Muslim suicide bombers are Wahhabis." [14]

William Kristol, editor of *The Weekly Standard* and chairman of the Project for the New American Century — a conservative nonprofit organization dedicated to American global leadership — told a congressional subcommittee last May: "The Saudis have been deeply implicated in the wave of suicide bombers that have attacked Israeli citizens — and American citizens in Israel — in recent years. [Yet,] initial Saudi official reaction has been to deny the link." [15]

Scrutiny turned to hostility in some camps as the Saudi government dragged its feet in acknowledging the hijackers' origins and stemming the flow of Saudi donations to Muslim charities thought to be supporting al Qaeda and other terrorist organizations.

"Saudi Arabia is a corrupt, totalitarian regime at sharp variance with America's most cherished values, including religious liberty," Bandow, of the Cato Institute, testified on Capitol Hill last June. "By any normal assessment, Americans should care little if the House of Saud fell, as have other illegitimate monarchies, such as Iran's peacock throne. Except for one thing: Saudi Arabia has oil. For this reason, Washington has long been hesitant to treat Saudi Arabia the way Washington treats most other nations." [16]

But it's not just conservative supporters of Israel who condemn Saudi Arabia's post-Sept. 11 conduct. "One way [Saudi rulers] have held power is to allow and even encourage some of the extremists," says Weisbrot, one of the Bush administration's most vocal liberal critics. "Look at how long it took them — and how much pressure it took — for them to even freeze the assets of these people. So it's understandable that somebody should make a stink over that. The criticism is just a logical outcome of the Saudi government's gross hypocrisy."

Anti-Saudi criticism mounted still further in November, when it was reported that Princess Haifa, wife of the Saudi ambassador to Washington, Prince Bandar bin Sultan, had donated money to Saudis connected with the Sept. 11 hijackers. Although there was no suggestion that the princess had knowingly funded anti-American terrorists, the scandal prompted the Saudi government to launch a public-relations campaign on U.S. television aimed at quelling anti-Saudi sentiment.

However, some Middle East experts say the criticism of the House of Saud is overblown. They note that in the 1980s the Reagan administration asked the Saudis to help get Islamic fundamentalists to join U.S.-supported "freedom fighters" trying to expel the Soviet Union from Afghanistan. Bin Laden and many of his followers received U.S. training, weapons and support, as did future members of Afghanistan's oppressive Taliban regime, which sheltered al Qaeda before being driven from power by a U.S.-led coalition after Sept. 11.

"We found that utilizing Islamic motivation to rid a Muslim country of the infidel Soviets was very convenient," says Walter L. Cutler, president of the Meridian International Center think tank and U.S. ambassador to Saudi Arabia in the late 1980s. "We worked very closely with not only the Saudis but also a lot of other Arab governments in trying to get the Soviets out of Afghanistan. It was still the Cold War, and when that was crowned with success in 1989 we tended to relax a bit and focus more on walls falling down in Berlin than we did on what was going on elsewhere."

Cutler says American critics of Saudi behavior fail to recognize that charitable giving is central to the Islamic faith. "We have a right to expect the Saudis to be more accountable," he says. "But one has to realize that when Muslims give to charity it is not within their religious or cultural tradition to check up on where every rial is going. That is almost counter to the spirit of giving."

The Saudis themselves are baffled by the degree of U.S. hostility, says the University of Maryland's Telhami. "From the Saudi point of view, they've been extremely cooperative in the war on terrorism," he says. "They don't know what the United States wants them to do, other than crack down on charities. We have to recognize that these charities are an important part of life in Saudi Arabia, and that most of them pose no danger and are truly peaceful."

Some critics even advocate pressuring the regime to adopt domestic reforms, liberalizing the education system, affording greater civil rights to women and granting freedom of religion to non-Muslims in the country, including American military personnel based there.

"We're a tolerant country that allows Muslims to worship freely," says Bandow of the Cato Institute. "It's outrageous that U.S. soldiers aren't allowed to publicly worship according to their own faith when they're over there to defend the Saudis. On issues like that we have to be much more pushy with the [Saudi] government."

But defenders of strong U.S.-Saudi ties point out that during the Cold War the United States maintained close diplomatic relations with plenty of regimes with even weaker democratic credentials than the Saudis — as long as those regimes were anti-communist. The totalitarian regimes of Augusto Pinochet's Chile during the 1970s and Shah Mohammad Reza Pahlavi in Iran are but two examples. Even Hussein's Iraq enjoyed cordial relations with the United States for most of the 1980s, when he was fighting Iran, then considered one of America's principal enemies.

In any event, some experts warn, critics of Saudi Arabia's rulers should consider the likely alternative to the current regime. "Even though we would like to see greater economic, social and political reform in Saudi Arabia, we should bear in mind that there could be something much worse in power in Saudi Arabia," Cutler says. "I'm talking about a real Taliban regime, one that might not mind cutting off exports of oil for awhile if it thought that could bring down Western civilization and do huge harm to our economy.

"So we should think twice before we open fire with both barrels at the Saudis," he continues. "They have been very cooperative out of self-interest and out of valuing the relationship with the United States. We need their oil, and they need our security."

Can the United States greatly reduce its dependence on Persian Gulf oil?

Ever since the painful 1973 Arab oil embargo, politicians and conservationists have declared reducing U.S. dependence on Middle East oil a vital national priority. At the height of the oil crisis of 1978-79, President Jimmy Carter introduced an array of proposals aimed at improving auto fuel economy, developing alternative-energy sources and stocking a strategic reserve of crude oil to soften the blow of future oil cutoffs.

But relatively low oil prices since the early 1980s have dampened Americans' enthusiasm for saving energy, especially gasoline. Gone are the days when U.S. consumers opted for fuel-efficient Japanese cars, nearly driving the Big Three Detroit automakers out of business after gasoline prices skyrocketed in the 1970s. Today the cars of choice are SUVs and other large gas-guzzlers. And because U.S. oil production has been declining since reaching its peak in 1970, a growing portion of America's thirst for oil is being met by imports. Since the 1973 oil embargo, in fact, U.S. oil imports have increased from 36 percent of consumption to more than 50 percent today.

Alternative sources of oil from Nigeria to the North Sea have come on line to diminish reliance on the Persian Gulf region, while new technology is tapping the potential oil wealth of the Caspian Sea and other sources. "The development of deep-water technology has enabled us to drill under thousands of feet of water, which has led to some dramatic discoveries in the Gulf of Mexico and particularly West Africa," says the API's Felmy. "Also, the development of seismic technology has improved our ability to find the oil. The combination of those two technologies has been very important to our efforts to diversify oil sources."

Nevertheless, the world's largest known crude reserves still lie under the deserts of Saudi Arabia, Iraq and other states in the region. And many oil experts say energy independence is neither possible nor urgent, because the United States — by far the world's largest single consumer of crude — is just one player in a huge, interdependent oil market. "Independence from foreign oil is impossible because more than half of our oil supplies are imported today," says Lichtblau of the Petroleum Industry Research Foundation. "So there's no way we could become independent; neither is it necessary or even desirable to try."

"Most industrial countries are net importers of substantial amounts of oil," Lichtblau explains. "Japan, South Korea and the European countries — with the exception of the United Kingdom — are all net importers of much more of their oil supplies than we are. That's been the nature of the world oil market for many decades, and it's not going to change because there's plenty of oil around."

Lichtblau downplays the potential threat to U.S. energy supplies of political instability in the Middle East. "These countries that sell us the oil must sell it," he says. "It's their principal or only source of foreign exchange. So we are interdependent with Saudi Arabia, and to a lesser degree with Iraq, Kuwait and the United Arab Emirates."

In addition, three Western Hemisphere producers — Canada, Mexico and Venezuela — rank among the top-four suppliers, along with Saudi Arabia, of oil imports into the United States. "Venezuela right now has trouble, but normally it must sell oil in order to survive, as must Mexico."

Still, many experts say the United States should do more to wean itself from its dependence on foreign oil. "I'm very much in favor of our developing a serious, long-term strategic plan for reducing our dependence on imported oil from wherever," says Cutler of the Meridian International Center. "We tend to worry about the Middle East, with possible boycotts and instability in that region, but look at some of the other major suppliers." Besides the industrywide strike in Venezuela, unrest in Nigeria, Colombia, Indonesia and other oil-supplying countries puts those sources at risk as well, he points out.

But energy security is not simply a question of foreign supplies, Cutler emphasizes. There is much the U.S. government and consumers could do to reduce demand for oil, he says. "We should have started back in 1973, when we had the first oil crisis, to reduce our consumption of oil, no matter what the source," he says. [17]

But consumer demand for uneconomical vehicles appears stronger than ever. The recent North American International Auto Show in Detroit featured such behemoths as a 16-cylinder, 1,050-horsepower Cadillac. [18]

"Here we are worried about being vulnerable to energy shortages," Cutler says, "but so far we have failed to take energy security seriously."

BACKGROUND

Strategic Commodity

Blessed with abundant energy supplies, the United States enjoyed a distinct advantage over other emerging industrial powers from the Industrial Revolution well into the 20th century. [19] Coal powered the factories and railroads during the 1800s, and the discovery of vast oil deposits in Texas in the early 1900s paved the way for a new revolution that would be based on the gasoline-powered automobile.

Henry Ford's innovative manufacturing system of mass production brought the cost of personal autos within reach of many Americans. That led to a boom in auto sales that prompted massive highway building and shaped patterns of suburban development that ensured the dominant

1900s–1940s *The United States and Europe discover and extract oil in the Middle East.*

1927 British-dominated Iraq Petroleum Co. becomes one of Persian Gulf region's first significant oil exporters after the discovery of a major Iraqi oil field at Kirkuk.

1933 Standard Oil Co. of California (Socal) obtains a 60-year concession for exclusive rights to oil in eastern Saudi Arabia, breaking Britain's control over the region's oil resources and securing a major source of cheap oil for U.S. consumers.

1948 The creation of Israel after World War II fosters enduring conflict with neighboring Arabs.

1950s–1970s *Middle Eastern nations take possession of their oil fields, enabling Organization of Petroleum Exporting Countries (OPEC) to assert control over the global oil market.*

1970 U.S. oil production peaks at 11.3 million barrels a day, but growing subsequent demand sparks increasing need for imports.

1973 Saudi Arabia and other Arab OPEC members impose an oil embargo against the United States in retaliation for its support of Israel in the October 1973 Arab-Israeli War.

1974 The United States and other industrial countries establish the International Energy Agency (IEA), which requires member countries to stockpile oil to minimize the impact of future supply disruptions.

1975 The Energy Policy and Conservation Act establishes Corporate Average Fuel Economy (CAFE) standards mandating an increase in auto fuel economy to an average of 27.5 miles per gallon by 1985 and authorizes the creation of the Strategic Petroleum Reserve.

1978–1979 Islamic revolutionaries topple the shah in Iran, a major oil producer and U.S. ally, and install an anti-American Islamic government.

1980s–1990s *The United States, with help from Saudi Arabia and other Arab countries, recruits religious Muslims to help expel Soviet forces from Afghanistan.*

September 1980 War between Iran and Iraq breaks out. The eight-year war sparks oil shortages and price increases that contribute to recession in the United States.

1991 A U.S.-led military coalition forces Iraq to retreat from its occupation of neighboring Kuwait. The Soviet Union collapses, eliminating the United States' chief adversary during the previous half-century and eroding OPEC's hold on world oil markets by making some of the world's most promising oil reserves — under and around the Caspian Sea — available to world markets.

2000s *Terrorism prompts changes in U.S. oil diplomacy.*

April 2001 Bush administration's energy plan calls for more oil production in the United States, including Alaska's Arctic National Wildlife Refuge (ANWR).

May 2001 President Olusegun Obasanjo of Nigeria, the fifth-largest U.S. oil supplier, meets with President Bush in the first White House visit by an African leader since Bush took office.

Sept. 11, 2001 Nineteen hijackers — 15 of Saudi origin — crash commercial aircraft into the World Trade Center and the Pentagon in the worst act of terrorism ever on U.S. soil.

place of oil in the country's energy mix.

While the United States developed its industrial economy with few initial concerns about energy, other industrial nations were forced to look outside their boundaries to meet their growing demand for oil. The 1908 discovery of a vast oil deposit in Iran focused European attention on the region surrounding the Persian Gulf as a promising source of crude. European demand for oil took off on the eve of World War I, when Winston Churchill, then First Lord of the Admiralty, converted Royal Navy ships from domestic coal to oil.

The quest for oil became a primary focus of energy-poor Europe's policies toward the oil-rich Middle East in the early 20th century, particularly in the Persian Gulf region. But Britain quickly consolidated a near-monopoly over Middle Eastern oil fields, edging out Germany and other European competitors by negotiating exclusive production concessions with the region's kings and sheikhs. After the discovery of a major oil field at Kirkuk in 1927, the British-dominated Iraq Petroleum Co. became one of the region's first significant oil exporters.

America's presence in the region began in earnest in the early 1930s. Even though the United States still had plenty of oil to satisfy domestic demand, the strategic importance of controlling access to the world's major oil sources was becoming increasingly apparent as European powers jockeyed for influence in the Middle East. After the discovery of another large field, in the Persian Gulf island nation of Bahrain in 1932, geologists from Standard Oil Co. of California (now ChevronTexaco) began searching for deposits in neighboring Saudi Arabia. In 1933, Standard Oil obtained from King Abdul Aziz (known as Ibn Saud) a 60-year concession for exclusive rights to oil in eastern Saudi Arabia, breaking Britain's control over the region's oil resources and securing a major source of cheap oil for American consumers.

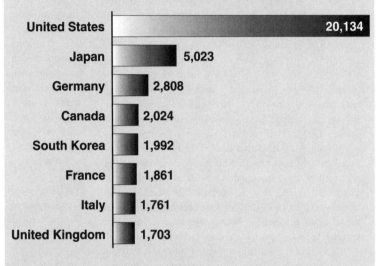

U.S. Oil Use Dwarfs Other Nations'

The United States used more than 20 million barrels of oil in August 2002, or more than all the petroleum used by seven other industrialized nations in the Organization for Economic Cooperation and Development (OECD).

Petroleum Consumption, August 2002
(In thousands of barrels)

United States	20,134
Japan	5,023
Germany	2,808
Canada	2,024
South Korea	1,992
France	1,861
Italy	1,761
United Kingdom	1,703

Source: Energy Information Administration, *Monthly Energy Review*, December 2002

As the immensity of Saudi Arabia's oil reserves became apparent, Standard Oil negotiated a six-year extension to its original concession and extended its rights over almost 80,000 square miles of Saudi territory. The American concession underwent several ownership changes and in 1944 was renamed the Arabian American Oil Co. — Aramco. By then, all the major U.S. oil companies — including the predecessors of ExxonMobil and ChevronTexaco — had interests in the Saudi concession.

Americans' reliance on the family car for commuting and other daily needs was well established by the time demand for gasoline and other petroleum products began to outstrip domestic supplies. In 1970, American oil production reached its all-time peak of 11.3 million barrels a day and began its inexorable decline as domestic deposits began to run out of easily recoverable oil. As population growth, economic prosperity and suburban development continued to fuel U.S. consumers' demand

New Attack on Greenhouse Gases

In 1992, the first President George Bush and other world leaders met in Rio de Janeiro, Brazil, to sign the historic Framework Convention on Climate Change — the first international agreement that recognized the environmental threat posed by petroleum and coal use.

But concern over the cost of complying with the treaty soon mounted in the United States, by far the world's largest oil consumer and emitter of so-called greenhouse gases. In 1997, the Senate went on record opposing the 1997 treaty that implemented the Rio agreement — the Kyoto Protocol — by calling for mandatory reductions in greenhouse gases. Scientists widely agree that the gases released by burning oil and other carbon-based fuels trap the sun's heat inside Earth's atmosphere like a greenhouse, causing a gradual but potentially disastrous warming.

In January 2001, within days of taking office, the current President Bush reversed his campaign pledge to support controls on global warming and renounced the Kyoto Protocol. Arguing that mandates would harm the U.S. economy, he called instead for further research into global warming and economic incentives to encourage individuals and industries to voluntarily reduce carbon emissions.

This January, Canada became the 100th nation to ratify the Kyoto treaty, leaving the United States as the only major industrial power refusing to accept the protocol's mandate to reduce greenhouse emissions. Meanwhile, the Bush administration has launched its promised research into the causes of climate change — causes that most of the world has agreed lie with fossil-fuel use.

Frustrated by the president's refusal to begin reducing carbon emissions, Sens. John McCain, R-Ariz., and Joseph I. Lieberman, D-Conn., introduced a bill on Jan. 8, 2003, calling for mandatory greenhouse-gas reductions. The emission caps, which would apply to all sectors except agricultural and residential energy use, are less stringent than those laid out in Kyoto. By 2010, carbon emissions would have to decline to the level reported in 2000; by 2016, they would have to fall to the 1990 level — about 12 percent below the current U.S. emission level. By comparison, the Kyoto Protocol requires industrialized countries to cut their carbon emissions an average 5 percent below 1990 levels by 2012.

"Today we take the first step up a long mountain road — a road that will culminate with this country taking credible action to address the global problems of our warming planet," Lieberman testified at a Jan. 8 hearing before the Senate Commerce, Science and Transportation Committee. "The rest of the world is now taking on the

---

for gasoline-driven automobiles, oil imports slowly rose as a portion of the country's total energy supply, from 2.2 million barrels a day in 1967 to 6 million barrels a day in 1973. Over the same period, imports as a share of total U.S. oil consumption rose from 19 percent to 36 percent, the vast majority from the Middle East. [20]

'73 Oil Embargo

But the era of cheap Middle Eastern oil soon came to an abrupt halt. Resentment over the Western powers' exploitation of their precious resource and opposition to the creation of Israel in 1948 fueled a broad movement of Arab nationalism that spread from Egypt to the major oil producers. Over the next two decades, Saudi Arabia, Iraq, Iran and smaller states surrounding the Persian Gulf expelled Western oil companies, nationalized their oil fields and created state-run companies to take over oil production.

In 1973 the Saudi government assumed a 25 percent stake in Aramco and expanded its ownership to 100 percent in 1976. In 1989, the last vestige of American control over Aramco ended when American John J. Kelberer ceded the presidency of the company to a Saudi, Ali Naimi. The Saudi government describes this event as a key moment in national self-determination: "Thus the oil of the kingdom, which had lain for so long beneath Saudi Arabia's deserts and which then for decades had been exploited by foreign interests, became at last a national resource controlled and managed by those under whose soil it lay." [21]

In addition to resenting Western control of the region's oil supply, Saudi Arabia and other Arab countries were outraged by U.S. support of Israel during the 1973 Arab-Israeli War. In retaliation, Saudi Arabia led several other Arab countries in a five-month oil embargo that caused nationwide gasoline shortages in the United

challenge this problem presents. The United States, as the world's largest emitter of the gases and the home of the world's strongest economy, must not have its head in the clouds."

Transportation, which is fueled almost exclusively by oil products — gasoline and diesel — accounts for about a third of U.S. greenhouse emissions. The bill would apply to oil producers and refiners, as well as to automakers, who would be allowed to buy and sell credits earned under the Corporate Average Fuel Economy (CAFE) program, which requires carmakers to achieve an average 27.5 miles per gallon across their fleets. Manufacturers that fail to meet the standard would be allowed to buy credits from automakers that produce more fuel-efficient cars.

The bipartisan nature of the McCain-Lieberman bill has prompted cautious optimism about its prospects for passage by the new, Republican-controlled Congress. "The admin-

Sens. John McCain, R-Ariz., and Joseph I. Lieberman, D-Conn., introduced legislation early this month calling for mandatory greenhouse-gas reductions.

istration suggests that little or nothing can be done to reduce emissions," said Senate Minority Leader Thomas A. Daschle, D-S.D. "The Senate will lead the United States to address the problem of global warming since the president is unwilling to." [1]

But the impact of such efforts on the United States' enduring dependence on oil imports may be limited, says oil analyst John Lichtblau, chairman of the Petroleum Industry Research Foundation in New York City. "More efficient automobiles would reduce gasoline consumption and have a positive impact on the environment," he says. "It also probably would reduce somewhat our oil import dependence, but not by very much."

---

[1] See Eric Pianin, "Reductions Sought in Greenhouse Gases," *The Washington Post*, Jan. 9, 2003, p. A4.

States. As the leading producer in OPEC, Saudi Arabia convinced the other members to reduce their exports, causing a quadrupling of world crude oil prices to about $12 dollars a barrel and demonstrating OPEC's control of the world oil market.

The United States and other industrial countries quickly responded to the embargo in 1974 by establishing the International Energy Agency (IEA), which helped coordinate supplies among nations and required member countries to stockpile enough oil to last for three months.

For its part, the U.S. government responded with a flurry of programs to conserve energy, including a largely unsuccessful program to develop alternative fuels for automobiles and equally unsuccessful oil-price and allocation controls. The 1975 Energy Policy and Conservation Act established "Corporate Average Fuel Economy" (CAFE) standards mandating an increase in auto fuel economy to an average of 27.5 miles per gallon

by 1985. The act also authorized creation of the Strategic Petroleum Reserve, an underground repository aimed at cushioning the impact of future oil shortages. In 1977 the Energy Department was created to consolidate energy-related functions into a single, Cabinet-level agency.

More Instability

The U.S. conservation efforts did not insulate the economy from a second "oil shock" in 1979, caused by increasing turmoil in Iran and OPEC's announcement that it would raise prices.

World crude spot prices skyrocketed in early 1979, as buyers snapped up product before OPEC's price hikes went into effect. Spiraling gasoline prices produced long lines at service stations, which shortened their hours and limited purchase quantities. Some localities restricted gasoline purchases according to whether the buyer's license plate ended in odd or even numbers.

AFP Photo/Luke Farazza

Israeli Prime Minister Ariel Sharon meets with President Bush at the White House last Oct. 16. Arabs widely see the Bush administration as heavily favoring Israel in the ongoing exchanges of violence between Israel and the Palestinian Authority, led by Yasser Arafat.

In Iran, oil production plummeted by 4 million barrels a day in early 1979 after the shah's government was overthrown by religious extremists. And on Nov. 4, militant students overran the U.S. Embassy, taking more than five dozen Americans hostage for more than a year — a crisis that lasted for the rest of Carter's presidency and further accentuated how vulnerable America was due to its dependence on Middle Eastern oil.

The outbreak of the eight-year Iran-Iraq War in September 1980 further reduced Persian Gulf oil output. By 1981, total OPEC production had fallen to 22 million barrels a day, 7 million less than in 1978. At the same time, prices shot up from around $14 a barrel in early 1979 to more than $35 in early 1981. It was not until 1983 that oil prices stabilized at around $28 a barrel. [22]

By the early 1980s, many oil deposits in the United States were running low, and producers had capped off thousands of wells as the cost of extracting the hard-to-reach dregs of these "marginal" well exceeded the revenue they could generate. But with world oil prices soaring and foreign supplies tight, American producers reopened many marginal wells, especially after President Ronald Reagan abolished Nixon-era domestic price controls within days of taking office in 1981.

High oil prices also prompted the United States and other industrial countries to seek new foreign oil sources outside OPEC and develop new technologies to detect and extract oil from previously inaccessible deposits. Deep-sea oil rigs began tapping huge underwater deposits in the North Sea and the Gulf of Mexico, and Alaska's frigid North Slope became a major source of oil. As these sources came on line, the share of world oil production controlled by OPEC shrank from 50 percent in 1978 to 30 percent by 1985. By increasing imports from Canada, Mexico, Britain and other non-OPEC countries, the United States was able to cut its dependence on OPEC sources by an even greater margin, from 82 percent to 41 percent over the same period.

As still more alternative sources of crude came on line, OPEC gradually lost its power to control world oil output and prices. OPEC's leading producer, Saudi Arabia, acted as the group's "swing producer," and tried to prop up oil prices by cutting its own output, from 10 million barrels a day in early 1981 to just 2.3 million barrels a day by mid-1985. But even this drastic action failed to significantly buoy oil prices, and Saudi Arabia resumed normal production to win back market share. Other OPEC members followed suit, and oil flooded the world market, depressing oil prices to less than $10 a barrel by the end of 1985.

Low oil prices had a mixed impact on U.S. producers and consumers. Once again, producers could no longer afford to extract oil from marginal wells, which they shut down. Consumers lost the price incentive to conserve energy, as cheap gasoline encouraged sales of increasingly large, gas-guzzling vehicles. The sport-utility vehicle, with its appeal as a youthful, off-road vehicle, became an instant hit among American consumers. Classified as "light trucks," SUVs were not covered by even the lax CAFE standards for passenger cars, which remained at their 1985 levels. The popularity of SUVs has slowed improvement in the fuel efficiency of the American auto fleet.

Persian Gulf Crisis

A third spike in oil prices occurred after Iraq invaded neighboring Kuwait on Aug. 2, 1990. The United Nations approved an embargo on oil exports from both countries — removing more than 4 million barrels a day from world markets. By September, the price of crude had risen from about $16 a barrel before the invasion to around $36 a barrel.

But unlike earlier supply shortfalls, this one was short-lived, thanks to the new non-OPEC sources of oil that had come on line in Central America, Western Europe and Africa. Plus, the United States and other International Energy Agency members now had emergency supplies to cushion sudden cutoffs. As a result, the U.S.-led Persian Gulf War to expel Iraq from Kuwait in early 1991 had little impact on oil markets, despite the near-destruction of Kuwait's oil fields by retreating Iraqi forces, who set them afire as they left.

The 1980s also had seen a shift in U.S. diplomatic relations in the Persian Gulf that helped dampen the impact of the oil embargo. Saudi Arabia and Iran, enemies of the United States and its allies at different times during the 1960s and '70s, shared America's opposition to Hussein and boosted oil production during the Gulf War. Iran had suffered enormous casualties during its eight-year war with Iraq in the 1980s; Saudi Arabia feared Hussein's destabilizing influence in the region, especially inside its own kingdom, where dissidents were fomenting unrest. The Saudi government even allowed the United States to station troops on Saudi territory during the war — a decision bin Laden would later cite as his main grievance against the House of Saud.

The Soviet Union's 1991 collapse dramatically impacted oil diplomacy. Besides eliminating the United States' chief Cold War adversary, it further eroded OPEC's influence by making some of the world's most promising oil reserves, located under and around the Caspian Sea, available to world markets. Chevron, Amoco and other U.S. producers quickly formed joint-production projects with the former Soviet countries of Kazakhstan and Azerbaijan.

As American oil companies developed production facilities in the region, the U.S. government pursued diplomatic ties with the Caspian Sea nations in hopes of ensuring access to this promising new source of oil. The

U.S. government also spearheaded a plan to build an oil pipeline from the Caspian oil fields through Turkey, a NATO ally, to the Turkish port of Ceyhan on the Mediterranean Sea.

Meanwhile, Russia's need for foreign exchange prompted it to maximize oil exports from its own vast oil fields.

In the 1990s, the relative stability of oil supplies and prices was a boon to the global and U.S. economy, which was experiencing astounding prosperity and growth. But as the booming '90s progressed, the United States was quietly but inexorably losing the quest for energy independence. Falling domestic oil production and rising demand fueled by low oil prices pushed U.S. imports to 9.1 million barrels a day in 2000 — triple the imports in 1985.

CURRENT SITUATION

Sept. 11 Aftermath

The terrorist attacks on the World Trade Center and the Pentagon added a new and lethal twist to U.S. relations with the Muslim world. "I was surprised by the nature of the attack," says Cutler of the Meridian International Center, who as ambassador to Saudi Arabia became aware of rising Islamic extremism long before the attacks. "There was a pretty clear trail left by al Qaeda, but nobody was anticipating a dramatic strike in the heart of America."

Despite endless U.S. efforts to negotiate peace between Israel and Palestinian leaders during the 1990s, antipathy toward the United States had grown throughout the region because of U.S. support of Israel, Cutler says. "Underneath it all there was a kind of love-hate relationship toward the United States," he says. "Together with admiration of our technology and universities, there were feelings of inadequacy and vulnerability to the West going back generations, and this all came together after Afghanistan."

Because the United States was instrumental in driving the Soviet army out of Afghanistan, many Saudis and other Middle Easterners resented the United States, blaming them for the rise of al Qaeda. Al Qaeda grew out of the resistance movement in Afghanistan, notes Telhami of the University of Maryland. "We solicited the help of Saudi Arabia, Egypt and other allies, asking them specifically to recruit fanatical believers of Islam to fight the infidel communists. Of course, it was inadvertent, and people didn't understand the consequences of mobilizing a force of that sort, but the Saudis and the Egyptians have some reason to be frustrated with America's forgetting that part of history."

Aggravating this sense of frustration, Telhami says, is what Arabs see as the Bush administration's abandoning the lead role previous administrations had played in advancing the Arab-Israeli peace process. President Bush has instead appeared to come down heavily on the side of Israeli Prime Minister Ariel Sharon in the ongoing exchange of violence between Israel and the Palestinian Authority led by Yasser Arafat. Bush has undermined Arafat's authority in the decades-old dispute by calling for new Palestinian elections as a necessary pre-condition for peace.

Bush's decision to step back from an active role in mediating Arab-Israeli tensions has fed anti-American opinion throughout the Middle East. Telhami says surveys consistently place the Arab-Israeli conflict at the top of the list of Arab concerns. "They look at the United States through the prism of the Arab-Israeli issue," he says. "So while the United States is angry at Arab Muslims over issues that the Arabs think they are not centrally to blame for, they are very frustrated that the United States is not responding to their most immediate and pressing concern."

U.S.-Saudi Relations

Opinion polls and commentators suggest that Americans continue to blame Saudi Arabia for contributing, at least indirectly, to the rise in Islamic extremism and for not cooperating fully with the Bush administration's war on terrorism. According to an online survey in early December, 69 percent of respondents answered "no" to the query, "Is Saudi Arabia a true friend of the United States?" [23]

"The House of Saud must end the Faustian bargain it originally made with the country's extremist Wahhabist sect," columnist Jim Hoagland wrote in *The Washington Post*. [24]

"The Bush administration and the Saudis have done a masterful job of turning attention away from . . . the trail that leads to the possibility that a foreign government provided support to some of the Sept. 11 hijackers," said Sen. Bob Graham, D-Fla., then-chairman of the Senate Intelligence Committee. [25]

The Saudi government, meanwhile, is trying to smooth over its damaged relations with the United States. Adel al-Jubeir, foreign policy adviser to Crown Prince Abdullah, came to Washington in December to defend the kingdom's record on fighting terrorism and denounced anti-Saudi sentiment as part of a campaign that "borders on hate."

"We believe that our country has been unfairly maligned," al-Jubeir said. "We believe that we have been subjected to criticism that we do not deserve. We believe that people have been misinformed about Saudi Arabia and what Saudi Arabia has done, or, frankly, that people have lied about what we have done and what we allegedly have not done." [26]

On Jan. 11, the Saudis convinced OPEC to increase the group's daily oil production by 1.5 million barrels in an effort to thwart a significant increase in oil prices in the event of war in Iraq. The move was welcome news in Washington, where the U.S. economy is in a year-long slump, and a prolonged rise in oil prices, which already exceed $30 a barrel, could tip the economy into a recession.

Saudi Arabia also has taken the politically risky step of agreeing to allow the Pentagon to use its airspace and air bases in the event of war with Iraq, including a command center that would provide vital coordination for air attacks. [27] Since the Gulf War, the Saudi government had barred U.S. forces from conducting bombing strikes in retaliation for Iraqi attacks against U.S. and British planes that patrol no-fly zones in northern and southern Iraq. But after the U.N. Security Council resolution of Nov. 8, 2002 — which demanded that Iraq fully account for its weapons of mass destruction and cooperate with U.N. inspectors — the Bush administration, after weeks of diplomatic negotiations, persuaded the Saudis to rescind that restriction in case of war with Iraq. [28]

The Bush administration has stood by Saudi Arabia throughout the criticism. During the crown prince's visit to Bush's ranch last April, the president spoke of "the strong relationship" between the two countries. "Our partnership is important to both our nations," Bush said. "And it is important to the cause of peace and stability in the Middle East and the world."

On Dec. 13, Secretary of State Powell announced a program to encourage economic, political and educational changes in Saudi Arabia and other Arab countries. The U.S.-Middle East Partnership Initiative, with an initial funding of $29 million, would focus on improve-

Should the U.S. demand more support from Saudi Arabia?

YES — William Kristol

Chairman, Project for the New American Century; Editor, The Weekly Standard

From Testimony before the House International Relations Subcommittee on the Middle East and South Asia, May 22, 2002

It is time for the United States to rethink its relationship with Riyadh. For we are now at war . . . with terror and its sponsor, radical Islam. And in this war, the Saudi regime is more part of the problem than part of the solution.

The case for re-evaluating our strategic partnership with the current Saudi regime is a strong one. Begin with the simple fact that 15 of the 19 participants in the Sept. 11 attacks were Saudi nationals. That's something the Saudis themselves could not initially admit. A large proportion — perhaps as high as 80 percent, according to some reports — of the "detainees" taken from Afghanistan to Guantanamo Bay are Saudis. And although Osama bin Laden has made much of his antipathy to the Saudi regime, his true relationship with the royal family is certainly more complex and questionable. . . .

The Saudis also have been deeply implicated in the wave of suicide bombers that have attacked Israeli citizens — and American citizens in Israel — in recent years. Again, initial Saudi official reaction has been to deny the link. . . .

But even more important [is] the Saudi regime's general and aggressive export of Wahhabi fundamentalists. . . . Wahhabi teachings, religious schools and Saudi oil money have encouraged young Muslims in countries around the world to a jihad-like incitement against non-Muslims. The combination of Wahhabi ideology and Saudi money has contributed more to the radicalization and anti-Americanization of large parts of the Islamic world than any other single factor. . . .

Clearly, the long tradition of quiet diplomacy with the Saudi monarchy no longer serves American purposes. The royal family has taken silence as consent in its strategy of directing Arab and Islamic discontent away from the House of Saud and toward the United States, Israel and the West. This is a strategy inimical to American security and a dangerously crippling problem in President Bush's war on terrorism. . . .

Only by applying pressure can we encourage whatever modernizing movement there may be within the royal family and the armed forces while isolating the radical Wahhabi clerics and their supporters. Prince Abdullah is sometimes seen as a reformer. We should give him every incentive to reform the current Saudi regime, and the main such incentive would be to tell him, privately and publicly, that the status quo is unacceptable.

NO — F. Gregory Gause III

Associate Professor of Political Science, University of Vermont

From testimony before the House International Relations Subcommittee on the Middle East and South Asia, May 22, 2002

We expected our friends to stand with us after Sept. 11, without question and without hesitation. Since the Gulf War, we have counted Saudi Arabia in the camp of our friends. . . .

[T]he Saudis are strategic partners who share a number of common interests with us. We can work with them when those interests coincide, as they frequently do. The Saudis' first reaction to any policy choice is not, "How can we help the Americans on this?" but, "How can we help, or at least not hurt, ourselves?" In this, Saudi Arabia is like almost every other country in the world. Those who thought otherwise, who put the Saudis in the "friends" category, have swung to the other extreme and now come close to labeling them as "enemies." This is equally mistaken. . . .

We have pressed the Saudis for more open intelligence sharing, with some positive results, and we should continue to press them on that score. In short, we have gotten what we need, even if we have not gotten all that we want from the Saudis during the first phase of the war against terrorism. . . .

Those who call for American pressure on the al-Saud to open up their political process should be careful what they wish for. Saudi cooperation on Iraqi and Arab-Israeli issues will be more, not less, difficult to achieve if the Saudi public has a greater say in the country's foreign policy. If you are worried about the level of anti-Israeli rhetoric in the Saudi press, permitting more press freedom will not solve your problem. . . .

Moreover, any elections in Saudi Arabia now would be won by people closer to bin Laden's point of view than to that of liberal democrats. . . .

There is an active debate in Saudi Arabia, predating Sept. 11, about the need to reassess the educational system in light of the changing world economy. Pressure from the United States on this issue will only work against those in Saudi Arabia who seek reform.

Americans can offer advice if asked. In general, however, Washington ought to resist suggesting that it knows better than the Saudis themselves how to manage their society.

What would come after al-Saud rule, if reformist openings lead to revolutionary fervor, would not be an improvement from the point of view of either American interests or American values.

ments in the status of women. "Until the countries of the Middle East unleash the abilities and potential of their women, they will not build a future of hope," he said. [29]

Some experts say the Saudi government has made progress in reforming its institutions and warn against weakening Washington's close diplomatic relations with the House of Saud, because the alternative could be a Taliban-like regime.

"The country is changing, but it's important to the Saudis, and it should be important to us, that this change be evolutionary and not revolutionary," says Cutler of the Meridian International Center. "Because, if sometimes we're critical of the Saudis, let's not help move them into a situation where we would say, 'My God, what have we done?'"

OUTLOOK

Oil Diversification

While maintaining close relations with Saudi Arabia, the Bush administration has expressed concern over the reliability of Middle Eastern oil supplies. Shortly after taking office in January 2001, Bush and Vice President Cheney introduced an energy plan they said would reduce U.S. vulnerability to future oil shortages. [30]

To the dismay of environmentalists, who prefer reducing the high demand for petroleum products through higher energy taxes and incentives to develop alternative power sources, the Bush plan focuses on increasing oil supplies. Among other things, it calls for opening public land, most controversially in the 23-million-acre Alaskan Arctic National Wildlife Refuge (ANWR) to oil exploration and production. But critics say even if the Republican-dominated Congress approves the plan this year, ANWR oil would do little to reduce U.S. dependence on foreign oil, because production would not begin until 2011 and would only add an estimated 800,000 barrels a day to U.S. crude output — enough to reduce from 62 percent to 60 percent the share of foreign oil used by American consumers in 2020. [31]

The Bush plan also calls for continuing the diversification of foreign oil sources under way since the 1973 Arab oil embargo. A prime target for this effort is West Africa, which already supplies about 12 percent of U.S.

oil imports and could double that share over the next decade or so. [32] Nigeria currently accounts for the bulk of U.S. oil imports from West Africa, making it the fifth-largest supplier of crude, behind Canada, Saudi Arabia, Mexico and Venezuela. [33]

But some analysts fear that by simply increasing reliance on West African oil without promoting economic development and government reform in that beleaguered part of the world, the Bush administration risks repeating the same mistakes previous administrations have made in the Middle East. Nigeria and the other regional producers — Angola, Equatorial Guinea, Chad, Cameroon and the Republic of Congo — are beset with government corruption, internal strife and extreme poverty. As corrupt leaders siphon off Western oil-company payments with no public oversight, the region's population sinks ever deeper into poverty, setting the stage for the kind of unrest that has afflicted other countries that rely heavily on oil exports.

"Anybody can see that if we're going to rely on Africa as an alternative source of supply, then we mustn't fall into the same trap that we're trying to extricate ourselves from in Saudi Arabia," said international financier George Soros, who is calling for changes in securities law to force oil companies to make public their investments in foreign countries. [34]

Russia and the Caspian Sea region also are promising sources of non-Middle Eastern crude. Their current combined production of 9 million barrels a day is expected to increase by half eventually. Russia is eager to maximize oil exports to improve its ailing economy, while U.S., European and Russian oil companies are developing production facilities and pipelines to carry Caspian oil to ports on the Mediterranean and Black seas.

The promise of Russian oil and Russia's tolerance of the growing U.S. oil-industry presence in the Caspian — a region of Russian strategic interest even after the Soviet Union's fall — have been a key focus in the Bush administration's rapprochement with Russian President Putin.

The U.S. interest in Russian oil even trumps the widespread U.S. misgivings about Putin's brutal supression of dissent in the breakaway province of Chechnya.

"The growth of oil supplies from Russia and the Caspian can be one of the most important new contributions to stability in world oil markets — especially in the face of non-OPEC declines elsewhere," said Yergin of

Cambridge Energy Research Associates. "By working with the Russian government to facilitate energy development, the U.S. government can make one of its most important contributions to energy security." [35]

Latin America, a third major area of potential new oil development, is closer than other foreign suppliers. It takes just five days to ship oil from Venezuela to the United States, compared to about 45 days from the Persian Gulf. But, as in West Africa and the Middle East, oil production in several Latin American countries has come at a price. Pipeline construction and oil spills have polluted pristine jungle habitat in Ecuador, threatening indigenous communities. An ongoing civil war and rampant drug trade jeopardize Colombia's oil production, while the oil industry faces an uncertain future in Brazil, where the country's newly elected populist president, socialist Luiz Inacio Lula da Silva, has vowed to review his country's social and economic policies.

In Venezuela — Latin America's leading oil producer and the world's fifth-largest oil exporter — the striking oil workers claim leftist President Chávez is mismanaging the oil industry by resisting calls to increase oil production to slow rising world oil prices.

"The management of [the state-run oil company] wants to produce 6 million barrels a day, which is what the United States wants them to do," says Weisbrot of the Center for Economic and Policy Research. "Chávez has taken a different strategy, which is probably better for Venezuela, which is to obey the OPEC quotas as much as he can and produce a lower amount. Venezuela is actually better off with lower levels of production at a higher price, a fact that no one in the United States is considering because we just want more oil and cheaper oil."

Iraqi Wild Card

Despite the upheavals in Venezuela, the greatest source of uncertainty in world oil markets, however, is Iraq. U.N. weapons inspectors are scheduled to report their findings from the ongoing search for weapons of mass destruction in Iraqi on Jan. 27. Even if they report no evidence of violations, the Bush administration, which is massing troops, ships and weapons in the region, may dismiss their conclusions and proceed with an invasion.

The impact of a war against Iraq would depend on its duration, outcome and effect on the region's other oil producers. "If the war lasts three days — we've blown everything up, we've found all the weapons of mass destruction, the U.N. is coming in and everybody's happy — the oil-price impact could be pretty modest," says Amy Myers Jaffe, a senior energy adviser at the Baker Institute.

"But suppose the campaign turns out to be a little bit more drawn out," Jaffe continues, "and the U.S. military does what it's done in the past — knocks out electrical power stations. That's going to slow down the resumption of Iraq's exports, which would make for a less optimistic scenario."

Some analysts say their biggest concern is the chance that Iraq's oil production will be interrupted by war before Venezuela resumes production. "It will be a much tighter and much more expensive market if both of these countries are out at the same time," says Lichtblau of the Petroleum Industry Research Foundation. "This is entirely possible, because we don't know when the Venezuelan situation will actually improve to the point where they can again become normal oil exporters. Even if the strike ended in a week or two, it would take them maybe another four or five weeks, or longer, to get back to where they were before Dec. 2."

Meanwhile, critics charge that the Bush administration's desire for Venezuela's oil makes it more than a passive bystander in the crisis. When opposition leaders staged a coup against the democratically elected Chávez last April 12, Washington refrained from condemning the action. The coup failed two days later, but the administration continues to support the strikers' demand for early elections to replace the leftist Chávez.

With so much attention focused on the Middle East and the potential for war with Iraq, Washington's diplomatic initiatives in Venezuela have attracted little attention. But that may soon change. Nineteen liberal members of Congress recently sent a letter of support to Chávez, decrying "unconstitutional" plans to hold early elections in the South American nation.

"The purpose of the letter is to express to the democratically elected president of Venezuela that that there are members of Congress who believe in the principles of our own country," said Rep. Maurice D. Hinchey, D-N.Y., the letter's author. "Our country is supposed to respect democratic policies and principles, but this administration doesn't seem to understand that." [36]

NOTES

1. From remarks after the meeting in Crawford on April 25, 2002.

2. Energy Information Administration, *Monthly Energy Review*, December 2002, pp. 49, 55.

3. See Jeff Gerth, "Bribery Inquiry Involves Kazaks Chief, and He's Unhappy," *The New York Times*, Dec. 11, 2002, p. A16.

4. Human Rights Watch, "World Report 2003." See also Warren Vieth, "U.S. Quest for Oil in Africa Worries Analysts," *Los Angeles Times*, Jan. 13, 2003, p. A1.

5. Gaffney testified June 20, 2002, before the House International Relations Committee.

6. Bush's comment was in answer to a reporter's question on Oct. 21, 2002.

7. Thomas L. Friedman, "A War for Oil?" *The New York Times*, Jan. 5, 2003, p. A11.

8. See, for example, "Protesters Denounce U.S. Navy Presence," *Chicago Tribune*, Dec. 27, 2002.

9. Pew Research Center for the People & the Press, "How Global Publics View Their Lives, Their Countries, the World, America," released Dec. 4, 2002.

10. Robert Fisk, "What the U.S. President Wants Us to Forget," *The Independent* (London), Sept. 10, 2002, p. A17.

11. Speaking with host Tim Russert on NBC's "Meet the Press," Dec. 29, 2002.

12. "Guiding Principles for U.S. Post-Conflict Policy in Iraq," James A. Baker III Institute for Public Policy and Council on Foreign Relations, December 2002.

13. Daniel Yergin, "A Crude View of the Crisis in Iraq," *The Washington Post*, Dec. 8, 2002, p. B1.

14. Schwartz's book, *The Two Faces of Islam*, is described by Ira Rifkin, "Author Sees Terrorist Roots in Saudi Religious Code," *The Washington Post*, Jan. 11, 2003, p. B9.

15. From testimony before the House International Relations Subcommittee on the Middle East and South Asia, May 22, 2002.

16. Bandow testified on June 12, 2002, before the House Government Reform Committee.

17. For background, see Mary H. Cooper, "Energy Security," *The CQ Researcher*, Feb. 1, 2002, pp. 73-96.

18. See Brock Yates, "Car Talk," *The Wall Street Journal*, Jan. 9, 2003, p. A10.

19. For a comprehensive history of oil diplomacy, see Daniel Yergin, *The Prize* (1991).

20. *Ibid.*, p. 567.

21. From a Saudi government information Web site, www.saudinf.com.

22. U.S. Department of Energy, Energy Information Agency, "Petroleum Chronology of Events 1970-2000," www.eia.doe.gov.

23. From a Dec. 6, 2002, survey at www.doubtcome.com.

24. Jim Hoagland, "Saudi Arabia's Choice," *The Washington Post*, Dec. 1, 2002, p. B7.

25. Quoted in "U.S. Sen. Graham Critical of Bush Administration, Saudi Arabia," *Dow Jones International News*, Dec. 3, 2002.

26. Speaking at a press conference at the Saudi Embassy in Washington, Dec. 3, 2002.

27. See Thomas E. Ricks, "American Way of War in Saudi Desert," *The Washington Post*, Jan. 7, 2003, p. A1.

28. See Michael R. Gordon, "Iraq's Neighbors Seem to Be Ready to Support a War," *The New York Times*, Dec. 2, 2002, p. A1.

29. See Edward Walsh, "Powell Unveils U.S.-Arab Initiative," *The Washington Post*, Dec. 13, 2002, p. A22. For background on women's rights, see David Masci, "Emerging India," *The CQ Researcher*, April 19, 2002, pp. 329-360; Kenneth Jost, "Rebuilding Afghanistan," *The CQ Researcher*, Dec. 21, 2001, pp. 1041-1064; and Mary H. Cooper, "Women and Human Rights," *The CQ Researcher*, April 30, 1999, pp. 353-376.

30. For background, see Mary H. Cooper, "Energy Policy," *The CQ Researcher*, May 25, 2001, pp. 441-464.

31. Energy Information Administration, "The Effects of the Alaska Oil and Natural Gas Provisions of H.R. 4 and S. 1766 on U.S. Energy Markets," February 2002.

32. See Warren Vieth, "U.S. Quest for Oil in Africa Worries Analysts," *Los Angeles Times*, Jan. 13, 2003, p. A1.

33. Energy Information Administration, "Nigeria," January 2002.

34. Quoted in Vieth, *op. cit.*

35. Yergin testified June 20, 2002, before the House International Relations Committee.

36. See Jonathan Riehl, "House Liberals Defend Leftist Venezuelan President Chávez," *Congressional Quarterly Daily Monitor*, Jan. 14, 2003.

BIBLIOGRAPHY

Books

Schwartz, Stephen, *The Two Faces of Islam: The House of Saud from Tradition to Terror*, Doubleday, 2002.
The author, a convert to Islam, blames Wahhabism — Saudi Arabia's strict interpretation of the faith — for instilling hatred of Western values in young Arab men.

Telhami, Shibley, *The Stakes: America and the Middle East*, Westview Press, 2002.
A University of Maryland political scientist writes that so long as the United States is viewed in the Middle East as arrogant, pro-Israel and supportive of authoritarian regimes such as Saudi Arabia, it will not win the war on terrorism.

Yergin, Daniel, *The Prize: The Epic Quest for Oil, Money, and Power*, Simon & Schuster, 1991.
This Pulitzer Prize-winning history of the oil industry provides a comprehensive review of how oil shaped U.S. foreign policy toward the Middle East. Yergin is president of Cambridge Energy Associates and former chairman of the Energy Department's Task Force on Strategic Energy Research and Development.

Articles

"Don't Mention the O-Word," *The Economist*, Sept. 14, 2002.
Fears that a U.S.-led invasion of Iraq would disrupt global oil supplies are exaggerated, according to this overview of Middle Eastern oil supplies, because Iraqi oil exports are already low.

Morse, Edward L., and James Richard, "The Battle for Energy Dominance," *Foreign Affairs*, March/April 2002, pp. 16-31.
Efforts to buy oil from suppliers outside the Middle East have intensified since the Sept. 11, 2001, terrorist attacks, putting Russia in a position to surpass Saudi Arabia in coming years as the world's leading exporter.

Ottaway, Marina, "Reluctant Missionaries," *Foreign Policy*, July-August 2001.
Oil companies are drawing criticism for polluting the environment and tolerating human-rights abuses in countries where they operate. But oil companies are not in a position to effect human-rights reforms, the author writes.

Ratnesar, Romesh, "The Unending War," *Time*, Dec. 9, 2002.
Critics question the Bush administration's cordial relations with Saudi Arabia after revelations that the wife of its U.S. ambassador contributed to charities that may have ties to al Qaeda.

Vieth, Warren, "U.S. Quest for Oil in Africa Worries Analysts, Activists," *Los Angeles Times*, Jan. 13, 2003, p. 1.
The Bush administration's search for more secure sources of oil is leading it to the doorsteps of some of the world's most repressive regimes: the petroleum-rich countries of West Africa.

Reports and Studies

Congressional Budget Office, "Reducing Gasoline Consumption: Three Policy Options," November 2002.
Tightening fuel-efficiency standards for cars, raising the federal tax on gasoline and setting carbon-emission limits on companies that produce cars and other gasoline-powered products would reduce U.S. energy dependence and emissions of gases linked to global warming.

Friends of the Earth, Taxpayers for Common Sense and the U.S. Public Interest Research Group Education Fund, "Running on Empty: How Environmentally Harmful Energy Subsidies Siphon Billions from Taxpayers," 2002.
Three advocacy groups argue the U.S. government is impeding the development of alternative-energy sources by spending more on fossil fuel research than it devotes to developing renewable-energy sources and encouraging energy efficiency.

James A. Baker III Institute for Public Policy and Council on Foreign Relations, "Strategic Energy Policy Challenges for the 21st Century," 2001.
Before the next crisis erupts, the U.S. government should urgently overhaul its international energy policy with a view toward achieving energy independence, according to this report.

National Intelligence Council, "Global Trends 2015: A Dialogue about the Future with Nongovernment Experts," December 2000.
The CIA's research branch predicts that Asia will replace North America as the world's leading energy-consumption region and account for more than half the world's total increase in demand for oil by 2015.

Natural Resources Defense Council and Union of Concerned Scientists, "Dangerous Addiction: Ending America's Oil Dependence," January 2002.
The report calls on the government to reduce U.S. dependence on Middle Eastern oil by tightening fuel economy, providing tax credits to buyers of hybrid vehicles and providing incentives to speed the development of hydrogen-powered fuel-cell cars.

For More Information

American Petroleum Institute, 1220 L St., N.W., Washington, DC 20005; (202) 682-8000; www.api.org. A membership organization representing U.S. oil and natural-gas companies that provides information about the industry and oil-supply forecasts.

Energy Information Administration, U.S. Department of Energy, 1000 Independence Ave., S.W., #7B058, Washington, DC 20585; (202) 586-8800; www.eia.doe.gov. Provides data, forecasts and analyses on all U.S. energy sectors.

Human Rights Watch, 350 Fifth Ave., 34th floor, New York, NY 10118; (212) 290-4700; www.hrw.org. A non-profit advocacy group that issues detailed reports on human rights around the world.

International Energy Agency, 2001 L St., N.W., #650, Washington, DC 20036; (202) 785-6323; www.oecd-wash.org. This branch of the Organization for Economic Cooperation and Development provides information on industrial countries' emergency stockpiles of oil.

Middle East Institute, 1761 N St., N.W., Washington, DC 20036; (202) 785-1141; www.mideasti.org. This non-profit educational organization provides information on the Middle East in an effort to increase Americans' knowledge and understanding of the region.

7

AFP Photo/Yoshikazu Tsuno

A homeless man finds shelter in one of the many parks and gardens in Tokyo. Japan's unemployment rate has doubled in the past decade, triggering a jump in homelessness. Last year alone, homelessness spiked 25 percent.

From *The CQ Researcher*,
July 26, 2002.

Japan in Crisis

David Masci

O n the surface of Japan's orderly society, all appears to be well. Most streets are clean, the crime rate is relatively low and people are generally polite and cooperative. Throngs visit fashionable shopping districts, and many live comfortably in tidy, elegant suburbs.

But under the patina of harmony and affluence, all is not as it seems. "There's a lot more pain in Japan than people are willing to admit or talk about," says Eugene Mathews, an expert on Japan at the Council on Foreign Relations in New York City. "There is a sense of paralysis and great despair."

Indeed, many experts say Japan is in a crisis. A near-continuous recession for more than a decade has cost hundreds of thousands of jobs — devastating in a country where lifetime employment with a single company traditionally has been central to the social compact. One result of the rise in unemployment: Homelessness is up, rising 25 percent in the last year alone, according to the Health, Labor and Welfare Ministry. [1]

The nation's historically low crime rate also has been rising rapidly — 12 percent last year — although it is still nowhere near American or European levels. [2]

Even Japan's much-vaunted educational system, once the envy of the world, is now seen as an anachronism that fosters rote learning instead of the creativity and independent thinking needed in today's competitive global economy. "Our whole school system now seems antiquated because it's good at producing bureaucrats and middle managers, but not the entrepreneurs that Japan needs right now," says Mariko Ikehara, director of the Washington office of CNET, a Japanese public service cable-TV station.

131

Land of the Rising Sun

The ancient Japanese, unaware of any lands east of their own, called their realm Nippon — "Land of the Rising Sun." The California-sized island nation is home to about 127 million people — nearly half the population of the United States.

Japan at a Glance

Population: 126,771,662 (July 2001 estimate)

Ethnicity: Japanese, 99.4 percent; Koreans, 0.6 percent

Life Expectancy: 80.8 years

Fertility Rate: 1.4 children are born to each woman. (2.06 in the United States)

Religion: Buddhism and Shinto, 84 percent; secular and smaller sects, 16 percent.

Total Area: 152,200 square miles. (About the same as California and Germany)

Gross Domestic Product: $3.15 trillion. (2000 estimate)

Monetary Unit: The yen. One dollar equals about 116 yen.

Major Industries: Among the world's largest manufacturers of autos, electronic products, steel, ships and chemicals.

Government: Japan is a parliamentary democracy with a bicameral legislature. The 252 members of the upper house (Shang-in) are elected for six years, while the 480 members of the lower house (Shugi-in) serve for four years. The prime minister, who is elected by the lower house, leads the government. The chief of state is the emperor, a largely ceremonial office currently held by Emperor Akihito.

Sources: CIA World Factbook; The World Almanac (2002).

Yet only a decade ago, scholars and journalists on both sides of the Pacific saw Japan as the world's new great power and a model society. In books such as *Japan as Number One* and *The Rise and Fall of the Great Powers*, they predicted that Japan would soon rival or even sur- pass the United States as an economic and geopolitical superpower.

Today, however, bookstores in both countries carry volumes explaining what went wrong in Japan, and newspaper editorials exhort the Japanese to adopt American-style economic reforms and business practices. "We used to say that Japan had third-rate politicians but a first-rate economy," Ikehara says. "Now, everything is third-rate."

Despite the pessimism, Japan's still boasts the world's second-largest economy behind the United States. And it is still home to some of the world's most successful and innovative companies, like Toyota, Sony and Honda. But the island nation is drowning in debt and seemingly incapable of sustained growth.

Much of the trouble can be traced to Japan's banking system, which lent trillions of dollars to land developers and other businessmen during the high-flying 1980s — when unparalleled economic growth sparked gravity-defying spikes in stock and real estate prices. When the "bubble" burst in the early 1990s, massive loan defaults saddled the banks with almost unimaginable losses. (*See story, p. 136.*)

Economist Adam Posen of the International Institute for Economics in Washington, D.C., is among the analysts who believe Japan's banking system could collapse by year's end, creating economic chaos. Others think the banks could continue to limp along for another two or three years. But all agree that unless the government of Prime Minister Junichiro Koizumi bails out the banks — and soon — they will crumble under the weight of their non-performing loans.

The banks' troubles have left them with little cash, making them less likely to extend new loans — even to creditworthy borrowers — thus sending the economy into more of a tailspin. [3] The cash shortage has also triggered deflation, or falling prices, further hurting Japan's already battered economy. Lower prices mean that businesses earn less for selling goods and services. Moreover, since a scarcity of money makes it more valuable, borrowers have a harder time paying back loans.

And debt problems aren't limited to the private sector. The government's 8 percent annual budget deficit shows no sign of decreasing. Total public debt is now nearly 160 percent of the annual gross domestic product (GDP) — more than three times the U.S. government's debt rate and by far the highest level in the developed world.

AFP Photo/JiJI Press

Prime Minister Junichiro Koizumi follows a Shinto priest during his controversial visit last April to Tokyo's Yasukuni Shrine — resting place for 2.5 million Japanese war dead, including former Prime Minister Hideki Tojo and other convicted war criminals from World War II.

When he was elected 18 months ago, Koizumi promised to fix the banking system, bring the budget under control and make the political process more open and responsive. But so far, he has been unable to make meaningful changes.

Many Japan-watchers blame Koizumi's inability to effect change on the country's political system. The prime minister's own Liberal Democratic Party (LDP)

— which has been in power almost continuously since 1955 — stifles any attempt at radical change and owes its long rule to support from Japan's many entrenched special interests. But others note that Koizumi came into power with an 80 percent approval rating and a mandate for change, both of which they say he squandered in his first year and a half.

However, the prime minister has been able to make a few changes, most notably to Japan's military posture. The country's constitution — imposed by occupying American forces after World War II — prohibits the armed forces from engaging in combat outside Japan. But following the Sept. 11 attacks on the United States, Koizumi convinced the Diet, or parliament, to ease some of the strict limits on the military by allowing naval vessels to provide non-combat support for U.S. forces in the Middle East.

Many Japanese citizens, as well as U.S. Japan-watchers, want the country to scrap the constitutional ban on sending troops into combat. As the largest pro-Western democracy in Asia and a key American ally, Japan should contribute to multilateral military actions, they argue, such as the current efforts to fight terrorism in Afghanistan.

But others say the so-called Peace Constitution has served Japan well and should not be changed. "We can do other things, non-military things, to help, like give humanitarian assistance," says Mariko Tamanoi, a Japanese national teaching at the University of California at Los Angeles (UCLA).

Debate over the country's proper military role, of course, stems from Japan's aggression before and during World War II, when the Japanese attacked China, the United States and many other countries throughout Asia and the Pacific. Some observers say Japan — in stark contrast to Germany, its former wartime ally — has yet to fully atone for its wartime actions, including the Bataan death march and other unspeakable atrocities.

But Japan's greatest challenge lies not in coming to grips with its past but in charting a path into an uncertain future. In the coming decades, the Japanese will have to grapple with the economic and social costs of an aging population, as well as increasing competition from neighboring Asian countries. As Japan deals with its past, present and future, here are some of the questions being asked:

Is substantial economic reform possible under Japan's current political system?

When Koizumi swept to victory last April 26, he had assets any politician would envy — striking good looks, charisma and extensive political experience. But perhaps his greatest strength was that he came to office having convinced the public that he could change the country and end its persistent recession.

Talk of bold reforms marked Koizumi's first months. He promised to overhaul the tax system, deal with the banking crisis and control Japan's massive budget deficits. He also pledged to show no favoritism to Japan's sacred political cows — most notably farmers, the construction industry and small-business owners — and the old leaders of his own party. The tantalizing promises netted Koizumi astounding 80 percent approval ratings — a level of popularity unparalleled in the nation's modern political history.

But today, more than a year after the election, few of Koizumi's proposals have been enacted. Moreover, his approval rating has dropped since the beginning of the year by half — to 40 percent — as hopes fade that he could revive the economy and effect systemic change.

Some analysts say Koizumi's dreams of reforming Japan never really stood a chance against the country's entrenched ruling party, special interests and powerful bureaucracy. But others remain hopeful. "The Japanese political system is capable of reform and change," says Steven Vogel, an associate professor of political science at the University of California at Berkeley. "It may not be easy, but it's possible."

Koizumi's popularity gave him a golden opportunity to make meaningful changes, Vogel and others contend. "He had real room to maneuver and space to make real reforms because he was so overwhelmingly popular," he says. "But he squandered it."

Indeed, the prime minister's critics say, Koizumi could have tackled what many consider Japan's most pressing problem: the banking crisis. "With his

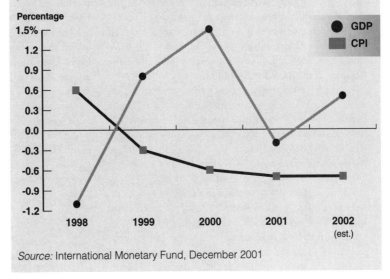

Signs of a Struggling Economy

Japan's moribund economy is reflected in the lackluster gross domestic product (GDP) and recent years of deflation, or falling prices, tracked by the consumer price index (CPI).

Percentage

Source: International Monetary Fund, December 2001

immense popularity in the beginning, Koizumi could have tried to reform the banking sector, but essentially he has done nothing about this," says Edward J. Lincoln, an expert on the Japanese economy at the Brookings Institution.

Instead, the prime minister ignored the facts and declared the banking situation much less serious than it is, according to Lincoln and others. "He basically said it wasn't that big of a problem by grossly underestimating the amount of bad loans the banks had and then said they could deal with it themselves by writing these loans off over the next three years," Lincoln says.

Koizumi's critics also say he lacks both a clear agenda and a genuine commitment to reform. "I don't think he really understands what the problems are and so doesn't know what to do to solve them," Vogel says.

"He put himself forward as 'Mister Reform' because that's what the people wanted," Lincoln says. "Beyond the rhetoric, I don't think he has concrete ideas on how to tackle the real problems facing Japan."

But others say the prime minister faces structural obstacles that would hamstring even the most dedicated or persuasive reformer. "Given the way things work in

Banking System Faces Collapse

During the 1980s, Japanese banks were among the world's largest and most profitable. But today, the industry is headed for a total meltdown.

"The banking system is on the verge of collapsing, and many of Japan's biggest banks are already technically bankrupt," says Edward J. Lincoln, an expert on the Japanese economy at the Brookings Institution.

Although estimates vary, most private analysts say the nation's banks have between $1 trillion and $2 trillion in bad loans on their books, an amount equal to between 20 percent and 40 percent of Japan's gross domestic product (GDP). By contrast, the value of bad loans during America's savings and loan crisis in the late 1980s and early '90s represented 5 percent of the U.S. GDP.

"I think [Japan's] system will begin to collapse in the next six months," predicts Adam Posen an economist at the International Institute for Economics.

But others say predictions of imminent collapse may be premature. "There are a lot of non-performing loans, and, of course, that's bad," says Miles Fletcher, a professor of history at the University of North Carolina at Chapel Hill. "But people have been talking about the dire condition of Japan's banks for almost a decade and they haven't collapsed yet."

The roots of Japan's banking crisis lie at the heart of the system that vaulted the country from a post-World War II basket case into an economic superpower. After the war, the economy was micromanaged by an army of government bureaucrats, who directed and oversaw every industrial sector.

Banks were often directed to lend money to certain parts of the economy — like steel or petrochemicals — deemed by government officials as crucial to the country's economic health. The usual factors that lending institutions consider, such as whether the loan would be put to good use or paid back, often were set aside in favor of political considerations.

---

[1] Information on the Atlantic Basin is found in Energy Information Administration, *International Energy Outlook 2002*, pp. 35-36.

Japan, it's hard to blame Koizumi," says Marie Anchordoguy, a professor of political science at the University of Washington at Seattle. "Koizumi had a mandate from the people, without the power to carry out that mandate."

Japan's problems "have nothing to do with economics but everything to do with the political system," says Frank Gibney, a professor of political science at Pomona College in Claremont, Calif. Indeed, Koizumi's biggest obstacle is his own party, which has dominated Japan since the mid-1950s, he adds.

"Members of the LDP are so tied to special interests they won't do anything to go against them, even if it's clearly in the interests of the society as a whole," agrees Tsuneo Watanabe, a Japan specialist at the Center for Strategic and International Studies (CSIS).

The special interests contribute huge amounts to keep certain Diet members in office. "Basically, each special interest has at least 20 or 30 members of the Diet, usually in the ruling party, that are in their pocket," Gibney says. "These members can be counted on to jam up any effort that threatens whatever interest is supporting them."

The construction industry ranks among the biggest offenders, Gibney says. To keep their firms busy and profitable, the industry presses the government to spend billions on unnecessary infrastructure projects every year, he says. "They pass these huge economic-stimulus bills that fund the building of roads in remote areas or bridges that are not needed," Gibney says. "But, of course, this spending ultimately does nothing to end the recession."

Moreover, because its opposition parties are usually weak, Japan essentially is a one-party state, critics point out. "There are other political parties, but there's really no practical alternative to the LDP," Anchordoguy says. "And, even so, these parties are often filled with old LDP guys."

Thus, the ruling party has little incentive to respond to the will of the people, she says. "The LDP can afford to ignore the voice of the Japanese people because they know there is nowhere else to turn."

"The system is comparable to the command economy in the old Soviet Union in the sense that market forces aren't really the major consideration," says Tsuneo Watanabe, a fellow at the Center for Strategic and International Studies.

The system worked remarkably well through the 1980s. Indeed, the Japanese model of directing the economy was often touted as the wave of the future. But government officials during the 1980s nudged banks to lend massive amounts of money to the construction and real estate sectors, which were growing almost exponentially. The almost complete collapse of real estate prices in the early 1990s left banks holding hundreds of billions in bad loans. Moreover, many other businesses that had nothing to do with construction had borrowed money to invest in real estate, widening the circle of heavily indebted businesses.

Since then, according to Lincoln, the government has largely ignored the problem. "They say that there are $300 billion in bad loans and the industry can solve its own problems," Lincoln says. But Japan's banks are beyond self-help, he contends. "Prime Minister Koizumi needs to go on TV, declare a national emergency and tell the Japanese people that everything that they've heard about the banks, including from his own government, is untrue."

Watanabe agrees, arguing that the banks should be nationalized. "They need to take over all of the banks and close the ones with too many bad loans on their books and clean up the ones that can be revived," he says. The government should finance part of the cleanup by selling the banks' assets, he says, with the rest coming from the taxpayers. In a few years, the banks would be fiscally healthy and could be resold to private investors.

The cleanup costs would surpass the hundreds of billions in taxpayer funds needed to resuscitate the banks. "Thousands of companies would be forced into bankruptcy because their loans would be called in," Lincoln says. "The construction and real estate industries would suffer the most, but retailing and manufacturing would also have some bankruptcies."

Such a radical overhaul would lead to a near doubling in unemployment, Lincoln predicts, from the current 5.5 percent rate to about 9 percent.

"It would be very painful, but in the years following [the bankruptcies] the people laid off would be reabsorbed back into more productive parts of the economy, and the rate of unemployment would drop."

Should the Japanese military be allowed to engage in combat missions overseas?

After Sept. 11, Japan joined other close U.S. allies in pledging support in the war against terrorism. But unlike the others — including Japan's former World War II ally, Germany — Japan was constitutionally blocked from providing combat forces. *

Koizumi immediately pushed a bill through the Diet that allowed the nation's armed forces to assist allies overseas — but only in a non-combat capacity. By November, three Japanese ships were in the Indian Ocean, providing logistical and supply help to the U.S. Navy.

The limits on Japan's armed forces stem from its 1947 constitution — a pacifist document drafted largely

by the United States — whose Article 9 decried war and initially prohibited Japan from even maintaining a military. But the prohibition — written when memories of World War II carnage were still fresh — soon fell victim to the realities of the Cold War. Prodded by the United States, Japan in 1954 set about creating a "self-defense force" that could help the Americans stave off Soviet aggression. Japan has since built a small, but state-of-the-art, military.

The Japanese have been chipping away at Article 9 for years. The changes often come when a world crisis like Sept. 11 creates pressure for Japanese military assistance. And yet Japanese forces are still prohibited from direct combat, to some extent because of public opposition. According to a recent poll, only 42 percent of the Japanese favor allowing their forces to join others in military actions that include combat. [4]

Many experts dismiss Article 9 as an anachronism with no real purpose except to handicap Japan's efforts to be a responsible world power. "No one wants the constitution changed to allow for military aggression," says

---

* Because the United States needed Germany to be a partner in the North Atlantic Treaty Organization, Germany was allowed to build a military after World War II, but it, too, was prohibited from deploying troops overseas. That prohibition was lifted in the mid-1990s, when Germany participated in peacekeeping operations in Bosnia. Today, Germany's chancellor can send troops into overseas combat, but only after obtaining parliament's approval.

National Debt Has Doubled

Japan's national debt has more than doubled since its lowest point in 1991. It is projected to reach more than 150 percent of the country's annual gross domestic product (GDP) in 2003 — about triple the relative size of the U.S. government's debt and by far the highest in the developed world.

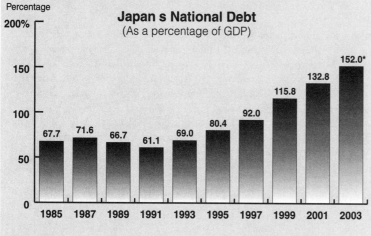

Japan s National Debt
(As a percentage of GDP)

* Projected

Source: "Statistical Annex," Organization for Economic Cooperation and Development, 2002

world," says William Breer, an expert on Japan at the CSIS. "It would give them a seat at the table that they don't have right now because they can't commit troops."

For instance, the Japanese tried to play an important role during the Persian Gulf War by contributing $13 billion to the allied effort, Breer points out. But even with such a large sum of money, "Japan was not taken seriously," he says.

Finally, opponents of Article 9 say that abolishing the ban on combat will help Japan exorcise the ghosts of its militaristic past. "If Japan could show both itself and the world that it is a responsible military power, then it would finally be able to move on from its history," says Pempel.

But proponents of the prohibition say one of the enduring lessons of World War II is that Japan should eschew the use of the military to solve problems. "The pacifist movement and the pacifist impulse is still very popular in Japan for a reason," says UCLA's Tamanoi. "Japan suffered so much during wartime, especially with the allied bombing of Tokyo and other cities. But we also remember that we bear responsibility for these tragedies because we started the conflict."

CSIS's Watanabe, "but the overseas ban on combat missions must be lifted so Japan can take her place along with the United States and other nations in peacekeeping operations and other multilateral missions."

"Japan has a moral obligation, as a prosperous nation, to help others, and that includes peacekeeping," says T. J. Pempel, director of the Institute of East Asian Studies at the University of California at Berkeley. "So in a place like East Timor in 1999, Japan should have been there with combat troops, helping to protect the East Timorese," he adds, referring to an Australia-led peacekeeping mission to the island, which was then part of Indonesia.*

Allowing Japan to send soldiers into harm's way will pay handsome geopolitical dividends, say critics of the current system. "Japan would increase its influence around the

Instead, the Japanese should focus on continuing to contribute to peacekeeping and other missions in non-military ways, Tamanoi and others say. "Japan can do many things to pull its weight in ways that don't involve the military," she says. "For example, in Afghanistan, we have sent many people to provide humanitarian assistance, such as digging wells."

Such endeavors would be much more useful than military assistance, says Miles Fletcher, a professor of history at the University of North Carolina at Chapel Hill. "They just don't really have a big military that they can project far from home, so I don't see them making much of a difference, beyond symbolism," he says.

Thus, opponents of lifting the ban insist Japan would probably gain little influence from taking on military

* Japan did send 600 non-combat soldiers to East Timor, which since has achieved independence.

missions. "Given what they could contribute, I really doubt they would all of a sudden acquire all of this new influence if they allowed their armed forces to engage in combat," Fletcher says. "They'd have to have a huge military buildup in order to make a difference.

Moreover, say supporters of Article 9, removing the ban on combat could bolster nationalist forces in Japan — a vocal minority that wants to move the country toward a more aggressive foreign and military policy. "If the nation began thinking more in military terms, you could end up encouraging the wrong people," Fletcher says. "The pacifist constitution is a check on these tendencies."

Should Japan do more to atone for its wartime past?

World leaders routinely visit memorials dedicated to their war dead, but for Japan — a nation whose only major recent war ended in defeat and ignominy — honoring the fallen can be very complicated.

Japan's major war memorial, the Yasukuni Shrine, holds the remains of more than 1 million soldiers, sailors and airman who died in service to the emperor during World War II. Honoring their sacrifice is not controversial. But the shrine also contains the remains of 12 people executed by the United States in the late 1940s as war criminals.

As a result, Yasukuni has become a litmus test for Japanese politicians. Visiting the shrine pleases the country's nationalists, who say that it is correct and natural for their leader to honor those who served the nation in war.

Prime Minister Koizumi has visited the shrine twice since taking office, once last August and then again this past April. But while the pilgrimage mollified nationalists, many Japanese criticized it as a repudiation of Japan's post-World War II pacifist policies.

The visit has also drawn fire from countries attacked by Japan before and during the war, particularly China and Korea, where millions perished. Honoring war criminals is grossly insensitive to the memories of the victims of Japan's wartime aggression, the two nations claim.

The controversy is just the tip of a larger ongoing debate in Japan and throughout much of Asia over how Japan handles its wartime past. Although Japan no longer threatens its neighbors, critics claim events like the Yasukuni visit show that the Japanese, unlike the Germans, have not fully accepted their culpability for the horrors they perpetrated before and during World War

II. "I just don't think that they've come to grips with what they did, as a nation," says the University of Washington's Anchordoguy. "It's hard to look at what they've done since then and argue that they've been accurate and responsive on this."

Anchordoguy and others point to the fact that Japanese textbooks downplay or try to mitigate the country's aggressive and brutal behavior during the period. For example, last year, the South Korean government complained that many Japanese textbooks do not even mention that tens of thousands of Asian women, many from Korea, were forced into sexual slavery by the Japanese military during World War II. [5]

"German textbooks portray the war and Germany's role in it in an accurate light," Pempel says. "But in Japan the Ministry of Education has pushed textbook publishers to 'balance' the view of the Japanese as aggressors by reminding students of such things as the fact that there was white colonialism in Asia."

Critics also dismiss apologies for the country's past aggression offered by Japan's prime ministers. "Sure, they've made these half apologies saying that they regret this or that," says the University of Washington's Anchordoguy. "They haven't really made heartfelt apologies to these countries. If they made a good faith effort at contrition, they would mollify many of these countries, like China."

But others say the critics, both Japanese and foreign, are hypersensitive. "Japan totally subjugated itself to the victorious allies, paid reparations to the countries we conquered and has been the most peaceable nation on Earth since World War II," says Yoshishisa Komori, editor-at-large at *Sankei Shimbun*, one of Tokyo's largest daily newspapers. "What else do people want?"

"I think the Japanese are getting a bit of a bum rap on this whole thing," agrees the University of North Carolina's Fletcher. "Sure, there is still a lot of ignorance and apathy among the Japanese about the war, but there's a lot of the same in the United States and elsewhere too, so we can't really use that as proof that they haven't done enough."

Japan has gone to great lengths to face its past, apologizing to every nation it invaded and paying some of those countries reparations, according to Komori, Fletcher and others. In some cases, such as China, Japanese prime ministers have apologized on more than one occasion. "They've issued all kinds of apologies to

CHRONOLOGY

Before 1850 *European efforts to influence Japan lead to 200 years of isolation.*

1543 Portuguese traders arrive in Japan, followed by the Spanish and Dutch.

1580s Trade with Europe expands. Some Japanese convert to Christianity.

1603 A military dictatorship, or shogunate, unifies the country.

1622 The shogunate drives Christianity and European commerce from Japan. For the next two centuries, Japan bars foreigners.

1850-1945 *Japan opens up to the West and quickly modernizes. Expansionism ultimately leads to war with the Allies and defeat.*

1853 Commodore Matthew C. Perry forces the Japanese to open diplomatic and trade relations with the United States. European states establish similar treaties soon after.

1868 The shogunate collapses and Emperor Meiji becomes ruler of Japan.

1894 Japan and China go to war over Korea. Japanese forces destroy the Chinese military, and Korea comes under Japanese sway.

1905 Japan defeats Russia in a war over Manchuria.

1937 Japan conquers eastern China, slaughtering thousands of civilians in Nanjing.

Dec. 7, 1941 In a surprise attack on Pearl Harbor, the Japanese destroy much of the U.S. Pacific fleet. The United States joins the war against Japan and the Axis.

1942 Japan is defeated at Midway. The Allies begin pushing Japanese forces back toward Japan.

1945 Japan surrenders after atomic bombs devastate Hiroshima and Nagasaki. U.S. troops occupy the country until 1952.

1946-1990 *Japan becomes Asia's pre-eminent economic power.*

1947 Under American guidance, the country adopts a new constitution establishing democratic institutions, guaranteeing individual rights and forswearing war.

1951 Japan signs Mutual Security Assistance Pact with the United States.

1955 The Liberal Democratic Party (LDP) is formed.

1965 The Japanese economy begins growing 11 percent a year.

1968 Japan surpasses West Germany to becomes the world's second-largest economy, behind the U.S.

1973 The Arab oil embargo hurts Japan's economy but gives Japanese automakers a toehold in the U.S. market.

1989 Japan's Nikkei index has tripled in value since 1986.

1991-Present *A decade of recession stalls Japan's economic miracle.*

1991 Nikkei stock index has lost nearly two-thirds of its value since 1989.

1993 The ruling LDP loses power for the first time since 1955. It returns to power in 1995.

April 26, 2001 Junichiro Koizumi becomes prime minister, promising reforms.

Aug. 13, 2001 Koizumi sets off controversy by visiting Yasukuni Shrine, where Japanese war dead are interred, including World War II war criminals.

Oct. 29, 2001 In response to Sept. 11 attacks on the U.S., the Diet authorizes the deployment of Japanese forces overseas in a non-combat capacity.

May 31, 2002 For the fourth time since 1996, Japan's credit rating is downgraded.

most of these countries, but it never seems to be enough," says Breer of CSIS.

According to Breer, the apologies usually fall on deaf ears because countries like China and Korea use Japan's wartime guilt to put the country's leaders on the defensive. "Other nations, especially China, are reluctant to put it to rest because it gives them political leverage over the Japanese," he says. "It gives them a wonderful political and diplomatic button to push anytime they want anything from the Japanese. So, of course, they don't want to give it up."

The country's defenders insist the Japanese are not afraid to face the grim reality of what they did. For instance, Fletcher says, Japanese historians have examined various atrocities committed by Japan during the years right before and during World War II, including the infamous "Rape of Nanjing," which led to an estimated 200,000 Chinese deaths and countless rapes and other human rights abuses. [6]

Finally, supporters say, the proof is in the pudding. Japan has turned from an aggressive, imperialist power into a tolerant democracy and model world citizen. "Japan has made such great strides, politically, economically and otherwise and they should feel proud of the kind of country they've created," Mathews of the Council on Foreign Relations says.

BACKGROUND

The Rising Sun

The Japanese have always perceived foreigners with a mixture of fascination and fear. But throughout much of Japan's history, fear — often justified — has trumped curiosity. Even today, 150 years after the country was "reopened" to the world, many Japanese still view foreigners, or *gaijin*, with trepidation.

Europeans first came to Japan in the middle of the 16th century, when competing warlords (or shoguns) ruled the country. Portuguese traders and missionaries arrived first, quickly followed by the Spanish and Dutch. By the 1580s, the newcomers were engaging in a brisk trade in silks, silver and gold, and about 150,000 Japanese — 2 percent of the population — had converted to Christianity. [7]

But in the following decades, Japan was unified under one warlord, and encroaching European influence was deemed a threat to the new state. Both Christianity and foreign commerce were suppressed. By the 1640s, Christianity was heavily proscribed and foreigners largely expelled from the country. For the next 200 years, Japan existed in virtual isolation.

By the 1840s, Western encroachments in the rest of Asia, especially China, were increasingly threatening to Japan. Its isolation ended in July 1853, when American Commodore Matthew C. Perry sailed into Tokyo Bay with four warships. The overwhelming power of the then-modern naval vessels forced the Japanese to accede to some American terms — namely the opening of diplomatic and trade relations with the United States. Soon, other European countries had wrested similar treaties from the Japanese. [8]

Partly as a result of Western incursions, an already weak Japanese shogunate began to totter and eventually collapsed. In 1868, he was replaced by an emperor, a hereditary office that had been largely symbolic until then.

The 16-year-old Emperor Meiji transformed Japan. He largely abolished the old feudal social order in favor of a more egalitarian model, legalized private ownership of land and replaced a crushing taxation system — which had kept many average Japanese in penury — with a more progressive tax structure.

Japan also instituted a crash modernization program, aimed at bringing the nation up to American and European standards. Shipyards, telegraphs, railroads and factories were built at a rapid pace. [9] The emperor also created a Western-style financial system — with a convertible currency, stock exchange and central bank — and overhauled the military using modern Western methods and weapons.

Meanwhile, the Japanese harkened back to the past to glorify the emperor. Meiji became the head of the state Shinto religion — a Japanese offshoot of Buddhism — and was declared a living god.

But peasants, vestiges of the old aristocracy and others opposed at least some of the modernization. In the 1870s several armed rebellions broke out, which were put down by the new government.

Yet the unrest led to a partial democratization of the political system and establishment of an independent judiciary. In 1889, a new constitution was enacted, creating an assembly with limited legislative powers, elected by wealthy male Japanese men. [10] Despite these reforms,

Women and Immigrants to the Rescue?

Of the many social and economic problems that Japan faces, the rapidly aging population is perhaps its most daunting challenge.

Coupled with a shrinking pool of young people, the burgeoning elderly population is "already a huge problem, and it's just going to get worse, much worse, as time goes on," says Yoshihisa Komori, editor-at-large at *Sankei Shimbum*, a daily newspaper in Tokyo.

Already, 17.2 percent of the population is over 60, one of the highest rates in the industrialized world. [1] By 2050, a whopping 42.3 percent of the population will be 60 or older. [2] By contrast, only 26.9 percent of the U.S. population will be in that age category by mid-century.

At the same time, the Japanese are having fewer children because birth rates in the Land of the Rising Sun have been dropping since the 1960s. In the 1970s, Japan's fertility rate fell below 2.1 births per woman, the number needed to maintain the population at its current size. Today, the fertility rate is a mere 1.41. [3]

Several factors explain the alarming statistics. First, the Japanese citizen lives an average of 81.5 years — longer than the residents of most other developed countries — thanks to Japan's traditionally healthy diet and excellent health-care system. [4]

Low birth rates are caused in part by a drop in the rate at which the Japanese marry. Many young Japanese women prefer to live at home with their parents and work, rather than to tie themselves to a husband and children in a country where women are still expected to be homemakers after marriage. In addition, women traditionally are expected to care for their husband's parents, as well as their own, making marriage even less attractive. The average age for marriage among Japanese women has increased from 22 in 1950 to 26 today. At the same time, the divorce rate rose 50 percent from 1990 to 1998. [5]

The impact of having fewer children and more seniors will wreak social havoc. The cost of providing the current, generous level of health care and pensions will rise dramatically, even as the number of working people shrinks. Indeed, by 2050, the ratio of working-age people to dependents — both children and the aged — is expected to approach one-to-one. [6]

If current trends continue, say experts, pension benefits will have to be cut and the retirement age increased. "Everyone understands that the current pension system will not survive," says Shinji Fukukawa, chief executive officer of the Dentsu Institute for Human Studies, a Tokyo think tank. [7] Indeed, the Japanese government is already running huge annual budget deficits, making any social-service spending increases in coming years unlikely.

Some experts say there are several ways to mitigate the coming demographic crisis. Japanese women comprise an

---

[1] The worldwide average is 6.9 percent and 14.3 present in the industrialized countries. *World Population Prospects: The 2000 Revision and World Urbanization Prospects:* The 2001 Revision, Population Division of the Department of Economic and Social Affairs of the United Nations Secretariat, http://esa.un.org/unpp/index.asp?panel=2.

[2] *Ibid.*

[3] *CIA World Factbook*, www.cia.goc/cia/publications/factbook/

[4] *Ibid.*

---

[5] Figures cited in Sonni Efron, "Japan's Demographic Shock," *Los Angeles Times*, June 25, 2002.

[6] *Ibid.*

---

most political power in Japan still rested with the emperor and a clique of elder statesmen around him.

Imperial Overreach

By the end of the 19th century, Japan had become a modern power with typical modern-power ambitions: It wanted to expand its influence and acquire territory.

Throughout the 1880s, Japan and China each maneuvered to become the dominant power in nearby Korea,

wrangling that in 1894 pushed the two countries into war.

The Sino-Japanese conflict, which lasted only nine months, resulted in China's complete defeat. In subsequent peace talks, Japan gained control of the island of Taiwan and the southern part of the northern Chinese province of Manchuria and became the primary foreign influence in Korea. [11]

However, Japan soon found itself facing another Asian power. In the years after the victory over China,

underutilized segment of the work force. Only 60 percent of single women have a job, and only half of all married women work outside of the home. "Women are still subjected to a lot of discrimination in Japanese society," says Mariko Tamanoi, an associate professor of anthropology at the University of California at Los Angeles. "To a great extent, they are still banned from business and government."

"Women are really an untapped resource in Japan," agrees Marie Anchordoguy, a professor of political science at the University of Washington. Japan needs to open up opportunities for women so they can be more productive members of society, she adds.

Yet some would say that Japan's working women are already carrying more than their share of the workload: Many married women only work part time because they are solely responsible for keeping house and caring for both the children and the elderly. [8]

The country needs to encourage employers to be more flexible with its male employees, Anchordoguy says. "We need to allow men to be able to come home and participate in family life so women are not the only caregivers," she says. "This would free up a lot of women to go out, find

Residents of a Japanese nursing home are entertained by a visiting musician. Today, 17 percent of the Japanese population is over 60 — one of the highest rates in the world. By 2050 the level is expected to reach 42.3 percent, producing what some have called a "demographic crisis of epic proportions."

work and lead their own lives."

Experts also argue that Japan cannot tackle its demographic trouble without overhauling its very restrictive immigration policy. Currently, less than 1 percent of Japan's population is foreign-born (compared to more than 10 percent in the United States), and many are ethnic Japanese from Latin America, where many emigrated in the early 20th century.

Accepting newcomers who are not ethnic cousins is difficult for the Japanese. "They've never really accepted foreigners because, unlike us, they consider themselves an ethnic group as well as a state," says Edward J. Lincoln, a senior fellow for foreign policy studies at the Brookings Institution. "As a result, you've got fourth-generation Koreans in Japan who don't yet have citizenship and are discriminated against."

According to Lincoln, to sustain the economy and support the growing numbers of retirees Japan must open its borders to new immigrants. "They need 500,000 immigrants a year if they really want to have enough workers," Lincoln says. "Will they do it? I'm not sure the Japanese are flexible enough to accept new people coming and staying."

But the Japanese don't really have a choice, says Miles Fletcher, a professor of Asian studies at the University of North Carolina at Chapel Hill. "They need these new people, so they're going to have to change their values," he says. "They're going to have to become a multiethnic society."

[7] Figures cited in "Consensus and Contraction," *The Economist*, April 18, 2002.

[8] Figures cited in *ibid.*

Russia tried to clip Japan's wings by forcing the Japanese to return to China the portion of Manchuria it had occupied and trying to mitigate Japan's influence in Korea. Tensions between the two countries boiled over in 1904 when war broke out. Unlike China — whose days as a great power were long past — Russia was a key player in world affairs. Most statesmen and diplomats predicted the Russians would crush the Japanese.

But to the shock of many, Japan beat the Russians, sinking the czar's Pacific fleet in a surprise attack in 1904. The following year, Japan also destroyed the enemy's huge Baltic fleet — which had been moved to the Pacific — leaving Russia without a sizable navy. [12] A peace treaty negotiated by the United States confirmed Japan's primacy in Korea and its influence in southern Manchuria.

The Russo-Japanese War put Japan on the geopolitical

AP Photo

U.S. Gen. Douglas MacArthur, who helped put Japan on the road to economic and political recovery after its defeat in World War II, allowed Emperor Hirohito to remain on the throne.

to set up a puppet state, Manchukuo, with the last Chinese emperor as its titular head. [13]

In the next five years, Japan built up its military might and edged closer to Nazi Germany and away from its former World War I allies — the United States, Britain and France. In 1937, Japan entered into a full-scale war with China, invading south from its Manchurian territories. The Japanese army eventually conquered much of eastern China.

World War II

In 1940, Japan officially entered World War II on the side of the Axis allies, Germany and Italy. That year, the Japanese conquered the northern half of French Indochina, greatly expanding Japan's territories in East Asia, and called for the creation of a "Greater East Asia Co-Prosperity Sphere" uniting China, Korea and other parts of the region under Japanese control. The announcement was tantamount to a public declaration of the country's territorial ambitions. [14]

But while Japan sought an Asian empire, the United States had a presence throughout much of Asia and was also a major Pacific power. As the 1930s wore on, the two countries' interests were increasingly at cross-purposes.

The U.S. government wanted to prevent Japan from becoming the dominant power in resource-rich Asia. The U.S. economy depended on raw materials from Europe's Southeast Asian colonies — like Holland's Indonesia, Britain's Malaysia and Burma and France's Vietnam and Cambodia.

Moreover, news accounts of Japanese atrocities, especially in the Chinese city of Nanjing, helped turn American public opinion against Japan. But Japan resented U.S. efforts to take the moral high ground, especially since the United States still held the Philippines and other colonies in the Pacific. Indeed, many Japanese thought their country was liberating Asia from white imperialism. Resource-poor Japan also viewed its new Asian colonies as its only avenue to economic self-sufficiency.

By 1941, relations between Japan and the United States had seriously deteriorated and talk of war was in the air. America had imposed severe economic sanctions against Japan after its invasion of China and other aggressive actions. For the Japanese, the sanctions only confirmed Japan's need for extensive colonies to ensure economic self-reliance. As the year came to a close, the Japanese decided that a bold gamble on their part was needed to resolve the standoff.

map. The Great Powers, which had dismissed the island nation as an Asian upstart, now began to treat it as an equal.

In 1914, shortly after World War I broke out, Japan declared war against Germany and occupied its interests in China and on some South Pacific islands. After the war, Japan was one of the "big five" powers at the Versailles peace conference and was given a permanent seat in the newly formed League of Nations, the precursor to the United Nations.

As Japan was integrating into the world community, ultranationalists at home were gaining strength and influence. They sought to check the growing trend toward democracy, elevate the emperor and the Shinto religion to an even higher level in society and accelerate Japan's dominance of Asia. By the early 1930s, parts of the military were openly hostile to civilian rule.

In 1932, the elected Japanese prime minister was assassinated and a new government composed of military men and nationalists took power. That same year, Japan expanded its holdings in Manchuria, using the province

On Dec. 7, 1941, the Japanese navy destroyed much of the U.S. Pacific fleet in a surprise dawn raid at its Hawaiian headquarters at Pearl Harbor. On the same day, Japanese forces invaded the Philippines as well as British and European colonies in Asia.

The Japanese did not think the attacks would lead to the total defeat of the United States. Instead, they hoped to cripple American naval power and confidence, leading to a quick armistice and peace talks on Japan's terms.

But the attack on Pearl Harbor, though a stunning surprise, accomplished none of its objectives. America's most valuable naval vessels, its aircraft carriers, survived because they were not in port when the attack occurred. Moreover, the American government and people, far from being cowed into peace talks, demanded total war against Japan.

America's economic and technological superiority made it unlikely that Japan would prevail in an all-out war. Indeed, within a year of the attack — before the full force of American industry could be felt — the U.S. military had already turned the tide. At an engagement near Midway Island in early June 1942, American naval forces destroyed much of Japan's aircraft-carrier fleet.

By 1943, the Americans were pushing Japan back toward its home islands. The following year, U.S. forces began massive bombing raids against Japan itself. The war ended on Sept. 2, 1945, less than a month after the Americans dropped atomic bombs on the Japanese cities of Hiroshima and Nagasaki, killing an estimated 190,000-210,000 people.

Some historians said that the devastation caused by these new weapons of mass destruction convinced the Japanese that any hopes of fighting to even a stalemate were unrealistic. But others said the Japanese were on the verge of surrendering and that the bombings were inhumane and purely retribution for Pearl Harbor.

Post-War Recovery

After the surrender, the United States set out to completely reorder Japanese society to prevent future military aggression. The Japanese armed forces were dissolved and all munitions factories converted to civilian use. More than 4,000 Japanese officers were found guilty of war crimes and 700 were executed. Tens of thousands of nationalist officials were purged from the government. [15]

In the interest of social stability, Emperor Hirohito was retained as the country's symbolic leader, but he was no longer to be considered divine. In addition, Shintoism was disestablished as the state religion.

U.S. forces under the command of Gen. Douglas MacArthur occupied Japan from the time of its surrender until 1952. Initially, they focused on helping the Japanese house, clothe and feed themselves. The war, and especially allied bombing, had destroyed much of the country, leaving millions homeless and hungry.

By 1947, MacArthur had imposed a new constitution on Japan, establishing a British parliamentary political system under the symbolic leadership of the emperor. The document contained many of the guarantees contained in the U.S. Constitution, such as freedom of worship and speech. In addition, it committed Japan to pacifism, renouncing war as an instrument of international relations and prohibiting the maintenance of a military. [16]

Japan signed a formal peace treaty with the United States and its allies in 1951. In it, Japan gave up all claims to China, Korea and other territories it conquered before or during the war. The treaty also acknowledged Japan's right to defend itself against foreign aggression, the first crack in the pacifist constitution ratified only four years before. [17] Just hours after accepting the peace treaty, the Japanese signed the Japan-United States Mutual Security Assistance Pact, which linked Japan's military policy to America's aims in Asia. Three years later, Japan's armed forces were resuscitated as "self-defense forces."

Meanwhile, Japan was beginning to experience some normalcy on other fronts. Elections first took place in 1947, with many parties jockeying for power. Although party squabbling and collapsing coalitions characterized the first seven years of Japanese politics, one man, Yoshida Shigeru, held office as prime minister during most of the period from 1948 until 1954.

The economy also was beginning to pick up, helped by more than $2 billion in U.S. assistance. Under the leadership of its Ministry of International Trade and Industry (MITI), Japan began rebuilding its shattered economy. Export industries — notably electronics, automobile manufacturing and steel — began to expand rapidly after receiving low-interest loans and other special treatment. This led to higher exports and greater economic growth. The Korean War (1950-1953) also helped the economy in these early years, as the United States bought large quantities of Japanese goods to help supply its armed forces stationed in nearby Korea.

By 1954, the average Japanese income had returned to its mid-1930s level. Four years later, living standards had risen another 27 percent. [18] In the 1960s, the country's GDP increased at an almost unparalleled rate. Indeed, in the second half of the decade, GDP was galloping an average of 11 percent each year. [19]

With economic growth came a new political stability. In 1955, Japan's two largest conservative parties merged to form the LDP. Several socialist parties also merged in 1955 to become the largest opposition group in the Diet. Another major party, Komeito, or Clean Government, was formed in 1964.

The LDP dominated politics during the post-war decades, largely because of Japan's ever-burgeoning economy. So long as the standard of living continued to rise, voters saw no reason to punish the ruling party.

But the LDP's popularity was based on more than just a consistently growing economy. It built rock-solid support among various sectors of Japanese society — notably farmers and small-business men — by assiduously catering to their political desires. Farmers, for instance, were protected from cheaper food imports. Small businesses likewise benefited from rules that contained the growth of large retailers.

In short, the LDP tried to be all things to as many Japanese as it could — a particularly effective formula in a consensus-driven country like Japan. Plus, the party's policies were producing a harmonious and prosperous society. Indeed, by the 1980s, Japan was enjoying a level of prosperity fast becoming the envy of the world. Even the United States began to worry about being outpaced by its protégé.

Economic Dynamo

On almost every economic front, the Japanese were beating their American and European competitors. Its electronic companies, including Sony and Matsushita (owner of the Panasonic brand) put most competitors out of business and produced the bulk of the world's consumer electronics goods, such as televisions, stereos and VCRs. Rising oil prices in the 1970s gave Japanese automakers like Toyota and Honda — which specialized in small, fuel-efficient cars — a foothold in the U.S. market, which Japan exploited by marketing reliable and increasingly upscale cars. Japanese steel, ships and memory chips also dominated world markets.

In addition, Japanese manufacturing practices became the world's quality standard, making their products much sought-after, even as the country's home market was protected from outside competition. Companies like Sony and Toyota reaped huge profits.

Export success overseas and protected markets at home drove the stock and real estate markets through the roof. In the four years from 1986 to 1989, the Nikkei index of leading stocks tripled in value, rising from 13,000 to 39,000. [20] Meanwhile, property values rose so high that the imperial palace and grounds in downtown Tokyo were worth more than all the real estate in California.

But by the end of 1989, the Japanese miracle began to grind to a halt. Western nations, led by the United States, were in a recession. New, low-cost competitors from South Korea and other Asian countries were taking market share and profits away from Japanese companies. The result was a spiral into recession.

With profits down, the Nikkei plunged, losing 65 percent of its value in a year and a half. [21] Since the stock market boom had fueled the real estate boom, land prices began to plummet. Soon, many developers and speculators were bankrupt, leaving the country's banking system with more than $1 trillion in bad loans. As a result, banks stopped lending, further adding to the economy's woes.

The LDP tried to bring the country out of recession by enacting massive new public-spending programs aimed at jump-starting the economy. But the efforts only led to brief spurts of economic growth.

By 1993, the Japanese were frustrated with the LDP's inability to end the recession. The party's standing dropped further when LDP bigwigs were implicated in several damning bribery scandals. Voters turned to opposition groups, including new parties formed by LDP defectors. By August, a seven-party coalition was running the country — the first non-LDP government since its formation in 1955.

But the newcomers also proved ineffective. During the next two and a half years, the coalition devoted most of its energies to political infighting and did not address the nation's problems. In 1996, the LDP retook power under the leadership of the charismatic Hashimoto Ryutaro.

Hashimoto promised to clean up the banking system and restore Japan's economic health. But his policies — which included more spending and a tax cut to stimulate the economy — also proved ineffective. [22]

While 1998 election losses did not oust the LDP, disappointment within the party led to Hashimoto's resig-

Should Japan revise its constitution to allow Japanese forces to engage in combat missions?

YES Ted Galen Carpenter
Vice president, defense and foreign policy studies, Cato Institute

Written for the CQ Researcher, July 2002

Article 9, the "pacifist clause" in Japan's constitution, has outlived whatever usefulness it may have had when it was adopted at the insistence of the United States after World War II.

Japan is now the only major power that does not play a security role commensurate with its political and economic status. Even Germany, the other principal defeated power in World War II, has sent peacekeeping troops to the Balkans and Afghanistan. Tokyo cannot forever limit its security role to cheerleading for U.S. military exertions.

A more vigorous Japanese role in East Asia is essential. North Korea poses a significant security problem, and there are concerns about China's rising power and ambitions. A militarily capable, assertive Japan is indispensable for stability and an effective balance of power. Otherwise, the United States ends up shouldering all of the region's security burdens by default.

In recent years, Japan has moved away from a rigid interpretation of Article 9. The 1997 revisions to the defense guidelines of the U.S.-Japanese alliance allowed Japan's Self-Defense Forces (SDF) to help U.S. forces repel a security threat in the western Pacific. Four years later, the Diet adopted anti-terrorism legislation allowing the SDF to play a similar role outside the western Pacific theater.

But one must not overstate the significance of those mildly encouraging changes. In both cases, the SDF is only empowered to provide non-lethal, logistical support to U.S. forces — not engage in combat operations — unless Japan itself is under attack. That restriction needs to end.

Many argue that if Japan played a more active military role it would upset its East Asian neighbors, who still remember the outrages committed by imperial Japan in the 1930s and '40s. But that argument oversimplifies reality.

Several of Japan's neighbors -including Australia, Singapore, Taiwan and the Philippines — have signaled unmistakably in recent years that they would accept, perhaps even welcome, a more assertive Japan to balance China's growing power.

It is time for Japan to fully rejoin the ranks of the great powers, and the United States must help with that transition. Washington should make it clear to Japan and to its neighbors that it would welcome the repeal of Article 9.

NO David Krieger
President, Nuclear Age Peace Foundation

Written for the CQ Researcher, July 2002

Article 9 of the Japanese constitution is a statement of intent and limitation, highly unusual in the constitution of any state and particularly in that of a powerful nation such as Japan. In it, Japan renounces war as a "sovereign right" and further renounces "the threat or use of force as a means of settling disputes."

This article was accepted by Japanese leaders after World War II under pressure from the occupying U.S. forces. But for more than 50 years Japan has retained and supported this constitutional provision against internal nationalist forces and, ironically, against pressure from the United States, which wants Japan to accept more military responsibility in its alliance with the United States.

The intent of Article 9 was to transform Japan from a warlike, aggressor nation into a peaceful nation. In this sense, the article has been very successful. For more than half a century — despite international pressure — Japan has forsworn participation in war.

However, it has developed extremely powerful self-defense forces and sent Self-Defense Force ships to the Indian Ocean to provide refueling and other logistical support to British and U.S. forces in the war in Afghanistan.

Article 9 conforms to international law as set forth in the United Nations Charter. If all states relied only on self-defense forces and adopted their own version of Article 9, war would be effectively abolished as a sovereign right. This would clearly be a step forward in a world of increasingly powerful and destructive weapons.

As the first nation to experience the effects of nuclear weapons, Japan has a special responsibility to be a messenger to the world of the need to end the Nuclear Age. Article 9 is, in part, a way of fulfilling this responsibility.

Article 9 is helping to establish a new international norm necessary to assure the continuation of civilization. Should Japan amend Article 9 to allow it to participate in multilateral military missions, including combat duty, it would signal to the world that the renunciation of war and force is not practical and has failed.

The Japanese people need to hold to the high ideals of their constitution and help lead the world out of the Nuclear Age and into a new age, in which conflicts are settled without force. Japan's, or any nation's, status as a great nation need not rest on military prowess.

Unemployment Doubles

Japan's unemployment rate has doubled during the nation's long recession, a devastating development in a country where lifetime employment with a single firm is central to the social compact.

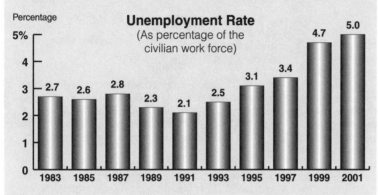

Source: Organization for Economic Cooperation and Development, 2002.

nation and the elevation of several caretaker prime ministers. During the tenure of the second leader, Mori Yoshiro, the LDP's popularity dropped to new lows.

In March 2001, Mori resigned, and the party searched for a new leader. For a time, it looked as though Hashimoto might make a political comeback, but Koizumi, who had the support of the party's rank and file, beat him, promising "a total reversal of the past." [23]

CURRENT SITUATION

An Important Friendship

When the last U.S. troops left Japan in 1952, the two countries had already signed a mutual-security treaty charging America with protecting Japan in case of attack. In exchange, the Japanese promised to allow U.S. military bases in the country.

In the ensuing decades, Japan's security policy remained tied to the American military. The new Japanese Self-Defense Force essentially supplemented the U.S. defense of the country.

Although the military relationship between the two countries has been generally good, tensions exist. The United States routinely prods Japan to beef up its armed

forces, especially when U.S. military power is stretched thin, such as during the 1991 Persian Gulf War. And the Japanese have been troubled by the occasional misconduct of American servicemen, as occurred in 1995 when three U.S. Marines were convicted of gang-raping a teenager on the island of Okinawa, where most U.S. forces are based.

Still, most experts agree that security relations between the two remain on a sound footing. "Military relations between the two countries are very strong," the University of California's Pempel says. "I see no real threat to that in the near future."

Indeed, in 1996, when the relationship was last subjected to a thorough mutual review, both countries declared it in robust health. "The U.S. and Japan essentially said they were on the same page militarily and that they were happy with the way things were going," Pempel says.

More recently, the U.S. war on terrorism has prompted the Japanese government to expand its security cooperation with the United States. Besides allowing Japanese forces to support U.S. forces in the Indian Ocean near Afghanistan, the Diet also allowed the country's military to protect U.S. forces in Japan. "There's no question that the events of Sept. 11 have propelled Japan toward a more active security role with the United States," says Vogel, of the University of California. "And of course that has pleased the Americans."

On economic matters, relations between the two countries have been on a less secure footing. During the 1980s, American politicians and others worried that an increasingly successful Japan would eventually dominate the U.S. economy. The Japanese purchase of American icons like Columbia Studios and New York's Rockefeller Center fed fears that "Japan Inc." — as the country was often called — would supplant America as the world's pre-eminent economic power. Moreover, as Japanese companies were aggressively exporting products and investing overseas, the Japanese prevented foreign competition in their home market. U.S. producers of goods ranging from rice and apples to automobiles were prevented from making significant inroads into the Japanese market.

Today, economic tensions between the two nations remain, but for very different reasons. No longer the economic juggernaut it was in the 1980s, Japan has seen its economic prospects sink so low that the United States is now chiding the government for not making its economy more competitive.

Other issues also cause tension. For instance, the Bush administration's abrogation of both the Kyoto Protocol on Global Warming and the Anti-Ballistic Missile (ABM) Treaty have been unpopular in Japan. [24]

Even the vaunted security alliance may be buffeted in the coming decade, as the war against terrorism inevitably leads the United States to ask Japan to carry a greater share of the responsibility for regional defense. "I think things will be fine in the short term, because of the momentum in Japan created by Sept. 11," Vogel says. But, he adds, trouble may come when America looks to Japan to significantly enhance its military capability to better supplement American power in the region.

"Because of politics and the peace constitution, I'm not sure the Japanese will want to upgrade their forces and expand their military's mission," he says. "This could cause a real increase in tension."

Economic Trouble

On May 31, Japan's creditworthiness was downgraded two levels by Moody's, an influential U.S. credit-rating firm. The rating measures a country's ability to pay its debts.

While the new A2 rating implies that Japan is still likely to pay back the money its government has borrowed, it puts the creditworthiness of the world's second-largest economy far below most other advanced economies and on par with Botswana and Estonia. [25]

The downgrade was the fourth endured by Japan since 1998 and reflects the size of the government's debt, now nearly triple that of the United States. But the lower rating is also a sign of the economy's fundamental weakness.

The Japanese now refer to the 1990s as the "lost decade," when the country's once-mighty economy was mostly contracting, with only short bursts of growth. The decade before had been the nation's best, with high corporate profits and ever-rising stock and real estate markets.

But in the early 1990s, the bubble burst. The Nikkei index has lost three-quarters of its value since its 1988 high. [26] The real estate market has fallen even further:

Commercial real estate prices in Japan's six biggest cities have dropped 84 percent since 1991. [27]

The current decade also may be lost, some economists say. Last year, the country's economy shrank by 1.9 percent. In the first quarter of 2002, GDP decreased by a whopping 4.8 percent. [28] Even though the economy is expected to grow about 1.3 percent in 2003, few see an end to the overall trend toward recession.

The economic gloom can be puzzling to Americans, who see Japanese corporations like Sony, Toyota and Honda as world leaders in manufacturing. However, the successful multinationals produce less than 10 percent of Japan's economic output.

"The other 90 percent has some bright spots — like the convenience-store sector, which is very competitive — but, overall, most of the country's business sectors are not competitive at all," says the Brookings Institution's Lincoln. "Many industries in Japan — like the construction, real estate, agricultural and hotel sectors — have been made inefficient by government protection and coddling."

That "protection and coddling" include trade barriers and what Lincoln calls government-subsidized "informal cartels" that allow companies to edge out even domestic competitors.

Deflation, another major problem facing Japan, has caused prices for goods and services to drop from 1 to 2 percent a year over the last three years, a situation that creates difficulties for everyone. Deflation, caused by a shortage of currency in circulation, causes prices to fall and reduces the average person's assets. Workers suffer because employers ultimately cut wages, even as the cost of servicing a mortgage or other consumer debt rises because money is worth more. [29]

Businesses suffer, too. "Companies get less for the goods and services they provide," says Posen of the International Institute for Economics. "At the same time, they may have debt payments to make or wage agreements with unions that prevent them from cutting wages." To stay afloat, some businesses are forced to cut back and some "just go under," he says.

According to Posen, deflation has been caused in part by the Bank of Japan's refusal to print more currency and create inflation. The central bank's unwillingness to act is based on the belief that sparking even mild inflation will ease pressure on the government to tackle the country's greatest short-term problem: the huge number of bad loans at the nation's banks.

"The cost of servicing debt would decrease, providing some breathing room for the banks," Posen says. "The [central] bank is playing a game of chicken with the government, saying it won't deal with the deflation problem until the government begins to take on the bad-loan crisis at the banks."

But Posen thinks the central bank's policy is misguided. "Ignoring one problem isn't a way to solve another," he says.

Still, there is some good news amid the gloom. Thanks to the weaker yen, Japanese exports are more attractive overseas, particularly in America, which may be coming out of its own recession. Thus, profits for Japanese manufacturers are expected to grow by an astonishing 43 percent this year. [30]

OUTLOOK

Epic Crisis Ahead?

History teaches that Japan is capable of instituting rapid change, from its breakneck industrialization in the middle of the 19th century to the miraculous recovery from devastation in the middle of the 20th. But experts are divided over whether Japan can emerge from its current economic and social slump anytime soon.

Some, like the University of California's Pempel are "increasingly pessimistic. They have these huge economic problems," he says, "but, they show absolutely no sign of even starting to deal with them anytime soon."

"It will be at least a decade before they've sorted out the structural problems with their economy," says Brookings' Lincoln. "And even if they manage to eventually deal with their economy in the next 10 years, they face a demographic crisis of epic proportions."

Many say the projected graying of Japan's population is the next big challenge casting a long shadow over the future. "Their population is going to be falling and aging at the same time," says Lincoln. "This just doesn't bode well for Japan remaining a vibrant economic force in the world."

Moreover, the pessimists say, the country lacks a tradition of encouraging entrepreneurial risk-taking that produces new industries that could help create new wealth. "Japan is behind and it's falling further behind in information technology and biotechnology," Pempel says, "because they don't push this entrepreneurial spirit like we do in the United States.

Moreover, says UCLA's Tamanoi, Japanese society is not well positioned to embrace globalization. "It's a very closed society, with a difficult language and complicated social rules and mores," she says. "It just doesn't seem like it will fit easily into the global economy."

But others see Japan's long-term future as quite bright. "Japan is going to come back and come back strong," the University of California's Vogel says. "The next few years are going to be very tough as they sort out their economic troubles — especially the banks. But afterwards, they will be strong again."

Vogel and others are optimistic because, for all its recent troubles, Japan is still, at its heart, a strong and competitive country. "All of the fundamentals are still there," says Mathews of the Council on Foreign Relations. "They have a hard-working, highly educated populace and some of the world's most competitive companies. There's no reason why they shouldn't bounce back."

According to Mathews, Japan is transitioning from its past reliance on manufacturing to new, service-oriented industries, as the United States did in the 1970s and '80s. "The future for Japan lies in industries like financial services," he says. "No other country in Asia has anything like the capital that Japan does. It will rely on these kinds of industries to stoke its prosperity."

NOTES

1. "Out of Site, Out of Mind," *Yomiuri Shimbun*, May 28, 2002.

2. Figure cited in "Crime Rate in Japan on the Rise," *The Globe and Mail*, Dec. 22, 2001.

3. For background, see Christopher Conte, "Deflation Fears," *The CQ Researcher*, Feb. 13, 1998, pp. 121-144.

4. Figure cited in "Poll Shows 57 Percent Favor Revision of Constitution," *The Yomiuri Shimbun*, April 5, 2002.

5. "Japan's Sins of Omission," *The Economist*, April 14, 2001.

6. James L. McClain, *Japan: A Modern History* (2002), p. 449.

7. Robert Dolan and Robert Worden (eds.), *Japan: A Country Study* (1992), p. 24.

8. Richard Tames, *A Traveller's History of Japan* (1993), pp. 115-117.

9. Marius B. Jansen, *The Making of Modern Japan* (2000), p. 374.

10. *Ibid.*, pp. 389-395.

11. Louis G. Perez, *The History of Japan* (1998), p. 120.

12. Jansen, *op. cit.*, p. 440.

13. *Ibid.*, p. 586.

14. *Ibid.*, p. 633.

15. Dolan and Worden, *op. cit.*, p. 60.

16. *Ibid.*, pp. 306-318.

17. McClain, *op. cit.*, pp. 557-558.

18. Figures cited in Tames, *op. cit.*, pp. 180-181.

19. Figures cited in *ibid.*, p. 184.

20. Figures cited in McClain, *op. cit.*, p. 601.

21. *Ibid.*

22. *Ibid.*, pp. 604-605.

23. Quoted in "A New Face for Japan," *The Economist*, April 26, 2001.

24. For background, see Mary H. Cooper, "Transatlantic Tensions," *The CQ Researcher*, July 13, 2001, pp. 553-576.

25. Jason Singer, "Moody's Downgrades Japan's Credit Rating by Two Levels to A2," *The Wall Street Journal*, June 3, 2002.

26. John Grimon, "What Ails Japan?" *The Economist*, April 18, 2002.

27. *Ibid.*

28. Conte, *op. cit.*

29. Figures cited in "Economic and Financial Indicators," *The Economist*, June 1, 2002.

30. "The Bottom Line," *The Economist*, April 27, 2002.

BIBLIOGRAPHY

Books

Jansen, Marius B., *The Making of Modern Japan*, Harvard University Press, 2000.
An emeritus professor of Japanese history at Princeton University presents a detailed chronicle of Japanese history from 1600 to the present, emphasizing the various forces working for and against modernizing the country through four centuries.

McClain, James, *A Modern History of Japan*, W.W. Norton, 2002.
A professor of history at Brown University describes the panorama of Japanese history from the beginning of the 17th century to the present. His chronicle of the country's political and social transformation after World War II is particularly clear and insightful.

Tames, Richard, *A Traveller's History of Japan*, Interlink Books, 1993.
A prolific author of books on Japan has written an engaging, concise history of the Japanese.

Articles

Brooke, James, "Japan Braces for a 'Designed in China World,'" *The New York Times*, April 21, 2002, p. A1.
No longer just a venue for cheap manufactures, China is now a haven in Asia for high-technology research and development, eroding Japan's last real competitive advantage in the region.

Efron, Sonni, "Japan's Demographic Shock," *Los Angeles Times*, June 25, 2002, p. A12.
The article examines the implications for Japan of its rising elderly population and looks at options, like increasing immigration, which could help mitigate the cost of caring for increasing numbers of seniors.

Gibney, Frank, "Koizumi Spirals Down," *Los Angeles Times*, Feb. 11, 2002, p. B11.
A professor of political science at Pomona College criticizes Prime Minister Junichiro Koizumi for being indecisive and not pursuing reform vigorously enough.

Grimond, John, "What Ails Japan?" *The Economist*, April 18, 2002.
The British magazine's most recent survey on Japan explores how the country's political and economic systems are failing the Japanese. The author concludes that Japan may have to endure a catastrophe even greater than the banking crisis before both the people and the political elites take the kinds of steps needed to overhaul the country.

Kruger, David, "Despite Failures, Japan's Koizumi Revives Office," *The Wall Street Journal*, April 30, 2002, p. A15.

Kruger argues that although Prime Minister Junichiro Koizumi has failed to push through his promised reforms, he has made some important changes, including strengthening the office of prime minister and expanding the role of Japan's military since the Sept. 11 terrorist attacks on the United States.

Landers, Peter, Jason Singer and Phred Dvorak, "Silver Lining? Amid Japan's Gloom, Corporate Overhauls Offer Hints of Revival," *The Wall Street Journal*, Feb. 21, 2002, p. A1.
As politicians dither on economic reform, some Japanese companies are trying to deal with the near-continuous recession by laying off workers and redirecting other employees to more productive operations.

"The Politics of Nationalism," *The Economist*, April 25, 2002.
The article describes Prime Minister Junichiro Koizumi's April visit to the Yasukuni Shrine, where Japanese war criminals are interred along with other World War II servicemen.

Struck, Doug, and Kathryn Tolbert, "In Japan, a Growing Gap Between Haves and Have-Nots," *The Washington Post*, Jan. 4, 2002, p. A22.
According to Struck and Tolbert, "Japan's unrelenting decade-long recession is increasingly . . . exposing a host of social strains and removing the mythical cloak of equality."

Williams, Michael, and Phred Dvorak, "Japan Seethes Over Comparisons to Botswana," *The Wall Street Journal*, May 13, 2002, p. C1.
The recent downgrading of Japan's creditworthiness to the level of Botswana has touched off a firestorm of anger and protest in the country.

Reports

Hwang, Balbina, and Brett Shaefer, "Assessing the Looming Financial Crisis in Japan" *The Heritage Foundation*, March 26, 2002.
Two Heritage Foundation analysts urge the United States to push Japan to reform its banking sector. Failure to take action, they say, could lead to a financial meltdown that ultimately drags the world economy into recession.

For More Information

Center for Strategic and International Studies, 1800 K St., N.W., Suite 400, Washington, DC 20006; (202) 887-0200; www.csis.org. Provides information on global issues, including Japan's role in the world economy and its security relationship with the United States.

Council on Foreign Relations, 58 East 68th St., New York, NY 10021; (212) 434-9400; www.cfr.org. Generates ideas and educates the public about foreign policy.

Institute of East Asian Studies, University of California at Berkeley, 2223 Fulton St., Suite 2318, Berkeley, CA 94720-2318; (510) 642-2809; ieas.berkeley.edu. Offers a broad range of courses and programs on East Asia and hosts the Center for Japanese Studies.

Institute of International Economics, 1750 Massachusetts Ave., N.W., Washington, DC 20036-1903; (202) 328-9000; www.iie.org. A private, nonprofit, nonpartisan research institution devoted to the study of international economic policy, including that of Japan and East Asia.

8

Foreign Aid After Sept. 11

Mary H. Cooper

Women wait to receive food aid from the U.N. in December 2001 in Kabul, Afghanistan. The nation has been devastated by earthquakes, a three-year drought and 23 years of war — including six months of U.S. bombing to rout terrorists. The U.S. and other rich nations pledged in January to provide $4.5 billion in aid to the nation of 23 million people.

From *The CQ Researcher,*
April 26, 2002.

Most would agree that Afghanistan needs help. Devastating earthquakes, a three-year drought, Taliban oppression and 23 years of war — including six months of U.S. bombing to rout out terrorists — have reduced much of the country to rubble.

The United States and other rich nations pledged in January to provide $4.5 billion in aid to the landlocked country of 23 million people. "We will help the new Afghan government provide the security that is the foundation for peace," President Bush told Interim Afghan Prime Minister Hamid Karzai at a joint news conference in the White House Rose Garden on Jan. 28. "The United States will continue to be a friend to the Afghan people in all the challenges that lie ahead."

But almost three months later, Karzai is still waiting. Only about $360 million of the promised aid has arrived from the United States and other donors. Meanwhile, Karzai's government is relying on outside help to pay salaries for teachers and doctors, plant crops and rebuild gutted roads, bridges and buildings. [1]

"If the international community is really serious in seeing Afghanistan secure, it must help [us] begin reconstruction of infrastructure projects — the first of which is roads," Karzai said on April 10. But, he added, "When we speak about these projects, no one is interested." [2]

Although Afghanistan is in the spotlight these days, it is hardly the only nation needing assistance. Over the past decade of unprecedented prosperity in the United States and other industrialized countries, the gap between the world's wealthiest nations and its poorest has widened relentlessly. Today, about half the world's pop-

Aid Is Sliver of U.S. Budget Pie

Contrary to popular perception, U.S. aid to other countries makes up a tiny slice — less than 1 percent — of overall U.S. government expenditures. Moreover, only a fraction of that amount gets into the hands of the poor. According to the Congressional Research Service, foreign aid recipients spend 87 percent of military aid and 90 percent of food aid purchasing U.S. goods and services.

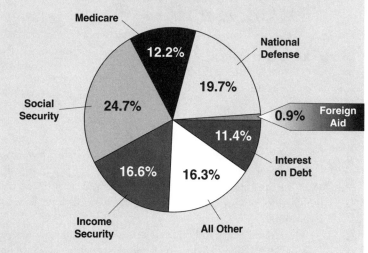

Bush Administration Budget Requests, 2003

- Medicare: 12.2%
- National Defense: 19.7%
- Foreign Aid: 0.9%
- Interest on Debt: 11.4%
- All Other: 16.3%
- Income Security: 16.6%
- Social Security: 24.7%

Note: Does not add to 100% due to omissions of minor expenditures.

Source: Congressional Research Service

Foreign aid, or official development assistance (ODA), has gotten something of a bad reputation in the United States, for a variety of reasons. For one thing, during the Cold War a large portion of foreign aid was used for geopolitical and strategic purposes — primarily to halt the spread of communism. As a result, U.S. tax dollars often ended up lining the pockets of corrupt but pro-U.S. dictators who often spent it on lavish lifestyles or stashed millions in Swiss bank accounts.

In the 1980s, for example, the United States sent large sums of aid to Somalia, Sudan and Liberia. "It was going to those countries to fight communism, and the people at the top of the system were ruthless and corrupt," says David Beckmann, president of Bread for the World, a Christian, grass-roots advocacy network that fights hunger. "That money may have helped fight the Cold War, but it didn't help poor people."

Indeed, many projects failed economically, or wreaked environmental havoc.

ulation lives on less than $2 a day, according to the World Bank. One person in six — about a billion people — lives on less than $1 a day. [3]

As the gap was widening, the levels of foreign aid donated to developing countries for roads, schools, clinics and economic development have actually decreased in recent years. Since peaking at $65.5 billion in 1990, aid has shrunk by 20 percent, falling to $53.1 billion in 2000. [4] Although the United States, the world's richest country, gives the second-largest dollar amount in foreign aid, after Japan, it actually gives less than any other industrialized country when measured as a portion of its economic output — just 0.1 percent of gross national product (GNP). (*See chart, p. 167.*) By contrast, the United States spent 20 times that much — 2 percent of GNP — to help rebuild postwar Europe under the Marshall Plan. [5]

Despite the failures and questionable criteria for targeting assistance, foreign aid advocates cite stunning examples of how it has improved living standards in much of the developing world.

"Since 1960, life expectancy in poor countries has increased 20 years — to the mid-60's — and adult illiteracy has dropped by more than half," writes Nicholas H. Stern, chief economist and senior vice president for development economics at the World Bank. In addition, he points out, economic growth rates in poor countries are up, and the number of people in extreme poverty is falling. "Of course, there have been failures as well as success, and too many countries, particularly in sub-Saharan Africa, have been left out," he writes. "Yet the overall picture of development is surely one of success." [6]

Some analysts sense that public support for foreign aid in the United States has grown since the Sept. 11 ter-

Israel and Egypt Get Most U.S. Aid

The United States is giving more than $4.5 billion in military and economic aid to Israel and Egypt this year — about 30 percent of America's $15.3 billion aid program (bar graph). More than half of all U.S. aid went to the Middle East in fiscal 2000, and less than one-third went to Africa and Eastern Europe (circle graph).

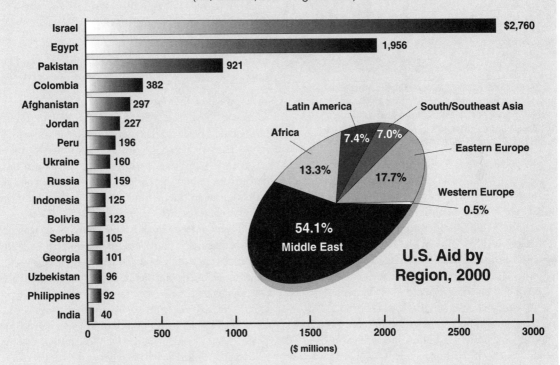

Leading Recipients of U.S. Foreign Aid, 2002
(in $ millions, excluding food aid)

Country	$ millions
Israel	$2,760
Egypt	1,956
Pakistan	921
Colombia	382
Afghanistan	297
Jordan	227
Peru	196
Ukraine	160
Russia	159
Indonesia	125
Bolivia	123
Serbia	105
Georgia	101
Uzbekistan	96
Philippines	92
India	40

U.S. Aid by Region, 2000

- Africa 13.3%
- Latin America 7.4%
- South/Southeast Asia 7.0%
- Eastern Europe 17.7%
- Western Europe 0.5%
- Middle East 54.1%

Sources: World Bank, "World Development Report 2000" (pie chart); Congressional Research Service (bar graph)

rorist attacks on New York City and the Pentagon. [7] "Polling has always shown that most Americans don't like the idea of foreign assistance," says Rep. Jim Kolbe, R-Ariz., chairman of the House Appropriations Subcommittee on Foreign Operations, which oversees the U.S. foreign aid budget. "But since Sept. 11, people understand that foreign assistance is a vital piece of the whole budget, and there's more willingness to increase spending on foreign assistance."

President Bush recently proposed increasing U.S. foreign aid by $5 billion by the year 2006, to be kept in a special account separate from current development assis-

tance allocations of about $11 billion. The new aid would be limited to countries that prove they are reforming their economies and ending corruption — part of a worldwide trend among donor countries to demand more so-called transparency, or proof that aid dollars are being used appropriately and effectively.

"The goal is to provide people in developing nations the tools they need to seize the opportunities of the global economy," Bush said in announcing the proposed increase on March 14. "In return for this additional commitment, we expect nations to adopt the reforms and policies that make development effective and lasting."

U.S. aid to Israel has become increasingly controversial, as a sign held by a Palestinian demonstrator makes clear at an Israeli Army checkpoint outside Jerusalem in March 2001. Israel has been the leading recipient of U.S. aid for many years and received $2.7 billion in economic and military aid this year.

The following week, at a United Nations-sponsored global development conference held in Monterrey, Mexico, Bush and 50 other heads of state endorsed the U.N.'s so-called Millennium Development goals of halving world poverty by 2015, as well as combating AIDS and other diseases, improving literacy, women's rights, maternal and child health and environmental quality. The World Bank estimates that it will cost up to $60 billion a year in additional foreign aid to meet those goals.

Bush's proposed $5 billion increase in foreign aid spending pales when compared to his $369 billion request for defense spending for next year, an increase of $38 billion, or 11 percent, over the previous year. But given the low current allocations for aid programs, foreign aid advocates welcome the president's announcement.

"We applaud the president for making this new commitment to overseas development assistance," says Mary McClymont, president of InterAction, an alliance of about 160 U.S.-based humanitarian non-governmental organizations (NGOs) that work to alleviate poverty in some 100 countries. "It obviously signals the administration's recognition of the importance of addressing poverty, disease and hunger around the world, and we see it as a significant step forward."

But even if Congress approves the president's foreign aid boost, the United States has a long way to go before meeting the Millennium Development goals and a U.N.

plea for donor nations to spend the equivalent of 0.7 percent of GNP on foreign aid.

"Bush's request would probably bring us to something like 0.2 percent of GNP," Kolbe says. "And that's still way, way behind where the rest of the world thinks we ought to be. But it would be the first time we would have seen more than five years of sustained increases in the foreign assistance budget."

As Congress debates the president's proposal to increase U.S. aid, these are some of the issues lawmakers will consider:

Would boosting U.S. foreign aid help to combat terrorism?

In the wake of the terrorist attacks of Sept. 11, many Americans have asked whether changes in U.S. foreign policy could deter similar aggression in the future. The immediate policy response was President Bush's "war on terrorism" — military action in Afghanistan to hunt down those responsible for planning the attacks and the formation of an international coalition of governments willing to beef up their counterterrorism policies.

But some analysts say that more should be done to prevent what they see as the root causes of terrorism — poverty, hunger, illiteracy and substandard living conditions — that foment resentment of America and its unequaled wealth. Development assistance, they say, is the most effective policy tool available to improve those conditions. "We will not create a safer world with bombs or brigades alone," said World Bank President James D. Wolfensohn, who has called on the United States and other wealthy donor nations to double their foreign aid contributions. While poverty does not necessarily lead to violence, he said, it can "provide a breeding ground for the ideas and actions of those who promote conflict and terror." [8]

"There is a very strong correlation between instability, armed conflict and terrorism on one hand, and poverty and hunger on the other," says Per Pinstrup-Andersen, director general of the International Food Policy Institute. "Poor people are much more likely to seek solutions that involve conflict, and conflict is quite likely to result in poverty and hunger."

The correlation between poverty and conflict has only strengthened with the globalization of information via television, cinema and other media, he says. "People living in hunger, poverty and hopelessness can now see how the rest of the world lives," he says. "We cannot have stability in this world simply by sending in the military when the poverty is so widespread and so severe, and when the inequalities are greater than they ever have been in human history."

However, skeptics point out that none of the 19 suspects involved in last fall's attacks fit the profile of typical foreign aid beneficiaries. They were neither poor nor illiterate, and, in fact, most were the children of middle-class professionals. Their leader, Osama bin Laden, whose whereabouts remain unknown, was a wealthy Saudi businessman who enjoyed close links to the royal family until he was expelled from Saudi Arabia for his anti-government activities.

"The assertion that terrorism is fomented by poverty is a really superficial, materialist assertion," says Nicholas N. Eberstadt, a political economist at the American Enterprise Institute (AEI). "The last time I looked, Costa Rica didn't have a terrorism problem, and Northern Ireland did, yet Costa Rica is poorer than Northern Ireland. There are many reasons to be in favor of poverty alleviation, but the assertion that it is anti-terror medicine is just the latest of the Hydra-headed excuses for development assistance."

A more plausible explanation for anti-American, Islamic fundamentalist terrorism, Eberstadt says, has to do with the nature of the education systems and political leadership in much of the Arab world. "In closed, radicalized education systems or in un-free countries' state propaganda machines, there is an extraordinary amount of anti-Israel, anti-U.S., anti-West invective. There is a more immediate connection between cohorts of would-be terror operatives and this perverse educational function than between them and life expectancy, infant mortality, literacy and per-capita income."

But there appears to be a growing consensus that foreign aid is just as essential an instrument of national-security policy as military forces, diplomacy and intelligence-gathering. "You can't think of these as separate little entities, as though they were somehow unrelated to each other," Kolbe says. "Frequently, we can use the foreign-assistance budget as a first line of defense so we don't have to send in the troops. Had we been successful politically in staying involved in Afghanistan in the 1990s, perhaps a strong foreign-assistance program there might have meant the Taliban wouldn't have come to power, and that might have meant there wouldn't have been such a friendly home for the al Qaeda terrorists."

Bono, lead singer of the Irish group U2, meets President Bush at the Inter-American Development Bank in Washington, D.C., last March, where Bush announced he was asking Congress to increase U.S. foreign aid by $5 billion. The rock superstar has become a leading advocate of aid to poor nations.

This view unites Democrats who have long supported foreign aid with Republicans who have recently altered their traditional views that aid is a waste of taxpayers' money. For example, Senate Select Intelligence Committee Chairman Richard C. Shelby, R-Ala., recently called for a new Marshall Plan to help combat terrorism, not only in Afghanistan but also throughout Central Asia, including India and Pakistan. [9] "I call it helping people fight the roots of terrorism, fight what causes people, out of desperation, to listen to messages they wouldn't ordinarily listen to," Shelby said during a recent trip to the region. [10]

President Bush has joined the call for a boost in aid targeted to help combat terrorism. But, as with U.S. aid policy during the Cold War, his foreign aid focus during the war on terrorism is clearly on national security rather than poverty alleviation. As part of a $27.1 billion emergency supplemental budget request he sent to Congress on March 21, Bush asked for $372.5 million in Foreign Military Financing — grants to foreign governments specifically earmarked to buy military equipment and services, primarily from U.S. contractors. Other than U.S. military contractors, the main beneficiaries of the new aid money, if Congress approves it, would be

Where the Money Goes

The United States spent about $15 billion on foreign assistance in 2001, including more than $11 billion on traditional developmental and humanitarian aid. President Bush's proposed new Millennium Challenge calls for an additional $5 billion in aid over the next three years for countries that prove they are reforming their economies and ending corruption.

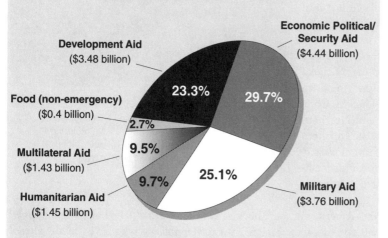

Composition of U.S. Aid, 2001

Development Aid ($3.48 billion) — 23.3%
Economic Political/ Security Aid ($4.44 billion) — 29.7%
Food (non-emergency) ($0.4 billion) — 2.7%
Multilateral Aid ($1.43 billion) — 9.5%
Humanitarian Aid ($1.45 billion) — 9.7%
Military Aid ($3.76 billion) — 25.1%

Major Categories of Foreign Assistance

Development Aid	Fosters sustainable, broad-based economic progress and social stability in developing countries.
Economic Political/ Security Aid	Helps meet special U.S. economic, political or security interests, including providing cash grants to help countries stabilize their economies.
Military Aid	Helps U.S. friends and allies acquire U.S. military equipment and training.
Humanitarian Aid	Funds emergency disaster aid and the refugee program administered by the State Department.
Multilateral Aid	Finances multilateral development projects, in combination with contributions from other nations through international organizations like the U.N. Children's Fund (UNICEF) and the World Bank.
Food (non-emergency)	Provides U.S. agricultural commodities to developing countries, as well as technical advice and training; known as the Food for Peace program.

Source: Congressional Research Service, "Foreign Aid: An Introductory Overview of U.S. Programs and Policy," April 6, 2001

Pakistan ($75 million), Afghanistan ($50 million), Turkey ($28 million) and the Philippines ($25 million) — all countries active in the war on terrorism. Indeed, during a recent trip to Latin America Bush argued that terrorism must be eliminated before other forms of assistance can be effective. "You can't alleviate poverty if there's terror in your neighborhood," he said." [11]

However, some supporters of increasing foreign aid caution that using it to enhance international security could backfire. "The primary objective should be to eliminate poverty, hunger and hopelessness, because that's how we can achieve our self-interest goals, namely international stability," Pinstrup-Andersen says, pointing out that when U.S. aid during the Cold War was used to prop up corrupt, profligate, anticommunist governments, it did little to help the poor.

"It is very important that we clearly identify poverty eradication as the ultimate goal," he says. "The positive payoffs to us in the United States and Europe will be more stability, more trade and less pressure on our borders" from immigrants fleeing poverty.

Is foreign aid a waste of taxpayer dollars?

Treasury Secretary Paul O'Neill stunned participants at the World Economic Forum in February when he summarily dismissed the utility of foreign aid. "Don't talk to me about compassion," he said. "I've seen with my own eyes babies born into the dust, and I know about Africa. We have spent trillions of dollars on overseas aid, but we have precious little to show for it." [12]

O'Neill's comments unleashed a torrent of criticism from foreign government officials, NGO leaders and others, who since Sept. 11 have been pressing for a large increase in development assistance. "This is the kind of rhetoric that somebody as bright as Paul O'Neill should not be using because I think he knows better, or he ought to know better," says Pinstrup-Andersen, who attended the meeting. "He really made himself and the United States look pretty bad. It took Bono * to correct him. Paul O'Neill has not reviewed the evidence if he argues that development assistance has been useless."

Aid advocates cite a large body of evidence demonstrating the effectiveness of development assistance. They point to countries like Chile, Korea and Thailand, which used international aid to establish thriving industrial economies. More recently, Uganda — wracked by civil war and famine during the 1960s and '70s — has emerged as one of sub-Saharan Africa's success stories, thanks to economic reforms introduced by the government and more than $1 billion in loans from the World Bank. [13]

But opponents point to another compelling body of evidence that appears to justify O'Neill's skepticism. Haiti has received more than $1 billion in World Bank loans, and the International Monetary Fund (IMF) has lent the country $150 million in the last 20 years. But more than 80 percent of the island's population still lives in dire poverty, a significant jump from 65 percent 15 years ago. And living standards in much of sub-Saharan Africa have not improved, despite the tens of billions of dollars invested by international donors over the past 40 years, in large part because much of it was stolen by corrupt dictators. [14]

U.S. officials readily acknowledge that some of the waste and inefficiency in the U.S. foreign aid program can be traced to U.S. policy itself. "As one who oversaw foreign aid during the Cold War, I can say that we gave assistance to those who were seen as being in our camp," said former Secretary of State Madeleine K. Albright. "We saw assistance through that prism." [15]

A woman hawks clothing on a garbage-filled street in Port-au-Prince, Haiti, one of the world's poorest nations. Haiti has received more than $1 billion in World Bank loans over the years, but more than 80 percent of the island's population still lives in dire poverty. The nation's per-capita gross national product is about $300.

World Bank President Wolfensohn echoed that sentiment during the recent Monterrey conference. "Too much money has been squandered in the past by decisions born of politics, not development," he said.

Foreign aid also has been wasted due to mismanagement and honest mistakes about what works and what doesn't in alleviating poverty. The World Bank, for example, for many years spent money on large infrastructure projects, such as building huge hydroelectric dams, in hope of attracting foreign investors and thus fueling overall economic growth. But these costly "mega-projects" often had little positive impact, beyond providing electricity for impoverished rural areas. In fact, some had negative impacts — such as when dams displaced ethnic groups from their tribal homelands.

* Bono, the lead singer of the Irish rock group U2, has become a leading advocate for aid to poor nations. He attended the economic forum, where he hobnobbed with billionaire Bill Gates and other high-profile delegates and campaigned for debt relief for Africa and other poor regions.

Micro-loans for Poor Women Go Farther

If foreign aid donors have learned anything over the past half-century of development assistance, it is that smaller is often better.

The World Bank and other development banks and multilateral agencies were designed, in part, to fund mammoth construction projects in poor countries. The hope was that big infrastructure improvements would lure foreign business investment, thereby creating jobs and invigorating local economies. But dams, roads and bridges alone were not enough. Many fell into disuse, and now many expensive projects are crumbling in the deserts, mountains and jungles of Africa, Asia and Latin America.

Donors have since discovered that it's often more effective to build wealth from the ground up. Small projects that improve living conditions among the poor — coupled with government reforms that enable change to take root — are proving much more effective antidotes to poverty than mega-projects. And nowhere is the need greater than among the world's poor women.

"In many rural economies, a lot of the men have left to work in the city," says Nancy Barry, president of New York City-based Women's World Banking. "Sometimes they send money home, and sometimes they don't." Even when men are present in the household, Barry says, "in a lot of cultures, the women do most of the work in agriculture, and the men are involved in counting the money and drinking tea."

Women's World Banking, which Barry has headed since 1990 after spending 15 years at the World Bank, is at the forefront of the "micro-lending" movement. Since the late 1970s, the bank and its affiliate organizations have helped more than 12 million poor people in more than 40 developing countries by lending them small sums of money to set up businesses selling food, clothing and other goods.

Despite their inferior status, Barry says, poor women are ideal candidates for micro-loans, which rarely amount to more than a few hundred dollars. "Women tend to put any increased income directly into building their business and into the mouths, medicines and schoolbooks of their children," she says. "For men, it's much more of a boom-or-bust thing than an organic buildup of a business, and there's a lot more waste that ends up happening in less-than-productive behavior involving alcohol and non-household activities."

Women also tend to be reliable clients, Barry says. "Poor people, in general, but particularly poor women, have had no access to institutional finance, so they take those loan obligations very seriously," she says. Barry cites the experience of Bank Rakyat Indonesia, a large commercial bank in Jakarta that provides more than 2 million micro-loans, about a quarter of them to women. During the East Asian financial crisis of the late 1990s, she says, when the bank had to write off all of its corporate loans and half of its loans to medium-sized industry, "the micro-finance portfolio didn't skip a beat."

Enabling women to gain a stake in a country's economy has a ripple effect that extends beyond individual house-

"We have learned once and for all there are no magical elixirs, [and we] should leave aside some of our past arrogance," writes William Easterly, a World Bank senior economist who has been on leave since publishing a controversial assessment of the bank's track record. "The problem of making poor countries rich was much more difficult than we thought." [16]

Echoing O'Neill, Easterly complains that foreign aid has left many of the world's poor still living in chronic poverty. But aid workers and NGO leaders say many of the defects in aid allocations have been overcome since the Cold War ended, enabling the United States and other donors to focus more squarely on the development needs of recipient countries.

"So much of what was provided was arguably bad for poor people, but that's changed," says Beckmann of Bread for the World. "Since the end of the Cold War, the industrialized countries no longer care about fighting communism, and all of the large-scale official agencies have very clearly improved the quality of what they do." Thus, he says, although international aid levels dropped suddenly at the end of the Cold War, the donors — including the World Bank, the regional development banks, the U.S. Agency for International Development (USAID) and the U.N. Development Program (UNDP) — are serious about using available aid money more effectively.

The worldwide spread of democracy over the past two decades and anti-corruption campaigns have helped

holds. Barry cites the case of Bangladesh, a conservative Muslim country long considered one of the world's worst economic basket cases. "Prior to micro-lending, these women didn't come out of their houses," Barry says. "But nowadays, thanks to active government support of economic growth, more than 80 percent of poor Bangladeshis now have access to micro-loans, compared with the global average of 5 percent. In the process, women's living standards have improved noticeably.

"Micro-lending creates confidence and a sense of solidarity," she says. "By building the economic base of a household or a community women gain a real sense that they have a stake in the future of their country."

As women gain economic clout, however limited, it becomes more socially acceptable for them to play a greater role in society, which improves conditions throughout society. Economic empowerment and declining infant mortality rates have contributed to a recent decline in birthrates in some of the world's poorest nations. [1] Economic empowerment also encourages women to influence the political makeup of local and national governments. "Micro-lenders

Margaret Mugabane raises rabbits in Wanyange, east of Kampala, Uganda. Micro-loans from the Foundation for International Community Assistance (FINCA) helped her and other local women open businesses.

do not tell women how to vote," Barry says, "but they definitely tell them to vote. In Bangladesh, women did not vote before. By voting, these women have changed the complexion of elections."

The experience in Bangladesh offers hope to another conservative Muslim country. Barred from education and work, girls and women in Afghanistan were held as virtual prisoners inside their homes during the six-year rule of the fundamentalist Islamic Taliban movement.

Despite their plight, Barry hopes Afghan women will take advantage of micro-lending. Although they are still absent from male-dominated public markets, she says, "Afghan women are very active in a whole range of microbusinesses, such as stitching and other things they can do within their homes." Unlike many other countries mired in poverty, she says, "in Afghanistan, entrepreneurship is alive and well."

---

[1] See Barbara Crossette, "Population Estimates Fall as Poor Women Assert Control," *The New York Times,* March 10, 2002.

reduce foreign aid waste, Beckmann adds. "Back in the 1960s and '70s, most developing countries were dictatorships, but people in many countries have pushed from below to establish democratic rights and accountability," he says. The changes have made it easier for aid to reach its intended beneficiaries, including those in some of the poorest countries in sub-Saharan Africa.

"If somebody steals money, and you're in a country where you can complain about it and not get thrown in jail, that person is less likely to steal money," Beckmann says. "So, although they've still got a long way to go, there are now grass-roots or church-led campaigns to reduce corruption in a number of African countries."

President Bush appears to have taken O'Neill's comments seriously. He stipulated in his call for a new foreign aid account that it would be targeted toward countries that won't allow the money to be stolen or wasted on projects that will not appreciably improve living standards.

Bush's initiative has won broad initial support. "He's correct in saying it isn't just a matter of how many dollars we spend," Rep. Kolbe says. "We've spent hundreds of billions of dollars in Africa, and most of those countries are worse off than they were before. A handful are doing quite well now without assistance. Why are they better off? Not because they got assistance and other countries didn't, but because they used it effectively."

World Bank

The World Bank helped build this hydroelectric project in Ghana. The bank credits foreign aid with dramatically increasing life expectancy, adult literacy and economic growth in many poor countries, but much of sub-Saharan Africa and Asia has not shared the prosperity. Bank President James D. Wolfensohn recently called on the U.S. and other wealthy nations to double their aid contributions.

In Kolbe's view, the more demanding criteria for allocating aid are in the best interests of both donors and recipients: "To put it in its starkest terms, if you have $100 to spend on foreign assistance and you have two countries — one where the money is going to disappear into the pockets of politicians and not do anything, and another where the $100 is going to start an economic program and make people's lives a little bit better — which one would you give it to? Give it where you can actually make a difference in people's lives."

While targeting foreign aid to democratic, well-run governments makes obvious sense to U.S. taxpayers, it may spell trouble for millions of poor people unlucky enough to have governments that do not pass muster. Unfortunately, the world's poorest people typically languish in corrupt or war-torn countries, such as Haiti, Sudan or Somalia.

In Haiti, for instance, "There's nothing we can do until the government isn't totally corrupt, and there are elements of governance that protect human rights," Kolbe says. "Until those basic things are in place, we can only offer humanitarian assistance, such as feeding people and providing health care. We can't do the things that can improve Haitians' lives until they're ready to accept it."

Does U.S. foreign aid go to the most effective programs?

Not counting military assistance, the United States is spending about $11 billion in foreign aid this fiscal year, which ends Sept. 30. Of that, $1.4 billion goes to two countries — Israel ($720 million) and Egypt ($655 million) — to help achieve Middle East peace as set forth in the 1979 Camp David accords. In comparison, the United States sends less than $2 billion to all of sub-Saharan Africa, home of some of the world's poorest nations. Overall, Israel and Egypt receive about $4.5 billion in U.S. aid — by far the biggest portion.

Some experts say the money the U.S. spent on achieving peace in the Middle East — about $70 billion over the past 20 years — has been a good investment. "Have our allocations to Egypt encouraged development in Egypt?" Eberstadt asks. "I don't think so. But the Camp David monies did prevent a general war in the Middle East for 20 years, and I would say that is money pretty well spent for the United States."

Many aid advocates disagree with Eberstadt about the money being well spent, given the ongoing Israeli-Palestinian conflict. But they insist much of the remaining foreign aid is being spent on efficiently run economic-development programs. For example, if you don't count aid to Israel and Egypt, and military assistance to Afghanistan, Pakistan and the rest of South Asia, Pinstrup-Andersen says, "quite a large share of what's left is allocated for poverty eradication."

Based on a half-century of experience assessing the effectiveness of development programs, several types of programs have proved particularly helpful in improving living standards in poor countries. For example, the so-called Green Revolution, in which agricultural research funded by the United States and other donors produced faster-growing, disease-resistant species of rice, wheat and other grains, helped reduce hunger and enabled parts of South and Southeast Asia to become self-sufficient in grains, and thus to develop vibrant economies.

Another success story is the famine early-warning system set up in East and Southern Africa in the 1980s by USAID, the U.N. and local governments. "This system has made a major change in how the world works," Beckmann says. "People still die of famine today, but it's political famine — because someone is trying to kill them. Nature-induced famines don't kill people any more."

Moreover, improved health care, especially for children, has significantly reduced mortality and sickness in much of the developing world. In the early 1980s, the United Nations Children's Fund (UNICEF) — with support from USAID, other donor nations and numerous NGOs — began intensive campaigns promoting immunization, growth monitoring, breast-feeding and anti-diarrheal oral rehydration therapy. The U.N. estimates that the number of children who die each year has declined from roughly 14 million in 1995 to about 11 million in 2000. [17]

"Even if we had spent $50 billion a year for 20 years and achieved nothing else except the Green Revolution, the child-survival revolution and the end of fatal, nature-induced famine," Beckmann says, "I would feel that we'd used our money pretty well."

Combating the spread of HIV/AIDS, which has killed 25 million, mostly African people, is a new USAID objective. [18] Even Sen. Jesse Helms, R-N.C., — who has often opposed foreign aid appropriations as throwing money down a "rat hole" — recently endorsed the new goal. He proposed increasing aid by $500 million to help prevent the spread of the dread disease from mothers to children in Africa.

"I know of no more heartbreaking tragedy in the world today," he wrote, "than the loss of so many young people to a virus that could be stopped if we simply provided more resources." [19]

Some experts say education programs yield the biggest bang for the funding buck. "If you educate children, you will have children who are able to care for themselves and their families and create wealth," says Kolbe, who also supports economic-assistance programs that pay for small physical improvements on the local level. "I'm not talking about massive, World Bank infrastructure projects like dam construction, but simple things like lining irrigation ditches, putting wells in, things that can allow people to grow their own food and maybe sell a little bit of it on the side and get a little more cash. These are things that can make a difference."

The biggest obstacle to ensuring that aid only goes to the most effective programs, Pinstrup-Andersen says, is the lack of control over the money once it is transferred to recipient countries or agencies. "We have virtually no control over how governments allocate their own money," he says.

For example, he explains, if the United States boosts spending on primary health care in a country, the recipient government can then spend that money on something else. "The only way to confront this problem," he says, "is to pick developing countries [with] a transparent allocation process for money they have at their disposal within the country."

Donors also fail to accurately assess a recipient's ability to absorb and effectively distribute donated funds. "Development aid tends to go in very high concentrations to the poorest countries, which is really a very silly way to allocate the money," says Nancy M. Barry, president of Women's World Banking, a New York-based nonprofit devoted to increasing poor women's economic access through micro-lending. (*See sidebar, p. 160.*) "Often money is pushed into countries where the objectives are clearly political without demonstrating the country's absorptive capacity."

But another obstacle to effective foreign aid has more to do with domestic U.S. policies. Most food aid, for example, comes from surplus American farm commodities, like wheat, rice and dairy products. Under U.S. law, American farmers receive support payments for their commodities when excess production pushes prices for their goods below a given level. But U.S. agricultural subsidies can negatively impact food aid recipients.

"Most of the assistance that NGOs get from the government consists of surplus food," says Pinstrup-Andersen. "The NGOs can then sell this food in developing countries to generate funds, which they can then use for their development projects. [But] when they sell American surplus food in a country where 75 percent of the poor people depend on agriculture, they're killing the market for local producers."

BACKGROUND

The Marshall Plan

It was not until the end of World War II that foreign aid emerged as a key ingredient of U.S. foreign policy. Following the Allied victory against Nazism, Europe lay in ruins. Responding to Europe's call for help, the United States and other countries established the International Monetary Fund (IMF) and the International Bank for Reconstruction and Development — better known as the World Bank — on Dec. 27, 1945.

CHRONOLOGY

1940s-1960s *The United States leads the world in foreign aid spending.*

Dec. 27, 1945 The U.S. and other countries establish the two main multilateral institutions involved in debt relief and economic development — the International Monetary Fund (IMF) and the International Bank for Reconstruction and Development — the World Bank.

June 5, 1947 Secretary of State George C. Marshall calls for a massive infusion of economic assistance to help rebuild Europe after World War II. Calling "hunger, poverty, desperation and chaos" the main enemies of democracy, he says economic assistance is the best way to restore "the confidence of the European people in the economic future of their own countries."

April 2, 1948 President Harry S. Truman signs the Economic Cooperation Act authorizing the Marshall Plan.

Nov. 3, 1961 President John F. Kennedy, warning that the economic collapse of poor nations "would be disastrous to our national security, harmful to our comparative prosperity and offensive to our conscience," calls for a renewal of U.S. commitment to development assistance. The Foreign Assistance Act creates the U.S. Agency for International Development (USAID) to administer development assistance.

1970s-1980s *The United States stresses the use of foreign aid to deter the spread of communism and promote peace in the Middle East.*

1979 Under the Camp David accords, the United States agrees to boost aid to Israel and Egypt in return for their agreement to cease hostilities. Most of the aid is in the form of military assistance used to procure U.S. weapons.

1984 President Ronald Reagan institutes the "Mexico City policy," barring the government from contributing aid to any foreign non-governmental organization involved in abortion for reasons other than rape, incest or threat to the mother's life.

1990s *U.S. foreign aid decreases after the Cold War ends.*

1990 Global spending on foreign aid peaks at $65.5 billion and begins a 20 percent decline, to $53.1 billion by 2000.

1997 Sen. Jesse Helms, R-N.C., who has long dismissed foreign aid as throwing money down a "rat hole," tries unsuccessfully to downsize USAID and fold it into the State Department.

2000s *The attacks on New York City and the Pentagon on Sept. 11, 2001, spark new interest in foreign aid as a potential deterrent to terrorism.*

Jan. 28, 2002 After joining other rich nations in pledging $4.5 billion in aid to Afghanistan, President Bush promises Interim Prime Minister Hamid Karzai that the United States "will continue to be a friend to the Afghan people in all the challenges that lie ahead."

March 6, 2002 World Bank President James D. Wolfensohn calls on the United States and other wealthy donor nations to double their foreign aid contributions.

March 14, 2002 President Bush proposes creating a supplemental development-assistance fund that would provide $5 billion a year by 2006 and be available only to countries that "adopt the reforms and policies that make development effective and lasting." The proposed increase comes in addition to Bush's request for a $5 billion increase in foreign aid for fiscal 2003.

March 18-22, 2002 Meeting at a United Nations-sponsored global-development conference in Monterrey, Mexico, Bush joins 50 other heads of state in endorsing the U.N.'s Millennium Development goals: halving poverty by 2015, as well as improving literacy, women's rights, maternal and child health and environmental quality and combating AIDS and other diseases. The World Bank estimates that meeting the sweeping goals will cost up to $60 billion a year in foreign aid.

March 24, 2002 Sen. Helms softens his crusade against foreign aid by calling for a new, $500 million program to help prevent the spread of HIV/AIDS from mothers to children in Africa.

But American policymakers feared that the Soviet Union, America's wartime ally, would take advantage of Europe's weakness to expand westward before the two new multilateral institutions could provide the assistance Europe needed to get back on its feet. George F. Kennan, a diplomat in charge of long-range planning for the State Department, called for a policy of "containment" aimed at preventing both Soviet territorial expansion and the spread of communism into Western Europe.

Complementing Kennan's plan — which would shape U.S. Cold War strategy over the next 45 years — Secretary of State George C. Marshall called for a massive infusion of economic aid to help rebuild Europe's war-ravaged industry and infrastructure and thus save the continent's democratic institutions. In a commencement speech at Harvard University on June 5, 1947, Marshall defined "hunger, poverty, desperation and chaos" as the main enemies of democracy. (*See excerpt, p. 168.*) He recommended aid as the best way to restore "the confidence of the European people in the economic future of their own countries."

On April 2, 1948, President Harry S. Truman signed the Economic Cooperation Act, which authorized the rapid infusion of American funds to rebuild Europe. By the time it ended, on June 30, 1951, the Marshall Plan — as America's first foreign aid program was known — had proved a resounding success, both in terms of resuscitating European markets and discouraging the spread of communism. Recipient governments used the $13 billion disbursed during the four-year life of the program to quickly rebuild factories, roads and other key infrastructure, fueling Europe's economic "miracle" of the 1950s and '60s by creating jobs and demand for European goods. Although European Communist parties also thrived during this period, the Soviet Union never expanded west of the "iron curtain" dividing Eastern and Western Europe.

The Marshall Plan's rapid success prompted President Truman to proclaim foreign aid as a key component of U.S. foreign policy. In January 1949 — the year Marshall Plan spending peaked at the equivalent of more than $50 billion in today's dollars — Truman announced a "bold new program" to provide aid to developing countries as well.

But foreign aid took a back seat to the military dimension of U.S. policy during the administration of Truman's successor, Dwight D. Eisenhower (1953-61),

as foreign aid spending remained flat amid heavy spending on the Korean War.

Under President John F. Kennedy (1961-63), foreign aid resumed a prominent place in U.S. foreign policy. Shortly after taking office, Kennedy called for a renewal of U.S. commitments to development assistance, proclaiming that the economic collapse of poor nations "would be disastrous to our national security, harmful to our comparative prosperity and offensive to our conscience." (*See excerpt, p. 169.*) Later that year, Kennedy launched the Alliance for Progress, a multilateral campaign aimed at boosting economic and military aid to Latin America to counter the appeal of revolutionary politics on the continent. The United States agreed to supply or guarantee $20 billion in the effort.

On Nov. 3, 1961, Kennedy unified U.S. foreign aid programs under USAID, a new, semiautonomous agency within the State Department charged with administering long-range economic and social aid efforts.

In proposing the new initiative, embodied in the 1961 Foreign Assistance Act, Kennedy argued for foreign aid in terms that shape today's debate on the issue: "Widespread poverty and chaos lead to a collapse of existing political and social structures, which would inevitably invite the advance of totalitarianism into every weak and unstable area. Thus our own security would be endangered and our prosperity imperiled. A program of assistance to the underdeveloped nations must continue because the nation's interest and the cause of political freedom require it."

Reform Efforts

The 1961 Foreign Assistance Act provided only general criteria for disbursing foreign aid. In the early 1970s, support for foreign aid programs waned as the nation was embroiled in controversy over the U.S. role in Vietnam War and the unfolding Watergate scandal, which brought down President Richard M. Nixon (1969-73). Critics also charged that U.S. aid was being wasted on ineffective projects that did little to advance American foreign policy interests. In 1971, the Senate rejected a bill authorizing foreign assistance for fiscal 1972 and '73 — the first time either house of Congress had failed to pay for foreign aid programs since the Marshall Plan.

In 1973 Congress amended the Foreign Assistance

The Myth of U.S. Generosity

A huge gap exists between the public's perception of U.S. spending on foreign aid and the reality. Polls show that Americans believe several myths about foreign aid, including that the U.S. government spends much more on foreign aid than it actually does. One survey suggested a majority think 15 percent of their tax dollars goes for foreign aid. That's about 15 times more than the actual figure — 0.9 percent. [1]

"People don't believe you when you tell them just 1 percent of the budget goes to foreign aid," says Steven Kull, director of the Program on International Policy Attitudes (PIPA) at the University of Maryland. "One person recently told me there had to be a cover-up."

The public also believes the United States provides more money for foreign aid than other rich countries do — as much as 60 percent more, Kull says. In fact, the United States ranks last among the world's 22 wealthiest countries in terms of the percentage of economic output earmarked for development assistance.

Americans also don't think very highly of foreign aid. "People seem to have the sense that we've done so much for the world — including the Marshall Plan, U.S. participation in World War II and our defense of other countries during the Cold War — that they mistrust the information when they're told the truth," Kull says. "There's also a concern about whether the money's wasted. When asked how much of our foreign aid spending they thought ended up in the pockets of corrupt government officials overseas, the median estimate was 50 percent."

In reality, most American foreign aid ends up in the pockets of U.S. businessmen. By law, a large proportion of U.S. development aid must be spent on American goods and services. According to a 2001 study by the Congressional Research Service, recipients of U.S. foreign aid spend 87 percent of military aid and 90 percent of food aid on American services and goods, such as military equipment and training or surplus agricultural commodities. The law even requires that 75 percent of all food aid be shipped by U.S. carriers. [2]

The perception gap persists over the forms of assistance that make up, or should make up, the U.S. foreign aid budget. "By far, the most popular reason for giving aid is to address hunger and disease," Kull says. "The least popular reason for giving aid is to increase influence over other countries. And the form of aid that was the least popular of all is aid to Israel and Egypt." In fact, the two countries receive nearly a third of all U.S. foreign aid. (*See graph, p. 155.*)

The Sept. 11 terrorist attacks on New York and the Pentagon may have enhanced Americans' perception that foreign aid is a way to deter terrorism. Asked by PIPA to consider various "possible approaches for trying to reduce the problem of terrorism," an overwhelming 86 percent of respondents said they favored "building goodwill toward the United States by providing food and medical assistance to people in poor countries." Almost as many — 80 percent — said they favored "building goodwill toward the U.S. by helping poor countries develop their economies." [3]

Indeed, Kull found broad support for doubling foreign aid to achieve the United Nations' Millennium Development goal of cutting global hunger in half by 2015. "There was overwhelming support for that goal, even if it cost every American $50 a year," he says. "That would be more than enough to double U.S. foreign aid spending."

The overall message Kull hears from Americans he polls: "We're ready to do our fair share. If other countries will do their part, we'll do our part, too."

---

[1] The poll was taken in 1995 by the Program on International Policy Attitudes (PIPA), a joint program of the Center on Policy Attitudes and the Center for International and Security Studies at the University of Maryland's School of Public Affairs.

[2] Curt Tarnoff and Larry Nowels, "Foreign Aid: An Introductory Overview of U.S. Programs and Policy," Congressional Research Service, April 6, 2001.

[3] PIPA survey, Nov. 6, 2001.

Act to channel U.S. bilateral aid to specific categories of need in the poorest countries, such as agriculture, family planning and education. In 1979, another reform effectively shifted the authority to administer most economic-development funds from the secretary of State to the USAID director, while the secretary retained authority over the Economic Support Fund (EFS), an account earmarked for security assistance.

During the presidency of Ronald Reagan (1981-89), U.S. funding of family-planning programs became a lightning rod for foreign aid critics. Anti-abortion activists charged that U.S. funds were supporting China's draconian population policy, which reportedly included the use of forced abortions and sterilization of couples that violated the country's rule limiting family size to one child. In 1984, the Reagan administration instituted the "Mexico City policy," named for the site of the second U.N. intergovernmental conference on population and development, which barred the government from contributing aid for family planning to any foreign non-governmental organization offering or funding abortions for reasons other than rape, incest or threat to the mother's life. The ban included groups that provided abortions with their own funds or counseled women on abortion.

Despite repeated efforts to reform the U.S. foreign aid program, criticism continued to plague it, and funding for USAID slowly fell. In 1988 a House Foreign Affairs Committee report listed the main complaints, some of which are still heard today. Foreign aid programs are too dispersed to be effective, the report concluded, and so numerous that they "cannot provide meaningful direction or be effectively implemented."

In addition, numerous restrictions on how funds will be used — such as requiring that aid help boost exports of U.S. commodities, goods and services — force administrators to focus on "anticipating how assistance will be used, rather than on how effectively it has been used," the report said.

U.S. Aid Share Is Least Generous

The United States ranks last among other industrialized countries when aid contributions are measured as a portion of the nation's economic output, or gross national product (GNP). However, the U.S. gives the second-largest dollar amount in foreign aid, after Japan. Only Denmark and four other nations meet the U.N.'s longstanding contribution target of 0.7 percent of GNP.

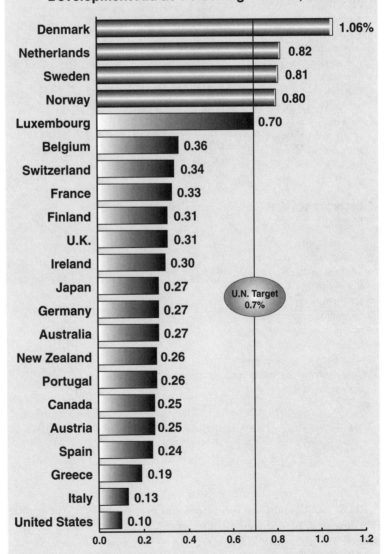

Development Aid as Percentage of GNP, 2000

Source: Organization for Economic Cooperation and Development, 2001

'There Is No Escaping Our Obligations'

Secretary of State George C. Marshall and President John F. Kennedy both played key roles in the development of U.S. foreign aid policy. Marshall's commencement speech at Harvard University in 1947 formed the framework for U.S. assistance in the economic recovery of Western Europe following World War II — the celebrated Marshall Plan. In 1961, Kennedy signed the Foreign Assistance Act into law, establishing the U.S. Agency for International Development (USAID) and ushering in a new era of U.S. foreign aid policy.

The following are excerpts from Marshall's Harvard address and Kennedy's remarks at the USAID bill signing. [1]

Secretary of State Marshall:

"The people of [the United States] are distant from the troubled areas of the Earth, and it is hard for them to comprehend the plight and consequent reactions of the long-suffering peoples, and the effect of those reactions on their governments in connection with our efforts to promote peace in the world.

Secretary of State George C. Marshall's plan to help rebuild Europe's economy after World War II was designed to restore political stability and peace.

Courtesy of the George C. Marshall Research Library, Lexington, Virginia

"In considering the requirements for the rehabilitation of Europe, the physical loss of life, the visible destruction of cities, factories, mines and railroads was correctly estimated, but it has become obvious during recent months that this visible destruction was probably less serious than the dislocation of the entire fabric of European economy.

"The truth of the matter is that Europe's requirements for the next three or four years of foreign food and other essential products — principally from America — are so much greater than her present ability to pay that she must have substantial additional help, or face economic, social and political deterioration of a very grave character. The remedy lies in breaking the vicious circle and restoring the confidence of the European people in the economic future of their own countries and of Europe as a whole.

"Aside from the demoralizing effect on the world at large and the possibilities of disturbances arising as a result of the desperation of the people concerned, the consequences to the economy of the United States should be apparent to all. It is logical that the United States should do whatever it is able to do to assist in the return of normal economic health in the world, without which there can be no political stability and no assured peace.

---

[1] Marshall Foundation and U.S. Agency for International Development.

"U.S. public support for helping poor people remains strong, but the public does not view the aid program as doing this effectively," the report concluded. "The public has very little concept of the aid program as an instrument of foreign policy, used to advance U.S. interests." [20]

The report recommended repealing the Foreign Assistance Act and drafting a new law establishing more focused criteria and goals for foreign aid. But the new proposal became so bogged down in new earmarks for spending, paperwork requirements and rules for allocating aid that it failed to become law. A later effort to rewrite the

"Our policy is directed not against any country or doctrine but against hunger, poverty, desperation and chaos. Its purpose should be the revival of a working economy in the world so as to permit the emergence of political and social conditions in which free institutions can exist.

"Such assistance, I am convinced, must not be on a piecemeal basis as various crises develop. Any assistance that this government may render in the future should provide a cure rather than a mere palliative. Any government that is willing to assist in the task of recovery will find full cooperation, I am sure, on the part of the United States government. Any government which maneuvers to block the recovery of other countries cannot expect help from us."

President John F. Kennedy in 1961 proposed creating the U.S. Agency for International Development to improve the nation's "awkward and slow" aid program.

President Kennedy:

"No objective supporter of foreign aid can be satisfied with the existing program — actually a multiplicity of programs. Bureaucratically fragmented, awkward and slow, its administration is diffused over a haphazard and irrational structure covering at least four departments and several other agencies. The program is based on a series of legislative measures and administrative procedures conceived at different times and for different purposes, many of them now obsolete, inconsistent, and unduly rigid and thus unsuited for our present needs and purposes. Its weaknesses have begun to undermine confidence in our effort both here and abroad.

"Although our aid programs have helped to avoid economic chaos and collapse . . . it is a fact that many of the nations we are helping are not much nearer sustained economic growth than they were when our aid operation began. Money spent to meet crisis situations or short-term political objectives . . . has rarely moved the recipient nation toward greater economic stability.

"To fail to meet those obligations now would be disastrous; and, in the long run, more expensive. For widespread poverty and chaos lead to a collapse of existing political and social structures, which would inevitably invite the advance of totalitarianism into every weak and unstable area. Thus, our own security would be endangered and our prosperity imperiled. A program of assistance to the underdeveloped nations must continue because the nation's interest and the cause of political freedom require it.

"The answer is that there is no escaping our obligations: our moral obligations as a wise leader and good neighbor in the interdependent community of free nations — our economic obligations as the wealthiest people in a world of largely poor people, as a nation no longer dependent upon the loans from abroad that once helped us develop our own economy — and our political obligations as the single, largest counter to the adversaries of freedom."

1961 law — proposed by President George Bush (1989-93) — met a similar fate and ultimately went down in defeat after some lawmakers objected that it gave the executive branch too much power in allocating foreign aid.

President Bill Clinton (1993-2001) also tried to rewrite the Foreign Assistance Act. The 1994 Peace, Prosperity and Democracy Act would have replaced the law with a new account structure for foreign aid, which would have merged several separate programs under a single funding account. Like most previous reform proposals, it failed to win congressional approval. No further efforts to amend the law have emerged.

In 1997, then-Chairman Helms of the Senate Foreign Relations Committee proposed merging USAID into the State Department. Although Congress approved the portion of his proposal that weakened and merged the Arms Control and Disarmament Agency and the U.S. Information Agency into the State Department, lawmakers balked at stripping USAID of its autonomy.

U.S. Aid Programs

Over the past half-century, Cold War political objectives, natural disasters and several devastating famines in South Asia and sub-Saharan Africa have all helped shape U.S. foreign aid programs. To address these needs, six basic categories of aid programs have emerged: [21]

- **Economic aid with U.S. political and security objectives** — The biggest slice of U.S. foreign assistance goes to advance American foreign-policy goals. Half of these funds — $2.2 billion in fiscal 2002 — are funneled through the Economic Support Fund to support the Middle East peace process. Israel and Egypt receive most of this money in exchange for their support of the 1979 Camp David accords. They may use the funds to build development projects, pay for imports of U.S. goods through the Commodity Import Program, pay off foreign debt and implement economic-policy reforms. After the fall of the Soviet Union in December 1991, two new programs were added to this category: SEED (1989 Support for East European Democracy Act) and the Freedom Support Act (1992 Freedom for Russia and Emerging Eurasian Democracies and Open Markets Support Act), designed to help Central Europe and the newly independent states of the former Soviet Union develop democratic institutions and free-market economies. Finally, this category includes funds for law enforcement, training and equipment to combat terrorism, narcotics, crime and weapons proliferation.
- **Military assistance** — The second-largest component of foreign aid — often excluded from assistance totals — consists of funds to help U.S. friends and allies build their armed forces and buy American military equipment and training. Like ESF funding, most foreign military financing goes to Israel and Egypt. A highly controversial program in this category, which provides training for foreign

military personnel, was used during the Cold War to bolster anti-communist and often dictatorial regimes like that of Chilean Gen. Augusto Pinochet, who used U.S. expertise to violently suppress dissent. The military-aid program also supports non-U.N. peacekeeping forces in Africa.

> "The goal is to provide people in developing nations the tools they need to seize the opportunities of the global economy. In return for this additional commitment, we expect nations to adopt the reforms and policies that make development effective and lasting."
>
> —*President Bush, announcing new aid and tougher demands for accountability*

- **Bilateral development assistance** — These programs support the traditional, long-term focus of most USAID programs — economic development and improved living standards in developing countries. They include spending on economic reform, private-sector development, creation of democratic institutions, environmental protection, family planning and health care. This category also includes debt relief for the poorest countries and funding for the Peace Corps, the African Development Foundation and other institutions active in developing nations.
- **Humanitarian economic assistance** — Three programs are designed to alleviate the kinds of humanitarian emergencies that bilateral assistance tries to prevent. Most of these funds go to the State Department's refugee program, which contributes to the U.N. High Commissioner for Refugees and the International Committee of the

Red Cross. USAID administers two other humanitarian programs providing relief to victims of manmade and natural disasters. Some of that assistance comes in the form of emergency food assistance, the Food for Peace program often known by its legislative moniker, PL 480.

- **Multilateral assistance** — Less than one-tenth of all U.S. foreign aid funds are combined with contributions from other donor countries to finance multilateral development projects administered by international organizations like UNICEF and UNDP, as well as multilateral development banks like the World Bank, the Asian Development Bank, the African Development Bank, the Inter-American Development Bank and the European Bank for Reconstruction and Development. However, due to longstanding opposition among conservative legislators to U.S. support of multilateral organizations, the United States is behind in its scheduled payments to some of these organizations, although not nearly so much as in previous years.

- **Non-emergency food aid** — The Food for Peace program provides U.S. agricultural commodities to developing countries. Food aid is funneled through private, voluntary organizations or multilateral organizations like the World Food Program. It also provides technical advice and training to farmers.

Poverty Increased in Africa, South Asia

The number of people worldwide in extreme poverty — living on less than $1 a day — dropped from 1.27 billion in 1990 to 1.17 billion in 1998, with much of the decline occurring in Latin America, East Asia and the Pacific region. Meanwhile, extreme poverty continued climbing in sub-Saharan Africa, South Asia and Eastern Europe/ Central Asia.

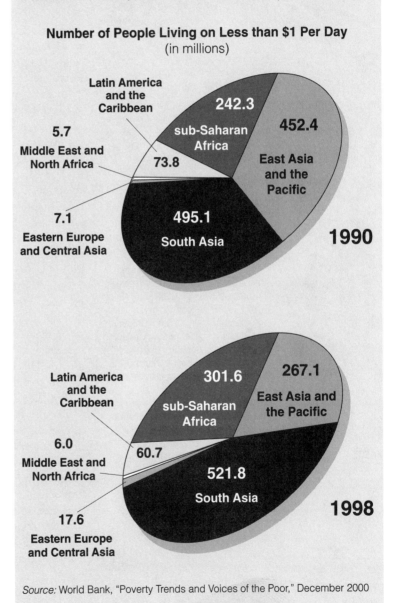

Source: World Bank, "Poverty Trends and Voices of the Poor," December 2000

AFP Photo/Joel Robine

AFP Photo/Behrouz Meri

AFP Photo/Michelle Quintaglie

The Scourge of Drought and Warfare

The skeletons of dead livestock attest to the drought that devastated war-torn southeast Ethiopia in 2000 (top). Afghan children wait for food being distributed by the U.N. Children's Fund (UNICEF) at the Maslakh refugee camp in western Afghanistan in December 2001 (middle). A malnourished youth at a hospital in Bukavu, Democratic Republic of Congo, is among the thousands of people displaced by warfare in recent years. Living standards in sub-Saharan Africa have improved little over the past 40 years, in large part because corrupt dictators stole billions of dollars in aid.

CURRENT SITUATION

Appeals for Aid

Since the Sept. 11 terrorist attacks, calls have mounted to reverse the downward trend of the past decade in global development assistance. In November, the World Health Organization (WHO) led the charge with an appeal to raise $2.5 billion in aid for victims of humanitarian crises.

"Afghanistan is not a unique case," said Paul Grossrieder, director general of the International Committee of the Red Cross, which launched the appeal with WHO. "Several countries, such as Sudan and the Democratic Republic of the Congo, are now in the same situation as Afghanistan before Sept. 11."

Estimating that at least 30 million people were living in perilous conditions in conflict zones around the world, he said, "Substantial support is needed to provide water, food, medicines and other essentials these populations need to survive. Addressing these problems now means preventing greater crises tomorrow." [22]

In February, King Abdullah II of Jordan said a Western-backed economic-revitalization plan for the Muslim world was the key to deterring fundamentalist Islamic terrorism. "Today's Muslim population is mostly young," he said. "Too many live in poor environments that steal hope and breed despair. The international community can contribute to a more tolerant environment by providing financial assistance to bolster economic and social reform." [23]

Shortly after Sept. 11, Gordon Brown, Britain's finance minister, asked the developed world to double its level of assistance — to $100 billion a year. After U.S. Treasury Secretary O'Neill rejected that proposal in February, World Bank President Wolfensohn suggested that donor countries could phase in the increases to soften the blow on their budgets and still come up with the additional $60 billion a year he said it would cost to meet the U.N. Millennium goals. "It is time to recognize that in this unified world, poverty is our collective enemy," he said. [24]

Because it is the world's richest nation and contributes the smallest portion of its GNP to foreign aid of all 21 industrial nations, aid supporters are looking to the United States to make the biggest boost in spending. For instance, InterAction's 160 NGO groups have asked President Bush to double U.S. spending on overseas assistance.

InterAction President McClymont said the group wants a doubling of seven basic accounts over the next five years: programs that support basic health care, education, jobs and business skills, hunger reduction, refugee and disaster response and improving the status of women and girls. "We think those are all top priorities for helping people come out of poverty, but when you account for inflation and population growth, those accounts are actually $1 billion less than they were 10 years ago," she pointed out. "So clearly, we're in the ditch and we have a long way to go."

Bush's Priorities

Since Sept. 11, the Bush administration has been sending mixed signals about the role foreign aid should play in overall U.S. foreign policy. In early February, Treasury Secretary O'Neill rejected the mounting calls for large increases in American aid spending, after questioning the utility of foreign aid. But in mid-March, Bush appeared to contradict that position when he proposed establishing a new fund to aid well-governed countries, which would boost overall aid spending by some 50 percent by 2006.

Apart from that proposal, Bush has requested $16.1 billion in foreign aid for fiscal 2003, an increase of around $5 billion over current levels. But the administration continues to support some controversial restrictions on aid introduced by past Republican presidents, notably opposition to funding of U.N. Population Fund (UNFPA) programs, which critics charge use donations to fund abortions in China. This year Bush decided to withhold $34 million already approved by Congress for the UNFPA this year. Because the United States has been the agency's largest donor, withholding the money will severely curtail its ability to meet the growing global demand for contraceptives.

"Today we are faced with a paradox," said Thoraya Obaid, the fund's executive director, who denied the abortion charges. "The need for reproductive health services is great and growing. At the same time, the funding for such services is declining." [25]

The military war on terrorism has complicated the debate over foreign aid in several ways. Citing difficulty finding enough money through the State Department to pay Pakistan for its support of U.S.-led military operations in Afghanistan, the Defense Department is now seeking authority to set up its own foreign-assistance account. As part of a $14 billion request in supplemental spending for 2002, the Pentagon asked for $130 million to create an autonomous account to fund military assistance to foreign governments without going through normal State Department channels.

Despite the relatively modest initial funding request, the Pentagon's initiative alarms some lawmakers. "The concerns this raises are less about the sums requested than about the troubling precedent it would set," said Sen. Patrick J. Leahy, D-Vt., chairman of the Senate Appropriations Foreign Operations Subcommittee, which oversees foreign aid spending. "And that makes this a controversial proposal." [26]

The war on terrorism also is complicating the job of aid workers on the ground in Afghanistan, where chaotic conditions, compounded by recent earthquakes, have drawn U.S. servicemen into the relief effort. While pro-

> ## "Today we are faced with a paradox. The need for reproductive health services is great and growing. At the same time, the funding for such services is declining."
>
> *—Thoraya Obaid*
> *Executive Director,*
> *U.N. Population Fund*

viding relief services, soldiers dress in Afghan civilian clothes to make them less vulnerable to sniper fire. But the practice exposes civilian aid workers to attack by hostile forces who may assume they are actually U.S. military personnel. In a letter to National Security Adviser Condoleeza Rice, representatives of 16 NGOs protested that allowing soldiers to work out of uniform "significantly increases the security risks of every humanitarian worker in that country." [27]

Bush's recent proposal to boost foreign aid was his strongest indication of support for foreign aid since he came to office. The proposed aid fund, which would begin in 2004 and provide $5 billion a year by 2006, would be earmarked for countries that fight corruption, respect human rights, open their trading markets and spend an adequate portion of their budgets on social services. "We'll apply these criteria fairly and rigorously," Bush promised.

Would increasing foreign aid reduce terrorism against the United States?

YES — Madeleine K. Albright
Former Secretary of State; Professor, School of Foreign Service, Georgetown University

From Testimony Before Senate Foreign Relations Subcommittee on International Operations and Terrorism Feb. 27, 2002

We all know the objections to spending more on international affairs. . . . Developing countries, we are told, are rife with crooks, and where there is no honesty, there is no hope. A couple of weeks ago, Secretary [of State Colin] Powell testified before this committee. He said, "We can no longer invest in places . . . where you cannot be sure the money will be well spent."

I agree with that caution, but [it] should not become a rationale for inaction. Over the years, we have learned how to design international programs that reward merit, while providing incentives for the reluctant to clean up their act.

And I have seen our investments pay off, helping to destroy nuclear warheads and safeguard nuclear materials; training thousands of people in counterterrorism; intercepting narcotics; strengthening democratic institutions; raising life expectancy; cutting infant mortality; defeating smallpox. . . .

The time has come to replace the old myth with truth. Our international assistance programs . . . are not money down a rat hole. They are poison down the snake hole of terrorism; helping to choke off the hatred, ignorance and desperation upon which terrorism feeds.

There should be no more excuses. After all, we are at war. But still we hear the excuses. We are told we can't afford to increase significantly our investments in overseas education and family planning, battling AIDS and vaccinating children [or] our support for international peacekeeping or for securing Russia's nuclear arsenal. . . .

To all this I would reply with a diplomatic term of art — "balderdash." Today, on a per-capita basis, Americans contribute only about $29 per year through official channels to developing free societies. . . . This puts us dead last among industrialized countries. . . .

It is sad, but not surprising, that a recent survey found that our country is almost resented as much as it is admired overseas. The reason is not the extent of our power, the pervasiveness of our culture, or the tilt of our policies in the Middle East.

We are resented because much of the world believes we are rich and do not share, and because they believe we are intent on widening the gap between haves and have-nots. . . .

We need to be bold now in developing and financing a new generation of initiatives — with democracy-building as a priority — to correct misapprehensions and win the battle of ideas.

NO — Richard Perle
Chairman, Defense Policy Board; Fellow, American Enterprise Institute

From Testimony Before Senate Foreign Relations Subcommittee on International Operations and Terrorism Feb. 27, 2002

The idea that poverty is a cause of terrorism, although widely believed and frequently argued, remains essentially unproven. That poverty is not merely a cause, but a "root cause" . . . is an almost certainly false, and even dangerous idea, often invoked to absolve terrorists of responsibility or mitigate their culpability. It is a liberal conceit, which, if heeded, may channel the war against terror into the cul de sac of grand development schemes in the Third World and the elevation of do-good/feel-good NGOs [non-governmental organizations] to a role they cannot and should not play.

What we know of the Sept. 11 terrorists suggests they were neither impoverished themselves nor motivated by concerns about the poverty of others. After all, their avowed aim, the destruction of the United States, would, if successful, deal a terrible blow to the growth potential of the world economy. Their devotion to Afghanistan's Taliban regime, which excluded half the Afghan work force from the economy and aimed to keep them illiterate as well as poor, casts conclusive doubt on their interest in alleviating poverty.

Poverty — or poverty and despair — is the most commonly adumbrated explanation for terrorism abroad — and crime at home. Identifying poverty as a source of conduct invariably confuses the matter. We will never know what went through the mind of Mohammed Atta as he plotted the death of thousands of innocent men, women and children, including a number of Muslims. We do know that he lived in relative comfort as did most, perhaps all, of the 19 terrorists. . . .

If we accept poverty as an explanation, we will stop searching for a true, and useful, explanation. We may not notice the poisonous, extremist doctrine propagated, often with Saudi oil money, in mosques and religious institutions around the world.

If we attribute terrorism to poverty, we may fail to demand that President Mubarak of Egypt silence the sermons, from mosques throughout Egypt, preaching hatred of the United States. As you authorize $2 billion a year for Egypt, please remember that these same clerics are employees of the Egyptian government. . . .

So when you hear about poverty as the root cause of terrorism, I urge you to examine the manipulation of young Muslim men sent on suicidal missions by wealthy fanatics, like Osama bin Laden, whose motives are religious and ideological in nature and have nothing to do with poverty or privation.

Should Congress allow Colombia to use U.S. anti-drug military aid to combat insurgencies?

YES   Otto Reich
Assistant Secretary of State, Bureau of Western Hemisphere Affairs

From testimony before House International Relations Western Hemisphere Subcommittee hearing on Colombia, April 11, 2002

What happens in Colombia is of vital importance to all of us in the United States. Terrorism and narcotics trafficking not only exact a terrible human toll in Colombia, but their effects are felt here as well. The FARC [Revolutionary Armed Forces of Colombia], the ELN [National Liberation Army] and the [paramilitary] AUC all have been designated as foreign terrorist organizations by the United States; all three threaten a wide range of U.S. interests.

Colombia is the source of 90 percent of the cocaine consumed in the United States and is a significant supplier of heroin to the U.S. market. The FARC and the AUC are intimately involved in this trade.

The ongoing attacks [by these groups] on Colombia's democracy have had a tremendous cost within Colombia. The AUC has killed two legislators over the past 12 months, while the FARC has kidnapped six, including presidential candidate Ingrid Betancourt. Three thousand Colombians were killed by terrorist violence in 2001; nearly as many were kidnapped.

President Andres Pastrana took the initiative in 1999 with the launch of the five-year, $7.5 billion Plan Colombia. This plan calls for substantial social investment; judicial, political and economic reforms; modernization of the Colombian armed forces and renewed efforts to combat narco-trafficking.

Since July 2000, the U.S has provided Colombia with $1.7 billion in assistance. We also provided Colombia and our other Andean partners with trade benefits. . . .

In the counterterrorism supplemental submitted on March 21, we seek new, explicit, legal authorities that would allow our assistance to Colombia, including assistance previously provided, to be used "to support a unified campaign against narcotics trafficking, terrorist activities and other threats to its national security."

The request for new authority does not signify a retreat from our concern about human rights nor an open-ended U.S. commitment in Colombia. It expressly recognizes that we intend to use the new authority consistent with the human rights conditions relevant to our assistance to Colombia's armed forces and the 400-person cap on U.S. military personnel.

As far as the [Occidental Petroleum Corp.] pipeline, the primary beneficiary of the pipeline is the government of Colombia. It derives most of the income. And, by the way, we are the consumers of a lot of that oil. To the extent that we can protect that pipeline and other infrastructure in Colombia, we might succeed in lowering the price of oil.

NO   Rep. Ron Paul, R-Texas

From testimony before House International Relations Western Hemisphere Subcommittee hearing on Colombia, April 11, 2002

Some people describe our policies in Colombia as a slippery slope, and that may be true, but sometimes I think we're approaching a cliff on involvement there.

In 1979, we had a grand announcement at Camp David — the accord for peace in the Middle East. But since then, it has cost us $300 billion, and now we're in the midst of chaos and war.

There are a lot of people in this country that aren't any more optimistic about what's happening down in Colombia than they were in horror about what happened in the Middle East.

They've been fighting down [in Colombia] a long time — since the civil war broke out in 1964. We're getting involved in civil war, and to pass this off as something current, dealing with terrorism, dealing with 9/11, I think, is just really, really a stretch.

I represent a rather poor district in Texas. I have never had one individual come up and say, "You know, I really need to be further taxed because I like what you're doing in Colombia."

Let me tell you, I get dozens and dozens of people saying, "What are you doing down in Colombia spending our money?" And they're very concerned and not optimistic at all.

I don't see the moral justification. I don't see the constitutional justification for this. And this notion that we boost this up in words of terrorism when we're dealing with civil factions and civil wars, I think, is a real careless definition of what terrorism is all about and what this world is facing today.

But I'm wondering whether we might have an amendment to this bill that would deal with some equity in it. It was pointed out that if we could only get [Colombia's] oil running, it would help the government and it would alleviate some of our financial burden.

Well, that's a circuitous argument, but I was wondering, since it's not only the government that's going to benefit down there to keep the oil running, but it's Occidental Oil Corp. that's going to benefit.

So, we're down there, we're being the police force for Occidental. Now, if Occidental, all of a sudden, makes a lot more profits, do you think it would be proper — and this is a question — do you think it would be proper for us to then tax Occidental to reimburse us for going down there and securing their oil pipeline?

Colombian soldiers patrol near Vista Hermosa in February after the Revolutionary Armed Forces of Colombia (FARC) kidnapped a Colombian senator. On March 22, President Bush asked Congress to allow Colombia to use U.S. military aid to help pay for its war against the 17,000-man guerrilla group, which the U.S. calls a terrorist organization.

International Response

International reaction to Bush's new aid proposal has been mixed. While welcoming any increase in U.S. funding, representatives of NGOs, other donor nations and multilateral agencies say the world's richest nation could, and should, contribute more to global poverty-alleviation efforts.

Bush's decision to condition allocation of the new money on recipient countries' good governance practices is broadly welcomed. "This is something that the NGO relief and development community has been calling for, for a long time," says McClymont of InterAction. "So for us it was very good news and a very strong first step."

But she agrees with many experts who are concerned about the way the administration defines its criteria for allocating the money. "In light of our knowledge and experience on the ground, we believe it is critical that we be involved in helping set the criteria for which countries will receive this new money," McClymont says.

Other experts are more skeptical about Bush's new initiative. "This new approach sound good, but as with most new formulas in the aid world, it will not be a magic bullet," writes Thomas Carothers, vice president for studies and founder and co-director of the Democracy and Rule of Law Project at the nonprofit Carnegie Endowment for International Peace. [28]

Citing the relatively large amounts of aid now going to Russia, Afghanistan and Pakistan — all of which have far to go in advancing democratic institutions and the rule of law — Carothers questions whether the administration will really rule out potential aid recipients that it considers important allies in advancing U.S. security interests. This concern also extends to the kinds of reforms that will determine a country's eligibility for American assistance. Citing Tunisia, which has continued to exercise political repression even as it has undertaken effective economic reforms, Carothers writes, "There is a risk that democracy will get lost in the reformist wash."

Finally, Carothers worries that making government reforms a condition of aid will exclude the world's neediest from American largess.

"The larger part of the 40 or 50 poorest countries in the world — most of which depend heavily on foreign aid for their basic survival — are poor reformers," he writes. "Are we and other donors really ready to walk away from them, greatly magnifying human suffering, and to direct aid primarily to good reformers, which tend to need the aid much less?" (*See "At Issue," p. 174.*)

Some analysts who welcome Bush's plan to increase foreign aid are skeptical of its impact on global poverty, because other U.S. policies may thwart economic progress in the developing world. For instance, in Monterrey, Bush reiterated his call for free trade as a key to development. "When nations close their markets, and opportunity is hoarded by a privileged few, no amount — no amount — of development aid is ever enough," he said.

But two weeks earlier Bush had imposed tariffs on imported steel in an effort to help the ailing U.S. steel industry. Although the tariffs would exempt most poor nations, Bush's action was broadly criticized because it could lead to a global trade war that could impede developing countries' ability to enter global markets.

Critics say this policy is not only inconsistent but also harmful to the very countries the United States purports to help through its foreign aid program.

The United States and other rich countries "use their trade policy to conduct what amounts to robbery against the world's poor," states a new report by the aid group Oxfam International. The report cites figures showing that developing countries exporting goods to wealthy countries "face tariff barriers four times higher than those encountered by rich countries. Those barriers cost them $100 billion a year — twice as much as they receive in aid." [29]

OUTLOOK

Hot Issues

Two issues are likely to stir considerable debate this year as lawmakers take up the Bush administration's foreign aid request for 2003 — aid to Colombia and contributions to family-planning programs.

On March 22, Bush formally asked Congress to allow Colombia to use U.S. military aid — which currently can only be used to curtail cocaine production — to help pay for its war against the Revolutionary Armed Forces of Colombia (FARC), a 17,000-man guerrilla group the United States deems a terrorist organization. Critics say the action could move the United States dangerously back in the direction of using aid to support counterinsurgency efforts in Latin America. "Though everybody seems to be tracking on the same wave length over aid to the Middle East," Rep. Kolbe predicts, "aid to Colombia is going to be very controversial." (*See "At Issue," p. 175.*)

Another contentious issue is funding for U.N. Population Fund family-planning programs.

"Although this is a very minor detail in the whole world of foreign assistance, it is threatening to come back with a vengeance now, because the president has not released the $34 million budgeted for UNFPA," says Kolbe.

Although that amount is an increase over the $25 million level allocated to the agency over the past six years, Kolbe says it's far below historical levels. "But the pro-life people don't want to spend that amount of money," he says, "so this has some potential for being a very contentious issue in the hearings this year."

Kolbe does not see Congress doubling the foreign aid budget, an overriding goal of many NGOs and multilateral agencies.

"I don't think you'll find Congress amenable to making any kind of commitment to an exact percentage of assistance," he says, but it does want to see foreign aid dollars "effectively spent."

With midterm elections only six months away, prospects for early consideration of Bush's latest call to boost foreign aid to well-governed countries are uncertain at best.

"There is a tendency to be thrilled by this promise of a major increase in assistance, pop open the champagne corks and call it quits," McClymont says. "But, of course, that isn't called for. If nothing else, we have given the president an assurance of a real constituency out there in support of increased humanitarian and development assistance.

"But we must continue to make sure that the administration does indeed request this new money in the coming years and that the Congress approves it."

NOTES

1. See Pamela Constable, "Afghanistan's Rebirth Imperiled by Its Past," *The Washington Post*, April 8, 2002. For background, see Kenneth Jost, "Rebuilding Afghanistan," *The CQ Researcher*, Dec. 21, 2001, pp. 1041-1064.

2. Quoted by Mark Turner, "Karzai Urges Donors to Fulfill Pledges," *Financial Times*, April 11, 2002.

3. See Jon Jeter, "Less Than $1 Means Family of 6 Can Eat," *The Washington Post*, Feb. 19, 2002.

4. Organization for Economic Cooperation and Development (OECD), "ODA Steady in 2000; Other Flows Decline," Dec. 12, 2001.

5. For background, see Mary H. Cooper, "Reassessing Foreign Aid," *The CQ Researcher*, Sept. 27, 1996, pp. 841-864.

6. From a letter to the editor, *The New York Times*, March 31, 2002. The World Bank is a multilateral institution and the largest source of low-interest loans and grants to fund development in poor countries.

7. For background, see David Masci and Kenneth Jost, "War on Terrorism," *The CQ Researcher*, Oct. 12, 2001, pp. 817-848.

8. From a speech delivered March 6, 2002, at the Woodrow Wilson International Center in Washington, D.C. For background on anti-Americanism, see Mary H. Cooper, "Hating America," *The CQ Researcher*, Nov. 23, 2001, pp. 969-992.

9. For background, see David Masci, "Emerging India," *The CQ Researcher*, April 19, 2002, pp. 329-360.

10. Quoted by Brandt Ayers, "We Need New Marshall Plan," *Sunday Gazette Mail* (Charleston, W. Va.), April 7, 2002.

11. Bush spoke on March 23, 2002, in Lima at a joint news conference with Peruvian President Alejandro Toledo.

12. O'Neill spoke at the forum, held Feb. 1-4, 2002, in New York City. See Jeremy Warner, "U.S. Treasury Secretary Sheds No Tears for Poor," *The Independent* (London), Feb. 4, 2002.

13. See John Cassidy, "Helping Hands," *The New Yorker*, March 18, 2002, pp. 60-66.

14. See Daniel Altman, "As Global Lenders Refocus, a Needy World Awaits," *The New York Times*, March 17, 2002.

15. Albright spoke April 10, 2002, at a press conference following a development assistance conference held by the William Davidson Institute, a nonprofit research institute affiliated with the University of Michigan that promotes business development in emerging markets.

16. William Easterly, *The Elusive Quest for Growth* (2001), quoted in Ken Ringle, "Bank Shot," *The Washington Post*, March 20, 2002.

17. See Elizabeth Olson, "U.N. Says Millions of Children, Caught in Poverty, Die Needlessly," *The New York Times*, March 14, 2002. Also see Brian Hansen, "Children in Crisis," *The CQ Researcher*, Aug. 31, 2001, pp. 657-688.

18. For background, see David Masci, "Global AIDS Crisis," *The CQ Researcher*, Oct. 13, 2000, pp. 809-832.

19. Jesse Helms, "We Cannot Turn Away," *The New York Times*, March 24, 2002.

20. The "Hamilton-Gilman Report," House Foreign Affairs Committee, 1989, quoted in USAID, "A History of Foreign Assistance," Jan. 15, 2002. The report's main authors were Reps. Lee Hamilton, D-Ind., and Benjamin A. Gilman, R-N.Y.

21. Material in this section is based on Curt Tarnoff and Larry Nowels, "Foreign Aid: An Introductory Overview of U.S. Programs and Policy," Congressional Research Service, April 6, 2001.

22. Speaking at WHO headquarters in Geneva, Switzerland, Nov. 7, 2001.

23. Quoted in Associated Press Newswires, "World Forum Briefs," Feb. 4, 2002.

24. From a speech at the Woodrow Wilson Center, March 6, 2002.

25. Quoted by Barbara Crossette, "U.N. Agency on Population Blames U.S. for Cutbacks," *The New York Times*, April 7, 2002.

26. Quoted by Bradley Graham, "Pentagon Seeks Own Foreign Aid Power," *The Washington Post*, April 8, 2002.

27. See Edward Walsh, "Aid Groups Fear Civilian, Military Lines May Blur," *The Washington Post*, April 3, 2002.

28. Thomas Carothers, "The New Aid," *The Washington Post*, April 16, 2002, p. A19.

29. Oxfam International, "Rigged Rules and Double Standards," April 10, 2002.

BIBLIOGRAPHY

Books

Easterly, William, *The Elusive Quest for Growth*, MIT Press, 2001.
A World Bank economist now on leave describes what he sees as misguided bank policies over the past half-century that wasted billions of dollars while doing little to improve the living standards of most people in the developing world.

Lancaster, Carol, *Transforming Foreign Aid: United States Assistance in the 21st Century*, Institute for International Economics, 2000.
A former deputy administrator of the U.S. Agency for International Development (USAID) reviews the goals of American foreign aid since the end of World War II and examines aid's potential to further U.S. interests in the new century.

Articles

Diamond, Jared, "Why We Must Feed the Hands that Could Bite Us," *The Washington Post*, Jan. 13, 2002.
The author of *Guns, Germs and Steel: The Fates of Human Societies*, calls on the U.S. government to boost funding of long-range initiatives to improve living standards in the developing world and thus reduce the risk that anti-American terrorism will recur.

Epstein, Helen, "Time of Indifference," *The New York Review of Books*, April 12, 2001, pp. 33-38.
A public-health expert reviews four recent books that describe the inequities in access to global health care that are deepening between rich and poor, as privatization of public-health systems leaves the poor to fend for themselves.

LaFranchi, Howard, "Foreign Aid Recast as Tool to Stymie Terrorism," *The Christian Science Monitor*, Feb. 26, 2002.
Investing more aid in human potential may go a long way toward deterring terrorism.

Marsden, Keith, "An Economist's View: Poverty Did Not Cause the Terror Attacks," *Transition*, July-September 2001, p. 3.
The "basic roots" of terrorism lie not in poverty but in the neglect in Arab countries of secular education, which has permitted the spread of Islamic terrorism.

Marshall, Andrew, "The Threat of Jaffar," *The New York Times Magazine*, March 10, 2002, pp. 44-72.
The author describes the rise of Jaffar Umar Thalib, an Indonesian Muslim cleric whose radical Islamic movement rivals Osama bin Laden's al Qaeda in its zeal to destroy Western institutions.

Talbott, Strobe, "The Other Evil," *Foreign Policy*, November/December 2001, pp. 75-76.
Former President Bill Clinton's deputy secretary of State argues that the war on terrorism will fail unless coupled with a new war on poverty to reduce the conditions that create anti-U.S. sentiment and enable terrorism to flourish.

Towell, Pat, "Supplemental Spending Plan May Unleash Battle Over Control," *CQ Weekly*, March 23, 2002, pp. 812-813.
President Bush has requested $1.2 billion in additional foreign aid spending for this fiscal year, with most of it earmarked for Afghanistan, Turkey, Jordan and Pakistan.

Reports and Studies

Bread for the World Institute, "Foreign Aid to End Hunger," 2001.
Bread for the World, which lobbies Congress to help reduce hunger, calls on the Untied States to allocate an additional $1 billion a year in aid to Africa, where hunger is "deep, pervasive and widespread."

International Bank for Reconstruction and Development, "The Role and Effectiveness of Development Assistance," March 11, 2002.
The World Bank offers a positive assessment of foreign aid's effectiveness in reducing poverty and improving access to health care and employment over the past half-century. Among other successes, it cites a 20-year increase in life expectancy in developing countries and a reduction in adult illiteracy from 47 percent to 25 percent.

Oxfam International, "Rigged Rules and Double Standards: Trade, Globalisation, and the Fight Against Poverty," 2002.
Current trade rules, the aid group's report concludes, allow rich countries to dominate world trade by keeping out cheap imports from poor countries.

Paarlberg, Robert L., "Governance and Food Security in an Age of Globalization," International Food Policy Research Institute, February 2002.
Developing-country governments can do more than international donors to reduce hunger by providing peace, the rule of law, clean water, roads, electrical power and funding to raise domestic farm productivity.

U.S. Agency for International Development, "United States Government Initiatives to Build Trade-Related Capacity in Developing and Transition Countries," October 2001.

This report summarizes USAID's initiatives to help developing countries gain access to the world trading system to sell their products overseas.

For More Information

American Enterprise Institute for Public Policy Research (AEI), 1150 17th St., N.W., Washington, DC 20036; (202) 862-5800; www.aei.org. A research and educational organization that studies trends in a broad range of policy fields, including foreign aid and foreign policy.

Bread for the World, 50 F St., N.W., Suite 500, Washington, DC 20001; (202) 639-9400; http://www.bread.org. A Christian citizens' movement that works to eradicate world hunger; organizes and coordinates political action on issues and public policy affecting the causes of hunger; interests include domestic food-assistance programs and international famine relief.

InterAction, 1717 Massachusetts Ave., N.W., Suite 701, Washington, DC 20036; (202) 667-8227; http://www.inter-action.org. Provides a forum for exchange of information among private U.S. voluntary agencies on development-assistance issues, including food aid and other relief services, migration and refugee affairs; monitors legislation and regulations.

International Bank for Reconstruction and Development (World Bank), 1818 H St., N.W., MC 12-750, Washington, DC 20433; (202) 477-1234; http://www.worldbank.org. An international-development institution funded by membership subscriptions and borrowings in private capital markets; encourages the flow of public and private foreign investment into developing countries through loans and technical assistance; finances economic-development projects in agriculture, environmental protection, education, public utilities, telecommunications, water supply, sewerage, public health and other areas.

International Food Policy Research Institute, 2033 K St., N.W., Washington, DC 20006; (202) 862-5600; http://www.ifpri.org. Analyzes the world food situation and suggests ways of making food more available in developing countries; provides various governments with information on national and international food policy; sponsors conferences and seminars; publishes research reports.

Oxfam America, 26 West St., Boston, MA 02111; 617-482-1211; info@oxfamamerica.org. Funds disaster relief and self-help development projects, primarily at the international level, including food and agriculture programs; supports grass-roots and community efforts to combat hunger; conducts an educational campaign and debt relief for foreign countries.

Program on International Policy Attitudes (PIPA), 1779 Massachusetts Ave., N.W., Suite 510, Washington, DC 20036; (202) 232-7500; www.pipa.org. A joint program of the Center on Policy Attitudes and the Center for International and Security Studies at the University of Maryland's School of Public Affairs that researches American public attitudes on foreign-policy issues.

United Nations Development Program (UNDP), One United Nations Plaza, New York, NY 10017; (212) 906-5558; http://www.undp.org. Funded by voluntary contributions from member nations and non-member recipient nations; administers and coordinates technical assistance programs provided through the United Nations system; seeks to increase economic and social development in developing nations.

William Davidson Institute, University of Michigan, 724 East University Ave., Wyly Hall, First Floor, Ann Arbor, MI 48109-1234; (734) 763-5020; www.wdi.bus.umich.edu. A research and educational organization that supports the transformation of emerging market economies into advanced economies through research, education and outreach initiatives.

Women's World Banking, 8 West 40th St., 9th Floor, New York, NY 10018; 212-768-8513; www.swwb.org. A nonprofit financial institution founded in 1979 and devoted to increasing the economic access of poor women around the world, largely through micro-financing.

9

Rebuilding Iraq

David Masci

Shiite demonstrators in Baghdad demand a government run by Muslim clergy rather than American-backed political appointees. U.S. and British forces working to democratize Iraq after toppling the dictatorship of Saddam Hussein also face criticism for not quickly restoring security and basic services.

From *The CQ Researcher*, July 25, 2003.

When U.S. and British soldiers toppled Saddam Hussein nearly four months ago, there was widespread hope that delivering the country from a brutal dictator would spark a smooth and peaceful transition to democracy.

Some positive changes have occurred. Today, Iraqis are much freer to speak, worship and assemble than they were under Hussein's repressive regime. And many top members of that regime, most notably Hussein's sons Uday and Qusay, have either been killed or captured. But for the most part, the result the coalition had hoped for hasn't occurred — at least not yet.

Much of Iraq remains without water or electricity; American and British soldiers are still being attacked and killed, almost on a daily basis. And the United States is mistrusted and even hated by some Iraqis, in part for failing to improve basic conditions fast enough.

But some recent changes have sparked new hope that Iraq may soon be on the path to both stability and democracy. Most important, on July 12, 25 prominent Iraqis gathered in Baghdad to form the country's first decision-making body since the war ended.

"There are defining moments in history," said Sergio Vieira de Mello, the United Nations' (U.N.) special representative to Iraq. "For Iraq, today is definitely one of those." [1]

The United States and Britain chose the council's members and can overrule its decisions. But in an effort to jumpstart the transition to self-government, the allies also empowered the group, known as the Council of Governance, to appoint ministers, create a budget and help form a commission to write a new constitution.

And the council has already acted, abolishing Hussein-decreed holidays and authorizing the creation of a war-crimes tribunal to try

Most Iraqis Are Shiite Muslims

Although a majority of Iraqis are Shiite Muslims, the country was ruled during Saddam Hussein's regime by Sunnis, who belong to the larger of the two major branches of Islam. The Kurds — an ethnic group with its own language and culture — occupy the oil-rich northwestern part of Iraq.

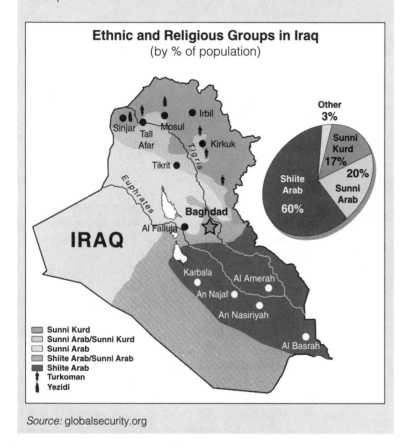

Ethnic and Religious Groups in Iraq
(by % of population)

Sinjar
Tall Afar
Mosul
Irbil
Kirkuk
Tikrit
Baghdad
Al Falluja
IRAQ
Karbala
Al Amerah
An Najaf
An Nasiriyah
Al Basrah

Tigris
Euphrates

Other 3%
Sunni Kurd 17%
Sunni Arab 20%
Shiite Arab 60%

- Sunni Kurd
- Sunni Arab/Sunni Kurd
- Sunni Arab
- Shiite Arab/Sunni Arab
- Shiite Arab
- Turkoman
- Yezidi

Source: globalsecurity.org

high-ranking members of the old regime.

The members represent a cross-section of Iraq's diverse population — from its large Kurdish minority in the north to Sunni strongholds in the center to the great Shiite Arab population's in the south. Freedom fighters newly returned from exile are represented, as are tribal leaders who survived the Baath Party's repressive 35-year reign and intellectuals who opposed the dictator.

Creation of the council reflects what Bush administration officials say is the halting but steady progress made since Hussein's regime collapsed on April 9. They note that more than 150 newspapers have been estab-

lished throughout the country and that all of Iraq's cities and a majority of its towns have elected local governments. Schools and universities have reopened, and for the first time in decades, citizens have been free to practice their religions and even hold public demonstrations.

Some Iraqis have used these new freedoms to protest the coalition's efforts and the continued presence of U.S. troops in Iraq. An outside report, prepared by the Center for Strategic and International Studies (CSIS), argues that much of the public dissatisfaction is linked to a lack of information and urges the Coalition Provisional Authority (CPA) to use television and radio to more effectively publicize its intentions and goals to the Iraqi public.

The head of the CPA and America's point man in what the allies call the "liberation" of Iraq is L. Paul Bremer III, a youthful, 61-year-old State Department veteran with a reputation for working hard and getting the job done. But even the most optimistic analysts admit that the task faced by Bremer and his 600-person civilian staff could take at least several years and cost billions of dollars. Currently, the United States is spending about $5 billion a month for military and reconstruction efforts.

First and foremost, the deteriorating security situation must be reversed. Sniper, mortar and grenade attacks have killed 47 American and British troops since May 1, when President Bush declared that "major combat" in Iraq had ended. The violence has kept the 160,000 American and British troops in the country on a combat footing, making it harder for them to interact with and gain the trust of Iraqi civilians. Moreover, with the troops on high alert, they have been largely unable to help repair the country's damaged infrastructure.

Bremer and U.S. military officials have maintained that the violence — which is primarily limited to a triangle-shaped area north and west of Baghdad dominated by Hussein loyalists — is containable. On June 30, Secretary of Defense Donald H. Rumsfeld echoed that view, arguing that the resistance "was not anything like a guerrilla war or organized resistance." [2]

But on July 17, Gen. John Abizaid, the new head of U.S. forces in Iraq, seemed to contradict the secretary when he said that American forces were facing "a guerrilla-style campaign." [3] And so far, the various steps they have taken to reduce the number of attacks, such as periodic security sweeps to round up suspected dissidents and confiscate weapons, have been unsuccessful.

The CSIS report, commissioned by the Pentagon and released on July 17, contends that the coalition has three months to "turn around the security situation." The document adds: "The 'hearts and minds' of key segments of the Sunni and Shi'a * communities are in play and can be won, but only if the CPA and new Iraqi authorities deliver in short order." [4]

U.S. officials vow to bring the security situation under control, pointing to the July 22 killings of Saddam's sons as the kind of step that will reduce future attacks and increase the Iraqi public's willingness to cooperate with coalition forces. "We've seen an increase in informants coming forward to our military, to our intelligence people and to our police in the last three weeks, and this is an obvious example of a culmination of that," Bremer said of the brothers' deaths on July 22. "I would hope this will encourage other Iraqis to come forward." [5]

From 'Cradle of Civilization' to Dictatorship

The world's first civilization flourished in Mesopotamia (modern-day Iraq), which later became a great center of Islamic learning. In about the 16th century, the Ottoman Turks absorbed Iraq into their huge empire. After the Ottoman collapse in 1918, Iraq became a British protectorate and then in 1932 an independent kingdom. A military coup overthrew the monarchy in 1958 and formed a "republic." In 1968, the Arab-nationalist Baath Party took power, leading to the rise of Saddam Hussein in 1979. Following Hussein's ouster in April 2003 by a U.S.-led invasion, coalition forces in Iraq have been restoring degraded infrastructure and paving the way for the establishment of a freely elected government.

Area: 168,753 sq. miles (about the size of California)

Population: 24.7 million (2003 est.)

Capital: Baghdad (pop. 5,772,000)

Major Rivers: Tigris and Euphrates

Natural Resources: petroleum, natural gas, phosphates, sulfur

Geography: mostly broad plains; reedy marshes with large flooded areas along Iranian border in south; mountains along eastern and northern borders with Iran and Turkey.

Life Expectancy: 67.8 years

Ethnic Groups: Arab 75%-80%, Kurdish 15%-20%, Turkoman, Assyrian or other 5%

Religion: Muslim 97% (Shiite 60%-65%, Sunni 32%-37%), Christian or other 3%

Industries: petroleum, chemicals, textiles, construction materials, food processing

Agriculture: wheat, barley, rice, vegetables, dates, cotton; cattle, sheep

Sources: CIA World Factbook; www.world-gazetteer.com

But some analysts contend that Bremer might have contributed to the current instability when he disbanded the Iraqi army and prohibited some 30,000 members of Hussein's Baath Party from holding government posts. Clearly many of the attackers are regime loyalists from the armed forces and the former ruling party.

At the same time, some Iraqis and Iraq-watchers applauded a recent U.S. announcement that the military would recruit Iraqis, including former soldiers, for a paramilitary force that would help American troops keep order and root out resistance. Likewise, many argue that some Baathists currently prohibited from government

* This is an alternate spelling for Shiite.

Members of Iraq's newly established national governing body — the first since U.S.-led forces ousted Saddam Hussein — hold an inaugural meeting on July 13 in Baghdad. The council is expected to appoint ministers, pass a budget and prepare the country for a constitutional convention in early September.

service should be allowed to contribute their talents and skills to rebuilding the country, arguing they only joined the party because it assured them of a job. But others contend a new Iraqi government would be tainted by the presence of Baath Party activists and leaders.

Restoring power, water and other services poses another huge challenge for Bremer. Utilities in many cities were never adequately repaired after they were damaged during the first Persian Gulf War in 1991. So, in effect, the United States inherited infrastructure problems that existed even before it launched its invasion. Moreover, Iraqi looting of copper wire and other newly installed parts and sabotage of power plants, oil pipelines and other facilities have hindered the re-establishment of electricity, engendering widespread anti-coalition sentiment and dissatisfaction.

While citizens have not been polled scientifically, anecdotal accounts in news reports reflect growing resentment. "At least we had power and security" before the war, said Baghdad shopkeeper Uday Abdul al-Wahab. "Democracy is not feeding us." [6]

Indeed, the CSIS report warned of "rising anti-Americanism in parts of the country." Some experts argue that the United States is exacerbating the problems by not devoting enough resources to the rebuilding effort. For instance, the CSIS report noted that while "significant progress" has been made, the civil authority is underfunded and overstretched. [7]

Many Iraq-watchers also blame the security and infrastructure problems on poor post-war planning by the United States and its allies. In the first weeks after the war, violence and looting often went unchallenged by allied troops and a civilian administration that did not want to look like an occupying power.

"They really didn't think through what would happen when Saddam fell, and they pieced together a [postwar] plan very quickly," says Judith Yaphe, a senior research fellow at the National Defense University.

But Bremer counters that it is unrealistic to expect a smooth transition to stability and democracy given Iraq's recent, totalitarian past. "Saddam took 35 years to run the place down, and it's not going to take 35 days to fix it," he said. "People need to be patient." [8]

Meanwhile, giving the U.N. a greater role in Iraq would speed up the reconstruction process, according to some experts. Although the U.N. is providing about $1 billion in humanitarian assistance to Iraqis, these experts contend that handing over the country's civil administration to the U.N. would transform the reconstruction from what is perceived as an American occupation into an international effort, which might be more successful in eliciting assistance from other countries.

For now, however, the United States and Britain remain firmly in control, arguing that they are best positioned to restore stability and foster the growth of democracy. And although some scholars question whether Iraqis — after living for years in a totalitarian state — are culturally prepared for democratic rule, American officials and others remain optimistic that the country will make the transition, if fitfully.

As Americans, Iraqis and others look to the country's future, here are some of the questions they are asking:

Can Iraq be transformed into a stable, pro-Western democracy?

President Bush has often chided critics of his Iraq policy as being overly pessimistic about the country's prospects for democracy. "The Iraqi people are fully capable of self-government," he told a largely Arab-American audience in Dearborn, Mich., in April. "Every day, Iraqis are moving toward democracy and embracing the responsibilities of active citizenship." [9]

Although U.S. and British officials are still in charge, the new, interim, national council has been given real — if limited — power. In addition, municipal councils have been elected in most cities and large towns. By September, Bremer said on July 15, a group of Iraqis will convene to draft a new constitution and set the stage for elections and democracy.

But many Middle East experts say building democratic institutions will take a long time. "The holding of a free, general election is the culmination, not the inauguration, of a process of democratization," says Bernard Lewis, a professor of Near East studies at Princeton University and author of *The Crisis of Islam: Holy War and Unholy Terror.* "Remember, our own democracies in the West took centuries to develop. Democracy doesn't come in a sort of do-it-yourself kit with a manual of instructions."

Others go further, arguing that Iraq's totalitarian past leaves it unprepared to even begin democratization. "To have a real chance at democracy, you need to have a strong civil society," says Ray Jennings, a senior fellow at the U.S. Institute for Peace, a federally funded think tank that promotes peaceful conflict resolution. "So, we're going to have to rehabilitate Iraqi civil society, and that's going to take time."

Jennings points out that during decades of brutal, authoritarian rule, the trappings of civil society — from a free press and free speech to independent interest groups — were eliminated. Dissidents were exiled, jailed or murdered by the government.

As a result, there is a huge "political vacuum" in Iraq, says Tom Carothers, director of the Democracy and Rule of Law Project at the Carnegie Endowment for International Peace. "A lot of the people who might normally step forward aren't available.

"It's not like the fall of the Berlin Wall, where at least you had societies that had had some experience of democracy or were exposed to democratic ideas," Carothers adds. "People in Iraq have no experience with these things. They have no real experience even working together."

Some scholars also maintain that radical Islam could be a hurdle, especially since some Iraqi Shiite clerics and others have called for theocratic rule of Iraq. According to Lewis, some of the problem stems from the Islamic view that church and state are interconnected. "The relationship between government and religion is much stronger and more basic in Islam than it is in Christianity," he said. "There is a sort of interpenetration of government and religion in Islam." [10]

The outlook is so bleak, pessimists say, that drafting a constitution and even holding elections might not lead to democracy. "It's very possible that Iraq will be given a constitutional framework of some sort in the coming years, but it still probably won't be democracy," says Vivian Hart, a professor of political science at the University of Sussex in England who specializes in democratic development. "Real democracy has to come from the people. It's not something you can impose on them."

Indeed, a future democratic experiment could be imperiled by the fact that it was the United States and not the Iraqi people that drove Hussein from power, notes Stephen Zunes, a professor of politics at the University of San Francisco. "This will make them much less enthusiastic about creating something new to take the place of Saddam," Zunes says.

But more optimistic experts say the Iraqi people are hungry for a change to a more open, democratic system. "There really is a pent-up demand on the part of the public for new freedoms," says Frederick D. Barton, a senior adviser at CSIS. "And they understand what those basic freedoms are, by the way. They want freedom of speech, worship and movement."

Yaphe, at the National Defense University, agrees. "It's very clear that they want representative government," she says. "They want it even if they don't ultimately know what all of that entails."

Adds Barton: "Their desire for freedom and democratic change are the most important underpinnings. You can leave it to the technocrats to write a constitution and run the elections."

Indeed, some argue that Iraqis are among the best qualified to embrace democracy in the Arab world because they are the best educated. "Baghdad is the Arab world's intellectual hub, and Iraqis are the intellectual cream of Arab society," says Abdulaziz Sachedina, a professor of religious studies at the University of Virginia. "Even under Saddam, Iraqis understood the need for a strong civil society and hoped for representative government."

Sachedina points to the recent return to Iraq of Sharif Ali Bin-al-Husayn — successor to the country's deposed Hashimite king — as a sign that Iraq is ready for democracy. "You'll notice that he said he was in favor of representative democracy, of a constitutional monarchy," he says. "It's a sign he understands the Iraqi people are not looking for another dictatorship and will not settle for anything less than democracy."

Reviving Iraq's Oil Industry Is No Easy Task

Iraq's black gold is flowing again. On July 13, a British Petroleum tanker in the southern port city of Basrah carried out the first shipment — 2 million barrels — of freshly pumped oil since the war ended. The following day, another 2 million barrels were loaded onto a Chevron-Texaco tanker, and Royal Dutch Shell is slated to take another shipment near the end of the month.

But while these and other scheduled shipments represent an important first step for the petroleum industry, Iraq is not likely to be a major player in the international oil market any time soon.

Iraq has the world's second-largest oil reserves after Saudi Arabia. But years of economic sanctions and neglect, coupled with recent looting and sabotage, have left the country's once-vaunted petroleum industry in deep trouble.

Currently, under American supervision, Iraq is producing an average of 600,000 barrels a day, a substantial drop from the 2.5 million barrels it was producing daily before the war. [1] According to the Centre for Global Energy Studies, a London-based energy think tank, Iraq should be able to pump 3 million barrels a day within three years if its oil infrastructure is restored. [2]

More than half of the country's crude comes from the vast oil fields near the northern city of Kirkuk, and most of the rest comes from fields near Basrah, in the south.

Before this year's war, American officials worried that Saddam Hussein would set the country's oil wells ablaze, as Iraqi forces did while retreating from Kuwait during the Persian Gulf War in 1991. But in the recent conflict, only a few wells were set afire, which were quickly put out by American engineers.

Given the small scale of war-related damage sustained by the oil industry, the United States and Britain had hoped to quickly bring oil production back to pre-war levels, but production has been hindered by lack of electricity to run the pumps and equipment. [3]

Post-war sabotage and looting by Iraqis themselves have also taken a toll. Iraq's 4,000 miles of pipelines have been repeatedly damaged by resistance fighters and illegally tapped by thieves. [4] The major line between the northern fields and Turkey is still out of service due to two attacks that damaged it. "Pipelines are very soft targets," says Robert Ebel, an energy analyst at the Center for Strategic and International Studies. "It doesn't take a rocket scientist to figure out where you can do the most damage, both physical and psychological, with the minimum amount of effort and the minimum chance of being caught."

The United States has begun using helicopters to patrol long stretches of pipelines in remote areas. It also has hired local tribesmen near the lines to watch for saboteurs. Even so, most experts contend that the pipelines remain vulnerable.

Sharing the Wealth

If daily production does reach 2 million barrels, only 1.3 million barrels would be available for export. Iraq needs about half a million barrels a day to feed its own petroleum needs, and 200,000 barrels of crude a day must be reinjected into the ground to keep the pressure high enough for the oil to keep flowing out of existing wells.

Tapping the nation's oil wealth is important for both the United States and the Iraqis. The coalition is planning to use revenue generated from oil sales to pay for at least half of the $7 billion reconstruction budget for the rest of the year, and the U.S. administrator in Iraq, L. Paul Bremer III, has indicated that petroleum exports would fund an even greater portion of

---

[1] Figure cited in "Iraq's Post-Conflict Reconstruction," Center for Strategic and International Studies, July 17, 2003, p. 8.

[2] See www.cges.co.uk.

[3] Faisal Islam and Oliver Morgan, "Pipe Dreams of Iraqi Oil," *The Observer*, July 13, 2002, p. 3.

[4] Warren Vieth and Alissa J. Rubin, "Iraq Pipelines Easy Target for a Saboteur," *Los Angeles Times*, June 25, 2003, p. A1.

Should the U.N. play a greater role in Iraq's reconstruction?

After the United States and Britain gave up on winning U.N. approval for military action in Iraq earlier this year, many analysts wondered whether the world body would have any role to play in post-war Iraq. When the conflict ended though, President Bush and other American officials indicated the United Nations could assist with humanitarian concerns, such as distributing food and water.

the budget in 2004. The Bush administration is considering using future oil sales as collateral to borrow money to pay for reconstruction, including rebuilding the oil infrastructure. [5]

Currently, the revenue from oil sales goes into the Development Fund for Iraq, a coalition-controlled account that funds the country's reconstruction. American officials also expect some of the money from oil sales to be used to pay reparations to Kuwait for damage sustained during the Persian Gulf War.

Recently Army Corps of Engineers personnel met with Iraqi oil officials and private contactors to map out a strategy for bringing production up to 3 million barrels. The United States plans to spend $1 billion to upgrade infrastructure in both northern and southern fields.

Overall, experts say, long-term prospects for oil production are good. According to the Central Intelligence Agency, Iraq has known oil reserves totaling 113.8 billion barrels, and much of the western half of the country has not yet been explored. [6] According to the U.S. Export-Import

Iraq's Oil and Gas Reserves

Oil and gas fields are scattered throughout eastern Iraq; the western desert remains undeveloped. At least six major refineries and oil and gas pipelines are in operation.

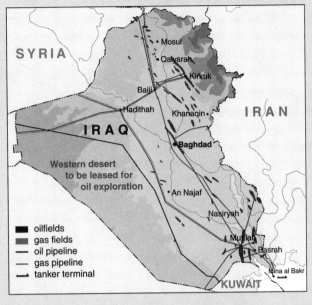

Source: *Petroleum Economist*, February 2003

Bank, Iraq could eventually be producing 5 million barrels per day. [7]

In the months before the war began, President Bush and other administration officials repeatedly said Iraq's oil would be used to "benefit the Iraqi people." This was a clear rebuke to former Iraqi President Saddam Hussein, who used the country's oil wealth to build a huge military and a network of lavish palaces.

Once Iraq attains self-government, the coalition plans to completely turn over the oil industry to the Iraqi government. How the Iraqi people will share in this great wealth is still to be decided.

In a recent column in *The New York Times*, Bremer proposed two possible ways future oil earnings could be distributed to the citizenry. "One possibility would be to pay social benefits from a trust financed by oil revenues. Another could be to pay an annual cash dividend directly to each citizen from that trust." [8]

[5] Warren Vieth, "U.S. May Tap Oil for Iraqi Loans," *Los Angeles Times*, July 11, 2003, p. A1.

[6] See *CIA World Fact Book* at: http://www.odci.gov/cia/publications/factbook/print/iz.html.

[7] Vieth, *op. cit.*

[8] L. Paul Bremer, "The Road Ahead in Iraq — And How to Navigate It," *The New York Times*, July 13, 2003, p. A13.

The U.N. role was expanded somewhat after the Security Council agreed to lift U.N. economic sanctions against Iraq on May 22.

The resolution also called for the appointment of a special U.N. representative for Iraq, charged with overseeing U.N. operations and representing the world body's interests. The day after the vote, the current U.N. High Commissioner for Refugees, de Mello, was appointed to the post.

Supporters of a greater U.N. role in Iraq's reconstruction point to the continuing chaos plaguing the country as the most obvious, but not the only, reason for more U.N. involvement.

"Iraq is a very big country, and the United States can't do it alone," says Johanna Mendelson-Forman, senior program officer at the U.N. Foundation, the Ted Turner-funded aid organization that works with the United Nations.

In fact, Mendelson-Forman and others say, the U.N. is the best-qualified organization to lead the post-war reconstruction. "They have the kind of experience doing the sorts of things we need done in Iraq," says Andy Pugh, a public-policy analyst at the international aid group CARE. "They've tackled nation building in places like Bosnia, East Timor and Kosovo."

And in Iraq in particular, U.N. supporters contend, the organization's tremendous expertise is currently being underutilized. "There were 1,000 U.N. people in the country before the war," says the CSIS's Barton. "These people would be invaluable in areas like aid distribution and in telling us who we can and cannot trust among the local population."

Moreover, getting the U.N. more involved could lend the reconstruction effort the international legitimacy it now lacks. "The United Nations conveys a legitimacy that the American occupying army simply cannot," Mendelson-Forman says. "When the U.N. is there, it says that the world community supports this."

Such legitimacy could also result in more aid to Iraq. "If the U.N. leads, the Europeans and others will give more aid and put more people on the ground," Pugh says.

"U.N. backing is especially important if you want to bring in upcoming, second-tier powers like India, Brazil and Mexico, because they take the U.N. very seriously," adds Mendelson-Forman.

Finally, the world body would convey legitimacy for the reconstruction effort among the Iraqis themselves, say supporters of more U.N. involvement. "For aid agencies like CARE, working under U.N. leadership gives us a mantle of neutrality," Pugh says. "It's much easier for us to work closely with local groups if we tell them we're working under U.N. leadership than it would be if we were operating under the U.S. or the coalition. Local people would certainly trust us more."

But the Carnegie Endowment's Carothers contends that giving the U.N. an administrative role in Iraq would make an already difficult situation worse. "Right now,

we have the freedom to make quick decisions," he says. "You bring in the United Nations, and that's over."

"Precious time would be lost if we tried to internationalize this," agrees Jennings. "It took the United Nations two years to get an administration running in Kosovo, which is, after all, a small country with only 2 million people." Iraq, by comparison, has nearly 25 million people.

In addition, critics say, the U.N. has failed at nation building in the past. "When people say the U.N. has a 'unique experience' in this area, I say: 'Yes, they have a unique experience at failing,' " says Christopher Preble, a historian at the Cato Institute, a libertarian think tank. "East Timor [formerly part of Indonesia] descended into chaos [under U.N. administration], and Bosnia and Kosovo are not closer to multi-ethnic democracy now than they were when the U.N. arrived," he says.

"Because the U.N. is a large bureaucracy staffed by people from all over the world, with different agendas and perspectives, they tend not to understand the local situation on the ground very well," says Rachel Belton, a consultant on international issues who is writing a book on nation building. Such an unwieldy bureaucratic structure makes the U.N. the wrong organization to establish the kind of institutions and values that will ultimately lead to democracy, she adds.

Others question whether the United Nations actually would add legitimacy to reconstruction efforts. "If the U.S. solves the country's practical problems, we'll have all of the legitimacy we need," Preble says. "Nothing succeeds like success."

And even those critics who agree that the world body would convey legitimacy argue that such benefits would be more than outweighed by the organization's shortcomings. "You don't want to obtain more legitimacy at the cost of doing the job well," Belton says.

Should Baath Party members be purged from the civil service and other public positions?

Within a week of his arrival in Iraq, U.S. administrator Bremer announced that up to 30,000 senior Baath Party members would be banned from government posts. The new policy, Bremer wrote on May 16, would help ensure that the country's next government is "not threatened by Baathist elements returning to power and that those in positions of authority in the future are acceptable to the people of Iraq." [11]

Under Bremer's plan, the top four ranks of current party members will be removed from any public office. In addition, 2,000 senior managers who run the country's ministries, universities, hospitals and large corporations will lose their jobs if they were active party members.

Bremer's predecessor, Lt. Gen. Jay Garner, had been criticized for reinstating high-ranking Baathists at public facilities, such as universities and government ministries. In one controversial incident, Garner reversed his decision to appoint Ali al-Janabi, a high-ranking Baathist before the war, as interim minister of health after Iraqi doctors demonstrated against his appointment.

However, removing 30,000 officials still leaves 94 percent of the 1.5 million Baath Party members that were in power in Hussein's Iraq, so no one realistically suggests banning all of them. That would leave ministries, businesses, schools, hospitals and other public facilities empty or understaffed.

Even the most hardline anti-Baathists concede that many people who joined the party did so to get or keep a job and not for ideological reasons or out of loyalty to Hussein. During his regime, party membership was often a requirement on job applications.

Indeed, some Iraq-watchers worry that removing so many senior officials will make an already unstable situation worse by stripping ministries, organizations and companies of their most capable employees. "Whatever Bremer might be saying now, he's going to have to reverse himself somewhat and dip into the Baath Party higher-ups to get things done," says Jennings of the Institute of Peace. "These are the people who have insight into how things work in a way that no one else does."

The University of Virginia's Sachedina agrees. "This is a very hasty step," he says. "We need them because they understood the nuances of the system and so, at the very least, we should be using many of them in the transition."

Sachedina also says Bremer did not take into account the compromises that people, even high-ranking Baathists, had to make living under Hussein. "When I was visiting Iraq over the years, many Baathists, including senior people, confided they did not believe in what they were doing," he says. "But what choice did they have?"

Sia Jawad, a political science professor at Baghdad University, echoed those sentiments. "A lot of them were good people," he said. "A lot of them had nothing to do with killing or torturing or eliminating people." [12]

But others argue that pushing Baathists out sends exactly the right message to recently liberated Iraqis. "Getting rid of these people lets everyone else know why we fought this war," consultant Belton says. "It adds legitimacy to our cause because local people see that we're actually taking down the old order."

Supporters of Bremer's purge also contend that leaving too many high-ranking Baathists in power would endanger the gains Iraqis have made since Hussein's fall. "Coalition forces paid a big price to get rid of Saddam," says Hilal Aboud al-Bayati, a professor of computer science at Baghdad University. "If these people are left in office, they are capable of killing liberty again."

The Baath Party wasn't just a political organization that backed Hussein. Purge supporters say it was a conscious imitator of what many consider the greatest evils of the 20th century: fascism and communism. "The ancestry of the Baath may be found not in the Middle East, not in Islam, not in Arabism but in the Nazi Party and the Communist Party, two sources of inspiration," Princeton's Lewis recently wrote. These ideologies were introduced into Iraq during its time as a European protectorate after World War I, he adds. [13]

Finally, a well-educated nation like Iraq doesn't need ideologically tainted people to rebuild and run the country, says the Carnegie Endowment's Carothers. "The Baath Party doesn't have the only reservoir of talent in the country," he says. "Most of these tasks can be taken on by the many talented and learned Iraqis who didn't become Baathist bigwigs."

But others wonder whether Bremer's goal is realistic. "It's a good idea, but we really don't know who the real top Baathists are," Barton, of the CSIS, says. "I've seen vetting processes in other places, and I can tell you that it's very hard to do. And I've seen nothing from our people [in Iraq] that leads me to believe that they will do it any better."

BACKGROUND

Nation Building

During the 19th and early 20th centuries, while European states were gobbling up much of Africa and Asia, the United States engaged in comparatively little overseas conquest. Except for establishing colonies in the Philippines and Cuba after the 1898 Spanish American

CHRONOLOGY

March-April, 2003 *Coalition forces invade and conquer Iraq. Looting and guerrilla warfare follow the end of major combat.*

March 17 Retired Gen. Jay Garner arrives in Kuwait to begin planning Iraq's post-war reconstruction.

March 20 The coalition ground offensive begins.

April 9 U.S. forces move into central Baghdad. Saddam Hussein's regime collapses.

April 10 Looters lay seige to Baghdad.

April 14 The last major city in Iraq, Hussein's hometown of Tikrit, falls to American troops.

April 15 Garner meets with Iraqi opposition leaders in Ur.

April 18 Iraqis stage a peaceful, anti-American demonstration in Baghdad.

May 2003 *Continued chaos in much of Iraq prompts the United States to appoint a new administrator.*

May 1 President Bush declares an end to major combat operations in Iraq.

May 3 Baghdad schools reopen.

May 6 The United States replaces Garner with L. Paul Bremer III, a former State Department official.

May 12 Bremer arrives in Baghdad.

May 14 U.S. troops are authorized to shoot looters.

May 16 Bremer announces that 30,000 Baath Party activists will be ineligible to serve in government posts.

May 22 U.N. Security Council votes 14-0 to lift economic sanctions against Iraq.

May 23 The U.N. appoints Sergio Viera de Mello as its special representative in Iraq.

May 29 British Prime Minister Tony Blair visits Iraq.

June-Present *Continued violence prompts the United States to alter its post-war strategy.*

June 18 U.S. forces capture Hussein's top aide, Abid Hamid Mahmoud al-Tikriti.

June 29 Bremer says that the continued attacks will not hinder reconstruction.

July 2 President Bush says "Bring 'em on" when asked about Iraqi resistance fighters.

July 4 The United States offers a $25 million reward for information leading to Hussein's capture. The same day, a tape purporting to be the dictator's voice is broadcast on Arab radio.

July 9 Gen. John Abizaid takes control of U.S. forces in Iraq, replacing Gen. Tommy Franks.

July 10 Franks tells members of Congress that U.S. troops will remain in the country for the foreseeable future.

July 13 An interim council of 25 prominent Iraqis meets for the first time in Baghdad.

July 16 The new council authorizes formation of war-crimes courts to try high-ranking members of Hussein's government.

July 16 Abizaid admits that the U.S. is in a "classic guerrilla-type war" in Iraq.

July 17 In a speech before a joint session of Congress, British Prime Minister Tony Blair defends the coalition invasion of Iraq and predicts the country will successfully transition to democracy.

July 22 In what military officials called a "fierce gunbattle," coalition forces killed Hussein's sons, Uday and Qusay — "further assurance that [Hussein's] regime is gone and won't be back," said an administration spokesman.

September Iraqis are slated to hold a convention to draft a new constitution.

War, the U.S. government focused primarily on taming its western frontier and creating a continent-wide nation.

The emergence of the United States as a superpower after the Second World War shifted America's priorities to a more global focus and established its reputation as a nation that helps rebuild its vanquished enemies. Indeed, by 1959, America's nation-building impulses were great enough to warrant a spoof — the British film "The Mouse That Roared." In it, a tiny European country declares war on the United States in hopes that it will be vanquished so the generous Americans will rebuild the defeated country.

The reputation was based on what most scholars consider the most successful nation-building exercise ever — the reconstruction of the defeated Germany and Japan after World War II. Americans occupied Japan for seven years and set out to entirely remake huge sectors of the society. Tens of thousands of military and government officials were purged from the public sector. Business conglomerates were broken up and labor unions were allowed to form.

The emperor was retained as ceremonial head of state, but a new American-drafted constitution was imposed on the population, creating a British-style parliamentary system of government with a bicameral legislature and a prime minister. The document contained many of the guarantees found in the U.S. Constitution, such as freedom of worship and speech. In addition, it committed Japan to pacifism, renouncing war as an instrument of international relations and prohibiting the maintenance of a military. Cold War concerns later prompted the United States to allow Japan to establish a "self-defense force."

Many of the same changes occurred in West Germany, which was controlled by America and her allies while the Eastern third of the country was controlled by the Soviets. Denazification of the business and public sector went hand-in-hand with the creation of a new parliamentary system of government based on a Western-style constitution.

Both Japan and Germany were transformed into and remain stable and wealthy democracies.

In the early 1950s, the United States helped to defend South Korea from an invasion by Chinese and North Korean communists, and then maintained a huge military and political influence after the war ended. For more than three decades under U.S. tutelage, South Korea developed a sophisticated market economy but remained essentially a military dictatorship. In the 1980s, South Koreans created genuine democratic institutions. Indeed, they recently even elected a new president who ran on an anti-U.S. platform due to a dispute over America's policy on North Korea.

An ostensibly similar situation led to a different result in South Vietnam, in part because the United States did not successfully contain a communist insurgency from North Vietnam, as it had in South Korea. During the war, the U.S.-backed government in the South was only marginally democratic — and very corrupt. Three years after American troops pulled out of the country in 1972, South Vietnam was invaded by the North, which unified the two countries into one communist dictatorship.

The debacle in Vietnam — coupled with subsequent humiliations in other countries under American influence, notably Iran and Lebanon — led to a reappraisal of nation building. Many experts, especially on the left, began to see it as an act of imperialism. [14]

But by the early 1990s, American self-doubt was on the wane. The country's greatest enemy, the Soviet Union, collapsed in 1991. The same year, the United States won a stunning victory in the Persian Gulf War. Then-President George Bush declared a "new world order" in which "freedom and respect for human rights find a home among all nations."

His first opportunity to enforce the new order occurred in Somalia in 1991. U.S. forces arrived to provide security to humanitarian efforts to feed millions of starving people who were denied access to aid because of feuding warlords. But what had started out as an aid mission soon morphed into a nation-building exercise when the United States and its allies decided to eliminate warlord-based strife and set the country on a more stable course. On Oct. 3, 1993, 18 Army rangers were killed in an effort to capture a warlord, a tragedy made more painful when an American soldier's corpse was filmed being dragged through the streets of Mogadishu, the country's capital.

The disaster in Somalia, recently portrayed in the film "Black Hawk Down," prompted then-President Clinton to pull American forces out of the country. Once again, the idea of nation-building was called into question, and for several years afterwards the United States did not involve itself in any similar effort, including in 1994, when more than 1 million people died in an ethnic genocide in Rwanda.

Contracts to Rebuild Iraq Raise Eyebrows

In the coming years, the reconstruction of Iraq may end up costing the United States tens of billions of dollars, most of which will go to private firms. Although only a small portion of that money has been spent so far, controversy already has broken out over how some of the funds have been awarded, and to whom.

At the eye of the storm are two big contracts awarded by the U.S. Army Corps of Engineers without soliciting competitive bids to Halliburton — a giant oil services and construction firm formerly run by Vice President Dick Cheney. Critics allege the firm may have used its high-powered political connections to win lucrative deals and that the U.S. taxpayer may be left holding the bag.

The first contract was awarded to a Halliburton subsidiary, Kellogg, Brown and Root (KBR) in December 2001, more than a year before the war in Iraq began. The Corps tapped KBR to provide housing, recreation, food, sanitation and laundry services to troops in Iraq — a deal with no spending ceiling and awarded without open, competitive bidding.

The second contract called for KBR to repair and upgrade Iraq's oil infrastructure immediately after the war, including dousing any fires and assessing the petroleum industry's capacity. Signed in March 2003, the deal had a ceiling of $7 billion, but it, too, was approved without competitive bidding.

So far, KBR has received more than $800 million from the two contracts — $596.8 million for troop services and $213 million for oil-well support. [1]

Normally, the U.S. government must seek competitive bids before issuing contracts. But agencies can waive the requirement if national-security interests are at stake and quick action is required. The waiver allows an agency to narrow the field of competitors to those with prior experience and the necessary security clearances.

Critics of the deals contend Halliburton's connection to Cheney may have automatically given it the inside track. "No one is suggesting that Dick Cheney ordered that contract," says Charles Lewis, executive director for the Center for Public Integrity, a government accountability advocacy group. "The problem is that he doesn't have to do anything; everyone in the Pentagon knows that Halliburton is Dick Cheney's company."

Moreover, critics worry the open-ended nature of the two contracts could lead to abuses. According to Rep. Henry A. Waxman, D-Calif., ranking minority member of the House Government Reform Committee, the lack of limits on time and funding structures the contracts "in such

---

[1] Figures cited in "Halliburton Contracts in Iraq Exceed $800 million," *Los Angeles Times,* June 21, 2003, p. A5.

But by 1995, the United States, along with its NATO allies, was trying to create peace in the former Yugoslav republic of Bosnia, after ethnically driven genocide had claimed nearly 250,000 lives. [15] And in 1999, the United States and its NATO allies again found themselves embroiled in a conflict in Yugoslavia, this time in the Serb province of Kosovo. Intense bombing by American and allied warplanes prevented the Serbs from "ethnically cleansing" the area of its Muslim majority. [16]

American and European troops still occupy Bosnia and Kosovo, keeping a fragile peace between the Muslims, Croats and Serbs who live in Bosnia and the Muslims and Serbs who inhabit Kosovo. In both places, the United Nations has established shaky multi-ethnic governments and, with NATO help, stopped the killing.

But governing and other institutions are still very weak, and ethnic divisions have not died.

Afghanistan

The terrorist attacks in the United States on Sept. 11, 2001, focused American attention on Afghanistan, where the Islamic fundamentalist Taliban regime was harboring the al Qaeda leaders who perpetrated the attacks. By the end of the year, the Taliban had been routed and the United States and its Afghan allies were in charge of the country. [17]

Decades of war and underdevelopment had left Afghanistan without much in the way of physical infrastructure or civil society. Instead, the country is a loose collection of ethnic tribal groups, most of them poor but well armed. [18]

a way as to encourage . . . increase[s] [in their] costs and, consequently, the costs to the taxpayer." [2]

Military officials refute the claim. In a letter to Waxman, Lt. Gen. Robert Flowers, chief of engineers at the Corps, argued that in both cases Halliburton was chosen because it had extensive experience and was the best contractor for the job. For instance, with regard to the oil contract, Flowers noted that KBR had put out 350 oil fires in Kuwait during the 1991 Persian Gulf War. He added: "Only KBR, the contractor that developed the complex, classified contingency plans, could commence implementing them on extremely short notice." [3]

Flowers said the deals were open-ended because they were designed to cover "worst-case scenarios" that never came to pass. [4] The contracts will soon be re-tendered for open bidding, he pointed out, and, in fact, the Corps has already solicited bids for two contracts worth $1 billion to resuscitate Iraq's oil industry.

The Halliburton controversy may be the tip of the iceberg. Future issues loom that could muddy upcoming bidding.

Contracts made with the old regime are a major concern. When the war began, the Iraq government had inked an estimated $57.2 billion in contracts with firms from Russia, China, Holland, France, Egypt and elsewhere,

mostly to upgrade energy and telecommunications sectors. The vast majority of the contracts, roughly 90 percent, were signed with Russian firms. [5]

On May 22, the United Nations Security Council passed a resolution ending economic sanctions against Iraq. Under that resolution, Secretary-General Kofi Annan is charged with determining the fate of the outstanding contracts. Russian officials have said they will not consider helping the United States rebuild or police Iraq until the status of their contracts is resolved.

Meanwhile, France, Germany and other nations that refused to join the alliance to oust Saddam want their companies to be allowed to bid on future contracts, especially if they contribute funds to the reconstruction effort. But the Bush administration has shown no interest in including those nations in the bidding, and all of the contracts handed out so far have gone to U.S. firms.

Of those, the largest — a $680 million contract to repair and rebuild the country's infrastructure — has gone to the U.S. construction firm Bechtel. [6] The U.S. Agency for International Development, which is charged with handing out most of the reconstruction contracts, also has awarded contracts to administer Iraqi harbors and airports and to rebuild the educational and health systems.

---

[2] Quoted in Stephen J. Glain and Robert Schlesinger, "Halliburton Unit Expands War-Repair Role," *The Boston Globe,* July 10, 2003, p. A1.

[3] Quoted in Byron York, "All Smoke, No Fire," *National Review*, July 14, 2003.

[4] Glain and Schlesinger, *op. cit.*

[5] Figures cited in "Reconstructing Iraq: A Guide to the Issues," The Open Society Institute, May 30, 2003, p. 47.

[6] For a complete list of all USAID Iraq-related contracts, see www.usaid.gov/iraq/activities.html.

In the 18 months since the Taliban fell, much progress has been made in Afghanistan. Over 2 million refugees have returned to the country, a sign that people are optimistic about the future. Afghanistan has a new currency and a new president — Hamid Karzai — elected by a representative grand council. Roads are being built, shops are opening; some cities even have a mobile-phone system. [19]

But the country has yet to recover from some of its most severe problems, most notably a widespread lack of security. Warlords, each with his own army, are still the dominant force outside of the capital, Kabul. As a result, in many parts of the country security is still tenuous and citizens are robbed and even killed with great frequency.

The United States, along with its allies and the U.N., says it is trying to address these problems. For instance, allied soldiers are training the first recruits in a new, projected 70,000-person Afghan army. And plans are in place to hire tens of thousands of Afghan men, many of whom are currently fighting for one warlord or another, to upgrade the country's road system.

Many already have accused the United States of losing interest in Afghanistan at a time when the country is still very fragile and, in many places, still fraught with violence and instability.

Indeed, Americans admit that the 9,000 U.S. combat troops in the country are specifically there to hunt down terrorists and remaining members of the old regime. "Our troops are not here to build a nation, but to fight al Qaeda and the Taliban," says America's ambassador to Kabul, Robert Finn. "A lot of people would like them to be used for nation building, but that is not why they are here."

From Garner to Bremer

The appointment of Garner to administer Iraq immediately after the war was accompanied by high hopes. After all, the general had led the successful U.S. effort to help the Kurds of northern Iraq after the Persian Gulf War in 1991.

But this time the now-retired Garner did not earn high marks. Within a month, the White House had replaced him — a favorite of Secretary of Defense Rumsfeld — with Bremer, the State Department's choice.

Garner's brief tenure atop the new civil administration was marked by rampant disorder and confusion. As U.S. soldiers stood by, looters robbed government buildings of everything that could be carried away — from toilets and file cabinets to electrical wiring. Public services were restored slowly and in some places not at all. At first, administration officials, including Rumsfeld, attributed the disorder to the natural exuberance of a long-oppressed people who were now free. And the slow return of services was blamed on the decrepit state of Iraq's infrastructure.

But as the weeks passed and the situation in many places did not improve, the administration came under increasing criticism that it had neglected post-war planning. Actually, the administration had been planning for a post-Hussein Iraq at least since January, when Garner was chosen. But unlike the painstakingly detailed war plan, the post-war plan was sketchy.

"The war plan was there is spades," said Ron Adams, who served as Garner's deputy. "But we didn't see much post-conflict stuff in writing until we got into Kuwait," on March 17, two days before the war started. [20]

Critics also contend that the president and others relied on a rosy post-war scenario. "Our post-war planning was based on some very optimistic assumptions about what would happen when the shooting stopped," says the U.N. Foundation's Mendelson-Forman. "They relied heavily on diaspora intelligence," she adds, referring to Iraqi exiles, many of whom claimed that U.S. officials would be welcomed by nearly the entire population. "The [exiles] were in contact with people in the country, but they weren't on the ground, so their knowledge was limited."

The trouble caused by poor planning was compounded by a lack of assertiveness on Garner's part. In particular, the critics claim, the general did not want to appear too authoritarian. "I think he was so concerned about not appearing to be too overbearing that it undercut his own authority right from the start," says James A. Phillips, a research fellow at the Heritage Foundation.

To make matters worse, the general did not have any authority over U.S. forces in the country, giving him very little real power.

By the beginning of May, the administration decided that Garner had to go. In picking Bremer, Bush turned to a key player in the GOP foreign-policy establishment. In his 23-year career at the State Department, Bremer had served as the top counterterrorism official and ambassador to the Netherlands. He retired in 1989 and went to work at the consulting firm headed by former Secretary of State Henry A. Kissinger.

Bremer is known for his no-nonsense style and his capacity for hard work, a reputation that he has lived up to so far in Iraq. Since his arrival in Baghdad on May 12, wearing a business suit and army boots, Bremer has moved quickly on many fronts, from putting more military police on the streets to officially dissolving the Iraqi army and banning senior Baath Party members from government posts. Moreover, Garner's plan to quickly establish an Iraqi interim government was put on hold for a few months in order to send a message that Bremer himself would be making all decisions for the time being.

"He came in and wanted to show that there was a new sheriff in town," Phillips says.

While Bremer was working to establish a new U.S. administration in Baghdad, diplomats in New York were wrangling over how the international community should deal with an Iraq under American and British control. During the first three weeks of May, the Security Council debated whether the U.N. itself should play a key role in the country's reconstruction.

The same troika that had led the opposition to the war — France, Germany and Russia — argued that the international body should play a leading role in rebuilding Iraq. [21] But the United States and Britain disagreed. The Americans and British also wanted the U.N. to lift economic sanctions, imposed on the country by the United Nations after the Persian Gulf War, so Iraq could begin selling oil and using the funds for reconstruction. [22]

On May 22, the Security Council approved, 14-0, a resolution lifting the sanctions and giving the United States and Britain de facto control over Iraq's political and economic future. While the vote gave the United States almost all of what it wanted, it also gave the U.N. and other international organizations and countries permission to aid in Iraq's reconstruction. In addition, it provided for the United Nations to send a special representative to the country to represent the international body's interests.

CURRENT SITUATION

Security Troubles

In the final days of the war, the Iraqi army, like the regime it served, utterly collapsed. Those units that were not destroyed either surrendered or disintegrated.

The U.S.-British victory led Pentagon planners to predict that Iraq could be stabilized in a matter of months. Early assessments estimated that the United States could reduce its troop strength in Iraq to 30,000 by the fall — from about 150,000 at the end of the war.

But an upswing in guerrilla-style attacks against allied forces has dashed those hopes. Since Bush declared an end to major hostilities on May 1, 47 American and British troops have been killed by Iraqi hostile fire. New casualties are reported almost daily, often as the result of hit-and-run attacks on military convoys or sniper fire directed at soldiers guarding major facilities.

The attacks have been taking place mostly in Sunni-dominated areas in central Iraq — dubbed the "Sunni Triangle" by the Americans — stretching from Baghdad to Tikrit and Falluja. Hussein enjoyed substantial support in the region when he was in power. With a few exceptions, the violence has not spread either to the Shiite-dominated southern half of the country or to the Kurdish north, where a combination of coalition troops and indigenous security forces are keeping order.

Iraqi fighters have attacked U.S. troops in densely populated areas, using crowds and tall buildings to cover surprise attacks and aid in their escape. The tactic seems to be working: In most of the attacks the assailants have gotten away.

"When you're in the middle of a city, it's impossible to tell friend from foe," said Sgt. Lawrence Adams of the U.S. Army's First Armored Division. [23]

AFP Photo/Bullit Marquez

L. Paul Bremer III (center), the U.S. civilian administrator in Iraq, meets with tribal leaders on June 14. A former State Department official, Bremer says stabilization of the situation in Iraq will take time and patience.

American and British soldiers are not the only targets. On July 5, seven recruits for a new Iraqi police force were killed in an attack. Others seen as "collaborating" with the coalition have been attacked or threatened.

Adding to the destruction caused earlier by looters, resistance fighters have further damaged the country's fragile infrastructure, impeding coalition efforts to restore power and other services (*see p. 198*). In recent weeks, oil pipelines, electrical power plants and various infrastructure targets have been damaged or destroyed by saboteurs.

Despite the breadth and regularity of the attacks, most administration officials maintain the resistance will be contained. The attacks pose "no strategic threat to us," Bremer told Fox News on July 20, during a visit to the United States. Calling members of the resistance "professional killers" with ties to the old regime, Bremer maintained that the U.S. will slowly but surely root out and kill or capture them. [24]

This view was echoed earlier this month when President Bush now famously said: "Bring 'em on." The president added: "We've got plenty of tough force there right now to make sure the situation is secure." [25]

The Heritage Foundation's Phillips agrees that the situation is probably containable. "The fact that the Shia,

A U.S. soldier with the 1st Armored Division stands guard near a steel bridge in Baghdad newly built by the 16th U.S. Engineer Battalion. Protecting infrastructure from saboteurs distracts coalition forces from the task of rebuilding the country.

who make up 60 to 65 percent of the population, are not joining in is a sign that this is not some national uprising but the work of a group within the Sunni minority."

But many critics, and even some supporters, of the administration's post-war policy offer a less sanguine assessment. Indeed, many were stunned when, on July 16, Abizaid called the resistance, "a guerrilla-style campaign" that is becoming increasingly organized. [26]

And some worry that U.S. forces will continue to be "bled" of troops as small attacks continue. "I'm now concerned that we have the world's best-trained soldiers serving as policemen in what seems to be a shooting gallery," said Sen. Edward M. Kennedy, D-Mass., at a July 9 Senate Armed Services Committee hearing.

And others contend that things could get a lot worse. "What we're seeing is just the tip of the iceberg," says Charles V. Peña, director of defense policy studies at the Cato Institute. "This is a small part of a much larger resistance."

According to Peña and others, the attackers are most likely some of the more ardent supporters of the former regime. "We didn't truly defeat the Iraqi military, because many of the Republican Guard soldiers [elite Iraqi units] simply shed their uniforms, kept their guns and melted back into the population," he says. "So now we have thousands of guerrilla fighters poised to take us on."

Many analysts contend that much of the resistance so far was linked to the fact that Hussein and his sons were still at large. They argue that the July 22 killing of Uday and Qusay Hussein — who helped their father run the state's security apparatus and had a reputation for excessive cruelty — will help pacify the country.

"Uday founded and led the Fedayeen Saddam [paramilitary squads] and Qusay . . . controlled Iraq's intelligence and security forces," said Anthony H. Cordesman, a senior fellow at CSIS. "They were the symbols of the horror and abuses. [Their demise] will have a huge impact on the whole country." [27] Indeed, when their deaths were announced celebrations broke out all over Baghdad.

But others say the deaths, while important, do not represent a major turning point because Saddam himself is still at large. "The sons were important . . . but the father is the one who extracts retribution," said Sen. Jay Rockefeller, D.-W.Va. "We have to get him . . . The father is the symbol and the intimidator to the Iraqi people." [28]

Arab media recently broadcast taped messages from Hussein urging Iraqis to drive coalition forces out of Iraq.

"Obviously, as long as Saddam's fate is unknown, some of his followers are going to want to fight on," Phillips says.

Even with his sons gone, the mystery of Hussein's whereabouts may make ordinary Iraqis less likely to cooperate with coalition forces because they may fear the dictator and his Baath Party may return and exact revenge on those who helped coalition forces or spoke out against the regime. "When the American soldiers first came to Baghdad, we thought we would never hear from Saddam again," said Abdelrahim Warid, a shopkeeper. "Now we know he is in our midst — and that is very dangerous for us." [29]

In the past month or so, U.S. troops have stepped up their hunt for Hussein and dozens of his chief associates. A recently announced $25 million reward for information leading to Hussein's capture has spurred a flood of tips from locals, and American intelligence officials believe they may be close to locating him. [30] "They've made inroads and, yes, I think they may be getting closer," Phillips says.

Indeed, some of the material in the house where Hussein's sons were killed may provide intelligence on their father's whereabouts.

Meanwhile the United States is trying to stem the immediate violence by conducting raids in central Iraqi towns in search of weapons and Hussein sympathizers. A recent, three-day coordinated sweep through the area,

Should the U.S. withdraw from Iraq within the next year?

YES
Charles V. Peña
Director, Defense Policy Studies, Cato Institute

Written for The CQ Researcher, July 2003

Prior to going to war against Iraq, President Bush said, "we will remain in Iraq as long as necessary, and not a day more." That's an open-ended commitment. But if the United States can devise a plan and execute a military victory in three weeks, certainly the administration can do better with a plan for getting out of Iraq. Indeed, the United States must do better because the cruel irony is that the longer the U.S. military stays in Iraq, the more resentment against American occupation is likely to grow. And more troops sent to quiet the discontent means more targets to be shot at and killed.

Rather than linger, the United States should be setting a timetable for leaving. Here is a prescription for a relatively quick exit:

- Hand over governing power to an interim Iraqi council immediately. This was originally supposed to be done by the end of May, but is only now beginning to take shape.

- Have the interim authority create the framework for a newly elected Iraqi government in three months or less.

- Hold elections within the subsequent two to three months. This may seem ambitious, but it only took six months from the meeting in Bonn, Germany, that created a plan for a new Afghan government for Hamid Karzai to be elected as the new president in Afghanistan.

- Once a new Iraqi government is in place — which according to the prescribed schedule should take no longer than six months — withdraw U.S. military forces.

Most important, the United States must be willing to live with the result, which is not likely to be a perfect democracy. Liberating the Iraqi people from a brutal dictator and creating democracy may be a noble purpose, but U.S. national security demands only that the new government not harbor or support terrorists who would harm the United States.

Even an Islamic government would not necessarily be hostile to the United States. According to one Iraqi: "We thank the Americans for getting rid of Saddam's regime, but now Iraq must be run by Iraqis."

To prevent that gratitude from turning to resentment and hostility, we must have the wisdom to leave as quickly as possible. If we don't, the United States runs the risk of its own version of the Soviet experience in Afghanistan — Arabs and Muslims from the region could flock to Iraq to expel the American infidel.

NO
Gen. Tommy Franks
Former Commander, U.S. Army Central Command

From testimony before The House Armed Services Committee, July 10, 2003

Although security continues to improve, portions of Iraq are now, and will remain for some time, dangerous.

I think it's very important for us all to remember and continue to remind ourselves that the term "stability operations," which is what we're doing right now, does not infer that combat operations have ended. It does infer that major combat operations against enemy formations have ended. Military forces are still required to set conditions that will enable the evolution of Iraq.

Factors that will influence our force mix in the days ahead — that is, how many Americans are to be invested in Iraq for how long — will be subject to conditions that we see on the ground.

One of those conditions will be coalition-force contributions: How much international interest are we able to generate? What types and how many international forces will we be able to invest in this country? How quickly will we bring along Iraqi police forces and security forces to guard key infrastructure in that country? And how long will it take us to move forward and establish a new Iraqi army?

All these issues are under way as we speak. Ambassador [L. Paul] Bremer is working very, very hard to balance three key points. One is the establishment of governance — that is to put an Iraqi face on what we see in Iraq. Another is to move the economy forward and the third is to improve security. . . .

Underlying all security functions is the need to continue to conduct humanitarian assistance and the conduct of civil military operations, which we have been doing and will continue to do in order to improve the quality of life of the Iraqi people. It's possible to say that there will be no growth in the economy . . . until security improves.

My view is that we want to be there as long as it takes, an expression the president has used, and an expression that my boss [Secretary of Defense Donald H. Rumsfeld] has used. We want to be there for as long as it takes to have the Iraqis being able to operate with a form of governance that respects human rights as well as neighbors. But we don't want to be there a day longer than that.

And so, I anticipate that we will be involved in Iraq in the future, and sir, I don't know whether that means two years or four years. I just don't know.

dubbed Operation Sidewinder, nabbed 282 suspects and large caches of weapons and ammunition.

In addition, help is on the way. About 20,000 peacekeepers from 19 U.S. allies — including Poland, Italy, Ukraine and Spain — are arriving in Iraq and should be in place by mid-August. The United States also is asking other countries, like Turkey, to send soldiers. And some 31,000 Iraqi police officers are back on the job — about half the pre-war level — with more being added every day. [31]

Moreover, U.S. military planners have decided to recruit and quickly train an indigenous Iraqi paramilitary force to help American troops restore order. This new civil defense force will consist of about 6,800 men and will be ready for duty in early September, according to Gen. Abizaid.

"Over time, it'll free up an awful lot of American forces," said Abizaid. [32]

The Pentagon also is planning to hire and train a private Iraqi security force — including former members of the country's military — to guard up to 2,000 sites around the country. Military officials hope giving former soldiers gainful employment and replacing American troops with native soldiers will help reduce tensions in those parts of the country wracked by violence. [33]

For the time being, though, American and British troops will remain the primary peacekeepers in Iraq, with U.S. troop levels remaining at about 148,000 "for the foreseeable future," Gen. Tommy Franks, the just-retired commander of U.S. forces in the region, told the House and Senate Armed Services Committees. (See "At Issue," p. 197.) At the same hearing, Secretary Rumsfeld estimated the U.S. deployment would cost $3.9 billion a month.

Iraq's Infrastructure

Power blackouts were not unknown in pre-war Iraq, especially in those neighborhoods and towns that had resisted Hussein. But today, the situation in many parts of the country, especially the capital, is worse.

For instance, before the war, the average Baghdad resident could expect the power to work about 20 hours a day. In early July — during some of the hottest days of the year — residents were averaging less than half that.

Other services — such as water and sewage treatment — have yet to be fully restored in some areas, often because the power needed to operate those systems is not available.

Iraq's infrastructure problems have been exacerbated because of the poor state of the country's utilities before the war. Bombing during the Persian Gulf War and more than a decade of tough economic sanctions had left Iraq with a damaged infrastructure and few funds to repair it. The little money that did come into the country — through the U.N.-sponsored oil-for-food program and oil smuggling — was often used for other purposes.

Since the war ended, the looting and sabotage have only made the problems worse. Of 21 ministry buildings in Baghdad, 17 were rendered unusable by looters. [34] Subsequent attacks by Hussein loyalists against electrical stations, pipelines and other facilities have further complicated efforts to restore power and other services.

"Combat damage was comparably light," said Army Maj. Gen. Carl Strock, deputy director of operations for the CPA. "The real problem here is decades of neglect to this infrastructure, lack of investment in operations and maintenance and also the looting and sabotage." [35]

According to Strock, the United States has already committed about $1 billion "to several thousand projects" to repair and improve basic infrastructure, including $314 million to upgrade the electricity system. Army engineers and 39,000 Iraqi electrical workers are trying to boost the system's output. As a result, he predicts that by the end of July, power in Baghdad will almost be back to pre-war levels.* Water and sewer services should be at 80 percent of pre-war levels by October, the general says.

The money is part of $7 billion that the CPA estimates it will spend on reconstruction projects through the end of the year. More than half of the budget, about $4.2 billion, will come from Iraqi oil-export revenues, money found in Hussein's palaces after the war (about $1 billion) and funds from international bank accounts frozen since the Persian Gulf War. [36] The United States will provide the remainder, a figure some estimate could reach as high as $25 billion per year in the future. [37]

Other sorts of vital infrastructure also are being reconstituted. For example, all of the nation's 240 hospitals, many of which were badly looted, are now open and operational. In addition, all of the country's public schools are scheduled to reopen in the fall, with the CPA spending $62.5 million to help overhaul the educational

---

* The United Nations estimates that a complete overhaul of the nation's power grid could cost as much as $10 billion.

system. Much of this funding will pay for new textbooks to replace the pro-Hussein, anti-American books students were reading until earlier this year.

The United States also recently announced plans to reconstitute the country's financial sector. An American-style central bank has been established, which will be independent of the Finance Ministry. In addition, Iraq's currency — all of which contain a portrait of Hussein — will be replaced by new dinars, beginning Oct. 15. [38]

According to U.S. officials, replacing the old currency will improve confidence in the nation's money by offering notes in a greater variety of denominations, which also will be harder to counterfeit. But American officials admit that ridding the money supply of Hussein's visage is another justification for the change.

"There's no question that we've felt it was very unfortunate he was on the currency," said one official in Baghdad. [39]

OUTLOOK

Too Soon to Tell

Despite the problems facing U.S. and British soldiers and civilians working to rebuild Iraq, many experts are optimistic that, over the long term, it will develop into a stable and prosperous country.

"I don't think it's going to be some sort of perfect democracy, but Iraq — with its secular and well-educated population and its oil wealth — stands a good chance of creating a stable, representative system," says the Heritage Foundation's Phillips.

Others offer a more pragmatic, but still upbeat, assessment. "A majority of Iraqis [are] willing to be patient with the United States and tolerant of mistakes, so long as they see improvements on the ground, like their security and standard of living," says Jennings of the Institute of Peace. "I'm optimistic because I think those things are not going to be that hard to provide."

But others don't share their optimism. "I'm very pessimistic," CARE's Pugh says. "I fear that our chance to make it work may have already passed."

Pugh and others contend that the failure of American and British forces to restore order and basic services in the months following the war have eroded their credibility to the point where most Iraqis simply want them to leave. "These missteps have cost us dearly," Pugh says. "And things are going to get more complicated because you already have a very difficult political and ethnic situation in the country, and it's getting worse, not better."

The University of San Francisco's Zunes agrees, adding: "We've gotten ourselves into something a lot bigger than we realize, in part because we thought that military power was the only thing we needed before we went in there and didn't think about what Iraqis might think or do once we arrived."

According to Zunes, the continuing chaos, unrest and attacks against U.S. troops are only a sign of things to come. "It's quite possible that we will find the security situation continuing to deteriorate the longer we are there," he says. "We simply don't have the support of the Iraqi people, so whatever we do is going to be problematic."

Others argue that the United States was wrong to think that an outside power could come in and rebuild a country's infrastructure and society. "Japan and Germany were aberrations, because they were closed, utterly defeated societies, which made them easier to reshape," says National Defense University's Yaphe. "I don't think it's that the U.S. is bad at nation building. It's that no one is particularly good at it. It's just too difficult."

Finally, experts like CSIS's Barton say that it's too early to be optimistic or pessimistic, in large part because it's too early to tell whether the United States is willing to commit time and resources to what will almost certainly be a long-term project. "It's basically 50-50 at this point, and that hinges on whether we're willing to commit ourselves to it or not," he says.

Right now, momentum is not with the administration. Recent polls show that American support for the war has dropped in recent months. A July 10, *Washington Post*/ABC News Poll showed that only 57 percent of Americans believed that the war in Iraq was worth fighting, a drop of 13 points since the end of April.

Indeed, Barton remembers what America's most successful nation builder, Gen. George C. Marshall, said about his famed Marshall Plan. "Marshall said his greatest victory wasn't the plan itself, but convincing the American people that it was necessary," he says. "If the U.S. has the will to stay in Iraq and make it work, it will work. If we're not, it won't. It's that simple."

NOTES

1. Quoted in Rajiv Chandrasekaran, "Appointed Iraq Council Assumes Limited Role," *The Washington Post*, July 14, 2003, p. A1.

2. Quoted from "Fox Special Report With Brit Hume," June 30, 2003.

3. Quoted in "Iraq War Still Claiming Lives," *The Myrtle Beach {South Carolina] Sun-News*, July 17, 2003. p. 4.

4. "Iraq's Post-Conflict Reconstruction: A Field Review and Recommendations," Center for Strategic and International Studies, July 17, 2003, p. i.

5. Quoted in Eric Schmitt and Tom Shaker, "With Hussein's Heirs Gone, Hopes Rise for an End to Attacks," *The New York Times*, July 23, 2003, p. A1.

6. Quoted in Romesh Ratnesar and Simon Robinson, "Life Under Fire," *Time*, July 14, 2003, p. 22.

7. Center for Strategic and International Studies, *op. cit.*

8. Quoted in Ratnesar and Robinson, *op. cit.*

9. See the full text of the president's speech at: http://www.whitehouse.gov/news/releases/2003/04/iraq/20030428-3.html.

10. Quoted on "Weekend Edition Sunday," National Public Radio, May 11, 2003.

11. Quoted in Peter Slevin, "U.S. Bans More Iraqis From Jobs," *The Washington Post*, May 17, 2003, p. A1.

12. Quoted on "Morning Edition," National Public Radio, May 20, 2003.

13. Quoted in Jim Hoagland, "In Iraq, Don't Throw Chance for Indigenous Imput Out with Baath Water," *The Washington Post*, April 24, 2003, p. B7.

14. James Dao, "Nation Building: The Return of American Generosity," *The New York Times*, Nov. 24, 2002, p. A6.

15. Jason Horowitz, "A Contrite Pope Urges Reconciliation to Heal Bosnia's Scars," *The New York Times*, June 23, 2003, p. A9. For background on NATO, see Mary H. Cooper, "Future of NATO," *The CQ Researcher*, Feb. 28, 2003, pp. 177-200.

16. For background, see Kenneth Jost, "Democracy in Eastern Europe," *The CQ Researcher*, Oct. 8, 1999, pp. 865-888.

17. For background, see David Masci, "War on Terrorism," *The CQ Researcher, Oct.* 12, 2001, pp. 817-848.

18. For background, see Kenneth Jost, "Rebuilding Afghanistan," *The CQ Researcher*, Dec. 21, 2000, pp. 1041-1064.

19. "The Rebirth of a Nation," *The Economist*, Jan. 9, 2003.

20. Quoted in Ratnesar and Robinson, *op. cit.*

21. For background, see David Masci, "Confronting Iraq," *The CQ Researcher*, Oct. 4, 2002, pp. 793-816.

22. For background on economic sanctions, see Mary H. Cooper, "Economic Sanctions," *The CQ Researcher*, Oct. 28, 1994, pp. 937-960.

23. Rajiv Chandrasekaran and Molly Moore, "Urban Combat Frustrates Army," *The Washington Post*, July 8, 2003, p. A1.

24. Quoted from Fox News, Sunday, July 20, 2003.

25. Soni Effron and Terry McDermott, "'Bring Them On,' Bush Says of Iraqi Resisters," *Los Angeles Times*, July 3, 2003, p. 8.

26. Quoted in Tom Shanker, "U.S. Commander Says Year-Long Tours Are an Option to Combat Guerrilla Style War," *The New York Times*, July 17, 2001, p. A1.

27. Quoted in Laurie Goering and E.A. Torriero, "Deaths Expected to Increase Iraqis Confidence in Allies," *The Chicago Tribune*, July 23, 2003, p. A1.

28. Quoted in "Sons' Demise is Good," *Agence France Presse*, July 23, 2003.

29. Quoted in Rajiv Chandrasekaran, "Many Iraqis Fear Hussein is Plotting Return to Power," *The Washington Post*, July 7, 2003, p. A1.

30. Molly Moore, "Chasing Tips on Hussein," *The Washington Post*, July 12, 2003, p. A1.

31. Figure cited in Morton M. Kondrake, "Bush Must Counter Bad News From Iraq with Progress Reports," *Roll Call*, July 10, 2003.

32. Quoted in Vivienne Walt, "Iraq Unrest Grows," *The Boston Globe*, July 21, 2003, p. A1.

33. Douglas Jehl, "U.S. Considers Private Iraqi Force to Guard Sites," *The New York Times*, July 18, 2003, p. A1.

34. Ratnesar and Robinson, *op. cit.*

35. Quoted in Eric Schmitt, "Water and Electricity in Iraq Are Still Below Pre-War Levels," *The New York Times*, July 8, 2003, p. A14.

36. Steven R. Weisman, "U.S. Seeks Help with Iraq Costs," *The New York Times*, July 14, 2002, p. A6.

37. Figure cited in Jeff Gerth, "U.S. Is Banking on Iraq Oil to Finance Reconstruction," *The New York Times*, April 10, 2003, p. B14.

38. Rajiv Chandrasekaran, "U.S. Banishing Hussein From Iraq's Currency," *The Washington Post*, July 9, 2003, p. A13.

39. Quoted in *ibid.*

BIBLIOGRAPHY

Books

Mackey, Sandra, *The Reckoning: Iraq and the Legacy of Saddam Hussein*, W.W. Norton and Co., 2002.
Mackey, an expert on Persian Gulf states, examines Saddam Hussein's Iraq and argues that deposing the dictator could destabilize the country and the entire region.

Articles

"Making Peace With the U.N.," *The Economist*, May 22, 2003.
The article examines the negotiations that ultimately led the United Nations Security Council to lift sanctions against Iraq.

Bremer, L. Paul, "The Road Ahead in Iraq — And How to Navigate It," *The New York Times*, July 13, 2003, p. 13.
The U.S. administrator in Iraq lays out a plan to transform the country in the coming years, from the creation of the recently established interim council to the privatization of state industries.

Chandrasekaran, Rajiv, "Blackouts Return, Deepening Iraq's Dark Days," *The Washington Post*, July 3, 2003, p. A1.
The article details the difficulties the coalition is having in providing power, water and other basic services in certain parts of Iraq.

Crossette, Barbara, "How to Put a Nation Back Together," *The New York Times*, Nov. 21, 2001, p. A3.
An informative look at the lessons learned during past nation-building efforts.

DeYoung, Karen, "U.S. Sped Bremer to Iraq Post," *The Washington Post*, May 24, 2003, p. A1.
DeYoung reconstructs the events and decisions that led the administration to pull Gen. Jay Garner as head of Iraq's civil administration and replace him with L. Paul Bremer III.

Hoagland, Jim, "De-Baathification, Root and Branch," *The Washington Post*, April 24, 2003, p. A25.
A foreign affairs columnist argues in favor of a vigorous effort to rid Iraq's next government of Baath Party activists and loyalists.

Johnson, Scott, and Evan Thomas, "Still Fighting Saddam," *Newsweek*, July 21, 2003, p. 20.
The article examines evidence suggesting that the guerrilla-style war now being waged against U.S. troops in Iraq was planned before the conflict even began.

Oppel, Richard A., "Banking Overhaul and New Currency Planned for Iraq," *The New York Times*, July 8, 2003, p. A14.
The article details American plans to restructure Iraq's Central Bank and issue new currency (without Saddam Hussein's picture on it) in the fall.

Owens, Mackubin Thomas, "Post-War Iraq: The Big Picture," *National Review Online*, July 8, 2003.
A former Marine and professor at the Naval War College argues that the guerrilla war in Iraq is not the "quagmire" many analysts believe it to be. Patience, good intelligence and willingness to use force pre-emptively will allow the U.S. to root out and defeat the resistance.

Ratnestar, Romesh, "Life Under Fire," *Time*, July 14, 2003, p. 22.
An excellent overview of the situation on the ground in Iraq, including a brief history of the ongoing occupation and the trouble coalition troops and officials face as they try to piece a damaged and violent nation back together.

York, Byron, "All Smoke, No Fire: The Administration's Critics Are Wrong About Halliburton," *The National Review*, July 14, 2003.
The article argues that recent allegations of favoritism in the awarding of contracts in Iraq to Halliburton are ungrounded and politically motivated.

Zakaria, Fareed, "Iraq Policy is Broken, Fix It," *Newsweek*, July 14, 2003, p. 35.
A journalist specializing in foreign affairs argues that the United States should share decision-making in Iraq with other countries, like France and Germany, in exchange for their help in policing and rebuilding the country.

Reports

"Iraq's Post-Conflict Reconstruction: A Field Review and Recommendations," Center for Strategic and International Studies, July 17, 2003.
Asked by the Pentagon to assess the situation in Iraq today, a team from CSIS, led by former Deputy Secretary of Defense John Hamre, spent two weeks in country sizing up post-war problems and developing a list of recommended changes.

The Open Society Institute and the United Nations Foundation, *Reconstructing Iraq: A Guide to the Issues*, May 30, 2003.
The two grant-making foundations have produced a thorough primer on the issue facing post-war Iraq, from creating a new legal system to providing humanitarian relief.

For More Information

American Enterprise Institute for Public Policy Research, 1150 17th St., N.W., Suite 1100, Washington, DC 20036; (202) 862-5800; www.aei.org. Conducts conferences and debates and sponsors research on international affairs.

Carnegie Endowment for International Peace, 1779 Massachusetts Ave., N.W., Washington, DC 20036; (202) 483-7600; www.ceip.org. Conducts research on international affairs and American foreign policy.

Cato Institute, 1000 Massachusetts Ave., N.W., Washington DC 20001-5403; (202) 842-0200; www.cato.org. A libertarian research foundation.

Center for Strategic and International Studies, 1800 K St., N.W., Suite 400, Washington, DC 20006; (202) 887-0200; www.csis.org. Supports scholars who study a wide range of international and domestic security issues. Recently conducted an independent assessment of the situation in Iraq for the Defense Department.

Council on Foreign Relations, 58 East 68th St., New York, NY 10021; (212) 434-9400; www.cfr.org. One of the nation's premier foreign policy think tanks.

Middle East Institute, 1761 N St., N.W., Washington, DC 20036; (202) 785-1141; www.mideasti.org. Conducts research on the Middle East.

United Nations Foundation, 1225 Connecticut Ave., N.W., #400, Washington, DC 20036; (202) 887-9040; www.unfoundation.org. Funded by former media mogul Ted Turner; supports the United Nations and its charter.

10

Emerging India

David Masci

With teeming Bombay in the background, thousands of worshippers gather at a festival to pay homage to the elephant-headed Hindu god Ganesh. Eighty-one percent of India's 1 billion-plus population is Hindu, but there are also four other major religions, including Islam.

From *The CQ Researcher,*
April 19, 2002.

Sectarian violence has a long, unhappy history in India. Indeed, in the year of the nation's birth, 1947, more than 1 million Indians died in savage fighting between Hindus and Muslims. Such were the tensions between the two great religious communities that the Muslim nations of Pakistan and Bangladesh were carved from territory that was once part of India.

Early this year, another round of sectarian clashes rocked India and shocked the world. The trouble began on Feb. 28, when a Muslim mob in the western city of Godhra attacked Hindu extremists returning from the holy city of Ayodhya. The mob set the Hindus' train ablaze, killing 58 travelers — including more than a dozen children. [1]

In the weeks that followed, nearly a thousand more people, mostly Muslims, died in mob violence in Gujarat state in western India. Some of the victims were mutilated, including pregnant women. Others were trapped in their homes and burned to death. The Gujarat state government, under the control of the Hindu nationalist Bharatiya Janata Party (BJP), reacted sluggishly in stopping the rioting. Hindu extremists justified the attacks as revenge for the 58 who died in Godhra.

"Now, it is the end of toleration," said Harish Bhai Bhatt, the firebrand leader of the Hindu World Council, a fundamentalist Hindu group close to the BJP believed to have incited the anti-Muslim violence. [2]

"This kind of narrow appeal to religious sentiment is, I'm afraid, part of India," says Sumit Ganguly, a professor of government at the University of Texas at Austin, which has a noted South Asia studies program. "One would hope that the horror of the Gujarat riots

203

A Crowded, Troubled Land

India has one-sixth of the world's people but only 2 percent of the land. Conflict between India's majority Hindus and 125 million Muslims led to the creation of Muslim Pakistan and Bangladesh from territory once part of India. Meanwhile, separatists are battling for independence in Kashmir, in northern India.

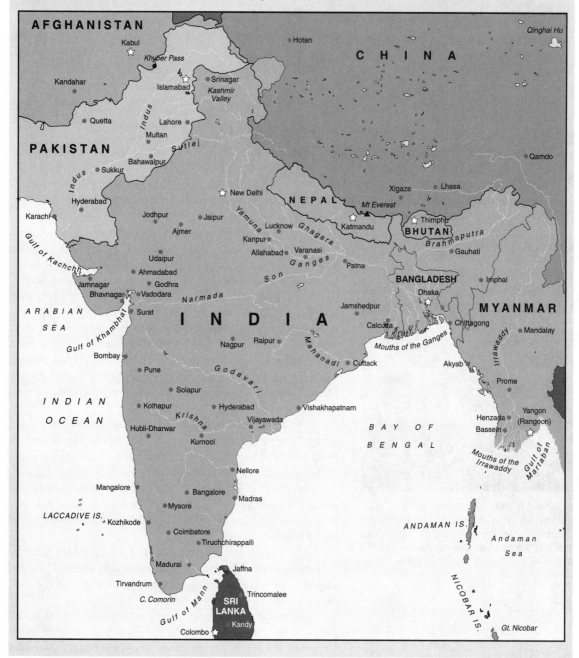

India at a Glance

Area: 3.3 million sq. km., slightly more than one-third the size of the United States.

Population: 1.03 billion, as of July 2001.

Population growth: 1.5 percent per year, or 3.04 children per woman.

Infant mortality: 63.2 deaths per 1,000.

Religion: Hindu 81.3 percent; Muslim 12 percent; Christian 2.3 percent; Sikh 1.9 percent; the remaining 2.5 percent includes Buddhists and Jains.

Languages: English is used for political and business communica-tion. Hindi is the largest indigenous tongue, spoken by 30 percent of the people. Bengali, Urdu, Telugu and Tamil are among India's other 32 major languages.

Government: India's president is elected by Parliament and state legislatures for a five-year term and has only limited power. The most powerful political leader is the prime minister, who is elected by the lower house (*Lok Sabha*), which has 543 elected members serving five-year terms. All but 12 of the 245 members of the upper house, or Council of States (*Rajya Sabha*), are elected by the state and territorial legislatures. The president appoints the remaining 12.

Economy: The economy ranges from subsistence farming and handicrafts manufacturing to thriving software and biotechnology industries. The country also has large service and manufacturing sectors, including textiles, chemicals and finance. The gross domestic product was $474 billion in 2001, and the per-capita GDP was around $500. About 35 percent of the population lives below the poverty line.

Communications hardware: 27.7 million telephones, 2.9 million mobile phones and 43 Internet service providers serving 4.5 million users, in 2000.

Sources: CIA World Factbook; The Economist: Country Briefings.

But the sprawling multiethnic nation is comprised of many other Indias — some of them clearly more focused on the future.

In the same month that Hindus and Muslims were clashing in Gujarat, the Indian Space Research Organization tested a rocket engine for a new satellite-launching vehicle near the southern city of Bangalore, home of the nation's vibrant technology sector. In addition to high-tech software companies, India's so-called Silicon Valley is also host to other cutting-edge industries, like biotechnology and telecommunications. [3] In March, CEOs from some of India's biggest information-technology companies met to discuss establishing India's version of the famed Media Lab at the Massachusetts Institute of Technology, to research future technologies. [4]

That rockets and media labs coexist with savage sectarian violence "is one of the ironies of India's muddled march into the 21st century," Shashi Tharoor, an Indian social critic and novelist, wrote recently in *The New York Times*. Despite the country's technologically inspired vision of the future, it appears "shackled to the dogmas of the past," he noted. [5]

But given India's diversity and vast size — the population exceeds 1 billion — perhaps the irony is not so surprising. "India is a country the size and complexity of Europe," with distinct regions and ethnic groups that speak 32 major languages and thousands of dialects, says Harold A. Gould, a noted India scholar at the University of Virginia's Center for South Asian Studies. And, although 81 percent of the population is Hindu, there are four other major religions in India, including Islam; the nation's

would wake us up and make us stop this, but I fear that it won't."

Although ethnic and religious tolerance has been one of the hallmarks of modern India since its inception, Hindu-Muslim troubles are still a part of India's present.

Controversy Over Kashmir

In the majority-Muslim Kashmir region at India's northern tip, separatists in the Kashmir Valley want either to form a new state or become part of Pakistan. India has been fighting several Pakistani-backed Kashmiri separatist groups in the last 25 years, and thousands of combatants and civilians have died in the conflict. Pakistan took control of the western third of Kashmir (dark area, at left) after a 1947 war with India.

Source: http://www.jammu-kashmir-facts.com

belief in socialism and economic self-sufficiency stunted the new nation's economic growth during the 1960s and '70s, a time when Taiwan, South Korea and other Asian nations were developing more rapidly. Partly as a result, India remains desperately poor, with a $500 per capita GDP — about one-twentieth of South Korea's — and about the same as Nigeria and Kenya. [6]

In the past decade, however, India has instituted striking economic reforms, selling off many publicly owned industries and allowing the private sector to compete in areas once monopolized by the government. The nation also has begun to forge a new relationship with the world's leading democracy and sole superpower, the United States.

The new, warmer Indo-American relationship — bolstered by India's enthusiastic support for the U.S. war against terrorism — comes after years when the former Soviet Union was India's closest great-power ally.

The combination of economic reforms and closer ties to the West has fostered newfound optimism among many India-watchers. Some even see India becoming an economic and geopolitical powerhouse in the coming decades.

"India will soon be a great power, and if the economy really picks up, it could be a superpower at some point as well," says Ashutosh Varshney, a political science professor at the University of Michigan at Ann Arbor.

But to some experts, the death toll in Gujarat is a bloody and particularly troubling reminder of the obstacles ahead. They view the riots as an indication that India is losing its dedication to multiculturalism and secularism. They blame the current coalition government — led by the BJP — for shifting the country away from religious tolerance and toward Hindu chauvinism. "The government has created the conditions that allowed this

125 million Muslims comprise 12 percent of the population. "India is basically Europe with a central government," he adds.

Like the 15-member European Union, India is a relatively recent creation, born after nearly two centuries of British rule. The leaders of India's independence movement — Mohandas K. Gandhi and Jawaharlal Nehru — are famous the world over as the architects of a non-violent revolution that wrested the country away from the most powerful empire of its day.

Gandhi and Nehru set India on a democratic path, and today it is the world's most populous democracy. But their

kind of horrible violence to happen," Ganguly says, by blatantly favoring the Hindu majority.

But optimists say India's strong democratic process will keep the BJP from turning India into a Hindu state, to a large extent because appealing to Hindu chauvinism will not win it enough votes to remain in power. In fact, they note that party leaders have already rejected extremists' demands that a new Hindu temple be constructed on the site in Ayodhya where the mosque was destroyed. (*See "At Issue," p. 225.*)

The conflict over Kashmir is another flashpoint. Some Kashmiris believe their distinct language, culture and identity justify seceding from India to either form a new state or become part of Pakistan. (*See "At Issue," p. 224.*)

India has been fighting several Pakistani-backed Kashmiri separatist groups, and thousands of combatants and civilians have died in the conflict in the last 25 years. But the violence is not confined to the disputed province. On Dec. 13, 2001, two of the separatist groups attacked the Indian Parliament building; 14 security guards and terrorists were killed.

The majority Muslim province at India's northern tip also has prompted two wars with Pakistan, which claims the territory. Since both India and Pakistan are nuclear powers, the situation in Kashmir could conceivably wreak havoc of global proportions. [7]

Meanwhile, an increasingly assertive India argues that it is well on the way to becoming one of the world's great economic and military powers and, as such, deserves a permanent seat on the United Nations Security Council, beside the United States, Russia and other heavyweights.

As India strives to solve tough domestic problems and play a greater role on the world stage, here are some of the key issues being debated:

Is India's commitment to secularism and pluralism waning?

In 1992, Hindu activists in the northern city of Ayodhya tore down the Babri Masjid, a Muslim mosque built, they claim, on the place where their god, Ram, was born. That incident sparked a wave of sectarian violence across India that year that left more than 3,000 dead.

But while the destruction of the mosque and the riots shocked the nation and the world, they had a long-term political impact at home, bringing a wave of new support for Hindu nationalist parties, most notably the BJP.

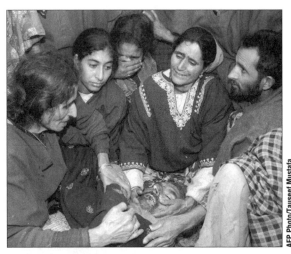

AFP Photo/Tauseef Mustafa

Neighbors grieve over a man killed in a firefight between Indian soldiers and Kashmiri separatists. Muslim Kashmir has been fighting for independence from India for more than two decades.

The BJP's leaders, including Prime Minister Atal Behari Vajpayee and even the more hard-line Home Minister L.K. Advani, have condemned the most recent sectarian violence in Gujarat and supported a court order preventing Hindu fundamentalists from building a temple to Ram on the site where the mosque was destroyed nearly 10 years ago.

But many say that the BJP and its core supporters — mainly Hindu chauvinists — helped create today's atmosphere of intolerance. "The prime minister and home minister . . . back in 1992 . . . threw gasoline on the fire that's still burning," says Richard Lariviere, dean of the College of Liberal Arts at Texas. Indeed, some India-watchers argue that the latest violence indicates the general direction in which India has been heading for more than a decade — away from a tolerant, secular society and toward one in which the Hindu majority suppresses minority rights. "This really reflects the long-term decline in India's commitment to secularism and the ability of the government to remain a neutral force in society," says Texas' Ganguly.

Indian author and social critic Pankaj Mishra agrees, claiming India's current leaders have moved the country in "the opposite direction" of the pluralistic state created by Gandhi and Nehru. "What was once quickly identified as unreasonable and aberrant — Hindu majoritari-

Economy Has Steadily Increased

India's gross domestic product (GDP) has grown eightfold over the past three decades, to more than a half-trillion dollars.

($ billions)

India's Gross Domestic Product
(In $ billions)

Year	Value
1970	62.9
1975	112.4
1980	173.5
1985	222.1
1990	310.9
1995	347.3
2002 (projected)	532.5

Source: "The World Economic Outlook Database," International Monetary Fund, December, 2001, available at http://www.imf.org/external/pubs/ft/weo/2001/03/ data/index.htm

anism — enjoys a growing influence and legitimacy as the ruling ideology of the Indian government," he wrote recently in *The New York Times*. [8]

Pessimists like Ganguly compare the situation in India today to America's "Jim Crow" period. "This is like the South in the 1930s and '40s, when whites could commit acts of violence against blacks and the police would not intervene," he says. "In India, we have case after case of Muslims being attacked, and the police just sit back and do nothing."

Pessimists contend that these incidents are driving a greater wedge between the two communities, creating the prospect of radical polarization. "Unfortunately, I think it's inevitable that Hindu and Muslim attitudes will change in India, that an ever larger wall will exist between these two communities," Lariviere says. "You can't have this kind of horror without that kind of impact."

But, optimists counter, several factors could prevent India's leaders from ultimately destroying the secular state, most notably the population's inherent support for an open society. "The BJP may have whipped up enough

people to come to power over this, but most Indians don't really want anything like this," says Huma Malik, a fellow at the Center for Strategic and International Studies (CSIS). "Most Indians like a system that accommodates everyone."

Tharoor, the author of *Riot* and other popular novels, agrees that most Indians prefer living in a tolerant country. "Pluralism is intrinsic to Indian society. It emerges from its geography and its diverse culture," he says. "And as for Hindus and Muslims, in general they live together and get along in most places."

In addition, Tharoor says, Hindu nationalists will not succeed because the Hindu majority they envision does not really exist. "There is no majority community in India," he says. "Your region, caste, language and other factors all help create your identity." *

Finally, optimists argue, Indian democracy is an inherent safeguard against any party that might want to push an extremist agenda. "You can't come to power and keep power by suppressing other parties and interests," says Philip Oldenburg, associate director of the Southern Asia Institute at Columbia University. He notes the BJP received only a quarter of the vote in the last election and rules in coalition with 25 other parties. "Forming large coalitions moderates the ruling party and pushes the extreme wing to the sideline," Oldenburg explains. "There is an enormous premium on being in or near the center of the political spectrum, because that's the only place from which you can really govern."

In fact, Prime Minister Vajpayee and even Home Minister Advani are seen as much more moderate than leaders of the World Hindu Council and other groups fighting to rebuild the Ram temple. "The government has come out against building this temple, against its

---

* The Indian Constitution outlawed discrimination based on caste, but it still plays a major role in Indian society. (*See glossary, p. 222.*)

core supporters," says Dana Robert Dillon, an Asia expert at the Heritage Foundation. "This clearly shows that [Vajpayee and Advani] understand they cannot appease their extremist Hindu wing and stay in power."

Should Kashmir be allowed to secede from India?

In addition to triggering two wars between India and Pakistan — in 1947 and 1971 — Kashmir has brought the two countries to the brink of armed conflict on several other occasions. Even during calm times, the heavy troop presence both sides maintain on their mutual border occasionally leads to skirmishes.

The dispute over Kashmir began with the birth of both countries in 1947. Pakistan — created specifically as a home for Muslims living in British India — believed then, as it does now, that majority-Muslim Kashmir should be part of Pakistan. Indeed, Pakistan conquered roughly a third of Kashmir in the 1947 India-Pakistan war. [9]

Today's dispute involves the Kashmir Valley, a part of the Indian-controlled province with a mostly Muslim population. Two other parts of the territory, Jammu and Ladakh, have primarily Hindu and Buddhist majorities, respectively, and are not in dispute.

A Pakistani-backed, separatist insurgency against Indian rule began in Kashmir in 1989. India has responded with a mixture of tough military crackdowns and promises of greater self-determination. But none of these strategies has quelled the violence, which so far has cost more than 30,000, mostly civilian, lives.

Some India-watchers contend that the Kashmir problem has one basic solution: independence for the Muslim part of the province. "Kasmiri-speaking people have wanted to be free of India and independent for a long time, and they should be," says Oldenburg at Columbia University. "The Kashmiri people have their own culture and their own national feeling, and they want to be independent."

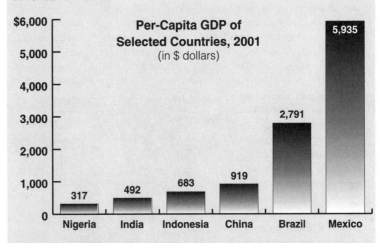

Per-Capita GDP Near the Bottom

When compared to other populous developing countries, India's per-capita gross domestic product (GDP) comes out near the bottom — and, at less than $500, is roughly one-seventieth the average American's income.

Per-Capita GDP of Selected Countries, 2001
(in $ dollars)

Country	Per-Capita GDP
Nigeria	317
India	492
Indonesia	683
China	919
Brazil	2,791
Mexico	5,935

Source: "The World Economic Outlook Database," International Monetary Fund, December, 2001, available at http://www.imf.org/external/pubs/ft/weo/2001/03/ data/index.htm

Timothy Crawford, a post-doctoral fellow at the Brookings Institution, points out that Kashmir's unique status was recognized when India and Pakistan were founded. "The Indians promised the Kashmiris could decide their ultimate fate in a plebiscite, and then backed away from the promise," he says.

But Marshall Bouton, president of the Chicago Council on Foreign Relations, argues that allowing Kashmir to secede could create a "domino effect," possibly prompting other groups, such as the Sikhs or Tamils, to abandon India. "This would be such a blow to the whole idea of India as a multiethnic state," says Bouton, an expert on the region.

CSIS's Malik, herself a Pakistani, agrees. "With a country as diverse as India, letting one part go would have a disastrous effect on the larger whole," she says. "All of a sudden, the Sikhs and others would be saying that they want their own states, too."

Kashmir's secession could also lead to a violent backlash against the 125 million Muslims who would remain in India, Bouton warns. "To admit that the only

For India's Women, a Hard Life

All the world knows of former Prime Minister Indira Gandhi and other accomplished Indian women. But out of the limelight, life for most women in India holds hardship rather than fame and glamour.

Often married off by their late teens, many toil for abusive husbands and in-laws, powerless to make even the most rudimentary decisions for themselves. Thanks to neglect, violence and malnutrition, Indian women typically live to age 63, compared to 72 among Chinese women and 82 for American women. [1]

Indian women routinely suffer from domestic abuse. A recent United Nations survey found that 65.3 percent of Indian women have been subjected to some form of domestic violence. The most common reason for the abuse: meals not prepared on time. [2]

Even worse, statistics indicate that more and more women are being kidnapped, raped and killed. Indeed, each year thousands of women are murdered — often burned to death in faked kitchen fires — by their husband and his family when they feel that the dowry collected from the wife's family is insufficient. Killing a wife allows the husband to remarry and, hopefully, collect a better dowry.

Women in rural India fill their water jugs. Life for most women in India is unremitingly difficult. The average woman in India dies at age 63, and more than 65 percent suffer domestic abuse, according to the United Nations.

Recent statistics show that between 1999 and 2001 the number of reported dowry-related deaths rose almost 4 percent — to 6,220 in 2001 — despite new laws requiring criminal investigations into the sudden death of a new bride and imposing stiff sentences on anyone involved in dowry murder. [3]

Indian women also suffer significant discrimination outside the home. The average Indian woman earns 60 percent of what men in the same job earn, and women occupy only 3 percent of the management positions in the business sector. Moreover, only 54 percent of women are literate, compared with 76 percent of men. [4]

Perhaps the most chilling statistic is India's man-woman ratio. Currently, there are only 933 women for every 1,000 men. Other societies typically have about 5 percent more women than men. [5] The shortage of women reflects not only their lower life expectancy but also the widespread practice in India of aborting female fetuses and, to a lesser extent, female infanticide.

Boys are more prized in India because they don't require their families to pay a dowry when they get married. Dowries — outlawed since 1961 but still

---

[1] Cited in Kalyani Menon-Sin and A.K. Shiva Kumar, "Women in India: How Free? How Equal," *United Nations Report,* 2001.

[2] *Ibid.*

[3] "Dowry Deaths, Abuse Among Women on the Rise," *The Times of India,* March 9, 2002.

[4] Cited in "Women Rally Against Inequities, Exploitation," *Dow Jones News Wires,* March 8, 2002.

[5] Menon-Sin and Kumar, *op. cit.*

Muslim-majority state in the country cannot be part of a multiethnic country would embolden Hindu chauvin-ists," he says, "and raise the prospect that India's Muslims would not be accepted."

widely paid — can cost up to $1,000, or two years' wages for the average Indian. Boys offer another economic advantage: They bring their wives to live in their parents' house, which allows both of them to contribute to the family income. The economic hardships associated with having girls leads to an estimated 2-5 million aborted female fetuses every year. [6]

The Indian Constitution bans all gender-based discrimination, and several laws — such as those punishing dowry deaths — now guarantee women's rights. "There were many laws passed in the 1990s regarding the physical, economic and social position of women in the family, in the workplace and in the public sphere," says Partha Chatterjee, director of Calcutta's Centre for Studies in Social Sciences. "These were among the most progressive laws anywhere. But actual practices on the ground have not necessarily changed much."

Chatterjee says old prejudices often make the police and other authorities loath to enforce a law that raises a woman's status. "When women go to the state authorities, prevailing practices and prejudices within the [police] administration or the courts work to deprive them of the protection," she says. As a result, many domestic abuse and dowry-death cases have been inadequately investigated or dismissed.

Female Life Expectancy

Indian women live about 20 years less than U.S. females. Poor women in India, in particular, often do not have access to education or health care and are subject to gender-related violence.

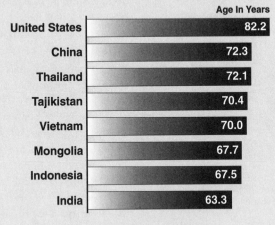

	Age In Years
United States	82.2
China	72.3
Thailand	72.1
Tajikistan	70.4
Vietnam	70.0
Mongolia	67.7
Indonesia	67.5
India	63.3

Source: Human Development Report 2000

Ignorance and fear among women themselves also hinders improvements in their lot, Chatterjee says. "Often, women are not aware of their rights," she contends. "Even when they are, they often do not have the courage or the resources to flout the authority of family or community power structures and seek the protection of the law."

While huge problems persist, Indian women are becoming more politically active. Women's groups established in every major city and even in some rural areas routinely sponsor women's-rights demonstrations and rallies.

To celebrate International Women's Day on March 8, thousands of women demonstrated and held panel discussions around the country, speaking out against violence and exploitation and demanding new laws to protect women and expand their opportunities. [7]

In New Delhi, the capital, India's first lady, Usha Narayanan, joined the activists, saying India could not become a modern, prosperous state without dramatic improvements in the lives of women.

"The upliftment of women by widening opportunities for their full participation in every area of activity will be the harbinger of sustainable development," Narayanan told activists. "Development, if not engendered, is endangered." [8]

---

[6] Cited in S. N. M. Abdi, "God Help Us to Save Baby Girls, Says Minister," *South China Morning Post,* June 25, 2001.

[7] *Ibid.*

[8] Quoted in *ibid.*

Michigan's Varshney agrees that secession would spark "a serious backlash against Muslims all over India, because many people are still smarting at the loss of Pakistan in 1947."

Indian Prime Minister Atal Behari Vajpayee heads the Hindu nationalist Bharatiya Janata Party, which leads India's coalition government. Vajpayee, 77, faces re-election next year.

But independence supporters doubt it will lead to fragmentation. "No other state in India has anything like this depth of feeling about independence," Oldenburg says. "There has been a Kashmiri independence movement since 1931. There is no other region like this."

Crawford agrees that India would survive as a country if it lost Kashmir. "Kashmir has always been a disputed territory and is on the periphery of India," he says, "so losing it would not disrupt the geographic continuity of the country like [losing] some other territory might."

Crawford also doubts that losing Kashmir would destroy India's attempts to create an open, multicultural society. "Will India's fundamental character be destroyed by this? I don't think so," he says. "India came into possession of Kashmir under very dubious circumstances, so the idea that it is crucial to the Indian experiment, to Indian nationhood, is wrong."

But secession opponents say independence would be worse than the status quo. "If Kashmir were to gain its independence, it would be a very small country wedged in between two very powerful, hostile states," says the University of Virginia's Gould. "It would just end up as a pawn in a great power game."

As for handing the province over to Pakistan, that "would be a total disaster for the Kashmiris" as well as the Indians, he says. "Pakistan has been plagued by chaos and has gone from one military dictatorship to another, so I don't think Kashmir would benefit from becoming part of Pakistan."

Should India have a permanent seat on the U.N. Security Council?

At a recent United Nations debate on the future of the Security Council, India's deputy representative to the U.N. proposed expanding the number of permanent council members. The current council is "unrepresentative and anachronistic," A. Gopinathan argued, and should be revamped to better reflect the increasing importance of India and other large, developing states. [10]

It's an old argument. Indeed, India and other big, Third World countries, such as Brazil and Nigeria, have been seeking seats for decades.

As the body that decides on issues of war and peace, the Security Council is widely considered the most important part of the U.N. Ten seats are filled by member states elected by the General Assembly to two-year terms. But the United States, Russia, China, the United Kingdom and France sit on the council permanently, an arrangement that hasn't changed since the world body was established at the end of World War II, in 1945. Each of the five permanent members has the power to veto any action by the council.

Michigan's Varshney argues that it is absurd to deny a country with a billion people a place on the powerful council when England and France — with roughly 5 percent of India's population — are members. "The Security Council's power structure is based on the power framework of the 1940s, when India wasn't even a country and Britain still had a huge empire that included India," Varshney says. "But that framework is no longer relevant and hasn't been for years."

Oldenburg agrees. "If India had been an independent state when the council was created in 1945, it certainly would have gotten a seat based on population alone," he says. "Today, they are every bit the equal, and then some, of Britain or France, be it militarily, economically or politically."

Indeed, Oldenburg adds, India's influence reaches throughout South Asia. "They basically govern or have great influence over a billion and a half people — if you include countries like Pakistan, Bangladesh and Sri Lanka — or about a quarter of the world's population," he says. "That has to count for something."

Moreover, proponents say, India's geopolitical importance is only going to grow as its population and economy continue to expand. (*See graph, p. 208.*) "India is only going to become more important, not less," Varshney says.

But Ganguly says population shouldn't be the only criterion for a permanent seat. "Just because they have a billion people doesn't mean they automatically deserve a seat," he says. "For one thing, they have to get their house in order before they take on these new responsibilities that affect other countries."

For Ganguly, that means solving the Kashmir problem. "If they have their own province trying to break away, how can we ever expect them to deal fairly with a situation like Kosovo?" he asks, referring to international efforts three years ago to assist Serbia's Muslim-majority province. "If [India] had been sitting on the council in 1999, it would have vetoed any effort to help in Kosovo out of fear of setting a bad precedent for Kashmir."

In addition, Ganguly says, India is still catching up to the rest of the world economically. "To be a real power in this world, you need to have real economic power," he says. "And, frankly, India's economy is not yet a great-power economy. They need years of growth before they reach that point."

Opponents also cite India's brazen development and testing of nuclear weapons as a reason to reject it as a permanent council member. "I expect permanent members of the Security Council to make real contributions to world security, [including] reducing dangers of weapons of mass destruction, particularly nuclear weapons," says Michael Krepon, founding president of the Henry L. Stimson Center, an international-security think tank in Washington.

While India has not sold nuclear technology to rogue regimes like Iran and Iraq, it has refused to submit to international limits or safeguards on its own nuclear program, which exploded the country's first nuclear device in 1974. "India is not acting responsibly, because they haven't accepted any restraints on their nuclear weapons," Krepon says "They should sign the Nuclear Test Ban Treaty and the Non-Proliferation Treaty before they're considered for a seat at the high table." [11]

Michigan's Varshney argues, however, that opposition based on India's nuclear program is unfair, since all five permanent members have nuclear weapons, and India's program is clearly necessary for self-defense. "India has to pay attention to two potentially hostile nuclear powers on its borders, Pakistan and China," he says. "They live in a very tough neighborhood and need to be free to pursue a legitimate nuclear deterrent."

But opponents claim that even if India were to deserve a seat, adding the country would almost certainly be detrimental to the Security Council as an institution. "Basically, the only way India would ever come on the council is as part of a group of new countries, like Brazil and Japan, that also have longstanding and valid claims to a seat," Krepon says, adding that, at the same time, existing members are unlikely to give up their seats. "So all of sudden you'd have 10 [permanent] members of the Security Council, each with a veto. It's already unwieldy with just five veto-wielding members. Imagine what things would be like with 10. Nothing would ever get done."

BACKGROUND

5,000 Years of History

Dating back almost 5,000 years, India's incomparable civilization has left a legacy ranging from the decimal system and cotton weaving to ancient methods of meditation and the game of chess.

The first cities and literate societies in South Asia sprang up along the Indus River in western India in around 2500 BC. By the second millennium B.C., pastoral tribes from Central Asia known today as Aryans had arrived on the subcontinent. They spoke a primitive form of Sanskrit and worshiped gods who evolved into the Hindu pantheon. [12]

By 500 B.C., the Aryans had conquered most of northern and much of central India, establishing several regional kingdoms. The northern invaders brought domestic agriculture and built towns and cities throughout India.

Indian civilization developed during much of this period. The great Hindu epic, *The Mahabharata*, was written, and Buddhism was established. The country's caste system probably formed during this era.

Many large and small hereditary kingdoms rose and

1900-1945 *After more than a century of colonial rule, the British hold over India begins to wane.*

1905 The Indian National Congress (the Congress Party) calls for a boycott of British-made goods to protest the division of the province of Bengal. The boycott is a success.

1919 The massacre by the British of 379 people in the Punjab sours Indian public opinion against European rule.

1920 Mohandas K. Gandhi assumes leadership of the Congress Party. He advocates non-violent resistance to British rule.

1940 The Muslim League calls for the partition of India into separate Muslim and Hindu states.

1945-1965 *India gains independence from Great Britain and commits itself to tolerance and multiculturalism.*

June 3, 1947 The last British viceroy, Viscount Louis Mountbatten, announces a plan to partition India into Hindu and Muslim states.

Aug. 15, 1947 India is declared an independent state. Jawaharlal Nehru becomes the country's first prime minister.

Fall 1947 Creation of Pakistan leads to severe violence between Hindus and Muslims. More than 1 million people are killed.

1948 Gandhi is assassinated by a Hindu extremist.

1964 Nerhu dies in office.

1966-1990 *Nehru's daughter and grandson dominate Indian politics; India becomes self-sufficient in food production following its "Green Revolution."*

1966 Nehru's daughter, Indira Gandhi, becomes prime minister.

1974 India tests its first nuclear weapon.

1975 Amid domestic turmoil, Mrs. Gandhi declares a state of emergency. Press freedom is curtailed, and political opponents are jailed.

1977 Mrs. Gandhi lifts the state of emergency but is voted out of office.

1979 India becomes self-sufficient in grain production.

1980 Mrs. Gandhi is restored to office as prime minister. Her son and political heir, Sanjay, dies in a plane crash.

1984 Mrs. Gandhi is assassinated by Sikh militants. Her son, Rajiv, becomes prime minister and promptly wins election for a new term.

1989 Rajiv is defeated. V.P. Singh becomes prime minister.

1991-Present *Hindu-Muslim violence helps bring Hindu nationalists to power.*

1991 Rajiv Gandhi is assassinated by a Tamil extremist while campaigning to regain the prime minister post. The new prime minister, Narasimha Rao, institutes sweeping free-market reforms.

1992 A Hindu mob destroys the Babri Masjid mosque in Ayodhya. Thousands die in sectarian rioting that follows.

1998 The Hindu nationalist Bharatiya Janata Party wins a plurality of votes and forms a government under Prime Minister Atal Behari Vajpayee. India tests nuclear weapons in response to Pakistan's first nuclear test.

Sept. 12, 2001 India offers the United States use of its military bases in the war against terrorism.

Feb. 28, 2002 The killing of 58 Hindus in Godhra by Muslims sets off a new wave of sectarian violence. More than 800 are killed, mostly Muslims.

fell throughout the subcontinent during the ensuing centuries. The largest and most enduring were the Mauryan and the Gupta dynasties, which ruled over much of northern India in the third century B.C. and from 320 A.D. to 550 A.D., respectively. The peace and prosperity brought by the Guptas helped foster innumerable achievements in art, architecture and literature. [13]

Around the 10th century A.D., Islamic invaders from the north and west began penetrating into South Asia and gradually established control over north India. In the early 16th century, incursions of central Asians known as the Mughals defeated the ruling Muslim dynasty. Under Babur and his successors, the Mughals swept over most of the subcontinent. Within a century and a half, they had conquered all but the southernmost tip of India.

Under a series of great Mughal rulers — including Akbar and Shah Jahan — much of northern India was converted to Islam. Mughal rule was marked by many cultural achievements, including the building of the famed Taj Mahal, as a tomb for Shah Jahan's wife. But by the beginning of the 18th century, the empire was falling apart, weakened and eventually destroyed by both internal rebellion and invasions from Persia. The collapse of the Mughal Dynasty occurred just as the European presence in India was growing.

The Raj

European involvement in India coincided with the Mughal invasion. The Portuguese explorer Vasco da Gama reached Calicut in southern India in 1498, and the Portuguese established a colony in Goa in 1510. By the middle of the 17th century, chartered trading companies from Britain, Holland and France also had established small outposts on the subcontinent, the most famous of which was the British East India Company.

The British began expanding inland in the mid-18th century. At first, they looked for sources of spices, opium, cotton and other valuable commodities needed for trade. They gradually expanded their control over these areas by training and employing Indian soldiers (called sepoys) and forming ties with powerful merchants and rulers. [14]

By 1800, the British controlled a substantial patchwork of territories. But the perceived threat from the French during the Napoleonic Wars of the early 19th century and later the expansionist policies of Czarist Russia prompted the English to begin expanding their domain. By the 1850s, the East India Co. ruled most of the subcontinent, either directly or through alliances. [15]

In 1857, sepoys mutinied near Delhi, sparking a revolt across much of northern India. "The Great Mutiny" shocked the British, who were largely unaware of the depth of resentment their conquest of the subcontinent had engendered among the local population. The British harshly suppressed the rebellion, which dramatically altered the attitudes of both groups toward each other. [16] The East India Co. was replaced by direct British rule, and Queen Victoria became the empress of India.

Before the rebellion, the British had been relatively open with Indians, but they quickly became insular and xenophobic. European houses were segregated from the general population and set away from large native settlements in what became known as cantonments. And the British mixed far less socially with Indians — even those who were well-educated or from aristocratic families.

For Indians, especially those educated in the West or at Western-oriented schools, the post-rebellion years were a time of growing national identity. In 1885, elite civil servants, journalists and other Indian professionals formed the Indian National Congress, later known simply as the Congress, or Congress Party. It was the progenitor of the party that ruled India for more than four decades. At first, the group only petitioned the country's British ruler, known as the viceroy, and the Parliament in London for reforms aimed at increasing Indians' rights.

By the early 20th century, though, the Congress Party was expressing growing nationalist sentiments. In 1905, the party faced its first test, calling on all Indians to boycott British-made goods to protest the partition of Bengal into largely Hindu and Muslim provinces. The move was widely seen as another effort by the British to quell nationalism and maintain their hold on the country using "divide-and-rule" tactics.

The boycott was a success, and the partition eventually was reversed. For the first time since the mutiny 50 years before, Indians had risen up successfully against the British.

During World War I, Indians provided invaluable support to the British, sending 1.3 million soldiers to Europe and elsewhere. [17] To reward the wartime loyalty, the British in 1917 announced their intention to move toward self-government for India. But only two years later, Parliament passed new laws giving British authorities in India greater latitude to quell unrest — including censorship, detention without trial and arrest without warrant.

India's Ticking Population Bomb

Agrim clock stands in the center of the northern Indian city of Lucknow, ticking out a steady and troubling beat: 33 births per minute, 2,000 an hour, 48,000 a day.

If India's population clock is supposed to be a warning, it has not entirely been heeded. India grew by 181 million people in the last decade, to more than 1 billion, and is expected to grow another 14 percent this decade. [1] If present trends continue, India will overtake China as the world's most populous country by mid-century. [2]

Still, India has made great strides in population control. The desperately poor country has halved the rate of live births in the last 50 years, from six per woman in 1950 to three in 2000.

Meanwhile, India still must struggle to maintain the vast population it already has, in a nation about one-third the size of the United States (which has only a quarter as many people.) But the country has made great strides in achieving food self-sufficiency since the 19th and early 20th centuries, when famines claimed tens of millions of lives.

Beginning in the 1960s with the Nobel Prize-winning research of American scientist Norman Borlaug, India initiated a "Green Revolution," dramatically improving agricultural productivity. Better seeds, fertilizer, pesticides,

farming techniques and land reform vastly increased yields of cereals and other crops.

Today, India is the world's third-largest food producer and regularly produces a grain surplus. Nonetheless, one in every three Indians still goes hungry at least some of the time — a problem that is especially acute with children. "Even today . . . more than 2.7 million children die of hunger each year," said Manju Sharma, secretary of India's Department of Biotechnology. [3]

In fact, more than half of all Indian children under age 4 suffer from malnutrition, and 30 percent of all newborns are underweight, according to the World Bank. [4] A 2001 United Nations Children's Fund (UNICEF) report found that half of all Indian children have suffered stunted growth. [5]

To solve the problem, the government is enthusiastically supporting India's "Green Revolution: Version 2.0," which relies on genetically modified (GM) crops to once again dramatically increase yields. Despite the global controversy surrounding GM foods, Indian farmers are expected to plant protein-fortified potatoes, Vitamin A-filled rice and insect-resistant cabbage in the coming years.

"Food security is a challenge," Sharma said. "If you look at genetically modified products, there are several positive

---

[1] Celia W. Dugger, "India Uses Varied Tactics to Reduce Population Growth," *The New York Times,* July 8, 2001.

[2] "Population Growth to Spell Boomtime for Retailers," *Business Standard,* Feb. 16, 2002.

[3] Quoted in Arvind Padmanabhan, "Enter GM Food, Exit Hunger and Malnutrition," *The Economic Times,* March 29, 2002.

[4] Kathleen Kenna, "India's Growing Pains," *The Toronto Star,* Sept. 9, 2001.

[5] *Ibid.*

The new laws led to widespread protests throughout the country, culminating in the shooting of 379 people by the British. The incident shocked India, radicalized opposition to the British and soured any good feeling that might have endured from wartime cooperation and the self-government proposal.

Fight for Independence

By this time, Mohandas K. Gandhi had arisen as a new leader in the Congress Party. Educated in Britain, Gandhi had cut his political teeth in South Africa, where he worked on behalf of indigent Indian laborers. By

1920, he had returned to India and become a party leader.

Gandhi, later known as the nation's beloved Mahatma, or "Great Soul," also saw the fight for independence from Britain as an opportunity to improve Indian society. He sought to build a new India that would be pluralistic, tolerant and self-sufficient. [18] To accomplish his aims, Gandhi turned the Congress into a mass movement.

In the early 1920s, he helped lead the party on a campaign of non-violent civil disobedience (*satyagraha.*) Gandhi urged his countrymen to boycott British goods,

factors — yield is better, the nutritional value improves and wastage declines sharply." [6]

But increased food production is not enough, experts say. India also has to continue trying to lower birth rates.

Some of the earlier gains were achieved through mass-sterilization programs that often bordered on coercion, especially in the mid-1970s, when then-Prime Minister Indira Gandhi suspended democracy and forced many poor Indians to be sterilized.

Population Growth Is Slowing

India's population growth rate has been slowing since 1950, but its population is still expected to increase fourfold, from 358 million to 1.5 billion people by 2050.

	Past and Projected Population	Population Growth Rate
1950	358 million	1.69%
2000	1 billion	1.52
2015	1.2 billion	1.11
2025	1.3 billion	0.92
2050	1.5 billion	0.41

Source: "World Prospects: The 2000 Revision," U.N. Population Division, Feb. 28, 2001.

example, poor people who get sterilized are given priority in housing, loans and other state services. The policy has worked; local women have only an average of 2.1 children, well below the national average. [7]

But, experts say, the greatest hope for improving population control lies in changing attitudes. That is already happening in parts of the country. Even some of India's rural poor — who traditionally have many children — have come

Today, the central government has stopped forcing poor people to be sterilized and has even stopped setting sterilization targets. Instead, it and many of India's states are focused more on providing education and access to contraceptives. States like Kerala and Tamil Nadu, for example, are educating girls about family planning.

Still, some of India's most populous provinces still encourage and reward sterilization. In Andra Pradesh, for

to view smaller families as a way to improve the next generation's prospects.

"We cannot afford to educate more than two," said G. Ramanamma, an Andra Pradesh farmer whose wife was sterilized after their second child was born. "I do not want my children to grow up to be farm laborers like us. I want them to get jobs." [8]

---

[6] Quoted in Padmanabhan, *op. cit.*

[7] Dugger, *op. cit.*

[8] Quoted in *ibid.*

---

discard Western dress, refuse to pay taxes and resign from government jobs. Equally important, he fought for improvements in the lives of India's huge, impoverished rural population. Gandhi's high principles, accompanied by personal asceticism and piety, made him increasingly popular as the 1920s wore on. [19] Other Congress leaders emerged at this time as well, including Nehru, who later became India's first prime minister and the founder of its greatest political dynasty.

During the late 1920s and early '30s, Gandhi and the Congress alternately agitated against and negotiated with the British. In the 1935 Government of India Act,

London gave the provinces in India autonomy. In the first provincial elections following the new law in 1937, the Congress Party won control of more areas than any other group and solidified its position as India's dominant nationalist group.

After the viceroy declared war on Germany for India without consulting the Congress, the party withdrew from provincial governments and refused to support the war effort. In 1942, it launched a nationwide "Quit India" movement ending cooperation with Britain. This action prompted the authorities to arrest 60,000 Congress members, including Gandhi and Nehru.

Mohandas K. Gandhi, known as the Mahatma ("Great Soul"), led a non-violent independence movement that helped wrest India from British control in 1947 and set the new nation on a path toward a democratic and secular society.

At the same time, another major political party, the Muslim League, decided to support the British war effort. Led by Mohammad Ali Jinnah, the league spoke for the country's Muslims, more than a quarter of India's population. In 1940, the league called for India to be divided into two states, one for Muslims and one for Hindus. "Jinnah believed that Muslims would not get a fair shake from the Hindu majority in the post-independence India that was coming," says Bouton of the Chicago Council on Foreign Relations. "For him, the only solution was a Muslim homeland in South Asia — Pakistan."

As the war dragged on, the British tried to placate political forces by promising greater autonomy for India once the conflict ended. But by war's end in 1945, the British hold on India clearly was tenuous, and the only question was how it would best manage its exit.

Meanwhile, the Congress did little to allay Muslim fears. For his part, Jinnah showed little interest in moving away from his goal of a separate Muslim state. The gap between the two communities widened when rioting broke out in Calcutta in August 1946 and spread throughout much of the country, killing thousands of Muslims and Hindus.

Fearing a civil war, the last British viceroy, Viscount Louis Mountbatten, on June 3, 1947, announced plans to partition the country at independence. Pakistan would occupy two Muslim-majority areas on the western and eastern peripheries of British India.* On Aug. 15, India became independent, and Nehru gave one of the most famous political speeches of the 20th century, declaring that the new nation had a "tryst with destiny."

A New Nation

The first step in India's new destiny was a violent one. Partition led millions of Hindu and Muslim refugees to flee India for Pakistan, and vice-versa. The mass migrations turned violent, and an estimated 1 million people died. To make matters worse, the two countries went to war in the fall of 1947 over Kashmir. The war ended in a cease-fire on Jan. 1, 1949, with Pakistan taking control of a third of the disputed province.

More tragedy occurred. On Jan. 30, 1948, Gandhi was assassinated by a Hindu fanatic upset with the Mahatma's efforts to reach out to the tens of millions of Muslims remaining in India.

In spite of these early difficulties, Nehru began to move India forward on several fronts. He and his colleagues in 1950 adopted a democratic constitution. In India's first general election in 1952, the Congress won a sweeping victory. Nehru also pressed many social reforms. He pushed laws through India's Parliament aimed at improving the status of women in society. The minimum marriage age was raised from 12 to 15, and women were given the right to divorce their husbands and inherit property. (*See sidebar, p. 210.*)

In the international arena, Nehru made India a leader in the so-called Nonaligned Movement, comprised largely of newly independent African and Asian states that did not want to choose sides in the Cold War. But

---

* Eastern Pakistan became Bangladesh in 1971.

he tilted India toward the Soviet Union, supporting the communist state even after it invaded Hungary in 1956.

Educated at Oxford, the popular Nehru was a champion of both democracy and socialism. During his 17-year tenure as prime minister, Indian democracy strengthened, and the society became more open and tolerant. But Nehru also nationalized much of India's heavy industry, a move that many economists think slowed the country's economic development in the decades following independence.

Nehru died in office in 1964 and was replaced by his only child, Indira, two years later. Indira Gandhi (Gandhi was her husband's last name; he was not related to the Mahatma) proved to be a vigorous, decisive leader, but less democratic than her father. She also won plaudits in 1971 when India defeated Pakistan in a war that enabled East Pakistan to gain its independence as Bangladesh.

But the cost of the war, coupled with rising oil prices in 1973-74, hurt the Indian economy. Mrs. Gandhi's once stratospheric popularity plummeted as strikes and civil disobedience campaigns plunged the country into turmoil. On June 25, 1975, Gandhi declared a state of emergency and suspended civil rights. During the next 19 months, she jailed thousands of her political opponents and instituted a forced sterilization program among the poor to curb the nation's high birth rate.

Democracy was restored in January 1977, and Gandhi promptly lost a general election. Fortunately for her, factional infighting divided her political opponents, and she regained power in the 1980 general election. But many historians believe Gandhi's push for centralization hurt India.

"She weakened the democratic institutions, like regional parties, that could have helped diffuse the problems and ended up encouraging extremists," Bouton says, including armed Sikh militants.

In May 1984, Sikhs occupied their religion's holiest site, the Golden Temple in the city of Amritsar. Mrs. Gandhi responded by ordering the military to storm the temple, killing hundreds of Sikhs. The move restored order but also alienated millions of once-loyal Sikhs. On Oct. 31, Gandhi was assassinated by two Sikhs in her bodyguard detail. In the days that followed, several thousand Sikhs were killed in revenge riots across the country. [20]

Mrs. Gandhi had been grooming her son Sanjay to lead the Congress Party when she retired. But Sanjay died in a plane crash, and her other son, the less politi-

Jawaharlal Nehru served as India's prime minister from independence in 1947 until his death in 1964, when his only daughter Indira became prime minister.

cally minded Rajiv, found himself atop India's ruling party after her death. [21] Although a relative newcomer to politics, Rajiv at first won over many hearts and minds with his sincere efforts to tackle India's pressing problems. However, his popularity dipped as he proved an ineffective leader.

During his five years in office, the Congress Party's popularity ebbed, hurt by corruption scandals and the failure of an Indian peacekeeping mission to neighboring Sri Lanka. Rajiv Gandhi lost power in the November 1989 election and, like his mother, was felled by an assassin — while campaigning for re-election in 1991. Rajiv was killed by a Tamil extremist, angry that Indian soldiers had fought against Tamil separatists during the peacekeeping mission to Sri Lanka.

Two major developments have dominated the last decade in India. Prime Minister P.V. Narasimha Rao and

The Booming Technology Sector

India's technology industry has grown into a $12.2 billion behemoth in just six years. Two-thirds of the revenues come from sales of software and software services — which have jumped eightfold since 1995. Most of the rapid growth in software sales resulted from exports, many to the United States.

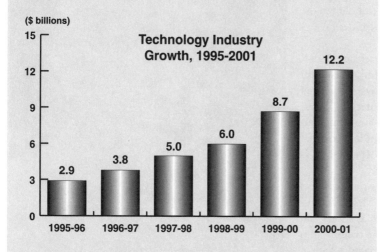

($ billions)

Technology Industry Growth, 1995-2001

1995-96	1996-97	1997-98	1998-99	1999-00	2000-01
2.9	3.8	5.0	6.0	8.7	12.2

Source: India's National Association of Software and Services Companies. Document can be found at http://www.nasscom.org/it_industry/indic_statistics.asp

Finance Minister Manmohan Singh instituted sweeping economic reforms in 1991. And Hindu nationalism emerged as a political force, culminating in the election of Prime Minister Vajpayee and the BJP in 1998 — six years after the destruction of the Ayodhya mosque.

CURRENT SITUATION

Economic Reform

While Nehru's socialist policy had some initial success, economic growth in India was anemic in the 1960s and '70s when compared with many other countries in Asia. During that period, India's gross domestic product (GDP) increased by 3.5 percent annually, far less than the GDPs in the thriving economies of Southeast Asian "Tigers" like South Korea and Taiwan. [22]

Moreover, Nehru and his successors did not succeed in their stated goal of producing a more egalitarian society. By the late '70s, half of all Indians still lived at or under the poverty line, and the gap between rich and poor had actually grown.

During the '80s, modest reforms spurred a small jump in economic growth, but some of the increase had been achieved by borrowing from abroad, and in 1990 India faced a balance of payments crisis.

"Basically, they had 10 or 12 days' worth of foreign reserves left and were in deep trouble," says Makul Majumdri, a professor of economics at Cornell University.

The crisis forced the country to change. The International Monetary Fund offered India a loan to increase foreign reserves in exchange for promised free-market reforms. Economic liberalization commenced almost immediately, but was codified and expanded the following year, in 1991.

India then embarked on a major program of economic reform, initiated by then-Prime Minister Rao and Finance Minister Singh. The reforms steered India away from the Gandhi-Nehru-inspired socialism that had shaped the country's economic policy for 40 years and helped India throw off its protectionist and statist cloaks. Tariffs were slashed from 300 percent in 1991 to 50 percent four years later. Foreign investors were allowed to purchase majority stakes in Indian companies, and whole sectors of the economy were opened to private-sector ownership. [23]

Much has changed during the nearly 12 years since the reform process began. India's economy has grown at an average rate of about 6 percent. And there are now nearly 200 million middle-class consumers, who help drive domestic growth and make India a more tempting destination for Western investment. [24]

And there have been dramatic success stories, particularly in the software industry, which has been growing more than 50 percent a year since the early 1990s. Software is now an $8.3 billion industry, accounting for 15 percent of the country's exports. It could reach $50 billion by 2008. [25]

The boom began in Bangalore. By the mid-1990s, software firms like Microsoft and Oracle had set up research facilities in and around the city to take advantage of large numbers of highly educated workers who could write software code for a fraction of the salaries paid their American counterparts.

"In the 1950s, the government began to emphasize science and technology and set up institutes to train large numbers of people," Mujumdri says. "We are really reaping the benefits of this now."

Software firms have spread from Bangalore and elsewhere, to Hyderabad, New Delhi and other Indian cities. The industry now consists mainly of domestically owned firms.

Indian firms are making headway in other high-tech sectors, including computer-related services, telecommunications and biotechnology. Indeed, many economists predict that biotechnology will duplicate the kind of phenomenal growth rates witnessed in the software industry. The country already has 30 firms and a biotech market worth an estimated $1.5 billion. [26]

Moreover, says Kiran Mazumdar Shaw (owner of Biocon, India's largest biotech company), the country's universities are graduating 20,000 people with biology-related degrees every year, creating an attractive work force for both foreign and domestic research firms. [27]

Amid all of the good news, however, economists say the country's economic reform is far from complete and that huge challenges remain. For instance, laws governing foreign investment still impose severe limits on foreign firms. These difficulties, combined with bureaucratic red tape and corruption, bad roads and stifling labor laws, scare away potential domestic and foreign investors.

Investment from abroad has actually dropped in recent years, from $3.5 billion in 1997 to $2 billion in 2000. [28] Corporate giants like Bell South and Vodaphone have left India after years of trying to build a presence in the market.

"The Indians still think they're doing you a big kindness by allowing you to invest in their country," says Alan Heston, a professor of economics at the University of Pennsylvania. "The system needs to be much more open to outside money."

In addition, Majumdri says, the country needs to dramatically improve its infrastructure and streamline and reform its bureaucracy.

"We need better roads, more telephones and better ports and airports so goods can be moved around, and

AFP Photo/Indranil Mukherjee

Students learn how to surf the Web at a free Internet clinic held at a stadium in Bangalore — known as India's Silicon Valley. India has long stressed science and technology education, and now boasts a burgeoning high-tech sector.

businesses have confidence that they can function here," he says. "We also need to cut back the bureaucracy and simplify many of the regulations and laws that make it hard for a company to set up a business."

For example, Majumdri points out, obtaining an export license can require up to 250 official signatures. "This is ridiculous, of course, and so damaging to the business climate," he says. "It also leads to a lot of petty corruption."

Another problem facing India, experts say, is the continuing role of the state in the economy. While the reforms opened once-closed sectors of the economy to private firms, 43 percent of all business assets still are owned by the government, according to a report last year by McKinsey & Co., a consulting firm. Indeed, many of the country's major industries, from power generation to banking, still have a sizable government presence.

The government routinely announces the names of firms that will be privatized or partially privatized. Sometimes the efforts are successful, as with the recent sale of 25 percent of VSNL (India's international telephone carrier) to a private company. In other cases, efforts come to naught. The recently announced sale of 40 percent of money-losing Air India to a consortium led by Singapore Airlines fell through after domestic political and union opposition forced the company to withdraw its bid. [29]

From Bollywood to Viceroy — an Indian Glossary

Bollywood — The name given to the film industry in Bombay, which produces even more movies each year than its namesake, Hollywood. Although India's movie studios churn out more than 800 features a year, most are from the same mold: larger-than-life, formulaic dramas that offer audiences large dollops of romance, action, music and dancing.

Caste — The caste system is nearly as old as Indian civilization. It is a hereditary system of social classes that restricts the occupations of members and their ability to associate with those in other castes. There are thousands of different kinds of castes in India today, but all are believed to have come from the system of four great castes (also known as *Varnas*) described in ancient Hindu writings. The four *Varnas* are *Brahmins* (priests and scholars), *Vaishyas* (merchants), *Kshatriyas* (soldiers and rulers) and *Shudras* (the farmers and laborers at the bottom of society.) Although the caste system has been perceived as rigid, some Indians have moved between castes, and the status of certain castes has changed over time. Today, discrimination based on caste is illegal, and democratic ideals and globalization have further weakened the caste structure, but it is still an influential force in Indian society. For instance, even though their lives are improving, members of the lowest caste, known as *Dalits* (see below) or "untouchables" still face discrimination, sometimes deadly, in many parts of India.

Constitution — The Indian Constitution, which took effect in 1950, guarantees equal rights for all Indians, regardless of religion, caste or ethnicity. The document also sets social policy goals, such as a living wage for all workers and subsidized health care.

Dalit — A term meaning "The Oppressed," for members of India's lowest caste, also known as "untouchables." Dalits traditionally do the jobs — such as slaughtering animals — deemed unsuitable for members of higher castes. In recent decades, *Dalits* (the name they prefer) have benefited from a sweeping affirmative-action effort to give them entrée into all segments of Indian society.

Hinduism — Unlike many religions, Hinduism does not have a single system or creed. It is more like a collection of traditions and beliefs. In addition, Hindus (unlike the followers of most other faiths) do not believe that their religion is the only revealed truth and that all other religions are wrong. There are thousands of gods in the Hindu pantheon, including Brahma the Creator, Vishnu the Preserver and Siva the Destroyer. Animals are frequently associated with Hinduism. Some gods have animal characteristics or forms — like the popular elephant god Ganesha. But the most important creature to Hindus is the cow, which is revered for its usefulness and peaceful nature.

Jainism — A religion founded in around 500 B.C. (about the same time as Buddhism), Jainism is practiced by

Many economists criticize the piecemeal approach to privatization, arguing that the government needs to be more aggressive about getting out of the economy. But the University of Pennsylvania's Heston contends that it is unrealistic to expect a country with so much poverty to throw many people out of work — the inevitable result of privatizing many state firms at once.

"It's impossible to do this quickly because it would be too unpopular," he says. "The best we can hope for is a gradual shift from state to private ownership, which is what they're doing."

U.S.-Indian Relations

Since independence, India's relations with the United States often have been marked by mutual wariness and estrangement. "It's been a dialogue of the deaf," the

University of Michigan's Varshney says. "Neither country has really tried to pay attention to the other's legitimate concerns."

As the largest and most significant European colony to achieve independence after World War II, India saw itself as a bulwark against Western imperialism, particularly the geopolitical dominance of the United States.

For its part, the United States added to the tensions by forming a close, Cold War alliance with India's long-standing rival, Pakistan, even selling sophisticated U.S. weapons and providing training and other assistance to India's enemy. At the same time, India cultivated a close, long-term relationship with the Soviet Union, which did not sit well with Washington.

As recently as 1998, Indian nuclear testing rocked Indo-U.S. relations, setting off American government

millions of Indians, especially in the northern part of the country. Its tenets include charity, non-violence and self-control. Mahatma Gandhi was influenced by its teachings, although he was not a Jainist.

Mahabharata — One of India's two great religious epics, along with the *Ramayana*. Begun in the last millennium before Christ and completed in the centuries just after, it is five times as long as the Bible. The poem's narrative heart concerns the rivalry between two family dynasties, but it is a treasure trove of legends, philosophy, wisdom and history.

Maharajahs — The Hindu princes who ruled over hundreds of kingdoms within India, the largest of which was Kashmir. During the years of British rule, these princes, along with their Muslim counterparts, Nawabs, had titular authority over one-third of India. These territories were absorbed into India and Pakistan after independence in 1947.

Nehru-Gandhi Dynasty — India's greatest political family was founded by Jawaharlal Nehru, who ruled as prime minister from 1947 until his death in 1964. Nehru's daughter Indira Gandhi and grandson Rajiv Gandhi (both took Indira's husband's last name; they are not related to Mohandas K. Gandhi, the Mahatma) dominated politics until the late 1980s. Rajiv's wife Sonia heads the Indian National Congress Party — India's largest opposition party.

Raj — The word, which means "kingdom" or "reign," was used to describe the system of British rule in India until independence in 1947.

Sanskrit — The language of the Aryan invaders who conquered India more than three millennia ago. Much of India's greatest literature was originally written in Sanskrit and is the basis for Hindi, Urdu and many of the county's other major languages.

Sati — The once common practice among Hindu widows of burning themselves to death on the funeral pyres of their deceased husbands. The practice was prohibited by the British during their rule over India and has slowly died out. According to the Indian government, the last recorded instance of Sati occurred in 1988.

Satyagraha — The method used by Mohandas K. Gandhi and his followers to bring about social and political change through the use of non-violent resistance, such as non-cooperation and boycotts. The word is a combination of the Hindu words for "truth" and "holding firmly." Gandhi began forming and applying these principles while working on behalf of Indian laborers in South Africa, where they met with only limited success. The experience taught him that non-violent tactics required patience. His campaigns of strikes and non-cooperation took almost 30 years to pry the country loose from Britain.

Sikhs — A monotheistic religion founded in the Punjab in the 15th century that combines elements of Hinduism and Islam. Sikh men do not cut their hair or beards but instead wear them tightly wrapped in turbans. While India's 20 million Sikhs make up just 2 percent of the population, they comprise 25 percent of the nation's army.

Viceroy — The de facto ruler during the British occupation of India. The viceroy held immense power and was answerable only to the British government in London.

---

protests and prompting the United States to impose economic sanctions on India.

But relations between the two countries have warmed considerably since then. For one thing, the mutual suspicion fostered by the Cold War mindset is fading, along with the memory of the now-defunct Soviet Union. "The end of the Cold War has slowly changed the priorities in both countries," Varshney says. "They are both largely beyond that old rivalry now."

In addition, U.S. relations with Pakistan had cooled considerably in the last decade — at least until Sept. 11 — because Pakistan developed nuclear weapons in the late 1990s and supported the Taliban and other radical Islamic elements in Afghanistan. [30] By pulling away from Pakistan, the United States found it easier to improve contacts with India.

Indo-U.S. relations received a tremendous boost when then-President Bill Clinton visited India for five days in March 2000 — the first visit by an American president in 22 years. Clinton scored a public relations homerun during the trip. Speaking at the Asia Society in New York a few weeks later, Indian Finance Minister Yashwant Sinha said the charismatic president's trip had swept away 50 years of misperceptions. [31]

The momentum toward better relations fostered by Clinton has been maintained by his successor, President Bush.

"The Bush administration has shown a real interest in India from the very beginning," says the University of Texas' Ganguly. "They recognized that it was important in a number of ways and shouldn't just be viewed as another nuclear threat."

Should India allow Kashmir to become an independent state?

YES
Rep. Edolphus "Ed" Towns, D-N.Y.
Written for the CQ Researcher, April 2002

In April 1948, the United Nations (U.N.) Security Council adopted a resolution that called for a plebiscite on Kashmir's independence. The following year, the U.N. Commission on India and Pakistan adopted two separate resolutions reiterating the need for a plebiscite. At the time, India promised to comply with the resolutions to help burnish its democratic image.

Unfortunately, to date no free and fair vote has taken place. In the 50 years since India's failure to honor its commitment, there have been three wars, numerous near-wars, tens of thousands of deaths, countless human rights violations, and an entire region has been paralyzed by the ebb and flow of this highly polarizing conflict.

Today, India, the largest democracy in the world, fails the "democracy test" beyond its borders, maintaining control of Kashmir through an occupying force of more than 500,000 troops. The time is right for India to make good on its commitment and hold an internationally supervised plebiscite on independence for Kashmir.

In December of 2001, India accused Pakistan of backing a group of five suicide terrorists who attacked the Indian Parliament and killed nine people. The attack brought India and Pakistan to the brink of war yet again. Tensions eased only after concerted pressure by the United States, and Pakistan decided to take a harder line on terrorist organizations within its borders.

The freezing and thawing of tensions between India and Pakistan has become all too familiar, but the presence of nuclear weapons on both sides of this regional conflict — as well as the utter failure of India's military answer to this political problem — demands that India finally fulfill its historical commitment.

Clearly, the situation in South Asia is a volatile one, and Kashmir is at the eye of the storm. However, the first step toward any attempted resolution must include an India-sponsored plebiscite to determine the will of the Kashmiri people. Only then will it be possible for all of the parties to sit down and work out a political solution.

After more than five decades of a failed military approach, it is time for a political solution. Too many lives have been lost, and too many atrocities have been committed for the situation to continue. The time for an internationally supervised plebiscite on independence for Kashmir is now.

Rep. Towns has spoken out frequently on the floor of the House of Representatives in favor of Kashmiri self-determination.

NO
Harold A. Gould
Visiting Scholar, Center for South Asian Studies, University of Virginia

Written for the CQ Researcher, April 2002

History and political reality ordain that this cannot happen. Before partition, Kashmir was one of the many "princely states" that dotted the Indian subcontinent — some minuscule and others as large as European countries. The creation of India and Pakistan as independent nations included an understanding that none of these princely states would fully retain their sovereignty, but would have the right to choose annexation either by India or Pakistan. Kashmir was the only state that presented potentially intractable affiliation problems.

Compelling geo-strategic, political, cultural and religious reasons led both India and Pakistan to lay claim to Kashmir. Because of its predominantly Muslim population and a contiguous border with the newly emergent "Islamic state" of Pakistan, Pakistani leaders believed they were legally and logically entitled to absorb Kashmir.

However, multiethnic and secular India believed it also had a right to annex Kashmir — a state ruled by a Hindu monarch whose population included the Hindu-majority region of Jammu and the Buddhist-majority Ladakh region. In addition, Kashmir's Muslims were distinct — both by sect and ethnicity — from the Punjabi Muslims who politically dominated Pakistan.

The wars that erupted between India and Pakistan over Kashmir in 1947, 1965 and 1971 revolved around these fundamentally different perspectives, undoubtedly interlaced with Cold War strategic preoccupations. Neither India nor Pakistan seriously considered valid the claims of the Kashmiri people for a separate sociopolitical identity. They have always envisioned the Kashmiris falling within either of the two larger countries while enjoying some form of quasi-autonomy.

Amid current political realities, however, the reconstitution of Kashmir to its pre-partition dimensions is inconceivable. Neither side will ever allow a genuine plebiscite. Thus, settlement of the Kashmir imbroglio will in the end involve a "Second Partition of India" along the so-called "Line of Control," which runs between Azad Kashmir — a Pakistani puppet state — and the Kashmir Valley/Jammu/Ladakh region, which is now irrevocably under Indian suzerainty.

Within each, the Kashmiri people will be compelled to negotiate a political status for themselves that maximizes their rights and interests as a separate people. The attainment of absolute independence is a myth that cannot be realized either by Kashmiris themselves, by Indo-Pakistani rapprochement, or by foreign intervention.

Should Hindus be allowed to rebuild the temple at Ayodhya?

YES   World Hindu Council of India,
www.vhp.org

April 2002

There is a deliberate attempt being made by those who control the written and visual means of communication in our society to pervert the essence of Hindutva (Hinduism). The Shri Rama Janmabhoomi movement is no exception to this agenda. Shri Rama is one of the most important persons in the galaxy of personalities at the core of our culture and civilization. He is a unique and unequaled symbol of our oneness, of our integration, and of our aspiration to live a life of higher values. He is uniformly worshipped by all as an ideal person full of virtues. He has represented for thousands of years the ideal of just conduct. It would be no exaggeration to say that in India everyone knows the story of Shri Rama.

The Shri Rama Janmabhoomi movement is not merely one of construction of a temple, but a resurgence of our culture and civilization. A temple at the Shri Rama Janmabhoomi will focus the minds of the people to achieve this goal. It would not merely be a place of worship, but a symbol of our great past and a beacon for the future.

In 1528 A.D., Babur, an Islamic invader, destroyed the temple at Shri Rama Janmabhoomi and then had the Babri structure built on its ruins. Such acts of vandalism have happened to many other indigenous places of worship all over the world. Thus, the Babri structure was a monument of our slavery, and becomes a political structure, and not a religious one.

Hindus have made numerous sincere efforts to get the site back in a peaceful manner. They were frustrated not so much by an obscurantist Muslim leadership but by those who pretend to wear the badge of secularism proudly on their sleeves. While one can rationalize such behavior in the case of the politicians, it is dangerous when the intellectuals adopt the same agenda.

Legal cases seeking to get the site back have been filed almost since the beginning of India's independence from colonial rule. These cases, unfortunately, are dragging on with no end in sight. Even though Hindus kept on making efforts to get the site back right from the destruction of the temple in 1528, the Shri Rama Janmabhoomi movement has come to the center stage of our national life only in the mid-1980s. It was the result of a denial of the fulfillment of legitimate Hindu sentiments. It was also a reaction to the practice of secularism, in which the opinions of the Hindus were not only ignored but also trampled upon.

Hindus are asking for the return of the [site] not as a special favor to them, but because justice should be done. The [site was] forcibly appropriated from them, by those who wished to destroy the Hindu civilization and culture.

NO   Amberish K. Diwanji
Senior associate editor, rediff.com

April 2002

While many might actually welcome a new Ram temple as the end of a dispute that has wracked the secular and moral fabric of India, it is far more likely that a temple on the disputed site will only open a Pandora's box for similar demands.

And such demands can be insatiable.

The VHP [a right-wing Hindu organization] has already set its eyes on the mosques at Varanasi and Mathura that adjoin important Hindu temples, while some other radicals now see buried temples where the Taj Mahal, the Qutub Minar and the Jama Masjid stand.

At this rate, almost every standing mosque or structure with an Islamic link can and will be seen as having been built on the ruins of some ancient temple. Competing Hindu outfits will each see success in the number of mosques or other structures that can be brought down to build a Hindu temple or edifice.

This has the potential of devastating India. It simply cannot be allowed under any circumstances.

Thus, a solution must be found to the Ram temple, a solution that is just, fair and which ends the dispute rather than becomes the harbinger of further conflicts.

There is no guarantee that a Ram temple will actually end the Hindu-Muslim divide. If anything, a temple is guaranteed to once more stir up communal passions, something that the politicians will love, since they stand to gain from it.

A Ram temple will whet the appetite of the VHP and its allies, who will then seek to do an encore on other mosque sites. Even if the VHP and allies give a guarantee that they will desist from further claims and settle only for a Ram temple, what is the surety that other groups not under the control of the VHP will also be bound by such a promise? Just as the VHP does not speak for all Hindus, it does not speak for all fanatical Hindu groups.

Perhaps the best alternative is to create a monument to honor Mangal Pandey, the man whose revolt sparked the 1857 War of Independence (also called the Sepoy Mutiny).

Going a step further, a monument could be built to hail all the greats who participated in that famous war — Pandey, Rani Laxmibai of Jhansi, Nana Sahib, Tantya Tope, Bahadur Zafar Shah, etc. It would be a tribute to Hindu-Muslim unity, given that the Indian forces went into war with the dual battle cry of "Har Har Mahadev" and "Allah-o-Akbar" (both mean God is Great).

AFP Photo/Prakash Singh

Muslims at a New Delhi mosque pray during the Eid festival, marking the end of the holy month of Ramadan. Predominantly Hindu India has the world's third-largest Muslim population, after Indonesia and Pakistan, numbering 125 million people.

Texas' Lariviere agrees, adding, "interest in India really took off after Sept. 11, for obvious reasons."

Indeed, the terrorist attacks on New York City and the Pentagon and the subsequent military response in Afghanistan dramatically raised India's profile among American policymakers. As Southern Asia's 800-pound guerilla, India has been able to offer the United States military, intelligence and political assistance in Afghanistan and other parts of South and Central Asia.

But beyond the war on terrorism, the U.S. and India both have pressing reasons to improve ties, experts say. For the United States, India's huge population and expanding economy act as a potential counterweight to communist China, America's new strategic competitor. "India is very important in our strategy toward China," says Gould of the University of Virginia.

However, India need not challenge China militarily to counter its influence, Gould says. "We don't need to help India become a military superpower, but just encourage their better natures," he says. "Helping nurture Indian democracy and the Indian economy will reduce China's capacity to influence other countries [in the region] because these states will see India as a better alternative and emulate it."

For India, the U.S. is already a market for its exports and a source of investment and knowledge, as evidenced by America's role in the phenomenal growth of the country's software industry. "They know they need the United States to help them grow, economically," Ganguly says. And, he points out, the Americans have an interest in growing that economy, because access to more than a billion consumers presents untold opportunities for U.S. corporations.

In addition, Ganguly says, India knows that good relations with the United States are necessary if it is to become an important player on the world stage. "The United States is the dominant country in the world, and Vajpayee knows that India will not become a great power unless relations with the U.S. are on a firm footing."

The converging interests of India and the United States — the war on terrorism and economic growth — both are likely to strengthen ties between the two countries well into the future. "We're heading toward a more mature friendship," Varshney says. "We will have the kind of good relations that can accommodate serious disagreements without severely damaging those relations."

But good relations won't automatically turn India into an American dependent or even a close ally, says the CSIS's Malik. "India has lived with colonization for years, so I don't think that they will ever accept a subservient role, even with the United States," she says. "They are unlikely to challenge the U.S., as China does, and are more likely to want to be partners, but it will have to be as an equal partner."

Varshney agrees, arguing that India probably will not become a close American ally, like Britain or Japan.

"Friendship can be affectionate, without intimacy," he says. "I think the Indians, because of their history, are too wary of U.S. domination to become intimate with the Americans. They will, however, welcome sincere and deep friendship."

OUTLOOK

A New Superpower?

Predicting the future is especially hard when it comes to India, says novelist Tharoor. "India has always had a habit of exceeding expectations and falling short of them at the same time," he says.

He notes, for instance, that the widespread predictions in 1947 that democracy would quickly give way to authoritarianism have not proven true. Today, Indian democracy, while far from perfect, is real and vibrant. Yet, spasms of horrifying sectarian violence not commonly associated with democratic states still afflict the country, Tharoor points out.

In spite of these warnings, some India-watchers are willing to predict that India will overcome its problems to become a great regional power in the coming decades. "If you just look at how far India has come in the last 50 years, you'd be amazed," says Columbia University's Oldenburg. "And the spread of education and communication is accelerating the kinds of changes that they need to advance.

"Of course, India is already a power in South Asia," says Dillon of the Heritage Foundation. "But they will soon have the economic, political and military clout to be a 'great power' — the country everyone else has to come to when they have a concern or want to get anything done in the region. India would be a real player on the world stage."

But there's a caveat, Dillon warns. "They have to continue pursuing the kind of economic reforms that they began with in 1991, or they won't get very far," he says. "You need wealth to have real power, and unless they continue to grow at a solid pace over the next 25 years, they won't be able to afford to be a great power."

The University of Texas' Ganguly agrees. "A lot really hinges on the economy," he says. "If India continues in the direction of reform, I feel confident they will become a real economic powerhouse and, by extension, a great power "But if they let reform go, they will not realize their great-power ambitions."

But Tharoor's vision for the India of tomorrow is broader. In a region fraught with underdevelopment and dictatorship — as in China or Pakistan — India must seek to be more than just powerful, he says.

"India has already been 'a player' on the world stage with its leadership of the non-aligned movement during the Cold War," Tharoor says. "With our liberal democracy and our high-tech economy, we should seek to be an example, a beacon, to other countries in the region and elsewhere. That should be our ambition."

NOTES

1. Celia W. Dugger, "Fire Started on Train Carrying Hindu Activists Kills 58," *The New York Times*, Feb. 28, 2002.

2. Celia W. Dugger, "Hindu Justifies Mass Killings of Muslims in Reprisal Riots," *The New York Times*, March 5, 2002.

3. "Indigenous Cryo Engine Successfully Test-Fired," *The Hindu*, March 31, 2002.

4. "IT Bigwigs to Discuss Private Participation in Media Lab," *Business Standard*, March 30, 2002.

5. Shashi Tharoor, "India's Past Becomes a Weapon," *The New York Times*, March 6, 2002.

6. Figure cited in theeconomist.com, "Country Briefing: India." For background, see Kenneth Jost, "Democracy in Asia," *The CQ Researcher*, July 24, 1998, pp. 625-648.

7. For background, see Rodman D. Griffin, "Nuclear Proliferation," *The CQ Researcher*, June 5, 1992, pp. 481-504.

8. Quoted in Pankaj Mishra "Hinduism's Political Resurgence," *The New York Times*, Feb. 25, 2002.

9. "The Stand-off at the Roof of the World," *The Economist*, Jan. 17, 2002.

10. Quoted in "India Calls for U.N. Security Council Expansion," *Press Trust of India*, March 12, 2002.

11. For background, see Mary H. Cooper, "Non-Proliferation Treaty at 25," *The CQ Researcher*, Jan. 27, 1995, pp. 73-96, and Mary H. Cooper, "United Nations at 50," *The CQ Researcher*, Aug. 18, 1995, pp. 729-752.

12. James Heitzman and Robert L. Woodson, *India: A Country Study* (1996), p. 4.

13. *Ibid.*, pp. 12-15.

14. James Morris, *Heaven's Command: An Imperial Progress* (1973), pp. 74-76.

15. Heitzman and Woodson, *op. cit.*, p. 30.

16. Morris, *op. cit.*, pp. 218-248.

17. Heitzman and Woodson, *op. cit.*, p. 40.

18. James Morris, *Farewell to Trumpets: An Imperial Retreat* (1978), pp. 279-285.

19. *Ibid.*, p. 281.

20. Shashi Tharoor, *India: From Midnight to Millennium* (1997), p. 38.

21. *Ibid.*, p. 37.

22. Cohen, *op. cit.*, p. 95.

23. *Ibid.*, p. 171.

24. Figure cited in Manjeet Kripalani, "India: Luring Investors Will Take Real Change," *Business Week*, June 4, 2001.

25. Stephen Cohen, *India: Emerging Power* (2001), pp. 102-103.

26. Cited in "India's Firmentation Queen," *The Economist*, Aug. 30, 2001.

27. *Ibid.*

28. "Unlocking the Potential," *The Economist*, May 31, 2001.

29. "Why India's Economy Needs Faster Privatization," *The Economist*, Sept. 6, 2001.

30. For background, see Kenneth Jost, "Rebuilding Afghanistan," *The CQ Researcher*, Dec. 21, 2001, pp. 1041-1064; David Masci, "Islamic Fundamentalism," *The CQ Researcher*, March 24, 2000, pp. 241-264, and David Masci and Kenneth Jost, "War on Terrorism," *The CQ Researcher*, Oct. 12, 2001, pp. 817-849.

31. Cohen, *op. cit.*, p. 268.

BIBLIOGRAPHY

Books

Cohen, Stephen P., *India: Emerging Power,* **Brookings Institution Press, 2001.**
A senior fellow at the Brookings Institution argues that India is becoming, along with China and Japan, one of the most important states in Asia.

Heitzman, James, and Robert L. Worden, *India: A Country Study,* **U.S. Government Printing Office, 1996.**
Part of a Library of Congress series, this superb, massive study provides an excellent background to the country.

Khilnani, Sunil, *The Idea of India,* **Farrar, Straus and Giroux, 1997.**
A professor of political science at the University of London examines the achievements of India's first 50 years, with special focus on the country's democracy, which has survived and even thrived over the years.

Kux, Dennis, *India and the United States: Estranged Democracies, 1941-1991,* **National Defense University Press, 1992.**
The New York Times called the retired U.S. ambassador's account "the definitive history of Indo-American relations."

Tharoor, Shashi, *India: From Midnight to the Millennium,* **Arcade Publishing, 1997.**
A noted novelist and social critic paints a portrait of India today that focuses on the country's many ironies.

Articles

"Enter GM Food, Exit Hunger and Malnutrition," *The Economic Times,* **March 29, 2002.**
An examination of efforts in India to plant genetically modified (GM) crops to increase food production.

"Himalayan Brinkmanship," *The Economist,* **Jan. 4, 2002.**
An excellent overview of the tense situation in Kashmir, including historical background.

"India's Fermentation Queen," *The Economist,* **Aug. 30, 2001.**
An examination of India's emerging industries, focusing on the growing biotechnology sector.

"Unproductive," *The Economist,* **Sept. 6, 2001.**
This look at ongoing efforts to reform India's economy points out that while the country has made great strides since reforms began more than 10 years ago, much needs to be done, especially increasing the rate of privatization.

Chellaney, Brahma, "On the Same Side: India's Strategic Shift," *The Asian Wall Street Journal,* **Oct. 1, 2001, p. A12.**
A professor of security studies at the Center for Policy Research in New Delhi contends that as the U.S. becomes more involved in the region, especially after the Sept. 11 terrorist attacks, it is likely to become closer to India.

Dugger, Celia W., "India Uses Varied Tactics to Reduce Population Growth," *The New York Times,* **July 8, 2001, p. A18.**
Dugger looks at how different states in India are trying to cope with the country's growing population, among them Andhra Pradesh province, which both encourages sterilization and uses education and access to voluntary contraception to reduce the birth rate.

Kenna, Kathleen, "India's Growing Pains — But Poverty Chokes Hopes," *The Toronto Star,* **Sept. 9, 2001.**

An excellent profile of the troubles spawned by India's huge impoverished population. Kenna pays special attention to efforts at providing adequate nutrition and health care for children.

McGeary, Johanna, "Person of the Century: Mohandas Gandhi," *Time*, Dec. 31, 1999, p. 118.
McGeary chronicles Gandhi's life and beliefs, concluding that he "shines as a conscience for the world."

Mishra, Pankaj, "Hinduism's Political Resurgence," *The New York Times*, Feb. 25, 2002, p. A21.
The article explores the roots of the Hindu nationalist movement and its successes in recent years. It examines whether the movement will turn India into a de facto Hindu state.

Tharoor, Shashi, "India's Past Becomes a Weapon," *The New York Times*, March 6, 2002, p. A21.
The novelist and social critic concludes that the Hindu chauvinists who incited crowds to violence recently in Gujarat "are profoundly disloyal to the religion they claim to espouse, which stands out not only as an eclectic embodiment of tolerance but also as the only major religion that does not claim to be the only true religion."

Reports

Menon-Sen, Kalyani, and A.K. Shiva Kumar, "Women in India: How Free? How Equal?" The United Nations, 2001.
The report looks at health, education, labor, legal rights and other areas, such as women's low life expectancy and rising domestic violence against women.

For More Information

Arms Control Association, 1726 M St., N.W., Suite 201, Washington, DC 20036; (202) 463-8270; www.armscontrol.org. Conducts research into arms-control issues and seeks to broaden public interest in the subject.

Asia Foundation, 465 California St., 9th Floor, San Francisco, CA 94104; (415) 982-4640; www.asiafoundation.org. A private, nonprofit, non-governmental organization working to advance the mutual interests of the United States and the Asia-Pacific region.

Asian Studies Center, The Heritage Foundation, 214 Massachusetts Ave., N.E., Washington DC 20002; (202) 608-6081; www.asianstudies.org. Studies economic and security issues in the Asian region.

Brookings Institution, 1775 Massachusetts Ave., N.W., Washington, DC 20036; (202) 797-6000; www.brookings.edu. A public-policy research organization that seeks to bridge scholarship and public policy. Brookings' foreign policy studies department includes scholars on South Asia.

Center for South Asian Studies, University of Virginia, P.O. Box 400169, 110 Minor Hall, Charlottesville, VA 22904; (434) 924-8815; www.virginia.edu/~soasia/. Conducts research and offers courses on South Asian politics, cultures and languages.

Center for Strategic and International Studies, 1800 K St., N.W., Washington, DC 20006; (202) 887-0200; www.csis.org. Provides strategic insights on international issues to political and other leaders.

Chicago Council on Foreign Relations, 116 South Michigan Ave., 10th Floor, Chicago, IL 60603-6097; (312) 726-3860; www.ccfr.org. Provides the general public a forum for the consideration of significant international issues bearing on American foreign policy, including the situation in South Asia.

Institute for Food and Development Policy, 398 60th Street, Oakland, CA 94618; (510) 654-4400; www.foodfirst.org. Works to address root causes of hunger and poverty in countries like India.

Kashmir Study Group, 1875 Palmer Ave., Larchmont, NY 10538; (914) 834-0400; www.kashmirstudygroup.net. Comprised of politicians and scholars committed to finding a solution to the Kashmir question.

South Asia Regional Studies, 3600 Market St., Suite 501B, Philadelphia, PA 19104-2653; (215) 898-7475; www.southasia.upenn.edu. Supports the study of issues related to India and South Asia.

Southern Asian Institute, International Affairs Building, 420 West 118th St. New York, NY 10027; (212) 854-5406; www.columbia.edu/cu/sipa/REGIONAL/SAI. A major center for the study of South Asia, including culture, language, history, economics and politics, based at Columbia University.

11

Trouble in South America

David Masci

A funeral procession for 17 peasants reportedly killed by the Revolutionary Armed Forces of Colombia (FARC) wends through San Carlos on Jan. 19, 2003. The Bush administration is seeking $537 million from Congress for Colombia this year, partly to help protect an oil pipeline from attacks by the guerrillas. Political turmoil in much of South America has some experts worried about the survival of democratic gains made in the 1980s and '90s.

From *The CQ Researcher*, March 14, 2003.

L a Paz means "peace" in Spanish, but Bolivia's capital was anything but peaceful on Feb. 12, when thousands of angry citizens marched to the center of the city. At one point during the ensuing melee, striking police officers and army troops sent to keep order fired at each other.

By the next day, 29 people were dead, seven government ministries had been ransacked, scores of businesses looted and large downtown sections of the city set ablaze. Protesters even rushed the presidential palace, forcing President Gonzalo Sánchez de Lozada to make his escape by hiding in an ambulance.

The protests were sparked by Sanchez's decision, later rescinded, to raise taxes and cut government spending in order to secure International Monetary Fund (IMF) loans. Aid is desperately needed in the poor Andean nation, where nearly three-quarters of the 8 million people live at or below the poverty line.

Economic and political turmoil has wracked much of South America in recent years, sending protesters into the streets in Argentina, Peru and Venezuela, often with violent results.

"There's a sour mood throughout much of the continent right now," says Michael Shifter, a professor of Latin American studies at Georgetown University and vice president of Inter-American Dialogue, a Washington think tank. "There's a sense that the economic and political models they'd been relying on for years are not working."

Venezuela is perhaps the best example of such failure. President Hugo Chavez — whose 1999 election reflected voter dissatisfaction with the existing government — has responded to massive strikes with dictatorial tactics, such as arresting opponents. (*See sidebar, p. 242.*)

231

Democratic Nations, Elected Leaders

South America's remaining dictatorships evolved into democracies in the last two decades, including those in Brazil, Argentina, Paraguay and Chile. Today, every leader on the continent has either been elected by direct popular vote or by a parliament or other elected body. Brazil, the continent's largest and most populous nation, recently elected the popular Luiz Inácio Lula da Silva — widely known as Lula.

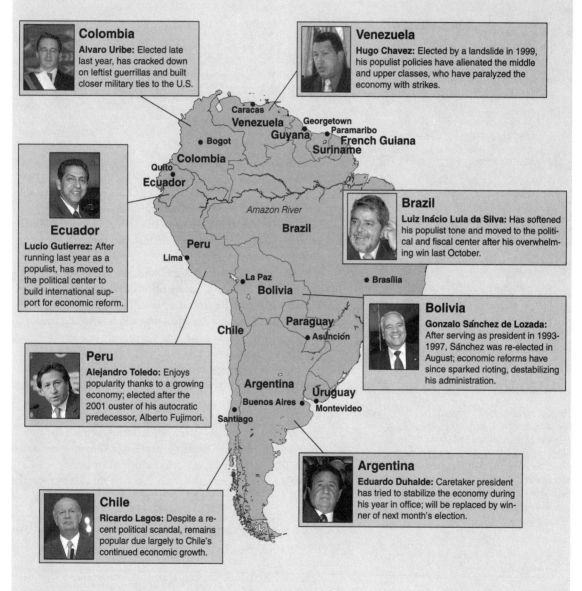

Colombia

Alvaro Uribe: Elected late last year, has cracked down on leftist guerrillas and built closer military ties to the U.S.

Venezuela

Hugo Chavez: Elected by a landslide in 1999, his populist policies have alienated the middle and upper classes, who have paralyzed the economy with strikes.

Ecuador

Lucio Gutierrez: After running last year as a populist, has moved to the political center to build international support for economic reform.

Brazil

Luiz Inácio Lula da Silva: Has softened his populist tone and moved to the political and fiscal center after his overwhelming win last October.

Peru

Alejandro Toledo: Enjoys popularity thanks to a growing economy; elected after the 2001 ouster of his autocratic predecessor, Alberto Fujimori.

Bolivia

Gonzalo Sánchez de Lozada: After serving as president in 1993-1997, Sánchez was re-elected in August; economic reforms have since sparked rioting, destabilizing his administration.

Argentina

Eduardo Duhalde: Caretaker president has tried to stabilize the economy during his year in office; will be replaced by winner of next month's election.

Chile

Ricardo Lagos: Despite a recent political scandal, remains popular due largely to Chile's continued economic growth.

Caracas, Venezuela, Georgetown, Paramaribo, French Guiana, Guyana, Suriname, Bogot, Colombia, Quito, Ecuador, Amazon River, Brazil, Peru, Lima, La Paz, Bolivia, Brasília, Paraguay, Chile, Asunción, Argentina, Buenos Aires, Uruguay, Montevideo, Santiago

Source: Freedom House, 2000, "Freedom in the World, 1999-2000"

Brazil and Argentina Dominate South America's Economy

South America encompasses 13 countries totaling more than 350 million people. Portuguese is spoken in the largest country, Brazil. Most of the rest speak Spanish. About 80 percent of South Americans are Roman Catholic, but in recent years evangelical Protestants have converted millions.

Economic Data, 2002

Country	Population	Gross Domestic Product (GDP)*	Per capita GDP*	Inflation	Main industries
Argentina	37.8 million	$382 billion	$10,202	41.0%	Food processing, motor vehicles, textiles, petrochemicals
Bolivia	8.4 million	$21.4 billion	$2,600	2.5	Mining, tobacco, handicrafts
Brazil	176.0 million	$1.3 trillion	$7,500	12.5	Aircraft, motor vehicles, steel, cement
Colombia	41.0 million	$255 billion	$6,300	7.0	Textiles, food processing, chemicals
Chile	15.5 million	$153 billion	$10,000	2.5	Mining, steel, cement
Ecuador	13.4 million	$48.6 billion	$3,997	12.5	Timber, petroleum, plastics
French Guiana	182,333	$1 billion	$6,000	2.5	Construction, shrimp processing, timber
Guyana	698,209	$2.5 billion	$3,600	6.0	Sugar, textiles, mining
Paraguay	5.9 million	$26.2 billion	$4,600	7.2	Sugar, cement, timber
Peru	27.9 million	$132 billion	$4,800	1.5	Mining, oil, steel, food processing
Suriname	436,491	$1.5 billion	$3,500	5.9	Mining, timber, food processing
Uruguay	3.4 million	$31 billion	$9,200	3.6	Food processing, heavy equipment, chemicals
Venezuela	24.3 million	$146.2 billion	$6,100	31.2	Petroleum, mining, motor vehicles

* All GDP and per capita GDP numbers are calculated in purchasing power parity, or the amount of goods and services purchasable in local currency.

Sources: CIA World Book, 2002; news reports (for inflation)

In Argentina, Bolivia and other countries, economic troubles have discredited political elites and traditional political parties to the point that some South America-watchers fear for the survival of democracy on the continent. Although few believe South America will return to the military dictatorships of the 1970s, some feel that new populist leaders like Chavez may subvert the democratic gains of the 1980s and '90s just to stay in power. [1]

Much of the trouble stems from the troubled world economy, which has been in a slump since the turn of the millennium. The region's gross domestic product (GDP) shrank by more than 1 percent last year, and a similar drop is expected this year, according to Shifter and others.

But some analysts also blame the big multilateral lending institutions, in particular the IMF, for many of the continent's woes. The IMF and the World Bank lend tens of billions each year to South American nations, giving the banks tremendous influence over economic policy.

Critics of the big lenders say they impose "a one-size-fits-all" economic regimen — including tight monetary

Brazil's Rags-to-Riches President

His life story sounds like a rags-to-riches Hollywood movie: Born into abject poverty, Brazil's Luiz Inácio Lula da Silva — known simply as Lula — has risen from shining shoes to the nation's highest office.

The miracle of Lula's incredible success is not lost on his fellow citizens, who love him with a passion usually reserved for religious leaders or rock stars. Even before he was officially declared the winner of the country's presidential election on Oct. 27, the streets of Brazil's largest city, São Paulo, were crowded with pro-Lula revelers.

Lula did not disappoint his supporters, winning more than 60 percent of the vote against his government-supported opponent. Indeed, the landslide marked another chapter in his remarkable life: The triumph came after four previous unsuccessful runs for the presidency.

"This is a historic victory because, finally, it represents the will of the people," said Gabriel Brasileiro, a São Paulo social worker. "People want wealth distributed more fairly, and I'm sure Lula will adopt a more social stance right from the start." [1]

But restoring the country's sagging economy while eliminating its crushing poverty will be no easy task for the 56-year-old former factory worker.

Born the son of impoverished farm workers, he dropped out of school after the fifth grade to help support his family. For the next decade, Lula did factory work, often as a lathe operator.

At 22, Lula joined a union and quickly became a labor activist. He was elected president of a metalworkers' union when he was 30, and by 1980 he had come to national attention after leading several successful strikes. The following year, he formed the Workers Party, bringing together several leftist groups under one banner.

In 1985, Brazil's military dictatorship ended, and Lula ran for president. He lost the first election, as well as the next three, but on each try his share of the vote rose. Still, few believed he would ever get more than 35 or 40 percent of the vote because of his leftist ideology.

Indeed, in his first four campaigns, Lula unabashedly espoused large increases in social spending while criticizing big business, free trade, the International Monetary Fund (IMF) and the United States. He even dressed like the workingman that he was, in casual clothes instead of the business suits most political leaders wear.

For the 2002 election campaign though, Lula changed his stripes — literally. In addition to donning pinstripe suits, candidate Lula moderated his positions, sounding less like the fiery populist of yore and more like the kind of calm, left-of-center democrat one might find in Europe. During the campaign, he reversed his earlier opposition to the proposed Free Trade Area of the Americas and even supported the strict conditions for a new $30 billion IMF loan negotiated by then-President Fernando Henrique Cardoso.

The move won him new support from the country's political center, which had feared the former union leader would lead Brazil to economic ruin. Still, bankers and business leaders were less convinced, leading to a 35 percent drop in the value of the country's currency, the real, and a drop in Brazil's stock market as it became clear Lula would win.

But Lula has surprised the doubters so far. He has stayed within budgetary constraints imposed by the IMF deal and journeyed to Washington even before he was inaugurated to discuss policies, privatization and trade liberalization — that does much more harm than good in countries with fragile economies. They point to Argentina, where they say IMF policies helped cause and exacerbate a fiscal crisis of immense proportions.

But IMF officials say the fund tailors its advice to fit each country's situation. "One-size-fits-all is a big myth," says Tom Dawson, chief spokesman for the IMF. "We're always accused of not caring what [other countries] think, but we look closely at every individual country and try to help them fashion policies to suit their needs." Other experts blame the region's problems on government corruption and inefficiency.

The United States, meanwhile, is hoping to jump-start the region's economies with the proposed Free Trade Area of the Americas (FTAA) treaty — which would encompass all of North and South America plus most of the Caribbean. The U.S. proposal for the FTAA, unveiled in February by U.S. Trade Representative Robert Zoellick, would phase out all tariffs for treaty signatories between 2005 and 2015.

Zoellick and other free-trade advocates contend that eliminating trade barriers will promote long-term growth in South America, as countries gain greater access to the giant U.S. market. But some in the region worry that large American multinational corporations will use free

free trade with President Bush. He also picked an economic team known for its commitment to fiscal responsibility. Consequently, the stock market has fully recovered and the *real* has regained about half its lost ground.

At the same time, the new president has not forgotten his leftist supporters, announcing a new campaign, Zero Hunger, to help Brazil's poorest. The food-assistance proposal would spend nearly $1.5 billion over the next four years to help 46 million of the country's 176 million citizens.

"He's really trying to take the middle road of economic and fiscal stability on one side and poverty reduction on the other," says Michael Shifter, vice president for policy at Inter-American Dialogue, a Washington think tank.

So far, the balancing act seems to be working, Shifter and others say. Certainly everywhere the new president goes, crowds cheer him.

But huge challenges remain. Brazil faces a crippling public debt of more than a half-trillion dollars — about 42 percent of the country's $1.2 trillion gross domestic product (GDP). At 12 percent, inflation is also creeping up too high,

Luiz Inácio Lula da Silva, Brazil's populist president in pinstripes, moderated his leftist positions — and his attire — after his victory.

economists say. In addition, the public pension system is running huge deficits, and the tax system is not taking in enough revenue.

Lula has pledged to reform pensions and taxes, but that may be difficult given that his Workers Party has only 18 percent of the seats in parliament. He also wants Brazil's economy to grow at 5 percent this year, (more than twice last year's increase) — a tall order considering the sputtering global economy.

Still, Brazil's new president has been underestimated his whole life. And supporters and foes alike acknowledge his unique ability to work with different groups.

"All his political life, he's been a good negotiator," says John Welch, chief Latin American economist at the New York branch of WestLB, a German bank. "Maybe he can pull this one off, too."

---

[1] Quoted in Tony Smith, "Music and Victory in the Streets of Brazil," *The New York Times*, Oct. 27, 2002, p. A6.

trade to overwhelm smaller South American businesses and despoil the continent's environment — especially the vast Amazon basin, whose rain forests are being threatened by loggers and agricultural interests.

America's other major regional policy initiative is "Plan Colombia" — a multiyear program to provide military assistance to the Colombian government. Colombia is in the grip of a brutal, decades-long, civil war fueled by drug money, involving both left-wing guerrillas and right-wing paramilitary soldiers. In recent years, U.S. aid has shifted its focus from just the narcotics trade to countering the guerrillas as well.

Human rights activists and others criticize the new

aid, slated to be more than $500 million this year, because the Colombian army is closely linked to the paramilitaries, who — like the guerrillas — have been charged with committing atrocities against civilians. "The concern is that the Colombian military has links to paramilitaries who have committed atrocities, and that those involved at the highest level have not been brought to justice," said Sen. Patrick J. Leahy, D-Vt. "Neither the Colombian military leadership nor the [Colombian] attorney general has shown the will to end the impunity." [2]

Supporters counter that to bring peace to Colombia the army must be strong enough to rein in both sides and restore order.

Some experts are cautiously optimistic that Colombia, along with the continent's other nations, will overcome its problems in the coming decades. Indeed, some optimists say that with its rich resources and new democratic traditions, South America will become a stable and prosperous region over the next 20 years.

"There's no doubt that South America has great untapped potential," says John Williamson, a senior fellow at the Institute for International Economics, a think tank in Washington.

Even in the here and now, the news is not all bad. Brazil's popular, new president is grappling valiantly with the nation's crippling public debt and the social problems that have created its large underclass. And in Chile, democracy and the economy have flourished since military dictator Gen. Augusto Pinochet stepped down nearly 15 years ago.

As South America-watchers look to the future, here are some of the questions they are asking about the continent today:

Are IMF policies partly responsible for South America's current economic woes?

According to a recent World Bank report, South America's GDP will shrink by 1.1 percent this year — its worst performance in 20 years. [3] The decline is driven not only by the limping world economy but also by Argentina's fiscal collapse and economic problems in Brazil, Venezuela and other nations on the continent (see p. 248).

But some economists say the IMF bears some of the responsibility for these problems, much more than other international lenders like the poverty-fighting World Bank and much smaller Inter-American Development Bank. "When you look at South America as a whole, the [fund] really has mishandled things," says Sarah Anderson, director of the Global Economy Project at the Institute for Policy Studies, a Washington think tank. "Especially in a place like Argentina, where they forced an austerity program on them as their economy was collapsing, you see that they've often been a negative force in many places."

During the 1990s, the IMF and other international financial institutions pushed most of South America to adopt the so-called Washington Consensus — a set of policies aimed at liberalizing economies by removing trade barriers, privatizing state-owned industries and opening financial markets to foreign capital.

Left-leaning critics of the IMF like Anderson say the measures exposed South America's fragile economies to often-destructive forces that have usually fallen hardest on the poor and middle class. "Basically, there has been this experiment where they've forced these countries to implement tight fiscal policies and open trade and monetary policies regardless of what was happening on the ground, and it has failed," says Mark Weisbrot, co-director of the Center for Economic Policy Research, a Washington think tank.

"During the 20 years between 1960 and 1980, South America's economy grew 75 percent," he says. "In the next 20 years, between 1980 and 2000, when they were supposedly doing the right thing according to the IMF, their economies grew a total of 6 or 7 percent."

Weisbrot says the IMF pushed a one-size-fits-all policy that didn't take into account individual countries or their economic situations at the time. "So you had countries cutting [government] spending even though they were in a recession," he says. "That's usually disastrous, which is why we in the United States don't do it. But that's what's happening right now in Argentina."

Such criticism is "nonsense," says IMF spokesman Dawson. "The Washington Consensus calls for flexible currency-exchange rates, and yet when Argentina told the fund that they were going to have a fixed rate, we accepted it as the right policy," he says. "So much for one-size-fits-all. Our policies are based on a nuanced, case-by-case analysis."

And, despite economic turmoil in many South American countries, Washington Consensus policies have generally had positive results, Dawson claims. For instance, he says, the IMF, through loans and advice, has helped set Chile on a stable course. "And they've paid off their IMF loans ahead of schedule."

A different example of an IMF success is its push for South American countries to privatize industries. "Of course, there have been setbacks, but in general, the privatized companies lowered prices and offered better service to consumers, and that's good," says Williamson, whose ideas inspired the Washington Consensus.

Defenders of the multilateral lending institutions say South America's troubles are largely homegrown. "They're not doing the things good governments should do to make their economies grow," says Julia E. Sweig, a senior fellow at the Council on Foreign Relations, a New York City think tank. "For instance, they don't have adequate tax systems and often use VAT [value-added taxes]

taxes — which are very regressive — to raise revenue." In addition, South American governments tend to spend beyond their means and waste much of their revenue on inefficiency and corruption, she says.

Indeed, IMF Research Director Kenneth Rogoff argues, countries that have been spending beyond their means often criticize the fund when it forces them to confront the obvious: that government budgets must be more in line with revenues. "Blaming the fund for the reality that every country must confront its budget constraints is like blaming the fund for gravity." [4]

But some conservative critics of the international funding institutions blame the continent's problems on the lenders' unwillingness to use their leverage to force South America's countries to make needed systemic changes.

"The IMF has turned into a savings and loan for these countries by perpetually providing money for them no matter what they do," says Stephen Johnson, a senior fellow at the Heritage Foundation. As a result, he says, "the people who run these countries think they can live off the IMF's largess forever, without ever having to really work out their problems. Until the [IMF] is willing to really hold their feet to the fire and cut them off, you won't see South America undertaking the real reforms that they need."

Ian Vasquez, director of the Project for Global Economic Liberty at the libertarian Cato Institute, agrees. The IMF "basically made a bad situation worse by encouraging borrowing and undisciplined spending," he says, pointing to its recent loan to tottering Argentina.

"They stopped lending to Argentina for a year, and I thought maybe they'd turned a corner," he says. "But they blew it when they gave [Argentina] another loan just a year later in spite of the fact that the Argentines hadn't really done anything to warrant more money."

Is South America in danger of retreating from the democratic gains made since the early 1980s?

South America's successful shift to democratic rule over the past two decades has been widely celebrated. Beginning in the early 1980s, several of the continent's largest and most important countries — among them Argentina, Brazil and Chile — replaced military rulers with democratically elected leaders and legislatures.

But in the last two years, severe political turmoil in several Latin democracies has thrown those democratic gains into question. In Argentina, five presidents came and went in a tumultuous two-week period at the end of 2001. The leaders of Peru and Ecuador have been forced from office, and in Venezuela, President Chavez's heavy-handed tactics have prompted his political opponents to respond in kind.

Meanwhile, public support for democracy in South America is faltering. In Brazil, Colombia, Paraguay and Chile, fewer than half the respondents to a 2002 poll favored democracy over other forms of government. [5]

Some observers say South American democracies have been hurt by their new, largely leftist leaders, who they say used the ballot box to seize power and then showed little respect for democratic institutions once in office. "There is no doubt South American democracy is in crisis," says Angel Rabasa, a senior policy analyst at the Rand Corporation, a think tank in Palo Alto, Calif. "You have a trend away from real democratic institutions and toward leftist, authoritarian leaders."

Chavez is widely seen as this group's chief offender. Shortly after his election, he convened a constituent assembly that replaced the elected Congress and reshuffled the Supreme Court. Indeed, says Constantine Menges, a senior fellow at the conservative Hudson Institute, "Chavez has gone further than that, creating paramilitary groups to intimidate and even shoot his opponents." Recently, Chavez arrested political opponents who organized a crippling, nationwide strike late last year.

But Chavez' critics have used undemocratic means to push their agenda as well. Last April, business leaders and some military units briefly deposed Chavez in a coup, only to see him returned to power days later by other elements in the armed forces.

Elsewhere, the situation is little better, according to Menges and Rabasa. They point to Argentina, where a revolving-door presidency has damaged the office to the point that the winner of the May presidential election probably will be severely weakened, possibly creating a power vacuum. In Ecuador, they note, the president is a populist former army officer who was elected after a coup he helped engineer. The governments of Bolivia and Peru also are shaky, with the presidents of both countries in danger of being deposed.

Pundits link the instability to recent economic troubles. "The failure of market-oriented reforms in places like Ecuador and Argentina has led to the [negative] reaction against the governing institutions that are responsible," Rabasa says. "They turn to populists like Chavez."

But others point out that most South American countries, even those in economic trouble, still enjoy robust democratic systems. "In most places they're not getting the guns out, the military is staying in its barracks and they're resolving their differences peacefully with elections," says the Council on Foreign Relations' Sweig.

"With the exception of Chavez in Venezuela, I don't think they're backtracking," agrees Peter Hakim, president of Inter-American Dialogue. "Although many people have lost confidence in their institutions and their leaders, democracy is still the rule."

Hakim disagrees with the notion that the continent is turning toward leftist, populist, authoritarian leaders like Chavez. In Brazil, he points out, newly elected President Luiz Inácio Lula da Silva, widely known as Lula, has forsaken his populist roots to become a pragmatic centrist. (*See sidebar, p. 234.*) "The real story in Brazil isn't of a leftwing firebrand, but of a person who has become much more moderate in power," Hakim says. "Since he was elected, he hasn't tried to tear down his predecessor's more conservative policies, but has accepted them and even built on them."

For instance, Lula has adopted the previous administration's policy of creating government surpluses each year to pay down Brazil's large foreign debt, Hakim points out. "This is very hard for him because it constrains his ability to spend money and to enact new programs," he says. "But he's done it, and he's even proposed running higher surpluses in order to pay down more debt."

In Ecuador, another recently elected populist, Lucio Gutierrez, also has moved toward the political and economic center, winning plaudits from the IMF and the Bush administration for his fiscal belt-tightening and other reforms.

Moreover, optimists say, most South Americans want to have nothing to do with the kind of populism that has wracked Venezuela. "Chavez scares a lot of people, and they want to avoid becoming anything like what Venezuela has become," says Johnson of the Heritage Foundation. "For example, what's happened in Venezuela has had an effect on Peru, where President Alejandro Toledo may not be popular, but he's muddling through in part because people value stability and don't want to sink into chaos."

Should the United States continue aiding Colombia's fight against leftist guerrillas?

Colombia is South America's most violent country — under siege by leftist guerrillas, rightist paramilitary groups and narco-traffickers. In the last decade, 30,000 Colombians — mostly civilians — were killed. Last year alone, 3,000 people were kidnapped. [6]

Newly elected President Alvaro Uribe Velez is trying to contain the violence with a get-tough policy, targeted especially against the country's 18,000-member left-wing guerrilla group, the Revolutionary Armed Forces of Colombia (FARC). [7] Established in 1964 as the military wing of the Colombian Communist Party, FARC has since largely shed its political agenda to focus more on organized criminal activities like kidnapping and drug-trafficking.

Uribe virtually reversed the policies of his predecessor, Andres Pastrana, who devoted most of his tenure to unsuccessfully trying to negotiate a peace agreement with FARC, even ceding control to the guerrillas of a "safe haven" the size of Switzerland in southeastern Colombia.

Uribe's about-face won strong support from the Bush administration, which casts the country's troubles as a part of the broader war on terrorism. "After Sept. 11, the Bush administration changed its whole focus worldwide to fighting terrorism, so it makes sense that they would see the [Colombian] government's battle against the FARC as a struggle against terrorism," says Rand's Rabasa.

But the United States was helping Colombia even before 9/11. Since 1997, the United States has given Colombia $2 billion — including $411 million last year — to beef up its anti-narcotics and law-enforcement capabilities. [8] But the Sept. 11 terrorist attacks on New York and the Pentagon prompted the U.S. to up the ante.

When Secretary of State Colin L. Powell visited Bogotá on Dec. 4, he announced the administration would seek $537 billion from Congress for Colombia this year, including $98 million for counterinsurgency training. The administration also has sent 60 Special Forces soldiers and intelligence operatives to help train the country's army. [9]

The aid is largely to help the Colombian army protect an oil pipeline from the frequent disruptions by guerrilla attacks. Still, the new emphasis on helping Colombia fight guerrillas is a break from the past, when military aid solely targeted anti-drug efforts.

Some experts applaud the administration's help fighting FARC and other groups, saying that without U.S. aid, Colombia could implode, becoming a state without a real governing authority. Then they warn, the chaos could spread to less stable neighbors, like Venezuela, throwing the region into further turmoil.

"Colombia might very well collapse unless we strengthen the army enough to fight the leftist guerrillas and the right-wing paramilitaries," says the Council on Foreign Relations' Sweig. "Already they don't control half the country, so something needs to be done to restore government control."

"The problem is getting worse and will continue to get worse if something isn't done," agrees Heritage's Johnson. "Any army's job in [such] a situation is to guarantee public safety and the rule of law. The only way they're going to do that in Colombia is to push the FARC back."

And repelling the FARC is the only real option, aid supporters say. "Pastrana's efforts to talk to the FARC ended in failure, because the FARC really weren't interested in making peace," Rabasa says. "The government has exhausted all possibilities and now they have to fight them."

Colombia has only about 40,000 combat soldiers, compared with more than 20,000 leftist, mostly FARC guerrillas and about half that many paramilitaries. The military largely controls the urban areas and some well-populated parts of the countryside. But large swaths are without either a military or civil presence.

Rabasa and others say the U.S. should be doing more, given the army's small size and the task ahead. "Basically we are training and equipping a battalion to guard the oil pipeline," he says. "While that helps, the army is going to need more resources and training from the Americans if it is going to retake control of the country."

But others say beefing up the Colombian military is counterproductive, because they see the war as unwinnable. "Everyone knows that you're not going to end this thing militarily," says Sanho Tree, a fellow at the Institute for Policy Studies.

Effective counterinsurgency usually requires 10 times as many troops as the rebels, he says. "Colombia is the size of Texas and California combined and has about 40,000 soldiers to deal with almost as many insurgents," he says. "The New York City police have almost as many people to deal with in an area a fraction of that size."

Opponents of aid also argue that America's Colombia policy eerily parallels the early years of U.S. involvement in Vietnam. "This has quagmire written all over it," Tree says. "And just as they were saying about Vietnam in the early 1960s, some American hard-liners say we need to help the Colombian military achieve a few big victories to strengthen its position at the bargaining table. That's how we got deeper into Vietnam, and look what happened."

More important, say critics of U.S. aid, the Colombian army has a record of human rights abuses and deep ties to right-wing paramilitary vigilante groups formed in the early 1980s to fight FARC and other guerrillas. "The Colombian military created the paramilitaries and has maintained strong ties to them, even after the government declared them illegal in 1989," says Robin Kirk, a senior researcher with Human Rights Watch and author of the best-selling 2003 book *More Terrible Than Death: Massacres, Drugs, and America's War in Colombia.*

The military "subcontracted out its dirty war against the leftists to the paramilitaries," says Kirk. Indeed, paramilitary groups devote most of their energy and resources to killing civilians suspected of sympathizing with the FARC, she says, rather than the guerrillas themselves.

"The paramilitaries are believed responsible for 70 percent of the human rights abuses in the country," Tree adds. "These are not good guys."

But supporters of aid say U.S. assistance will help the army disassociate itself from the paramilitaries and improve human rights in Colombia. "The army has supported and worked with the paramilitaries [because] they haven't had the resources to combat the guerrillas on their own," Johnson says. "By strengthening the army, you will make them less dependent on the paramilitaries."

In addition, aid proponents say, the U.S. can use military aid to assure that the Colombian military cleans up its human rights record. "When we've pulled aid — as in Guatemala in the 1970s — things went haywire, and the military committed horrendous abuses," Sweig says. "But when we've used aid to slowly change an army — as we did in El Salvador in the 1980s — things got better."

But Kirk disagrees. "Aid and training never solved a human rights problem," she says. "In El Salvador, soldiers who received full training by the United States went on to commit massacres and atrocities."

CHRONOLOGY

16th-18th Centuries *European explorers conquer South America.*

1498 Italian explorer Christopher Columbus, sailing under a Spanish flag, lands in Venezuela, becoming the first known European to see South America.

1500 Portuguese explorer Pedro Alvares Cabral discovers Brazil.

1510 The first African slaves arrive.

1530 Spaniard Francisco Pizarro begins the conquest of the Inca.

1776 The American Revolution inspires South Americans to consider their own independence.

19th Century *South American states become independent.*

1811 Venezuela declares independence, but Spain reasserts its authority in 1815.

1816 Simón Bolívar helps Venezuela resist Spain. . . . Argentina declares independence.

1819 Bolívar liberates Colombia.

1821 Bolívar frees Venezuela and Ecuador.

1822 Brazil becomes a separate state with a Portuguese king.

1823 The U.S. adopts the Monroe Doctrine to keep Europe out of hemispheric affairs.

1888 Brazil abolishes slavery.

1900-1980 *Dictators rule over economic growth and urbanization.*

1914 World War I halts immigration into South America.

1946 Juan and Eva Perón assume power in Argentina.

1948 The U.S. helps establish the Organization of American States (OAS).

1964 A Brazilian coup ousts the elected president.

1973 Gen. Augusto Pinochet overthrows Salvador Allende, Chile's elected president.

1980-Present *Democracy and free markets proliferate.*

1985 Brazil returns to civilian rule.

1989 Pinochet loses a referendum and civilian rule in Chile is restored. . . . Carlos Menem wins Argentina's presidency and institutes free-market reforms.

1994 Fernando Cardoso becomes Brazil's president and institutes free-market reforms.

1998 Populist Hugo Chavez is elected president of Venezuela.

2001 Eduardo Duhalde becomes president of Argentina after the country's slide into recession. . . . Businessmen mount a coup against Chavez on April 12. He returns to power in two days.

May 2002 Alvaro Uribe becomes president of Colombia, promising to crack down on guerrillas.

October 2002 Luiz Inácio Lula da Silva becomes president of Brazil on his fifth try.

December 2002 Businesses and the national oil company begin a two-month strike in Venezuela demanding Chavez's resignation.

January 2003 Venezuela's strike ends; Chavez arrests some strike leaders and forces the state oil company to resume operations.

February 2003 Protests in La Paz, Bolivia, over tax hikes and spending cuts almost bring down the government.

April 2003 Presidential elections are scheduled in Argentina to replace Duhalde.

BACKGROUND

Discovery and Conquest

Christopher Columbus discovered what is now Venezuela during his third voyage to the New World in 1498. He was soon followed by fellow Italian, Amerigo Vespucci (after whom the Americas were named) and Pedro Alvares Cabral, a Portuguese sailor who discovered Brazil in 1500.

The Europeans who followed these first explorers into South America found an array of cultures and societies. The largest and most technically sophisticated of these indigenous groups were the rapacious Inca, who had used their formidable military and organizational skills to forge a vast empire of 12 million people encompassing much of the Andes Mountains and the Pacific coast.

By contrast, there were the peaceful Guarani, who raised crops in the jungles of central South America. Other areas supported groups ranging from stone-age hunter-gatherers to large-scale agricultural and fishing communities.

The conquest of South America began in earnest in 1530, when Spaniard Francisco Pizarro led a small band of well-armed troops against the Inca. Cunning, skill and vastly superior weaponry helped Pizarro and later conquistadors bring down the huge empire. [10] Old World diseases, like smallpox, also played a role, wiping out millions of potential Inca adversaries. The future Peru, Ecuador, Bolivia and Venezuela soon lay in Spanish hands.

Meanwhile, the Portuguese were consolidating their hold over Brazil. Incursions into the colony by French, English and Spanish adventurers prompted the king of Portugal to grant huge tracts of the territory to rich patrons who promised to colonize and protect the area for Portugal in exchange for the right to exploit the land and its people.

Spanish rule was more centralized. A Council of the Indies — located in Spain and comprised of the king, aristocrats and lawyers — made general policy, which was then carried out by an appointed viceroy, who ruled over the continent from Lima, Peru, through a hierarchy of colonial administrators. [11]

By 1600, the economy of colonial South America flourished on gold and silver mining and large plantations that produced cotton, tobacco and sugar for export.

But while Spanish and Portuguese rule made fortunes for many Europeans, it brought misery to the continent's native peoples. Millions succumbed to diseases that had been common in Europe for centuries but were unknown in the Americas, and hence devastating. [12] Millions more were ultimately drafted for forced labor in mines, plantations and other ventures.

Viewing the Indians as potential converts, the Catholic Church urged the Spanish crown to prohibit the mistreatment of indigenous people. Its missionaries fought for their basic human rights, but European settlers resisted the reform efforts.

But the forced-labor system eventually collapsed as more and more Indians died from disease, overwork and the abuses meted out by their Spanish and Portuguese overlords. Many of the Indians who survived became sharecroppers on large European-owned plantations known as haciendas. In turn, millions of African slaves were brought in to do work originally performed by the Indians.

During the 18th century, Spanish kings tried several times to reform the administration of their New World colonies. In an effort to decentralize authority, South America was broken into three territories — the Viceroyalties of New Granada (now Venezuela) in the north, Peru along the Pacific coast and Rio de la Plata (Argentina) in the south. Many trade barriers also were lifted, which helped stimulate the continent's economy.

Push for Independence

In the late 18th century, increased prosperity expanded South America's middle and upper classes — the descendants of the early European settlers and mixed-race mestizos. But prosperity did not trickle down to the continent's Indian or black populations, intensifying the region's social stratification. As the wealth of the new elites grew, so did their wish to run their own affairs. Desire for greater autonomy was further strengthened by revolutions in the 1770s and '80s in the United States and France and by the revolutionary theories of the Age of Enlightenment, which held the sovereignty of the individual as a primary tenet.

But the independence movement simmered for decades before being brought to a boil in the early 1800s, during the Napoleonic wars that engulfed Europe. In 1796, Spain joined France in a war against England. The alliance cut the Spanish off from their New World colonies because the English navy was powerful enough

Venezuela's Leader Hangs onto Power

Venezuela's feisty President Hugo Chavez prefers to stand and fight — even in situations where others might have retreated or resigned.

Within the last year and a half, he has weathered a coup attempt that forced him from office for two days and outlasted a two-month nationwide strike that shut down the entire country. "Chavez actually thrives in situations like this," says Stephen Levitsky, a professor of government at Harvard University. "He's at his best when he's fighting an enemy."

If that is true, President Chavez has had many opportunities lately to be "at his best." Roughly two-thirds of Venezuelans — from almost all sectors of society, including organized labor, business and parts of the military — oppose his leadership. But while his political obituary has been written more than once, Chavez has always managed to confound conventional wisdom and bounce back.

The recent strike, for instance, was initially seen as a huge victory for his opponents. Businesses everywhere were shuttered — at an estimated economic cost of $50 million a day. [1] Many workers at the state-owned oil company — which provides half the government's revenues, 80 percent of the country's exports and is America's fourth-largest foreign supplier of oil — went on strike, completely shutting down the entire industry. [2]

The strikers, led by a coalition of business and labor leaders, demanded that Chavez step down or at least submit his four-year-old rule to a free and fair referendum. The president didn't budge. Instead, he waited until the strikers were so financially strapped they had to reopen their businesses. As for the all-important state oil company, Petroleos Venezuela, Chavez fired 16,000 striking workers — about 40 percent of its workforce — and set the rest to work restarting production.

Chavez may have won his latest political battles, but the victories may turn out to be pyrrhic. Inflation has reached more than 30 percent, and unemployment is expected to reach the same level by June. The economy shrank by 9 percent last year and is expected to decline 20 percent this year. Latin America has never seen such a dramatic economic contraction, said Organization of American States (OAS) Secretary-General Cesar Gavira — "not even during a civil war." [3]

Moreover, Petroleos is unlikely to return to its pre-strike production level of 3.1 million barrels of oil a day, because the loss of hundreds of experienced workers has hobbled the firm, analysts say. "It will not be the company it once was," said Mazhar al-Shereidah, an oil economist in Caracas, Venezuela's capital. [4]

Petroleos is not the only company in danger of foundering. More than 5,000 private firms have gone bankrupt since Chavez was elected four years ago, and hundreds of others are about to follow suit. "The feeling we have," one business leader told *Newsweek*, "is that this man wants to do away with the private sector altogether." [5]

But Guillermo Garcia Ponce, the Stalinist coordinator of the Political Command of the Revolution — an advisory committee chaired by Chavez — says that rather than wanting to shut down private business, Chavez wants to improve capitalism, so it's "not subject to globalization or U.S. interests." [6]

Venezuela's democracy also has suffered a series of blows since Chavez came to office in 1999. Most notably, in 2000, he pushed through the election of a new Assembly that dismissed and replaced the existing Congress and reshuffled the Supreme Court. The president also expanded the powers of his own office, granting himself the right to rule by decree in matters affecting the economy and crime.

More recently, Chavez arrested some of the strike leaders and promised to put them on trial. Many fear that he will also curb press freedoms.

Venezuela was not always in such a chaotic state. In the 1970s, as one of Latin America's oldest democracies and richest economies, Venezuela was hailed as a model for the rest of the continent. With plentiful supplies of oil, a solid middle class and a strong multiparty democracy, many believed Venezuela would be the first to join the ranks of the developed world.

But plummeting oil prices in the 1980s and '90s sent the petroleum-dependent economy into a tailspin. Falling standards of living eventually led to riots and, in 1992, two coups, one led by then-Col. Chavez.

In 1999, Chavez swept into power as a fiery populist promising a revolution on behalf of the lower and working classes and against the country's wealthy elite. But the new

---

[1] Ginger Thompson, "Strike's Efforts Tear at Social Fabric," *The New York Times*, Jan. 16, 2003.

[2] Juan Forero, "Venezuela's Lifeblood Ebbs Even as it Flows," *The New York Times*, Feb. 26, 2003, p. C1.

[3] Quoted in Phil Gunson, "Out for Revenge?" *Newsweek*, Feb. 24, 2003.

[4] Forero, *op. cit.*

[5] Gunson, *op. cit.*

[6] *Ibid.*

president's heavy-handed tactics failed to jump-start the economy, and by 2001 the former paratrooper was deeply unpopular, except among the very poor.

But if Chavez made mistakes, so did his opponents. In April of 2002, members of the business community joined elements in the military to depose the president. Within 48 hours, Chavez had rallied much of the army to his side and was back in power.

The United States, which traditionally condemns military takeovers of democratically elected governments, appeared to acquiesce to Chavez's overthrow, earning widespread international criticism. In fact, Chavez later alleged that the United States was behind the coup, a charge vehemently denied by U.S. officials. [7]

Meanwhile, the administration continues to support the strikers' demand for early elections, and, with Chavez returned to power, relations between the two countries have been strained.

The two sides have never seen eye-to-eye. Chavez's consistently anti-American rhetoric — such as calling the U.S. assault on Afghanistan as great a crime as the Sept. 11 terrorist attacks in New York and the Pentagon — has irked the United States. Chavez also raised American ire by pushing for the Organization of Petroleum Exporting Countries to limit production and raise world oil prices.

Critics of Chavez say that he will only get more authoritarian as Venezuela's economy continues to decline and he becomes even more unpopular. They point out that he is a close friend and admirer of communist Cuban dictator Fidel Castro (who has advised the Venezuelan president) and allegedly supports leftist guerrillas in neighboring Colombia.

"The defeat of the opposition in the strike is allowing him to consolidate a leftist dictatorship and that will con-

President Hugo Chavez, a former paratrooper, survived a two-day coup and outlasted a recent strike that brought Venezuela to a standstill.

AFP Photo/Juan Barreto

tinue," says Angel Rabasa, a senior policy analyst at the Rand Corporation, a Palo Alto, Calif., think tank.

But others argue that the opposition is trying, by hook or by crook, to oust a democratically elected president because he is fighting for the poor and not tending to the interests of the country's elites. "His radical rhetoric favoring the poor over the privileged has alienated the middle class," wrote Steve Ellner, co-editor of the 2003 book *Venezuelan Politics in the Chavez Era: Class, Polarization and Conflict.* [8]

The OAS — along with regional heavyweights like the U.S., Mexico and Brazil — is trying to fashion a negotiated settlement to the country's crisis, possibly an agreement to hold a referendum on the president's rule at the midpoint of his term (August of this year) as is allowed under the country's constitution.

Chavez has largely dismissed the efforts of the OAS as the "meddling" of outsiders. [9] Moreover, while he has said he would submit to a vote in August, many Venezuelans don't believe him.

"They are convinced that in August, when the constitution contemplates a referendum on the president, the government will resort to delaying tactics and dirty tricks," said Moses Naim, former Venezuelan minister for trade and industry and editor of *Foreign Policy* magazine. [10]

Levitsky, at Harvard, agrees that Chavez is unlikely to submit himself to a vote for the simple reason that he would almost certainly lose. "He's deeply unpopular right now, so I just can't see him winning a vote that was fair," he says. "Instead, I think he's going to keep trying to tough it out."

[7] Scott Wilson, "Chavez Raises Idea of U.S. Role in Coup; Interview Suggests Rocky Road Ahead," *The Washington Post*, May 5, 2002, p. A20.

[8] Steve Ellner, "Venezuela on the Brink," *The Nation*, Jan. 13, 2003, p. 5.

[9] Quoted in David Buchbinder, "Slowly, Chavez Isolates Himself from the World," *The Christian Science Monitor*, March 5, 2003, p. 7.

[10] Quoted in Moises Naim, "Hugo Chavez and the Limits of Democracy," *The New York Times*, March 5, 2003, p. A23.

to virtually halt Spanish shipping to and from the Americas.

In 1806, the British invaded Argentina and captured Buenos Aires. The Argentines soon organized an armed resistance and drove the foreigners from the city.

But what had seemed a victory for Spain was short-lived. By taking matters into their own hands, the Argentines gained new confidence that they could run their own affairs. Meanwhile, Spain was slowly being absorbed into Napoleon's empire. In 1807, the French leader replaced the Spanish king with his brother and invaded Portugal. The move provoked an uprising by the Spanish, leading to five years of brutal war.

With Spain in turmoil, Venezuelan elites — led by revolutionary leader Francisco de Miranda — took the opportunity to declare independence, creating a constitutional republic in 1811. [13] But bickering within the revolutionary camp (which included a young army officer named Simón Bolívar) and Spanish attempts to reassert authority after Napoleon's defeat in 1812, led to the downfall of the new Venezuelan republic by 1815.

While many revolutionary leaders (including Miranda) were captured, Bolívar escaped to Jamaica, where he began organizing resistance to Spain. In 1816, he returned to a remote part of Venezuela, where revolutionary support was still strong, and organized an army.

In the following years, Bolívar (with British assistance) handed the Spaniards a series of stunning defeats, conquering Colombia in 1819, Venezuela and Ecuador in 1821. [14]

Other parts of the continent were cutting their European bonds at the same time. In Argentina, those who had resisted the British in 1806 slowly pulled away from Spain, first appointing a Congress to rule in the king's name in 1810 and finally declaring independence in 1816. An Argentine army under the leadership of José de San Martin marched north and west, liberating Chile and Uruguay. San Martin also tried to liberate Peru, but it was Bolívar and his lieutenant, José Antonio de Sucre, who ultimately freed the area from Spanish rule in 1823.

Brazil was liberated with much less fighting, in part because the revolution was led by the heir to Portugal's throne, Dom Pedro, who had originally come to South America to escape Napoleon's invasion of his country. In 1822, Dom Pedro resisted calls from Portugal for his return and declared Brazil independent and himself king. [15]

New Troubles

Political chaos and continuing social imbalances characterized the post-independence period. Contrary to the high expectations that followed independence, there was little change in the ills of colonial South America — such as slavery and poverty among Indians and the working class — after Spanish and Portuguese rule had ended. The powerful landowners and urban elites who ran the newly independent states used their new power to advance their own positions, ignoring the great majority of the citizenry.

The cornerstones of good government — such as the rule of law and orderly transfer of political power — were absent in most of the new states. Warlords (called *caudillos*) and violent bands were common in many areas. Established landowners — able to acquire more property through government connections — grew richer while the peasants were forced to pay ever-higher taxes.

By the middle of the 19th century, South American political thinkers were desperate to reverse the continent's downward trajectory. Looking to the United States and Great Britain for inspiration, they noticed the relationship between both countries' political and economic systems and began to see economic advancement as the way to greater political stability and freedom.

The new focus on economic development in the 1850s and '60s came at a propitious time: Foreign investors from Europe and the United States had begun to enter the South American market, attracted by the continent's abundant natural resources and agricultural potential. Over the next 60 years, huge tracts of land were cleared for grains, sugar and later coffee, and cattle ranching became a huge industry, especially in Argentina. Foreign investors also helped develop the continent's mineral wealth.

In some countries, strong new leaders emerged. In Brazil and Argentina, governments established stability and order. Roads, bridges and railroads were built — often by foreigners — further facilitating commerce.

The economic boom also attracted immigrants mostly from Europe. By the end of the century, hundreds of thousands were arriving each year, many from Italy and Spain as well as northern Europe. Argentina, for instance, received 1.2 million Italian and 1 million Spanish immigrants before 1914. After World War I, immigrants began arriving from Asia. More than 200,000 Japanese came to Brazil between 1920 and 1940.

New wealth and the new immigrants brought a push to modernize society. Slavery was finally eliminated — Brazil was the last nation to act, freeing its slaves in 1888. [16] New universities sprang up, and more and more children entered primary school. Brazil, Chile, Argentina and other countries cast off dictators and kings to become republics.

By the early 20th century, South America had become a major exporter of raw materials and agricultural commodities — minerals from Chile and Bolivia, grain and beef from Argentina and coffee from Brazil. About the same time, heavy industry was developing, particularly in the southern half of the continent, triggering a population shift to urban areas. Brazil's São Paolo, for instance, grew from a large town of 65,000 in 1890 to a metropolis of 350,000 by 1910.

Urbanization brought a newfound sense of entitlement on several levels. Workers unionized and began demanding not only better pay but also pensions and other benefits from the government. By the 1930s, many countries had created large social-welfare schemes and nationalized major sectors of their economies to protect industrial workers.

Relations With U.S.

On a broader level, countries began to seek more independence from the United States, whose enormous economic and military power had made it influential throughout the continent. The Monroe Doctrine of 1823 initially had helped establish U.S. supremacy in the Western Hemisphere, discouraging further incursions by European powers. Moreover, American intervention in Mexico, Central America and the Caribbean in the opening decades of the 20th century made South Americans even more distrustful of U.S. intentions. [17]

Relations improved during the 1930s, with President Franklin D. Roosevelt's Good Neighbor Policy, which pledged the U.S. would not interfere in the continent's affairs. World War II helped cement better ties, as the United States turned to South America to help supply its war effort, bringing new prosperity to the region. In 1948, the United States helped found the Organization of American States (OAS) to promote development and democracy throughout Latin America and the Caribbean.

Despite widespread progress, some countries could not make the transition to stable democratic rule. Strongman Getulio Vargas led Brazil in the 1930s and '40s. In 1946, Juan Perón and his charismatic wife Evita came to power in neighboring Argentina, promising to

solve the nation's social ills by nationalizing industry and spending lavishly on social programs.

Vargas and Perón eventually were deposed and both countries returned to more democratic systems. But by the 1960s and early '70s, Brazil, Argentina, Chile, Uruguay and Peru had succumbed to authoritarian and often brutal military dictatorships. Despite its stated preference for democracy, the United States often supported dictators as bulwarks against the spread of communism on the continent.

In addition to being repressive, most of the strongmen — with the exception of Chile's Augusto Pinochet — proved to be poor stewards of the economy. Economic mismanagement and corruption led to runaway inflation, particularly in Brazil and Argentina, and a high level of foreign debt.

By the early 1980s, many of the military regimes had become highly unpopular. Argentina's junta — which "disappeared" thousands of leftist opponents — gave up power in 1983. The military had been discredited over its mishandling of the economy and its humiliating loss in the Falkland Islands war, in which Argentina invaded a British possession off its coast, only to be expelled by the Royal Navy and Marines. Brazil's military handed back power to civilians in 1985. Chileans, tired of Pinochet's dictatorial rule, voted the general from power in 1989.

During the 1990s, democracy and free markets thrived in South America. In Argentina, popular President Carlos Menem tamed hyperinflation and brought the country almost a decade of sustained economic growth. Fernando Cardoso worked similar economic magic in Brazil, first as finance minister and then as president. In Peru, President Alberto Fujimori destroyed a crippling Maoist rebellion by the Shining Path guerrillas and set the economy on a more stable footing.

However, the decade ended on a sour note. Menem left office accused of corruption, while Argentina's economy slid into a deep recession. A corruption scandal also drove out the increasingly authoritarian Fujimori.

CURRENT SITUATION

Free-Trade Proposal

Since the Sept. 11 terrorist attacks in the United States and the ongoing confrontation with Iraq, South American diplomats and political leaders have complained about

U.S. neglect of the region. But the United States hasn't been entirely distracted.

In addition to sending U.S. aid to Colombia, the United States has been leading the negotiations to create a free-trade zone linking North and South America and the Caribbean — 34 countries stretching from the Antarctic to Canada. The Free Trade Area of the Americas (FTAA) was first proposed in 1994, but the idea has received little attention until recently.

On Feb. 11, the United States presented its opening negotiating stance, offering to eliminate tariffs on 65 percent of imports from other FTAA countries as soon as the treaty took effect in 2005. American textile tariffs, long regarded as unfair by South American competitors, would be phased out over the next five years. By 2015, all treaty signatories would eliminate all tariffs. [18]

"The U.S. has created a detailed road map for free trade in the Western Hemisphere," said U.S. Trade Representative Zoellick. "We've put all our tariffs on the table, and we now hope our trading partners will do the same." [19]

Many trade analysts applaud Zoellick for moving the process forward, but they caution that negotiations could take a long time. "I think it's overly optimistic to set a 2005 deadline for completing the treaty," says the Cato Institute's Vasquez. "There are a lot of sensitive issues and things that will be hard for each country to give up."

Indeed, many signs do not auger well for the treaty's early completion. The U.S. has tarnished its free-trade credentials in the past year, reinstating farm subsides and imposing steel tariffs on many countries, including big steel makers in Brazil, in an effort to protect its own ailing industry.

For its part, South America has a mixed-to-poor record on free trade, with many countries employing high tariffs to protect uncompetitive industries. The major free-trade zone on the continent — Mercusor, encompassing Brazil, Argentina, Uruguay and Paraguay — has fallen on hard times.

The problems began in 1999, when Brazil decided to allow its currency to decline in value, making its exports much cheaper. The move devastated trade with the other big Mercusor member, Argentina, because its currency was pegged to the dollar, keeping it artificially high, and hence its exports very expensive. The zone was also rocked by last year's economic crisis in Argentina, which shuttered much of the country's industry and left its consumers with little money to spend on imports.

On the other hand, the news for free-traders is not all bad. In December, the United States sealed a free-trade deal with Chile, probably South America's most market-oriented economy. South Americans can also look to their Latin cousin to the north, Mexico, where relatively open trade with the U.S. and Canada — spurred by the North American Free Trade Agreement (NAFTA) — has generally been judged a success, leading to increased foreign investment and sustained economic growth for that country. [20]

Finally, Brazil's Lula, formerly a vocal opponent of the FTAA, has shifted his position since taking office late last year. "In order to grow, Brazil needs to increase the amount of its foreign trade," he told an audience at the National Press Club in Washington on Dec. 10. "And the FTAA, in our view, can represent a genuine opening up of the U.S. and Canadian markets."

Lula's newfound willingness to negotiate a free-trade agreement is a big step forward for supporters of FTAA, given that Brazil is South America's largest economy.

Few dispute that better access to the North American market would offer South Americans tremendous opportunities. But opponents of the trade zone worry that it also could devastate already fragile South American economies.

Local farmers and businesses could be hurt — and possibly bankrupted — by a flood of cheaper imports from the more competitive north. Millions of people could lose their jobs, their businesses or their farms, if U.S. multinationals move in with cheaper, better products. "We cannot compete with them," said Ermel Chavez, an activist in Ecuador. "We'll become nothing more than consumers." [21]

The Institute for Policy Studies' Anderson agrees: "Many people down there see free trade as a way for the big American companies to expand their access to and investment in their market in order to make greater profits without improving the standard of living of local people."

Indigenous groups and environmentalists also oppose the pact because they fear it could spur the kind of development (such as mining and logging) that would damage the continent's environment. Concern is especially great over the Amazon basin.

"I was just in Ecuador, where there is a strong, indigenous movement and a strong sense these wild places need to be protected as a resource for these indigenous people who make their living off the land," Anderson says. "The people I talked to think [the FTAA] will simply be an

Should the United States continue aiding Colombia's counterinsurgency efforts?

YES Stephen Johnson
Senior Policy Analyst for Latin America, The Heritage Foundation

Written for The CQ Researcher, March 10, 2003

Just as Colombia is making progress in its fight against violence, terror and drug trafficking, it would be a mistake to withdraw assistance for its counterterrorism efforts.

Despite having one of South America's longest-running continuous democracies, Colombia has had weak governments and a minimal state presence outside urban areas. Civil conflicts triggered a rural communist insurgency in the 1960s. Meanwhile, marijuana, heroin and cocaine production flourished in the uncontrolled countryside. By the mid-1990s, U.S. counternarcotics aid had helped Colombia defeat its major drug cartels. But when allegations surfaced that President Ernesto Samper had received campaign contributions from one of the kingpins, the United States halted assistance. In the ensuing disarray, Colombian rebels joined with remaining drug producers and took over where the cartels left off.

With the election of President Andrés Pastrana, aid was restored under a bilateral agenda called Plan Colombia. But Pastrana spent most of his term trying to achieve a cease-fire by allowing the largest rebel group, the Revolutionary Armed Forces of Colombia (FARC), to occupy a huge safe-haven in the middle of Colombia. FARC grew from 10,000 to 18,000 troops and began collecting between $50 million and $100 million a month from drug trafficking, extortion and kidnapping. Today, guerrillas — and the paramilitary forces that have risen up to fight them — cause up to 3,500 brutal deaths a year and hundreds of millions of dollars in infrastructure damage, not to mention the public costs of pursuing them.

Last year, newly elected President Alvaro Uribe embarked on an ambitious program to retake the countryside, curb drug trafficking, strengthen public institutions and provide public security. With a decline in coca cultivation, he is already achieving some success. Because America's drug demand fuels much of the problem, the United States should help meet these goals. Counterterrorism aid must be part of the mix. Failure to leverage Colombia's homegrown efforts could easily destabilize the wobbly northern Andean region and lead to terrorist violence in neighboring countries.

Bipartisan consensus exists for continuing military aid, but critics point out that Colombia's security forces still commit human rights abuses, albeit fewer than in the past. Yet, leaving Colombia to the mercy of narco-terrorists is no option. The only alternative is to help the government disarm these criminals and protect innocent citizens — especially when it is beginning to make progress.

NO Jason Hagen
Associate for Colombia, Washington Office on Latin America

Written for The CQ Researcher, March 10, 2003

U.S. taxpayers should ask what their $2 billion has achieved in Colombia. I have yet to see many positive results: The drug supply has not been curtailed, the country has become more violent and the ranks of the poor are swelling.

Meanwhile, anti-terrorist rhetoric from both governments is drowning out the complexity of the conflict. Instead of providing much-needed creativity, the United States is digging its heels into very hostile terrain alongside a new administration in Colombia that seems committed to repeating historical errors.

Most analysts, including me, see negotiations as the only way to resolve the conflict. But those who believe the country can be pacified through military means should at least be honest with the math. Classic counterinsurgency doctrine requires 10 soldiers for every insurgent in order to win on the battlefield. Right now, the Colombian military has up to 60,000 soldiers ready to be deployed, and the government does not have the money to pay for additional regular soldiers. There are approximately 35,000 illegal, armed guerrillas.

Will the United States provide the missing 290,000 troops for jungle warfare?

Colombian social spending has dried up because the government is devoting its slim resources to the war. Even in areas the government has designated as security priorities, promised social assistance has not arrived. This is a tremendous oversight, considering that more than 60 percent of Colombians make less than $2 a day, roughly 6 percent of the population has been forcibly displaced from their homes and unemployment is nearly 20 percent.

Having soldiers on every corner means little to a family that cannot afford bread. If even a tiny fraction of these desperate people join the insurgency for a paycheck or for political reasons, the guerrilla threat will continue to grow. Colombia and the United States should be investing heavily in social and economic programs to prevent this from happening.

Elements of the Colombian military continue to maintain ties with an illegal paramilitary force that the United States regards as a terrorist organization. Turning a blind eye to terror in order to fight terror is neither morally acceptable nor a smart strategy to bring peace to Colombia.

Rather than waste years dabbling in an intractable conflict — at the cost of thousands of lives and billions of dollars — the United States should put its considerable diplomatic weight behind a peace process.

opening for big foreign companies to exploit the forest, and that average people will not benefit."

Free-trade supporters counter that while these concerns are legitimate, they should not stand in the way of open trade. "At the end of the day, when you argue against free trade, you are arguing against modernization," Vasquez says.

Vasquez admits that dislocations will occur as industries large and small struggle to compete in the new, more open environment. But, he argues, many of those who lose jobs and businesses will find new opportunities as other, more competitive sectors of the economy expand.

Most important, Vasquez says, free trade will benefit all South Americans, especially the poor, by driving down the prices of many goods and services. "When you protect industries from competition, prices stay higher than they should, which is a big deal in South America where so many people are poor."

Shaky Economies

Argentina's economic collapse at the end of 2001 has raised fears of a continentwide meltdown. And indeed, some other countries, including Uruguay, Venezuela and even Brazil, look to be in danger of sliding into a full depression.

The continent's gross domestic product (GDP) shrank by roughly 1 percent last year and is expected to do so again this year as Argentina and Venezuela undergo painful economic contractions, along with other nations. According to the Economic Commission for Latin America, a United Nations-sponsored think tank in Santiago, Chile, poverty in the region is also high, with 44 percent of Latin Americans now poor, nearly half of them living in extreme poverty. [22]

And inflation, once the bane of Brazil and many other South American countries, is creeping back up after years in check. Atop the watch list are Argentina and Venezuela, currently tackling annual inflation rates of nearly 41 percent and 31 percent, respectively. At 12.5 percent, consumer price increases in Brazil are also considered too high. [23]

Argentina is still in deep trouble, with its economy contracting 11 percent last year — its fourth annual consecutive decline in GDP. The country is continuing to struggle through an economic crisis that saw a quarter of its population out of work, private bank accounts frozen and government defaulting on its loan obligations.

In January, the IMF rode to the rescue, giving Argentina a $6.8 billion loan that would enable it to service its debt to the IMF and other lenders through August. But the agreement (which has yet to be ratified by the country's Congress) would impose strict fiscal discipline on Argentina. For instance, under the plan, subsidies on energy and other staples would be cut, which would hurt the poor and could lead to renewed riots and other forms of social instability.

"I don't think anyone really doubts that in the short term, it's going to be pretty rocky for Argentina," says Inter-American Dialogue's Shifter. "I think it will be at least a few years before they're able to turn a corner and get back on their feet."

The other big economy of the region, Brazil, is in better shape, but there is the real risk of an Argentine-style collapse. The economy grew only 1.5 percent last year, and the currency, the *real*, lost 35 percent of its value. [24]

But there are signs of improvement. At 3.4 percent, fourth-quarter GDP growth was higher than the other three quarters, and agricultural exports have surged due to the weaker currency. [25]

Like most other South American countries, Brazil has a high public debt — running at about 56 percent of GDP. In exchange for an IMF loan last year, Brazil agreed to cut government spending in order to pay some of it off. The problem now facing Lula, the country's charismatic president, is that many of the cuts must come from social programs, hard for a leader who campaigned on a platform of helping the poor. [26]

In the continent's Andean region in the north and west, the situation is not much better, possibly worse. "I think this is the most troubled part of the continent," Shifter says. "It's sort of an axis of upheaval."

Deep political turmoil has wracked the economy of oil-rich Venezuela, which shrank about 9 percent last year. [27] And as President Chavez tightens his grip on the country, more stores and factories are expected to close as members of the business community (which vehemently opposes the president) leave the country.

Economists agree that Colombia, with abundant natural resources and a well-educated populace, has great economic potential. But the civil war has prevented foreign and domestic investment while prompting Colombia's best and brightest to emigrate. As a result, the economy grew at only 1.6 percent last year. [28]

Ecuador and Bolivia also are facing civil strife, caused

in part by slow economic growth. Among the poorest countries in South America, each grew at about 2.5 percent last year, not fast enough for a developing country to greatly improve the standard of living for most citizens. [29]

Economic troubles throughout the continent are leading to a re-examination of the free-market policies that South Americans embraced, in some places, as early as the 1980s. "After 10 or 15 years of operating with free-market policies, paradise hasn't come," says Julio Carrion, an economist at the University of Delaware. "People are starting to wonder whether the gospel is as good as advertised."

"People are really tired of the current formula because it hasn't paid the dividends they'd hoped for," Georgetown University's Shifter says. "At the same time, they don't want to go back to the discredited socialist policies of the 1970s either."

South Americans are beginning to look for something that combines the best of both policies, Shifter says. "They are groping right now, looking for a mix of the state and the market to solve their problems."

Shifter believes that Brazil's new president is making the first attempt to move in a new direction. "Lula represents the best hope for this middle ground," he says. "He's moderated his attitude toward free trade and the IMF, but he's also committed to dealing with Brazil's poverty."

But others say the problem is not free-market policies but the unwillingness or inability of South American leaders to implement them. "Beginning in the 1980s and picking up steam in the '90s, all of these leaders tried free-market reforms because they'd literally tried everything else, and nothing had worked," says Cato's Vasquez.

"It worked just like it was supposed to, with inflation down and growth up, but none of these guys, like [Argentina's] Menem and [Peru's] Fujimori were really free-marketers. So they abandoned the reforms once the economies picked up and the pressure was off."

Fighting Poverty

The search for a new economic path also reflects the continent's stubbornly high poverty rates. In Brazil, 50 million people — almost a third of the population — live at or below the poverty line, and 19 percent of all households still lack running water. [30] In Argentina, the economic crisis has driven the number of people in poverty from roughly one-third of the population to nearly one-half in the last 18 months. And in the desperately poor Andes region, countries like Ecuador have poverty rates as high as 80 percent.

The World Bank, the world's largest anti-poverty institution, made $4.4 billion in social-development loans to Latin America in 2002. The loans ranged from $200 million to improve access to higher education in Colombia to $600 million to help poor Argentine families make ends meet.

"We lend money for so many things — to improve health care by building clinics in rural areas or education by building schools or training teachers," says Christopher Neal, a World Bank spokesman. Other activities include environmental protection, land distribution and improving the way governments deliver services.

In exchange, Neal says, "we ask countries to make government reforms by, say, improving transparency," or public accountability. For instance, he says, the bank might help the government publish information about government procurement on the Internet so citizens can understand and monitor how and where public money is being spent.

The Inter-American Development Bank (IDB) also makes poverty-alleviation and economic-development loans to South American countries. The IDB lent Latin American countries about $8 billion last year — 40 percent of which went directly for anti-poverty programs like building low-income housing or hospitals in poor areas.

Aid organizations are often criticized for being ineffective, given that South America's poverty rates are still shockingly high. But the World Bank's Neal points out that the situation in South America has been steadily improving, especially on certain key social-development indicators. "Life expectancy for the region in 1990 was 68; 10 years later it was 70," he says. Infant mortality and illiteracy rates have also dropped during the same period, he says, from 41 deaths per thousand births to 29, and from 16 percent illiteracy to 12 percent.

Neal argues that poverty is sometimes driven up by outside factors, such as the slumping world economy or the historic and intransigent lack of widespread land ownership in rural areas throughout the continent. Efforts at land reform in the 1970s and '80s failed in most Latin countries, and today institutions like the development banks focus on funding programs that buy land from large property holders and sell it to poor farmers.

Moreover, lenders like the World Bank and IDB can only be effective in those countries with adequate governing institutions, Neal says. "If a government is not functioning well, it's hard to have an impact, because you need to work with effective local institutions to be able to make a difference."

OUTLOOK

New Leaders

Since the late 19th century, South America has been seen as a continent long on potential, both economically and politically, but short on actual results. Argentina actually achieved first-world living standards in the early 1900s, only to fall far behind the United States and Europe by the middle of the century.

Some experts believe the continent will continue failing to live up to its potential in the coming decades, largely because South Americans do not yet have the political maturity needed to create prosperous societies.

"They're going to muddle along for the time being because they don't really have a vision for the future aside from each person's desire to increase their individual wealth," says Johnson of the Heritage Foundation. "Many people in South America don't understand that their personal prosperity is tied to that of their neighbors and of society as a whole, so they don't push hard enough for the kind of change they need, like strong legislatures and judiciaries and a government that actually listens to people."

But others say South Americans will begin to make the changes needed to make their societies work. "It is more likely than not that they will do the things they need to do, like continuing to liberalize their markets, reform labor laws and battle corruption," says Williamson of the Institute for International Economics. "South America will end up looking like North America. If you look at countries like Singapore, they went from being poorer than South America is now to developed-country living standards in less than 30 years. So it is possible."

Inter-American Dialogue's Sifter agrees that the future is bright, in part because the next generation of leaders will be very different from the current crop.

"I've met with a lot of the people who are in their 30s and 40s and are going to be running things soon, and I can tell you that these people are very impressive," he says. "They understand that governments have to be honest and effective and responsive, and that's what they're working for."

NOTES

1. For background, see Kenneth Jost, "Democracy in Latin America," *The CQ Researcher*, Nov. 3, 2000, pp. 881-904.

2. Quoted in Thomas Ginsberg, "Latin Battleground," *The Philadelphia Inquirer*, Dec. 12, 2002, p. A1.

3. Figure cited in "Praying for a Happier New Year," *The Economist*, Dec. 19, 2002.

4. Kenneth Rogoff, "The IMF Strikes Back," *Foreign Policy*, January/February 2003, p. 38.

5. Poll cited in "Democracy Clings On in a Cold Climate," *The Economist*, Aug. 15, 2002.

6. Figures cited in "More Order and Less Law," *The Economist*, Nov. 7, 2002.

7. *Ibid.*

8. Juan Forero, "Colombia Will Tie Aid Request to Terror," *The New York Times*, Feb. 10, 2003, p. A6.

9. Steven R. Weisman, "Powell Says U.S. Will Increase Military Aid for Colombia," *The New York Times*, Dec. 5, 2002, p. A14.

10. Jared Diamond, *Guns, Germs, and Steel: The Fates of Human Societies* (1997), pp. 67-81.

11. Edwin Williamson, *The Penguin History of Latin America* (1992), pp. 91-92.

12. Diamond, *op. cit.*, pp. 210-211.

13. Williamson, *op. cit.*, p. 217.

14. *Ibid.*, p. 223.

15. Rex Hudson (ed.), *Brazil: A Country Study* (1998), p. 37.

16. *Ibid.*, p. 53.

17. Williamson, *op. cit.*, pp. 322-327.

18. Neil Irwin, "U.S. Seeks to End Many Tariffs," *The Washington Post*, Feb. 12, 2003, p. E1.

19. Quoted in *ibid.*

20. For background, see Mary H. Cooper, "Rethinking NAFTA," *The CQ Researcher*, June 7, 1996, pp. 481-504, and David Masci, "Mexico's Future," Sept. 19, 1997, pp. 817-840.

21. Quoted in Edmund Andrews, "Outside the Halls of Power, Many Fear Free Trade," *The New York Times*, Nov. 3, 2002, p. C4.

22. Figures cited at www.eclac.cl.

23. *CIA World Book*, 2002.

24. Tony Smith, "Brazil: Growth Despite Turmoil," *The New York Times*, Feb. 28, 2003, p. W1.

25. *Ibid.*

26. "Gruel Before Jam," *The Economist*, Feb. 13, 2003.

27. Figure cited in Marc Lifsher, "The Andean Arc of Instability," *The Wall Street Journal*, Feb. 24, 2003, p. A13.

28. Figure cited in *ibid.*

29. Figure cited in *ibid.*

30. "Three Square Meals a Day," *The Economist*, Feb. 20, 2003.

BIBLIOGRAPHY

Books

Easterly, William, *The Elusive Quest for Growth: Economists' Adventures and Misadventures in the Tropics,* **MIT Press, 2002.**
A former World Bank economist concludes that aid programs for the developing world fail because people and institutions respond to incentives, not penalties.

Kirk, Robin, *More Terrible Than Death: Massacres, Drugs, and America's War in Colombia,* **PublicAffairs, 2003.**
A Human Rights Watch researcher chronicles the human toll of Colombia's drug war.

Skidmore, Thomas E., and Peter H. Smith, *Modern Latin America,* **Oxford University Press, 2000.**
The authors, who teach history at Brown University and political science at the University of California at San Diego, respectively, explore social and political trends in South America.

Williamson, Edwin, *The Penguin History of Latin America,* **Penguin U.S.A., 1993.**
A professor of Hispanic studies at the University of Edinburgh focuses on 19th-century independence movements.

Articles

Bussey, Jane, "U.S. Trade Chief Offers Zero Tariffs," *The Miami Herald,* **Feb. 12, 2003, p. 1.**
U.S. Trade Representative Robert Zoellick's offer to eliminate tariffs in the Western Hemisphere by 2015 is detailed.

Andrews, Edmund L., "Outside the Halls of Power, Many Fear Free Trade," *The New York Times,* **Nov. 3, 2002, p. C4.**
Andrews examines the debate over the proposed Free Trade Area of the Americas, focusing on the critics' concerns.

Bluestein, Paul, "IMF's 'Consensus' Policies Fraying," *The Washington Post,* **Sept. 26, 2002, p. E1.**
The article details the small but growing number of economists who oppose the "Washington Consensus" due to South America's anemic growth rates.

Forero, Juan, "How Venezuelan Outlasted His Foes," *The New York Times,* **Feb. 6, 2003, p. A6.**
The article explores the character traits that help President Hugo Chavez survive political turmoil.

Jost, Kenneth, "Democracy in Latin America," *The CQ Researcher,* **Nov. 3, 2000, pp. 881-904.**
Jost details the strengths and weakness of the democracies that have arisen in South America in the last two decades.

Kristof, Nicholas D., "The Next Africa," *The New York Times,* **Dec. 10, 2002, p. A35.**
Kristof concludes from South America's many troubles that it is "quietly falling apart."

Lifsher, Marc, "The Andean Arc of Instability," *The Wall Street Journal,* **Feb. 24, 2003, p. A13.**
Lifsher explores the extreme poverty and political turmoil in the Andean region.

"Lula's Burden of Hope," *The Economist,* **Jan. 2, 2003.**
Brazil's new president is committed to helping the poor but constrained by IMF spending requirements.

"**More Law, Less Order,**" *The Economist*, Nov. 7, 2002.
The article asks whether Colombian President Alvaro Uribe's get-tough policies will undermine civil liberties.

Naim, Moises, "**The Washington Consensus: A Damaged Brand,**" *The Financial Times*, Oct. 28, 2002.
The editor of *Foreign Policy* magazine argues the free-market prescriptions of the Washington Consensus are worth considering, despite all the criticism.

Stiglitz, Joseph E., "**Argentina, Shortchanged; Why the Nation That Followed the Rules Fell to Pieces,**" *The Washington Post*, May 12, 2002, p. B1.
A former chief economist at the World Bank argues that the orthodox economic prescriptions imposed on Argentina by the Washington Consensus helped derail its economy.

Tobar, Hector, "**The Good Life is No More in Argentina,**" *Los Angeles Times*, Feb. 18, 2003, p. 1.
The piece details Argentina's slide into economic chaos and the impact the country's depression is having on its once well-to-do populace.

Reports

Human Rights Watch, "A Wrong Turn: The Record of the Colombian Attorney General's Office," November 2002.
The advocacy group alleges the attorney general failed to adequately prosecute members of the military for human rights abuses.

World Bank, *Global Economic Prospects and the Developing Countries 2003: Investing to Unlock Global Opportunities*, December 2002.
The report looks at Latin America's economy in 2002 and the prospects for growth in the coming years, focusing on the impact of Argentina's financial collapse.

For More Information

Center for Economic and Policy Research, 1621 Connecticut Ave., N.W., Suite 500, Washington, DC 20009; (202) 293-5380; www.cepr.net.

Council on Foreign Relations, The Harold Pratt House, 58 East 68th St., New York, NY 10021; (212) 434-9400; www.cfr.org.

Council on Hemispheric Affairs, 1730 M St., N.W., Suite 1010, Washington, DC 20005; (202) 216-9261; www.coha.org.

Institute for International Economics, 1750 Massachusetts Ave., N.W., Washington, DC 20036; (202) 328-9000; www.iie.com.

Inter-American Development Bank, 1300 New York Ave., N.W., Washington, DC 20577; (202) 623-1000; www.iadb.org.

Inter-American Dialogue, 1211 Connecticut Ave., N.W., Suite 510, Washington, DC 20036; (202) 822-9002; www.iadialog.org.

International Bank for Reconstruction and Development (World Bank), 1818 H St., N.W., Washington, DC 20433; (202) 473-1000; www.worldbank.org.

Organization of American States, 17th St. and Constitution Ave., N.W., Washington, DC 20006; (202) 458-3000; www.oas.org.

Washington Office on Latin America, 1630 Connecticut Ave., N.W., Suite 200, Washington, DC 20009; (202) 797-2171; www.wola.org.

12

Aiding Africa

David Masci

Protected by a Nigerian peacekeeper, Liberians unload U.N. food aid in the port city of Monrovia. Civil wars have devastated Liberia and other African countries in recent years, as have AIDS and famine. Corruption and economic stagnation also have taken a toll. Now the United States and other industrial nations are calling for new infusions of international humanitarian and development aid.

From *The CQ Researcher,*
August 29, 2003.

Sitting on his velvet throne in a crisp, white suit, Liberian President Charles Taylor looked every bit the African strongman. But Taylor's position on a recent August morning was anything but secure. After six violent and chaotic years, he announced he was stepping down and going into exile in Nigeria.

"I have accepted this role as the sacrificial lamb," he said, comparing himself to Jesus Christ and vowing one day to return. [1]

Taylor had been pressured for months, by the United States and most of the rest of the international community, to leave his utterly devastated country, which has seen tens of thousands of civilians die during more than a decade of civil war.

"He was in every way bad for his country, and his departure is long overdue," says Ali A. Mazrui, chancellor of Jomo Kenyatta University of Agriculture and Technology in Thika, Kenya, and a respected Africa scholar. "This is especially good news because Africa has had so many leaders like Taylor, but few of them have ever resigned."

But while Taylor's resignation is unusual, the hallmarks of his rule — authoritarianism, violence and brutality — are all too common in sub-Saharan Africa. Since the late 1950s and early '60s, when most African colonies achieved independence from Europe, scores of repressive dictators have come and gone, from the late Idi Amin of Uganda to Zaire's Mobutu Sese Seko.

Their legacy of underdevelopment, corruption, desperate poverty and violence continues to hobble Africa. The nearly 700 million inhabitants of sub-Saharan Africa are the poorest in the world, with a per-capita gross-domestic product (GDP) of $460 — just over a dollar a day. African life expectancy also is the world's

Successes Amid the Crises

Many of sub-Saharan Africa's 48 nations are struggling with life-and-death challenges, such as political instability, war, desperate poverty, famine and the spread of HIV/AIDS. But there are success stories as well: Angola emerged last year from a 25-year civil war, and Kenya and Nigeria both held elections after years of authoritarian rule.

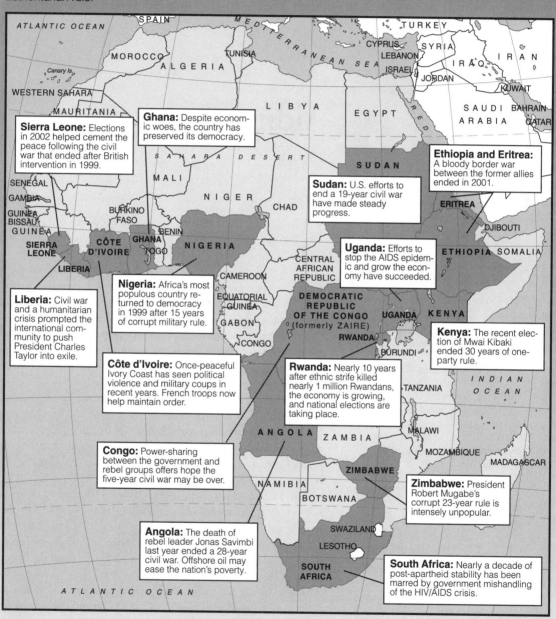

Sierra Leone: Elections in 2002 helped cement the peace following the civil war that ended after British intervention in 1999.

Ghana: Despite economic woes, the country has preserved its democracy.

Ethiopia and Eritrea: A bloody border war between the former allies ended in 2001.

Sudan: U.S. efforts to end a 19-year civil war have made steady progress.

Uganda: Efforts to stop the AIDS epidemic and grow the economy have succeeded.

Liberia: Civil war and a humanitarian crisis prompted the international community to push President Charles Taylor into exile.

Nigeria: Africa's most populous country returned to democracy in 1999 after 15 years of corrupt military rule.

Kenya: The recent election of Mwai Kibaki ended 30 years of one-party rule.

Côte d'Ivoire: Once-peaceful Ivory Coast has seen political violence and military coups in recent years. French troops now help maintain order.

Rwanda: Nearly 10 years after ethnic strife killed nearly 1 million Rwandans, the economy is growing, and national elections are taking place.

Congo: Power-sharing between the government and rebel groups offers hope the five-year civil war may be over.

Zimbabwe: President Robert Mugabe's corrupt 23-year rule is intensely unpopular.

Angola: The death of rebel leader Jonas Savimbi last year ended a 28-year civil war. Offshore oil may ease the nation's poverty.

South Africa: Nearly a decade of post-apartheid stability has been marred by government mishandling of the HIV/AIDS crisis.

Source: Economist.com

Quality of Life Lowest in Sub-Saharan Africa

Sub-Saharan Africa ranks lowest among other regions in several categories used to measure quality of life, including life expectancy, child mortality and access to clean water.

Selected Regions	Population (in millions) 2001	Life expectancy at birth (in years) 2001	GNP per capita (in $US) 2001	Under-5 mortality rate (per 1,000) 2001	Percent with access to clean water 2000
Sub-Saharan Africa	674	46	$460	171	58%
East Asia & Pacific	1,823	69	900	44	76
Europe & Central Asia	475	69	1,970	38	91
Latin America & Caribbean	524	71	3,580	34	86
Middle East & North Africa	301	68	2,220	54	88
South Asia	1,378	63	450	99	84

Source: 2003 World Development Indicators database, World Bank, April 13, 2003

lowest — and falling even lower, dropping from 50 years in 1990 to 46 in 2001.

The decline in lifespan is largely due to HIV/AIDS, which has killed millions in southern and eastern Africa and is still being largely ignored by governments in several affected nations. Now the disease is rapidly spreading into West Africa.

Meanwhile, rulers with little or no democratic legitimacy govern more than half of all African states, even though Zambia, Malawi and several other African countries made the transition to democracy during the 1990s. While some experts point to recent elections in Kenya as evidence that the trend toward elections and freedom continues, others contend that the push for democratic change has largely stalled.

Either way, democratic reform is often hindered by instability, which has plagued many parts of the continent since independence. Civil war, revolution and even genocide have been all too common since African countries began governing themselves roughly 40 years ago.

In the last 10 years alone, wars have been fought in, among other countries, Sierra Leone, Liberia, Congo, Angola, Sudan and Rwanda. Even Côte d'Ivoire (Ivory Coast), once a bastion of stability in West Africa, has recently descended into a bloody civil war.

Since the end of the Cold War, Africa's internecine fighting has occurred largely unhindered by the West, even when the blood-letting reached horrific proportions. In Congo alone, an estimated 3 million people have died from fighting and starvation in a civil war that has embroiled eight other countries. An earlier tragedy in Rwanda, where a 1994 genocide led to an estimated 1 million deaths, also provoked little action from the developed nations.

Lately though, the world community has been paying more attention to African conflicts. Earlier this year, about 8,000 peacekeepers (mostly from France) arrived to try to stop the fighting in Congo. In addition, British forces entered Sierra Leone in 1999 to stop a civil war.

Similarly, the world community had been calling in recent months for the United States to intervene militarily to stop the civil war in Liberia and ensure the flow of humanitarian aid. After more than a month of indecision, President Bush on Aug. 14 finally sent 200 Marines and dozens of helicopters to Monrovia, Liberia's capital, to back up a much larger contingent of Nigerian peacekeepers already there.

The president's hesitation over sending troops to Africa on a humanitarian mission stemmed in part from the deadly 1992 U.S. experience in Somalia, where a military intervention to help feed famine victims thrust American troops into the middle of a civil war.

AFP Photo/Eric Ferferberg

Young workers carry dirt out of a gold mine in the Democratic Republic of Congo. Economists say most African economies are much too dependent on exporting price-sensitive commodities like gold.

Eventually, 44 Americans died, and the rest of the force was hastily pulled from the country.

Critics of humanitarian intervention say U.S. blood should not be spilled in places like Somalia and Liberia, where American strategic interests are not clear-cut. "We need to focus our military on those areas where we have big interests and allow regional powers to deal with these smaller peacekeeping operations," says Jack Spencer, a senior defense-policy analyst at the Heritage Foundation.

But advocates of intervention contend that saving innocents from violence and starvation — and preventing war and political chaos from spreading to other countries — is in America's strategic interest. "We should understand by now that letting problems fester can lead to horrible consequences," says Joseph Siegle, a senior fellow and Africa expert at the Council on Foreign Relations,

noting that al Qaeda terrorists have taken advantage of instability in countries like Somalia, Sudan and, most notably, Afghanistan to recruit and train converts.

Many experts see the deployment of U.S. troops in Liberia as the latest in a series of recent Bush administration actions reflecting almost a sea change in U.S. attitudes about Africa's political, economic and strategic importance. Since the Sept. 11 attacks almost two years ago, the White House has proposed a number of ambitious aid programs, ranging from promoting democratic change and open markets to easing the continent's AIDS crisis.

Indeed, many experts see Bush's recent five-nation trip to sub-Saharan Africa — only the second by an American president — as a sign of America's new interest in the long-neglected continent. In Botswana and Uganda, the president visited AIDS clinics to underscore his recent $15 billion commitment to fighting the disease that has already claimed 20 million Africans and infected 30 million more. And during a speech in Nigeria, Bush stressed the need for both African and Western countries to reverse the continent's history of poverty, instability and underdevelopment.

"Working together," the president said, "we can help make this a decade of rising prosperity and expanding peace across Africa."

The president's emphasis on cooperation is reflected in a proposed U.S. development-assistance program pending before Congress that would reward countries that make political and economic strides. In 2002, he announced a $5 billion aid package for countries that create more democratic, open and accountable societies. Called the Millennium Challenge Account, the new program has been bolstered by promises of more aid from European and other prosperous nations.

But some Africa-watchers contend that foreign assistance often does more harm than good in Africa, feeding corruption and warping the very market forces that could help lift Africans out of poverty. Like opponents of domestic welfare, critics of foreign aid charge that it creates a damaging dependency, robbing recipients of the incentive to solve their own problems.

The opposing sides in the aid debate do agree on one thing: Much work needs to be done before Africa can begin living up to its enormous potential. And all agree that the West, and the United States in particular, have an important role to play.

As policymakers debate Africa's future, here are some of the questions they are asking:

Should the U.S. intervene militarily in Africa to stop wars and humanitarian crises?

The recent civil war in Liberia has renewed the debate over whether American troops should intervene in African countries that are not considered strategically important.

The dilemma has confronted the United States only in the last decade or so — particularly since the end of the Cold War.

Traditionally, Africa has drawn more attention from European powers, most notably Britain and France, which colonized much of the continent in the late 19th and early 20th centuries. Even the rise of the United States as a superpower after World War II and the breakup of Europe's colonial empires did not lead to direct American military involvement in sub-Saharan Africa. Instead, the United States, then embroiled in the Cold War with the Soviet Union, limited its role to providing money and arms to African countries — often run by corrupt dictators — or rebel forces fighting communist or socialist governments.

But the fall of the Soviet Union in 1991 left the United States as the only nation on Earth able to deploy large numbers of troops in distant theaters. In addition, cable television and later the Internet brought far-off humanitarian crises into Americans' living rooms 24 hours a day, often sparking widespread demands for action.

Such factors drew the United States in 1992 to its first and so far, only major, humanitarian intervention in Africa. That year a bloody civil war in Somalia had led to widespread famine and American troops were called on, as the lead nation in a United Nations-sponsored coalition, to help feed millions of people and stabilize the country.

At first, the mission succeeded. But efforts to stabilize the country put American soldiers in the middle of a chaotic civil war. After 44 Americans died, and a U.S. soldier's body was dragged through Mogadishu, President Bill Clinton withdrew all the U.S. troops.

Two years later, Clinton faced a similar choice in tiny Rwanda, where tribal tensions between the Hutus and Tutsis were threatening to erupt. But still smarting from the Somalia debacle, the United States and other allies didn't aid Rwanda, and an estimated 1 million people eventually were killed in the worst ethnic genocide in recent history.

Rwanda is often cited by supporters of humanitarian military intervention as an example of what can happen when a chaotic situation is allowed to continue. "I was in an airport hangar waiting to go into Rwanda when the mission was scrapped, and I've never felt good about that," says Army Special Forces Maj. Roger Carstens, a member of the Council on Emerging National Security Affairs, a private think tank. "If sending 2,500 troops in can make a situation like that better and save the lives of millions of people, it seems like a pretty good trade-off, if you ask me."

Carstens and others argue that intervening in trouble spots like Rwanda can prevent them from destabilizing neighboring countries, something that commonly occurs. Indeed, Rwanda's troubles spilled into Burundi and Congo, stoking the flames of Congo's long-running civil war.

"These sorts of humanitarian conflicts are the main source of instability in the world because they move across borders through refugee flows, through slower economic growth and through warfare itself," says the Council on Foreign Relations' Siegle. "Avoiding that has to be in our strategic interest."

As a result, Carstens says, it is folly to say that humanitarian crises like the current troubles in Liberia are not in America's strategic interest. "After 9/11, everything is a strategic interest more or less, especially if it is in a state of chaos," he says. "Look at Afghanistan: When ignored and left to its own devices, it became a haven for drug smugglers and terrorists."

In Carstens' view, African trouble spots could, like Afghanistan, turn into direct threats to American security. "When you look at failing states like Congo and Liberia, you have to remember that we now live in a world where terrorism and weapons of mass destruction have taken on a global dimension," he says. Some experts even say Liberia's Taylor may have laundered money for al Qaeda. [2]

But others counter that while crises like those in Rwanda and Liberia are tragic and even important to the United States, they do not represent the sort of strategic interests that American soldiers should risk their lives protecting.

"The United States has a unique role to play in the world, and that is keeping the big peace, doing the sort of things that other countries can't do," says the Heritage Foundation's Spencer. "Our job is to deter aggression and promote stability in strategically important regions like Europe, the Middle East and Asia, not respond to every flareup everywhere."

Five Nations Owe More Than $100 Billion

The five sub-Saharan nations with the most national debt owe more than $100 billion, mostly to donor nations and multilateral lenders like the World Bank. Most Africa-watchers contend that the prospects for poverty reduction in these and other African countries will remain bleak until much or all of their debt is forgiven. But some advocates of debt forgiveness argue it should only be granted to countries that successfully move to democracy and open markets.

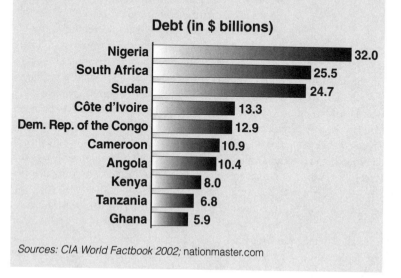

Debt (in $ billions)

Country	Debt
Nigeria	32.0
South Africa	25.5
Sudan	24.7
Côte d'Ivoire	13.3
Dem. Rep. of the Congo	12.9
Cameroon	10.9
Angola	10.4
Kenya	8.0
Tanzania	6.8
Ghana	5.9

Sources: CIA World Factbook 2002; nationmaster.com

As for sending American troops to Liberia, syndicated columnist Charles Krauthammer said recently on Fox News, "In principle, it's a bad idea because foreign policy is not social work. There are a lot of bad guys in the world, but we don't spend our blood and treasure going after all the bad guys. We go after bad guys who are our enemies. . . . The military is to defend the United States, it's not to do relief." [3]

Moreover, Spencer adds, the American military is not trained to do the kind of work necessary to stabilize a Rwanda or Liberia. "U.S. ground forces are trained to fight and win wars, not to do peacekeeping duties," he says.

Opponents of humanitarian missions also contend that they deter other nations capable of doing peacekeeping missions from undertaking them. "We need to stop communicating to the rest of the world that the U.S. has a responsibility to do this because we've created an expectation that we will intervene," says Christopher Preble, director of foreign-policy studies at the Cato

Institute. "In most of these situations, there are local and regional powers that have a role to play, and we should let them play it."

For instance, Preble says, Nigerian troops delayed their entry into Liberia by more than a month due to expectations that the United States might intervene. "I got the sense that they were ready to go into Liberia [in June,] but then they decided to wait because they thought we might go in."

But Princeton Lyman, former U.S. ambassador to Nigeria and South Africa, says expectations of U.S. intervention don't delay other countries from carrying out their responsibilities. "No one expected us to go into Congo or Sierra Leone, and we didn't," he says. "Instead, the French and British went in, as they should have."

Even in Liberia, Lyman points out, the Nigerians only delayed their deployment because the United States was very publicly considering intervention. "Bush went all over Africa saying we might go in, so of course the Africans waited until a decision was made."

Will Africa's recent democratic gains be sustained and expanded?

In the 1990s, many African countries made substantial steps toward democratic reform. In Zambia, for instance, longtime dictator Kenneth Kaunda stepped down after losing multiparty elections in 1991. Similar events occurred in Malawi, South Africa and Nigeria. [4]

But Africa's march toward democracy has by no means been smooth, and much of the continent remains mired in dictatorships or quasi-democratic systems that do not give citizens much voice in state affairs. For instance, nations such as Eritrea, Congo and Sudan have repressive, authoritarian governments. And in some places — notably Zimbabwe — governments that once had at least some trappings of democracy have largely lost them.

According to the democracy-advocacy group Freedom House, only 18 of the 48 countries in sub-Saharan Africa are electoral democracies. And of those, only 11 received the organization's highest rating of "free," meaning they respect citizens' full political and civil rights. [5]

Some experts argue that Africa's 1990s trend toward democracy has lost momentum and that the continent is unlikely to make substantial progress on democratic reform in the foreseeable future.

"There is no question that the democratization process that was moving forward in the mid-1990s has stalled today," says George Ayittey, a professor of economics at American University and president of the Free Africa Foundation, which promotes democratic change on the continent.

Robert Rotberg, director of the Program on Intrastate Conflict at the Kennedy School of Government at Harvard University, agrees that Africa's momentum toward democratization has slowed. "I don't think we can say that there is some democratic blossoming in Africa right now," he says. "Until some of the states that are large and influential, like Congo and Sudan, begin going democratic, it will be hard to say that the trends are running in the right direction."

Part of the problem, Ayittey says, is that many African governments are making cosmetic changes just to please aid donors, but are not committed to real democracy. "Many have twisted the rules of the game and then stood for elections, knowing full well that they would win," he says, citing countries like Togo, where the electoral process has been "rigged" to ensure the continuation of the current ruling clique. "That's not democracy."

Moreover, Rotberg says, the ruling elite is perfectly willing to ignore the popular will in order to preserve its privileges. "There is a growing middle class in Africa, and it wants the same things that middle classes in other parts of the world want, including a say in how their country is run," he says. "But you have a determined group of elites ready and willing to stand in the way to protect what they have."

Over the longer term, says Ayittey, a native of Ghana, Africa will continue to be "democracy poor" until local media are truly free. "If Africans really want to reinvigorate democracy, they need to reinvigorate the media," he says. "This is the best way to expose government wrongdoing and cronyism and hold them accountable."

AFP Photo/Issouf Sanogo

Nigerian President Olusegun Obasanjo votes in the presidential election last April. Nigeria is among several African countries that made the transition to democracy in the 1990s, including Zambia and South Africa.

By Ayittey's count, however, only eight countries have a truly free media. "So, you see, they have a long way to go."

But Charles Cobb, senior diplomatic correspondent for AllAfrica.com, a news-gathering organization, says the dire assessment by Ayittey, Rotberg and others is unwarranted. Although Africa is still far from its democratic potential, the trend remains positive, he contends. "On balance, I'd say they are going in the right direction," Cobb says.

Ambassador Lyman agrees, arguing that difficulties in a few countries like Liberia, Zimbabwe and Congo have blinded many people to the progress being made on the continent.

In Kenya, for instance, a new, freely elected president, Mwai Kibaki, has just taken power after 39 years of one-party rule under former president and strongman Daniel Arap Moi. Even in war-torn Congo, Lyman says, a government of national unity has been formed between the sitting government and rebel groups, and an election is to be held in the next two years. "There's real reason to hope there."

Cobb and Lyman also see positive signs that bode well for long-term democratic prospects on the continent. For instance, military coups are becoming much less common, both say, in large part because most African countries now ostracize governments that have taken power by force.

"Coups are just no longer acceptable in institutional Africa," Cobb says. "They recently had coups in Chad and Sao Tome, and African institutions like the African Union pressured these guys to back down and restore civilian rule, and they did. That's progress."

Meanwhile, on a more local level, optimists note, Africans are taking charge of their own future and not leaving it in the hands of corrupt leaders. "There's a great increase in civil-society groups," Cobb says, referring to churches, anti-corruption groups, environmental organizations, labor unions and the like. "These groups are increasingly making a difference all over Africa."

Michelle Carter, deputy regional director for East and Central Africa for the aid group CARE, says the impact of the groups was especially apparent in last year's election in Kenya. "In Kenya, you had a situation where the people were holding their leaders accountable, and it made a real difference," she says. "The rise of these civil-society groups is relatively new, but it is spreading throughout Africa."

Is the foreign aid that goes to Africa generally effective?

Nearly half of all Africans live in dire poverty. And only 15 percent live in an environment conducive to economic growth and development. [6] Such bleak statistics have helped Africa gain more aid from the developed world in recent years.

The United Nations got the ball rolling in 2001 with its Millennium Development Goals, a series of objectives aimed at cutting world poverty in half by 2015. [7]

Then in March 2002 President Bush weighed in with his own development initiative, the Millennium Challenge Account (MCA), targeted at rewarding Third

World countries that meet certain political and economic standards. Only countries with democratically elected governments that protect human rights and foster open markets are eligible for the aid, expected to total $5 billion over the next three years. Much of the MCA funding will likely go to Africa. [8]

The case for increased foreign assistance gathered more momentum at the G-8 summit near Calgary, Canada, in June 2002, when Russia and the world's seven biggest economies — Japan, Germany, France, Britain, Italy, Canada and the United States — pledged an additional $6 billion in aid for Africa beginning in 2003. The G-8 leaders also pledged to phase out domestic subsidies to their own farmers, which make it hard for Africa's agricultural sector to compete on the international market.

A year later, at the next G-8 summit in Evian, France, several African leaders, including South Africa's President Thabo Mbeki and Nigeria's Olusegun Obasanjo, were invited to speak to the United States and its great-power allies as part of a Third World delegation. [9] The move was meant to underscore the importance of listening to and helping Africa and other underdeveloped regions.

A little more than a week before that meeting, on May 21, Bush pledged $15 billion over five years to combat the AIDS epidemic killing hundreds of thousands throughout sub-Saharan Africa each year. [10] Congress later authorized the money but has yet to appropriate the funds.*

African leaders, aid workers and others applaud these recent steps, arguing that reducing poverty and creating prosperity will require massive new infusions of aid. Moreover, they say, much more money will be needed to meet the U.N.'s ambitious goals. Indeed, U.N. Secretary-General Kofi Annan has called on the world's rich countries to double their development assistance. The total is currently about $50 billion per year — down more than 20 percent from its 1990 peak of $65.5 billion. [11]

But others point out that Africa has received hundreds of billions of dollars in aid over the last four decades, only to slip further into poverty. "The goal of aid, that being sustainable economic development, has not been met," says Paolo Pasicolan, a trade analyst at the

---

* The House has appropriated $2 billion of the $3 billion Bush requested for the first year of the five-year plan. The Senate has yet to act.

Heritage Foundation. "Most African countries are poorer now than when we began giving them assistance after they became independent 30 or 40 years ago."

As William Easterly, a professor of economics at New York University and a senior fellow at the Center for Global Development, noted recently in *Forbes* magazine, "Africa is the most intensive recipient of foreign aid of any continent on the globe. . . . Yet Africa's growth in output per person has declined from 1.5 percent per year in the 1960s and 1970s to zero in the 1980s and 1990s. Meanwhile, foreign aid to Africa increased from 7 percent of its income in the 1960s and 1970s to 16 percent in the 1980s and 1990s." [12]

The reason for the failure, critics say, is that aid doesn't help poor countries, it actually hurts them. "As a general rule, foreign aid is not an effective way to promote prosperity," says Cato's Preble. "Indeed, it makes things worse because it strengthens the very institutions that thwart prosperity."

Preble believes that giving money to African governments or even non-governmental organizations (NGOs) damages the only mechanism that will allow Africans to economically better themselves: the free market. "Everything governments do becomes politicized, and how and what they do with the money is based on political considerations."

For instance, he says, "When we give money to a government to establish a bank to lend money to small-business men, its lending practices will inevitably be based on political considerations." Private banks, by contrast, lend to those businesses they believe will succeed, he adds.

At the same time, Preble contends, establishing a government bank with cheap foreign aid discourages the development of private banks. "If the government is lending money at low rates, private banks won't be able to compete. It would be stupid for them to try."

Others argue that aid creates a damaging dependency for African countries. "Developing countries, especially in Africa, have become much too dependent on aid," Pasicolan says. "It's very much like welfare."

Indeed, Pasicolan and others point out that in many African countries, aid often makes up a huge share of the government budget. In Malawi, for instance, 40 percent of government spending comes from foreign aid. In Zambia and Uganda, the figure is even higher. [13]

The best thing the United States and other developed countries can do for Africa is not to give them more aid but open their domestic markets to the continent's products. "The trade barriers we put up are doing great harm to African countries," Preble says. "We need to eliminate agricultural subsidies and tariffs if we really want to help them."

Aid opponents cite a recent *New York Times* column in which Amadou Toumani Toure and Blaise Compaore, the presidents of Mali and Burkina Faso, call on the U.S. and the European Union to end their domestic subsidies for cotton producers, arguing the subsidies have effectively shut African farmers out of the world cotton market and are helping to impoverish people in rural areas. [14]

But others counter that foreign aid, for all its problems, has helped Africa tremendously. "Things in Africa are not good right now," says Ambassador Lyman. "But if we didn't have aid, I guarantee there would be much more human suffering than there has been."

CARE's Carter agrees. "For all that's wrong, many indicators in Africa in areas like education and health are higher today than they were 50 years ago, and that's due to aid. No question about it."

Carter and others point to U.N. statistics showing that in several areas from infant mortality to literacy, African countries have been making progress. For example, infant mortality has dropped in Uganda from 110 per 1,000 births in 1970 to 79 in 2001. Meanwhile, the percentage of young Ugandans who can read and write has risen from 70.1 percent in 1990 to 79.4 in 2001. [15]

But, according to some supporters, foreign aid is only as good as the policies of the countries that receive it. A recent study by World Bank economists David Dollar and Craig Burnside found that "aid has a positive effect on growth in a good policy environment." [16] In other words, countries with sound monetary policy, the rule of law, open trade and other hallmarks of developed economies will be able to put foreign aid to good use.

Jerry Wolgin, the World Bank's principal economist for Africa, says that although the Dollar and Burnside study sounds obvious, it has helped make aid more effective. "Donors are getting better at putting their money in countries with good environments," he says, adding that there are between 12 and 15 states in Africa, such as Botswana and Ghana, that currently make the grade and would qualify for aid under MCA standards.

On the flip side, Wolgin says, countries without a good aid environment will get help to develop one. "So,

1950s-1960s *Europe's colonies in Africa gain independence, often peacefully.*

1957 Ghana becomes the first British colony to gain independence.

1958 France offers its 14 colonies in sub-Saharan Africa independence or semi-autonomy within a new "French Community." Within two years, all but one former colony opt for independence.

1960 Africa's most populous state, Nigeria, gains independence. Kenya, Uganda and other British territories become free over the next five years.

1965 Efforts by Britain to negotiate a power-sharing agreement between blacks and whites in Rhodesia fail, and the white minority declares independence, sparking an uprising by the black majority.

1970s-1980s *Cold War rivalry and economic mismanagement hurt most African states.*

1975 Mozambique and Angola gain independence from Portugal and almost immediately plunge into civil wars.

1980 Minority-white rule ends in Rhodesia, which is renamed Zimbabwe. But white Afrikaners continue to oppress South Africa's black majority under the apartheid system of legal discrimination and segregation.

1990-Present *Much of the continent embraces democracy while it grapples with challenges like economic stagnation, ethnic violence and HIV/AIDS.*

1990 South African opposition leader Nelson Mandela is freed from prison by President F.W. de Klerk after 27 years. Negotiations over the transition to black majority rule begin.

1991 Zambia's president for 30 years, Kenneth Kaunda, is defeated in free elections. . . . Two Marxist dictators in Africa's so-called Horn, Mohammed Siad Barre of Somalia and Mengistu Haile Mariam of Ethiopia, are overthrown by homegrown rebellions.

1992 American aid efforts in Somalia end in failure, and U.S. troops are pulled from the country.

1994 Ethnic tensions in Rwanda erupt into genocide, killing an estimated 1 million people. South Africa, Mozambique and Malawi hold free elections.

1997 Congo's Mobutu Sese Seko is ousted.

1999 Congress passes the Africa Growth and Opportunity Act, aimed at spurring exports from Africa to the United States. . . . Nigeria holds its first successful multi-party elections after 15 years of army rule. . . . The number of people living with HIV/AIDS in sub-Saharan Africa reaches 25 million.

2001 Ethiopia and Eritrea fight a bloody border war.

March 2002 President Bush proposes the Millennium Challenge Account, a new U.S. aid program aimed at rewarding poor countries that promote democracy and enact sound economic policies. . . . Angola's rebel leader, Jonas Savimbi, is killed, ending his country's 28-year civil war.

June 2002 A G-8 summit in Canada focuses on alleviating Africa's poverty.

December 2002 Kenya's ruling party loses its 30-year grip on power in the wake of the country's first free election in decades.

May 21, 2003 President Bush pledges $15 billion over five years to combat the AIDS epidemic in Africa. Congress later authorizes the money but has yet to appropriate the funds.

July 2003 President Bush visits five nations in sub-Saharan Africa. His trip is only the second by an American president.

August 2003 Liberian President Charles Taylor goes into exile under pressure from the United States and other nations, and a small American force joins Nigerian peacekeepers in an effort to bring stability to the war-torn country.

for example, in Sierra Leone, where they currently have weak institutions, we're sending experts to help train government officials," he says. "We're helping them bring themselves up to a point where they can put development aid to good use."

Also on the good-news front: Some donors are beginning to reverse the longstanding practice of tying most of their foreign aid to purchases of domestic goods and services, leaving little actual money in the hands of recipients. For instance, foreign aid from Britain no longer must be spent on British products and contractors.

BACKGROUND

Out of Imperialism

During the 19th and early 20th centuries, the British and French — the world's two greatest colonial powers — conquered huge chunks of sub-Saharan Africa. Germany and Italy also grabbed pieces here and there, and even small states, like Belgium and Portugal, seized territories that were many times larger than their own.

European colonizers brought much that was both good and bad to Africa. The English and French, for instance, built roads, railroads and other infrastructure and created a native civil service to assist them in running their territories.

But all the colonizers exploited the land and its people. Some, like the Belgians, literally killed and maimed millions as they stripped their huge colony, Congo, of its natural resources.

But Europe's role as Africa's overseer was short-lived, largely due to the Second World War, which dramatically weakened most of the colonial powers. Many of Africa's masters — notably France and Belgium — had been occupied by Germany. Even Britain, one of the victors, emerged from the conflict considerably diminished. In short, Europe could no longer afford the cost of maintaining vast colonies far from home.

Meanwhile, even before the war ended, the world's new great power, the United States, had been pressuring the Europeans to divest their colonies in Africa and elsewhere.

As a result, independence came to many parts of Africa without the violence that often precedes a colony's separation from its mother country. In more cases than not, power was transferred smoothly and even amicably.

By the late 1940s, the British Colonial Office had begun transferring some governing authority to local elected councils in Africa. It was the first step toward self-government and eventually led to the formation of political parties in each of Britain's colonies. [17]

The establishment of a genuine political process in British Africa led to an independence "domino effect" that began in 1957 in Ghana. Three years later Nigeria — the most populous African country — gained its freedom, and tiny Sierra Leone followed suit in 1961. Over the next five years, Uganda, Tanzania, Kenya and Gambia would all become independent via the peaceful transfer of power. *

The 14 French colonies in West and Central Africa also began to gain more and more autonomy in the late 1940s and '50s, electing local officials and even sending representatives to the French parliament. [18] By 1956, Francophone Africa was largely self-governing, although Paris still controlled the colonies' finance, defense and foreign policies. [19] France hoped to make this arrangement permanent when in 1958 it offered its African possessions two choices: total independence or autonomy within a new "French Community." Colonies that chose autonomy would receive French aid and protection in exchange for continued French oversight of external and finance policy. [20]

Initially, almost all the territories chose continued close association with France. But within months, the new quasi-states began opting out of the community and declaring total independence.

By 1960, all but one of the Francophone countries in sub-Saharan Africa — French Somaliland — had rejected community in favor of independence. The same year, Congo formally declared itself a sovereign state, severing its formal association with Belgium.

Still, the great wave of decolonization did not leave Africa entirely free of white rule. Portugal employed increasingly repressive tactics to retain control of Portuguese Guinea, Angola and Mozambique. Soon, however, the three territories were in open revolt, and by 1970 Lisbon had to maintain 150,000 troops in Africa to hold onto its possessions. [21]

---

* Beginning in 1952, Kenyans rose up against the British in the bloody Mau Mau uprising. But it had been quelled by the time the country won its freedom in 1963.

Leaders Target Bribery and Corruption

When Kenya's minister of local government, Karisa Maitha, found a briefcase with $62,500 outside of his Nairobi office recently, he did something that is unusual in Africa: He found the man who left it, a local developer, and threw him and his money out of the building. [1]

It is so rare for an official in Africa to turn down a bribe, especially such a large one, that Maitha's gesture made headlines in Kenya and beyond. From the lowliest bureaucrat or police officer to cabinet ministers and presidents, bribery and corruption are woven into the fabric of life. Indeed, African civil servants' salaries are the lowest in the world, partly in expectation that paychecks will be supplemented by bribes.

Citizens who need a phone installed, a form processed or a traffic violation overlooked simply slip the appropriate official a little baksheesh. The same holds true for multinational corporations and rich businessmen, who often see kickbacks as part of the price of doing business.

But the custom may be changing, at least in some parts of Africa. In Kenya, recently elected President Mwai Kibaki has launched a "zero corruption" initiative that already has caused Kenya's chief justice, central bank chief and top tax collector to step down.

"Corruption has undermined our economy, our politics and our national psyche," Kibaki said. [2]

Other countries, including Ghana, Mozambique, Zambia and South Africa, also have launched anti-corruption drives. Zambia, which has been developing new standards of conduct for civil servants, recently put former President Frederick Chaluba on trial for allegedly plundering the state treasury during his two terms.

In South Africa, new laws now protect whistleblowers and require public disclosure of public spending. Moreover, a special anti-corruption unit — dubbed the Scorpions — has won fame by netting hundreds of allegedly corrupt officials, including top members of the ruling African National Congress (ANC) party. Indeed, at the end of July, the group was investigating charges that Deputy President Jacob Zuma took a $68,000 bribe from a French defense firm. [3]

But for all of this progress, Africa still ranks among the most corrupt places on Earth. A recent survey of 102 countries conducted by Transparency International, an anti-corruption group, found that many of the world's most corrupt nations were in Africa, including Nigeria, Madagascar, Kenya, Angola and Uganda. Of the 25 least-corrupt countries, only one, Botswana, was African. [4]

In Nigeria, for instance, bribery is rampant at all levels of society. "Nigerians say it is just a normal part of their lives, like anything else," says Chantal Uwimana, a Burundian, who is a program officer for Transparency

---

[1] "Minister Maitha Rejects Bag with a $62,000 Bribe," *The Nation* [of Kenya], April 5, 2003.

[2] Quoted in Marc Lacey, "A Sign of the New Kenya: A Briefcase Filled with Cash is Spurned," *The New York Times*, March 29, 2003, p. A6.

[3] "Just How Bad Is It, Really?" *The Economist*, Aug. 2, 2003.

[4] From Transparency International's "Corruption Perceptions Index 2002" at http://www.transparency.org/cpi/2002/cpi2002.en.html

---

A different but no less explosive situation prevailed in southern Africa. In South Africa, the descendents of 18th-century Dutch and German settlers, known as Afrikaners, held power over the territory's black majority. Upon achieving independence from Britain in 1948, the Afrikaners established a harsh, new system of formal racial segregation, known as apartheid ("apart"), in an effort to solidify their rule. Under apartheid, blacks were paid less than whites for the same jobs, restricted in where they could travel or live, prohibited from voting and generally not allowed to receive higher education or hold positions of authority in either government or business.

Meanwhile, just north of South Africa another white minority in another British colony was trying to retain its power and privileges. In the early 1960s, as it prepared to grant independence to what was then called Rhodesia, Britain tried to broker a power-sharing deal between whites and blacks. But the effort failed, and whites, though greatly outnumbered by the blacks, declared independence from the U.K. in 1965 and set about governing on their own.

Britain and most of the world community did not recognize Rhodesia's white-minority government, and soon the United Nations had imposed economic sanctions on the new country. Meanwhile, blacks began

International in Berlin. "They don't even wait until someone asks them for a bribe, but just pay it as if it was a normal fee."

Even in Kenya, with all of its recent efforts, bribery still costs the average citizen 20 percent of his salary, according to Uwimana. "They have to pay extra for everything — health care, education, police and judges."

But corruption hurts Africans in other ways as well. "Because of corruption, a significant amount of [foreign] aid doesn't reach its intended target," says George Ayittey, a professor of economics at American University and president of the Free Africa Foundation, which promotes democracy on the continent. "So much of [aid] is embezzled — an estimated 40 percent of World Bank loans in Ghana, for example — so the suffering continues."

In addition to foreign aid, oil and natural gas revenues are also frequently the targets of corruption. Nigeria sits on an estimated 25 billion barrels of petroleum and is Africa's largest oil exporter. Yet past governments and their allies have been accused of stealing about $30 billion in oil revenue and wasting much of the rest. [5] Meanwhile, Nigerian motorists often have to wait in line for gas.

"Oil has been a curse for Africa because it has completely undermined good governance," says Jerry Wolgin, the World Bank's principal economist for Africa. "There are just too many ways to get wealthy, too many temptations and so government officials focus on getting rich instead of doing their jobs."

But here too, some steps are being taken to ensure that oil wealth is used to good purpose. Chad, for example, recently agreed to allow the World Bank to oversee the spending of a new financial windfall from recent oil development. [6]

And in June, British Prime Minister Tony Blair threw his political weight behind efforts to get energy companies to disclose how much they are paying developing nations for oil and gas leases. So far, a number of companies, including British Petroleum and Royal Dutch Shell, have responded positively to the controversial initiative, though none have committed to full disclosure.

"It this succeeds, it will give people a sense of how much money their governments are getting, and that will make these governments more accountable for how they spend it," says Uwimana.

According to experts like Uwimana, Africans are growing more and more weary of corruption. But eliminating bribery and other dirty practices takes a determined effort starting at the top, says Stephen Hayes, president of the Corporate Council on Africa, a group promoting U.S.-Africa trade. "Tackling corruption of all kinds requires a genuine commitment from the leader of the government," he says.

Uwimana goes even further, arguing that anti-corruption efforts must be broad-based. "The commitment has to come from all parts of political society — executive, parliamentary and judicial as well as civil-society groups," she says. "Without that, you won't make real progress."

[5] Warren Vieth, "U.S. Quest for Oil in Africa Worries Analysts, Activists," *Los Angeles Times*, Jan. 13, 2003, p. A1.

[6] Daniel Fisher, "Dangerous Liaisons," *Forbes*, Aug. 28, 2003, p. 84.

actively fighting for independence from white rule, throwing the country into a civil war that lasted almost 15 years.

The Cold War

By 1970, sub-Saharan Africa was largely free of direct European rule. In less than 15 years, 42 new African countries had become members of the United Nations. Only the three Portuguese colonies, South Africa and Rhodesia were not ruled by black Africans.

But the speed and relative ease with which most African countries obtained independence belied the huge challenges they faced. Many of the new states had been left to govern themselves without enough skilled managers and technicians, both in government and business.

As Oxford University historian John Morris Roberts observes: "In practical terms, the speed of decolonization in Africa had often meant that there was little chance of finding native Africans in sufficient numbers to provide administrators and technicians for the new regimes, some of which continued for a time to rely upon white personnel. Similarly, the supporting structures of higher education, communications and armed forces were often nothing like so evolved as those in say, India; this, too, made new African nations even more dependent on foreign help." [22]

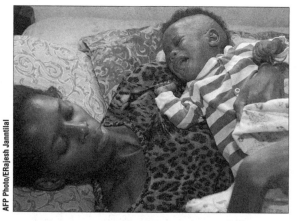

A South African woman with AIDS consoles her HIV-positive child. AIDS has killed some 20 million Africans and infected 30 million more in the last two decades. President Bush has pledged $15 billion over five years to combat AIDS in Africa, but Congress has yet to appropriate the funds.

And foreign "help" was always available. As the Cold War raged worldwide, it often had repercussions on the continent. The United States, Soviet Union, China and former colonial powers like Britain and France all jockeyed to gain influence in newly independent Africa. Often this led to economic and military backing for corrupt and even cruel leaders or support for a rebel group that was destabilizing the country.

In Congo, for instance, the Soviet Union and the United States each backed different sides in an internal conflict that began brewing literally as the country gained independence. The Soviets backed the newly elected prime minister, Patrice Lumumba, a fiery nationalist and socialist. The United States opposed Lumumba and eventually supported Army Chief of Staff Joseph Mobutu, who allegedly had Lumumba killed and eventually took control of the government. [23]

But Africa's problems were not entirely imported. Intertribal violence flared up in many new states, which often had been created without regard to traditional tribal boundaries. In eastern Nigeria, for instance, the Ojukwu tribe seceded in 1967, declaring the independent state of Biafra. Three years of bloody war ensued, leading to an estimated 1 million deaths — many from starvation — before the rebels surrendered. [24]

Tribalism often led states to abandon democratic principles in favor of authoritarian, usually military, rule.

So-called dictators for life, or strongmen, rose to power in many countries, including Zambia, Kenya, Ethiopia and Uganda, using the specter of intertribal violence as a justification for their heavy-handed rule. These regimes quickly became corrupt and often harshly repressive.

By the 1970s, the repression and corruption, often accompanied by socialist policies, eventually led to economic stagnation and decline. Ten years earlier, during the years immediately following independence, many African countries had experienced moderate economic growth. Rising prices for cocoa, cotton, gold and other commodities had boosted most African economies, which relied heavily on such exports. In addition, many states were bolstered by outside aid, usually spent on large infrastructure or prestige projects, like dams and universities.

But corrupt and inept governance eventually undermined the gains. In the early 1970s, a recession in the West sent world commodity prices plummeting. Africa was hit hard, and throughout the rest of the 1970s and '80s, the gross domestic product (GDP) of most African countries shrank. Between 1980 and '87, for instance, the continentwide GDP dropped an average of 2.6 percent per year. By contrast, Asian countries such as South Korea and Taiwan, which had been poorer than most parts of Africa just two decades before — were growing at a breakneck pace.

By 1989, 30 heavily indebted sub-Saharan African countries were being forced by the World Bank and International Monetary Fund (IMF) to submit to "structural adjustment" programs, or spending restrictions, in an effort to balance budgets and make their economies more market-oriented. But the spending limits also kept many economies in deep recession and hurt Africa's poor. [25]

The economic suffering was compounded by restrictions on political freedom. Only one state, Botswana, was judged in 1989 to be fully democratic. [26]

New Hope

The end of the Cold War in the early 1990s brought dramatic changes to Africa, especially in the political arena. Dictators who had been almost blindly propped up by the United States and Soviet Union began to lose their patronage.

Moreover, as Cambridge University historian David Reynolds writes, the spending limits imposed by the multinational lenders had a political impact as well: "Cutting government projects and slashing state jobs hit the patronage networks created by African rulers." [27]

Progress for Women, But Many Woes

Although African society is largely patriarchal, it is women who often form the social and economic backbone of their communities, doing a substantial portion of the daily work — as high as 80 percent by some estimates. [1]

"Women hold the family together," said Alicen Chelaite, Kenya's deputy assistant minister for gender, sports, culture and social services. "They are the managers — they manage the farm, the house, the children, the water, the firewood." [2]

At the same time, sub-Saharan Africa is a bastion of male chauvinism. Women in many parts of the continent routinely put up with sexual harassment, rampant discrimination in employment, polygamy, genital mutilation and domestic violence.

And yet, little is being done in many places to improve the lot of girls and women. For instance, throughout much of Africa there is a visible gender gap in education. Currently, girls make up 60 percent of all children on the continent who are not in school. [3]

"It's not that most African families don't want to educate their daughters," says Sofia Gruskin, an associate professor of international health and human rights at Harvard University's School of Public Health. "It's more a question of priorities. In most African countries, school fees are very high, and when a family can't afford to send all of their children, sons usually go first. The attitude is: Girls are going to be married away anyway."

Violence, especially rape, is another problem. In South Africa — called the "rape capital of the world" — health officials estimate a woman or girl is raped every 26 seconds, on average. And the numbers are rising. In 1994, the year of South Africa's first multiracial elections, 18,801 rapes were reported. In 2001, 24,892 cases were reported, considered a fraction of the actual number. [4]

And in countries like South Africa or Zambia, where 20 percent of the population between ages 18 and 35 is HIV positive, rape can do more than just physical and emotional damage to the victim: It can kill her. In fact, 58 percent of all HIV/AIDS victims in Africa are women. Since African men are more likely than women to have multiple partners, they also are more likely to infect more than one woman. [5]

Women in sub-Saharan Africa have many other health problems. For instance, according to the United Nations Development Program, they are 100 times more likely to die in childbirth than are women in Western countries. [6]

But there are signs of progress in a number of areas, especially on the political front. "You're seeing more women in real positions of authority, especially in Anglophone [English-speaking] Africa," Gruskin says.

Although there has been only one female president in Africa (Liberia's Ruth Perry, from 1996-1997), women now hold 30 percent of the parliamentary seats in Mozambique and South Africa, 26 percent in Rwanda and 24 percent in Uganda. [7]

More and more countries are also placing women in high cabinet positions, including Mozambique — where Luisa Diogo is minister of finance — and Nigeria, Senegal, South Africa, Botswana and Ethiopia.

Women are also fighting more forcefully and openly for their rights at the grass-roots level. In February, for instance, women from all over the continent met in Ethiopia to publicly denounce female genital mutilation, sometimes called female circumcision, a common practice in sub-Saharan Africa. [8]

And hundreds of civil-society groups have sprung up across Africa to address women's issues. One such group in Senegal surrounds the houses of men who have been accused of domestic violence against their wives or girlfriends and blows whistles to humiliate them and to call attention to the problem.

"This started in Senegal but is spreading all over Africa," Gruskin says. "It's really amazing what women are doing to improve their lives."

---

[1] Emily Wax, "Africa's Women Beginning to See Progress in Politics," *The Washington Post,* June 6, 2003, p. A14.

[2] Quoted in *Ibid.*

[3] Figure cited in "Human Development Report 2003," United Nations Development Program, 2003, p. 6.

[4] Vincent R. Okungu, "Culture of Sexual Violence Pervades Continent," allAfrica.com, Aug. 18, 2003.

---

[5] Kofi Annan, "In Africa, AIDS Has a Woman's Face," *The New York Times,* Dec. 29, 2003, p. D9.

[6] United Nations, *op. cit.*, p. 8.

[7] Figures cited in Wax, *op. cit.*

[8] For background, see Mary H. Cooper, "Women and Human Rights," *The CQ Researcher,* April 30, 1999, pp. 353-376.

One of the dictators' traditional levers of power was disappearing.

In a few cases, longtime dictators were violently overthrown. In 1991, for example, two brutal Marxists in Africa's so-called Horn, Mohammed Siad Barre of Somalia and Mengistu Haile Mariam of Ethiopia, were toppled by homegrown rebellions. And in 1997 Congo's Mobutu, long backed by the United States, was ousted by a rebel army led by longtime revolutionary Laurent Kabila.

Unfortunately, the abrupt changes left several countries no better off. Somalia descended almost immediately into civil war and famine. Likewise in Congo, Kabila's rule brought about a new and bloodier civil war.

But in much of the rest of Africa, the old order was swept away by more peaceful means. And often, the changes led to real improvements in people's lives. Between 1990 and 1995, 14 leaders were removed from power via the electoral process. Longtime strongmen like Zambia's Kaunda and Malawi's Hastings Banda were forced to step aside and make way for younger leaders who had built grass-roots political movements and enjoyed enormous popularity.

Perhaps the most significant and exciting of the new democratic transitions occurred in South Africa, where apartheid had continued despite the crippling effects of international economic sanctions and the end of white-minority rule in neighboring Rhodesia (renamed Zimbabwe) in 1980.

But South Africa's repressive white government could not withstand international pressure forever. By early 1990, when the nation's last white president, F.W. de Klerk, took office, the economy was reeling from the collapse of investment, international trade sanctions and high military expenditures needed to keep the increasingly rebellious black majority in line.

De Klerk immediately began preparing for the transition to majority rule. Within six months, he legalized the main opposition group, the African National Congress (ANC), and freed its iconic leader, Nelson Mandela, after 27 years in prison.

De Klerk and Mandela worked to shape a new, post-apartheid South Africa. The negotiations were marred by violence and threatened by both white and black extremists, but by late 1993 all sides had reached an agreement to hold elections in April 1994. [28]

The successful election marked the first time South Africans of all races voted. They elected Mandela as president and handed nearly two-thirds of the seats in the new parliament to the ANC. The white-dominated National Party became the chief opposition, and de Klerk was picked as deputy president. [29]

Despite the good news in South Africa and elsewhere, misery and death still burdened many parts of the continent. The same year South Africa held its first multiracial elections, tiny Rwanda exploded in horrific ethnic violence after a power-sharing agreement between the minority Tutsi tribe and majority Hutus broke down. The violence that followed left an estimated 1 million Rwandans, mostly Tutsis, dead — many hacked to death with machetes. A Tutsi rebel army, backed by Uganda, finally entered the country and restored order.

Today, the good news-bad news cycle that has characterized much of the post-independence period continues apace. Economic stagnation still grips the region, and civil wars continue to rage in Congo and Sudan. Even Zimbabwe and Côte d'Ivoire — once touted as examples of stability and economic success for the rest of Africa — recently have been plagued by civil unrest. Zimbabwe's economy has collapsed under the repressive rule of its longtime president Robert Mugabe. Meanwhile, ethnic violence has rocked Côte d'Ivoire, where only the presence of French and West African peacekeepers has allowed a fragile peace to take hold.

But some parts of the continent continue to make progress. In South Africa and in nearby Zambia, Botswana and Namibia strong democratic institutions have taken root and continue to grow.

Yet even there, the good news is tempered by other troubles. The new southern democracies recently have experienced both famine and an HIV/AIDS crisis that is affecting one in every five young adults in some areas and creating millions of orphans. [30]

CURRENT SITUATION

Slow Growth

The peaceful transfer of power throughout sub-Saharan Africa, coupled with rising prices for many African commodities, prompted many economists to predict the continent would outgrow Asia, Latin America and other parts of the developing world. Ghana, for instance, began the 1960s with a per-capita GDP nearly three times that of India.

Should Western donors impose strict conditions for African debt relief?

YES
George B.N. Ayittey, Ph.D.
Associate Professor of Economics, American University, President, Free Africa Foundation

Written for The CQ Researcher, August 2003

Africa owes more than $350 billion in foreign debt. Servicing that debt absorbs some 30 percent of export revenue, leaving scant resources to import critical materials for schools, hospitals and national development. About 80 percent of Africa's debt is owed to multilateral financial institutions, such as the World Bank, or to Western foreign-aid programs. But many of these aid programs failed in Africa because of mistakes made by both donors and the recipients.

Donors allocated aid to support Cold War allies and to woo various Marxist leaders from the Soviet bloc. They also tied aid — usually requiring the use of services offered by donor-country companies — reducing its effectiveness. As a result of those tie-ins, about 80 percent of U.S. foreign aid is spent in the United States. Foreign-aid allocations — cocooned in bureaucratic red tape and shrouded in secrecy — lacked transparency, and the people being helped were seldom consulted.

Meanwhile, African governments used loans to finance unproductive, grandiose projects of little economic value or simply squandered or embezzled the money. In many cases, the loans cannot be paid back because there is little to show for them.

But outright, unconditional debt relief would do Africa more harm than good: It would reward past, reckless borrowing behavior and make a mockery of any attempt to enforce accountability. If a person has accumulated a huge consumer credit-card debt, you don't just wipe off their debt and grant him access to the same credit cards without counseling.

Therefore, Africans would like to see the following conditions for debt relief:

- Full public accounting of external loans: The loans were contracted on behalf of the people, and they must know who took what loans and for what purpose.
- Repatriation of the loot stashed abroad by corrupt African leaders: The United Nations has estimated that in 1991 alone, more than $200 billion was siphoned out of Africa by the ruling elites.
- Debt relief should be restricted to the 16 African countries (out of 54) that are democratic; or,
- Debt relief should be given only to those countries with free media: Benin, Botswana, Cape Verde Islands, Ghana, Mali, Mauritius, Sao Tome & Principe and South Africa, according to Freedom House's 2003 Survey.

Without democratic accountability and a free intellectual environment to debate issues, debt relief to Africa would be meaningless.

NO
Michelle Denise Carter
Deputy Regional Director for East and Central Africa, CARE

Written for The CQ Researcher, August 2003

Poor countries pay rich countries nine times more in debt repayments than they receive in aid. In Ethiopia, where more than 100,000 children die each year from preventable illnesses like diarrhea, debt repayments amount to four times the amount of public spending on health services As a continent, Africa alone spends four times more to repay its debts than it spends on health care.

Obviously, debt burden continues to be a critical obstacle in Africa's development. Debt burden is a tangible symbol of both the vicious circle of poverty and the widening gap between the world's "haves" and "have-nots."

Strict conditions for debt relief do NOT help Africans, but simply stated, are another form of colonialism. In its poverty-reduction plans, Tanzania was given 157 policies as conditions for debt relief; Benin had 111. The donors decide what these conditions will be, and the donors decide satisfaction of compliance. Strict conditions make any and all reforms part of the donor agenda — with very little, if any, ownership by the recipient country. The Kenyan government, for example, promised many times to enact reforms in exchange for donors' resources, but those promises were broken. Who suffers? Poor people.

"Strings-attached" lending programs have failed to achieve substantial economic growth. Strict conditions are not only coercive but also highly ineffective. In fact, there is little or no evidence that attaching conditions reduces poverty. Too many times, the conditions imposed by donors punish poor performance on specific macroeconomic targets without consideration of appropriateness or capacity.

If donors are serious about reducing poverty in Africa, they cannot impose strict conditions for debt forgiveness. Better recommendations for debt forgiveness would include the promotion of good performance in broader poverty-reduction and development goals. In addition, donors should consider write-offs with no conditions for old unpayable debts and serious dialogue between poor countries and debtor governments, multilateral financial institutions and civil society on how to move forward on macroeconomic policies to further development and poverty reduction.

Donors should provide a platform for African success in reducing poverty that includes debt forgiveness, appropriate foreign aid and fairer trade practices. This will result in an Africa that can be more self-reliant and less dependent on the "generosity" of assistance from rich countries. This will also result in an Africa with a brighter future for generations to come.

AFP Photo/Marco Longari

A woman works in a new textile factory in Kampala, Uganda, one of several textile plants built recently in Africa to take advantage of a 2000 U.S. law allowing African countries to export to the United States without paying the usual tariffs.

But by the early 1970s, Africa's economic picture was bleak and getting bleaker. Widespread government mismanagement had created a business environment that discouraged foreign investors, who were needed to help Africa create an industrial base. Thus the continent was dangerously dependent on exports of coffee, cocoa, cotton, gold and other commodities that wildly fluctuated in price, even as other developing regions, particularly East Asia, were becoming low-cost exporters of manufactured goods.

"Most African countries were plagued by poor economic policies that discriminated against exporters," said Guy P. Pfeffermann, chief economist at the International Finance Corporation, an arm of the World Bank that promotes private foreign investment in the developing world. "The prevalence of often-inefficient state enterprises, horrendous red tape and uncertain macroeconomic policies generated investor uncertainty." [31]

Even in the booming 1990s, when most of the world was experiencing strong economic growth, most of Africa's economies failed to catch fire. There were some exceptions: Ghana, for example, grew at 6 percent for a few years.

Overall, however, per-capita income in sub-Saharan Africa actually declined by 0.2 percent from 1990 to 2001. Today, Africa remains the world's poorest region, with a per-capita GDP of only $460 per person, compared with $7,640 for Brazil and $36,410 in the United States. [32] In addition, life expectancy — at 46 years — is the world's lowest. [33] In industrialized nations, people routinely live into their late 70s.

Meanwhile, sub-Saharan Africa's share of global trade has dropped to a mere 1.6 percent, less than half the amount it had two decades ago. Similarly, its share of world investment plummeted from 4 percent in 1980 to 1.8 percent. [34]

Most economists blame Africa's economic troubles on a host of causes, but a woeful lack of good governance traditionally tops the list. "There's really no reason that any of these countries can't do well," says the World Bank's Wolgin. "All it takes is good government that is committed to the sorts of policies that promote growth."

For developing economies, promoting growth still means exports: matching foreign investment with cheap African labor. "They still don't have the same vision that Asian governments did when they began to grow" in the 1960s, Wolgin says. "For developing economies to really take off, they need to focus on exporting to the rest of the world."

Gearing up to export requires creating the right conditions for foreign investment, such as a stable currency, the rule of law and respect for property and contract rights, Wolgin says. "There also needs to be political stability," he adds.

Infrastructure is crucial as well. "It's not easy to transport things in Africa," Wolgin says, citing poor road and rail links. "And then once you reach the ports, you find that many of them don't work well either."

In addition, Africans themselves often lack the skills needed for success in a sophisticated, global economy. "Managerial expertise and organizational ability are lacking in many places," says Mazrui of Kenya's Jomo Kenyatta University. "They generally aren't being stressed by schools. The Europeans wanted Africans to do their chores, so they turned them into clerks. Unfortunately, this legacy of imperialism is still with us."

New Optimism

Some African countries — including Uganda, Mozambique and Ghana — are making great strides in opening up their economies to investment and growth. "A new generation of leaders in Africa is much more open to outside investment," says diplomatic correspondent Cobb. "The idea of African socialism, which kept many businesses away because they worried about having their factories nationalized, or whether they'd be able to repatriate their profits, is fading."

African leaders also are more willing to take responsibility for the continent's economic development. "They've turned a corner on this," Wolgin says. "Africans are beginning to recognize that their problems are theirs and not some outsider's responsibility."

Led by South Africa's Mbeki, African leaders have inaugurated the New Partnership for African Development (NEPAD), a framework for social and economic development. NEPAD's goals — such as government transparency, respect for human rights and greater openness to foreign investment — are not new. But there's a crucial difference: The plan is the handiwork of Africans, not imposed by donor countries, as in the past.

"We are taking responsibility for the success of the program," Mbeki said. "We can't say it's somebody else's plan. It's our plan." [35]

Meanwhile, the West has focused on boosting opportunities for African exporters. In 1999, the U.S. Congress enacted the Africa Growth and Opportunity Act, which allows most African goods to enjoy duty-free status. The law seems to be having the desired effect. Factories, particularly textile plants, have sprung up in Kenya, Uganda, Ghana and Ethiopia, creating jobs and earning foreign exchange for cash-strapped governments. [36] In Kenya, exports to the United States doubled in the first five months of 2003, from $38.5 million during the same period last year to $76.4 million. [37] Foreign investment also has quadrupled, from $14.9 million in 2000 to $60.6 million in 2002. [38]

Meanwhile, after years of stagnation, sub-Saharan Africa has been growing again — by 4.3 percent in 2001 and 3.2 percent last year, according to the United Nations Economic Commission for Africa (ECA) — a huge improvement over the 0.4 percent growth rate of the early 1990s. [39]

In 2003, Africa's GDP is expected to increase by 4.2 percent, the ECA predicts, even though the continent's largest and most sophisticated economy, South Africa, is only growing at a sluggish 1.5 percent. [40]

OUTLOOK

Bleak Future?

On July 8, the U.N. Development Program released its annual "Human Development Report," which measures living standards around the world.

Predictably, Africa fared poorly compared with the rest of the world. But the report also painted a bleak picture of the continent's long-term prospects, predicting that if current trends continue, sub-Saharan Africa will need roughly 150 years to meet the basic needs of most of its people. [41]

Such predictions are not surprising to American University's Ayittey. "The biggest reason Africa is in so much trouble is its leaders," he says. "They mismanage the economy and steal everything in the treasury and are not held accountable until someone comes along and kills them."

Unfortunately, there is little evidence that Africa's leadership deficit will be eliminated or even reduced in the coming decades, he says. "I'm not optimistic," he says. "For Africa, I see much of the same. It may even grow worse because these [leaders] are compounding already grave problems."

Trade analyst Pasicolan agrees. "There are still too many dictatorships and marginal democracies in Africa, and I don't see that changing any time soon," he says.

Moreover, some African leaders — including those who have been elected or are well-intentioned — are hamstrung by the past, Pasicolan points out. "They still blame Europe and the United States for their problems and think that they are responsible for solving Africa's problems," he says. "But look at Asian governments: They had a colonial period as well, but developed their own successful models in the post-colonial era that brought up people's living standards."

Others, though, wonder whether the problems Africa's leaders face are simply too enormous to handle. "You have this great wave of democratic reform and a real hope that they can make things right," says Hayes of the Corporate Council on Africa. "But it's going to be so hard because they have these crushing problems, like the disparity between rich and poor."

Diplomatic correspondent Cobb agrees. "The leadership in Africa is more open and more committed than ever," he says. "But look at the huge problems they face: high unemployment, massive slums, AIDS, a huge deficit in education. I just hope that they can act on their good intentions before they get overwhelmed."

Some scholars echo these views but argue that the prevalence of HIV/AIDS throughout much of the continent — more than any other factor — is likely to destroy Africa's chances for sustained development in the coming decades, particularly since the disease disproportionately impacts young adults, the most productive members of society. "There is every likelihood that AIDS will be a scourge for at least the next 15 or 20 years, and I can't imagine that will do anything but make matters worse," says the Kennedy School's Rotberg.

In parts of southern and eastern Africa, Rotberg points out, one in five adults has HIV or AIDS. To make matters worse, he notes, the disease is now spreading quickly in Nigeria and other parts of West Africa, where up to this point it hadn't been as bad.

Yet some experts are still optimistic about Africa's future. "Africans will be better off 10 or 20 years from now because they're learning how to better help themselves, and we're learning how to better help them," says the World Bank's Wolgin. "They've turned a corner on a lot of things, like not relying on military coups and learning that you can have a peaceful transfer of power."

Even AIDS, Wolgin says, is not an impossible obstacle. "The lesson of Uganda is that AIDS can be turned around," he says. The East African nation cut new HIV infections by more than half in the last 10 years through an aggressive education and condom-distribution program. [42]

Cato's Preble also thinks Africans themselves hold the key to their own success. "The people are getting a better sense of what they want and how to get it," he says. "On balance, this will inevitably push African governments toward a more democratic and prosperous future."

NOTES

1. Quoted in Somini Sengupta, "Leader of Liberia Surrenders Power and Enters Exile," *The New York Times*, Aug. 12, 2003, p. A1.

2. Frank P. Ardaiolo, "Liberia: U.S. Must Intervene," *The* [Rock Hill, S.C.] *Herald*, July 13, 2003, p. E1.

3. Quoted on "Fox News Sunday," July 6, 2003.

4. For background, see Kenneth Jost, "Democracy in Africa," *The CQ Researcher*, March 24, 1995, pp. 241-272.

5. Figures cited in "Freedom in the World: 2003," Freedom House; available at http://www.freedomhouse.org/research/index.htm.

6. Figures cited in "The Heart of the Matter," *The Economist*, May 13, 2000.

7. For a complete list of the U.N.'s development goals, see: http://www.un.org/esa/africa/africamillennium.htm

8. For background on the MCA program, see Steven Radelet, "Bush and Foreign Aid," *Foreign Affairs*, September/October 2003.

9. David Sanger, "G-8 Adopts Africa Aid Package, With Strict Conditions," *The New York Times*, June 28, 2003, p. A8.

10. Carolyn Skorneck, "AIDS Program Supporters Hope Senate Will Come Through with Full Funding for Program," *CQ Weekly*, July 26, 2003, p. 1876.

11. John Leicester, "Poor Nations Push the Rich for More Aid," The Associated Press, June 1, 2003. For background, see Mary H. Cooper, "Foreign Aid After Sept. 11," *The CQ Researcher*, April 26, 2002, pp. 361-392.

12. William Easterly, "Playing the Aid Game," *Forbes*, Aug. 11, 2003, p. 35.

13. Baffour Ankomah and Khalid Bazid, "Who Says Africa is Independent?" *New African*, July 1, 2003.

14. Amadou Toumani Toure and Blaise Compaore, "Your Farm Subsidies Are Strangling Us," *The New York Times*, July 11, 2003, p. A17.

15. "Human Development Report 2003," *United Nations Human Development Program*, 2003, pp. 264 and 272.

16. David Dollar and Craig Burnside, "Aid, Policies and Growth," *American Policy Review*, May 2000.

17. J.M. Roberts, *The Twentieth Century* (1999), p. 528.

18. *Ibid.*, pp. 528-529.

19. David Reynolds, *One World Divisible: A Global History Since 1945* (2000), p. 90.

20. John Reader, *Africa: A Biography of the Continent* (1998), pp. 645-646.

21. Figure cited in Roberts, *op. cit.*, p. 530.

22. *Ibid.*, p. 534.

23. Reader, *op. cit.*, pp. 656-662.

24. *Ibid.*, p. 670.

25. For background on Africa's structural-adjustment programs, see Kathy Koch, "Africa: Strategies for Economic Turnabout," *Editorial Research Reports*, Nov. 7, 1986, pp. 814-832.

26. Reynolds, *op. cit.*, p. 671.

27. *Ibid.*, p. 519.

28. Roberts, *op. cit.*, pp. 735-736.

29. *Ibid.*, p. 737.

30. For background, see David Masci, "Famine in Africa," *The CQ Researcher*, Nov. 8, 2002, pp. 921-944.

31. Guy P. Pfeffermann, "Africa's Investment Climate," International Finance Corporation, 1998. See http://www.ifc.org/economics/speeches/nov98.htm.

32. Economist.com

33. *Ibid.*

34. John Tagliabue, "Chirac to Call for a Shift from Battling Terrorism to Helping Poor Nations," *The New York Times*, June 1, 2003, p. A15.

35. Quoted in Sebastian Mallaby, "Africans to the Aid of Africa," *The Washington Post*, Sept. 23, 2002, p. A19.

36. Wilson F. Hunt Jr., "Trade With Africa," *The Chicago Tribune*, July 19, 2003, p. A24.

37. Figures cited in "Kenya Doubles U.S. Exports," *The Nation* [Kenya], Aug. 13, 2003.

38. "AGOA Exports Earn SH10 Billion," *The East African Standard*, Aug. 13, 2003.

39. See http://www.uneca.org/.

40. *Ibid.*

41. United Nations Human Development Program, *op. cit.*

42. Edwin Chen, "A Firsthand Look at Battle Against AIDS," *Los Angeles Times*, July 12, 2003, p. A3.

BIBLIOGRAPHY

Books

Freeman, Sharon, T., *Conversations with Powerful African Woman Leaders: Inspiration, Motivation, and Strategy*, American Small Business Exporters Association, 2002.
A business consultant who has worked in Africa profiles 11 African women who hold high-ranking government positions in their native countries.

Reader, John, *Africa: Biography of the Continent*, Knopf, 1998.
A research fellow at University College in London has written a thorough history of the African continent, from its geological formation to the post-independence period.

Articles

Beinart, Peter, "No Answer," *The New Republic*, July 21, 2003, p. 6.
The article examines the political impulses that drive American policy in Africa.

Cannon, Carl M., "Into Africa," *National Journal*, July 5, 2003.
An excellent overview of the continent's problems, written on the eve of President Bush's trip.

Cooper, Mary H., "Foreign Aid Since Sept. 11," *The CQ Researcher*, April 26, 2002, pp. 361-392.
Cooper explores the debate in the United States over foreign assistance.

Dickerson, John F., and Jeff Chu, "The African Bush," *Time*, July 2, 2003, p. 34.
The article chronicles President Bush's recent trip to Africa and details the hopes and expectations his visit created.

Gourevitch, Philip, "Africa Calling," *The New Yorker*, July 14, 2003, p. 29.
Gourevitch details the Bush administration's increasing involvement in Africa and the consequences for American foreign policy.

"A Region in Flames," *The Economist*, July 3, 2003.
An excellent overview of the recent civil wars that have been raging in Liberia, Sierra Leone and other West African countries.

Sachs, Jeffrey D., "A Rich Nation, A Poor Continent," *The New York Times*, July 9, 2003, p. A21.
The noted economist and director of the Earth Institute at Columbia University makes a plea for the rich world, especially the United States, to spend billions more helping impoverished Africa.

Stevenson, Richard W., "New Threats and Opportunities Redefine U.S. Interests in Africa," *The New York Times,* **July 7, 2003, p. A1.**
The article outlines the risks and potential benefits of increased American involvement in Africa.

Toure, Amadou Toumani, and Blaise Compaore, "Your Farm Subsidies Are Strangling Us," *The New York Times,* **July 11, 2003, p. A17.**
The presidents, respectively, of Mali and Burkina Faso, ask rich nations to end subsidies on cotton and other crops grown in Africa. Such subsidies, they say, are destroying Africa's agricultural sector and helping to keep the continent poor.

Walsh, Declan, "Liberia's War a Tangled Web," *The Boston Globe,* **July 31, 2003, p. A10.**
Walsh gives a good overview of the political forces at work pulling the small nation of Liberia apart.

Wax, Emily, "Africa's Women Beginning to See Progress in Politics," *The Washington Post,* **June 6, 2003, p. A14.**
Wax examines the routine hardships women in sub-Saharan Africa must endure, such as overwork and discrimination, and also charts their progress in the political realm.

Zakaria, Fareed, "Take the Lead in Africa," *Newsweek,* **Aug. 18, 2003, p. 35.**
A respected journalist and foreign-policy thinker argues in favor of sending American troops into Liberia.

Reports and Studies

Corruption Perceptions Index 2002, **Transparency International, 2002.**
The index ranks 102 countries in the world, from least to most corrupt. Most African states have high corruption indices.

Freedom in the World 2003: An Annual Survey of Political Rights and Civil Liberties, **Freedom House, 2003.**
An annual report on democracy and human rights in 192 countries, including sub-Saharan Africa.

Human Development Report 2003: Millennium Development Goals: A Compact Among Nations to End Poverty, **United Nations Development Program, 2003.**
A massive compendium detailing efforts to meet the United Nations Millennium Development Goals, which aim to halve poverty in Africa and elsewhere in the developing world by 2015.

For More Information

AllAfrica.com, 920 M. St., S.E., Washington, DC 20003; (202) 546-0777; www. allafrica.com. Provides African news from African news outlets.

CARE, 151 Ellis St., Atlanta, GA 30303; (404) 681-2552; www.careusa.org. One of the world's largest private humanitarian organizations.

Council for Emerging National Security Affairs, 1212 New York Ave., N.W., Suite 850, Washington DC 20005; (202) 289-7524; www.censa.net. A nonpartisan think tank founded in 1999.

Freedom House, 1319 18th St., N.W., Washington, DC 20036; (202) 296-5101; www.freedomhouse.org. Co-founded by Eleanor Roosevelt nearly 60 years ago, the non-partisan organization "is a clear voice for democracy and freedom around the world."

Heritage Foundation, 214 Massachusetts Ave., N.W., Washington, DC 20002; (202) 546-4400; www.heritage.org. The conservative think thank opposed U.S. military intervention in Liberia.

TransAfrica Forum, 1426 21st St., N.W., Suite 200, Washington, DC 20036; (202) 223-1960; www.transafricaforum.org. Lobbies on African issues and conducts educational training for minority students.

Transparency International, Otto-Suhr-Allee 97/9, 10585 Berlin, Germany; 49-30-343 8200; www.transparency.org. Monitors corruption around the world.

13

Torture

David Masci

AFP Photo/Issouf Sanogo

An Iraqi torture survivor, left, shows how secret police in Basra shocked him with electric wires. U.S. forces in Iraq are now seeking evidence of human rights abuses committed during Saddam Hussein's regime. More than 100 nations practice torture, according to human rights groups. The war on terrorism has sparked debate over the legality of U.S. interrogation methods.

From *The CQ Researcher*, April 18, 2003.

Just one day after British troops took control of Basra, in southern Iraq, the survivors of Saddam Hussein's torture chambers led reporters to an internal-security prison on the outskirts of town. In a room where a pair of electric cables hung from a wall, an Iraqi man pressed them to his ears and then his groin to show how shocks had been administered. [1] Others demonstrated how they were suspended from the ceiling, hands bound behind their backs.

Many had been arrested for participating in the three uprisings against Saddam's rule during the 1990s, others because they appeared too religious or simply spoke out against the regime.

"Thousands of people died here," said Ali Abu Hanief, who was held in the prison for a year. "Every one of us has a friend or relative who came here." [2]

Human rights groups have long criticized Iraq's regime for its brutality, a point graphically underscored by President Bush in his State of the Union address on Jan. 28. "International human rights groups have cataloged other methods used in the torture chambers of Iraq: electric shock, burning with hot irons, dripping acid on the skin, mutilation with electric drills, cutting out tongues and rape," the president said. "If this is not evil, then evil has no meaning." [3]

But Iraq is not an aberration. According to Amnesty International, torture is practiced in more than 100 countries to silence opponents, extract information or confessions and terrorize populations. "Torture is very common all over the world," says James Ross, a senior legal adviser for Human Rights Watch, an advocacy group based in New York. "We tend to think of it as something that is only used with high-profile political prisoners, but it takes place in criminal investigations and in other situations."

275

Torture Practiced on Five Continents

More than 100 countries on five continents allegedly practice torture, according to Amnesty International and the U.S. State Department. Although most nations accused of using torture are in the developing world, there are exceptions in Europe and elsewhere. Some human rights groups have accused the United States of torturing terrorism suspects, a charge American officials deny.

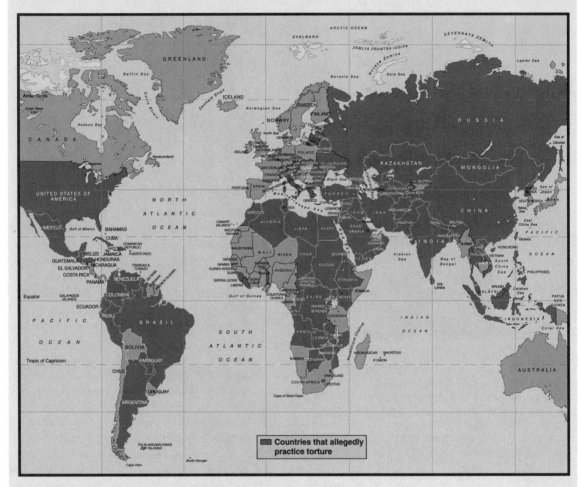

Sources: Amnesty International, U.S. State Department

The State Department's recently released "2002 Human Rights Report" says most of the countries that torture are in Asia, Africa and the Middle East. [4] Torture is less prevalent in Europe and North and South America, but not absent. In the Western Hemisphere, human rights groups frequently criticize Mexico, Cuba and Colombia for abuses. And in Europe, torture is widespread in Turkey and Bosnia-Herzegovina, according to the report.

It is a common misconception that torture only occurs in authoritarian or quasi-authoritarian states. Many Democratic governments have used — and still use — torture. British officials tortured anti-government militants during the decades-old conflict in Northern

Where Torture Is Severe

According to Amnesty International's 2002 Annual Report and the U.S. State Department, the following nations are among those cited for condoning widespread and particularly severe forms of torture:

Egypt: Torture in numerous detention centers includes electric shock, suspension by the wrists or ankles and threats of violence or rape.

North Korea: According to the State Department, "methods of torture routinely used on political prisoners included severe beatings, electric shock, prolonged periods of exposure, humiliations such as public nakedness, and confinement to 'punishment cells' too small for prisoners to stand upright or lie down."

China: Although torture is prohibited, in recent years thousands of members of the outlawed Falun Gong religious sect have been subjected to physical and psychological torture.

Colombia: All three sides in Colombia's civil war — the army, paramilitaries and left-wing guerrillas — routinely torture opponents.

Congo: Torture is practiced by all the combatants in the country's chaotic civil war.

Uzbekistan: The security services allegedly use suffocation, electric shock, rape and other sexual abuse.

Turkey: Military and law enforcement officials commonly use torture. Women detainees are routinely raped.

India: Torture is used in criminal investigations and in areas where political and sectarian violence is common, such as Kashmir.

Israel and Palestinian Authority: Both sides employ torture against opponents. A 1999 Israeli Supreme Court ruling outlawing torture has reduced, but not eliminated, the practice among the Jewish state's security services.

Sources: Amnesty International, U.S. State Department

In addition, torturers usually play mental games with their prisoners, such as telling them they already know the answers to the questions they are asking, or informing them that their families are in custody as well.

"There is almost always a psychological component: lying, shame, humiliation and threats," Iacopino says. "The purpose of torture is not just to hurt them, but to reduce them, to have power over them."

Some of these mental games are not, technically, torture, Ross says. "Lying to prisoners and telling them that you know certain facts are true or false is fine," he says. "But telling someone that you're torturing their children in the next room is wrong. That's torture."

Before the Sept. 11, 2001, terrorist attacks killed more than 3,000 people in the United States, the idea of Americans discussing the practicality or morality of torture would have been inconceivable. Yet with countries as diverse as the United States, Russia, the Philippines and Spain ramping up their anti-terrorism efforts, torture is being openly discussed and contemplated. Indeed, some say the boundaries for the uses of torture — and even the definition of torture itself — are becoming blurred.

In fact, in recent months the United States has been accused of torturing suspected terrorists being held at U.S. bases in Guantanamo Bay, Cuba, Afghanistan and Diego Garcia atoll in the Indian Ocean. U.S. officials acknowledge American interrogators are using "stress and duress" techniques to extract information from some of those prisoners, including leading members of the al Qaeda terrorist network, like Khalid Shaikh Mohammed, the supposed mastermind of the Sept. 11 attacks, who was arrested on March 1 in Pakistan.

"Stress and duress" puts psychological and physical pressure on suspects through methods such as sleep

Ireland, as did French authorities during Algeria's fight for independence in the 1950s and '60s.

Torture is still common in some democracies, notably India, where the military and police reportedly use it to control separatists in troubled regions like Kashmir. And Israel is widely thought to still use torture against suspected Palestinian terrorists, even though it was banned by the Supreme Court in 1999.

Torture methods vary widely, but there is a common thread. "Inevitably the person is beaten," says Vincent Iacopino, director of research at Physicians for Human Rights.

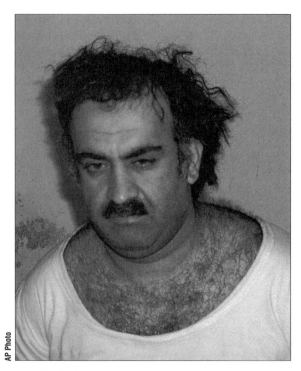

AP Photo

Khalid Shaikh Mohammed, considered the key planner of the Sept. 11, 2001, terrorist attacks, is being questioned by U.S. authorities reportedly using "stress and duress" techniques. He is shown moments after his capture in a raid in Pakistan on March 1.

deprivation, covering the head with a hood to cause disorientation and pinning prisoners in uncomfortable positions for hours. But U.S. officials and many security experts say these methods do not rise to the internationally accepted definition of torture.

They also contend that psychological and physical force shy of actual torture prompts many suspects to give up valuable information. "With many, many people it will work because everyone ultimately has a level of pain under which they will break," says security consultant Clinton R. van Zandt, former chief hostage negotiator for the FBI.

But human rights advocates and others say that subjecting someone to days without sleep or hours of physical discomfort meets the definition of torture set down by the United Nations. "Torture as defined by law is severe pain or discomfort, and these things seem to meet the test," says William F. Schulz, executive director of the human rights group Amnesty International USA.

Critics of U.S. policy also say the United States often has taken the easy way out: keeping its hands technically clean by sending some terrorist suspects to allies that use torture to question prisoners. [5]

The practice of using information gleaned under torture in other countries predates the Sept. 11 attacks. For instance, in 1995, Philippine security officials interrogated Abdul Hakim Murad, an alleged Islamic terrorist with information about a plot to blow up 11 U.S. airliners over the Pacific and fly another one into the headquarters of the Central Intelligence Agency in Virginia. Murad was later taken to the United States, where he was convicted based in part on evidence gleaned from his interrogation in the Philippines. He is currently serving a life sentence in federal prison. [6]

Schulz also disputes van Zandt's assertion that psychological or physical force extracts accurate information, arguing that prisoners will lie or make up facts to stop pain or other discomfort.

Human rights groups opposed to torture lobby governments around the world to abide by an international framework of treaties that outlaw the practice of torture. The cornerstone of the framework is the United Nations Convention Against Torture and Other Cruel, Inhuman or Degrading Treatment or Punishment, adopted in 1984 and ratified by more than 100 countries, including the United States.

In recent years, human rights advocates have adopted a new tactic: seeking the prosecution of leaders accused of torture and other abuses. Thus far, there only have been a few successes — most notably the extradition and trial of Serbian strongman Slobodan Milosevic.

Many activists want more world leaders held accountable for their actions, but others worry that widespread arrests would jeopardize international relations and geopolitical stability.

As experts and others look at all aspects of the practice of torture, here are some of the questions being asked:

Is the United States torturing suspected terrorists?

The U.S. government claims that it does not practice torture or condone its use by other countries. In fact, the State Department issues an annual report assessing and condemning other countries for using torture.

But critics allege the United States is using some of the same methods it deplores on terrorism suspects in U.S. custody overseas. "The State Department's human rights report on Iraq in 2001 lists 15 kinds of torture practiced by Saddam Hussein's regime, including prolonged sleep deprivation and verbal threats to family members," says Leonard Rubenstein, executive director of Physicians for Human Rights. "These are the same sorts of things allegedly being done by us."

However, U.S. officials maintain they treat prisoners lawfully. "We are in full compliance with . . . domestic and international law dealing with torture," White House spokesman Scott McClellan said on Dec. 27.

But according to *The Washington Post*, suspected terrorists in U.S. custody at Bagram air base in Afghanistan and Diego Garcia have been subjected to pain and emotional and physical stress.

Citing unnamed government counterterrorism officials, the story says prisoners have been held in painful, awkward positions or deprived of sleep for long periods. The officials also said that prisoners are often "softened up" by throwing them into walls or binding them in painful positions. "If you don't violate someone's human rights some of the time, you're probably not doing your job," said one of the officials. [7]

U.S. officials admit to using tough interrogation methods. "This is a highly classified area, but all you need to know is this: There was a 'Before 9/11' and there was an 'After 9/11,' " the CIA's coordinator for counterterrorism, Cofer Black, told a joint hearing of the House and Senate Intelligence committees last Sept. 26. "After 9/11, the gloves came off."

In "taking the gloves off," human rights activists say the United States may have crossed the line between ethical methods of interrogation and torture. "Torture is defined by international law as the administration of severe pain or discomfort," says Amnesty International's Schulz. "The torture convention even outlaws forms of severe stress or humiliation. So, of course, many of the things we hear about happening to these prisoners constitute torture."

But according to Anthony D'Amato, a professor of law at Northwestern University who has defended accused torturers, "There's a difference between torture and inhumane treatment. Causing someone stress or discomfort is not torture."

"Sleep deprivation or making someone stand in a certain position for a long time isn't torture," says security consultant Kelly McCann of Falmouth, Va., a CNN commentator and retired Marine major. Even causing

pain doesn't necessarily constitute torture, as long as it does not permanently harm the prisoner, McCann says. "There are things you can do, such as striking the common peroneal nerve on the leg, that can cause a lot of pain and won't do any damage," he says. "That seems perfectly reasonable to me."

McCann and D'Amato say the line between legitimate methods and torture is obvious. "You can't say exactly what it is, but you know it when you see it," D'Amato says. "[For example] holding a lit blowtorch to someone's feet is torture."

But according to Rubenstein, "if you are intentionally inflicting pain on someone, then you are torturing them. Period."

In addition, critics of the government's methods say, there is no difference between force that does or does not cause permanent damage. "The torture convention does not distinguish between temporary pain and permanent damage, nor should it," says Scott Silliman, director of the Center for Law, Ethics and National Security at the Duke University law school. "All pain, physical or mental, is torture, no matter how long it lasts."

But McCann counters that it is naive to try to apply such black and white definitions. "In the real world, people use force all the time in different situations," he says. "Do you know how many crackheads are kicked by the police? But that's not torture."

Andrew Bacevich, a former Army officer who teaches international relations at Boston University, agrees that strict definitions don't apply to the rough-and-tumble world of counterterrorism. "It's unrealistic to expect that, in the middle of a global war, we are going to treat deadly terrorists with all the traditional standards of chivalry," he says. "The urgency of the circumstances and the stakes will inevitably lead us to use methods that probably would not be acceptable at home but still do not amount to torture. We're not going to pull people's fingernails out."

But Americans need only ask themselves how they would feel if the U.S. POWs taken in Iraq were forced to endure sleep deprivation or physical or psychological pain, Rubenstein says.

"Everyone would be outraged," says Michael Greenberger, director of the Center for Health and Homeland Security at the University of Maryland at College Park.

Finally, if the United States is found to be using torture, its credibility will be nil when it tries to get other

U.S. Center Helps Survivors of Torture

For "John," a university-educated young man in West Africa, imprisonment for anti-government activism included torture. For five years, John was periodically incarcerated under inhumane conditions, surrounded by excrement and filth. He was beaten while suspended from the ceiling. His captors hit the soles of his feet and then forced him to walk on crushed stones.

When John learned he would be transferred to an even more brutal facility because he "hadn't learned his lesson," he went into hiding and eventually fled to the United States, where he was granted asylum.

"He was highly depressed — you could see it in his face and his body — this man had been severely affected by his torture," says Chuck Tracy, a clinical social worker at the Minneapolis-based Center for Victims of Torture (CVT). Founded in 1985 as the first U.S. rehabilitation center for torture survivors, the center treats 225 people a year from 70 countries.

Many torture survivors struggle with physical and emotional scars for a lifetime, while others achieve a semblance of recovery and return to a relatively normal life.

"The torturer's aim is to keep someone suspended in a time and place — in agony — for as long as they live," says Helen Bamber, founder of the Medical Foundation for the Care of Victims of Torture, in London. "I don't think of it as recovery from torture but as the process of recovery — it's a daily battle every morning for survivors."

Torture survivors suffer a range of problems, from post-traumatic stress disorder and depression to physical scarring and chronic pain. Each victim experiences torture differently, limited "only by the torturer's capacity to think of terrible and awful things to do," Tracy says.

Some survivors consider suicide, and many suffer panic attacks brought on by sights and sounds that remind them of their captivity and torture, says CVT Executive Director Douglas A. Johnson. In some of the most extreme cases, like that of Sister Dianna Ortiz, who was raped, burned and tortured by Guatemalan security forces, the abuse can produce amnesia-like effects, where the survivors cannot recall anything prior to their captivity and abuse. [1] (*See sidebar, p. 286.*)

The lingering physical effects of torture are often as difficult to overcome as the psychological. "Sometimes their

---

[1] Sister Dianna Ortiz with Patricia Davis, *The Blindfold's Eyes: My Journey from Torture to Truth* (2002).

---

countries to improve their human rights records, Rubenstein notes. "We've been a leader in the fight to stop torture, and we've had some real successes, but using that kind of moral leverage requires clarity on our part," he says. "With all of the ambiguity in the recent policy, we're losing that clarity, and our leverage."

Does torture extract reliable information from uncooperative suspects?

Experts agree that "breaking" someone through torture is possible. "Everybody breaks if it's no holds barred," says Stan Walters, a law-enforcement consultant and author of *Principles of Kinesic Interview and Interrogation.* "It's just a matter of when."

However, many of those experts maintain that forcing someone to talk through the use of torture does not produce useful information. "There is little reliable information to be gotten from someone who is screaming in agony," says Iacopino of Physicians for Human Rights.

"The information that you often get from people in pain is not credible, by definition," agrees Silliman. "Many people will say anything just to make the pain stop."

After the Sept. 11 terrorist attacks, U.S. intelligence officials said they had discounted warnings from al Qaeda prisoners in the Philippines about future attacks because the information had been obtained through torture. [8]

Moreover, Silliman and others say, torture and other forms of severe force are least effective against the very people with the most important information: resistance or opposition leaders and true believers. "The people most likely to have vital information just happen to be the people most likely to be steeled to torture," Rubenstein says.

"It's very hard to break people when they passionately believe in a cause," Silliman adds. "So what you get when you torture them, even severely, often turns out to be false information."

torturer will say, 'You're never going to physically recover from this.' One of the roles of the physician is to say, 'Well, they lied to you and this is OK now,' " Johnson says.

Recovery often begins with the therapist and survivor working up a history of their torture experiences. "One of the most important roads to resolution is recognition of the survivor's experiences," Bamber says. "Torture can hold someone paralyzed — trapped by memory and experience and nightmare, and those memories can be all-pervading." Tracy says his clients "often talk about the upsetting memories having control over them, rather than having control over their memories."

Recovery often means conquering those crippling memories. "The goal of recovery is for clients to be able to remember their torture without being overwhelmed by all sorts of negative feelings," Tracy says. Survivors feel they are making progress when they begin to have control over their memories.

While Bamber fears survivors never completely vanquish their memories of torture, she sees some hope for recovery. "Someone who survives, they have a resiliency, and . . . the therapist [must] try to retrieve that resilience and that part of the person that feels intact," she says.

For some survivors, a strong family upbringing may help them survive their torture and eventually recover, Tracy says. But Bamber thinks that people who had unstable childhoods often deal with torture more effectively.

Current events can also affect a patient's recovery, Bamber says. The CVT recommends that survivors not watch news coverage because it can trigger new nightmares and "re-traumatize" them, Johnson says.

Experts note that each survivor's response to torture is different, and as a result, there is no one-size-fits-all treatment. "We use music, drama, storytelling and alternative medicine, and we look on our philosophy as a holistic one — there is no pure science in torture rehabilitation," Bamber says.

Torture often attacks an individual's ability to form meaningful relationships, to trust other human beings, Bamber says. For that reason, some professionals think the mere act of forming a bond with their therapist may help some survivors recover.

"It rekindles their faith in their fellow man that not all people are like their torturer," Tracy says, "so I believe the relationship between therapist and client is curative in and of itself."

Following years of work and therapy, "John" resumed his education. He hopes to be a doctor and, so far, has received straight A's at a top state university.

"I'm very hopeful about survivors being able to recover," Tracy says. "That doesn't mean forget, but I do believe people can recover and get on with their lives and be relatively happy."

— *Benton Ives-Halperin*

But others say that physical and mental pressure is sometimes the only way to get prisoners to talk. "Of course it works," says Washington lawyer Robert Litt, a former deputy assistant attorney general during the Clinton administration. "The fact that so many people still use it suggests that it produces results."

Security consultant McCann agrees, but he cautions that torture alone is not effective. "You won't get what you want if you just apply pain," he says. "But when you couple that with things like vague threats and sleep deprivation, it can become overwhelming to someone."

Advocates of using force also contend that some or all of the information obtained with the use of stress, or even pain, can usually be verified. "When you're trying to obtain a confession, force is the wrong way to go, because we don't want people being forced to incriminate themselves," D'Amato says. "But when you're talking about getting information, it's very reliable, because you usually can confirm at least part of what was told to

you, and you can make sure the prisoner knows that."

"Inevitably, you'll have the ability to juxtapose what was said with other intelligence," agrees security consultant van Zandt. "So whatever someone tells you won't have to stand alone."

But opponents contend that anyone who finds value in torture or even "stress and duress" is simply trying to justify an immoral practice. "A strong psychological power allows someone to pretend that they are acting morally, that there is actually a reason for doing this," Iacopino says.

Should foreign leaders whose governments practice torture be subject to arrest?

When President Robert Mugabe of Zimbabwe was attending a summit in Paris in February, human rights activists unsuccessfully petitioned the French government to arrest him. [9] Mugabe's regime has been widely accused of torturing thousands of political opponents.

Human rights advocates argue the African leader should have been charged under both the international torture convention and French law.

The effort to arrest Mugabe reflects a relatively new and growing movement to hold leaders accountable for human rights violations. In 1998, for instance, former Chilean President Gen. Augusto Pinochet was held under house arrest in England for 16 months while a Spanish judge tried, without success, to have him extradited to Spain. The judge wanted to try Pinochet for torture, mass murder and other human rights violations against Spanish citizens in Chile during his 17-year rule. Similarly, human rights advocates tried unsuccessfully to get former Secretary of State Henry Kissinger arrested for alleged Vietnam-era crimes against humanity when he recently traveled to England.

Activists had more luck with former Serbian President Milosevic. He is currently standing trial in an international tribunal in the Netherlands for crimes against humanity allegedly committed against Croats, Muslims and others in the 1990s following the breakup of Yugoslavia.

In 1993, Belgium passed a law allowing anyone, including a sitting head of state, to be tried by Belgian courts for human rights abuses, regardless of whether the alleged crime had any connection to Belgium. [10] Since then, courts in Brussels have indicted Israeli Prime Minister Ariel Sharon and Cuban President Fidel Castro, among others. None has appeared in the dock, and the International World Court recently handed down a decision prohibiting the prosecution of sitting leaders.

Still, some activists maintain that being a head of state should not shield someone from prosecution for torture. "There should be no immunity when it comes to human rights abuses," says Frances Boyle, a professor of law at the University of Illinois, Champaign-Urbana. "We shouldn't be sending signals to leaders that they can act with impunity."

But foreign-affairs experts argue that arresting current leaders will make international relations difficult, if not impossible. Normal business between heads of state will be severely hampered, they say, weakening the world order.

"We live in a world of sovereign competing states, and those states need to exist in harmony for peace [to exist]," says Boston University's Bacevich. "But you can't have that harmony if leaders view themselves as targets."

Bacevich says activists mistakenly think international law can replace nation states as a force for stability and thus do not see the danger in arresting leaders. "That's very unrealistic, because international law doesn't have

the force to create international harmony and peace," he says. "So if they weaken nation states, they won't have anything to take its place. There will be a vacuum."

Others contend that it is overly paternalistic to have international bodies deciding what is acceptable behavior by a sovereign nation. "I don't believe in international jurisdiction," says Washington lawyer Litt. "Individual nations should take it upon themselves to police their internal political affairs, not some outside body."

Moreover, Litt fears that efforts to bring one or two leaders to justice could easily get out of hand. "If someone can arrest Robert Mugabe, then who's next?" he asks. "Some people think that what George W. Bush is doing to al Qaeda prisoners, and, of course, in Iraq are crimes against humanity."

But supporters counter that arresting sitting leaders will send exactly the right kind of message to brutal rulers. "We need to make it clear that torture is unacceptable, just like slavery is unacceptable, and that there can be no place in the international community for leaders who engage in torture," says Amnesty International's Schulz. "If the leader of another country cannot ever travel to other nations for fear of being arrested, maybe it's time for someone who doesn't torture people to take over."

BACKGROUND

Ancient Practice

History is filled with tales of torture, from the gruesome mistreatment of prisoners of war in ancient Mesopotamia (now Iraq) and Christ's flogging and crucifixion by the Romans to the torture chambers and gulags of the now-defunct Soviet Union.

Indeed, torture has often been employed by those claiming to be saving civilization and defended by great thinkers through the ages. The Greek philosopher Aristotle, for instance, endorsed torture as the most reliable way to extract information. [11] Even the Christian philosopher St. Augustine approved of its use.

Wall paintings and friezes from the earliest civilizations, in ancient Egypt and the Near East, depict scenes of enemies being abused in horrific ways. Even the freedom-loving Greeks employed torture, though usually against slaves, rather than citizens.

The Romans tried to regulate torture, creating a legal code governing how and on whom it could be used. Initially, only condemned prisoners and slaves who were defendants in criminal cases were subject to torture. Accused slaves could be beaten, whipped, stretched on the rack or burned with hot irons, as long as injuries did not cause death or permanent damage. The condemned also were subjected to abuse that included crucifixion and attack by wild animals. [12]

Over the centuries, the Romans expanded the kinds of people who could be legally tortured to include slaves who were witnesses in criminal cases and, by the fourth century, free people charged with a crime.

As the Roman Empire crumbled and Christianity became the dominant force in much of Europe, the practice of torture started to fade. Christians, who had suffered atrocities at the hands of the Romans, initially opposed torture. An assembly of cardinals formally condemned the practice in 384. [13]

By the height of the Middle Ages, however, the Catholic Church had found torture to be effective in the war against heresy. In 1252, Pope Innocent IV declared that torture was justified if used against heretics.

As courts of law were established in medieval Europe, civil authorities also began using torture to extract confessions from defendants. Previously, guilt or innocence often had been determined by trials of combat or endurance, the idea being that God would favor the innocent.

For the next 600 years, torture was used widely throughout Europe. As in ancient Rome, the practice at first was only used with certain segments of society. In many places, women, children, aristocrats and the clergy could not be tortured. But by the 16th century, most of the exemptions had fallen away. [14]

Among the more common torture devices during this era was the strappado, a machine that held victims aloft by a rope tied to their hands, which were bound behind their backs. Victims would be raised and then dropped halfway to the floor, in an excruciatingly painful jerking motion. People were also stretched on the rack or subjected to leg or thumb screws.

Reform Campaign

In the 18th century, as part of a broader campaign of penal reform, the use of torture was increasingly questioned and opposed. Enlightenment thinking, especially in Northern Europe, held that convictions should be obtained through investigation rather than forced confessions. Many said torture, like slavery, was a scourge that needed to be stamped out if society was to progress.

Zimbabwean President Robert Mugabe attends a summit meeting in Paris in February after human rights activists unsuccessfully tried to get France to charge him with torturing political opponents. The attempt reflects a growing movement to hold leaders accountable for human rights violations.

In 1754, Prussia became the first state to officially abolish torture. By 1800, most other European states had followed suit. In 1874, the French novelist Victor Hugo naively declared, "Torture has ceased to exist." [15]

But many European countries, including France, were still flogging and abusing prisoners. Moreover, Europeans were torturing the native peoples in their ever-expanding colonial empires. The Belgians terribly mistreated Africans in the Congo by the tens of thousands, often maiming and dismembering them. In many of these lands, especially in Africa and Asia, local authorities had used torture long before the Europeans arrived. [16] Meanwhile, Americans used whipping and other forms of torture to punish their African slaves or to keep them from escaping.

In the decades immediately before and after the turn of the 20th century, new ideas and institutions emerged aimed at creating a more humane world. For instance, in 1863, the International Committee of the Red Cross was founded in conjunction with the Geneva Conferences of 1863 and 1864, which set guidelines for the treatment of wounded prisoners of war. Other treaties established other humanitarian standards. [17]

20th-Century Horrors

Despite these good intentions, the 20th century saw the use of torture on a scale that few could have imagined. The

CHRONOLOGY

1700s-1800s *Some countries begin to ban torture.*

1754 Prussia becomes the first nation to outlaw torture. Within 50 years, most European countries ban the practice.

1863 International Committee of the Red Cross is founded in Geneva to promote humane treatment of prisoners of war (POWs).

1874 French novelist Victor Hugo declares, "Torture has ceased to exist."

1880 Belgium begins its conquest of the Congo, killing millions of Africans over the next four decades.

1900s-Present *Widespread torture by fascist and communist states sparks international anti-torture efforts.*

1917 Russian Revolution gives birth to communism. Millions of people are killed or tortured by later communist regimes in Russia, China and other nations.

1932 Adolf Hitler comes to power in Germany. Torture is widely used by the Nazis.

1945 War crimes trials for German and Japanese officials and military officers begin in Nuremberg and Tokyo.

1948 United Nations adopts the Universal Declaration of Human Rights.

1949 Convention Relative to the Treatment of Prisoners of War is adopted in Geneva, Switzerland; the treaty outlaws the torture of POWs.

1954 Algeria's war for independence from France begins, leading to the torture of thousands of Algerians.

1961 Amnesty International is founded in London.

1977 U.S. State Department's first "Report on Human Rights" details torture and other abuses in other countries.

1978 Human Rights Watch founded in New York.

Dec. 10, 1984 U.N. adopts Convention Against Torture and Other Cruel, Inhuman or Degrading Treatment or Punishment.

1985 Center for Victims of Torture (Minneapolis, Minn.) and Medical Foundation for the Care of Victims of Torture (London) are founded.

1988 U.N.'s Committee Against Torture is established to investigate allegations of abuse and monitor treatment of prisoners by nations at war.

1993 Belgium allows its courts to hear cases against the alleged perpetrators of atrocities, even those committed in other nations.

1992 Yugoslavia begins coming apart, sparking nearly a decade of war and human rights abuses.

1994 U.S. Senate ratifies U.N. Torture Convention.

June 26, 1997 U.N. declares International Day in Support of Victims of Torture.

1998 Former Chilean President Gen. Augusto Pinochet is put under house arrest pending extradition to Spain on charges he abused Spanish citizens in Chile during his 17-year rule. After 16 months, Pinochet is released for health reasons.

May 1999 Israel's Supreme Court bans use of torture.

Sept. 11, 2001 Terrorist attacks on the United States lead to the detention of terrorism suspects in the U.S., Afghanistan and elsewhere. Human rights advocates charge — and U.S. officials deny — that torture is being used to get information from detainees.

2002 Serbian strongman Slobodan Milosevic goes on trial in The Hague, Netherlands.

March 11, 2003 International Criminal Court formally opens in The Hague.

April 2003 American and British forces find evidence of widespread torture in Basra and other Iraqi cities.

increase was largely driven by the rise of communism and fascism — authoritarian ideologies embraced in many of the largest and most powerful nations in the world, notably the Soviet Union, Italy, Japan, Germany, China and Spain. In all of these countries, the state became supreme, and torture often was used to break resistance to the new order.

In the Soviet Union, for instance, tens of millions of farmers, intellectuals, priests and others were tortured, imprisoned or killed to stamp out "the individual" and make way for collective society. Just over a decade later, in an effort to "cleanse" and "purify" society, Nazi Germany subjected millions of communists, Jews, Gypsies and other "undesirables" to unspeakable punishments and medical experiments before killing them in concentration camps.

In many of these states, scientists were ordered to make torture even more excruciating: Drugs were developed to inhibit the body's ability to deaden pain. In Nazi concentration camps, doctors turned torture into a macabre branch of medical science, experimenting on prisoners to see how much pain and stress their bodies could endure before dying. [18]

As the depravity of Germany and other countries became widely known, a new movement emerged to end torture and human rights abuses.

"What happened in World War II sparked new ideas on how to stop torture," says Elisa Massimino, director of the Washington office of the Lawyers Committee for Human Rights. "Since then, these ideas have slowly gained acceptance."

"We've had a mushrooming of human rights laws since the war and as a result of the war," agrees Duke University's Silliman.

The first manifestation of these new ideas was the Universal Declaration of Human Rights. Adopted by the U.N. General Assembly in 1948, the declaration banned torture as part of a broader guarantee of right and freedoms. [19]

At the same time, however, the Cold War between the United States and the Soviet Union was beginning, leading to a series of small and large proxy wars around the globe. Regimes allied with both sides engaged in torture during these wars. In places like Indonesia, Greece, Cuba and Angola, officials supported and often trained by the U.S. or the Soviet Union abused or tortured real or perceived opponents.

Meanwhile, within the Soviet Union and its Eastern European allies, torture continued to be widespread, used against both political opponents and criminal suspects, although the death of Josef Stalin in 1953 put an end to some of the regime's worst practices.

Torture was also common in communist China, especially during the Cultural Revolution of the 1960s, when millions were subjected to physical and mental abuse.

But the belief that torture was limited to communist tyrannies and authoritarian regimes was dispelled in the late 1950s by revelations that France was torturing large numbers of Algerians, many of whom had risen up against their French colonial masters in a successful bid for independence.

Torture also sporadically occurs in the United States, where police officers have sometimes been accused of abusing criminal suspects. Perhaps the most high-profile case occurred in New York in 1997, when police beat and sodomized a Haitian immigrant named Abner Louima. In another famous incident, Los Angeles police brutally beat suspect Rodney King after a high-speed chase.

Several non-governmental organizations (NGOs) have formed in recent decades to fight torture in all countries. The first and most well known, Amnesty International, was founded in 1961 in London. It has developed several innovative methods to pressure countries to stop using torture. For instance, Amnesty International routinely organized mass letter-writing campaigns in which thousands of members write a country's leader demanding an end to torture. The group also sometimes "adopts" individual prisoners of conscience and lobbies for their release.

Human Rights Watch is another prominent anti-torture NGO, founded in New York in 1978 to investigate and publicize human rights abuses, including instances of torture.

International Law

The post-World War II era has seen the development of a substantial body of both international and domestic law banning torture. Both the United Nations Universal Declaration of Human Rights (1948) and the International Covenant of Civil and Political Rights (1966) — prohibit the use of torture against anyone for any reason. Moreover, the Geneva Convention of 1949 also bans the torture and humiliating treatment of prisoners of war.

International common law also prohibits torture. War crimes trials, starting with the Nuremberg and Tokyo tribunals of the late 1940s, have classified torture as a "crime against humanity."

'A Nightmare That Does Not End'

In 1987, Sister Dianna Ortiz, a young Ursuline nun from the United States, went to Guatemala as a missionary. While teaching children in the rural hamlet of San Miguel two years later, she was abducted by government security forces who accused her of aiding anti-government rebels. She was imprisoned at a secret detention center and raped and tortured until she escaped 24 hours later.

She spent the next decade trying to recover from her traumatic experience. She also tried, unsuccessfully, to find out who had tortured her and whether American officials had been complicit in the abuses then occurring in Guatemala.

Today, Sister Dianna is the director of the Torture Abolition and Survivors Support Coalition International, based in Washington, D.C. Recently, she was awarded a fellowship by Ashoka, a nonprofit organization that supports social entrepreneurs. Her unsparing account of her experience — *The Blindfold's Eyes: My Journey from Torture to Truth* — was published last year. Sister Dianna recently discussed her ordeal with *CQ Researcher* staff writer David Masci at her office.

On speaking out:

"One of the common messages that torturers say to survivors is that if we survive, no one will believe us. So it takes great courage to come forward because there's always that possibility that we won't be believed. . . . We live with these memories 24 hours a day, which is just one of the reasons why I believe that it's important to educate the public to speak out against torture and to break that silence that surrounds it. It's a plague and it's destroying lives."

On her shock at being tortured:

"I was aware that human rights violations occurred [in Guatemala], but I never thought, as an American, that I would experience them firsthand. . . . It was my first experience with any form of violence. I didn't know that people could be so evil."

On being tortured:

"Talking about it is almost like going back in time and reliving it. . . . On Nov. 2, 1989, I was abducted and put into a police car. I was blindfolded and taken to a military installation in Guatemala City. That's where the nightmare began, a nightmare that does not end, even to this day. During my detention, I was interrogated. I was burned with cigarettes over 111 times. I was gang-raped. I also heard other people screaming in the building. Those are screams that even to this day I can still hear.

"One of the most difficult parts of my torture was my encounter with another woman who had been severely tortured. At one point during my torture, I was taken to another room, and that's where I met her. Her breasts had been severed and there were maggots in her body. It was very horrible. I don't know how long we were there. They returned, and they had with them a video camera and a camera, and the policeman had a machete and he forced it into my hands, and I think at that moment I thought that finally this nightmare would end — that they were going to force me to use the weapon to end my life. But they forced me to . . ." Sister Dianna found it too painful to finish the story. In her book, she says the policeman held the machete in her hands and forced her to stab the woman repeatedly.

On her escape:

"At one point, I was returned to the room where I had initially been taken, and I became aware of another person in the room. They referred to him as their boss, Alejandro. . . . When I saw that he was not Guatemalan, I was shocked that someone with white skin was in the clandestine prison in Guatemala and could give orders to Guatemalan torturers. He told them that

---

But the seminal anti-torture document is the United Nations' 1984 Convention Against Torture and Other Cruel, Inhuman or Degrading Treatment or Punishment. The so-called Torture Convention defines torture as "any act by which severe pain or suffering, whether physical or mental, is intentionally inflicted on a person" to either obtain information or a confession, or to punish or coerce that person.

The convention, signed by 130 countries including the United States, also states that torture is not allowed under any circumstances, even during war or public emergency. In addition, it authorized the establishment of a Committee Against Torture to monitor signatory states' compliance with the convention. Formed in 1988, the committee receives reports from treaty signatories on their treatment of prisoners and reviews com-

I was an American and that my disappearance had become public. He eventually led me out of the building and put me into a Jeep and told me that he was going to take me to see a friend at the U.S. Embassy who was going to help me leave the country. I asked Alejandro if he was an American and he asked me why I wanted to know. The fact that he spoke Spanish with an accent and that his skin color was white conveyed to me that he was an American.

"I'm not sure what his plans were — whether he was going to take me to the U.S. Embassy or take me to another torture center. I just knew that I had to get away from him. At one point, at a stoplight, the Jeep stopped. The door was unlocked and I managed to get out."

Sister Dianna Ortiz was doing missionary work in Guatemala when she was abducted and brutalized by government security forces. She now runs a U.S. group that works to stop torture.

CQ Press/David Masci

On her recovery:

"I [had] so many reactions: nightmares, flashbacks and fear shadowed me everywhere. And I had trouble with my memory. I couldn't recognize the people who were closest to me before my torture. I couldn't articulate what was happening to me, because, in my mind, I thought I was going crazy. And people around me just hoped I would forget what had happened and get on with my life. But it was impossible to do that. . . .

"I became aware of the Kolver Center [a Chicago treatment facility for torture survivors]. The people there allowed me to be myself. I did not have to justify why I was drinking 24 cups of coffee a day to avoid sleep or nightmares or why I was showering so many times a day or why I refused to go out. And they also helped me understand that my reactions were normal reactions to an abnormal situation, and that torture was not primarily about Dianna Ortiz, it was about terror. It was about terrorizing communities and whole societies."

On her faith:

"After violating me, the policeman whispered in my ear: 'Your God is dead.' And he was right. My God died in that prison. Coming out of that experience, I have struggled because I was very angry with God. I could not understand why God had not intervened to stop the torture of people. . . . I had a faith crisis. My image of God changed. In a sense, God was reborn. The God I had known, the God of the sacraments, the God of scripture. . . . had been crushed. . . . Now I know that God is not responsible for people's actions. We're responsible for our own actions. We're responsible for each other."

On the widespread use of torture:

"Torture is a horrible instrument that destroys lives and is destroying lives. No one is immune. That's the message I want to get out: that it can happen to anyone. What happened in Iraq with Saddam is happening in Colombia, it's happening in Guatemala, it's happening in China. The only thing different is the name of the country."

plaints by individuals claiming to have been tortured.

It also monitors the treatment of prisoners around the world. But efforts by the U.N.'s Economic and Social Council to authorize and fund prisoner-monitoring activities were opposed last year by dozens of countries, including Japan, Australia and the United States.

American officials argued that allowing international monitors into U.S. prisons would violate the U.S. Constitution, which puts most of the American prison systems in the hands of individual states. Others say the U.S. government balked at monitoring because it did not want the committee demanding access to Camp X-Ray in Guantanamo Bay, where al Qaeda and Taliban prisoners are being held. [20]

Last year, American negotiators at the U.N. tried to find a compromise that addresses U.S. concerns but allows monitoring to go forward. But negotiations with supporters of strict monitoring, led by European countries, broke down in July. The U.S. responded by threatening to withhold its share of the cost of monitoring. Ultimately, the monitoring scheme was approved, with the U.S. abstaining.

Human rights officials are baffled at U.S. opposition, since the committee can only send monitors into countries that specifically give it permission to do so. Ross, the senior legal adviser at Human Rights Watch, says he understands why the United States opposes allowing monitors into American prisons, even though he wishes they would do so. "I don't understand why we would be opposed to monitors going to other countries," he says. "It doesn't make sense."

According to Ross, "Torture is a difficult problem to address [because] countries always deny that they are doing it. So, having monitors that can actually get into certain places and find out what's going on would be very helpful."

But American officials remain wary. In a recent letter, John Davidson, deputy U.S. representative to the Economic and Social Council, called the scheme "overly intrusive."

The United States has also refused to join or participate in the newly formed International Criminal Court (ICC), which is beginning to receive numerous torture and torture-related cases. [21] The court, which formally opened in The Hague on March 11, will have jurisdiction over political and military leaders who engage in torture and other human rights abuses.

American opposition to the ICC stems from a fear that U.S. military and civilian officials will be in danger of arrest every time the country sends troops to another country, even to participate in peacekeeping. "We are particularly concerned about the potential for politically motivated prosecutions in the framework of this court," said State Department spokesman Richard Boucher the day the court formally opened. [22]

But others say the ICC could significantly reduce torture worldwide. "It will send a very clear message that if you think you can torture your people with impunity, think again," says the University of Illinois' Boyle. "It takes the right approach — going after the big fish — the leaders who have the power to stop torture."

Duke University's Silliman agrees. "Traditionally, international law has differed from domestic law in one important way: There was no way to enforce it," he says. "Now with the ICC, we finally have a way to enforce international human rights law, and that is very important."

CURRENT SITUATION

Authoritarian Tool

Many of the more than 100 nations worldwide that still use some form of torture are authoritarian, like Syria or North Korea, or have weak or flawed democratic institutions, like Ethiopia. (*See map, p. 276.*)

"Countries with strong democratic institutions are much less likely to employ torture, because democracy leads to accountability," says Massimino of the Lawyers Committee for Human Rights. The lack of accountability often leads to a disregard for the rule of law and governing bodies that operate in secret, which in turn leads to torture, Massimino says. "Anywhere you have a legal system that's not transparent, where you can be detained indefinitely and without a lawyer, is a place that has the right conditions for torture."

Ross agrees. "When you have a free society, the press can publicize abuses and watchdog groups can investigate the government. It makes a difference."

Nations use torture for a variety of reasons. "In many cases it's an accepted and ingrained part of the criminal justice system and the legal system won't do anything about it," Massimino says. "It's the way things have always been done, so, why change?"

Some nations, like Iraq or Syria, abuse citizens to instill fear in those who might oppose the current regime. "They target individuals perceived as a threat to the regime," says Iacopino of Physicians for Human Rights. "With torture, you can silence that individual and send a message to anyone else. It's a cheap and effective way to keep control of the opposition."

Many countries, like China and Egypt, also allegedly use torture as an investigative tool in criminal cases. "In some places torture is a substitute for investigation and adjudication," Iacopino says. "It's a shortcut for the police."

"A lot of them do it out of frustration or as an easy way to get convictions," says Ross, who adds that many police forces are pressured to find criminals, but are not given the resources they need to do so. "If you go into police stations in many parts of the developing world, you see that they lack training and proper investigative tools, like equipment for fingerprinting or DNA identification," he says. "Professionalizing these people could go a long way toward helping to end torture by the police."

But more professional law enforcement isn't enough,

he says. "The political leadership needs the desire and will to fight it, because it's not easy to stamp it out," he says. "That means people who do it must be prosecuted."

Indeed, in Israel, strong public opposition to torture led to a landmark Supreme Court ruling. In May 1999 the court unanimously held that torture could not be used in interrogations of Palestinian detainees and other prisoners.

Still, while Israel's Shin Bet security agency is no longer allowed to use rough methods — which includes violent shaking (a practice that killed at least one Palestinian) and the "shabeh position" of bending someone backwards over a chair — some human rights advocates contend the government has not entirely abandoned torture.

Post-War Iraq

While hundreds of U.S. military personnel fan out across post-Saddam Iraq searching for weapons of mass destruction, another group of American soldiers is looking for a different kind of "smoking gun." The 75th Exploitation Task Force is charged with locating and documenting Iraqi crimes against humanity, including torture.

The task force includes members of the Army's Criminal Investigation Division. [23] If initial discoveries in the field are any indication, the task force will have a lot of work ahead of it. In a number of cities, U.S. and British troops have found evidence of torture, including an array of torture instruments and records. In Nasariya, for instance, U.S. Marines found cells with torture equipment and photographs of victims, including some who had been burned alive. [24]

President Bush has already publicly ruled out using international courts to try Saddam Hussein (assuming he is captured alive) and other members of his regime charged with war crimes. Instead, the administration has said that suspects will be tried by U.S. military courts or by tribunals established and manned by Iraqis.

"We will work with the Iraqi people to create an Iraqi-led process that will bring justice for the years of abuses that have occurred," said Pierre-Richard Prosper, U.S. ambassador-at-large for war crimes issues. "For the current abuses, the crimes, particularly against U.S. personnel, we believe that we have the sovereign ability and right to prosecute these cases. We are of a view that an international tribunal for the current abuses is not necessary." [25] The abuses include the apparent executions of U.S. prisoners of war.

But human rights groups say the U.S. should turn Iraqi war criminals over to an international tribunal, as has been done with war crimes suspects from the former Yugoslavia. "We don't want to look like we're having some sort of victors' justice," said Raj Purohit, legislative counsel for the Lawyers Committee for Human Rights. "We want to provide a credible trial for individuals."

Others contend that an international tribunal will help the U.S. advance Iraqi reconstruction and ease America's frayed relations with its allies. "An international trial — transparent, professional and conforming to accepted legal standards — would greatly advance efforts to reconstruct Iraq and restore damaged international relations," Amy Ross, an associate professor of geography at the University of Georgia specializing in human rights, wrote recently. [26]

U.S. Methods

The United States has detained more than 3,000 terrorism suspects since the Sept. 11 terrorist attacks. Most were captured during the 2001 war against the Taliban regime in Afghanistan, in raids in countries like Pakistan, or arrested in the United States for alleged visa violations.

About 650 of the less important alleged Taliban and al Qaeda members are being held in Guantanamo Bay in Cuba. A large group of higher-level suspects has been detained at Bagram air base, an American military facility in Afghanistan.

The United States government has not said how it is interrogating the prisoners, only that they are being treated humanely and not being tortured.

But statements from unnamed U.S. officials indicate the prisoners are being subjected to "stress and duress," a combination of physical and mental pressure.

According to an unnamed American official quoted in *The Wall Street Journal*, a component of "stress and duress" is disorientation, which makes a prisoner much less likely to be able to hold out against interrogators. "You deprive him of what he's used to and comfortable with," the official said. "You deprive him of his surroundings. You move him . . . geographically, physically, emotionally. You put him someplace he's unfamiliar with. You deprive him of food, water and sleep. You make morning night and you make hot cold." [27]

Prisoners can be shown falsified documents to make them confirm or deny something; they can be screamed at or threatened by interrogators. [28]

AFP Photo/Shane T. McCoy

Suspected members of the al Qaeda terrorist group and Afghanistan's Taliban are held under tight surveillance at Camp X-Ray at Guantanamo Bay, Cuba. Human rights activists say their harsh treatment amounts to torture.

Sleep deprivation is another tool used by American officials. The suspect is forced to stay awake, sometimes for up to four or more days, by using bright lights, noise and other stimuli. "When they do this to you, first you get angry," security consultant van Zandt says. "But then you become more and more disoriented, more susceptible to giving information."

Many analysts believe U.S. interrogators at Bagram and elsewhere are professionals, who are probably using very sophisticated means to get suspects to tell what they know. "I get the sense that they know exactly what they're doing and that they're doing this the right way," McCann says.

Doing it the right way usually means being patient, McCann and other experts say. "Unless you have some time-sensitive information that you need immediately, you need to be willing to take your time," van Zandt says.

Experts say an interrogator should take time to understand and bond with a suspect. He must also be able to "set aside his own personality and his own value systems and his own beliefs, and to assume the personality of the person he's interrogating," says law-enforcement consultant Walters. "They've got to be good communicators and great listeners."

According to Walters, interrogators should find areas of common ground — be they taste in food, movies or even politics. The idea is to make the suspect feel like it is his duty to talk to the authorities, he says.

But common bonds may not be easy to establish with suspected terrorists who hail from completely different countries and cultures. And many, like Khalid Shaikh Mohammed, may have time-sensitive information about the whereabouts of other suspects and the timing and targets of future attacks.

"A lot depends on circumstances: What do I need and how soon do I need it?" asks van Zandt. "If things aren't working very well or you have to hurry up, you get crude and you get crude quickly. And yes, you get physical."

Getting physical can entail several things. For instance, a suspect can be tied down and left in an uncomfortable position for hours. Interrogators quoted in the *Journal* and other newspapers also allude to the use of hitting ("a little bit of smacky face"), although not severe beating. [29]

Harvard Law Professor Alan M. Dershowitz said he understands why law enforcement and intelligence officials use force or even torture to extract sensitive information from terrorists. "I have little doubt that torture has, on occasion, prevented the deaths of innocent people," he told CBS' "60 Minutes."

But Dershowitz also says that if the United States is going to occasionally torture a suspected terrorist, it must do it in the open, and put certain safeguards in place. "If it's going to happen — and it is going to happen — we can't just close our eyes and pretend that we live in a pure world," he said. "Get a warrant, justify in front of the judge the fact that this is the only conceivable way to save thousands of lives which are imminently in danger." [30]

OUTLOOK

Human Nature?

Some experts are not surprised that torture still flourishes, despite the substantial body of international law and international NGOs dedicated to extinguishing the practice.

Should the United States torture terrorist suspects to gather information?

YES
Clinton R. Van Zandt
Security consultant, Fredericksburg, Va.

Written for The CQ Researcher, April 2003

In man's search for truth down through the ages, "trial by ordeal" often has been resorted to when a suspect refused to talk. In recent times, however, numerous nations and international bodies have legislated against the intentional infliction of pain or suffering in an attempt to gain information or a confession.

Most civilized people would say they oppose the inhuman or degrading treatment of another human being. But what happens when there is a so-called "ticking time bomb" — a situation when a suspect is thought to have time-sensitive information affecting the lives of thousands — or even millions — of people? When the ticking bomb is factored into the equation, the physical and psychological rules of engagement suddenly become a sticky sea of gray for many otherwise absolutists.

The U.S. once taught friendly governments how to extract information from prisoners by the use of coercive techniques known as "stress and duress." Interview strategies were designed to exhaust the individual's ability to resist while providing him with the rationalization he needed to cooperate.

In the war against terrorism, we seek to gain intelligence about our adversary of immediate as well as long-term strategic value. In both cloak-and-dagger missions and law-enforcement operations, there may come a time when our nation must quickly try to obtain information critical to the lives of millions of people from a person who refuses to talk.

To remain a nation based upon the rule of law, the United States needs to establish a court at the national level before which the government could argue that torture was essential to extract critical information. The court would be required to rule on the matter immediately, and if in agreement, it would be able to issue a "duress-interview warrant" allowing the authorities to do whatever was necessary to obtain the needed information from the prisoner. There would be no appeal process and no public or media scrutiny. The authority of the court would be absolute.

In short, the overriding public-safety issue would take precedence over a prisoner's human rights. Without such a mechanism, we are left with conventional methods of interrogation while watching the seconds on the time bomb tick away, as the only person who might know how to stop the clock remains mute and simply awaits our fate. And lastly, should time allow, we still need to verify and corroborate the information before we act on it.

NO
Vincent Iacopino, M.D., Ph.D.
Director of Research, Physicians for Human Rights

Written for The CQ Researcher, April 2003

Torture cannot be justified by any government, for any reason, despite recent reports of U.S. officials and others attempting to justify such practices. Torture is unequivocally prohibited in international law. This legal and moral imperative was established in the aftermath of Nazi war crimes as a rhetorical statement of moral and human identity. Under the U.N. Convention Against Torture, the United States is obligated to prohibit torture, ensure prompt and impartial investigations and prosecute perpetrators. Additionally, on countless occasions the State Department's Country Report on Human Rights Practices has criticized governments that torture, in some cases the same practices the U.S. is now accused of committing in its "war on terrorism."

Those now advocating the use of torture risk undermining principles of justice and the rule of law in what appears to be an unfortunate public display of arrogance and ignorance:

- Torture does not make any one person or society safer or more secure. States that torture undermine their authority and legitimacy. Also, U.S. sanctioning of any form of torture will escalate its already widespread use.
- Those currently arguing in the abstract for torture only under "special circumstances" or with "humane limitations" know very little of the horror they are prescribing. Even seemingly innocuous methods of torture such as hooding can be terrorizing, for example when combined with a mock execution or other psychological methods. Moreover, hypothetical "limits" on torture cannot be ensured in the absence of independent monitoring of all interactions with detainees and investigation and prosecution of all allegations of torture — conditions that torturers do not permit.
- Labeling torture as a "stress and duress" interrogation technique does not alter the brutality that it represents.
- "Ticking bomb" scenarios are naive, abstract fantasies that serve to assuage the moral conscience of perpetrators and collaborators.

Acts of terror must be prevented and punished. To consider using acts of torture that the world has deemed unacceptable under any circumstance is profoundly disturbing. Torture will never serve the interests of justice because it undermines the dignity of us all. We all lose when the "war on terrorism" ends up threatening the protection of human rights.

The United States must be neither silent nor, in any way, complicit with such practices, or, indeed, we risk losing that which we seek to preserve — our humanity.

"This really comes down to human nature," says Boston University's Bacevich. "Violence is a part of who we are, and the notion that it can be rendered virtually obsolete by rules or treaties is unrealistic."

Washington lawyer Litt doubts the situation will change any time soon. "When governments are threatened or believe they are threatened, they will resort to all kinds of violence to protect themselves. That's not going to change."

But Northwestern University's D'Amato argues that norms of behavior can change, if slowly. "When you look back 50 years," he says, "a lot of people found the whole idea of the Nuremberg trials, of making heads of state responsible for crimes, unacceptable. Today, almost everyone accepts these sorts of things. For example, when Pinochet was arrested in England, most people in Europe applauded the action. Things can change."

Some argue that globalization and the free flow of information and ideas will help stamp out torture. "In today's world, the two-way flow of information from a country to the outside world is increasing all the time, and that's making it harder and harder for regimes to hide what they're doing to their people," says Massimino of the Lawyers Committee for Human Rights. Conversely, people living in repressive states "are more and more likely to know what it's like to live in a free society, where torture is not practiced, and ultimately will demand something better for themselves," she says.

Other optimists contend that the trend toward making individual political and military leaders responsible for torture and other human rights abuses will help stem future abuses. "As we go further in this direction, we are going to see torture become less and less acceptable around the world," says Amnesty International's Schulz.

"Traditionally, international law has differed from domestic law in one important way — there was no way to enforce it," says Duke University's Silliman. "Now with the ICC, we finally have a way to enforce international human rights law and that is very important."

But Litt thinks Schulz and Silliman are unrealistic, because the kind of international law they are talking about will be hard to enforce. "International treaties and covenants are always much more impressive on paper than they are in real life," he says. "I just don't think that torture is going to be hemmed in by it all."

Security consultant McCann agrees, arguing that even liberal democracies like the United States will con-

tinue to use what some say amounts to low-grade levels of torture when they feel threatened, as they now do by terrorism. "Everyone here wants to have their cake and eat it, too," he says. "They like the high-minded rules about not treating anyone badly, and they also want to make sure we get the information we need from terrorists to protect ourselves. But you can't be nice and effective at the same time."

And in the end, McCann says, people will choose to let their government be effective. "If a bomb goes off in this country, people aren't going to want to know about the rules, they'll want results. So being nice isn't going to last."

NOTES

1. Susan B. Glasser, "Bearing Wounds, Shiites Return to Torture Chamber," *The Washington Post*, April 9, 2003, p. A1.

2. Quoted in Craig S. Smith, "Former Captives Recall Horror of Hussein's Prisons," *The New York Times*, April 9, 2002, p. B8.

3. The entire text of the speech can be found on: www.whitehouse.gov/news/releases/2003/01/20030 128-19.html.

4. The report is available on the State Department's Web site: www.state.gov/g/ drl/rls/hrrpt/2002/index.htm; Amnesty International's 2002 human rights report is at www.amnesty.org/alib/aireport/index.html.

5. Eyal Press, "In Torture We Trust?" *The Nation*, March 31, 2003, p. 11.

6. Peter Maas, "Torture Tough or Lite," *The New York Times*, March 4, 2003, p. A4.

7. Dana Priest and Barton Gellman, "U.S. Decries Abuse, But Defends Interrogations," *The Washington Post*, Dec. 26, 2002, p. A1.

8. Maria Ressa, "U.S. warned in 1995 of plot to hijack planes, attack buildings," CNN.Com, Sept. 18, 2001.

9. Peter Tatchell, "Why This Dictator Must Stand Trial," *The Edinburgh Evening News*, Feb. 21, 2003, p. 10.

10. Marlise Simons, "Human Rights Cases Begin to Flood into Belgian Courts," *The New York Times*, Dec. 27, 2001, p. A8.

11. Edward Peters, *Torture* (1985), p. 14.

12. John Conroy, *Unspeakable Acts, Ordinary People: The Dynamics of Torture* (2000), pp. 27-28.

13. *Ibid*, p. 28.

14. *Ibid*, pp. 29-30.

15. Peters, *op. cit.*, p. 5.

16. Ben Harder, "Ancient Peru Torture Deaths," *National Geographic.com.* April 29, 2002.

17. For background, see David Masci, "The Ethics of War," *The CQ Researcher*, Dec. 13, 2002, pp.

18. *Ibid*, p. 125.

19. For a full text of the Declaration, go to: www.un.org/Overview/rights.html.

20. Barbara Crossette, "U.S. Loses Bid to Alter U.N. Prison Check Plan," *The New York Times*, July 25, 2002, p. A4.

21. Simons, *op. cit.*

22. Keith Richburg, "International War Crimes Court is Inaugurated," *The Washington Post*, March 12, 2003, p. A18.

23. Judith Miller, "Special Team Seeks Clues to Establish War Crimes," *The New York Times*, March 30, 2003, p. B7.

24. Joseph Brean, "U.S., British Soldiers Find More Evidence of Torture," *The* [Toronto] *National Post*, April 10, 2003, p. A5.

25. Quoted in Tom Brune, "Trial Plan Called a Mistake," *Newsday*, April 9, 2003, p. A33.

26. Quoted in Amy Ross, "To Help World Heal, Haul Saddam Before a Global Court," *The Atlanta Journal Constitution*, April 9, 2003, p. 23A.

27. Quoted in Jess Bravin and Gary Fields, "How Do Interrogators Make a Captured Terrorist Talk?" *The Wall Street Journal*, March 4, 2003.

28. *Ibid.*

29. Quoted in *Ibid.*

30. Quoted on CBS-TV's "60 Minutes," Sept. 22, 2002.

BIBLIOGRAPHY

Books

Conroy, John, *Unspeakable Acts, Ordinary People: The Dynamics of Torture*, Random House, 2000.

A staff writer for the Chicago Reader, an alternative weekly, examines the history of torture since ancient Greece while trying to understand the motivations of torturers.

Dershowitz, Alan M., *Why Terrorism Works: Understanding the Threat, Responding to the Challenge*, Yale University Press, 2003.

A professor of law at Harvard University and well-known legal commentator argues that torturing terrorism suspects should be allowed. He proposes that courts issue "torture warrants" to bring some legal oversight to the process.

Ortiz, Sister Dianna, with Patricia Davis, *The Blindfold's Eyes: My Journey from Torture to Truth*, Orbis Press, 2002.

A Roman Catholic nun describes her brutal torture while working as a missionary in Guatemala.

Peters, Edward, *Torture*, Blackwell, 1996.

A University of Pennsylvania history professor looks at torture through the ages, including the philosophical cases both for and against the practice.

Articles

Bowcott, Owen, "Torture Trail to September 11," *The Guardian*, Jan. 24, 2003, p. 19.

Bowcott argues that torture, used for years by Arab regimes against Islamic militants, hardened their views and actually helped create the al Qaeda terrorist organization.

Bravin, Jess, and Gary Fields, "How Do Interrogators Make a Captured Terrorist Talk?" *The Wall Street Journal*, March 4, 2003, p. B1.

The article examines the methods used by American interrogators in questioning terrorism suspects like recently captured Khalid Sheikh Mohammed.

Burkhalter, Holly, "No to Torture," *The Washington Post*, Jan. 5, 2003, p. B7.

The U.S. policy director for Physicians for Human Rights argues that in torturing terrorism suspects the United States is eroding international humanitarian norms and inviting the future mistreatment of American prisoners.

Cooperman, Alan, "CIA Interrogation Under Fire; Human Rights Groups Say Techniques Could be Torture," *The Washington Post*, Dec. 28, 2002, p. A9.

Human rights groups say U.S. officials could be prosecuted in European and other courts for allegedly torturing terrorism suspects.

"Ends, Means and Barbarity," *The Economist*, Jan. 9, 2003.
The article argues the United States should reject the temptation to use torture in the war on terrorism.

Finn, Peter, "Police Torture Threat Sparks Painful Debate in Germany," *The Washington Post*, March 8, 2003, p. A19.
Frankfurt Police are under fire for threatening to use torture to force a kidnapper to reveal where he hid his victim.

Johnson, Reed, "The Art of Interrogation," *Los Angeles Times*, March 15, 2003, p. 1.
Johnson argues that psychological ploys and patience are better than torture at making suspects talk.

Priest, Dana, and Barton Gellman, "U.S. Decries Abuse, But Defends Interrogations," *The Washington Post*, Dec. 26, 2002, p. A1.
The article ponders whether some of the U.S. interrogation techniques used against alleged terrorists constitute torture.

Simons, Marlise, "Human Rights Cases Begin to Flood into Belgian Courts," *The New York Times*, Dec. 27, 2001, p. A8.
A 1993 law that allows Belgian courts to hear atrocity cases has prompted the filing of a large number of suits, including charges against 12 former and current world leaders.

Tatchell, Peter, "Why This Dictator Must Stand Trial," *Edinburgh Evening News*, Feb. 21, 2003, p. 10.
A British human rights advocate argues that the leaders of nations that practice torture should be charged with violating the U.N. Torture Convention when they leave their countries.

Taylor, Stuart, "Is It Ever Right to Torture Suspected Terrorists?" *The Atlantic*, March 8, 2003.
A longtime legal analyst explores the ethical and legal difficulties of using torture.

Reports and Studies

Amnesty International, *Annual Report*, 2002; www.amnesty.org/alib/aireport/index.html.
The largest human rights group in the world catalogs abuses, including in many cases torture, in 152 countries.

U.S. State Department, *2002 Human Rights Report*; www.state.gov/g/drl/rls/hrrpt/2002/index.htm.
The department's annual review of abuses in nations around the world.

For More Information

Amnesty International USA, 322 Eighth Ave., New York, NY 10001; (212) 807-8400; www.amnestyusa.org. The U.S. chapter of the human rights advocacy group.

Canadian Centre for the Victims of Torture, 194 Jarvis St., 2nd Fl., Toronto, Ontario, Canada M5B 2B7; (416) 363-1066; www.icomm.ca/ccvt.

Center for Victims of Torture, 717 East River Road, Minneapolis, MN 55455; (612) 627-4231; www.cvt.org. Web site home page lists more than 20 additional organizations for torture victims and their families.

Human Rights Watch, 350 5th Ave., 34th Fl., New York, NY 10118-3299; (212) 290-4700; www.hrw.org. Investigates human rights abuses around the world.

Medical Foundation for the Care of Victims of Torture, 96-98 Grafton Rd., Kentish Town, London NW5 3EJ; (020) 7813 7777; www.torturecare.org.uk.

Office of the High Commissioner for Human Rights, 8-14 Ave. de la Paix, 1211 Geneva 10, Switzerland; (41-22) 917-9000; www.unhchr.ch. An arm of the U.N.

Physicians for Human Rights, 100 Boylston St., Suite 702, Boston, MA 02116; (617) 695-0041; www.phrusa.org.

14

Ethics of War

David Masci

U.N. Secretary General Kofi Annan visits the Mulire Memorial honoring the estimated 1 million Tutsis and other Rwandans who were killed in the African country's 1994 genocide. Genocides and brutal civil wars in recent years have focused new attention on the wartime fate of civilians and captured combatants.

From *The CQ Researcher*, December 13, 2002.

L ondoner Zumrati Juma had not heard from her 22-year-old son Feroz for more than a year. After checking with the local police, and even the mosque where he worshipped, she began to think the worst. [1]

But in January she was stunned to learn that Feroz, a British citizen, was being held incommunicado by the United States. He had been transported, hooded and in chains, to the U.S. Naval Station at Guantanamo Bay, Cuba, where he remains. The Justice Department says he is a member of al Qaeda, the global terrorist group headed by Saudi exile Osama bin Laden. [2]

Feroz is one of 625 detainees at Guantanamo captured last fall during the U.S.-led campaign launched against al Qaeda and Afghanistan's ruling Taliban regime following the Sept. 11, 2001, terrorist attacks on New York City and the Pentagon. [3] For nearly a year, the detainees have been interrogated for information that might help prevent future terrorist attacks or aid in the capture of bin Laden and other terrorists.

Classifying the detainees as "unlawful combatants," the Bush administration has refused to grant them access to either lawyers or U.S. courts. It contends that since the detainees are foreign nationals being held outside the United States, they do not warrant such rights.

"Are we supposed to read [terror suspects] their Miranda rights, hire a flamboyant defense lawyer, bring them back to the United States to create a new cable network of 'Osama TV,' provide a worldwide platform for propaganda?" Attorney General John D. Ashcroft asked the Senate Judiciary Committee on Dec. 6, 2001.

But lawyers representing Feroz and 16 other detainees have sued in federal court, arguing the Bush administration has unlawfully

A Century of War Atrocities

More people died in violent conflicts during the 20th century than in any previous century — including millions killed through genocide. Several factors fed the bloodshed, including the rise of state-supported racism, population growth, the destructive power of modern weapons, competition for dwindling natural resources and the emergence of unstable states. Major contemporary atrocities cited by historians include:

The Armenian Genocide — From 1915-1923, an estimated 1.5 million ethnic Armenian Christians were killed in forced marches and executions carried out by the "Young Turk" government of the Ottoman Empire. The Turkish government continues to challenge the veracity of some facts surrounding the atrocity.

Ukraine's Forced Famine — In an attempt to subordinate the Ukrainian republic, the Soviet leader Josef Stalin induced a famine in the Ukraine from 1932-1933 that killed an estimated 5 million people. While some organizations do not recognize famine as genocide, the Russian government has denounced Stalin's campaign as genocide.

The Rape of Nanking — When Japanese military forces sacked the Chinese city in 1937, they raped 20,000 women, killed over 200,000 people and imprisoned thousands more in one of history's bloodiest rampages.

The Holocaust — Under Adolf Hitler's Nazi regime in Germany, an estimated 6 million Jews were systematically killed in an attempt to eliminate the Jewish race. Gypsies, dissidents, homosexuals and others were also persecuted, with estimates of the number killed ranging from thousands to 5 million.

Cambodia's "Killing Fields" — The communist Khmer Rouge took control of Cambodia in 1975 and systematically forced most of the people into labor camps, where they starved or were worked to death. Vietnamese nationals, Chinese, Muslims, intellectuals and Buddhist monks were also "cleansed" from Cambodian society. An estimated 1.5 to 2 million people died during Pol Pot's Khmer Rouge reign, which ended in 1979.

Bosnia — Bosnian Serbs in the former Yugoslavia began a murderous campaign of "ethnic cleansing" against Muslims and Croats in 1992, killing hundreds of thousands of men, women and children by execution, imprisonment and torture.

Rwanda — Ethnic Hutus slaughtered an estimated 800,000 members of the Tutsi ethnic minority and suspected Hutu collaborators between April and July 1994. Millions of Hutus and Tutsis fled the country.

Sources: The Campaign to End Genocide, http://www.endgenocide.org/genocide /20thcen.htm; Aryeh Neier, *War Crimes,* Times Books, 1998; Human Rights Watch

process of law," said Joe Margulies, of the Center for Constitutional Rights, one of the lawyers. [4] "The government says no court in the world may hear from my clients. Guantanamo is unique. It is utterly outside the law." [5]

The treatment of soldiers captured in warfare is one of the seminal issues addressed by the 1949 Geneva Convention and other treaties on the conduct of war.

These rules were developed in the 19th and 20th centuries, at the same time that new, more deadly weapons were being created. "War at its inception was a wholly barbaric business," says Paul Stevens, a former legal adviser to the National Security Council. "But as our ability to inflict mayhem increased, we began to recognize the need to find ways to stop or control the violence."

But while the rules of international humanitarian law only were developed over the past 150 years, efforts to regulate warfare date back to ancient times.

Indeed, three centuries after the rise of Christianity, the religion's first great political theorist, St. Augustine of Hippo, set out the conditions that needed to be met before a state could go to war. His theory of the "just war," later refined by St. Thomas Aquinas and others, mandates that war must be fought only for a good or just cause, by a legitimate authority and only as a last resort.

While the U.S. action in Afghanistan — dubbed Operation Enduring Freedom — was widely seen as ethically and politically defensible, many theologians and other observers say that U.S. action against Iraq, now being contemplated by the administration, would not meet the just-war test. They argue that although Iraqi leader Saddam

denied the Guantanamo prisoners their legal rights. "Intelligence gathering may go forward, detentions at Guantanamo Bay may go forward, but [not] without

Hussein is a brutal dictator who may indeed have biological and chemical weapons, there is no evidence that he directly poses an imminent threat to the United States.

"Before we justify going to war, we need to see that Iraq poses a clear and present danger, and I just don't see it," says Bob Edgar, general secretary of the National Council of Churches, which represents 50 million Christians. Before an attack is even considered, Edgar advocates the continued use of the weapons-inspection process and other non-violent means to bring Iraq into compliance with U.N. disarmament resolutions.

But others support the administration's contention that Iraq directly threatens the United States and its allies, as indicated by the failure of the decade-long, non-violent effort to disarm the oil-rich nation. In addition, war supporters point out, Hussein has repeatedly used weapons of mass destruction and is likely to do so again in the future. [6]

"If attacking Iraq doesn't meet the just-war threshold in some people's minds, nothing ever will," says Keith Pavlischek, director of the Civitas citizenship program at the Christian-based Center for Public Justice, in Annapolis, Md.

Ethical issues also surround the U.S. refusal to join the International Criminal Court (ICC), established in July to investigate war crimes.

Temporary war-crimes tribunals were used after World War II, when defeated German and Japanese leaders were tried for crimes against humanity. Currently, temporary tribunals in the Netherlands and Tanzania are prosecuting Yugoslavs and Hutus accused of committing atrocities during brutal conflicts in the former Yugoslavia and Rwanda. [7]

The United States has refused to support the ICC, arguing that it could become politicized and ultimately be used by unfriendly states to target U.S. soldiers and officials, even when engaged in peacekeeping missions. "[One cannot] answer with confidence whether the United States would now be accused of war crimes for legitimate but controversial uses of force to protect world peace," says John R. Bolton, under secretary for arms control and international security. (See "At Issue," p. 307.)

But human-rights activists and other supporters of the ICC counter that the administration's concerns are overblown and that a permanent judicial body will better enable the international community to hold mass murderers accountable for their genocidal crimes.

While experts disagree about the ICC, many on both

AFP Photo/Karen Sahib

U. N. weapons inspectors examine equipment on Dec. 9 at a factory near Baghdad that once produced chemical and biological weapons. The Bush administration contends that if Iraqi leader Saddam Hussein doesn't dismantle his alleged arsenal of weapons of mass destruction, an attack on Iraq would constitute a "just war" because the oil-rich nation poses an imminent threat to U.S. security.

sides accept the contention that future conflicts may prove even more brutal and unregulated than past wars. Powerful countries, they predict, will find themselves fighting rebels or non-governmental entities like al Qaeda, which are disinclined to follow generally accepted rules of humane warfare.

But human-rights activists argue that even though al Qaeda and Taliban soldiers do not entirely fit the image or definition of traditional fighters, they still should be granted prisoner-of-war status when captured by the United States or other coalition forces.

They point out that the Geneva Convention requires countries capturing combatants to presume they are POWs unless a legitimate tribunal decides otherwise.

The administration argues that the detainees do not warrant POW treatment — which might require their release, since the war in Afghanistan is largely over — because they have none of the trappings of regular soldiers, like uniforms and insignias. [8]

"The whole idea behind awarding someone POW status is that they look and act like soldiers, which means they behave differently than civilians," says David Rivkin, a former Justice Department official under for-

Civilians Bear the Brunt of Warfare

Despite several treaties and international agreements designed to protect them, civilians bear the brunt of most fighting around the world.

Indeed, since World War II, non-combatants have made up 90 percent of all war-related casualties. [1] And academics estimate that between 1900 and 1987, a staggering 169 million civilians and unarmed soldiers were killed during conflicts, compared with the 34 million soldiers killed in combat. [2]

In the past, armies often were expected to "live off the land," pillaging and killing innocents as they moved from one area to another. In some conflicts, such as the religiously motivated Thirty Years' War (1618-1648), civilians were the targets of military aggression, as Protestant and Catholic armies attacked non-combatants to stamp out "heresy."

Civilians were constantly targeted during World War II. All sides bombed civilian areas, sometimes to destroy vital industries but sometimes to "demoralize" enemy populations, like the German V-2 rocket bombing of London, the U.S. fire-bombing of Dresden or even the atomic bombing of Hiroshima and Nagasaki by the United States. The Germans and the Japanese took the brutality a step further, wiping out entire towns and cities, and, in Germany's case, establishing concentration camps to exterminate whole races and groups of people.

The war's horrors prompted the International Committee on the Red Cross (ICRC) to recommend an international conference in Geneva, Switzerland, to regulate conduct during war. One of the four articles of the 1949 Geneva Convention specifically seeks to protect civilians

and their property. The rules were refined and expanded in 1977 to protect civilians from the growing threat of terrorism. (*See box, p. 305.*)

"The civilian population, as such, as well as individual civilians, shall not be the object of attack," states Protocol I, from 1977. The protocol also outlaws terrorism during war: "Acts or threats of violence, the primary purpose of which is to spread terror among the civilian population [are] prohibited." [3]

In addition, the Geneva rules prohibit the kinds of attacks, such as carpet-bombing, most likely to cause excessive civilian casualties. They also prohibit armies from using civilians as human shields to advance strategic objectives.

The Geneva code does not *prohibit* attacks against legitimate military targets that may or are expected to cause so-called collateral damage and produce civilian casualties. But in these cases, commanders must do all they can to avoid hurting civilians.

Although the rules governing the treatment of civilians are clear and have been ratified by most nations, conditions for non-combatants have, if anything, gotten worse since World War II, because the Geneva rules are, essentially, unenforceable.

"While we have this nice-looking piece of paper that says all the right things, states feel free to ignore it and to act in what they see as their best interest because there's no enforcement mechanism, no way to hold them accountable," says Thomas Lynch, an attorney at the International Human Rights Law Group in Washington, D.C. "So protecting civilians comes down to a matter of convenience."

In addition, many conflicts of the last 60 years have taken place in the developing world, where armies are often

[1] "The First Casualty," *The Economist*, Aug. 25, 2001.

[2] Eric Deggans, "A history of man's inhumanity," *The St. Petersburg* [Fla.] *Times*, April 4, 2002, p. 2B.

[3] Quoted in Roy Gutman and David Rieff, eds., *Crimes of War: What the Public Should Know* (1999), p. 85.

mer Presidents Ronald Reagan and George Bush. "These guys were no different than other men in Afghanistan, where everyone is armed and dresses in the same way." [9]

As policymakers and ethicists from the United States and other countries seek to apply the moral standards for warfare to today's terrorism, here are some of the questions being asked:

Would an invasion of Iraq be a "just war"?

All the major religious traditions contain teachings on war, including Islam. Western views are influenced by the Christian notion of the "just war," conceived nearly 2,000 years ago by St. Augustine of Hippo. According to generally accepted principles, a "just war" should be:

disorganized, and non-uniformed soldiers blend in with the civilian population, a combination that often leads to the killing of many innocents.

In some recent wars, civilians have been specifically targeted. During the civil war in Bosnia in the former Yugoslavia, all sides, especially the Serbs, targeted non-combatants — often in an attempt to "ethnically cleanse" an area. Serb soldiers executed thousands of civilians and raped enemy women as a form of torture.

In Chechnya, a breakaway Russian province, up to 160,000 people, mostly civilians, have died since Russia sought to put down the uprising in 1994. [4] Russian troops have been accused of everything from indiscriminately shelling Chechen villages to routinely torturing and executing suspected rebel sympathizers.

African conflicts have been especially hard on civilians. Over the last 40 years, civil wars in Angola, Sudan, Mozambique, Nigeria and elsewhere have left millions of innocents dead. In Sierra Leone, an entire generation has been

One of the thousands of civilians deliberately maimed by rebels during Sierra Leone's brutal 10-year civil war casts his ballot in presidential elections in May. Although the Geneva Convention prohibits attacks on non-combatants, 90 percent of the casualties in recent wars have been civilians.

maimed by machete-wielding soldiers who cut off the hands and feet of suspected enemy sympathizers or their children.

Even the United States is not immune from allegations that it has indiscriminately killed civilians. During the Vietnam War, for instance, American planes carpet-bombed targets in Vietnam and Cambodia. Recently, scholars have unearthed evidence suggesting that American officers ordered pilots to bomb defenseless Korean refugees, killing hundreds. [5]

In a break from past atrocities, some recent mass killings of civilians, specifically in Bosnia and Rwanda, have led to prosecutions of some of the alleged perpetrators (*see p. 304*).

"The idea of individual responsibility is novel," Lynch says. "I can't say, but maybe it will begin to deter some people in the future from committing atrocities."

In fact, several potential atrocities have been prevented or at least mitigated by humanitarian intervention. For example, in Kosovo in 1999, a U.S.-led bombing campaign prevented Serbian attempts to ethnically cleanse the province of its Albanian majority. Likewise, the same year, the presence of Australian troops likely prevented mass killing in East Timor, an Indonesian province that became independent in May.

---

[4] Sabrina Tavernise, "Chechnya is Caught in Grip of Russia's Anti-Terror Wrath," *The New York Times*, Nov. 12, 2002, p. A1.

[5] "The First Casualty," *op. cit.*

- based on clear, legitimate or just aims;
- undertaken by a legitimate authority — such as a recognized government;
- not undertaken out of hate, greed or other base motives;
- prosecuted only as a last resort; and,
- likely to succeed.

Many U.S. church leaders are among those who contend that war with Iraq would not meet most "just-war" tests, mainly because they say justification for an attack is absent. (Some religions, like the Baptists, say it meets the test.)

"Is there clear and adequate evidence of direct connection between Iraq and the attacks of Sept. 11 or clear and adequate evidence of an imminent attack of a grave nature?" asks Bishop Wilton Gregory, president of the U.S. Catholic Conference of Bishops, in a Sept. 13 letter to President Bush.

Gregory and others say "no," adding that pre-empting threats that may or may not materialize sometime in the future doesn't constitute adequate justification. "Iraq has chemical and biological weapons and the ability to deliver them up to 400 miles," says Edgar of the National Council of Churches. "But Saddam Hussein hasn't used them for more than a decade, and it seems that the most likely way he will use them is by being backed into a corner by us — when we invade — and he has nothing to lose."

In addition, some church leaders say, an invasion of Iraq, at least at this point, also would not be a measure of last resort. "No one is trying to defend Saddam Hussein, because he's a dreadful person who has done dreadful things," says James E. Winkler, general secretary of the United Methodist Church. "But we have other ways to pursue our goal of disarming him." Among those, he says, are the U.N. weapons inspectors now searching for weapons of mass destruction in Iraq.

Winkler also questions the likelihood that invading Iraq would be successful. "I'm sure we can beat them militarily, but what happens afterward?" he asks. "Everyone knows that this will seriously threaten the peace and stability of the Middle East, because so many people would be unhappy with the United States going in and killing a lot of Iraqis."

But others counter that striking Iraq would clearly meet the just-war test, since Iraq has both the desire and capability to do great harm to the United States now or in the near future.

"It's clear that there is a case for just war here," says David Davenport, a research fellow at the Hoover Institution and past president of Pepperdine University, in Malibu, Calif. "If Saddam has weapons of mass destruction — and it's pretty clear from the evidence that he does — and there is a likelihood of his using them — and, again, it seems clear that he very well might, since he already has — then you have a just cause for going to war." *

Even if Iraq is not yet a direct threat to the United States, it could endanger important U.S. allies, say supporters of an invasion. "Israel and our Arab allies in the region are already in danger," says Pavlischek of the Center for Public Justice.

In addition, Pavlischek says, an attack against Hussein would not be premature because he has been given — and is still being given — chances to disarm and has thwarted all of them so far. "I'm not sure what we're supposed to do if Iraq doesn't disarm," Pavlischek says. "Do they need to be marching down Broadway before we do something?"

"In an era when we face the threat from weapons of mass destruction, the idea of last resort takes on a new meaning," Davenport says. "Sure, we can try to keep putting pressure on Saddam to accept inspections and disarmament, but my guess is that this may be one of the last chances we have to go in and really address this issue."

Such action would become much more risky if Iraq were to succeed in its long quest to make nuclear weapons — something that could be just a few years away — according to international arms-control experts. [12]

But Edgar questions why, after more than a decade of sanctions and international isolation, Iraq is suddenly perceived as a great threat that must immediately be destroyed.

"There's been little evidence that Saddam Hussein has moved out of the box we put him in after the Gulf War," he says. "In fact, the last time he used those weapons was in the late 1980s, which was when we were supporting him. What makes him such a threat right now, and makes it so urgent that we go to war?"

Are the detainees at Guantanamo Bay entitled to prisoner-of-war status?

Traditional warfare features enemy combatants wearing uniforms and fighting for a specific country. Under the Geneva Convention, when such soldiers are captured they are supposed to be declared prisoners of war, treated humanely and repatriated when the fighting ends.

But in the war against terrorism, the United States has been fighting a very different enemy. Al Qaeda is an organization, not a country, and those who fight for it come from many nations. Moreover, some of the countries that supplied most of al Qaeda's fighters — like Saudi Arabia, Egypt and Pakistan — are staunch U.S. allies.

---

* It is well-accepted that Saddam Hussein used chemical weapons to kill thousands of people — combatants and civilians — in the late 1980s war against Iran and against Iraq's own ethnic Kurdish population after the Persian Gulf War.

In the case of the Taliban, the United States and nearly all other countries refused to recognize it as the legitimate government of Afghanistan. In fact, some Taliban soldiers are not even from Afghanistan but from the same states that supplied fighters for al Qaeda.

The Bush administration has argued that the more than 600 Taliban and al Qaeda fighters held at Guantanamo are, in practice, receiving many POW rights, even though the administration says they do not qualify as POWs under the Geneva Convention. In addition, declaring them prisoners of war would require their release once the conflict ended, something administration officials argue could prove dangerous, since many are alleged terrorists who could attack the United States again if freed. Instead, the government has opted to classify them as "unlawful combatants" and to hold them indefinitely.

The administration announced on Nov. 17, 2002, that an unspecified number of the Guantanamo captives eventually would be tried before U.S. military tribunals, which do not offer all of the due-process protections usually available in American courts. It's unclear what will happen to the other detainees. [10]

Federal courts, so far, have rebuffed efforts by civil-liberties groups and others to change the detainees' status or to accord them the right to a lawyer and an appearance in court. At a recent hearing, the 4th U.S. Circuit Court of Appeals agreed with the government's contention that courts "may not second-guess the military's enemy-combatant determination. Going beyond that determination would require the courts to enter an area in which they have no competence, much less international expertise [and] intrude upon the constitutional prerogative of the Commander in Chief." [11]

But civil-liberties advocates argue that President Bush has no right to unilaterally declare that the Afghan war captives are not POWs, noting that the Geneva Convention specifies that soldiers captured during a conflict are presumed to be prisoners of war until otherwise judged differently.

"It's quite clear under the Geneva Convention that the U.S. has an obligation to declare all of these people at Guantanamo prisoners of war," says Vienna Colucci, director of the International Law Program at Amnesty International, a human-rights advocacy group based in London. "Under the treaty, there is a presumption that someone captured on the battlefield is a prisoner of war until a court decides otherwise."

"If the government wants to question someone's status, they're supposed to convene a competent military tribunal to decide," agrees Jamie Felner, director of U.S. Programs at Human Rights Watch, an advocacy organization in New York. "So the administration not only has ignored the presumption but also has failed to convene the tribunal."

But the administration and its supporters argue that the Geneva Convention covers the treatment of lawful combatants, but the Guantanamo prisoners are unlawful combatants. "People don't seem to think that the term 'unlawful combatant' is legitimate, but it is," says former National Security Council adviser Stevens, pointing out that international law recognizes that some fighters are not covered under the 1949 treaty.

Indeed, administration supporters dispute the notion that battlefield prisoners automatically deserve POW status until proven otherwise. "This presumption is only the case when you appear to qualify for POW status but something puts such a qualification into doubt," says former Justice Department official Rivkin. "So if you're captured and your uniform is hard to recognize because it's been so damaged in battle, then the presumption exists until we clarify your status."

But the Taliban and al Qaeda detainees did not meet the criteria for POW status, according to Rivkin and Stevens. "These guys are not part of a regular armed force, with uniforms and insignias and other trappings of a real army," Stevens says. "Even the Taliban didn't wear uniforms, were not all from Afghanistan and were virtually interchangeable with al Qaeda, who fought alongside them."

"The Taliban and al Qaeda were indistinguishable from all other Afghanis," Rivkin says. "They're supposed to wear uniforms because we're not supposed to shoot civilians."

In addition, Rivkin says, the detainees meet none of the other criteria for POW status, such as having a discernable chain of command. "Between [Taliban leader] Mullah Omar and the regional commanders and everyone else, there doesn't seem to be a hierarchy," Rivkin says. "As for al Qaeda, we don't know what their chain of command is."

Finally, POWs must represent a military that itself follows the rules of war. "Both groups have completely ignored the rules of war," Rivkin says, pointing out that they committed human-rights abuses against non-combatants before and during the war.

CHRONOLOGY

Before 1800s *Vague notions of the need to regulate war begin to take shape.*

4th Century St. Augustine of Hippo argues that countries should only go to war for good or just reasons.

13th Century St. Thomas Aquinas says states must have good intentions when waging war.

17th Century Dutch scholar Hugo Grotius sets out basic principles for the rules of war.

19th Century *The rise of mass media brings home the horrors of war and leads to international efforts to codify rules.*

1854-1856 The barbarity of the Crimean War shocks Europe.

1863 Reports from the front during the Civil War prompt President Abraham Lincoln to ask for military rules governing the conduct of the Army. Swiss banker Jean-Henry Dunant founds the International Committee of the Red Cross (ICRC) in Geneva, Switzerland.

1864 The ICRC sets out humane principles for dealing with the sick and wounded in battle.

1899 A second international convention on war is convened in The Hague, Netherlands.

1900-1999 *Unprecedented brutality and genocide lead to stronger rules of war and war-crimes tribunals.*

1929 ICRC adops rules for humane treatment of prisoners.

1939-1945 Millions of civilians in Europe and Asia die during World War II.

1945 Nazi and Japanese leaders face war-crimes tribunals.

1948 U.N. adopts Genocide Convention.

1949 Geneva Convention sets protocols for the treatment of civilians, prisoners and the sick and wounded.

1977 Protocols to the 1949 Geneva Convention protect civilians against terrorism and other acts of violence. U.S. refuses to sign, citing a reluctance to legitimize terrorists.

1992 Civil war begins in the Yugoslav Republic of Bosnia.

1994 Rampaging Hutus in Rwanda kill up to 1 million ethnic Tutsis and moderate Hutus.

1995 Tribunal in The Hague begins trials of war criminals accused of atrocities in the former Yugoslavia.

1997 The first war-crimes trial against an alleged perpetrator of the Rwandan genocide begins in Arusha, Tanzania.

July 17, 1998 A U.N. conference adopts the Rome Treaty, setting the stage for creation of the International Criminal Court (ICC).

1999 American-led bombing halts Serbian ethnic cleansing in Kosovo; Australian-led forces stop violence in East Timor.

2000-Present *U.S. confronted with new threats.*

Dec. 31, 2000 President Bill Clinton signs the Rome Treaty.

Oct. 7, 2001 Following the Sept. 11, 2001, terrorist attacks, U.S. confronts Taliban and al Qaeda in Afghanistan.

January 2002 The first prisoners from Afghanistan arrive at the U.S. Naval Station at Guantanamo Bay, Cuba.

February 2002 War-crimes trial of former Yugoslav leader Slobodan Milosevic begins.

April 11, 2002 The ICC comes into existence in The Hague, after 76 nations ratify the Rome Treaty.

May 6, 2002 President Bush nullifies U.S. approval of the Rome Treaty.

July 12, 2002 The U.N. Security Council unanimously exempts U.S. peacekeepers from ICC jurisdiction.

December 2002 Weapons inspectors return to Iraq.

Stevens agrees, adding that the detainees at Guantanamo were not soldiers but terrorists. "All of these people were part of a huge terrorist network, and I'm sorry, you don't treat terrorists the same way you treat men in uniform who are part of a real army."

But administration critics contend the detainees in Guantanamo meet the test. "The Taliban were the de facto government of Afghanistan because they controlled over 90 percent of the country, so the Taliban soldiers are soldiers for the government of a nation state and should be treated that way," Amnesty International's Colucci says. Even al Qaeda troops meet the definition of POWs, she and others say.

"The Geneva Convention recognizes that you have irregular armies and makes allowances for that," Felner of Human Rights Watch says. "The al Qaeda might not have all the trappings of a modern military, but we have declared war on them and should treat them as if we are at war with them."

"Al Qaeda forces were fighting alongside the Taliban to defend Afghanistan," Colucci adds. "They were part of their force structure and deserve POW status as well."

BACKGROUND

Ancient Rules of War

Attempts to regulate war probably are as old as warfare itself. The ancients, most notably the philosophically minded Greeks, were known to have debated the morality of going to war or killing civilians.

But such exercises were the exception, not the rule. Weak neighbors typically were legitimate targets, and civilian populations and prisoners of war were often treated with great brutality.

The advent of Christianity, with its elements of pacifism, brought forth new doctrines on warfare. St. Augustine of Hippo (354-430), the first great Christian theologian to tackle political matters, theorized that war could be justified under certain limited conditions. In what became known as the "just-war" theory, Augustine argued that war was legitimate if it was fought by a proper authority and for what was then considered a good cause, which in those days might have meant a Christian kingdom prosecuting a crusade against non-Christians.

During the Middle Ages, theologian and philosopher St. Thomas Aquinas refined Augustine's theory, adding the requirement that "belligerents should have a rightful intention, so that they intend the advancement of good, or the avoidance of evil." [13]

In the 17th century, the Dutch scholar Hugo Grotius used the just-war theory to broaden the code for regulating conflict. Grotius set down rules of war that would become standard in the ensuing centuries, including the humane treatment of prisoners and non-combatants. "I saw in the whole Christian world a license of fighting at which even barbarous nations might blush," he wrote in 1625, explaining his desire to set down rules of warfare. "Wars were begun on trifling pretexts or none at all, and carried on without any reference of law, Divine or human." [14]

It was not until the 19th century, however, that efforts to regulate war really gathered steam. The invention of the telegraph and the development of industrial printing processes in the first half of the 1800s made on-the-scene reportage and widespread dissemination of information from the battlefield possible for the first time.

First in the Crimean War pitting Britain and France against Russia in the 1850s and then in the U.S. Civil War a decade later, war correspondents depicted the horror and cruelty of battle, shocking both officials and civilians back on the home front. The disturbing dispatches prompted President Abraham Lincoln to order the War Department to draft rules governing the army's conduct during wartime. Issued in 1863, the rules mandated humane treatment of prisoners of war and the wounded. Historians consider it the first attempt by an army to regulate itself. [15]

The same year, the International Committee of the Red Cross (ICRC) was founded by Jean-Henry Dunant, a Geneva banker who had been "seized with horror and pity" by what he witnessed at the Battle of Solferino in 1859, during the war for Italian unification. Tens of thousands had died, mostly from untreated wounds. Dunant resolved to find a way to prevent similar tragedies in the future.

In 1864, the ICRC held its inaugural conference in Geneva, Switzerland, and adopted the "Convention for the Amelioration of the Wounded and Sick in the Armies in the Field," calling on all states to care for the wounded and sick on the battlefield — even if they

The near-total devastation of Hiroshima, Japan, remains evident three years after the United States dropped the first atomic bomb on the city on Aug. 6, 1945, killing 140,000 people. Three days later, a second atomic bomb killed 74,000 people in Nagasaki. Both sides bombed cities and other civilian targets during World War II.

had fought for the enemy — and not to attack medical personnel.

In 1899 and 1907, delegates from several countries met in The Hague, the Netherlands, to build on the foundation set down in Geneva in 1864. Under the "Geneva Codes" passed by these two conferences, armies were charged not to unnecessarily kill civilians or destroy or confiscate civilian property. Prisoners of war were to be treated with respect.

World Wars

Only a handful of countries ever ratified any of the three treaties, and during the subsequent global wars the conventions were largely ignored by all sides, including the allies.

During World War I, all sides used gas and other new weapons to kill and maim millions. And in World War II, German bomb and rocket attacks destroyed much of London, and allied forces targeted and killed hundreds of thousands of civilians in bombing raids over German and Japanese cities.

But it was German and Japanese atrocities committed during World War II that prompted the nations to meet again in 1949 to try to mitigate the ravages of future wars. The world had been stunned by Japanese brutality in East Asia and China — including the so-called Rape of Nanking — and by Germany's genoci-

dal efforts during the Holocaust to exterminate entire populations of Jews, Gypsies (the Roma) and others it deemed "undesirable." [16]

Delegates to the Geneva Convention of 1949 produced what is considered the most significant and comprehensive document on the laws of war. Its four parts, ultimately ratified by 188 states, mandated countries involved in hostilities to treat the sick and wounded, prisoners of war and civilian non-combatants humanely and with respect. [17] They also prohibited attacks on civilian targets or the use of methods of warfare likely to lead to high levels of civilian casualties, such as so-called carpet-bombing. [18]

The horrors of World War II also led to the first formal, well-regulated war crimes trials for defeated Nazi and Japanese leaders held responsible for genocide and other mass attacks against civilians. Throughout military history, victors often executed enemy leaders and even regular soldiers and civilians without a trial. Only after the allied victory in 1945 did the notion of trying the leaders of defeated enemies fully take shape.

While ad hoc war-crimes tribunals had occasionally been convened after past wars, even in the Middle Ages, the tribunals at Nuremberg, Germany, and Tokyo set the standard by which subsequent war crimes trials have operated. Notably, the trials were the first instance where individuals were prosecuted for "crimes against humanity" — atrocities against non-combatants on a large scale.

Beginning in November 1945, in Nuremberg, 21 top Nazis — including Luftwaffe head Herman Goering, armaments minister Albert Speer and Deputy Führer Rudolph Hess — were tried for crimes against humanity, for their part in the murder of millions of Jews and others during the war. All but two were convicted, and 11 were executed. Similar trials occurred in Tokyo against Japanese leaders for their roles in massacres in China and elsewhere, including Prime Minister Hideki Tojo, who ordered the attack on Pearl Harbor. He was convicted as a war criminal and executed in 1948.

The United Nations Genocide Convention of 1948 was an outgrowth of the trials. It outlawed genocide, defined as a premeditated attempt "to destroy, in whole or in part, a national, ethnical, racial or religious group." [19]

Since World War II, international affairs have been

Atrocities Lead to Rules of War

Since ancient times, man has tried to impose ethical rules on wartime behavior, spelling out morally acceptable reasons for waging war and rules for how they are fought and how prisoners and civilians treated. The modern movement to regulate war began gathering steam in the 19th century, after such innovations as the telegraph, photography and, later, radio and television, brought the starkness of the battlefield into people's living rooms. Major contemporary efforts to regulate war include the following treaties:

Instructions for the Government Armies of the United States in the Field, April 24, 1863 — Prompted by descriptions of the horrors of the Civil War, President Abraham Lincoln ordered the War Department to create rules of conduct mandating humane treatment of prisoners during wartime. The so-called Lieber Code was drafted by Francis Lieber, a law professor at Columbia College, and revised by a board of Army officers.

Convention for the Amelioration of the Condition of the Wounded in Armies in the Field, Geneva, Switzerland, Aug. 22, 1864 — The first Geneva Convention — drafted by the fledgling International Committee of the Red Cross after the brutality of the Crimean War — called on all nations to care for the wounded, including those of their foes, and not to attack medical personnel treating soldiers.

Convention II with Respect to the Laws and Customs of War on Land and its Annex: Regulation Concerning the Laws and Customs of War on Land, The Hague, July 29, 1899 — The first Additional Protocol built on the 1864 Geneva agreement by setting down rules prohibiting the mistreatment of captive combatants or those disabled by sickness, injury or other means.

Convention for the Amelioration of the Condition of the Wounded and Sick in Armies in the Field, Geneva, July 6, 1906 — The 1906 Geneva Convention replaced the 1864 Geneva agreement and used more precise language to define the rights of wounded combatants and non-combatants. Rights of voluntary aid organizations were expressly recognized for the first time, and rules were established for the burial of dead combatants.

Convention on the Prevention and Punishment of the Crime of Genocide, United Nations, Dec. 9, 1948 — Created in response to the atrocities of World War II, the so-called Genocide Convention outlawed abuse "committed with intent to destroy, in whole or in part, a national, ethnical, racial or religious group."

Geneva Convention, Aug. 12, 1949 — Four conventions adopted in 1949 are the most significant and comprehensive efforts to codify the laws of war. Ultimately ratified by 188 nations, the conventions mandate humane treatment of sick and wounded ground and sea forces, prisoners of war and civilian non-combatants. They also prohibit attacks on civilian targets or methods of warfare that would injure civilians.

Additional Protocols to the Geneva Convention, June 8, 1977 — Two Additional Protocols expanded the scope of the 1949 Geneva Convention to cover modern weapons and victims of internal conflicts and terrorism.

Rome Statute of the International Criminal Court, July 17, 1998 — This treaty called for the creation of the International Criminal Court (ICC) to investigate crimes against humanity and serve as a permanent war-crimes court. Seventy-six nations have ratified the treaty, but on May 6, 2002, the Bush administration withdrew earlier U.S. approval by the Clinton administration. The court is expected to go into operation in 2003.

Sources: Aryeh Neier, *War Crimes* (Times Books, 1998); International Committee of the Red Cross, http://www.icrc.org

---

largely driven by the competition between the capitalist United States and the communist Soviet Union and — to a lesser degree — by the struggle for independence by European colonies in Africa, Asia and elsewhere. Both factors sparked horrific conflicts around the globe, most of which were fought with little adherence to the Geneva Convention or any other humanitarian code or treaty. In conflicts from Cambodia, India and Pakistan to Afghanistan and Nigeria, civilians and combatants have been subjected to unimaginable brutality, and even genocide. [20]

Still, in some violent conflicts in the early 1990s, notably in Rwanda and Bosnia, the laws of war actually came into play in a meaningful way, even if only after the genocidal killing stopped. In both cases, some of the alleged perpetrators have been brought to trial and in some cases convicted and sentenced to prison.

Defiant former Yugoslav President Slobodan Milosevic makes his first appearance before the U.N. War Crimes Tribunal in The Hague, Netherlands, in July 2001. Milosevic is charged with crimes against humanity for his alleged role in atrocities committed in Bosnia, Croatia and Kosovo during the civil wars in the 1990s that broke up Yugoslavia.

CURRENT SITUATION

International Court

Since the Nuremberg and Tokyo trials, several tribunals have been established to deal with horrific acts committed during war, often by soldiers. Currently, in The Hague, former Serbian leader Slobodan Milosevic is defending himself against charges that he deliberately ordered Serbia's military and paramilitary forces to commit genocide and other crimes against Muslims in Bosnia, Croatia and Kosovo. The international tribunal trying Milosevic was created in 1993 specifically to prosecute alleged war crimes associated with the war in Bosnia.

Besides Milosevic, more than 100 others also have been indicted and are either being tried or have had their cases resolved. So far, 11 defendants have been convicted and have served or are serving sentences. [21]

Meanwhile, in Arusha, Tanzania, dozens of Rwandans are facing charges stemming from the 1994

genocide — perpetrated by ethnic Hutus and largely directed against members of the Tutsi ethnic group — that killed up to 1 million people in Rwanda. So far, the tribunal has worked more slowly than its counterpart in the Netherlands, trying only nine people and convicting eight.

The Yugoslav and Rwandan tribunals inspired the creation of a permanent war-crimes court. On July 17, 1998, a United Nations-sponsored conference in Rome established the International Criminal Court (ICC), effective in July 2002.

Of the 127 countries at the conference, the United States was among the seven to vote against the treaty. In the ensuing years, U.S. opposition to the court has only grown stronger. Earlier this year, the Bush administration threatened to withdraw American soldiers from U.N. peacekeeping missions and veto all future ones if the European Union and other strong ICC supporters did not exempt American peacekeepers from the court's jurisdiction. (*See "At Issue," p. 307.*)

A temporary compromise was worked out exempting U.S. troops for a year. In addition, the United States has been pursuing bilateral agreements with individual countries to prevent American troops or officials from being extradited to the court from their jurisdictions.

The administration is concerned that American soldiers and even civilian policymakers could be summoned before the tribunal by prosecutors and judges with political or anti-American agendas. They argue that even top American officials could be indicted, pointing to persistent efforts by human-rights activists and some judges in Europe to bring former Secretary of State Henry A. Kissinger to court for his alleged role in the bombing of Vietnam and Cambodia during the Vietnam War in the 1970s and the toppling of Chile's left-wing President Salvador Allende. [22]

"The administration's concerns are fully justified," says Ted Galen Carpenter, vice president for foreign policy and defense studies at the Cato Institute, a libertarian think tank. "This looks like a highly politicized body, and I could see them pursuing a politically motivated prosecution of U.S. officials."

More important, the ICC lacks many fundamental due-process guarantees provided in the U.S. Constitution and in American courts, he says, "things like unanimous verdicts, the right to confront witnesses and protection against double jeopardy."

Is President Bush's opposition to the International Criminal Court justified?

YES John R. Bolton
Under Secretary for Arms Control and International Security

From remarks to the Aspen Institute, Berlin, Sept. 16, 2002

The International Criminal Court (ICC) has unacceptable consequences for our national sovereignty. [Its] precepts go against fundamental American notions of sovereignty, checks and balances and national independence. [It] is harmful to the national interests of the United States and harmful to our presence abroad.

The United States will regard as illegitimate any attempts to bring American citizens under its jurisdiction. The ICC does not fit into a coherent international "constitutional" design that delineates clearly how laws are made, adjudicated or enforced, subject to popular accountability and structured to protect liberty. . . . Requiring the United States to be bound by this treaty, with its unaccountable prosecutor, is clearly inconsistent with American standards of constitutionalism. . . .

The ICC's authority is vague and excessively elastic, and the court's discretion ranges far beyond normal . . . judicial responsibilities, giving it broad and unacceptable powers. . . . This is most emphatically not a court of limited jurisdiction. Crimes can be added subsequently that go beyond those included in the [authorizing] statute. Parties to the statute are subject to these subsequently added crimes only if they affirmatively accept them, but the statute purports automatically to bind non-parties — such as the United States — to [those] new crimes . . . [which] is neither reasonable nor fair.

Numerous prospective "crimes" were suggested and commanded wide support from participating nations, . . . such as the crime of "aggression," which was included in the statute, but was not defined. . . . There seems little doubt that Israel will be the target of a complaint in the ICC concerning conditions and practices by the Israeli military in the West Bank and Gaza. Moreover, one cannot answer with confidence whether the United States would now be accused of war crimes for legitimate but controversial uses of force to protect world peace.

Our concern goes beyond the possibility that the prosecutor will indict the isolated U.S. soldier who violates our own laws and values by allegedly committing a war crime. Our principal concern is for our country's top civilian and military leaders — those responsible for our defense and foreign policy. They are the ones potentially at risk at the hands of the ICC's politically unaccountable prosecutor. . . .

The prosecutor will answer to no superior executive power, elected or unelected. Nor is there any legislature anywhere in sight, elected or unelected. . . . The Europeans may be comfortable with such a system, but Americans are not.

NO Heather B. Hamilton
Director of Programs, World Federalist Association, and Coordinator, Washington Working Group on the ICC

Written for the CQ Researcher, December 2002

Holding tyrants and war criminals accountable for their crimes not only serves America's national interest but also extends the legacy of U.S. moral leadership since Nuremberg. The International Criminal Court (ICC) is a response to the horrors of the 20th century, which demonstrated the incapacity of nation states alone to ensure justice for genocide, egregious war crimes or crimes against humanity.

America has little to fear from the ICC. The crimes covered by the court closely follow U.S. military law and were largely crafted by American military negotiators. U.S. soldiers and leaders need not fear the court, because they already play by its rules. Bill of Rights protections are guaranteed to suspects. . . . Without a Security Council referral, the limited jurisdiction of the court extends only to atrocities committed on the territory of — or by nationals of — countries that have accepted its jurisdiction (thereby ruling out cases against Israel, which is not a signatory).

Countries like the United States, with a functioning, independent judiciary will not see their nationals brought before the court, which is blocked from acting when a domestic court is willing and able.

The ICC is the "Court of the Democracies." Joining it means accepting its jurisdiction, where the vast majority of participating countries already respect the rule of law. Of the 85 states that are parties to the treaty, 65 percent are ranked by Freedom House as "totally free," and another 29 percent are "partly free." These democracies make up an oversight body that will elect (and can dismiss) judges and prosecutors, provide the budget and ensure accountability for the court's actions.

The administration's war on the ICC does not ensure protections from illusory threats, but only promotes the perception that America sees itself as above the rule of law and as uninterested in justice for genocide victims. Joining the ICC would allow the United States to oversee the election of U.S. judges and prosecutors, influence the workings of the court and hold accountable tyrants in Sudan, Iraq and other critical areas of concern.

But even without U.S. ratification, the United States would best be served by engaging with the court to ensure that it follows the carefully built-in safeguards and focuses on those cases — like Congo, Sudan, Burma — where justice is desperately needed.

Bosnian prisoners held by Serbs in the squalid Ternopolje prison camp in Prijedor, Bosnia, in the early 1990s show signs of starvation. International humanitarian law prohibits the mistreatment of civilians, but brutality toward non-combatants has been commonplace in recent conflicts throughout the world.

But supporters of the new court counter that administration concerns about politicization are overblown. "If you look at European countries like Spain and Belgium, where the courts have wide jurisdictional latitude to indict anyone they want, you'll find that none of them have ever indicted U.S. officials," says Todd Howland, director of the Robert F. Kennedy Center for Human Rights. "Given the power and influence of the United States, it seems unlikely that the ICC would be hauling in an American official unless it had a very good case against that person."

In addition, Howland says, while the ICC may not offer every protection afforded by a U.S. court, it basically follows the successful procedures used by the current war-crimes tribunals in the Netherlands and Tanzania, which the U.S. supports. "Look, no court is going to ever be perfect, and the ICC is going to have problems here and there," he says. "But this system has been successful so far, and that's why it's internationally accepted."

Even though the United States opposes the ICC, it supports ad hoc war-crimes tribunals to prosecute crimes associated with specific atrocities, like those in Rwanda and the former Yugoslavia. Most recently, the Bush administration said it would like to see Saddam Hussein and his inner circle charged with crimes against humanity — such as the gassing of Iraqi Kurds — if the regime falls. Hussein and about a dozen top officials — known as the "dirty dozen" — would likely be judged by an international tribunal specially established to dispose of Iraq-related cases, said White House officials. [23]

OUTLOOK

More Brutal Wars?

In his 2002 bestseller, *Warrior Politics, Atlantic Monthly* correspondent Robert D. Kaplan predicts that future wars will be more chaotic and vicious, and less regulated.

While international law likely will grow in significance because of its role in trade organizations and human-rights tribunals, Kaplan writes, it will play less of a role in the conduct of future wars because "war will increasingly be unconventional and undeclared, and fought within states rather than between them." [24]

Moreover, Kaplan predicts that wartime justice in future conflicts will not depend on international humanitarian law but on "the moral fiber of military commanders themselves." In other words, every army will be as humane or inhumane as its leader.

Former Justice Department official Rivkin agrees that warfare will become more anarchic. But he says the efforts to regulate war are not keeping pace with the new reality that Kaplan and others envision.

While adversaries like al Qaeda or the Bosnian Serbs don't generally obey international norms, new and more restrictive rules and limits are being imposed on the United States and other "war-fighting countries" like Britain, Israel and Australia, Rivkin says. "We've lost control of the process," he says, because the rules now are being made by humanitarian organizations like Amnesty International and international law professors. "These people are confining us more and more and giving our enemies more and more of a free hand."

Whether it is U.S. troops in Afghanistan or Israeli soldiers in the West Bank, the armies of the developed world are held to increasingly high standards while their adversaries brook no standards at all, he says. For example, Rivkin says, international human-rights activists are far more outspoken about civilian deaths due to Israeli incursions into Palestinian refugee camps than they are about Israeli civilian deaths due to Palestinian suicide bombers. [25]

"The pendulum needs to swing back a bit," Rivkin says. "We need to say: 'If you don't comply with the rules of war, we're going to take the gloves off.' "

The Hoover Institution's Davenport agrees that the rules of war "need to change to fit new realities. We're living in an age of terrorism, and my sense is that we're still acting defensively because we feel constrained by these rules."

But Howland of the Robert F. Kennedy Center for Human Rights says that ignoring the rules will simply make warfare more violent and horrific. "This idea that we should 'take off the gloves' is simply ridiculous," he says. "Doing that merely makes the conflict more brutal."

The solution is to bring everyone, even non-state entities, into the rulemaking process, Howland says. "This is a structural problem, not a problem with the rules themselves," he says. "You have these rebel groups and others who see the laws of war as Western constructs. We need to bring them in as parties to the process. We need to make the laws of war apply to everyone, not set a bad example by ignoring them ourselves."

NOTES

1. Glenn Frankel, "Road to Son's Freedom Paved With Anguish," *The Washington Post*, Nov. 30, 2002, p. A16.

2. *Ibid.*

3. For background, see David Masci and Kenneth Jost, "War on Terrorism," *The CQ Researcher*, Oct. 12, 2001, pp. 817-848, and Kenneth Jost, "Rebuilding Afghanistan," *The CQ Researcher*, Dec. 21, 2001, pp. 1041-1064.

4. Quoted in Neely Tucker, "Detainees Seek Access to Courts," *The Washington Post*, Dec. 3, 2002, p. A22.

5. For background, see David Masci and Patrick Marshall, "Civil Liberties in Wartime," *The CQ Researcher*, Dec. 14, 2001, pp. 1017-1040.

6. For background, see Mary H. Cooper, "Weapons of Mass Destruction," *The CQ Researcher*, March 8, 2002, pp. 193-216.

7. For background, see Kenneth Jost, "War Crimes," *The CQ Researcher*, July 7, 1995, pp. 585-608.

8. For a thorough defense of the Bush administration's position, see Lee A. Casey, David B. Rivkin Jr. and Darin R. Bartram, "The Laws of War: They Aren't POWs," *The Washington Post*, March 3, 2002, p. B3.

9. Anthony Dworkin, "British Court Attacks U.S. Policy on Detainees," crimesofwar.org., Nov. 7, 2002.

10. Susan Schmidt and Bradley Graham, "Military Trial Plans Nearly Done," *The Washington Post*, Nov. 18, 2002.

11. Tom Jackman and Dan Eggen, "'Combatants' Lack Rights, U.S. Argues; Brief Defends Detainees'

Treatment," *The Washington Post*, June 20, 2002, p. A1.

12. See "Strategic Dossier: Iraq's Weapons of Mass Destruction," International Institute of Strategic Studies, September 2002. www.iiss.org.

13. Quoted in Bill Broadway, "Challenges to Waging a "Just War," *The Washington Post*, Oct. 13, 2001, p. B9.

14. Quoted at www.orst.edu/instruct/phl302/ philosophers/grotius.html; the Oregon State University Philosophy Web site.

15. Aryeh Neier, *War Crimes: Brutality, Genocide, Terror, and the Struggle for Justice* (1998), p. 14.

16. For background, see Kenneth Jost, "Holocaust Reparations," *The CQ Researcher*, March 26, 1999, pp. 257-290.

17. International Committee of the Red Cross, www.icrc.org.

18. *Ibid.*

19. Quoted in "Convention on the Prevention and Punishment of the Crime of Genocide," 78 U.N.T.S. 277, Article II.

20. For background, see Mary H. Cooper, "Women and Human Rights," *The CQ Researcher*, April 30, 1999, pp. 353-376.

21. United Nations, www.un.org/icty/

22. For background, see "Harry Dunphy, "Incisive and Controversial, A Statesman Returns," The Associated Press, Nov. 28, 2002.

23. Peter Slevin, "U.S. Would Seek to Try Hussein for War Crimes," *The Washington Post*, Oct. 30, 2002, p. A1.

24. Robert D. Kaplan, *Warrior Politics* (2002), p. 118.

25. For background, see Mary H. Cooper, "Global Refugee Crisis," *The CQ Researcher*, July 7, 1999, pp. 569-592.

BIBLIOGRAPHY

Books

Gutman, Roy, and David Rieff, eds., *Crimes of War: What the Public Should Know*, W.W. Norton, 1999.
An encyclopedia with 140 entries concerning war crimes, including Bosnia, civilian immunity, genocide and prisoners of war.

Johnson, James Turner, *Morality and Contemporary Warfare,* **Yale University Press, 2000.**
A professor of religion at Rutgers University argues that "just-war" theory is not essentially a pacifist doctrine, as some theologians and others see it.

Neier, Aryeh, *War Crimes: Brutality, Genocide, Terror and the Struggle for Justice,* **Times Books, 1998.**
A Holocaust survivor and president of the Open Society Institute chronicles efforts to bring war criminals to justice, focusing on recent atrocities in the former Yugoslavia and Rwanda.

Reisman, W. Michael, and Chris T. Antoniou, eds., *The Laws of War: A Comprehensive Collection of Primary Documents on International Laws Governing Armed Conflict,* **Vintage Books, 1994.**
An excellent primer on international humanitarian law (IHL), including excerpts from the Geneva and Hague Conventions and U.N. Charter.

Walzer, Michael, *Just and Unjust Wars: A Moral Argument with Historical Illustrations,* **Basic Books, 2000.**
A professor of social science at Princeton University considers the moral implications of making war, using examples from ancient times to the 20th century.

Articles

"Judging Genocide: Prosecuting War Crimes," *The Economist,* **June 16, 2001.**
An excellent overview of the war crimes trials dealing with alleged atrocities in the former Yugoslavia and Bosnia and what the new International Criminal Court can learn from their successes and mistakes.

"The Prisoners Dilemma," *The Economist,* **Jan. 24, 2002.**
The article looks at the dispute over the rights of the Taliban and al Qaeda prisoners at Guantanamo Bay.

Frankel, Glen, "Road to Son's Freedom Paved With Anguish," *The Washington Post,* **Nov. 30, 2002, p. A16.**
Frankel explores lawyers' efforts to secure trials for the detainees from Afghanistan at Guantanamo Bay.

Kagan, Robert, "Europeans Courting International Disaster," June 30, 2002, p. B7.
A senior associate at the Carnegie Endowment for International Peace defends the administration's concerns about U.S. soldiers and officials being hauled before the International Criminal Court.

Lattin, Don, "Clerics Question Whether Pre-Emptive Iraq Strike Would be Just War," *The San Francisco Chronicle,* **Oct. 12, 2002, p. A16.**
Lattin provides an overview of religious leaders' opinions on whether a U.S. attack on Iraq would meet the "just-war" test.

Pavlischek, Keith J., "The Justice in Just War," *First Things,* **May 2000, pp. 43-47.**
A fellow at the Center for Public Justice contends many theologians mistakenly think that just-war theory is essentially a pacifist doctrine.

Slevin, Peter, "U.S. Would Seek to Try Hussein for War Crimes," *The Washington Post,* **Oct. 30, 2002, p. A1.**
Slevin details administration plans to establish an ad hoc war-crimes tribunal to try Iraqi President Saddam Hussein and his inner circle for crimes against humanity, including gassing his own people.

Sprague, Joseph C., "We Must Say 'No' to War with Iraq," *Chicago Tribune,* **Oct. 21, 2002, p. 16.**
A United Methodist bishop argues that an attack on Iraq would not meet "just-war" criteria.

Tammeus, Bill, "Viewing War Through the Lens of Theology," *The Kansas City Star,* **Oct. 13, 2002.**
Tammeus goes back to the ancient roots of just-war theory and explains how it is being applied differently in today's global conflicts.

Reports

"Myths and Realities about the International Criminal Court," Washington Working Group on the International Criminal Court, www.wfa.org/issues/wicc/factsheets/myths
The report argues the International Criminal Court (ICC) contains adequate due-process protections and will not become a "star chamber."

"The U.S. Response to the International Criminal Court: What Next?" *The Federalist Society,* **May 2002.**
Papers and documents outline U.S. concerns over how the ICC could mistreat U.S. soldiers and officials.

For More Information

American Non-Governmental Organizations Coalition for the International Criminal Court, (AMICC), United Nations Association, 801 Second Ave., 2nd Floor, New York, NY 10017-4706; www.amicc.org.html. The coalition supports U.S. approval of the International Criminal Court (ICC).

American Red Cross, 430 17th St., N.W., Washington, DC 20006-2401; (202) 737-8300; www.redcross.org The nation's leading humanitarian organization prepares and disseminates information on international humanitarian law.

Amnesty International USA, 322 8th Ave., New York, NY 10001; (212) 807-8400; web.amnesty.org. A worldwide organization that promotes human rights.

Cato Institute, 1000 Massachusetts Ave., N.W., Washington, DC 20001; www.cato.org. A public-policy research organization that advocates limited government and individual liberty.

Center for Public Justice, 2444 Solomons Island Rd., Suite 201, Annapolis, MD 21401; (410) 571-6300; www.cpjustice.org. A public-policy think tank that looks at issues from a Christian perspective.

Crimes of War Project, American University, 4400 Massachusetts Ave., NW., Washington, DC 20016-8017; (202) 885-2051; www.crimesofwar.org. A collaboration of journalists, lawyers and scholars dedicated to raising public awareness of the laws of war.

The Federalist Society, 1015 18th St., N.W., Suite 425, Washington DC 20036; (202) 822-8138; www.fed-soc.org. Promotes conservative and libertarian views in the legal profession.

Hoover Institution, Stanford University, Stanford, CA 94305; (650) 723-1754; www-hoover.Stanford.edu. A conservative think tank devoted to the study of politics, economics and international affairs.

Human Rights Watch, 350 Fifth Ave., 34th Floor, New York, NY 10118-3299; (212) 290-4700; www.hrw.org. An advocacy group that investigates and documents human-rights abuses around the world.

International Committee of the Red Cross, Washington Delegation, 2100 Pennsylvania Ave N.W., Suite 545, Washington, DC 20037; (202) 293-9430; www.icrc.org. From its Geneva headquarters, the ICRC promotes more humane wartime behavior.

International Institute for Humanitarian Law, La Voie Creuse 16, 1202 Geneva, Switzerland; 41 22 9197930; geneve@iihl.org. A private, nonprofit organization founded in 1970 to develop and disseminate the principles of international humanitarian law.

National Council of Churches, 475 Riverside Dr., Suite 880, New York, NY 11080; (212) 870-2227; www.ncc-cusa.org. A coalition of 39 Christian denominations in the United States.

The Robert F. Kennedy Memorial, 1367 Connecticut Ave., N.W., Suite 200, Washington, DC 20036; (202) 463-7575.; www.rfkmemorial.org. A charitable organization that works for a peaceful and just world through domestic and international programs that help the disadvantaged and oppressed.

15

Bush and the Environment

Mary H. Cooper

Smog envelops downtown Los Angeles shortly after sunrise in early September. President Bush's Clear Skies Initiative would cut by 70 percent power-plant emissions of three major air pollutants that contribute to smog and acid rain and cause respiratory and cardiovascular diseases. Bush would use market incentives — not current EPA-set mandates — to encourage utility operators to reduce emissions. Critics say the approach favors industry.

From *The CQ Researcher*, October 25, 2002.

President Bush had barely hung his Stetson on the White House hat rack before he launched into a series of controversial environmental policy changes.

In one of his first moves, he froze 175 executive orders and regulations that President Bill Clinton had issued just before leaving office in January 2001. Since then, the Bush administration has implemented many other environmental policies that critics say favor oil producers, loggers, electric utilities and other industries.

In another early action, Bush sought to lower the arsenic levels permitted in drinking water, but the administration later bowed to widespread protests and restored Clinton's stricter standards. Still, the pace of Bush's regulatory "rollbacks" has since picked up.

This year, for example, the administration lifted a ban on new oil and gas drilling in the Rocky Mountains, eased tough air-conditioner efficiency standards and formally designated Nevada's Yucca Mountain as a nuclear-waste repository — despite lingering safety concerns. In June, Bush announced a plan that critics say would weaken enforcement of Clean Air Act pollution limits. In August, the administration opposed a sweeping proposal by the World Summit on Sustainable Development to increase the use of solar power and other forms of renewable energy. The president also unveiled a controversial plan to reduce wildfire damage in national forests by waiving limits on logging.

In addition to rewriting regulations, Bush has made other controversial environmental decisions. Within weeks of taking office, he reversed a campaign pledge to push for limits on industrial emissions of carbon dioxide and other "greenhouse gases," which most scientists believe are causing a potentially catastrophic warming of

Air Quality Has Improved

The Clean Air Act has significantly reduced industrial emissions that contribute to smog and acid rain and cause respiratory and cardio-vascular diseases. From 1982-2001, for example, the required intro-duction of lead-free gas eliminated more than 90 percent of the lead in the air, and particulate matter dropped by half. Only carbon monoxide increased, largely due to the popularity of gas-guzzling sport-utility vehicles. President Bush's new Clear Skies Initiative adds mercury emissions to the list of targeted pollutants.

Major air pollutants affected by Clean Air Act	1982-2001	1992-2001
	(percentage increase or reduction)	
Nitrogen dioxide (NO_2)	+9%	-3%
Volatile organic compounds (form ground-level ozone)	-16	-8
Sulfur dioxide (SO_2)	-25	-24
Particulate matter	-51	-13
Carbon monoxide (CO)	0	+6
Lead	-93	-5

Source: Environmental Protection Agency, "Latest Findings on national Air Quality: 2001 Status and Trends," September 2002

Earth's atmosphere. [1] Bush also renounced the Kyoto Protocol, an international treaty calling for mandatory carbon emission reductions designed to slow global warming.*

Environmentalists say Bush's approach constitutes an unprecedented assault on the nation's commitment to protect the environment. "The Bush administration has the worst record of any presidential administration ever," says Gregory Wetstone, director of programs at the Natural Resources Defense Council (NRDC), an environmental advocacy group in New York City. "I don't think we've ever seen a more sweeping or potent assault on our bedrock environmental laws."

Conservatives, on the other hand, extol Bush's policies as innovative alternatives to bureaucratic red tape. "The Bush administration wants to emphasize the next genera-

tion of environmental policy," says Steven F. Hayward, a resident scholar at the American Enterprise Institute (AEI), a conservative think tank. That policy will produce "less of the old-style, command-and-control regulation" from Washington, he explains, and more use of markets, incentives and regulatory flexibility to enable companies "to get around some of the rigidities in the way we've implemented environmental laws for the last 30 years."

Environmentalists point out that those environmental laws — among them the Clean Air Act, the Clean Water Act and the National Environmental Policy Act (NEPA) — have produced cleaner air and water, reduced the public's exposure to toxic waste and rescued many species from the brink of extinction. Most of the laws were enacted in the early 1970s, after a nationwide grass-roots movement persuaded Congress to clean up pollution generated by decades of unregulated industrial development and to protect the environment from future damage. [2]

But environmentalists say the progress made so far — such as banning the pesticide DDT, installing "scrubbers" on coal-burning smokestacks and halting the discharge of industrial waste into waterways — was the easy part. They concede the second generation of environmental improvements — preventing "runoff" from farms and city streets into streams, saving endangered species indigenous to prime real estate and slowing global warming — will cost more and be politically harder to accomplish.

Conservatives complain that environmentalists ignore the escalating costs of complying with environmental regulations. Cost considerations are especially critical when considering such sweeping issues as global warming, they point out. For instance, the United States is the world's leading source of industrial greenhouse-gas emissions. In order to reduce emissions of those gases, America must shift away from fossil fuels — oil, coal and natural gas — thought to be the main source of those emissions.

---

* Most scientists agree that industrial emissions of carbon dioxide and a few other gases act like the glass in a greenhouse, trapping heat within Earth's atmosphere, a process that over time could melt glaciers, raise sea levels and radically alter the world's ecosystems.

"If the environmentalists wanted to argue that addressing global warming would require us to get rid of fossil fuels, that would be an honest debate," says Jerry Taylor, director of natural resources studies at the Cato Institute, a libertarian think tank. "But to argue that it won't have major economic dislocations or dramatically change a number of aspects of our economy is silly. The main reason we don't use renewable-energy sources today is that it's too expensive and it's not very useful for most purposes."

However, environmentalists contend that cost-effective energy-saving alternatives already exist but policymakers refuse to support them. "We can get carbon-dioxide reduction that would be significant at an acceptable cost," says Michael Oppenheimer, a professor of geosciences and international affairs at Princeton University and an expert on climate change. "The quickest, most effective thing that could be done in the United States is to improve the fuel economy of motor vehicles," which he says would produce immediate emissions reductions without being "inordinately expensive."

In fact, Oppenheimer says, improving fuel economy would help the economy by generating "efficiencies that would ripple through industry," as individual producers figure out the cheapest way to implement the caps. Instead, the Bush administration wants to increase domestic production of fossil fuels, he points out.

Of course, not all the administration's actions can be said to favor business interests in environmental disputes. Last December, for example, the Environmental Protection Agency (EPA) ordered General Electric Co. to pay nearly $500 million to dredge deadly polychlorinated biphenyls (PCBs) from the Hudson River. The decision ended a lengthy struggle with the company, which had dumped 150,000 pounds of the toxic chemical into the river over several decades. [3]

U.S. Leads in Greenhouse Gas Pollution

The United States emitted more greenhouse gases — which are believed to cause global warming — in 1999 than the total emissions from 151 developing nations. Texas was the leading U.S. polluter. President Bush's Clean Skies Initiative does not regulate carbon dioxide — the main greenhouse gas and a major component of emissions from coal-fired power plants. Instead, the Bush plan depends on voluntary industry participation. Critics of the Kyoto Protocol on global warming, which Bush rejected, say it gives overly favorable treatment to developing countries by exempting them from the first round of required carbon-dioxide emission cuts. But Kyoto supporters say developing nations produce relatively few carbon emissions.

State/ Pollution Rank in U.S.	1999 Emissions (mmtce*)	Population (in millions)	No. of developing countries with lower combined emissions	Combined population of these developing countries (in millions)
Texas/1	166.6	21.8	119	1,000.0
California/2	94.8	35.1	109	791.1
Ohio/3	69.8	11.4	103	736.6
Penn./4	64.0	12.3	101	733.6
Florida/5	60.8	16.8	100	714.2
U.S. Total	1,526.1	288.2	151	2,631.0

* mmtce = million metric tons of carbon equivalent. The two biggest sources of mmtce are electric utilities and transportation.

Source: "First in Emissions, Behind in Solutions: Global Warming Pollution from U.S. States Compared to More Than 150 Developing Countries," National Environmental Trust, 2002

And two weeks ago the EPA ordered the permanent shutdown and cleanup of Marine Shale Processors Inc., a hazardous-waste incinerator in rural Louisiana that had claimed it produced harmless recycled material for construction. Environmentalists said the plant was responsible for an outbreak of cancer among nearby residents in the 1980s. [4]

But on the most controversial issues — those with the biggest potential environmental and economic impacts — environmentalists say Bush has come down squarely on the side of industry. For example, following the reversal of national policy on global warming, strongly supported by energy producers, the president announced two major policy shifts that pit business interests against environmental-protection advocates.

Key Bush Officials' Ties to Industry

President Bush has filled several key policy positions with people who have strong ties to industries opposed to environmental-protection laws. Some of the appointees even advocated the repeal or weakening of the very laws they were hired to enforce.

Bush himself is a former executive with Harken Energy Corp., a Texas oil-drilling firm. He chose fellow oilman Dick Cheney, then CEO of the oil-services firm Halliburton Corp., as his running mate in his successful bid for the White House in 2000. He then picked many of his administration's other top officials from the energy, mining and timber industries, all of which have chafed under regulations designed to curb pollution.

Topping the list of appointees hostile to existing environmental-protection programs is Energy Secretary Spencer Abraham, a former U.S. senator from Michigan who in 1999 actually proposed abolishing the department he was picked to head barely two years later. Abraham — whose home state is the center of the U.S. automobile industry — also voted against stronger fuel-efficiency standards for cars and trucks and for cuts to federal funding aimed at spurring the development of less-polluting renewable-energy sources.

Abraham helped craft the administration's national energy policy, presented last year, which calls for increased domestic production of fossil fuels — oil, coal and natural gas — which when burned produce gases and other air pollutants thought to contribute to global warming. The plan also calls for opening more public land, including 2,000 acres of the Arctic National Wildlife Refuge (ANWR), to drilling and mining operations. The energy plan is currently under consideration in the Senate, where Democrats have refused to go along with drilling in ANWR. Abraham's lifetime environmental voting record earned a low 5 percent rating this year from the League of Conservation Voters. [1]

Meanwhile, oil and gas exploration and production is proceeding apace on other federal lands, especially in the Intermountain West, thanks to rulemaking changes backed by Interior Secretary Gale Norton. Norton came from the Denver-based Mountain States Legal Foundation, a conservative property-rights advocacy group headed by James Watt, President Ronald Reagan's controversial Interior secretary (1981-83). The foundation supports opening public lands to logging and mining and recently announced plans to file a suit to block the proposed new listing of a rare mouse under the Endangered Species Act, a law Norton is responsible for implementing. [2]

As Colorado's attorney general, Norton cut her agency's budget for enforcing environmental laws by a third. Since taking office, she has overseen a massive expansion of drilling for oil, gas and coal-bed methane in the Rockies, including on some national monuments. She withdrew a report from the Interior Department's Fish and Wildlife Service that was critical of mountaintop removal. The controversial coal-mining technique pollutes downstream water in much of Appalachia. Norton later delayed completion of a study on the technique's environmental impact. [3]

The records of other key Bush officials are less blatantly anti-environmental. Agriculture Secretary Ann Veneman, whose domain includes the Forest Service and such environmental issues as pesticide regulations and genetically modified food, worked for a law firm that fought President Clinton's proposed moratorium

---

[1] League of Conservation Voters, "Presidential Report Card," January 2002. Information in this section is based on this report unless otherwise noted.

[2] "Group Threatens Lawsuit to Keep Mouse Off Endangered List," Associated Press Newswires, Aug. 1, 2002.

[3] See John Raby, "Mining Study Not Expected Until February," Associated Press Newswires, Aug. 2, 2002.

The Clear Skies Initiative, which Bush proposed in February, would no longer require owners of older, coal-fired electric utilities and other plants to install modern pollution controls when they expand their facilities. In August, after one of the most devastating wildfire seasons in U.S. history, Bush announced plans to let loggers harvest large trees in fire-prone national forests in exchange for clearing highly flammable brush and small trees. To expedite the process, the president's

Healthy Forests Initiative would relax the public-comment requirements spelled out in NEPA and make it harder to use the courts to block timber-clearing projects.

Some of the provisions in both initiatives can be implemented through administrative changes, but Congress will have to approve most of the proposals.

As lawmakers consider changes to environmental policy, these are some of the issues they are considering:

on road building in national forests. But she has won praise from environmentalists for supporting farm-conservation programs, though to little avail. This year's farm bill actually cut some of those programs. [4] And Fran Mainella, director of the National Park Service, another Interior Department agency, won conservationists' praise for her management of Florida's state park system. Yet she also went along with Norton in reversing a Clinton ban on recreational snowmobiling in Yellowstone and Grand Teton national parks last summer. [5]

Conservationists have been critical of Interior Secretary Gale A. Norton, left, and EPA Administrator Christine Todd Whitman.

The Bush administration official with the most visible role in environmental policy enforcement is Christine Todd Whitman, head of the independent Environmental Protection Agency. As governor of New Jersey, Whitman had a mixed record on environmental issues. A strong supporter of so-called smart growth, she set up a program to save open space and discourage suburban sprawl. But she also loosened rules requiring industries to report their use and release of toxic chemicals. Since becoming EPA administrator, Whitman has continued to garner mixed reviews from environmentalists, who welcome some of her decisions, including one forcing General Electric to clean up its deposits of deadly dioxin from the Hudson River. But she is faulted for defending the Bush administration's loosening of rules requiring older power plants to install modern anti-pollution equipment. [6]

It is at lower echelons of government that less visible political appointees with industry ties are making some of the most sweeping changes to environmental policies through the rulemaking process. Agriculture Undersecretary Mark Rey, for example, was a longtime timber-company lobbyist before becoming the administration's top forestry official. Rey helped shape the president's Healthy Forests Initiative, which would let his former clients harvest more large, commercially valuable trees in national forests in exchange for agreeing to clear them of fire-prone undergrowth. Only about half the changes called for under the plan require congressional approval.

Deputy Interior Secretary J. Steven Griles was a mining and energy industry lobbyist before joining the department that oversees both industries' access to public lands. He has come under scrutiny for potential conflict of interest stemming from his alleged interest in firms that stand to benefit from such department decisions as the issuance of permits for mining and mountaintop removal. [7]

[4] See Jake Thompson, "Farm-State Lawmakers Rip USDA Officials," *Omaha World-Herald*, Sept. 24, 2002.

[5] See Michael Kilian, "Park Service Tweaks Snowmobile Policy; New Guidelines to Avert Total Ban," *Chicago Tribune*, June 27, 2002.

[6] See H. Josef Hebert, "Bid to Ease Pollution Standards Under Fire," *Houston Chronicle*, Sept. 4, 2002.

[7] See Eric Pianin, "Official's Lobbying Ties Decried," The Washington Post, April 25, 2002; and "Boxer Seeks Conflict Probe in Mine Ruling," *Los Angeles Times*, Oct. 5, 2002.

Should basic environmental laws be revised to reflect economic priorities?

Among the environmental-protection laws passed in the early days of the conservation movement, NEPA ranks as the most far-reaching, the cornerstone of environmental protection. A recent *New York Times* editorial called it "the Magna Carta of environmental protection and perhaps the most important of all the environmental statutes signed into law by Richard Nixon three decades ago." [5]

Designed to ensure public access to environmental policymaking, the 1970 law requires the government to carefully study the environmental impacts that likely would result from a federal project; consider the impact of alternatives; and take public comments into account before moving forward. A variety of federal projects, including

Controversy Surrounds Use of Public Lands

The federal government owns more than one-quarter of the total U.S. land area — including more than three-quarters of Nevada and two-thirds of Alaska. Policies governing the use of public lands for recreation and industry — mainly logging, mining and grazing — are highly controversial. President Bill Clinton's ban on snowmobiles in Yellowstone and Grand Teton national parks was among 175 regulations that President Bush put on hold after taking office. Clinton's ban on new road building on 60 million acres of national forests was blocked by a federal judge in Idaho to prevent "irreparable harm" to the timber industry.

Percentages of Federally Owned Land

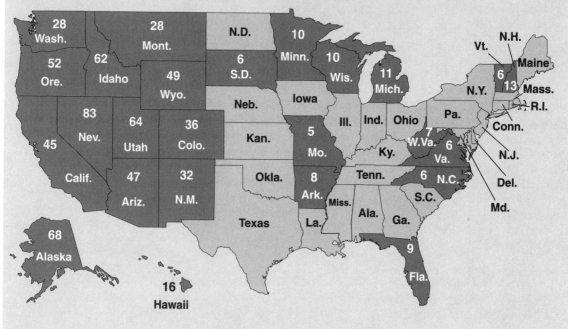

Note: States without percentages are 4 percent federally owned, or less.

Sources: www.anwr.org; Statistical Abstract of the United States

roads and dams, have been changed or halted as a result of NEPA-mandated environmental-impact statements.

But critics say NEPA has caused needless, costly delays of projects and discouraged well-designed policy initiatives. "Because of the straitjacket of a lot of environmental policy, the rulemaking process often leaves administrators in an either-or situation, where you're either going to apply a very tough rule or you decide to waive the rule for certain parties or get rid of the rule completely," says AEI's Hayward. "That results in mistakes like the Bush administration's arsenic decision, which was a complete political disaster."

Other critics say that by emphasizing public oversight, NEPA discourages the scientific assessment of environmental issues. "The law is overreaching and unconstitutional," says Taylor of the Cato Institute. "It makes environmental determinations based not on science or the public interest but on political gain. Anybody who thinks that the exercise of federal power in the environment is based on anything other than a political calculation about what will most appeal to the swing voter is living in a make-believe country."

In May, the Bush administration ordered the White House Council on Environmental Quality to conduct a review of NEPA, essentially inviting agencies to point out flaws in the law and suggest alternative language that may open the way for formal proposals to amend it. The council's task force has nearly completed its study of the environmental-impact statement process, which could include the drafting of new regulations.

"Laws get static over time," says Agriculture Undersecretary Mark Rey, who plays a key role in setting the Bush administration's public lands policy. While he recognizes the need for continued public involvement in policymaking, Rey says agencies need to meet that broad goal "by exploring new ways to involve the public in a good-faith and interactive effort." As the administration's top forestry official, Rey helped shape Bush's new forest-thinning plan, which would waive NEPA requirements for public input.

While the review process continues, the administration is using its executive power to make a broad array of changes to environmental policy with little public notice. "Rewriting laws requires a public process and an open debate," says the NRDC's Wetstone. "What we're seeing now is an effort to leave the laws largely on the books but render them for the most part empty words on paper, with little relevance for what polluters, mining companies and logging companies have to do in the real world."

Environmental laws set goals, such as keeping river, lake or ocean water safe for fishing and swimming. It is then up to executive branch agencies — such as the Interior Department or the EPA — to write regulations to enforce those goals. For instance, the EPA may set standards for maximum levels of water pollutants in a particular river. NEPA and the 1946 Administrative Procedures Act ensure a certain degree of public access to this rulemaking process, by requiring public hearings before any new regulations are adopted.

But the laws do not prevent agencies from making significant policy changes by simply issuing "guidance" on regulatory matters, without oversight. Critics say the Bush administration is purposely using this mechanism to avoid exposure to public scrutiny.

"We've seen big changes in forest policy and policy on snowmobiles in national parks that weren't even [advertised as] rulemakings," says Wetsone, who cites more than 100 separate actions by six federal agencies and the White House that were taken outside the rulemaking process. "Rulemaking requires a public process, while guidance can happen with almost no public process."

President Bush wants to spur domestic energy production by allowing more oil and gas drilling on public lands, including 2,000 acres in Alaska's vast Arctic National Wildlife Refuge (ANWR), above. Environmentalists say the United States should try to save energy by improving auto fuel efficiency, developing alternative fuels and reducing the burning of fossil fuels.

Critics of the current regulatory system say Bush has not gone far enough to change it. "The environmental regulatory state is pretty much on autopilot, a fact that most observers miss," says Taylor of the Cato Institute. "Environmentalists have every incentive to tell the public that every little squiggle in the regulatory process is a huge threat to the environment."

Will the administration's proposed clean-air measures improve air quality?

On Feb. 14, President Bush announced his new Clear Skies Initiative, which he said would greatly improve U.S. air quality and reduce the threat of global warming. "This new approach will harness the power of markets [and] the creativity of entrepreneurs and draw upon the best scientific research," Bush said. "And it will make possible a new partnership with the developing world to meet our common environmental and economic goals." [6]

The plan aims to cut by 70 percent power-plant emissions of three major air pollutants — nitrogen oxides, sulfur dioxide and mercury — that contribute to smog and acid rain and cause respiratory, cardiovascular and neurological disorders. But rather than relying on current EPA-set mandates, Bush would use market incentives to encourage utility operators to reduce emissions of the three pollutants. Bush's plan emulates an innovative pro-

Why Bush Backtracked on Kyoto

During the 2000 presidential campaign, then-Texas Gov. George W. Bush promised to set limits on the pollutant that most scientists say is mainly responsible for global warming.

But in one of his first acts after entering the White House, Bush abandoned that pledge, saying the scientific evidence linking carbon-dioxide emissions from fossil-fuel combustion was outweighed by the economic cost of curtailing fossil-fuel use throughout the U.S. economy.

Later, Bush announced he would not submit the Kyoto Protocol to the U.S. Senate for ratification. The United Nations agreement to cap carbon emissions that cause global warming had been signed by President Bill Clinton in 1997, along with the leaders of 175 other countries.

Bush's rejection of Kyoto was not surprising. Even Clinton never submitted it for Senate ratification because he knew he would be unable to garner the required two-thirds majority. U.S. industry has always been adamantly opposed to the protocol's terms, which set tougher carbon-dioxide emission targets for the United States — the world's largest source of greenhouse-gas emissions — than for any other industrialized country.

Critics say that achieving the treaty's emission targets would require a massive shift to non-fossil fuels, imposing unacceptable costs on the U.S. economy. They also oppose the protocol's favorable treatment of developing countries, which would be exempted from the first round of required carbon-dioxide emission cuts.

Finally, despite the consensus of hundreds of scientists from around the world who advised the United Nations on the threat of climate change, critics continue to say the evidence linking global warming to fossil-fuel use is not strong enough to warrant the economically disruptive remedies called for under Kyoto.

"Everyone accepts the fact that the planet's surface has warmed by about a degree Fahrenheit over the last 100 years," says Jerry Taylor, director of natural-resource studies at the libertarian Cato Institute. "But it turns out that the warming is quite a bit below what the computer models say should have occurred by now. What it means is that on a January evening in Yellowknife, Canada, instead of being 28 degrees below zero it might be 25 degrees below zero. It's very hard to spin disaster stories around that."

President Bush has acknowledged that global warming poses a threat, but he agrees with Kyoto critics that the protocol's remedies are too drastic. In February 2002, as part of his new Clear Skies Initiative to combat air pollution, he submitted an alternative plan for dealing with global warming. In place of the established limits on carbon-dioxide emissions set by the protocol, the Bush plan would seek an 18 percent reduction over the next 10 years in the United States' "greenhouse-gas intensity" — the amount of carbon dioxide emitted per dollar of gross domestic product. This change, he said, would come as technological advances enabled industry to emit less carbon dioxide without jeopardizing economic growth.

"This will set America on a path to slow the growth of our greenhouse-gas emissions and, as science justifies, to stop and then reverse the growth of emissions," he said. "This is the common-sense way to measure progress. Our nation must have growth. Growth is what pays for investments in clean technologies, increased conservation and energy efficiency." The president predicted that the plan would achieve the equivalent of "taking 70 million cars off the road." [1]

Supporters of the Kyoto process are dismayed by the administration's repudiation of the protocol. "Every other industrialized country, with the possible exception of Australia, has announced its intention to ratify and implement the Kyoto Protocol," says Michael Oppenheimer, a professor of geosciences and international affairs at Princeton University and an expert on climate change. "We have a situation where on the most significant environmental problem of this century the United States not only has

---

[1] Bush announced his Clear Skies Initiative Feb. 14, 2002, in a speech at the National Oceanic and Atmospheric Administration in Silver Spring, Md.

gram set up under 1990 amendments to the Clean Air Act that has successfully reduced acid rain in the Midwest and Northeast. The president's proposed "cap-and-trade" system would create markets in which less-polluting utilities could sell their pollution "credits" (based on the amount of pollution below the permitted maximum that they emit) to plants that exceed the caps but are unable or unwilling to invest in costly smokestack filters and other

abdicated leadership but also has essentially no plan for dealing with the problem. That will have the effect of significantly diluting global efforts to deal with the problem, and that inevitably means more global warming."

Bush made another major policy change affecting the global environment during his first weeks in office. In January 2001, he reinstated a ban on U.S. funding of international population programs that provide abortion services or counseling. The so-called "Mexico City" policy, strongly supported by anti-abortion activists, was first imposed by President Ronald Reagan and continued by the president's father, President George Bush senior. Critics charged that family-planning services are needed to slow the rapid growth of population in developing countries, where high population density poses threats to the environment and public health.

President Clinton resumed funding of population programs, but not of organizations that provide abortion services. For example, at the 1994 International Conference on Population and Development in Cairo, Egypt, the United States and other nations pledged to provide $17 billion a year on maternal-health programs.

Bush's action reversed that decision. In July, the Bush administration withheld $34 million in funds from the

U.S. Greenhouse Gases Increased

Total greenhouse-gas emissions — implicated in global warming — have risen 14.2 percent since 1990, according to the EPA. The dominant gas emitted was carbon dioxide, mostly from fossil-fuel combustion.

Increase in U.S. Greenhouse-Gas Emissions

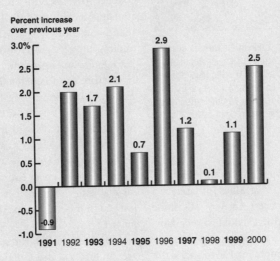

Percent increase over previous year

Source: "The U.S. Greenhouse Gas Inventory," Environmental Protection Agency, April 2002

U.N. family-planning organization because it works with Chinese authorities who are alleged to coerce women into undergoing abortions and sterilizations. Today, U.S. funding of maternal-health programs stands at about $500 million. [2]

On the other hand, Bush has continued another international environmental initiative supported by his predecessor. In 2001, EPA Administrator Christine Todd Whitman signed a treaty, negotiated by the Clinton administration, that calls for the global phaseout of 12 persistent organic pollutants (POPs). The pollutants — including dioxin, PCBs and DDT — break down slowly, can travel long distances and have been linked to cancer and birth defects.

The 50-nation Stockholm Treaty on Persistent Organic Pollutants would allow for the addition to

the list of new chemicals. But the enabling legislation Bush presented to the Senate for ratification in May lacks that provision. [3]

---

[2] See John Donnelly, "Maternal Health Survey Faults Cutbacks," *The Boston Globe*, Sept. 26, 2002.

[3] See Scott Lindlaw, "President Asks Senate to Ratify Treaty on Toxic Releases; Democrats Say His Plan Falls Short," Associated Press Newswires, May 7, 2002.

equipment to reduce their emissions.

"President Bush has a strong commitment to environmental protection, and this bill will not only accelerate the already improving air quality of our nation but

begin key reforms to regulatory programs which have hindered progress and impeded technological innovation," said Rep. Joe Barton, R-Texas, on introducing the legislation in the House on July 29, 2002.

Getty Images/David McNew

President Bush approved Yucca Mountain in the Nevada desert as the nation's repository for waste from nuclear-power plants. Environmentalists and Nevada officials had tried to block the site on health and environmental grounds. Pending approval by the Nuclear Regulatory Commission, more than 70,000 metric tons of nuclear waste will be shipped here beginning in 2010.

Environmentalists see the Bush plan as an attempt to get around existing law. "The Clear Skies Initiative is a legislative effort to weaken the Clear Air Act," Wetstone says. If the proposal goes forward, it "could be very damaging and have a dramatic impact on levels of pollution."

Especially troubling to environmental advocates is the plan's impact on so-called New Source Review (NSR) provisions in the Clean Air Act. Those measures require 17,000 older power plants, oil refineries and other facilities that were exempted from emission caps to comply with the caps if they modernize or expand their facilities, creating a new source of pollutants. Rule changes announced in June would eliminate the NSR requirements in all but the most flagrant cases of air pollution. (See "At Issue," p. 334.)

"New Source Review can and should be reformed to make it less bureaucratic," said Sen. John Edwards, D-N.C., chairman of the Senate Health, Education, Labor and Pensions Subcommittee on Public Health, at a hearing on Sept. 3, 2002. "But the need for reform should not be an excuse so that polluters can send more deadly pollution into the air without cleaning up. That's exactly what's happening here."

Industry has been so opposed to the NSR program that utilities were not expected to support the rest of the Clear Skies Initiative — the 70 percent reduction target

and the cap-and-trade program — unless the review program was weakened.

Bush submitted the plan to Congress in late July. "This is a very aggressive proposal to restructure environmental regulations," says A. Denny Ellerman, executive director of the Massachusetts Institute of Technology's Center for Energy and Environmental Policy Research. "The very ambitious targets for the three pollutants are clearly linked with relief from New Source Review."

Ellerman says Bush's market approach is a better way to reduce air pollution than the current hands-on, "command-and-control" system. "Instead of getting into this endless nitpicking over how exactly you're supposed to reach emission targets, the plan defines the general objective within the acceptable parameters and then lets the market or individual firms figure that out," he says.

The existing system assumes that the regulator knows how to reduce emissions most cheaply, which is never the case, he says. Under a cap-and-trade system, he adds, "Essentially we don't care what you do, just so you have a permit for whatever emissions you emit, and that's an inviolable rule. A market-based system would cost much less and in the end produce better environmental performance."

However, carbon dioxide — considered the main greenhouse gas and a major component of emissions from coal-fired power plants — is conspicuously missing from the list of air pollutants regulated by the Bush plan.

During the presidential campaign, Bush had promised to set carbon-dioxide emission limits. However, once elected, he backed off from that promise, saying it would hurt the economy. Indeed, this year for the first time in six years EPA's annual report on air-quality trends contains no mention of carbon dioxide. [7]

As an alternative to the carbon-dioxide emissions cuts mandated by the Kyoto Protocol, the Bush plan aims to reduce America's "greenhouse-gas intensity" — the amount of emissions created per million dollars of gross domestic product — from the current level of 183 metric tons to 151 metric tons by 2012. Industry participation in the effort would be voluntary.

"The approach taken under the Kyoto Protocol would have required the United States to make deep and immediate cuts in our economy to meet an arbitrary target," Bush said. [8] "It would have cost our economy up to $400 billion, and we would have lost 4.9 million jobs. As president of the United States, charged with safeguarding the welfare of the American people and American workers, I will not commit our nation to an unsound international treaty that will throw millions of our citizens out of work. Yet we recognize our international responsibilities. So in addition to acting here at home, the United States will actively help developing nations grow along a more efficient, more environmentally responsible path."

Supporters of international efforts to combat global warming say Bush's new policy will have little impact on carbon emissions in the United States — the world's largest source of industrial greenhouse gas output. "The plan to reduce slightly the carbon-dioxide emissions intensity of the U.S. economy effectively doesn't change anything," says Princeton geoscientist Oppenheimer. "On the whole, it appears that the Bush administration has effectively no policy on climate change — except to do nothing."

Would giving timber companies greater access to national forests help reduce wildfire damage?

In one of the worst wildfire seasons on record, 20 firefighters died last summer battling fires that scorched 6.5 million acres of national forests in the Western United States and destroyed hundreds of homes. To prevent similar outbreaks in the future, President Bush has proposed encouraging logging companies to clear highly flammable brush and small trees from 10 million acres of national forests that are especially prone to wildfires.

Scientists agree on the need for changes in longstanding fire-prevention strategies. For most of the 20th century, forestry officials tried to suppress all types of fire in the nation's forests. Visitors were constantly warned to put out campfires and extinguish cigarettes. Billboards nationwide featured the Forest Service's mascot, Smokey Bear, admonishing the public, "Only YOU can prevent forest fires."

But total fire suppression, it turns out, literally added fuel to the problem, by preventing the relatively small natural fires needed periodically to burn off undergrowth and allow tall-tree seedlings to mature. Abundant brushy vegetation, combined with the drought conditions of recent summers, set the stage for wildfires that quickly turned into unmanageable infernos engulfing vast tracts of forests, as well as the houses that have proliferated in them in the fast-growing Western states.

"The growth of [vegetation] on these stands of trees over the last 30 years has increased exponentially," says Undersecretary Rey. "As a consequence of substantial fire suppression, when a fire ignites in these stands it becomes cataclysmic, burning much more hotly and intensely."

Complicating the problem, he points out, is the fact that the five fastest-growing states are in the Intermountain West. "Everyone wants to build their homes out in the forests," he says, forcing firefighters to concentrate on saving human life and property instead of the kinds of "prescribed burns" that normally are set to clear small tracts of underbrush before they can cause uncontrollable fires.

On Aug. 22, as several large forest fires still raged, Bush unveiled a new plan to combat highly destructive wildfires. The Healthy Forests Initiative would waive NEPA-mandated environmental-impact statements for tree-thinning projects on 10 million acres of fire-prone federal land that is either near homes or watersheds or is infested by disease or insects. The plan would bar challenges to these projects through the Forest Service's normal administrative process or through the courts. The initiative also would relax regulations for forest-thinning projects on public land outside the 10 million high-risk acres. A judge asked to halt a particular logging project, for example, would have to consider potential wildfire damage if the tract were not logged, as well as the immediate environmental impact.

Finally, the plan would allow the Agriculture and Interior departments to enter into long-term "stewardship" agreements with logging companies and other private entities to harvest and sell large trees from public land, in exchange for clearing brush to reduce fire hazards. This provision, Rey says, also will help create markets for small trees that otherwise would have no commercial value.

For example, by allowing the government to sign longer-term tree-thinning contracts covering larger tracts of forest, the plan would allow companies to harvest enough three- to six-inch diameter trees to profitably turn them into laminated veneer. "If Congress will give us that authority to make that kind of transaction work," he says, "then over time much of that now valueless material will gain commercial value."

Environmental advocates express dismay over Bush's plan. "The Healthy Forests Initiative is going to be hugely damaging," says Wetstone of the NRDC. "We don't have that much old-growth forest left to protect, and to turn it over in a taxpayer-subsidized giveaway to logging companies is just tragic."

CHRONOLOGY

1970s *A grass-roots movement spurs environmental-protection legislation.*

1970 Congress passes Clean Air Act to curb industrial pollution. President Richard M. Nixon establishes Environmental Protection Agency (EPA) and signs National Environmental Policy Act (NEPA) ensuring public participation in the regulatory process.

1972 Clean Water Act requires industries and water-treatment facilities to stop dumping pollutants into rivers.

1973 Endangered Species Act authorizes EPA to list plants and animals threatened with extinction by habitat destruction or pollution.

1974 Safe Drinking Water Act authorizes EPA to set water-purity standards.

1977 Congress amends Clean Air Act to include the New Source Review (NSR) program, requiring companies to install state-of-the-art pollution-control equipment when they build a major new facility or upgrade an existing plant.

1980s *Anti-regulatory sentiment focuses on the costs of environmental protection.*

1980 Congress passes Comprehensive Environmental Response, Compensation and Liability Act — the Superfund law — requiring polluters to clean up toxic-waste sites.

1990s *The pace of new environmental laws slows.*

1990 Amendments to Clean Air Act require polluted cities to use oxygenated gasoline in winter and reformulated gasoline in summer to curb auto emissions; amendments also set up an innovative, market-based program to reduce acid rain by allowing cleaner industries to sell "pollution credits" to heavy polluters.

December 1997 United States and 175 other nations agree in Kyoto, Japan, to take steps to reduce emissions of carbon dioxide and other gases believed to cause global warming.

Nov. 12, 1998 Clinton administration signs Kyoto Protocol, committing the U.S. to cut its carbon emissions by 7 percent below 1990 levels by 2012.

February 1999 President Bill Clinton places an 18-month moratorium on new logging roads in national forests.

2000s *President Bush begins a rollback of environmental protections.*

January 2001 Upon taking office, Bush puts on hold some 175 Clinton administration environmental regulations.

May 17, 2001 Bush unveils plan to open Alaska National Wildlife Refuge to drilling and mining to boost domestic production of fossil fuels.

Jan. 11, 2002 Bush signs Small Business Liability Relief and Brownfields Revitalization Act encouraging private investment in redeveloping less-polluted waste sites by limiting developers' liability for future claims of injury.

Feb. 14, 2002 Bush announces Clear Skies Initiative to amend Clean Air Act and cut power-plant emissions of sulfur dioxide, nitrogen oxide and mercury by 70 percent by letting individual companies trade pollution credits. The administration later announces plans to let plants avoid installing pollution-control equipment when they modernize; plan does not address carbon dioxide, the main greenhouse gas implicated in global warming.

May 2002 Bush launches review of Clinton's moratorium on road building on 60 million acres of national forests.

June 2002 Administration reverses Clinton-era ban on recreational snowmobiling in Yellowstone and Grand Teton national parks. Interior Secretary Gale Norton halts Clinton administration plan to reintroduce grizzly bears to Rocky Mountains.

July 2002 Bush signs congressional resolution naming Nevada's Yucca Mountain as the nation's central repository for radioactive waste from nuclear power plants.

August 2002 Bush announces Healthy Forests Initiative, which would allow loggers to harvest more trees from national forests in exchange for clearing brush. The administration opposes proposal by World Summit on Sustainable Development to increase the use of renewable energy.

But conservatives argue that environmentalists forget that logging has always played a prominent role in the national forest system. "The Forest Service was created in 1898 for the purpose of supplying lumber to American business," says Michael Hardiman, legislative director of the American Land Rights Association, in Battle Ground, Wash., which opposes federal efforts to expand public land. "The Bush administration has seized on this forest-fire crisis to explain to the average person that chopping down trees in the national forests not only doesn't hurt the forests, but is actually a good idea."

Congress is now reviewing Bush's forest proposal. But Democratic lawmakers are torn between the need to prevent a replay of this year's devastating wildfires and reluctance to approve a measure that they say would weaken environmental protection. Even if Congress doesn't act, says Rey, the administration can accomplish about half of the plan's provisions by simply rewriting regulations that currently "bog the system down interminably."

Gale A. Norton, who as secretary of the Interior oversees most public land programs outside the Agriculture Department's Forest Service, echoed that theme recently in *The Washington Post.* "The program is a common-sense approach to reducing fuel loads in forests," she wrote. "The continuing threat to both people and wildlife is real. We must cut the red tape and restore the health of our forests." [9]

BACKGROUND

Status Report

The boom in heavy industry that began after World War II enabled the United States to become the world's leading economic power. Mining, steel, automaking, oil production and electricity generation fueled unparalleled economic growth. But they also took a heavy toll on the environment — polluting the air and water and releasing toxic waste that killed plant and animal life.

By the late 1960s, public concern over widespread pollution had sparked an environmental movement that would generate sweeping laws requiring industries to curb harmful emissions. The laws, and the regulations promulgated to enforce them, have had mixed results. Many environmental threats have been significantly reduced, but serious problems remain.

The following status report looks at the main environmental concerns addressed in the early laws and the Bush administration's actions since taking office in January 2001.

Air quality

The 1970 Clean Air Act, one of the first major environmental-protection measures, set emissions standards for almost 200 pollutants that contribute to smog. The law required factory and power-plant owners to install smokestack "scrubbers" to curb the release of small particles, known as particulate matter, and to reduce sulfur dioxide emissions, a product of fossil-fuel combustion that causes acid rain. Oil companies had to remove lead — which causes degradation of intelligence and the nervous system in children — from gasoline, and automakers were required to install catalytic converters in cars to reduce tailpipe emissions.

In 1977, Congress amended the Clean Air Act to include the New Source Review (NSR) program, designed to reduce emissions from older power plants, refineries and other industrial facilities that had been exempted from the stringent emission standards established for new plants. The NSR program required companies to install state-of-the-art pollution-control equipment when they built a major, new facility or modified an existing plant in ways that resulted in a significant rise in emissions.

Amendments enacted in 1990 strengthened the act by requiring oil companies to sell oxygenated gasoline in the winter to curb carbon-monoxide emissions and switch to reformulated gasoline in the summer to reduce ozone pollution in the most heavily polluted cities. [10] The amendments also strengthened emission standards for power plants and introduced a novel market-based emissions-trading program, which have succeeded in reducing emissions of sulfur dioxide and nitrogen oxide. [11] The amendments also authorized the EPA to address regional air-pollution sources, such as Midwestern power-plant emissions that contribute to smog and acid rain in Northeastern cities and forests.

Since 1970, the United States has seen a 25 percent drop in emissions of the six main air pollutants — nitrogen dioxide, ozone, sulfur dioxide, particulate matter, carbon monoxide and lead. [12] However, rapidly growing metropolitan areas, like Los Angeles, Houston and the Northeastern corridor, continue to experience unhealthy

AFP Photo/Steve Morgan

Glacial ice crashes into Alaska's Prince William Sound. Most scientists say industrial emissions of "greenhouse gases" are heating the atmosphere and eventually will melt glaciers and cause global flooding. President Bush contends his new Clear Skies Initiative would improve U.S. air quality and reduce global warming using voluntary market forces instead of regulatory mandates.

levels of air pollution. Moreover, the Clean Air Act's goal of eliminating air pollution from 158 national parks and wilderness areas has fallen far short of expectations. Ozone levels in Great Smoky Mountains National Park, for example, now rival those of Los Angeles during the summer months, according to a recent study by the National Parks Conservation Association. (*See graph, p. 333.*) [13]

The Clinton administration blamed much of the continuing air pollution on industrial facilities that refused to comply with emissions standards. It sued 51 power plants for violating NSR rules by making major improvements without installing modern smokestack scrubbers. Taking the opposite tack, the Bush administration

charged in June 2001 that NSR requirements discouraged utilities and factories from modernizing and announced plans to review the program.

On Feb. 14, 2002, Bush announced his initiative to amend the Clean Air Act and cut power-plant emissions of sulfur dioxide, nitrogen oxide and mercury by 70 percent. Bush's plan would let individual companies trade pollution credits in a nationwide emissions-trading system. By allowing companies to decide which plants to clean up, critics said the plan would weaken current provisions that protect air quality in national parks and curb cross-boundary air pollution.

On June 13, the administration announced its plans to relax NSR rules so that modernizing or expanding plants can avoid installing pollution-control equipment.

Although the Bush administration has overturned several rules introduced by President Clinton, it has retained a regulation calling for a 97 percent cut in sulfur levels in diesel fuel and a 95 percent cut in harmful emissions by diesel-powered trucks and buses beginning Oct. 1. The EPA also is developing a rule to extend the diesel standards to off-road vehicles, such as bulldozers and tractors. Diesel emissions cause lung cancer and asthma. [14]

Water Quality

For most of the country's history, factory owners built their plants next to rivers, which provided hydropower, ease of shipping and a handy repository for waste. Towns and cities also grew up along waterways, which also used them to dispose of sewage and other waste. By the 1960s, many lakes and rivers were too polluted to support fish and aquatic plants. In 1969, an especially foul, debris-laden section of Cleveland's oil- and chemical-choked Cuyahoga River actually caught fire, sparking indignant calls for the government to clean up the nation's waterways.

Congress responded with the 1972 Clean Water Act, which required factories, utilities and sewage-treatment plants to reduce toxic-waste discharges into waterways. Since then, water pollution from these easily identifiable sources has diminished, fish and wildlife have returned to many once-lifeless waterways and 60 percent of the nation's waters are clean enough to support fishing and swimming.

But runoff of fertilizers, pesticides and other toxic chemicals continues to pollute the remaining 40 percent of U.S. streams, rivers, lakes and coastal areas. The sources of these pollutants are widespread and

How Mercury Pollution Harms Humans

When U.S. power plants burn coal, they produce dangerous mercury vapors. Oxidants in the atmosphere turn vaporized mercury into water-soluble compounds. Rain and snow return the mercury compounds to lakes and streams, where they mix with bacteria to produce organic mercury (methylmercury) — which can cause brain and liver damage and heart problems; pregnant women, fetuses, children and subsistence fisherman are especially vulnerable. In the United States, coal-fired plants cause a third of all mercury emissions. President Bush's Clear Skies Initiative aims to cut by 70 percent the power-plant emissions of mercury, as well as other pollutants that contribute to smog and acid rain and cause respiratory and cardiovascular diseases.

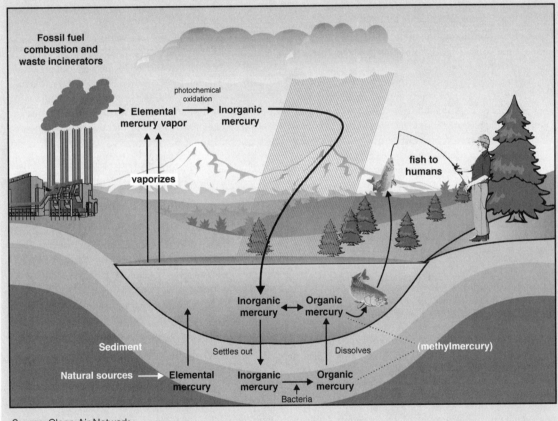

Source: Clean Air Network

hard to identify, including farms, suburban lawns and city streets and storm sewers. To reduce such so-called non-source pollution, the EPA in May proposed a water-quality trading policy similar to the administration's cap-and-trade policy for air emissions. It would allow states, private companies and farmers to trade or sell unused pollution-reduction credits to heavier polluters.

On May 3, the administration issued rules allowing coal companies to dump the rubble from mountaintop mining operations into surrounding streams, a practice the Clinton administration had barred. Critics of mountaintop removal, prevalent in Kentucky and West Virginia, say it exposes miles of Appalachian waterways to pollution from heavy metals and other toxic materials. A U.S. district judge had agreed with the Clinton admin-

The Hidden Power of Federal Regulations

Most federal policymaking involves both the legislative and executive branches of government. Congress passes the laws that lay out policy objectives, such as clean air. Then the executive branch, through its departments and agencies, sets the specific rules and regulations aimed at carrying out those objectives, such as the maximum allowable levels of air pollutants that power plants may emit without incurring sanctions. The third branch of government, the judiciary, comes into play when individuals or groups file suits alleging non-compliance with federal laws and regulations.

The rulemaking process itself can be highly complex. The 1946 Administrative Procedures Act required rulemaking agencies to publish a notice in the *Federal Register* * describing the proposed rule; allow the public to comment in writing on it; and give notice of the final rule and its effective date. The act also authorized the courts to review any rule that was challenged as illegal. 1 Subsequent laws have

---

* *The Federal Register* is published by the federal government every workday and is the legal document for recording and communicating the rules and regulations established by the executive branch. Executive agencies are required to publish in the Register in advance some types of proposed regulations.

[1] For a detailed description and history of the regulatory process, see *Congressional Quarterly's Federal Regulatory Directory*, 1999.

expanded the public's right to participate in the rulemaking process.

Presidents exercise considerable control over the regulatory system. They have the power to appoint like-minded individuals to head the departments and agencies that write the rules. Presidents also can effectively boost or curtail the effectiveness of regulatory enforcement by allocating more or less money to relevant agencies in their annual budget requests to Congress.

They also can issue directives to the regulatory agencies in the form of executive orders. President Ronald Reagan, for example, issued executive orders requiring all proposed regulations to undergo a cost-benefit analysis. No federal regulation could be adopted if it cost more to implement than the value of the benefits it would provide to society. President Bill Clinton reversed that policy with his own executive order.

By their nature, environmental-protection laws involve a large array of regulations. The 1970 Clean Air Act and the 1972 Clean Water Act, for example, rely on specific limits on the release of pollutants into the air and water. As a result, the Environmental Protection Agency (EPA) — created by President Richard M. Nixon in 1970 by executive order — uses regulations as a primary vehicle for administering these laws. According to one study, the EPA, with an enforcement budget of $4.2 billion in fiscal 2002, now spends more than any other agency to

---

istration's position and blocked the U.S. Army Corps of Engineers from issuing new permits for mountaintop removal. [15]

The Clean Water Act also provides protection for wetlands, which nurture the growth of new aquatic wildlife, filter pollutants and help prevent flooding. But development has destroyed more than half of U.S. wetlands, especially in coastal areas. Further destruction of wetlands seemed likely in the wake of the U.S. Supreme Court's January 2001 ruling that the law, which refers to "navigable waters," does not cover isolated bogs, pools and other bodies of water contained within a single state. The first Bush administration had adopted a policy of "no net loss of wetlands," requiring developers who drain and fill wetlands to build or protect additional wetlands. Conservationists charge that

the new wetland rules announced by the Corps of Engineers last year undermine that policy.

The Clinton administration launched a plan to restore the Florida Everglades, the country's largest wetland, which has been greatly reduced in size and polluted by runoff from surrounding cities and farms. The plan, the most comprehensive wetlands-restoration effort ever attempted in the United States, received the support of President Bush, whose brother, Jeb, is up for re-election in November as Florida's Republican governor. In January, the two brothers signed an agreement that ensures adequate water supplies to support the $7.8 billion, 30-year Comprehensive Everglades Restoration Plan. Critics say the plan postpones many key decisions about implementation until after the election. [16]

enforce federal regulations, accounting for a fifth of the total. [2]

Until recent decades, regulations played a relatively small part in government operations. Once confined to the field of commerce, such as the establishment of businesses and the rates they charged, regulations grew in scope and number as lawmakers created programs seeking broader social objectives, including environmental protection. By the late 1970s, the growth of regulations had sparked a heated debate between those who said they were necessary to force industries to stop polluting the environment, and others who blamed them for retarding economic growth.

President Reagan echoed the anti-regulatory message with his call to "get the government off our backs." His successor, President George Bush senior, oversaw a revival in regulatory activity following the passage of such laws as the Clean Air Act amendments of 1990. But he also set up a new office, the Council on Competitiveness, chaired by Vice President Dan Quayle, with a mandate to seek relief for American businesses from the growing number of regulations. Critics accused the council of engaging in "backdoor rulemaking" by failing to publicize its changes in regulations, as required by the 1946 Administrative Procedures Act.

[2] See Clyde Wayne Crews Jr., "Ten Thousand Commandments: An Annual Snapshot of the Federal Regulatory State," Cato Institute, 2002, p. 19.

Following President Clinton's election in 1992, anti-regulatory sentiment grew, helping the Republicans to gain control of the House in 1995. Central to the goal of the self-described Republican revolutionaries led by the House majority leader, Rep. Newt Gingrich, R-Ga., was the dismantling of environmental and other regulations. Clinton, too, joined the effort. His Executive Order 12866, "Regulatory Planning and Review," aimed to reduce existing rules by half and improve interagency coordination to reduce "red tape."

But after the 2000 election ensured Clinton's succession by an openly anti-regulatory administration, Clinton used his executive power to write scores of new environmental regulations during the closing days of his presidency.

Upon taking office, President Bush blocked most of Clinton's regulations while they were still in the public-comment phase. Although he later allowed some to take effect, critics say his administration is exploiting the relative obscurity of the rulemaking process to drastically weaken environmental-protection laws without public scrutiny.

"I think there's been an effort to avoid the public process," says Gregory Wetstone, director of programs at the Natural Resources Defense Council, an environmental advocacy group in New York City.

But supporters of Bush's extensive use of rulemaking to shape environmental policy say he is only responding to the need for a new approach. "The old way of doing things, with rulemaking from the EPA, has played itself out," says Steven F. Hayward, a resident scholar at the American Enterprise Institute. "We need to think of new ways of getting things done."

The nation's other main water-quality statute, the 1974 Safe Drinking Water Act, called on the EPA to set national standards for the purity of tap water provided by public water systems. Amendments enacted in 1996 require states to monitor the quality of groundwater, the source of most of the country's drinking water.

In 1999, however, the National Research Council reported that high levels of arsenic in drinking water put Americans at risk for cancer and urged the EPA to strengthen its standards for this dangerous pollutant. After setting aside a Clinton administration regulation tightening the arsenic standard, the Bush administration faced a storm of criticism and last October announced it would adopt the Clinton standard after all.

Since the Sept. 11 terrorist attacks, the Bush administration has focused on protecting the nation's 168,000 public drinking-water and 16,000 public wastewater systems from attack. On June 12, the president signed the 2002 Public Health Security and Bioterrorism Response Act, which includes measures to protect water supplies.

Meanwhile, EPA Administrator Whitman warned on Sept. 30 that the gains in water quality over the past 30 years are being jeopardized by delays in maintaining and replacing deteriorating water-treatment systems. As a result, the agency reported an increase in the number of estuaries, lakes, streams and rivers classified as "impaired" over the past two years. But many state and local governments, facing growing budget deficits, are asking the federal government to assume some of the financial responsibility for maintaining their water and wastewater-treatment systems. [17]

Toxic Waste

After addressing air and water quality, lawmakers turned to another major source of pollution: toxic-waste disposal sites. The 1980 Comprehensive Environmental Response, Compensation and Liability Act (CERCLA) — better known as the Superfund law — required the EPA to force the cleanup of toxic-waste sites. Under the "polluter pays" principle inherent in the law, industries that created toxic dumps must clean them up. To clean up sites where the polluter is unknown or unable to pay, the law created a Superfund, financed with a special corporate tax.

As it turned out, almost a third of all sites were "orphans," for which the polluter could not be identi-

> A 2001 study found that more than half the nation's 1,300 most-toxic waste dumps had either been cleaned up or no longer posed a threat to human health or the environment. The same study predicted, however, that the list of Superfund sites would grow by up to 50 sites each year over the next decade.

fied, and Superfund came under intense scrutiny as the cost of running the program ballooned to an average of $30 million per cleanup. As a result, Congress has not reauthorized the corporate tax imposed to fund Superfund activities since 1995, and insufficient financing has delayed cleanup operations.

Despite the setbacks, Superfund has begun to pay off. A 2001 study found that more than half the nation's 1,300 most-toxic waste dumps had either been cleaned up or no longer posed a threat to human health or the environment. The same study predicted, however, that the list of Superfund sites would grow by up to 50 sites each year over the next decade. [18]

Nonetheless, the administration announced in February it would not seek an extension of the Superfund trust-fund tax. It also reduced by half the number of sites to be cleaned up, a decision critics cited as another example of the Bush administration's desire to help industry shirk its legal responsibility. [19] Bush requested $1.3 billion — similar to spending levels since 1995 — to help cover program costs in fiscal 2003.

Under the aegis of the Superfund law, the EPA runs a special cleanup program for about 500,000 less-hazardous toxic-waste sites known as "brownfields." Because many of the sites occupy prime, urban real estate, businesses pressed the agency to relax its regulations barring their redevelopment. Fulfilling a campaign pledge, President Bush signed the Small Business Liability Relief and Brownfields Revitalization Act, on Jan. 11, 2002. The law encourages private investment in cleaning up and redeveloping brownfields, in part by limiting developers' liability for future claims of damages stemming from exposure to toxic materials on the sites.

Radioactive waste, chiefly spent fuel from nuclear power plants, is treated separately. For decades, utilities have stored radioactive waste on site, pending the creation of a permanent, central repository that the Energy Department promised to open by January 1998. Technical obstacles, safety concerns and political opposition slowed construction of the chosen site, a deep underground vault at Yucca Mountain in the Nevada desert 90 miles from Las Vegas.

Overriding the opposition of Nevada officials, who tried to block the site designation on health and environmental grounds, President Bush signed a resolution passed by Congress in July naming the site as the sole repository for high-level nuclear waste. Pending approval by the Nuclear Regulatory Commission, Yucca Mountain is expected to begin accepting the waste, which now exceeds 70,000 metric tons, in 2010. [20]

Public Land

Since President Theodore Roosevelt oversaw the creation of the first national parks, the nation's inventory of public land has grown to include more than one-quarter of the total U.S. land area. (*See map, p. 318.*) Most of this land is in the West, where policy governing its use fuels an ongoing debate. Public land has long been open to a variety of industrial and agricultural uses, including logging, mining and livestock grazing. The 1872 Mining

Law, for example, still allows mining companies to drill for hard-rock minerals on federal land for $5 an acre.

As the pace of residential and industrial development in the West quickened, however, policymakers began taking steps to protect public land. The 1964 Wilderness Act created the National Wilderness Preservation System to set aside some of the country's quickly disappearing pristine areas from all industrial use. Recreational uses of public lands also were restricted amid concerns that snowmobiles and other motorized vehicles were harming wildlife, causing erosion and polluting the air. Beginning in 1972, presidents have used executive orders prohibiting recreational snowmobile use in some national parks.

As one of his last environmental acts, President Clinton banned snowmobiles in Yellowstone and Grand Teton national parks. It was among the 175 regulations Bush put on hold after taking office. The administration later announced it would not block the ban, due to take effect in late 2003. But in June the National Park Service announced it would continue to allow snowmobilers into the two parks "with very strict limitations." In September the EPA required the makers of snowmobiles and other off-road vehicles to reduce their products' emissions. Conservationists say the new standards are too lax. [21]

Another Clinton initiative, a ban on road building on 60 million acres of national forests, has drawn strong criticism from the timber industry, which builds roads to reach remote stands of harvestable trees. Bush, who criticized the plan as detrimental to loggers, initiated a review of the ban in May 2002. Shortly thereafter, a federal judge in Idaho blocked the road-building ban, saying it would cause "irreparable harm" to the timber industry.

Bush's energy plan, announced in 2001, has fed pressure to open more public lands to drilling for oil and natural gas (*see p. 332*). His proposal to open a small part of the Arctic National Wildlife Refuge (ANWR) to drilling as a way to reduce growing U.S. dependence on foreign oil is stalled in the Senate, where the Democratic majority opposes the plan.

Meanwhile, environmentalists have challenged thousands of leases to drill for coal-bed methane in Wyoming's Powder River Basin on land managed by the Bureau of Land Management (BLM), charging that the agency granted permits in violation of NEPA. [22]

Rapid population growth, especially in the West, is sharpening a longstanding controversy over what kinds of recreational activities should be permitted on ecologically sensitive public land. Under the 1964 Wilderness Act, federal regulations prohibit "mechanized" activity in protected wilderness areas, barring not only off-road motorized vehicles but also mountain bikes and allowing only hikers and horseback riders. As demand for access to back-country recreation grows, conservationists are trying to protect more land as wilderness. A controversial bill introduced earlier this year by Sen. Barbara Boxer, D-Calif., for example, would set aside 2.5 million additional acres in California as wilderness. [23]

Endangered Species

In 1962, Rachel Carson's bestseller, *Silent Spring*, chronicled the devastating toll the popular pesticide DDT had taken on dozens of species of large birds, focusing public attention on the power that pollution had to drive vulnerable animals and plants to extinction. The 1973 Endangered Species Act addressed that concern by mandating the protection of threatened or endangered plants and animals.

Almost from the beginning, the law emerged as a lightning rod for an often-hostile debate between environmentalists, who invoked it to protect vulnerable habitat, and loggers, ranchers and other users of the land, who claimed such action would cost them their livelihoods.

More recently, the Defense Department added its voice to the critics of the law, arguing that it made it difficult to conduct vital training. Exercises involving naval sonar equipment have been linked to the death and injury of scores of whales and dolphins. [24] Congress rejected the Pentagon's request for exemption from the law, included in a defeated provision of the $29 billion supplemental appropriation for fiscal 2002 signed in August.

The Bush administration has come under attack from environmentalists over its handling of water allocation in the Klamath River basin of Northern and Southern California, home to several endangered salmon species. Thousands of salmon died after the administration acceded to farmers' demands for more irrigation water in late September, leaving insufficient water in the river to sustain the fish. [25]

In the late 1980s, conservationists sought to halt logging in the Pacific Northwest's old-growth forests in order to save the northern spotted owl from extinction.

Wildfires Spark New Policy

A firefighter monitors a backfire near Borrego Springs, Calif., in August (top). Spectators watch the 11-mile-long fire in California's Angeles National Forest in late September. Last summer, after wildfires killed 20 firefighters and scorched 6.5 million acres of national forests in the West, President Bush announced plans to let logging companies harvest large trees on 10 million acres of national forests in exchange for clearing flammable brush and small trees.

Since then, most controversies over the Endangered Species Act have centered on the Western states. [26] Some Western lawmakers, for example, opposed a Clinton plan to reintroduce 25 threatened grizzly bears into a 1.4 million-acre wilderness area of Idaho and Montana.

Although the plan resulted from a compromise among local residents, timber workers and environmentalists, Gov. Kirk Kempthorne, R-Idaho, denounced it as a way to force "massive, flesh-eating carnivores into Idaho" and filed suit to halt its implementation. On June 20, Interior Secretary Norton halted the reintroduction program.

CURRENT SITUATION

Energy Strategy

Despite calls to shift to less-polluting energy sources, the United States continues to rely overwhelmingly on fossil fuels to drive the economy. Oil-derived gasoline and diesel fuel power the nation's cars and trucks, and coal-fired power plants supply most of the electricity, while natural gas — the least polluting fossil fuel of all — heats a growing portion of houses and offices.

Domestic supplies of coal — the dirtiest fuel — are plentiful, and domestic and Canadian suppliers meet most of the demand for natural gas. But North American reserves of oil, the fuel in heaviest demand, are rapidly shrinking. For several years, the United States has had to import about 60 percent of the oil it consumes, largely from the politically unstable Middle East. As domestic oil supplies continue to dwindle, that portion can only increase over time. [27]

President Bush's solution to the country's energy needs is to spur domestic production. His energy plan, announced on May 17, 2001, would allow more oil and gas drilling on public lands, including 2,000 acres in Alaska's ANWR and wilderness areas in the Rocky Mountains, currently off-limits to industrial use. The plan also calls for greater reliance on coal and nuclear power. [28]

Environmentalists demanded that Vice President Dick Cheney, who headed the task force that produced the Bush energy plan, reveal records of the group's meeting with energy-business representatives while formulating the plan. Before taking office, Cheney was the chief executive of the Halliburton Co., an oil-services firm. The General Accounting Office, Congress' watchdog agency, sued to obtain the documents, but Cheney rejected the demands, saying the agency had no right to such sensitive information from the executive branch. [29]

The Republican-dominated House and the Democratic Senate produced different versions of energy legislation that conferees have so far been unable to merge into a compromise measure. In an effort to promote cleaner energy sources, a Senate proposal would require large utilities to use wind and other renewable energy sources to generate 10 percent of their electricity output. Another Senate plan would triple the use of ethanol, a corn product, as an additive to gasoline over the next 10 years. Senate conferees also have rejected the administration-backed proposal to allow oil drilling in ANWR. On Oct. 3, House conferees rejected a Senate proposal to require companies to disclose their emissions of greenhouse gases. It appears unlikely that House and Senate negotiators will overcome their differences over energy policy this year.

Meanwhile, the Bush administration is trying to advance another part of its energy plan — construction of new natural gas pipelines — by having all 10 federal departments and agencies involved in pipeline construction conduct simultaneous environmental reviews. [30]

Initiatives in Congress

Congress' focus on homeland defense and possible war with Iraq has given lawmakers little opportunity to work on either of the president's main environmental proposals. Legislation embodying the Clear Skies Initiative was introduced in the House on July 29 by Reps. Barton, R-Texas, and W.J. (Billy) Tauzin, R-La., and in the Senate by Sen. Bob Smith, R-N.H. But the proposals remain bogged down in the legislative impasse that has blocked passage of 11 appropriations bills, which will have to await lawmakers' return for a post-election, lame-duck session in November.

Congressional Democrats are focusing their criticism of the Republican clean-air proposal on its omission of any effort to curb carbon emissions. A Senate bill co-authored by James Jeffords, I-Vt., chairman of the Environment and Public Works Committee, and Sen. Joseph Lieberman, D-Conn., would impose mandatory caps on carbon-dioxide emissions as well as the three pollutants targeted by the Clear Skies Initiative. On Sept. 19, Senate Majority Leader Tom Daschle, D-S.D., announced his intention to give high priority to that bill when the 108th Congress convenes next year.

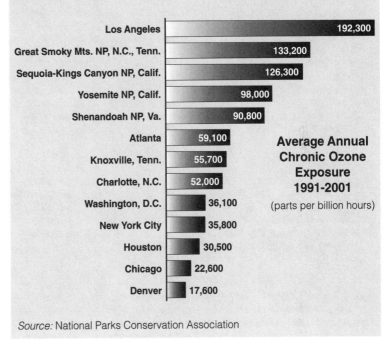

Some Parks More Polluted Than Cities

Ozone levels in four national parks were higher than in several major metropolitan areas, according to the National Parks Conservation Association. Since the 1970 Clean Air Act, the United States has seen a 25 percent drop in emissions of ozone and other major air pollutants. However, the act's goal of eliminating air pollution from 158 national parks and wilderness areas has fallen far short of expectations. Ozone levels in Great Smoky Mountains National Park, for example, now rival those in Los Angeles in the summer.

Los Angeles	192,300
Great Smoky Mts. NP, N.C., Tenn.	133,200
Sequoia-Kings Canyon NP, Calif.	126,300
Yosemite NP, Calif.	98,000
Shenandoah NP, Va.	90,800
Atlanta	59,100
Knoxville, Tenn.	55,700
Charlotte, N.C.	52,000
Washington, D.C.	36,100
New York City	35,800
Houston	30,500
Chicago	22,600
Denver	17,600

Average Annual Chronic Ozone Exposure 1991-2001
(parts per billion hours)

Source: National Parks Conservation Association

The president's Healthy Forests Initiative also has hit a roadblock. The Republican-dominated House approved the measure on July 17. But Democratic senators have blocked efforts by Sens. Larry E. Craig, R-Idaho, and Pete V. Domenici, R-N.M., to attach the plan as an amendment to the fiscal 2003 Interior Department spending bill. Many Democratic lawmakers from the fire-stricken West are torn between their constituents' calls for protection from future fires and their environmentalist supporters' strong opposition to the Bush plan. [31]

Even if lawmakers fail to overcome their differences to pass at least part of Bush's forest plan, many of its provisions to speed the regulatory process and curb the public's ability to halt individual logging projects are likely to take effect anyway. Agriculture Undersecretary Rey aims to

Should the government relax emissions rules on older power plants?

YES — Jeffrey Holmstead
Assistant Administrator, Environmental Protection Agency

From testimony before the Senate Health, Education, Labor and Pensions Subcommittee on Public Health, Sept. 3, 2002

There has been longstanding agreement among virtually all interested parties that the New Source Review program for existing [pollution] sources can and should be improved. For well over 10 years, representatives of industry, state and local agencies and environmental groups have worked closely with the Environmental Protection Agency (EPA) to make the program work better. In 1996, the EPA proposed rules to amend several key elements of the program [and since then] the EPA has had countless discussions with stakeholders and has invested substantial resources in developing final revisions to the program. . . .

EPA issued a report to President Bush on June 13 in which we concluded that the New Source Review program does, in fact, adversely affect or discourage some projects at existing facilities that would maintain or improve reliability, efficiency and safety of existing energy capacity. . . .

We now believe that it is time to finish the task of improving and reforming the New Source Review program. [When] we submitted our report to the president, we published a set of recommended reforms that we intend to make to the program. These reforms are designed to remove barriers to environmentally beneficial projects; provide incentives for companies to install good controls and reduce actual emissions; provide greater specificity regarding New Source Review applicability; and streamline and simplify several key New Source Review provisions.

To increase environmental protection and promote the implementation of routine repair and replacement projects, the EPA will propose a new definition of routine repairs. New Source Review excludes [routine] repairs and maintenance activities, but a multifactored, case-by-case determination must be made regarding what repairs meet that standard. This has deterred some companies from conducting certain repairs because they are not sure whether they would need to go through New Source Review. The EPA is proposing guidelines for particular industries, to more clearly establish what activities meet this standard. . . .

Overall, our reforms will [enable] industry . . . to make improvements to their plants that will result in greater environmental protection without needing to go through a lengthy permitting process. Our actions are completely consistent with key provisions of the Clean Air Act designed to protect human health and the environment from . . . air pollution.

NO — Carol M. Browner
Former Administrator, Environmental Protection Agency (1993-2001)

From testimony before the Senate Health, Education, Labor and Pensions Subcommittee on Public Health, Sept. 3, 2002

The administration's recent announcement of final and proposed changes to the New Source Review program abandons the concept of steady air-quality improvements promised in the Clean Air Act. Some have suggested that the administration's announced changes [were supported by] the Clinton administration. Nothing could be further from the truth.

There is no guarantee, and more importantly, no evidence or disclosure demonstrating that the administration's announced final or proposed changes will make the air cleaner. In fact, they will allow the air to become dirtier. The administration owes the American people a full analysis of the public-health and air-quality consequences of their announced final changes — not just an explanation of the flexibilities they are giving industry.

Since 1977, a key provision of the Clean Air Act has been New Source Review. It is an important and reasonable means of achieving pollution reductions — a recognition that older plants, if and when they modernize and increase their emissions, should be held to the same pollution standards as new plants. New Source Review thus tailors the technology requirements for individual facilities to the public health-based ambient air-quality standards — providing a backstop that a facility will not exacerbate pollution problems — and guarantees that facilities will employ state-of-the-art pollution controls when they are built or rebuilt.

Thus, New Source Review requires existing power plants, refineries and other industrial facilities to install modern pollution-control equipment only when they make a "major modification" to their facility and increase the emissions of the most commonly found air pollutants — nitrogen oxide, sulfur dioxide and volatile organic compounds — [which] contribute to significant public health and environmental problems, [ranging] from premature death to worsening asthma attacks and acid rain.

Not every change to a facility triggers a requirement to install pollution-control equipment. EPA regulations provide exemptions from New Source Review for routine maintenance, repairs and increases in operating hours or production rates. . . .

Older facilities that do not meet modern air-pollution standards continue to be a huge pollution problem for this nation. Seventy to 80 percent of all power-plant emissions come from facilities built before 1977. Compared to modern or updated plants, old power plants emit four to 10 times more pollution for every megawatt produced, creating dramatic, adverse health consequences. . . .

Is U.S. environmental policy on the right track?

YES President George W. Bush

From remarks on Earth Day, April 22, 2002, in Wilmington, N.Y.

I firmly believe that 32 years after [the first] Earth Day, America understands our obligation much more than in years past: That we must be careful of our actions. Good stewardship is a personal responsibility of all of us. And that's what's important for Americans to understand — that each of us has a responsibility, and it's a part of our value system in our country to assume that responsibility. . . .

Not only do people have responsibility, but so does your government. And the federal government has a big responsibility. And I accept [those] responsibilities. For three decades, we've acted with clear purpose to prevent needless and, at times, reckless disregard of the air, water, soil and wildlife. This commitment has yielded tremendous progress. Our lakes and rivers are much cleaner than they were on the first Earth Day. Limits on toxic emissions have greatly improved the quality of the air we breathe. The Clean Air Act has helped reduce acid rain and urban air pollution. We've done all this at a time when our economy and population grew dramatically . . . [showing] that we can expand our economy for the good of all of us, while also being good and conscientious stewards of the environment.

Some of the biggest sources of air pollution are power plants, which send tons of emissions into our air. Therefore we have set a goal: With Clear Skies legislation, America will do more to reduce power-plant emissions than ever before in our history.

We will reach [this] ambitious goal through a market-based approach that rewards innovation, reduces cost and, most importantly, guarantees results. Mine is a results-oriented administration. When we say we expect results, we mean it.

We will set mandatory limits on air pollution, with firm deadlines, while giving companies the flexibility to find the best ways to meet the mandatory limits. Clear Skies legislation [would] significantly reduce smog and mercury emissions, [and] stop acid rain. It will put more money into programs to reduce pollution . . . and less money into the pockets of lawyers and regulators. . . .

Americans have reached a great consensus about the protection of the environment: We understand that the success of a generation is not defined by wealth alone. We want to be remembered for our material progress . . . but we also want to be remembered for the respect we give to our natural world. This Earth Day finds us on the right path, gaining in appreciation for the world in our care.

NO Tom Daschle, D-S.D.
Senate Majority Leader

From a speech to the League of Conservation Voters, Sept. 19, 2002

Beginning with visionary leaders like Teddy Roosevelt and closing with a renewed recognition of our impact on the world around us, the 20th century was truly America's century of conservation.

As a new century unfolds, the question facing us is whether we will have the courage . . . to confront and defeat the threats to our global environment. For the first time, the answer to that question doesn't depend on science. The science on environmental issues and impacts is overwhelming, unequivocal and accepted. . . .

The answer hinges on one thing: leadership. Unfortunately, we haven't seen that leadership — at least not yet — from this White House. . . .

In the Senate, we've tried to use our majority to bring greater moral clarity to these moral issues. When they proposed opening the Arctic [National Wildlife] Refuge (ANWR) for drilling, we stopped them. We passed an energy bill that doesn't allow drilling in ANWR but does increase the amount of our energy we get from alternative and renewable fuels. When the administration tried to avoid issuing a strong rule to reduce arsenic in drinking water, we forced them to make that rule the law of the land. When they tried to cut the EPA's enforcement budget, we restored that money. . . .

We also believe that it is unacceptable for America to abdicate its responsibility to lead on the issue of global warming. Today, roughly 160 million Americans are breathing unhealthy air. In the space of five years, my part of the county has seen historic flooding and now a historic drought — something we can expect more of if we don't take steps to reduce the accumulation of greenhouse gases. [And] America is on the verge of a boom in power-plant construction. . . .

These things could be either a toxic combination or a historic opportunity. I choose to see this as an opportunity to lead — and that's why we're going to fight to enforce New Source Review requirements for power plants.

I believe we should go even further. I believe that we need to dramatically reduce the worst pollutants — sulfur dioxide, nitrogen oxides, mercury and carbon dioxide. So today, I want to make this pledge: If I have the privilege of serving as majority leader in the 108th Congress, we will put the environment back at the center of the national agenda, and a "four pollutants" bill will be high on my list of leadership priorities.

Bison and snowmobilers share a trail in Yellowstone National Park last January. President Clinton banned snowmobiles in Yellowstone and Grand Teton parks, but in June the National Park Service said it would continue to allow snowmobiles. The Environmental Protection Agency has since required manufacturers to reduce snowmobile emissions, but conservationists say the new standards are too lax.

complete these changes through the rulemaking process by the end of October. "The wheels of progress often turn slowly," he says, "but that's our hope and aspiration."

Because so much of the plan is likely to take effect outside the legislative process, environmental advocates who want to curb commercial logging in the national forests appear resigned to defeat. "These are ecosystems, and they're not going to just grow back," says Wetstone of the Natural Resources Defense Council. "It takes hundreds of years and the right kinds of conditions. We've already lost so much of our old growth on this continent that it's really a shame to see it frittered away. Healthy Forests is really about healthy tree stumps, because I think, sadly, that's what we're going to be left with."

For his part, Rey is optimistic that lawmakers will approve the forest plan in its entirety when they return to Washington after the November elections. "If not then, there's always the next session of Congress," he says. "These forests aren't going anywhere, except up in smoke."

Regulatory Review

Bush administration officials are not relying solely on Congress to change environmental policy. In September, the president issued an executive order to speed the NEPA-mandated environmental-impact statement

process for transportation projects that the administration deems high priority.

In addition, Congress is considering a bill introduced by Rep. Don Young, R-Alaska, that would "streamline" the environmental-impact statement process for specific projects, such as the expansion of runways at Chicago's O'Hare Airport and an electric utility in Arizona. The bill also would give environmental agencies and organizations only 30 days to comment on the environmental impacts of transportation projects.

"This bill would seriously undermine public health, endangered species and threatened wetlands by weakening natural resource laws," said Fred Krupp, executive director of Environmental Defense, an advocacy organization in New York City. "It makes the transportation objective paramount over natural-resource agencies' missions to protect public health and the environment." [32]

Even some conservative experts say that the move away from command-and-control regulations toward a market-based approach to environmental policy can only go so far. "The market approach works neatly for electric-utility plants, but after that it gets a lot harder," says Hayward of the American Enterprise Institute. "You'll never completely replace the regulatory system because there are a lot of environmental problems for which a market approach is very, very difficult to make work at all. I think the model that is going to evolve is not either pure markets or pure regulation, but some mix of the two."

Hayward predicts that the next major effort to change the regulatory system will focus on water quality. "We've pretty much done the big stuff with regulating pipes coming out of factories," he says. "Now what we're trying to get after is the much bigger problem of runoff from farm fields and streets." These "non-point" sources of water pollution are hard to identify, making it all but impossible for EPA regulators to enforce Clean Water Act limits on specific pollutants.

Meanwhile, the EPA is experimenting with market-based alternatives to water-quality regulations. When water pollution exceeded acceptable limits in North Carolina's Tar-Pamlico basin, EPA officials convened community leaders and farmers and agreed to assist them in finding ways to reduce runoff from fields and storm sewers. Although runoff pollution levels remain high in the basin, the effort has resulted in a slight improvement in water quality.

A similar effort is taking place along the Charles River in Massachusetts. "This approach is neither purely market nor purely regulatory," Hayward says. "I think that's the way the world is going, no matter what kind of administration we have."

Environmentalists insist that the regulatory system continues to offer the best means of ensuring water quality. They are especially troubled by Bush administration plans to review the Clean Water Act to determine which waters the law covers and which are exempt from its regulatory oversight. "I haven't heard any indication that the American public is up in arms looking for ways to reduce the coverage of the Clean Water Act because our waters are too clean," Wetstone says. "The reality is, this is one of the most popular and successful laws ever, but there's still a long way to go."

OUTLOOK

Election Impact

Environmental issues often figure prominently in campaign debates. But this year, counterterrorism efforts and the Bush administration's call for "regime change" in Iraq are likely to dominate.

"Environmental issues will be a very high priority in some areas, such as the Intermountain West and South Florida, where recreational access to public lands and private-property rights are a local concern," says Hardiman of the American Land Rights Association. But in most of the country, he says, "The war talk has pushed everything else further down the ladder, from health care to wilderness areas."

Some analysts say the Bush administration, rather than simply siding with industry on environmental issues, is actually vying for the support of voters who are open to new approaches to environmental protection.

"The environment has become a motherhood issue," says Ellerman of MIT. "Bush is playing for the environmental vote of the middle class — the soccer moms, the people who want to bring emissions levels down but who also want to get out of this system where you get into all these lawsuits. The Clear Skies Initiative has enabled them to inoculate themselves against Democrats' charges that they aren't doing anything on the environment."

Conservative analysts say Democratic candidates who support vigorous environmental-protection policies face an uphill struggle to get the attention of voters this year. "Environmental policy has the best chance of corralling votes when virtually nothing else is on the political agenda," says Taylor of the Cato Institute. In the wake of the Sept. 11 terrorist attacks, he says, "Voters probably care much more right now about security issues and the economy than they do about the environment."

Critics of Bush's environmental initiatives are hoping that voters will catch on to what they see as a quiet but deliberate assault on environmental regulations carried out while the public is preoccupied by the Sept. 11 attacks and their aftermath.

"With the distraction of the war on terrorism, I think [the administration] felt emboldened," says Wetstone of the NRDC. "There clearly has been an effort to try to keep this below the public radar screen, but the Bush administration's environmental initiatives are unpopular, and voters do care.

"History shows that people do have a way of catching on," he adds. "Whether they do in time for the congressional elections in November, I don't know."

NOTES

1. For background, see Mary H. Cooper, "Global Warming Treaty," Jan. 26, 2001, *The CQ Researcher*, pp. 41-64.

2. For background, see Mary H. Cooper, "Setting Environmental Priorities," *The CQ Researcher*, May 21, 1999, pp. 425-448; Mary H. Cooper, "Water Quality," *The CQ Researcher*, Nov. 24, 2000, pp. 953-976, and Mary H. Cooper, "New Air Quality Standards," *The CQ Researcher*, March 7, 1997, pp. 193-216.

3. See Eric Pianin and Michael Powell, "General Electric Ordered to Pay for Cleanup of Hudson," *The Washington Post*, Dec. 5, 2001.

4. See "EPA Orders Marine Shale Closed for Good," Associated Press Newswires, Oct. 7, 2002.

5. "Undermining Environmental Law," *The New York Times*, Sept. 30, 2002.

6. Bush presented his plan in a speech to the National Oceanic and Atmospheric Administration in Silver Spring, MD.

7. U.S. Environmental Protection Agency, "Latest Findings on National Air Quality," September 2002. See Andrew C. Revkin, "With White House Approval, E.P.A. Pollution Report Omits Global Warming Section," *The New York Times*, Sept. 15, 2002.

8. From Bush's Feb, 14, 2002, speech at NOAA.

9. Gale A. Norton, "A Better Plan for the Forests," *The Washington Post*, Sept. 17, 2002.

10. For background, see Mary H. Cooper, "Ozone Depletion," *The CQ Researcher*, April 3, 1992, pp. 289-312.

11. In U.S. Environmental Protection Agency, "Progress Report on the EPA Acid Rain Program," November 1999.

12. U.S. Environmental Protection Agency, *op. cit.*

13. National Parks Conservation Association, "Code Red: America's Five Most Polluted National Parks," Sept. 24, 2002.

14. See Eric Pianin, "EPA Links Lung Cancer, Diesel Exhaust," *The Washington Post*, Sept. 4, 2002, p. A4.

15. See Francis X. Clines, "Judge Takes on the White House on Mountaintop Mining," *The New York Times*, May 19, 2002.

16. See Michael Grunwald, "Plan to Revive Everglades Brings Renewed Dispute," *The Washington Post*, Dec. 29, 2001.

17. See "Whitman Says Water Treatment Needs Outstrip Funding," *The Washington Post*, Oct. 1, 2002. See also U.S. Environmental Protection Agency, "The Clean Water and Drinking Water Infrastructure Gap Analysis," September 2002.

18. Katherine N. Probst, David M. Konisky, Robert Hersh, Michael B. Batz and Katherine D. Walker, "Superfund's Future: What Will It Cost?" *Resources for the Future*, July 2001.

19. See Eric Pianin, "Democrats Assail Shift in Superfund Cleanup," *The Washington Post*, April 11, 2002.

20. For background, see Brian Hansen, "Nuclear Waste," *The CQ Reseacher*, pp. 489-504.

21. See John Heilprin, "Interior Department Originally Backed Tighter Snowmobile Emissions Rules, Letter Says," Associated Press Newswires, Sept. 25, 2002.

22. See "BLM to Re-Examine Thousands of CBM Leases," Associated Press Newswires, Aug. 31, 2002.

23. See "Mountain Bikers Up Against Calif. Conservationists," *The Washington Post*, Oct. 2, 2002.

24. For background, see Mary H. Cooper, "Threatened Fisheries," *The CQ Researcher*, Aug. 2, 2002, pp. 617-648.

25. See Brad Knickerbocker, "For Bush, Dollars and Cents Drive Land-Use Policies," *The Christian Science Monitor*, Oct. 2, 2002.

26. For background, see Mary H. Cooper, "Endangered Species Act," *The CQ Researcher*, Oct. 1, 1999, pp. 849-872.

27. For background, see Mary H. Cooper, "Energy Security," *The CQ Researcher*, Feb. 1, 2002, pp. 73-96.

28. For background, see Mary H. Cooper, "Energy Policy," *The CQ Researcher*, May 25, 2001, pp. 441-464.

29. See Neely Tucker, "Cheney-GAO Showdown Goes to Court," *The Washington Post*, Sept. 28, 2002.

30. See "USA: Bush Admin Will Speed Up Natgas Pipeline Permits," Reuters English News Service, Oct. 2, 2002.

31. See Eric Pianin and Juliet Eilperin, "At Loggerheads Over Forest Plan," *The Washington Post*, Oct. 9, 2002.

32. Environmental Defense, "Groups Criticize Bill to Limit Environmental Reviews of Highway Projects," Sept. 30, 2002.

BIBLIOGRAPHY

Books

Wilson, Edward Osborne, *The Future of Life*, Knopf, 2002.

An eminent Harvard naturalist makes an impassioned plea for a global strategy to protect Earth's natural resources using the best tools that science and technology can provide.

Articles

Adams, Rebecca, "Democrats Decry Bush's Clean Air Plan As Favoring Industry Over Environment," *CQ Weekly*, Aug. 3, 2002, pp. 2119-2120.

President Bush's market-based proposal would allow industrial polluters to buy and sell pollution credits to each other.

Arrandale, Tom, "The Pollution Puzzle," *Governing,* **August 2002, pp. 22-26.**

As federal environmental laws fail to achieve the desired results, some states are trying to improve environmental quality on their own.

Easterbrook, Gregg, "Hostile Environment," *The New York Times Magazine,* **Aug. 19, 2002, pp. 40-44.**

Among President Bush's top policymakers, Environmental Protection Agency (EPA) Administrator Christine Todd Whitman is the lone champion of basic environmental laws.

Goodell, Jeff, "Blasts from the Past," *The New York Times Magazine,* **July 22, 2001, pp. 30-64.**

Mountaintop mining, a controversial technique that pollutes water downstream, is likely to proceed because of the Bush administration's support of increased coal production.

Norton, Gale A., "A Better Plan for the Forests," *The Washington Post,* **Sept. 17, 2002.**

The Interior Secretary defends President Bush's Healthy Forests Initiative, a plan to speed removal of brush from fire-prone national forests by waiving public-comment and judicial-appeal procedures called for by the National Environmental Policy Act.

Speth, James Gustave, "Recycling Environmentalism" *Foreign Policy,* **July-August 2002, pp. 74-76.**

International efforts to protect the global environment have failed to slow the pace of deforestation and other threats.

Weinstein, Michael M., and Steve Charnovitz, "The Greening of the WTO," *Foreign Affairs,* **November-December 2001, pp. 147-156.**

Despite the criticism of "greens" who say globalization is accelerating environmental degradation, the authors document a series of World Trade Organization rulings suggesting that trade does not impede effective environmental regulation.

Wuerthner, George, "Out of the Ashes," *National Parks,* **September-October 2002, pp. 18-25.**

Since 2000, forest fires have devastated vast tracts of Western national forests. The author examines the pros and cons of fire suppression and the role of drought in wildfires.

Reports and Studies

Hayward, Steven F., and Julie Majeres, "Index of Leading Environmental Indicators," Pacific Research Institute, April 17, 2002.

A conservative think tank documents improvements in air quality, energy supplies, water quality and land conservation.

H. John Heinz III Center for Science, Economics and the Environment, "The State of the Nation's Ecosystems," Sept. 24, 2002.

The first of a series of reports on the nation's environmental health offers data on land, water and natural resources.

League of Conservation Voters, "Presidential Report Card," January 2002.

The nonprofit watchdog group examines the environmental record of Bush and his department heads after one year in office.

National Parks Conservation Association, "Code Red: America's Five Most Polluted National Parks," Sept. 24, 2002.

An advocacy group that seeks to protect national parks reports that air quality in several parks continues to deteriorate, rivaling in some cases smog levels of heavily polluted cities.

Natural Resources Defense Council, "Rewriting the Rules: The Bush Administration's Assault on the Environment," April 2002.

A leading advocacy group criticizes the administration for using regulatory changes to undermine environmental laws and examines its record since January 2000.

U.S. Environmental Protection Agency, "Latest Findings on National Air Quality: 2001 Status and Trends," September 2002.

EPA's periodic report on air quality departs from recent reports by failing to include among major pollutants carbon dioxide, the main "greenhouse" gas most scientists agree causes global warming.

For More Information

American Land Rights Association, P.O. Box 400, Battle Ground, WA 98604; (360) 687-3087; www.landrights.org. A conservative advocacy group that supports private-property rights and opposes federal efforts to limit access to public lands.

Cato Institute, 1000 Massachusetts Ave., N.W., Washington, DC 20001-5403; (202) 842-0200; www.cato.org. A libertarian think tank that supports efforts to relax environmental regulations, seen as costly and counterproductive.

Center for Energy and Environmental Policy Research, Massachusetts Institute of Technology, MIT E40-279, 77 Massachusetts Ave., Cambridge, MA 02139-4307; (617) 253-3551; web.mit.edu/ceepr/www. The center conducts economic analyses of corporate and public-policy issues involving environmental protection and energy production.

Environmental Defense, 257 Park Ave. South, New York, NY 10010; (212) 505-2100; www.environmentalde-fense.org. A national nonprofit group dedicated to protecting access to clean air and water, healthy and nourishing food and a flourishing ecosystem.

League of Conservation Voters, 1920 L St., N.W., Suite 800, Washington, DC 20036; (202) 785-8683; www.lcv.org.

An advocacy group that tracks administration policies and lawmakers' voting records on environmental issues.

Natural Resources Defense Council, 40 West 20th St., New York, NY 10011; (212) 727-2700; www.nrdc.org. A national advocacy group that studies and provides information on a wide array of environmental issues and policies.

Sierra Club, 85 Second St., 2nd Floor, San Francisco, CA 94105; (415) 977-5500; www.sierraclub.org. A leading environmental advocacy group that provides information on a wide array of current issues.

U.S. Environmental Protection Agency, 1200 Pennsylvania Ave., N.W., Washington, DC 20460; (202) 564-4700; www.epa.gov. Administers federal environmental policies and regulations and provides information on environmental issues.

U.S. Interior Department, 1849 C St., N.W., #6156, Washington, DC 20240; (202) 208-7351; www.doi.gov. As the main federal agency involved in conservation, manages most public land, except national forests, which are managed by the Agriculture Department.

16

Fighting SARS

Mary H. Cooper

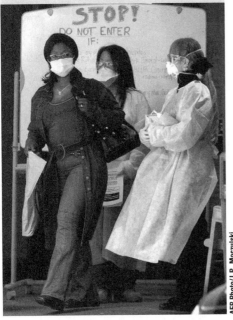

A visitor (left) passes nurses screening for SARS as she leaves Toronto General Hospital on June 11. SARS is the latest in a series of infectious-disease outbreaks that have appeared recently, such as West Nile virus. Since SARS hit China last fall, the pneumonia-like disease has killed some 800 people in 32 countries. In the United States, some health experts call SARS a wake-up call about underfunding of the public-health system.

From *The CQ Researcher*, June 20, 2003.

On March 7, a 63-year-old man went to the emergency room at Toronto's Scarborough Grace Hospital to get help when his chronic heart ailment flared up. What he got instead was a deadly infection from a patient in the next bed.

Nine days later, the man — officials only identify him as Mr. P — developed a rasping cough and high fever. When his wife took him back to the hospital, nurses whisked him into isolation while she went to handle the paperwork for her husband's admission.

Several weeks later, Mr. P and his wife had died, and 13 other people who had been in the hospital's admissions area with Mrs. P were seriously ill. Between them, the couple had spread their disease to 33 people.

As the world soon learned, Toronto was the epicenter of the outbreak in North America of a deadly, new disease now known as severe acute respiratory syndrome, or SARS. But at the time, the highly infectious disease had not been officially named or recognized.

By mid-June, health officials around the world had calculated SARS had sickened 8,464 people and killed 799 in 32 countries since it erupted the previous fall in China.

As it turned out, Mr. P had had the bad luck to be placed in a hospital bed next to the son of Canada's first recognized case of SARS — a 78-year-old woman who died from SARS shortly after returning to Toronto from Hong Kong.

SARS is the latest in a series of so-called emerging infectious diseases that have either appeared for the first time or occurred outside their endemic areas in recent decades, such as West Nile virus, Lyme disease and Legionnaire's disease. [1] Like Ebola hemorrhagic fever, which has killed about two-thirds of its 1,500 victims since first

SARS Death Toll Approaching 800

Since severe acute respiratory syndrome (SARS) first appeared in China last fall, at least 8,464 people have been infected, and 799 of them have died. Most cases occurred in China; cases elsewhere have been linked to persons who had recently traveled to Asia.

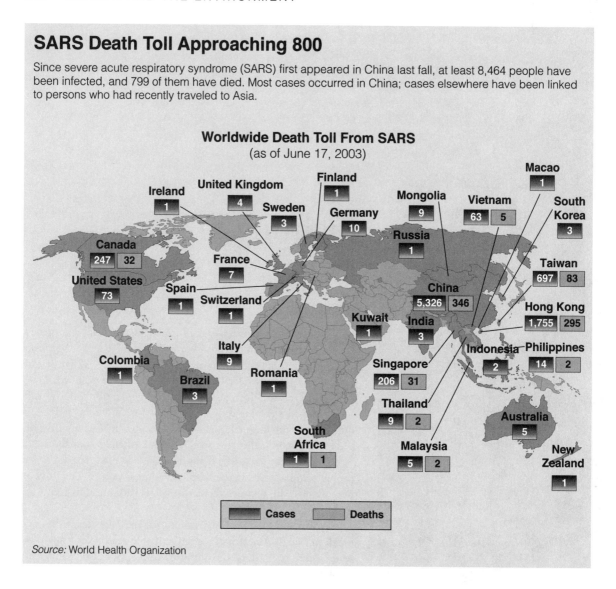

Worldwide Death Toll From SARS
(as of June 17, 2003)

Macao — 1
Ireland — 1
United Kingdom — 4
Sweden — 3
Finland — 1
Germany — 10
Mongolia — 9
Vietnam — 63 | 5
South Korea — 3
Canada — 247 | 32
France — 7
Russia — 1
Taiwan — 697 | 83
United States — 73
Spain — 1
Switzerland — 1
China — 5,326 | 346
Hong Kong — 1,755 | 295
Kuwait — 1
India — 3
Colombia — 1
Italy — 9
Indonesia — 2
Philippines — 14 | 2
Brazil — 3
Romania — 1
Singapore — 206 | 31
Thailand — 9 | 2
Australia — 5
South Africa — 1 | 1
Malaysia — 5 | 2
New Zealand — 1

Cases | Deaths

Source: World Health Organization

erupting in Sudan and Zaire in 1976, SARS is a new disease with no known vaccine or cure.

Public-health experts, who have long complained about inadequate funding in the United States, see the SARS outbreak as a wake-up call. "Public health is being asked to do more with less," Georges Benjamin, executive director of the American Public Health Association (APHA), told a congressional subcommittee in May.

Benjamin notes the Bush administration's proposed budget for fiscal 2004 would cut funding for the Centers for Disease Control and Prevention (CDC) by 8.5 per-

cent from its current level of $7.1 billion. "We believe that far more significant investments in public health will need to occur if we are to prepare the nation's public-health system to protect us from the leading causes of death, prepare us for bioterrorism and chemical terrorism and respond to the public-health crises of the day," Benjamin said. "We will always be one plane ride away, one infected person away and one epidemic away from a global tragedy." [2]

In addition, health experts worry that Americans may not be willing to accept quarantines and other drastic measures needed to stop a SARS epidemic in the United States. Some also say the World Health Organization (WHO) should have the power to intervene in any country that fails to take appropriate action in an infectious outbreak.

The main symptoms of SARS — initially a low-grade fever, followed by a dry cough and difficulty breathing — are also typical of pneumonia, making it difficult to diagnose quickly. On average, SARS kills about 15 percent of the people who contract it, but the fatality rate varies greatly by age: While children tend to have mild symptoms, SARS kills most of its victims over 60.

The disease is extremely contagious, especially in patients like Mr. P, known as "superspreaders." Mr. P and several highly contagious patients have infected far more people than is typical of other respiratory infections. "It's astounding that we don't have 80,000 or 800,000 cases of SARS, instead of 8,000," says Anthony S. Fauci, director of the National Institute of Allergy and Infectious Diseases in Bethesda, Md.

The SARS epidemic demonstrates both the best and the worst of the state of global public health. In China, where most cases have occurred, a precious opportunity to contain SARS was lost when health officials ignored for months reports that a virulent form of pneumonia was spreading in the southern province of Guangdong. By the time news of the outbreak reached infectious-disease agencies in other countries and WHO, which tracks global disease outbreaks, SARS had spread far beyond China's borders. *

"Clearly, the initial response in China left much to be desired," Benjamin says. "No one really knows what their motives were, but it certainly did not help at all and in some ways limited the capacity to contain this thing early on."

---

* Proposals to prevent a repeat of China's inaction on SARS were on the agenda for a WHO-sponsored global SARS conference scheduled for June 17-18 in Malaysia.

U.S. Has Had 73 SARS Cases, No Deaths

No one has died among the 73 people in the United States who have been infected with SARS, mostly recent visitors to Asia or Toronto. California has reported the highest number of cases.

Probable U.S. SARS Cases
(As of June 16, 2003)

Source: Centers for Disease Control and Prevention

On the positive side, the international scientific community — aided by the Internet, advances in medical research and an increasingly collaborative worldwide network of laboratories — quickly began trying to identify the new microbe and searching for diagnostic tests, vaccines and treatments. WHO and disease-control agencies around the world, including the U.S. Centers for Disease Control and Prevention (CDC) and National Institutes of Health (NIH), have taken the lead role in coordinating the assault on the disease.

"There are, from our perspective in Toronto, almost no good things to be said about SARS," said Allison McGeer, director of infection control at Toronto's Mt. Sinai Hospital. "The one good thing to be said about it is the phenomenal degree of collaboration and willingness to help among clinicians, epidemiologists and researchers around the world." [3]

Once they had determined that SARS was a distinct, new disease, scientists took just two weeks to identify the microbe as a novel form of coronavirus — similar to two relatively benign microbes that cause the common cold — and another two weeks to sequence its genome. By comparison, in the mid-1980s it took more than two

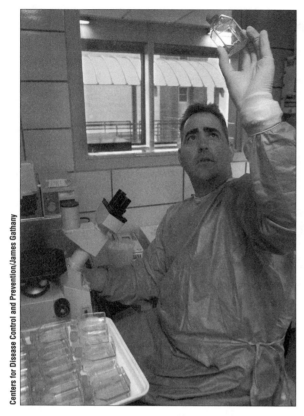

A Centers for Disease Control worker examines a container used in SARS research. Researchers think the virus originated in civets and raccoon dogs — wild animals considered delicacies in southern China — and jumped to humans working in live-animal markets.

years for scientists to identify the human immunodeficiency virus (HIV), the microbe that causes AIDS, and more than two years to sequence its genome.

"Think about how long it took us to figure out the AIDS virus, or for that matter legionella in 1976 and the hantavirus outbreak in New Mexico and Arizona just a couple of years ago," says Murray Lumpkin, principal associate commissioner of the Food and Drug Administration (FDA). "Once people began working on SARS, they came up with the coronavirus in a matter of weeks. The technology and the epidemiology were absolutely wonderful."

SARS actually has given U.S. health officials another reason to be pleased: There have been only 73 probable SARS cases in the United States — and no SARS-related deaths. "Toronto could just as easily have been Los Angeles or Chicago," Lumpkin says. "It just happened that Toronto is where the infected people landed." Thirty-two people have died from SARS in Canada so far.

While luck may help explain why the U.S. was spared a major SARS outbreak, experts also credit a heightened awareness of the infectious-disease threat in U.S. hospitals since the anthrax attacks that killed five people in the fall of 2001.

"Bioterrorism has been a catalyst for many different efforts in public health that are critical to diagnosing and catching all types of emerging conditions, whether they are introduced intentionally or not," says James G. Hodge Jr., deputy director of the Center for Law and the Public's Health at Johns Hopkins and Georgetown universities. "One of the things about SARS that is very consistent with a bioterrorist attack is that we don't know when it's going to happen. Also, we can't predict exactly how it's going to spread until we know more about the disease. In any event, the tools that we would use during a bioterrorist attack are the same ones that we'd use in response to SARS."

But heightened preparedness hasn't made the United States invulnerable to a deadly outbreak by a previously unknown agent like SARS. "I can imagine someone sitting for eight hours in an ER [emergency room] at a hospital before anybody figures out that they have a pneumonia that could really cause havoc," says Barry R. Bloom, dean of Harvard University's School of Public Health. "I would hope that that possibility is much reduced, but it's not out of the question."

Some public-health experts say the attention given to SARS is overblown, especially in light of a recent decline in the number of new cases worldwide. Compared with the world's big killers, SARS is a blip on the radar screen that distracts attention and precious resources from more lethal threats, they argue. "Our zero-sum approach to infectious-disease control means that resources are drawn away from big killers that do not rock international markets or inconvenience tourist itineraries," wrote Paul Farmer, a professor of medical anthropology at Harvard Medical School, noting that tuberculosis, AIDS and malaria kill 6 million people a year in the developing world. [4]

But those involved in the fight against SARS reject such criticism. "A blip on the radar screen is 25 cases of Ebola in Africa that go nowhere," says Fauci of the National Institute of Allergy and Infectious Diseases. "We don't know how bad SARS is going to get. How well we'll be able to control it will depend on public-health measures, luck and the development of vaccines and drugs. Thirty countries involved with 8,000 cases is not a blip on the radar screen. This is an international epidemic."

Fauci and many infectious-disease experts who gathered on May 30 for an NIH-sponsored conference on SARS research worry that the recent decline of new cases may be temporary, and that SARS may become an endemic seasonal disease, like influenza, that will return with a vengeance this winter.

As lawmakers hold hearings to determine how to prepare for a possible SARS outbreak in the United States, these are some of the questions they are asking:

Should WHO intervene in countries that fail to halt the spread of infectious diseases?

In 1948, soon after the United Nations itself was created, it established WHO to improve public health throughout the world. Based in Geneva, Switzerland, WHO monitors infectious diseases and helps national health agencies combat epidemics. The agency also issues travel advisories to areas with active infectious-disease outbreaks, as it did at the height of the SARS epidemics in China, Taiwan and Canada.

But WHO lacks enforcement powers, so it cannot dispatch health professionals to the site of potential public-health threats without the consent of the host country.

"WHO [can] monitor situations and put political pressure on countries to engage in responsible behavior, like they've done with China," says Hodge of the Center for Law and the Public's Health. "What they can't do — and what U.S. public-health authorities can do in the states — is go into a country like China and implement their own protective measures. They have no enforcement powers whatsoever." For many years, WHO's limited authority wasn't a big problem. Advances in medical technology, including the widespread use of vaccines and antibiotics — as well as improved sanitation and education in much of the world — helped the agency carry out its mission.

But globalization has brought changes that threaten WHO's ability to protect public health. While the expansion of world trade and international air travel, for example, has boosted economies worldwide, it also has greatly expanded the reach of potentially virulent microbes. Germs that once may have existed harmlessly in remote areas can now reach new habitats oceans away aboard container ships or in the blood of seemingly healthy travelers. Consequently, some critics of the global public-health sys-

tem say a more aggressive approach is needed to halt the spread of infectious diseases like SARS. [5]

"We live in an age where we're just not used to infectious diseases anymore," says David Gratzer, a Toronto physician and senior fellow at the Manhattan Institute, a conservative think tank in New York City. "If there is an outbreak in Asia today, it is very relevant to North America. Based on the SARS experience in Toronto, the best bet is to prevent the damned virus from crossing the Pacific in the first place. As soon as there's an outbreak, the overwhelming concern should be to see that the virus [does] not come here."

But, Gratzer says, WHO is not up to that task because not all of its members are willing to accept the economic and political consequences of owning up to a major disease outbreak in their own backyard. Leading health officials in China and Taiwan were fired for trying to cover up their SARS outbreaks, and all countries with significant SARS cases are paying a heavy price in lost trade and tourism revenues. (*See sidebar, p. 352.*)

"Countries have to reliably and honestly report [outbreaks]," Gratzer says. "WHO simply has too much of an honor-based system, and there's just no honor to be found in countries like China and scores of others."

That makes it imperative, he adds, for the government to "aggressively screen passengers for disease symptoms in our airports and theirs," ensuring that the screening is "up to our standards."

Some health experts say a new international treaty is needed to empower WHO to intervene in countries that don't report potential threats to global public health. A strengthened WHO could send teams of epidemiologists and clinicians to isolate and eradicate a disease outbreak before it spreads, just as weapons inspectors from the International Atomic Energy Agency investigate allegations that a member country has violated arms-control agreements. "Currently, the WHO can rely only on moral suasion," wrote Jerome Groopman, a professor of medicine at Harvard Medical School. "This is not a dependable lever to consistently move authoritarian governments. We need new agreements around public health similar to those [involving] nuclear, chemical and biological weapons." [6]

Under Groopman's proposal, countries that provided timely data on a communicable disease and unrestrained access for health inspectors would receive financial and logistical aid to stem the outbreak. Those that covered up an outbreak or blocked efforts to halt it would be held liable for the resulting economic and human costs. [7]

U.S. Privacy Rules Hide SARS Details

When a Canadian man was discharged June 3 from an Arkansas hospital after recovering from possible SARS, the state health department refused to identify the city, county or even the region of the state where the hospital was located — or the man's whereabouts before he got sick.

Officials would say only that they had contacted health agencies in areas where the man may have been before he checked into the hospital on May 22 and that those agencies were responsible for investigating any potential exposures to the deadly respiratory disease. [1]

In contrast, the names, gender, ages and hometowns of many SARS victims in Canada, Asia and elsewhere are common knowledge. Strict new U.S. patient-privacy rules account for the difference. The new rules — enacted as part of the 1996 Health Insurance Portability and Accountability Act, or HIPAA — went into effect on April 14, just as SARS cases began appearing in the United States.

Patient-privacy rights became a prominent issue in the United States in the 1980s, when the AIDS epidemic sparked such widespread panic that infected children were barred from school, and HIV-positive adults suffered discrimination, even after it was found that the virus was not transmissible through casual contact.

The HIPAA rules prohibit hospitals, doctors' offices, health plans and other entities that have access to individuals' health records from disclosing information in those records to anyone without that person's permission. Only public-health agencies have the right to the protected information in case of outbreaks of infectious diseases like tuberculosis, influenza and SARS.

But some state health agencies have interpreted HIPAA's mandate more strictly than others. For example, while Colorado, Massachusetts and Florida have released the age and gender of suspected SARS cases, and their counties of residence, others — including South Carolina and Arkansas — have not. Some concerned citizens argue that the secrecy violates their right to protect themselves and their families. "I'd like to see more information . . . to take every precaution to prevent it if possible," said Sam Turner, a resident of Greer, S.C. "Currently, it is possible my family has been exposed, and I wouldn't know because of information being withheld." [2]

But defenders of the new rules say they serve a dual purpose. "It's ethical to preserve patient anonymity, and it's ethical to not foster panic by not naming a city or locale," says Abraham Verghese, director of the Center for Medical Humanities and Ethics at the University of Texas Health Science Center in San Antonio.

Nevertheless, he adds, "I imagine that if a hospital in a given city had a major spread of the disease, that would not be something that they could or would keep quiet."

---

[1] See Greg Giuffrida, "Probable SARS Patient Recovered, Discharged," The Associated Press State and Local Wire, June 4, 2003.

[2] See Liv Osby, "State's SARS Secrecy Angers Some," *The Greenville* [South Carolina] *News,* April 27, 2003, p. 15A.

Hodge is among the experts who say a treaty to strengthen WHO would be rejected as a threat to national sovereignty, and not only by authoritarian governments like China. "Imagine WHO coming into a state out West and making decisions for the state authorities there," says Hodge of the Center for Law and the Public's Health. "I don't think that's going to fly in the United States, and if it won't fly here, how should we expect it to fly in less-developed countries?"

Gratzer also places little hope on the ability of a treaty to enhance WHO's authority. "Most international treaty negotiations stall," he says. In the absence of such a treaty, Gratzer calls for a "coalition of the healthy" — named after the "coalition of the willing" that joined the United States in its recent war against Iraq — to take matters into their own hands. "We need a coalition of the healthy who simply state that if you don't disclose early and effectively and honestly your outbreak to the relevant authorities, you're going to be slapped with huge sanctions, and you're going to bleed economically."

Would Americans accept draconian measures to stop the spread of a deadly epidemic?

Once China acknowledged the scope of the SARS outbreak, the government — and other affected countries —

imposed rigorous measures to contain the virus, including quarantining and isolating thousands of people.

Isolation, a less-drastic measure, involves separating infected patients from healthy people and other patients in a hospital setting. With highly infectious diseases like SARS, patients ideally should be placed in rooms with negative airflow to prevent the spread of the virus on airborne droplets released when a patient coughs. Doctors and nurses — who have proved especially vulnerable to infection from SARS patients — should be gowned and masked at all times.

Quarantine, a more radical — and controversial — measure, isolates healthy people who may have been exposed to an infectious disease during its incubation period (the time from exposure to onset of the disease) — 10 days, on average, for SARS. Authoritarian governments may encounter little resistance to quarantine, which generally requires individuals to stay at home. Indeed, Vietnam won praise for quickly suppressing its SARS outbreak last month, largely through rigorous isolation and quarantine.

"In [authoritarian] regimes, it's not that big a leap for a government to isolate and quarantine people," says Abraham Verghese, director of the Center for Medical Humanities and Ethics at the University of Texas Health Science Center in San Antonio. "People expect the government to be heavy-handed."

Even in more open societies, like Canada, public outcry over mandatory quarantines to contain SARS has been minimal. But some experts are concerned about how Americans would react to tough measures.

"Canadians are a lot less combative and a lot more civil about these sorts of things," says Toronto physician Gratzer. Even so, he recalls that enough Canadians broke quarantine during a smallpox outbreak in Montreal during the 1880s to spark an epidemic that killed 6,000 of the city's 100,000 inhabitants. Some Canadians also reportedly broke their SARS quarantine in recent weeks. [8] And Toronto authorities warned potential violators they would, if necessary, be "chained to a bed" to keep them away from the community. [9]

"Even when you have civic-minded people like Canadians, quarantine and isolation are pretty weak and blunt instruments to use," Gratzer says. In the United States, he predicted, "There's going to be one person who will use his right to go to the shopping mall and infect everyone there."

Exercising that right can have catastrophic results. In 1915, Irish immigrant Mary Mallon broke quarantine to return to work in New York City, only to be arrested and imprisoned. [10] Typhoid Mary, as she was better known, was blamed for spreading typhoid fever to household members where she worked as a cook.

"Quarantine has always been problematic because it takes away individual rights for the larger benefit of the community," Verghese says. "But if there is a major outbreak in this country, people will understand, even though those being quarantined will have a hard time with it." A recent poll supports that view. [11]

Scores of Americans, in fact, already have undergone voluntary quarantine in the 25 states with reported SARS cases. (*See map, p. 343.*) "Every identified case of SARS has gone through some level of isolation, and contacts of those persons have gone through some level of quarantine, and the response that most Americans provide in relation to these measures is very positive," says Hodge of the Center for Law and the Public's Health. "People are rational, and they recognize that isolation and quarantine, so long as it's as minimal as necessary and responsibly enforced in a way that's as non-intrusive as possible, will protect their families and friends from potential exposure, which is important to most people." Because people in quarantine receive close monitoring for possible signs of disease, Hodge says, "They also recognize that it's protecting themselves."

Hodge acknowledges that some Americans have resisted quarantine, including a Wisconsin man who balked at being questioned about his possible contacts with a SARS patient. "The authorities did have to call him in and basically sit him down and ask some critical questions of him," Hodge says. "So enforcement could be implemented very strongly if necessary to prevent a threat to the public's health. But in 99 percent of the cases, people adhere to isolation and quarantine measures because they know it's important for their own good to do so."

To deal with the 1 percent of Americans who might resist quarantine, President Bush recently signed an executive order authorizing immigration and customs agents at U.S. international airports to detain arriving passengers with SARS symptoms. In addition, federal and state laws authorize public-health officials to enforce isolation and quarantine. Even today, tuberculosis patients are routinely hospitalized against their will when they resist isolation and quarantine orders.

"It happens frequently enough that every health officer probably has experienced it," the APHA's Benjamin says. Nonetheless, he cautions that quarantine measures alone are unlikely to stop a massive SARS outbreak. "Apart from cabin fever, people break quarantine and isolation because provisions haven't been made for them to pick up their kids from school, deal with their job or shop for food," he says. "A social-support system must go with any kind of quarantine activity."

Can the public-health system protect Americans from infectious diseases?

Seventy-three people in half the states have contracted SARS — but no one has died from the disease. Health officials credit the zero-fatality rate to prompt medical attention. Moreover, officials say the United States has thus far escaped a full-blown SARS epidemic because rigorous isolation and quarantine measures were implemented.

Experts say the nation's brush with bioterrorism in 2001 — when a series of anthrax-laden letters killed five Americans — helped prepare the country for SARS. "We are much more prepared than ever before about odd things walking into the ER," says Bloom of the Harvard School of Public Health. "There have been rehearsals, and there's been training on all the major bioterrorism agents, so the docs who work at the front line are looking for things."

Indeed, Bloom says, the anthrax letters turned traditional clinical training on its head. "The theory used to be that if you hear hoofbeats, don't think zebras," he says, citing a recent line by bioterrorism expert Margaret Hamburg, vice president for biological programs at the Nuclear Threat Initiative. "Now the thinking is, if you hear hoof-beats, first rule out zebras. That's a complete change in mentality, and while I regret that it took bioterrorism to force it upon us, it's paying off today in the face of SARS."

Bloom worries, however, that the public-health system is being stretched thin, especially the CDC. "They have up to 500 people running all around the world working on SARS," he says. But that means 500 fewer people are working on other potential disease threats, he notes, because they have been reassigned to the SARS epidemic. To make matters worse, Congress cut the CDC's current budget for most infectious diseases by $10.5 million, he complains.

"That's just crazy," Bloom says. "At a time when we're worried about bioterrorism and emerging infections — as we ought to be — that's not the place the government should be saving money."

A recent Institute of Medicine report supports Bloom's concerns about U.S. preparedness. "The prevention and control of infectious diseases are fundamental to individual, national and global security," the report concluded. "Failure to recognize — and act on — this essential truth will surely lead to disaster. We must therefore continue to trumpet a message of urgency and concern." [12]

The General Accounting Office (GAO) also has found that preparedness for a major outbreak varies dramatically across the country. "[M]ost hospitals across the country lack the capacity to respond to large-scale infectious-disease outbreaks," the GAO reported. "Most emergency departments have experienced some degree of crowding and therefore in some cases may not be able to handle a large influx of patients during a potential SARS or other infectious-disease outbreak." [13]

Experts say the public-health system suffers primarily from inadequate funding. Last year, Congress allocated $940 million to help local health departments cope with emerging threats, including bioterrorism and naturally occurring infectious-disease outbreaks. [14] But essential public-health agencies have seen their budgets cut: The Bush administration would cut the CDC's funding by 8.5 percent in fiscal 2004.

"We can achieve a lot more in public health if we're willing to pay for it," Hodge says. "But right now, we're not, and as a nation we've suffered the consequences." Heart disease and cancer, for example, kill far more people in the United States than infectious diseases, Hodge points out. "We deal with chronic diseases in the United States as if these were acceptable outcomes," he says, "because the public-health community just is not equipped with the financial resources to prevent preventable causes of morbidity and mortality."

The lack of universal health insurance also undermines the public-health system, health advocates say, because it puts the nation's 41 million uninsured people at greatest risk if a deadly epidemic broke out in the United States.

"People are now beginning to recognize that the lack of universal health-care coverage is a major security issue in this country," says Benjamin of the APHA. "If you have insurance and you think you have SARS, you can call your doctor, who will arrange for the hospital to get you into an isolation room. But if you don't have health insurance and you show up unannounced at the ER, they won't be prepared for you, and they won't want you there because you're terribly contagious.

"This is not about not having the money," Benjamin concludes. "This is about priorities. We're now the only industrialized nation in the world without universal coverage."

BACKGROUND

Early Response

Infectious diseases have been a major scourge throughout human history and today account for about one in five deaths around the world. Early in the history of the United States, periodic epidemics of cholera, smallpox, yellow fever and other microbial diseases left tens of thousands of victims in their wake.

Before scientists discovered how germs spread disease, poor sanitary conditions in rapidly growing cities provided fertile breeding grounds for bacteria and viruses; animals also spread disease, like the mosquito that carries yellow fever.

Early Americans realized that epidemics tended to break out at ports of entry, where arriving slave ships introduced smallpox and yellow fever to North America. In 1796, New York passed the nation's first state public-health statute, which authorized offshore quarantine of passengers and crew aboard infected ships and on-shore "pest houses" to isolate the sick. Following a yellow-fever outbreak, Congress followed suit in 1798 by creating the U.S. Marine Health Service to extend port-quarantine authority throughout the country. [15]

The American public readily accepted quarantine — usually imposed on newly arrived immigrants and the urban poor — but it balked at mass immunization. In 1796, Edward Jenner, an English physician, discovered that exposing healthy individuals to material from cow-pox pustules protected them from deadly smallpox. [16]

But the nation's first compulsory-vaccination law did not pass until 1850, when Providence, R.I., required all schoolchildren to receive smallpox inoculations. And resistance to vaccines persisted in the United States, even after 1905, when the U.S. Supreme Court ruled in *Jacobson v. Massachusetts* that the need to protect the public health outweighed the rights of individuals to reject a medical procedure. [17]

The link between then-invisible germs and disease — first advanced by France's Louis Pasteur in 1862 — prompted slow but measurable improvements in public health, as communities across the United States adopted sanitation measures to prevent the spread of disease. But

advances in public health faced several lasting obstacles during the 19th century. Unlike most other industrializing nations, where central governments assumed leading roles in health care, public health in the United States evolved primarily as a local or state responsibility.

Meanwhile, the U.S. medical establishment jealously guarded the primacy of the individual doctor's role in health care to a greater extent than in Europe, resulting in a greater focus on treating individuals than on government policies aimed at improving health conditions of the public as a whole. Today's absence of national health insurance, a basic benefit in other industrial nations, grew out of that fundamental difference in focus.

"Friction between healers and preventers, between . . . independent doctors and government regulators would form [a] lasting theme of American public health," wrote journalist Laurie Garrett in a history of public health. "Not only was there no genuine federal leadership in public health in 19th-century America, few states had laws and policies that extended to all of their counties and cities." [18]

Fueled by the Industrial Revolution, the U.S. economy grew rapidly, bringing notable improvements in public health, as communities drained mosquito-infested swamps, built sewers, improved drinking water and cleaned streets of sewage and rubbish. As a result, death rates from such major killers as yellow fever, smallpox and cholera fell.

As immigration increased rapidly in the late 19th century, the federal government also expanded its public-health role to include the processing of immigrants at Ellis Island and other facilities. In recognition of its growing role, which also included supervising national quarantines and investigating epidemics, the old Marine Health Service was renamed the Public Health Service in 1912. [19]

But public-health advances had some unintended consequences. Clean water deprived infants of small immunizing doses of the virus that causes polio, leaving the population unprotected when the crippling microbe infected water supplies during several hot summers in the early 1900s. In 1916 polio, or infantile paralysis, erupted in the first of a series of epidemics that would continue until effective vaccines appeared in the early 1950s.

But the most alarming sign that the public was still vulnerable to deadly microbes despite advances in public health came in 1918: The first of three waves of Spanish influenza swept the globe in a three-year pandemic that killed 20-50 million people — 675,000 in the United States. From the first cases, which appeared at Camp

C H R O N O L O G Y

1900s-1920s *U.S. public-health system emerges.*

1905 U.S. Supreme Court rules in *Jacobson v. Massachusetts* that protecting public health outweighs the rights of individuals to reject a medical procedure.

1915 Mary Mallon — "Typhoid Mary" — is imprisoned after breaking quarantine in New York City and spreading typhoid fever.

1918-20 Spanish influenza sweeps the globe, killing 20-50 million people, including 675,000 in the United States.

1925 Geneva Protocol bans the use of chemical and bacteriological weapons.

1930s-1970s *Antibiotics and vaccines advance the war against infectious diseases.*

1932 Scottish scientist Alexander Fleming discovers penicillin, the first of a new class of drugs called antibiotics, which kill a vast range of microbes that cause such scourges as tuberculosis and syphilis.

1946 U.S. Communicable Disease Center (CDC) is set up in Atlanta to combat malaria, then prevalent in the South.

April 7, 1948 U. N.-affiliated World Health Organization (WHO) is founded in Geneva, Switzerland.

1951 U.S. schoolchildren receive polio vaccine developed by American researcher Jonas Salk. After 200 kids develop polio from a faulty batch of vaccine, a safer oral vaccine developed by American Albert Sabin is adopted in 1961.

1963 Measles vaccine is introduced and later (1969) combined with vaccines against rubella and mumps.

1968 Outbreak of Hong Kong flu, the latest in a series of periodic influenza epidemics, prompts the development of annual flu vaccines.

Jan. 22, 1975 President Gerald R. Ford ratifies the 1925 Geneva Protocol and the 1972 Biological and Toxin Weapons Convention.

1976 Ebola hemorrhagic fever, a deadly emerging viral disease, breaks out in Sudan and Zaire. Another new microbe causes Legionnaire's disease in the United States.

1980s-2000s *Emerging infectious diseases defy modern medicine.*

1980 CDC is renamed the Centers for Disease Control.

June 15, 1981 CDC reports the appearance of what will later be identified as acquired immunodeficiency syndrome — AIDS — a new disease that will kill more than 20 million people by the end of the century.

1992 CDC is renamed the Centers for Disease Control and Prevention.

2000 Fatal brain disorder is linked to the consumption of tainted British beef. "Mad cow disease" kills more than 130 people, mainly in Britain, before it is contained.

October 2001 Anonymous letters containing anthrax spores kill five people in the United States a month after the Sept. 11 terrorist attacks.

Nov. 16, 2002 First known case of severe acute respiratory syndrome — SARS — is reported in Guangdong Province, in southern China, but health authorities cover up the new disease.

January 2003 President Bush announces Project Bioshield, calling for spending $5.6 billion over 10 years on tests, drugs and vaccines to defend against bioterrorism.

March 5, 2003 An elderly Toronto woman dies of SARS after returning from Hong Kong, unleashing the disease's biggest outbreak outside Asia.

March 25, 2003 CDC tentatively identifies the microbe responsible for SARS as similar to the coronavirus that causes the common cold.

May 22, 2003 Toronto suffers a second SARS outbreak.

June 17-18, 2003 WHO holds the first global conference on SARS, in Malaysia.

Funston, an Army base in Kansas, the highly contagious flu traveled to Europe aboard vessels carrying American soldiers to World War I battlefields, to Spain where the flu's high death rate gave the disease its name, and throughout most of the rest of the world.

Although Spanish flu's fatality rate was only 2.5 percent — low for a major killer — the disease's near-global reach made it the deadliest plague in history. [20]

Technology Prevails

The first half of the 20th century saw rapid advances in the battle against infectious diseases with the exception of a resurgence related to poverty during the Great Depression of the 1930s. The discovery of penicillin in 1932 by Scottish scientist Alexander Fleming introduced antibiotics, a new class of drugs that kill bacteria — a vast range of microbes that cause such scourges as tuberculosis, syphilis, streptococcal pneumonia and typhoid fever.

Thanks to some 36,000 antibiotic products developed by the early 1950s, the incidence of tuberculosis plummeted by 91 percent between 1944 and 1970, while the death rate from pneumonia dropped 40 percent from 1936 to 1945. [21]

The broad support for multilateral institutions that arose from the ashes of World War II encompassed not only economic policy (the creation of the World Bank and the International Monetary Fund) and international relations (the U.N.) but also public health. On April 7, 1948, the U.N.'s World Health Organization was created to achieve the best health standards "for every human being without distinction of race, religion, political belief or economic or social condition." The organization's constitution went on to warn that "unequal development in the promotion of health and control of disease" is a "common danger" for all.

In 1946, a new U.S. Public Health Service agency was created, the Communicable Disease Center. (It was renamed the Centers for Disease Control in 1980 and the Centers for Disease Control and Prevention in 1992.) The Atlanta-based CDC was charged with helping states and localities combat malaria, then prevalent in the South.

But the expansion of the Public Health Service masked an unseen problem. While the antibiotics revolution brought dramatic improvements in public health, it undermined, ironically, the public-health sector itself, at least in the United States. Armed with pills to cure infectious diseases, private practitioners and hospitals

AFP Photo/Peter Parks

Workers in Beijing disinfect the waiting room of a deserted railway station in the fight against SARS, on May 25. The disease reportedly has decimated tourism in China, where more than half of the 8,500 SARS cases have occurred.

came to dominate the field of medicine, relegating preventive medicine to secondary status.

"The bacteriological revolution had played itself out in the organization of public services, and soon the introduction of antibiotics and other drugs would enable private physicians to reclaim some of their functions, like the treatment of venereal disease and tuberculosis," wrote sociologist Paul Starr. "Yet it had been clear, long before, that public health in America was to be relegated to a secondary status: less prestigious than clinical medicine, less amply financed and blocked from assuming the higher-level functions of coordination and direction that might have developed had it not been banished from medical care." [22]

Viruses — much smaller than bacteria and harder to identify and combat — were unaffected by antibiotic "magic bullets" like penicillin. Such viral killers as polio, measles and influenza continued unchecked until vaccines made from attenuated live viruses or killed viruses were developed. *

In 1955, schoolchildren across the country received the first polio vaccine developed by Jonas Salk, an American researcher. After 220 children contracted the disease through faulty vaccine production — Salk's vaccine used a killed virus vaccine, but the manufacturing

---

* Vaccines introduce just enough viral material into the body to trigger the production of antibodies to the targeted disease. The antibodies recognize and kill the virus during subsequent exposure.

SARS Sickens Global Economy

The SARS epidemic appears to be on the wane, but it continues to afflict the global economy. China, where more than half of the 8,460 SARS cases have occurred, has been especially hard hit.

Tourism and exports of consumer goods, the mainstay of China's economy, reportedly have plummeted, although few reliable statistics are available. Likewise, imports of electronics and other consumer goods have declined as fearful Chinese consumers have shunned shopping centers where such items normally are sold.

The falloff in Chinese sales has prompted cell-phone makers, like Finland's Nokia Corp. and Motorola Inc. of Illinois, to downgrade their growth forecasts. [1]

But SARS has given a lift to some economic sectors in China. Auto and bicycle retailers, for example, have enjoyed a small boom in sales from consumers wishing to avoid crowded trains and buses. [2]

SARS dominated the agenda at the 21-nation Asia-Pacific Economic Cooperation (APEC) conference in Thailand this month. The hardest-hit places outside China reportedly are nearby Hong Kong, Singapore and Taiwan, whose tourism- and export-driven economies are expected to shrink by 1-2 percentage points this year. [3] Retail sales in Hong Kong have dropped by 15 percent from last year, as residents have stayed away from shops and their jobs, and tourists have avoided the island altogether.

Even Australia — which has reported only five cases and no deaths from SARS — reported an 8 percent drop in export earnings in April, as tourists from SARS-affected Asian countries stayed home.

Beyond Asia, Canada has suffered the greatest economic fallout from SARS. In Toronto, where nearly all Canada's cases have occurred, nearly empty hotels and restaurants are slashing prices to lure tourists back.

"We usually get a lot of American tourists over Memorial Day — a holiday for you but not for us — but not this year," says David Gratzer, a Toronto physician. "The hotels are now running at about 20 percent capacity."

But, again, some industries stand to turn a profit from the outbreak. Drug and biotechnology firms are scurrying to be the first to develop diagnostic tests, vaccines and treatments for the new disease. Even before the World Health Organization confirmed that a novel coronavirus causes SARS, Artus GmbH — a small German biotechnology start-up — began supplying the first commercial test for the virus. [4]

Public and private laboratories, meanwhile, are rushing to patent the SARS virus. A private company could use such a patent to claim ownership of the virus itself and its component parts — assets that could produce a windfall if the disease spreads. The U.S. Centers for Disease Control and Prevention (CDC) itself is seeking the patent in order to keep the virus in the public domain. "The whole purpose of the patent is to prevent folks from controlling the technology," said CDC spokesman Llelwyn Grant. "This is being done to give the industry and other researchers reasonable access to the samples." [5]

Like other dread diseases, SARS has already ignited a flurry of hoaxes and folk remedies to ward off infection. In remote areas of China, people have set off firecrackers to fend off infection, and markets abound with herbs and roots said to confer immunity from SARS.

In the United States, the Food and Drug Administration (FDA) has warned at least eight individuals to halt false advertising for remedies they claim will protect against SARS. "We've been going after people who are out there touting all kinds of fraudulent products as protection from SARS," says Murray Lumpkin, the FDA's principal associate commissioner. "Their claims are totally unsubstantiated. It's nothing less than health fraud."

---

[1] See "Nokia Issues Sales Warning as SARS Impacts Industry," *The Wall Street Journal Online*, June 10, 2003.

[2] See "Economic Impact of New Disease, from Near Outbreak to Far Away," *The New York Times*, May 18, 2003, p. A12.

[3] See Jenny Paris, "APEC Will Focus on Impact of Disease on Flow of Goods," *Dow Jones Newswires*, June 2, 2003.

[4] See Vanessa Fuhrmans, "Agile Artus Sees Profit in Test to Detect SARS," *The Wall Street Journal Online*, June 10, 2003.

[5] Quoted in "SARS: Race to Patent Virus Renews Debate over 'Patents on Life'," NewsRx.com.

---

lab failed to kill the viruses — a safer oral vaccine developed in 1961 by Albert Sabin, another American, became the standard polio vaccine.

Within the next couple of decades, some of the most dreaded childhood diseases virtually disappeared from the industrial world. By 1990, vaccines for measles (introduced in 1963) and rubella and mumps (1969) had helped reduce the incidence of vaccine-preventable childhood diseases to 0.1 percent of all deaths in the United States, Western Europe and Japan. [23]

Meanwhile, despite the persistence of influenza epidemics — such as the 1957 Asian flu and the 1968 Hong Kong flu — the development of annual flu vaccines kept up with the virus' rapid mutation rate and reduced the disease's impact.

As microbes played a decreasing role in illness and death in the industrial world, the medical establishment virtually declared victory over infectious diseases and turned its attention to such chronic killers as cancer and heart disease.

New Diseases

Technology's seeming triumph over infectious diseases proved illusory. On June 15, 1981, the CDC's weekly report of global disease patterns reported the appearance of a mysterious illness that would become the leading infectious scourge of the late 20th century. Two years later, scientists identified the human immunodeficiency virus (HIV) as the cause of acquired immune deficiency syndrome, or AIDS.

But despite a multimillion-dollar research effort and the development of advanced antiviral drugs, modern medicine found no magic bullets to eradicate AIDS. By the late 1990s, the virus had killed nearly 20 million people worldwide — mostly in Africa — and become the leading cause of death among Americans ages 22-45.

Costly drug treatments have since helped prolong the lives of HIV-positive individuals in the developed world, but AIDS remains a leading killer in the Third World, particularly in Africa. While there are recent signs that the AIDS pandemic may be slowing, it is expected to continue devastating Africa, where more than 29 million people have HIV. [24]

Other new diseases — whether through first-time human exposure to existing microbes, new contacts with microbes that have caused disease outbreaks in the past or mutations of those germs — have cropped up at a rate of one a year since the 1960s. [25] Some of the more recent outbreaks in the United States include Legionnaires' disease, tick-borne Lyme disease, hantavirus pulmonary syndrome and mosquito-borne West Nile virus.

Rapid population growth has also brought humans into contact with some particularly lethal microbes. For instance, Ebola and other lethal viruses that cause rapid hemorrhaging and death have broken out in Congo, Gabon and other African countries. Meanwhile, exces-

sive antibiotic use over several decades began to take its toll, as many bacteria — including those that cause tuberculosis and food poisoning — have developed resistance to successive generations of antibiotics. [26]

Modern agricultural practices also have spawned new diseases, some of which have jumped the species barrier, passing from animal hosts to humans. In the mid-1980s, an anomalous form of a naturally occurring particle known as a prion began infecting and killing British cattle that had been fed beef byproducts. The resultant sickness, called mad cow disease, later infected and killed nearly 140 consumers of infected beef, mostly in Britain. [27] Industrial agricultural practices, such as crowding animals in feedlots and aviaries, have also caused periodic animal-to-human flu epidemics, including a 1997 outbreak of avian, or bird, flu in Hong Kong and a new variant that recently erupted in the Netherlands, Belgium and Germany. [28]

At the same time, several old diseases continue to take a heavy toll, especially in the poorest countries. Plague, which killed millions in Europe during the Middle Ages, erupted in India in 1994, killing 50 people. And despite the successful eradication of disease-bearing mosquitoes in much of the world, malaria continues to kill at least 1 million Africans each year, 90 percent of them children under age 5. [29]

Threat of Bioterrorism

Germ warfare, once a staple of warring nations, waned during the 20th century. Appalled at Germany's use of biological and chemical weapons during World War I, the United States and many other countries endorsed the 1925 Geneva Protocol banning the military use of chemical and bacteriological weapons. Concerned that the treaty would limit the wartime use of riot-control agents and pesticides, however, the U.S. Senate deferred action.

Nonetheless, over the next several decades, many countries, including the United States, continued to develop lethal microbes. President Richard M. Nixon unilaterally disbanded the U.S. bioweapons program in 1969, and later signed the 1972 Biological and Toxin Weapons Convention banning the production, stockpiling and use of microbes as weapons. President Gerald R. Ford then proposed that the Senate consider both the Geneva Protocol and the Biological Weapons Convention. The Senate unanimously approved both treaties, which Ford ratified on Jan. 22, 1975. [30]

Evidence that Iraq, Israel, Syria and other countries continued to develop bioweapons in violation of the con-

Basic Facts About SARS

Symptoms

- Fever greater than 100.4° F
- Headache
- Overall feeling of discomfort
- Body aches
- Mild respiratory symptoms
- Dry cough, trouble breathing

Timeline

- After seven days of illness, patients tend either to get better or have increasingly severe respiratory stress; death occurs after four or five weeks in 15 percent of patients. The disease kills more than half of its victims over 60.
- Virus can survive outside the body on ordinary surfaces for 16 days.

Who's at Risk?

- Travelers returning from countries where SARS has been reported.
- Health-care workers and family-caregivers in close contact with SARS patients.

How to Avoid SARS

- In SARS-affected areas, wash hands frequently and avoid close contact with large numbers of people.
- Avoid non-essential travel to China, Hong Kong, Taiwan or Singapore; observe precautions when traveling to Hanoi and Toronto.
- Family members caring for SARS patients should follow strict precautions for 10 days after symptoms have passed. Recovered patients should avoid school, work and other public areas for the same period.

Source: U.S. Centers for Disease Control and Prevention. [31]

vention prompted recent efforts to strengthen the bioweapons treaty. But the United States and other industrial countries have balked, saying proposals to enforce the ban through inspections could reveal drug companies' commercial secrets. [31]

In any event, the treaties have failed to prevent non-governmental belligerents from using deadly germs. In October 2001, just weeks after the Sept. 11, 2001, terrorist attacks on the World Trade Center and the Pentagon, the United States came under another non-conventional attack, this time from envelopes containing deadly anthrax spores. Mailed from a source that continues to elude authorities, the anthrax bacteria killed five people and sickened 13 others.

The Bush administration responded to the anthrax attacks with improvements in the CDC's disease-surveillance and emergency-response systems, while states and localities introduced federally funded programs to improve health-care workers' ability to quickly identify symptoms of rare diseases that could be caused by bioweapons.

CURRENT SITUATION

SARS Outbreak

Many of the factors that caused the resurgence of infectious diseases over the past decades converged when the SARS virus emerged last November. [32] The first person known to have contracted the disease was a man in Foshan, a city in China's Guangdong Province. Five more people died in that initial outbreak.

At that point, public-health experts say, the outbreak could have been contained by imposing isolation and quarantine at the source and alerting WHO and other global public-health agencies.

But China's authoritarian political system discourages the dissemination of bad news; indeed, a 1996 law decreed that highly infectious diseases should be classified top secret. [33] As a result, the outbreak went unacknowledged for months, eliminating the opportunity to isolate and eradicate the infection. It was not until Feb. 10, 2003, that WHO learned of the new disease from Promed, an online service that reports on outbreaks throughout the world. Thus, China not only caused the spread of SARS but also suffered its greatest impact — 5,326 infections, including 346 deaths, as of June 17.

On Feb. 21, an infected Chinese doctor, 63-year-old Liu Jianlun, carried the virus to neighboring Hong Kong, where he attended a wedding and spread it to several other visitors at the Metropole Hotel; some of them later carried it to Vietnam, Singapore and Canada. One of the ironies of the SARS epidemic is that a physician was one of the deadliest carriers of the new disease — a so-called superspreader, like Toronto's Mr. P. WHO traces more than half the total number of SARS cases worldwide to Liu, who died in early March. Partly because local authorities failed to initiate isolation and quarantine measures for two weeks after Liu was hospitalized, Hong Kong has had 1,755 SARS cases, including 295 deaths. [34]

Esther Mok, a 26-year-old former flight attendant, was one of three Singaporean women to develop SARS after staying at the Metropole. Most of the other 205 cases in Singapore, including 31 deaths, contracted the illness from Mok, who recovered. Singaporean authorities rapidly quarantined hundreds of people possibly exposed to SARS, enabling them to contain the disease.

Another Metropole visitor, American Johnny Chen, is believed to have spread SARS to Vietnam in late February. Before he died on March 13, Chen spread SARS to 62 people, mostly health-care workers who had treated him at the Hanoi French Hospital; five of them died. Nonetheless, the government's aggressive quarantine measures made Vietnam the first country to contain a SARS outbreak, according to WHO.

Sui-chu Kwan, 78, another Metropole visitor, carried SARS to Canada and became the first SARS death in North America when she died in Toronto on March 5. Her 43-year-old son and caregiver, Chi Kwai Tse, died of SARS on March 13 and is believed to have been the source of most early Canadian cases.

Meanwhile, on March 30, an elderly man died of SARS in Malaysia at Kuala Lumpur Hospital after returning from a vacation in Guangdong. A 26-year-old tour operator, who died on April 22 after visiting China and Thailand, was Malaysia's only other SARS death.

The first person to identify SARS as a distinct disease was Carlo Urbani, 46, a WHO physician hospitalized in Bangkok on March 11 after arriving from Hanoi, where he had been studying Chen's case. Urbani died in Bangkok, one of only two SARS fatalities in Thailand.

SARS returned from North America to Asia with Adela Catalon, 46, a Philippine nursing assistant who flew home from her job at a Toronto retirement home to care for her sick father. Both later died at a Manila hospital.

Taiwan reported its first SARS fatality on April 26, when a 56-year-old man died after visiting his brother in Hong Kong. Since then, 697 people have contracted SARS in Taiwan, and 83 have died. Taiwan blames its high SARS mortality rate on China, which continues to block Taiwan's membership in WHO, because the Chinese say it would be an implicit recognition of the island's independence. The Taiwanese say if Taiwan had been a member of WHO, the health agency could have intervened aggressively to help stop the spread of SARS. But critics blame the Taiwan authorities themselves for failing to control the infection. [35]

SARS Update

By the end of April, after placing some 10,000 people in quarantine, Toronto health officials announced they had contained the outbreak. On April 30, WHO lifted its advisory against travel to Toronto. But two weeks later, city officials announced SARS had returned, perhaps after lying dormant in four local hospitals. Once again, thousands of people were quarantined, and WHO put Toronto back on its list of SARS sites.

"Toronto has been very fortunate in that we've never had a community outbreak," says Gratzer, the Toronto doctor whose hospital has escaped infection with SARS. "It's existed almost entirely in the hospital system. But even though we've been so lucky, it takes a lot to contain a virus like this."

Indeed, besides placing thousands of people under quarantine at once, Toronto health officials shut down two hospitals and discontinued outpatient services for the rest. The outbreak's economic costs, especially to Toronto's tourism industry, are expected to reduce Canada's second-quarter economic growth by fully 1 percent.

"What we're seeing in Toronto is how a single case can wreak havoc," Gratzer says. "So while we've had it relatively easy, we're finding out how, in an age of jet travel, a problem in Guangdong is a problem in downtown Toronto."

Indeed, on May 22 Toronto suffered yet another SARS outbreak, apparently spread unnoticed before it was known that the virus can survive more than two weeks on surfaces like bedding or doorknobs. On June 10, Canadian health authorities closed a hospital to new patients in Whitby, Ontario, because of a possible new cluster of SARS cases there, the first outside Toronto.

Canada, site of the largest SARS outbreak to take place outside Asia, has reported 247 cases and 32 deaths from the disease.

U.S. Reprieve

The United States, meanwhile, continues to be relatively free of SARS, aside from a few suspected cases in hospital settings. Hospitals and clinics around the country are taking advantage of the reprieve to prepare for a potential future outbreak. Indeed, Benjamin of the American Public Health Association says the global epidemic, coming on the heels of the anthrax and Sept. 11 attacks, provided a needed wake-up call among U.S. health-care workers. "We're better prepared than we were two years ago, though we still have some work to do," he says. "There are some places that have done a lot, others that are just beginning and probably some that still haven't done anything" to prepare for a major disease outbreak.

While many urban hospitals are at the forefront of infectious-disease preparedness, Benjamin says city-dwellers should not necessarily expect to receive better care than those in small towns. "What matters in community preparedness is whether the people at the hospital 'get it' or not," he says. "Before the anthrax attacks, when I talked to health-care professionals about biological terrorism, they thought I was a nice guy but a little wacko. Today there's a lot more interest."

The nation's blood supply is also vulnerable to infectious diseases. Before scientists discovered HIV, the virus infected numerous people who had received transfusions of tainted blood. A less catastrophic contamination occurred last summer, when blood from donors with West Nile virus entered the blood supply.

"We don't know if SARS is blood-borne, but it is a virus, and a lot of viruses are," says Lumpkin of the FDA. To ensure that SARS does not infect the nation's blood supply, the FDA is screening donors for physical symptoms of the disease and questioning them about any recent travel to SARS-affected areas. "If you've been to a SARS-endemic area, you are not allowed to donate blood for 14 days after leaving that area," Lumpkin says. "If you've actually had a diagnosis of SARS, you're required to wait for 28 days after being declared free of the disease."

The FDA also is responsible for ensuring that hospitals have enough medical supplies to cope with a major disease outbreak. "When it comes to fluids, standard drugs and respirators, we're in pretty good shape," Lumpkin says. But some are concerned, he says, that there may not be enough N95 masks — which can block the small SARS viral particles — because there is such a high demand for them in Asia.

Fortunately, the number of SARS cases has continued to decline in most affected countries, though WHO continues to post warnings against unnecessary travel to Taiwan, where a new cluster of cases has occurred in a hospital, as well as Beijing and three other areas in China.

"There's very good news that the SARS epidemic is over its peak," said Henk Bekedam, WHO's representative in China. "Our conclusion is that SARS can be contained, [even though] we don't have a test, treatment or cure." [36]

Bush Response

At the top of the Bush administration's public-health agenda is the threat of bioterrorism. Last December, Bush announced plans to vaccinate about 500,000 health workers against smallpox. Thanks to a global effort to stamp out smallpox, the deadly viral disease no longer occurs naturally, but there is concern that bioterrorists may gain access to lab strains and deliberately release them, causing a global smallpox pandemic.

So far, however, the administration has failed to convince health workers that the risk of bioterrorism outweighs the risk of occasionally severe side effects from the smallpox vaccine. Only about 36,000 people have received the vaccine. [37]

"This is a beautiful example of the perception of risk," says Lumpkin of the FDA. "People feel that there's no real risk of getting smallpox. If you had an outbreak of SARS in this country, however, that perception would be very different."

Bush's focus on bioterrorism has shaped the administration's priorities for public-health spending as well. Since Sept. 11, 2001, Congress has approved administration requests for $1.1 billion in federal funds to help states improve communications and lab capacity as well as hospital preparedness for massive casualties in a bioterrorist attack.

In his January 2003 State of the Union address, Bush also announced Project Bioshield, a plan to spend $5.6 billion over 10 years to buy an arsenal of tests, drugs and vaccines to defend against bioterrorism. [38]

At the same time, the administration has called for cuts in public-health agency budgets that critics say will hamper the nation's ability to ward off infectious disease, whether intentional or, like SARS, naturally occurring. After increasing the National Institutes of Health's budget by around 15 percent in the past two years, the administration has called for an increase of only 2 percent in fiscal 2004, to $27.9 billion. [39]

Can the U.S. public-health system protect America from SARS?

YES   **Jerry Hauer**
Acting Assistant Secretary for public health Emergency Preparedness, Department of Health and Human Services

From testimony before the House Energy And Commerce Subcommittee On Oversight and Investigations, May 7, 2003

The Department of Health and Human Services continues to work vigorously to ensure that the nation is ready to respond to terrorism and other public-health emergencies. As we strengthen our public-health infrastructure against bioterrorism, we are simultaneously enhancing our ability to respond to emerging public-health threats. . . .

Despite the seriousness of the virus' impact worldwide, we have reason to be encouraged by the response to SARS, for several reasons. First, the identification of the agent that causes the disease was completed in record time. In contrast to diseases, including HIV, legionnella and Lyme disease, which took over a year or even longer to pinpoint, we have and continue to have daily videoconferences to share information, map the response and coordinate our activities. . . .

We are partnering with industry to organize a full-court press on vaccine development. We are taking maximum advantage of technology to facilitate information sharing. The map of the SARS genome was published on the Internet soon after it was successfully sequenced by an international team of laboratories led by [the Centers for Disease Control and Prevention] and Health Canada. Improvements in laboratory capacity and coordination that were made recently as part of our enhancing of our overall public-health emergency preparedness have contributed to the speed and accuracy with which we've responded to SARS. . . .

Although the situation in Canada appears to be coming under control, it is critical that we are prepared to confront an outbreak of SARS on U.S. soil. Our recent efforts to enhance the nation's preparedness to respond to a smallpox outbreak have laid the foundation for managing a potential SARS event in cities throughout the country. . . .

The bioterrorism-preparedness funding has made a material difference at the state and local levels. Over 90 percent of the 50 states and three municipalities that have been awarded funds have developed systems for 24/7 notification or activation of their public-health emergency-response plans. And 87 percent of these grantees have developed interim plans. . . .

These are truly challenging times for our department. I believe that we are up to the task, and we look forward to working closely with Congress to ensure that the nation is prepared to respond to bioterrorism and other public-health emergencies such as the SARS virus.

NO   **Dr. Georges Benjamin**
Executive Director, American public health Association

From testimony before the House Energy And Commerce Subcommittee On Oversight and Investigations, May 7, 2003

The SARS outbreak and others, including anthrax and West Nile, have . . . exposed gaps in our own public-health system in the United States. We are at a critical juncture in public health. For many years, experts have been warning us that our nation's public-health infrastructure is in disarray. Recent preparedness funding has provided for improvements in the public-health preparedness infrastructure; however, gaps remain. There still is a lack of adequate personnel and training [and] laboratory-surge capacity, and there are still holes in our communications networks. There remain serious gaps in our disease-surveillance systems. . . .

Perhaps never before has it been so important to shore up our public-health system. This system is being asked to support our response to some of the most threatening emerging diseases of our time and to prepare for diseases yet unknown. In this age when biological and chemical terrorism is added to the portfolio of public-health threats, we need to be assured that the system works, and works well. . . .

In the absence of a robust public-health system with built-in surge capacity, every crisis "du jour" also forces trade-offs — attention to one infectious disease at the expense of another, infectious-disease prevention at the expense of chronic-disease prevention and other public-health responsibilities. . . . public-health is being asked to do more with less. Unless we start supporting our public-health base in a more holistic way, we are going to continue to need to come to Congress for special emergency requests for funds as each new threat emerges. Funding public-health outbreak by outbreak is not an effective way to ensure either preparedness or accountability. . . .

It is time to think more strategically about the future of our nation's public-health system. . . . Because of their impact on society, a coordinated strategy is necessary to understand, detect, control and ultimately prevent infectious diseases. We believe that far more significant investments in public health will need to occur if we are to prepare the nation's public-health system to protect us from the leading causes of death, prepare us for bioterrorism and chemical terrorism and respond to the public-health crises of the day.

I hope we all recognize that this SARS event is not over, and that we still have a ways to go to ensure containment. In the future, we will always be one plane ride away, one infected person away and one epidemic away from a global tragedy. We cannot lower our guard, not today, not tomorrow.

The CDC has fared so poorly under the Bush administration that it has had to solicit funds from private donors to carry out its mission. The agency would suffer an actual reduction in funding in 2004 under the current budget request; its Center for Infectious Disease would see its budget fall from $343 million to about $332 million. [40]

"The administration's emphasis on bioterrorism has unquestionably strengthened our capacity to respond to terrorist threats, has left us a lot better prepared than we were two years ago and is paying off with SARS," says Bloom of the Harvard School of Public Health. "Having said that, how they can cut infectious diseases and the CDC budget is beyond my comprehension."

OUTLOOK

Promising Research

Researchers around the world took only a matter of weeks to identify the SARS coronavirus and sequence its genome. They have found that the virus probably originated in masked palm civets and raccoon dogs — wild animals considered delicacies in southern China, where the virus apparently jumped to humans working in live-animal markets.

Interestingly, there have been no reports of transmission to or between children. Researchers at the recent NIH conference on SARS suggested that children might be at least partially immune to the disease, or get milder symptoms than adults, just as they do with chicken pox and some other infectious diseases common in childhood.

Anecdotal evidence also indicates that immunosuppressed individuals, such as those with AIDS or undergoing chemotherapy, may also be less susceptible to SARS — suggesting the possibility that it is the individual's own immune response to the infection, and not the virus itself, that causes the severe and often fatal pneumonia-like symptoms.

But these are just hypotheses, and SARS remains largely a mystery. "We need a vaccine, and we need a better way to diagnose," says Fauci of the NIH. Currently, specimens from suspected SARS patients must be sent away for testing — a time-consuming process. "We need to get the next generation of user-friendly diagnostics that are readily available in the setting of the local hospital," Fauci says. "We have to see if drugs that we already have can be used to treat SARS. And there will be a whole array of vaccine initiatives aimed at preventing the disease."

The FDA is enlisting the drug industry to invest quickly in research to produce SARS tests, therapies and vaccines by streamlining its rules for drug testing and approval. "Obviously, this is not something we would do for every product," Lumpkin says. "But for true public-health emergencies like this — for serious and life-threatening illnesses that don't have good therapies available — absolutely. That's the way we do business, and SARS clearly fits into that category."

SARS Prognosis

As scientists search for diagnostics and therapies to test for and treat SARS, they also are working on a vaccine to prevent contagion in the first place. But vaccine research is notoriously slow and probably won't produce results for several years. "If we're really lucky and are able to rush it through, we may be able to have a big enough clinical trial in three years to get some reliable answers," Fauci says. "It could be three years, or it could just as easily be seven."

While the focus today is on SARS, Fauci and many other infectious-disease experts are more concerned about the potential for a deadly new influenza outbreak in the future. "We have our annual [flu] epidemics, which are bad enough," said Klaus Stohr, project leader for WHO's global influenza program. "More than a million people are dying every year from influenza."

In the industrial world, annual flu vaccinations help protect against major disease, but the world is past due for a major mutation of the flu virus that could render the vaccine useless, experts say.

"This vaccine, which we are producing now, will not be effective when the pandemic comes, and the pandemic will travel around the world within three to six months," Stohr warned. "Up to 50 percent of the population will be affected. Millions of people will die. This is something which we have seen in the past and, what is worse, it is going to lead certainly to a global health emergency because of the burden to the health-care system and to hospitals." [41]

One of the best defenses against such a pandemic would be an effective early-warning system that might enable health-care workers to isolate any new microbe before it escapes into the global community.

"Infectious diseases don't respect national boundaries," says Harvard's Bloom. "My lesson from the SARS epidemic is that if we want to protect ourselves, we need an early-warning system, whether it's a new global-surveillance network or upgrading the competence of national and regional labs, that can tell us what's happening anywhere in the world."

NOTES

1. For background, see Mary H. Cooper, "Combating Infectious Diseases," *The CQ Researcher*, June 9, 1995, pp. 489-512.

2. Benjamin testified before the House Energy and Commerce Subcommittee on Oversight and Investigations, on May 7, 2003.

3. McGeer spoke at a SARS conference held on May 30, 2003, at the National Institutes of Health in Bethesda, Md.

4. Paul Farmer, "SARS and Inequality," *The Nation*, May 26, 2003, p. 6.

5. See Rob Stein, "SARS Prompts WHO to Seek More Power to Fight Disease," *The Washington Post*, May 18, 2003, p. A10.

6. Jerome Groopman, "Global Warning," *The Wall Street Journal*, April 23, 2003, p. A22.

7. *Ibid.*

8. See "SARS Kills Man Who Broke Quarantine, Went to Work at Ont. Plant," Canadian Press Newswire, May 29, 2003.

9. See " 'Bed chains' for Canada SARS Violators," BBC News, June 1, 2003.

10. See Judith Walzer Leavitt, *Typhoid Mary* (1997).

11. The poll, conducted by Robert J. Blendon, professor of health polity and political analysis at the Harvard School of Public Health, was released May 21, 2003.

12. Institute of Medicine, "Microbial Threats to Health: Emergence, Detection and Response," March 2003, p. 7.

13. General Accounting Office, "Bioterrorism: Preparedness Varied Across State and Local Jurisdictions," April 7, 2003.

14. See Chris Conte, "Deadly Strains," *Governing*, June 2003, pp. 20-24.

15. Unless otherwise noted, information on the public-health system's history is based on Laurie Garrett, *Betrayal of Trust* (2000), pp. 268-485.

16. For background, see David Masci, "Smallpox Threat," *The CQ Researcher*, Feb. 7, 2003, pp. 105-128.

17. For background, see Kathy Koch, "Vaccine Controversies," *The CQ Researcher*, Aug. 25, 2000, pp. 641-672.

18. Garrett, *op. cit.*, p. 291.

19. For more information on the Public Health Service's development, see www.nlm.nih.gov.

20. See Ronald Kotulak and Peter Gorner, "After SARS, What Might Come Next?" *The Chicago Tribune*, April 27, 2003, p. A1.

21. Garrett, *op. cit.*, pp. 326-327.

22. Paul Starr, *The Social Transformation of American Medicine* (1984), cited in Garrett, *op. cit.*, p. 309.

23. Garrett, *op. cit.*, p. 334.

24. For background, see David Masci, "Global AIDS Crisis," *The CQ Researcher*, Oct. 13, 2000, pp. 809-832.

25. Kotulak and Gorner, *op. cit.*

26. For background, see Adriel Bettelheim, "Drug-Resistant Bacteria," *The CQ Researcher*, June 4, 1999, pp. 473-496.

27. For background, see Mary H. Cooper, "Mad Cow Disease," *The CQ Researcher*, March 2, 2001, pp. 161-184.

28. See Vanessa Fuhrmans, "Europe Struggles to Contain Outbreak of a Bird Flu Virus," *The Wall Street Journal*, May 16, 2003, p. A5.

29. See "Four Horsemen of the Apocalypse?" *The Economist*, May 3, 2003, pp. 73-74.

30. For background, see *Congress and the Nation*, Vo. IV, 1973-1976, p. 863, and http://dosfan.lib.uic.edu/acda/treaties and click on geneva 1 or bwc1.

31. For background, see Mary H. Cooper, "Weapons of Mass Destruction," *The CQ Researcher*, March 8, 2002, pp. 193-216.

32. The following account is based on a chronology that is continuously updated in *The Wall Street Journal Online*.

33. See Jonathan Mirsky, "How the Chinese Spread SARS," *The New York Review of Books*, May 29, 2003, p. 42.

34. See Ellen Nakashima, "SARS Signals Missed in Hong Kong," *The Washington Post*, May 20, 2003, p. A1.

35. See Jason Dean and Matt Pottinger, "Complacency in Taiwan Led to Revival of Spread of SARS," *The Wall Street Journal*, May 19, 2003, p. B6.

36. Quoted by Elisabeth Rosenthal, "SARS Epidemic Winding Down, Health Officials Say," *The New York Times*, June 5, 2003, p. A10.

37. See "Missing the Smallpox Goal," *The New York Times* (editorial), May 12, 2003, p. A24.

38. See Michael Barbaro, "Biodefense Plan Greeted with Caution," *The Washington Post*, May 2, 2003, p. E1.

39. See Ted Agres, "Funding 2004," *The Scientist*, Feb. 4, 2003.

40. See Peter Gosselin, "CDC Turns to Private Aid to Stay Healthy," *Los Angeles Times*, April 25, 2003, p. A1.

41. Stohr was interviewed on CNN's "In the Money," on June 8, 2003.

BIBLIOGRAPHY

Books

Garrett, Laurie, *Betrayal of Trust: The Collapse of Global Public Health*, Hyperion, 2000.
A journalist describes how underfunding has undermined the public-health system's ability to cope with human disease throughout the world, including the United States. Garrett won a Pulitzer Prize for her book *The Coming Plague*, about emerging infectious diseases.

Articles

Bloom, Barry R., "Lessons from SARS," *Science*, May 2, 2003, p. 701.
The dean of the Harvard School of Public Health calls on the United States to help strengthen the global public-health system to prevent the spread of infectious diseases like SARS.

"China Wakes Up," *The Economist*, April 24, 2003.
China is coming under fire for covering up the SARS outbreak and allowing the deadly disease to spread beyond its borders.

Conte, Christopher, "Deadly Strains," *Governing*, June 2003, pp. 20-24.
Seattle's public-health department is struggling to protect residents from infectious-disease threats in the face of dwindling federal support.

Donnelly, Christl A., et al., "Epidemiological Determinants of Spread of Causal Agent of Severe Acute Respiratory Syndrome in Hong Kong," *The Lancet*, May 5, 2003, pp. 1-6.
The authors helped define SARS' average incubation period, course and fatality rate by studying 1,425 SARS cases in Hong Kong. They found the fatality rate rises with patient age.

Gerberding, Julie Louise, "Faster . . . But Fast Enough?" *The New England Journal of Medicine*, May 15, 2003, p. 2030.
The director of the U.S. Centers for Disease Control and Prevention (CDC) calls on researchers to move as quickly in seeking vaccines and drugs to combat SARS as they did in discovering the virus that causes the disease.

Gratzer, David, "SARS 101," *National Review Online*, May 19, 2003.
Pointing to China's SARS cover-up, a Toronto physician urges the CDC and its Canadian counterpart, Health Canada, to require airports around the world to adopt exit screening.

Kristof, Nicholas D., "Lock 'Em Up," *The New York Times*, May 2, 2003, p. A35.
This column calling for strict isolation of anyone suspected of harboring a deadly infection sparked numerous letters to the editor. "If you disagree," Kristof writes, "how about if I visit your neighborhood the next time I'm back from an Ebola outbreak in Congo and feeling feverish?"

Lemonick, Michael D., and Alice Park, "The Truth about SARS," *Time*, May 5, 2002, pp. 48-57.
Fear of the deadly SARS virus has kept people away from markets in Asia and prompted travelers to cancel their vacation plans, causing a downturn in the global tourist trade.

McNeil, Donald G. Jr., "Help! I'm Stuck in Quarantine and I Can't Get Out!" *The New York Times*, June 1, 2003, p. D7.
A New York City resident who may have been exposed to SARS during a recent visit to Taiwan describes the difficulty of maintaining his 10-day voluntary quarantine.

Mirsky, Jonathan, "How the Chinese Spread SARS," *The New York Review of Books*, **April 30, 2003, p. 42.** China's oppressive political system, in particular its 1996 law classifying highly infectious diseases as top secret, caused health workers to deny the SARS outbreak for four months and enable its spread.

Shute, Nancy, "SARS Hits Home," U.S. News & World Report, May 5, 2003, pp. 38-44. The deadly disease's arrival in Toronto is cause for concern in the United States.

Reports and Studies

General Accounting Office, *Bioterrorism: Preparedness Varied across State and Local Jurisdictions,* **April 7, 2003.** The investigative arm of Congress found that most hospitals it studied "lack the capacity to respond to large-scale infectious-disease outbreaks."

Institute of Medicine, *The Future of the Public's Health in the 21st Century,* **Nov. 11, 2002.** The U.S. public-health system is ill prepared to deal with both chronic and emerging diseases, the IOM says.

__, *Microbial Threats to Health: Emergence, Detection and Response,* **March 18, 2003.** Released on the eve of the recent SARS outbreak, this IOM report calls for heightened preparedness in the United States and overseas to quickly detect and eradicate infectious diseases.

For More Information

American Public Health Association, 800 I St., NW, Washington, DC 20001; (202) 777-2436; www.apha.org. The largest organization of public-health professionals in the world represents 50,000 members from 50 related occupations.

Center for Law and the Public's Health, Johns Hopkins and Georgetown universities, 624 North Broadway, Baltimore, MD 21205; (410) 955-7624 (Hopkins); 600 New Jersey Ave. N.W., Washington, DC 20001; (202) 662-9373 (Georgetown); www.publichealthlaw.net. The center was founded in 2000 with support from the Centers for Disease Control and Prevention as a primary, national resource on public health law, ethics and policy.

Center for Medical Humanities and Ethics, University of Texas Health Science Center, 7703 Floyd Curl Dr., San Antonio, TX 78229-3900; (210) 567-0795; www.texashumanities@uthscsa.edu. The center uses literature, drama and the visual arts to integrate the humanities into medical education.

Centers for Disease Control and Prevention, 1600 Clifton Rd., Atlanta, GA 30333; (404) 639-3311; www.cdc.gov. The CDC is the lead federal public-health agency.

Food and Drug Administration, 5600 Fishers Lane, Rockville, MD 20857; (301) 827-5709; www.fda.gov.

National Institute of Allergy and Infectious Diseases, 9000 Rockville Pike, Bethesda, MD 20892; (301) 496-2263; www.nih.gov.

Nuclear Threat Initiative, 1747 Pennsylvania Ave., N.W., 7th Floor, Washington DC 20006; (202) 296-4810; www.nti.org. NTI seeks to reduce the risk of nuclear, biological and chemical weapons.

World Health Organization, CH-1211 Geneva 2, Switzerland; (41-22) 791-2111; www.who.int. The U.N. agency monitors infectious-disease outbreaks.